FROMMER'S

WONDERFUL WEEKENDS FROM SAN FRANCISCO

BY MARILYN WOOD

Macmillan • USA

About the Author

Marilyn Wood came to the United States from England to study journalism at Columbia University. The former editorial director of Macmillan Travel, she has also worked as a reporter, ranch hand, press officer, and book reviewer. In addition, Marilyn is the author of *Frommer's Wonderful Weekends from New York City, Frommer's London from $60 a Day,* and *Frommer's Toronto,* and a co-author of *Frommer's Canada.* Currently she's at work on other *Wonderful Weekends* guides.

MACMILLAN TRAVEL
A Simon & Schuster Macmillan Company
1633 Broadway
New York, NY 10019

Find us online at **www.frommers.com**
or on America Online at Keyword: **Frommers**

ISBN 0-02-861335-X
ISSN 1094-5490

Editor: Douglas Stallings
Production Editor: Kristi Hart
Design by Amy Peppler Adams—designLab, Seattle
Digital Cartography by Ortelius Design & John Decamillis

Manufactured in the United States of America

CONTENTS

GETAWAYS TO THE EAST: SACRAMENTO, THE GOLD COUNTRY, LAKE TAHOE & THE HIGH SIERRA

GETAWAYS TO THE SOUTH: MONTERY BAY, THE MONTEREY PENINSULA & BIG SUR

MAPS

Invitation to the Reader

In researching this book, I discovered many wonderful places—inns, restaurants, shops, and more. I'm sure you'll find others. Please tell me about them so I can share the information with your fellow travelers in upcoming editions. If you were disappointed with one of my recommendations, I'd love to know that, too. Please write to:

Marilyn Wood
Frommer's Wonderful Weekends from San Francisco
c/o Macmillan Travel
1633 Broadway
New York, NY 10019

A Disclaimer

Please be advised that travel information is subject to change at any time—and this is especially true of prices. We therefore suggest that you write or call ahead for information when making your travel plans. The authors, editors, and publisher cannot be held responsible for the experiences of readers while traveling. Your safety is important to us, however, so we encourage you to stay alert and be aware of your surroundings. Keep a close eye on cameras, purses, and wallets, all favorite targets of thieves and pickpockets.

SIX IMPORTANT TOPICS

Prices & Hours: Although I've made every effort to obtain correct and current prices and hours for the establishments and attractions, these can change swiftly and dramatically. Changes in ownership, changes in policy, and inflation can all affect this information. For prices beyond 1998, add about 5% to 10% to the given rates per year.

Reservations: These are a must on weekends. For accommodations, they should be made well in advance, particularly if you want to stay at a particular inn. In some cases they should be made as much as three months ahead and in exceptional circumstances when major festivals or events occur as much as a year. Dinner reservations, especially for Friday and Saturday, should also be made well in advance to avoid disappointment.

Minimum Stays: Most places demand minimum stays of two or three nights on weekends and four nights on holiday weekends. This information has not always been included, so check ahead. Note too that the reference to weekends in hotel listings means Friday and Saturday. Weekdays refers to Sunday night through Thursday night.

Deposits: These are often nonrefundable since they're the innkeeper's only defense against those folks who don't show up, especially when the weather is inclement. Always clarify this point when you book—and don't be a no-show.

Taxes: These are not included in the quoted rates. California state sales tax is 7.75%; many municipalities impose an additional percentage, so tax varies throughout the state. Hotel taxes almost always include additional tariffs.

The Definition of Weekends: In hotel and restaurant listings, weekend always refers to Friday and Saturday nights. In attractions listings, it refers strictly to Saturdays and Sundays.

Getting In & Out of San Francisco

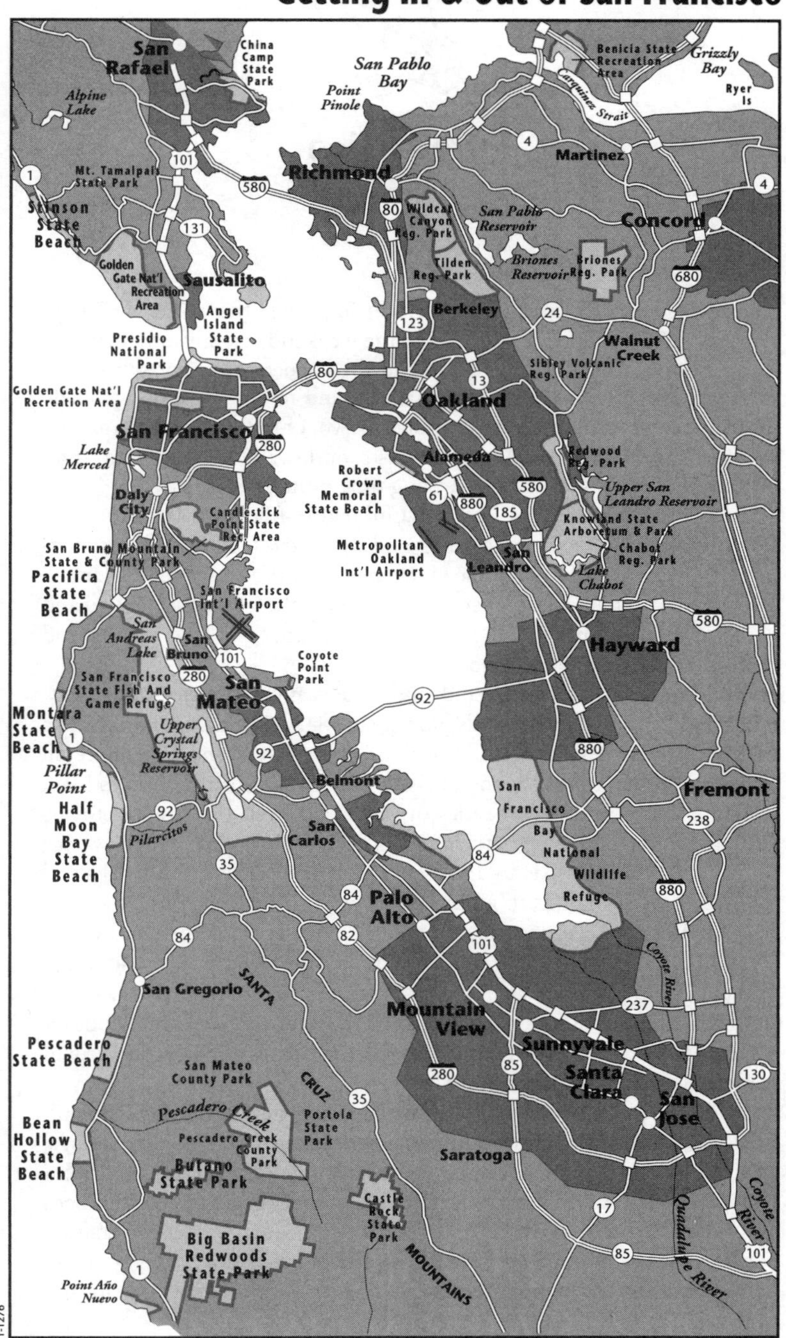

Introduction

Even if we live in the most beautiful, alluring city in the world, by Thursday most of us are looking forward to the weekend, eagerly anticipating a break from our busy work routine and the chance to get away from the tarmac, to relax, calm our jangled nerves, and rediscover who we really are. And that is what this book is all about: two- or three-day breaks among the lakes, or the mountains, or the forests, or down along the shore—and all within two to four hours of driving time from San Francisco.

So often, we forget that this beautiful nature-filled city is surrounded by many alluring, serene hideaways, and we head off for far-flung destinations. Northern California is one of the most beautiful places in the United States and a premier vacation spot. So why not take a weekend or two and explore what's around you in your own backyard, meet new friends, and revel in the beauty of the region.

There are country markets and fairs; rodeos; music; theater; apple, oyster, pumpkin, and wine festivals; flower shows; whimsical car races; and a myriad of other festive celebrations and events to attend. There are all kinds of unique museums and art galleries to visit; historic homes filled with the drama and personalities of those that lived there; ghost towns that haven't changed since they were abandoned 120 years ago; New Age retreats and mineral spas to discover; artists' and writers' residences and studios to view; fantastic architecture created for magnates by such brilliant architects as Julia Morgan and the Newsom brothers; and whole areas of countryside, shore, and mountains to explore by ballooning, cycling, gliding, hiking, camping, fishing, golfing, skiing, sailing, swimming, or doing whatever you relish and enjoy. Or you can simply opt for a rocking chair, a cocktail, and a broad veranda overlooking a verdant garden, the ocean, or the mountains.

And while you're enjoying all this, you can stay in old sea captains' homes; Victorian gingerbread fantasies with turrets and lacy trimmings; sybaritic coastal retreats; domed hideaways inspired by Russian architecture; or log cabin homes with huge, stone hearths. The choices are endless; so, too, are the delights of the table—juicy, sweet oystersfrom Tomales Bay; Sonoma lamb; California artichokes; Napa Valley wines—ingredients for the nation's finest cuisine that can be savored in airy dining rooms overlooking vineyard or ocean, in Gold Country saloons, or on picnics.

To arrange your weekend, though, in a way that suits your particular needs and quirks of personality, requires a certain amount of planning. When you only have two days, you need to know where you want to stay, and you can't waste precious moments circling around looking for a perfect picnic spot, or trekking to a well-regarded restaurant at Saturday noon only to find that it's closed.

This guide has been researched and written to forestall such problems and to deliver you, the weekender, from any such headaches, leaving you free to concentrate on roaming and fully enjoying your weekend your way. It is designed to help you, step-by-step, in the planning process. Each destination opens with a section that includes details about getting there by car, estimated driving times, and a list of any ultra-special seasonal events that you may want to plan your weekend around (or plan to avoid, depending on your attitude toward crowds).

After these opening sections, there follows a brief general introduction to the history and highlights of each region and then a detailed description of what your weekend is really all about: what to see, what to do, and what to explore. Inevitably, it's a very personal choice. Therefore, I have described the many choices available to you and offered some guidance about how to organize your two or three days and what I consider the real highlights of each destination.

You, of course, will pursue your own interests, whether they're architecture, historic houses, wine and food, antiques, graveyards, gardens, art galleries, museums, theater, bird-watching, or more active pursuits from windsurfing to skiing, swimming to golf, horseback riding to mountain biking. These last I have covered in an activities section at the end of each chapter (except in certain cases where it made more sense to place them at the end of each section in the chapter). In this section I have located public sports facilities wherever possible but make no claims to their quality and standards of service.

The problem of accommodations is tackled next, and while we're on the subject I cannot urge you strongly enough to make reservations, especially in peak seasons as much as five or six months in advance, *especially on weekends.* I have selected what I consider especially appealing accommodations, including a great number of inns and bed-and-breakfasts wherever they exist. In each case, I have endeavored to convey the atmosphere and type of lodging and treatment that a visitor can expect to receive. Rates are included, but I urge you always to check before you leave, because undoubtedly prices will have changed by the time this book reaches your hands. And do keep in mind that many inns have two- or sometimes three-night minimums on weekends. Although this does not pretend to be a camper's guide, I have included some camping ideas, usually state parks and other wilderness areas. Commercial campgrounds and trailer parks are not listed here.

Next, the problem of meals. I know an Englishwoman who built a very successful restaurant around the honest, nutritious breakfast that she served, and which can be difficult to find unless you know where to go—freshly squeezed juices, farm eggs, fine Canadian bacon, good spicy sausage, homemade breads, and muffins. Unless your accommodation provides breakfast, you, too, will have to search for a breakfast or brunch spot, and wherever I can, I've tried to help you out. Similarly, Saturday lunch can prove elusive—often restaurants close for lunch on Saturday—and so I have tried to find the best of those that are available. Often though, on a balmy Saturday you'll want to take a picnic somewhere overlooking the ocean or a river. Unlike France or England, where you can pull into a field and stretch out among the poppies with a fine bottle of wine, some garlic sausage, and a baguette, picnicking is not as easy in the United States. So I've tried to direct you to state parks and other idyllic settings for your leisurely meal *en plein air* and also, wherever possible, to the suppliers of your picnic fare.

For dinner I have described a selection of restaurants serving a diversity of cuisines for you to choose from. Hours and prices are all included to help your planning.

And finally, although many of the country destinations that appear in this book lack any rousing nightlife (which is precisely why you've chosen to go there), I have tried to include some nightlife options, if only a quiet, cozy convivial bar.

So let's weekend. T.H. White wrote, "The Victorians had not been anxious to go away for the weekend. The Edwardians, on the contrary, were nomadic." Let's copy the Edwardians.

GETAWAYS TO THE NORTH: MARIN, THE WINE COUNTRY & THE NORTHERN COAST

The Best of Marin County

Distance in Miles: Mount Tamalpais, 10; Muir Woods, 15; Stinson Beach, 20; Olema, 60; Sausalito, 8; Tiburon, 18; San Rafael, 19; Novato, 28

Estimated Driving Times: 40 minutes to Mount Tamalpais; 40 minutes to Muir Woods; 1 hour to Stinson Beach; 1¼ hours to Olema; 20 minutes to Sausalito; 45 minutes to Tiburon; 45 minutes to San Rafael; 1 hour to Novato

Driving: To get to Mount Tamalpais, Muir Woods, and Stinson Beach, cross the Golden Gate Bridge and take Highway 101 north to Highway 1. Highway 1, or the Shoreline Highway as it's often called, will take you to the Panoramic Highway, which leads to Pantoll Road. Pantoll Road will provide access via Ridgecrest Boulevard to the parking lot below Mount Tam's East Peak. If you continue along Highway 1, it will take you to Muir and Stinson Beaches.

If you're going directly to Point Reyes or Olema, the fastest route is via Highway 101 to Sir Francisco Drake Boulevard.

For Sausalito and Tiburon, take the Golden Gate Bridge (U.S. 101 north), then the first right after the bridge (the Alexander exit); Alexander becomes Bridgeway in Sausalito.

For Tiburon, take the Golden Gate Bridge (U.S. 101) to the Tiburon/Highway 131 exit, then follow Tiburon Boulevard all the way into town.

Ferry Service: It's also quite easy to get to Sausalito and Tiburon by ferry. Ferries of the **Blue & Gold Fleet** (☎ 415/705-5555) travel to Tiburon and Sausalito from Pier 43½ on a regular basis. The cost is $11 round-trip, half-price for children 5 to 11. The boat runs on a seasonal schedule; call for departure information.

Further Information: For information on what Marin has to offer, contact the **Marin County Convention & Visitors Bureau,** Avenue of the Flags, San Rafael, CA 94903 (☎ 415/472-7470). You might also try the **West Marin Chamber of Commerce,** P.O. Box 1045, Point Reyes Station, CA 94956 (☎ 415/663-9232).

Events & Festivals to Plan Your Trip Around

June: The **Mountain Play** has been a Mill Valley tradition for more than 90 years; the musical is performed in the amphitheater atop Mount Tamalpais. For information call the Mountain Play Association (☎ 415/383-1100).

The **Outdoor Antique Fair** in San Anselmo is a 1-day affair that brings together more than 150 vendors who spread their wares out in booths set up all around Creek Park. For information call the Antique Association (☎ 415/454-6439), which sponsors the event.

The **Dipsea Race** from Mill Valley to Stinson Beach has to be one of the toughest 8-mile runs anywhere—it crosses a mountain, after all. If the runners survive, they've achieved much. It's one of the oldest cross-country races in America having been run every year since 1905.

September: The **Sausalito Art Festival** turns the Labor Day weekend into an art free-for-all. It's a juried show, featuring works by 220 or so artists; the works are displayed under canvas in Marinship Park. There's also plenty of entertainment and good food. For information call ☎ 415/332-3555.

October: The **Mill Valley Film Festival** is an international event that has been held for 20 years. It features independent films, documentaries, and videos. Last year it opened with *Shine* and *Secrets & Lies*. Previous years saw the premier of Jane Campion's *The Piano*. An interactive media festival, children's film festival, and video festival are all held in conjunction with the film fest. For information call the Film Institute at ☎ 415/383-5256.

December: Since Point Reyes National Seashore is one of the premier bird-watching spots in all of California, a popular early winter activity is the Christmas Bird Count at the Point Reyes Observatory. Call ☎ 415/868-1221 for information.

For information on the areas around Mount Tamalpais, contact **Muir Woods National Monument** (☎ 415/388-2596); **Mount Tamalpais State Park** (☎ 415/388-2070 or 415/456-1286); or the **Stinson Beach Ranger Station** (☎ 415/868-0942). You might also contact the **Mill Valley Chamber of Commerce,** 85 Throckmorton Ave., Mill Valley, CA 94942 (☎ 415/388-9700).

For information about Point Reyes National Seashore, contact the **Bear Valley Visitor's Center,** located on Highway 1 just south of Olema (☎ 415/663-1092).

In the Sausalito/Tiburon area, contact the **Sausalito Chamber of Commerce,** P.O. Box 566, Sausalito, CA 95966 (☎ 415/331-7262); the **Tiburon Peninsula Chamber of Commerce** (☎ 415/435-5633).

To most of us, Marin County is synonymous with the California good life, albeit a life that emphasizes alternative lifestyles more than most. We imagine folks soaking in their hot tubs, eating healthy vegetarian meals, using solar energy, and experimenting with the latest in New Age and other alternatives. And there's good reason for thinking that way since the county manages to combine suburbia with environmental and social consciousness, making it quite possible to find outreach operations like Bread & Roses theater troupe that brings entertainment to the prison population.

Although the county contains what are in essence a string of wealthy bedroom communities, one-third of it is still miraculously reserved for nature—and brilliantly beautiful those reserves are, from Muir Woods and Mount Tamalpais to the Marin Headlands and the Point Reyes National Seashore. It's a blessing that so much has been retained for public pleasure, but it is a blessing that owes much to the citizens themselves who have fought to conserve these wild places.

The county's real history begins with the arrival of Sir Francis Drake aboard the *Golden Hind* in 1579, when he put in at what most historians assume is the often fog-shrouded, sandy (and eponymous) Drakes Bay. Here he was greeted by the local Miwoks as a god and brought gifts of fur and food. Little of historical interest happened thereafter for another 250 years until Mexico gained her independence from Spain in 1821, and the new Government dissolved the Mission system to make huge land grants to its favorites. One such land grant of 19,000 acres, Rancho Saucelito, was made in 1838 to Captain William A. Richardson, an English seaman who had married the daughter of the commandant at the Presidio Yerba Buena. The area was remade during and after the Gold Rush, when settlers who swarmed into the area ignored the Mexican land grants and staked their claims wherever they wished.

Although the aftermath of the Gold Rush ushered in an age of lumbering and papermaking, the mainstay of the economy continued to be dairy ranching and fishing. Not until 1937, when the Golden Gate Bridge opened, did the real struggle for Marin County's soul begin. The Marin Headlands had already been preserved by default when, after the Civil War, the military took over much of Rancho Saucelito. But after World War II, when the army's installations became obsolete, the Headlands were seriously threatened. Then the battle against development really began.

In 1964 an Eastern development company proposed to build the city of Marincello right on the Marin Headlands. The local residents fought the proposal and won. Then they went on to fight for the establishment of the Golden Gate National Recreation Area (1972), which incorporates 34,000 acres, including the Marin Headlands, Muir Beach, Muir Woods

Marin County

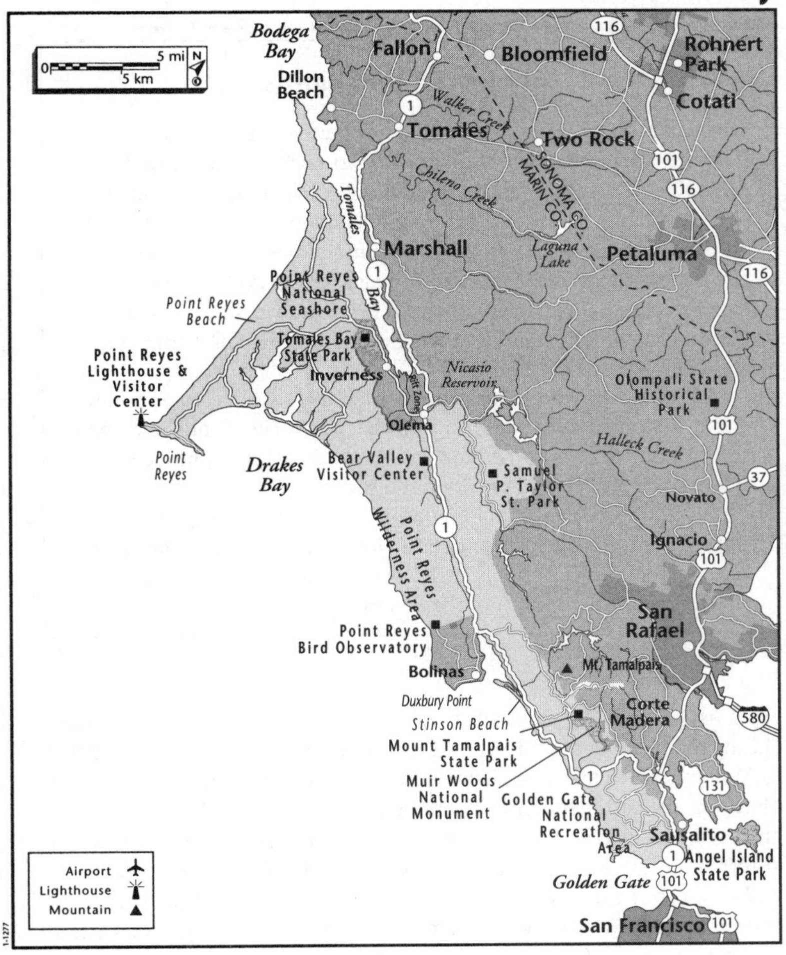

National Monument, and Point Reyes National Seashore. Thanks to their efforts that precious legacy can be enjoyed today.

LOWER MARIN COUNTY

SAUSALITO

Sausalito has some legendary history. A Spanish crew discovered this sheltered cove in 1775 and named it *Saucelito* after the "little willows" that they found here. In these early years, the wharf was used by many ship

Suggested Weekends

You will probably want to explore the county on several weekends. The most spectacular route would be to take the Shoreline Highway (Route 1) to Muir and Stinson Beaches, turning off to Bolinas at the southeastern arm of Point Reyes Peninsula, and then returning to the Shoreline Highway to visit Olema, Point Reyes Station, and the eastern or western shores of Tomales Bay. At Point Reyes Station you can access Point Reyes National Seashore via Sir Francis Drake Boulevard, which leads to Inverness and around the Peninsula to the Point Reyes Lighthouse.

Or you can head across the Golden Gate Bridge to Sausalito. From there you can climb up into the Marin Headlands and then loop around the Bay to Tiburon and Angel Island, stopping at Strawberry Point and Belvedere along the way.

Another weekend route might take you north along 101 to San Rafael, Santa Venetia, Ignacio, and Novato with sidetrips along the way to such Bayside spots as McNears Beach, China Camp, and Black Point at the mouth of the Petaluma River.

captains, particularly the English who built their homes on the hillsides. During the Mexican period, the 19,000+ acre Rancho Saucelito was granted to William A. Richardson, who had married the daughter of Ignacio Martinez, the commandante of Yerba Buena, in 1838. Richardson, an English seaman, was the first to pipe water from the hillside springs to a cistern and then onto a boat, in which he delivered it to San Francisco.

For most of the 19th century, the waterfront served as an anchorage and supply station for whalers and men of war. In 1855, though, Richardson sold a portion of his land, which was then resold to a ferry company that began a ferry link to San Francisco. Later, in 1875, the ferry schedules and routes were linked into the railroad that ran from Sausalito to West Marin. This is what made it easy for Sausalito to be discovered by San Francisco's nouveau riche, including William Randolph Hearst, who built a summer home here named Sea Point. The real working flavor, though, was provided by the Italian and Portuguese communities who fished for salmon, bass, herring, and shrimp from its wharves and worked in the town's hotels, restaurants, saloons, and gambling halls, the latter having sprung up in the 1890s when San Francisco banned track gambling.

The town was then known as a rambunctious, bawdy place where folks could have a swell time at such places as the Valhalla, a restaurant fixed up in fine style by the notorious madam Sally Stanford. The town's reputation as a good-time town continued even during Prohibition, when Baby Face

Nelson operated a bootlegging business from the Silva Mansion and Pretty Boy Floyd was supposedly the bartender at the Valhalla.

Although the trains and ferries both stopped running soon after the opening of the Golden Gate Bridge, the town continued to thrive as the waterfront was turned into a highly productive shipyard during World War II. It was these same piers that were rediscovered by the 1960s houseboating crowd of artists and writers, who turned them into rent-free homesites. Among the famous who made Sausalito such a legendary laid-back haven were Alan Watts and Jean Varda, who lived aboard the *Vallejo,* a converted ferryboat. Watts attracted Aldous and Laura Huxley, Allen Ginsberg, Fritz Perls, and many others to his Society for Comparative Philosophy. Today the houseboat crowd is still here clustered at the northern end of the Bridgeway in an area called **Marinship,** but increasingly they are embattled against developers. Walk or drive out to the area and stroll around. They certainly don't look like the homes of impoverished artists today.

Tourist Sausalito can be found along the **Bridgeway,** and by all means check out the galleries and stores along this street. Stop in at the **Venice Gourmet Delicatessen,** 625 Bridgeway (☎ 415/332-3544), to pick up a snack and enjoy it on one of the wooden benches that afford magnificent views of San Francisco.

The real Sausalito, though, can best be experienced by exploring the streets and hills behind the Bridgeway, where the residents do their shopping and eating and live in houses terraced into the steep hillside. So make the effort to go over to Bulkley Avenue and also to visit one of the restaurants set back up on the hills.

Also on the waterfront you may want to visit the **Bay Model Visitor's Center,** 2100 Bridgeway (☎ 415/332-3871), to view the model that engineers use to see what impact any changes in the water flow in San Francisco's Bay and delta will have. It's a scale model that reproduces the rise and fall of the tides, the flow of the currents, the proportions of salt to freshwater, and any resultant movement in the sediments. It is most interesting when it is operating, which is usually only once a month, so call ahead.

Hours: Summer, Tues–Fri 9am–4pm, Sat–Sun 10am–6pm; winter, Tues–Sat 9am–4pm. *Admission:* Free.

Lodging & Dining in Sausalito

Casa Madrona, 801 Bridgeway, Sausalito, CA 94965 (☎ 800/567-9524 or 415/332-0502, fax 415/332-2537), is the place to stay. It occupies a hillside perch with a magnificent view over the Bay. The core of the property is an historic 1885 Victorian containing 11 rooms, all furnished with handsome Victorian antiques. Some have fireplaces. More accommodations are located in cottages with woodburning stoves, rattan furnishings, a small desk, and hooked rugs on the pine floors. Each has a patio, and most have views of the bay. The rest of the rooms are newer hillside casitas, which are beautifully furnished in different colors and styles, from southwestern and Nepalese to French and Tuscan. My favorite is the Artist's Loft, which even has an easel and paints and brushes plus fireplace and large deck. All rooms have TV, telephone, and minibar. It's a full-service hotel with same-day laundry, room service and valet parking.

The hotel's restaurant, **Mikayla,** also has the best view in the house and some of the best dining around. Among the appetizers, the caramelized scallops with snap peas, jalapeño, and bacon are mouth watering. Each of the six or so main courses is finely prepared using local ingredients. There might be pan-roasted chicken breast with sweet corn sauce, or lamb chops with a pimento and lemon sauce, or seared salmon with fennel gratin. Prices range from $13.50 to $20. The Sunday brunch buffet is quite a spread and includes both egg dishes as well as roasts and shellfish, plus salads and several desserts. It's $19.50.

Rates: $135–$195 double.

As the name suggests, the **Alta Mira Hotel,** 125 Bulkley Ave, P.O. Box 706, Sausalito CA 94966 (☎ 415/332-1350, fax 415/331-3862), has great views of the city by the bay. It has a Mediterranean flavor with its large, triangular dining terrace and terra-cotta tile–roofed buildings. The nicest rooms are the one- and two-bedroom cottages and suites with views of the bay. They each have a fireplace and a balcony.

Rates: $90–$110 double without view, $115–$135 double with view, from $155 suite.

THE MARIN HEADLANDS

From Sausalito it's easy to explore one of the glories of Marin mentioned at the beginning of this chapter, the **Marin Headlands,** which sweep from the northern end of the Golden Gate Bridge northwest past Point Bonito, Rodeo, and Tennessee Beaches all the way to Muir Beach. Highway 1, or the Shoreline Highway, cuts across the Headlands at their northern end to Muir Beach. The only other roads are at the southern end, emanating from East Fort Baker. They are Conzelman Road and Bunker Road, at the end of which is the **Marin Headlands Visitor Center** (☎ 415/331-1540).

To reach East Fort Baker from Sausalito, take 2nd Street to Alexander, which will take you to the fort and the **Bay Area Discovery Museum,** on Bunker Road (☎ 415/332-9646), filled with hands-on discovery exhibits for kids.

Hours: Daily 9:30am–4:30pm. *Admission:* Free.

From here take Conzelman Road all along the Bay at an elevation that allows you to peer out over the towers of the Golden Gate Bridge to San Francisco. You can stop at several turnouts along the route or at **Battery**

Lower Marin County

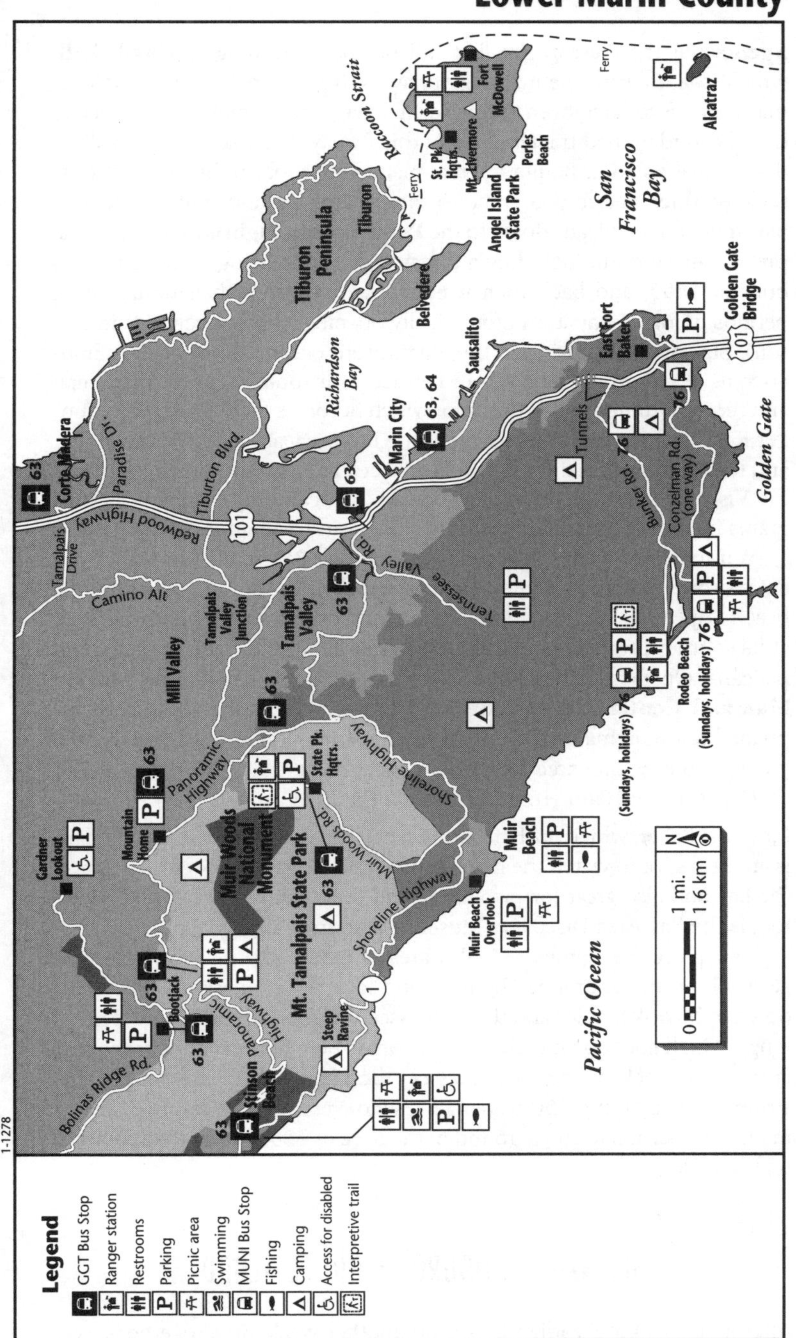

Spencer at the crest of the first hill before continuing to **Hawk Hill,** which is famous for the massing of hawks that occurs here in the fall. As many as 2,800 have been recorded in 1 day, and as many as 19 species have been identified traveling along this flyway. The road then nosedives down towards Point Bonita. A great picnicking spot can be found at **Battery Wallace** before you come to the parking lot and trailhead for the half-mile trail that leads down to the **Point Bonita Lighthouse** over some pretty hairy terrain, including a flimsy suspension bridge. This light was built in 1855, and back then it issued cannon every half hour during periods of fog. Today it is automatically operated (open weekends in season). Stay awhile to drink in the magnificent ocean view with San Francisco as a backdrop to the south. Retrace your route back to Conzelman and then continue around the loop, which becomes Field Road, then Bunker Road passing by Rodeo Lagoon, the Marin Headlands Visitor Center, and the Headlands Center for the Arts, back to East Fort Baker. Stop in at the Visitor Center for information on hiking, camping, and special programs including ranger-led walks in the Marin Headlands.

You may also want to drop down to Rodeo Beach, a short walk from the visitor center, to fly a kite or go beachcombing. The lagoon behind the beach is great for spotting loons, grebes, and other waterfowl. Bird Island, at its southern tip, is one of the best places along the coast to see brown pelicans. On the northern side of the lagoon is the **California Marine Mammal Center** (☎ 415/289-7325), to which wounded, sick, or orphaned sea mammals are brought for rehabilitation and release. Tour if you like, but be prepared to feel somewhat heartsick.

Hours: Daily 10am–4pm. *Admission:* Free.

East Fort Baker, which is often sunny when the western coast is fogged in, is an ideal spot to watch the many sailing and larger vessels cutting across the Bay and also great for picnicking and even fishing from a pier. Here, too, is the Bay Area Discovery Museum described above.

To explore the Tennessee Valley area of the Headlands, you'll need to get back on the Shoreline Highway and take the Tennessee Valley Road down to Miwok Stables and the Tennessee Valley Trailhead (about 2 miles long), which goes down to the beach. Somewhere out there under the surf is the shipwreck of the *SS Tennessee,* the namesake of the valley. This steamer was carrying 550 passengers, who were saved when the captain made the decision to run aground in the cove in 1853 rather than founder on the rocks.

BELEVEDERE, TIBURON & ANGEL ISLAND

After a visit to the Headlands—or on another weekend altogether—you can return to Highway 101 north to the turnoff that loops around the

Tiburon Peninsula, first to Belvedere and then to Tiburon. **Belvedere,** reached by Route 131, is a very tony island that is only 1 mile long and less than half a mile wide, connected to Tiburon by a causeway across the Belvedere Lagoon.

It is home to two yacht clubs—the San Francisco Yacht Club and the Corinthian Yacht Club—and also the historic **China Cabin,** 52 Beach Rd. (☎ 415/435-1853), the social saloon of the 19th-century ship *SS China,* which has been restored to its original sheen with brass and crystal chandeliers and plenty of 22-karat-gold ornamentation.

Hours: Wed and Sun 1–4pm. *Admission:* Free.

It's hard to believe that **Tiburon,** which today is filled with galleries, boutiques, and splendid homes with equally splendid views, was once a working-class town with cod fisheries and powder companies and a major stop for the railroad and passenger ferries, and also on the freight route from San Rafael to San Francisco. It was certainly a different place right up until the early 1960s, when 2,000 freight trains a month used to rumble through here. What remains today of that era are the railroad buildings, which have been converted into a condominium and shopping complex.

Ark Row, which shelters a cluster of boutiques and galleries, is named after the arks, or houseboats, that were kept at Belvedere Cove in the 1880s and '90s. They wintered in Belvedere Lagoon, and when that was filled in in 1940, Fred Zelinsky purchased some of them, dragged them up to Tiburon's Main Street, and put them on pilings. In 1955 the town's residents decided to restore Main Street, painting and restoring the facades of the historic buildings and making the waterfront an attractive scene. Today, from the decks of restaurants like Guaymas and Sam's Anchor Cafe, visitors can enjoy marvelous views of San Francisco across the Bay.

Stroll along Main Street, Ark Row, and Tiburon Boulevard. Besides the stores and galleries, visit **Windsor Vineyards,** 72 Main St. (☎ 415/435-3113), for some complimentary wine tasting.

Hours: Sun–Thurs 10am–7pm, Fri–Sat 10am–6pm.

Architecture buffs will appreciate the 1888 Carpenter Gothic church of **Old St. Hilary's** at Esperanza and Mar West streets, which is built out of redwood and Douglas fir. For information, call the Landmark Society (☎ 415/435-1853).

Hours: Wed and Sun 1–4pm.

Take the time to walk along the shoreline park that extends east from the downtown center and also to drive around the peninsula to see how lucky the people who live here are!

Besides the town attractions, visit the 900-acre **Richardson Bay Audubon Center and Wildlife Sanctuary,** 376 Greenwood Beach Rd. (☎ 415/388-2524), prime wetlands for migrating waterfowl. The headquarters is, by the way, the former home of Benjamin Lyford, an eccentric man who started the Eagle Dairy and claimed that his cows produced more milk because they were treated kindly.

Hours: Wed–Sun 9am–5pm.

From Tiburon you can board a ferry to **Angel Island,** which today, thanks to the efforts of conservationist Caroline Livermore, is a lovely state park to which you can take a bike and a picnic. Ride the trail around the island's perimeter, stop at Ayala Cove, climb to the summit of Mount Livermore, and explore some of the historic army buildings dating back to the Civil War at Camp Reynolds.

Angel Island is often called the Ellis Island of the West because it was the holding station for the Chinese who were awaiting clearance through immigration. Some of the inscriptions that they wrote while waiting for admission can still be seen on the walls in the park. During World War II more than 10,000 soldiers shipped out from Fort McDowell on the eastern side of the island. For information on the park call ☎ 415/435-1915. For information on ferry service from Tiburon call ☎ 415/705-5555.

Dining Only in Tiburon

Guaymas Restaurant, 5 Main St. (☎415/435-6300), specializes in regional Mexican cuisine from Guaymas, a fishing village famous for its shrimp. The specialties of the house are *camarones de Guaymas,* which are marinated in lime juice and cilantro and mesquite grilled. There are also plenty of exciting and unusual dishes found on the menu. To start, try the grilled prickly pear cactus with salsa and colija cheese, the little tamales filled with chicken and pumpkin seed sauce, or the pork with guajillo chile sauce. Follow with the delicious Pacific snapper sautéed with mushrooms, jalapeños, onions, tomato, and garlic and served on a banana leaf, or the slowly roasted pork with tomato, onions, cilantro, and serrano chiles. There are also a dozen mesquite grilled dishes to choose from, all of which can be accompanied by a side dish like grilled plantains. Prices range from $10 to $20. Desserts are varied and include a Mexican bread pudding with Kahlua ice cream and delicious fritters with drunken bananas and vanilla bean ice cream. The drinks list includes a dozen or so different tequilas.

Hours: Mon–Thurs 11:30am–9:30pm, Fri–Sat 11:30am–10:30pm, Sun 10:30am–9:30pm.

Sam's Anchor Cafe, 27 Main St. (☎ 415/435-4527), is a popular place to hang out, especially on the back deck overlooking the Bay. The food is traditional American—everything from burgers and steak sandwiches to crab cakes and broiled chicken breast with a barbecue sauce. Prices range from $7 to $17.

Hours: Mon–Thurs 11am–10pm, Fri 11am–10:30pm, Sat 10am–10:30pm, Sun 9:30am–10pm.

Sausalito, Marin Headlands & Tiburon
Special & Recreational Activities

Biking: You can mountain bike along the **Tennessee Valley Trail**, the **Bobcat Trail**, and the **Coyote Ridge Trail.** There are plenty of other trails in the area, on Angel Island in particular.

Bird-watching: See Hawk Hill, Bird Rock, Rodeo Lagoon, and the Richardson Bay Audubon Center descriptions, above.

Boating: You can rent Boston Whaler boats and waterbikes from **Captain Case Powerboat and Waterbike Rental,** 85 Libertyship Way #110A, Sausalito (☎ 415/331-0444).

Camping: There are several campgrounds in the Golden Gate National Recreation Area and Marin Headlands. **Bicentennial Campground,** near Battery Wallace, has three sites in a grove of trees that can be accessed by car; **Haypress** and **Hawkcamp Campgrounds** are hike-in, backcountry campgrounds. Call ☎ 415/331-1540 to make reservations and to obtain a permit for any of these.

Hiking: Easy trails to beaches have been mentioned above, but there are plenty of others. Two easy to moderate trails are the 1½-mile loop around the **Rodeo Beach Lagoon**, and the **Coastal Trail,** which starts from Rodeo Beach and links with the Wolf Ridge and Miwok trails back to the Marin Headlands Visitor Center for a total distance of about 4½ miles. Another moderate trail starts from the **Tennessee Valley Trail** and leads to Rodeo Beach via the Chaparral and Miwok trails; you can return to the Tennessee Valley Trail via the Coastal Trail. It's a total distance of a little more than 6 miles.

Horseback Riding: Miwok Stables, 701 Tennessee Valley Rd., Mill Valley (☎ 415/383-8048).

Kayaking: Sea Trek Ocean Kayaking Center, in Sausalito (☎ 415/488-1000), offers all day tours lead by naturalists.

FROM MOUNT TAMALPAIS TO STINSON BEACH

MOUNT TAMALPAIS & MUIR WOODS

Mount Tamalpais (2,571 feet high) was a sacred mountain to the Indians and to John Muir, and it remains so to many in and beyond the Bay area. It's an amazingly beautiful pleasure ground that lies only 10 miles from San Francisco and in fact includes three peaks: East (the tallest), Middle, and West. The name is thought to derive either from two Miwok words *tamal* (bay) and *pais* (mountain), or from Spanish, with the first a reference to the local Indian tribe and the second meaning a barren rocky place.

In 1896 an 8-mile narrow gauge railroad incorporating 281 curves ran from Mill Valley to East Peak, taking tourists to the ocean vistas at the top of the Mountain along the "crookedest railroad in the world." Fire destroyed the railroad in 1929 and, while the tracks remain, a paved road, the Panoramic Highway, now provides access almost to the top of the Mountain where you can stop in at the **visitor center** to find out about special nature and other programs led by the rangers. The amazing vistas are still there. On a clear day from East Peak, you can see Mount Shasta and Mount Helena to the north, Mount Diablo to the east (and the Sierras in the distance), and Mount Hamilton as well as San Francisco Bay to the south. Today **Mount Tamalpais State Park,** 801 Panoramic Hwy., Mill Valley, CA 94941 (☎ 415/388-2070), covers 6,204 acres and surrounds the famous Muir Woods.

The park and watershed offers more than 170 different trails and fire roads covering more than 200 miles. If you want to explore the magic of the mountain—which can best be done by hiking—then I recommend picking up a copy of Barry Spitz's *Tamalpais Trails,* which will help chart your way.

There are four man-made lakes on the mountain, all dammed, the largest being Alpine Lake and the highest and smallest being Lake Lagunitas. Many creeks course down the mountain, the most important being Lagunitas Creek, which is dammed in four places and holds a substantial portion of the region's water supply. Waterfalls abound, too, in season, while hundreds of wildflowers can be found blooming at different seasons—star lilies, trillium, morning glories, California buttercups and poppies, fuchsias, Indian paintbrushes, lupines, and irises. In spring the mountainsides are swathed in brilliant blue sky lupine, and you can walk across the hillside down to the sea at Stinson Beach and other points and wonder at the beauty of it all.

Summer fogs are normal from June through August; September is usually sunny and fog-free as October may be unless the winter rains begin early. January is usually the wettest month with December and February not far behind, followed by November and March, although this weather prediction is not an exact science. Facilities include camping and an outdoor amphitheater, site of the traditional annual Mountain Play, astronomy workshops, and other naturalist programs.

At **Muir Woods National Monument,** off Panoramic Highway (☎ 415/388-2596), you can walk the 6 miles of trails under the cool canopy of coastal redwoods and admire the lush sword fern and other plants that grow on the forest floor. These trees were saved from a developer in 1908 by Congressman William Kent, who purchased the 560 acres and named them after his friend John Muir, one of the nation's first ardent conservationists. The parking lot is always jammed on weekends, so you'll need to exercise some patience if you come by car rather than hiking in from Mount Tam or some other point. Similarly, the main trails will be crowded. If you want to enjoy some peace of your own in this cathedral of trees, get off the main trail.

Mill Valley, which is the intellectual center for Marin County, lies at the foot of Mount Tam. It's named after the old 1836 sawmill that still stands in Old Mill Park, but the town wasn't formally laid out until 1890 by Joseph Eastland. Back then, any visitors who came to town came to ride the railroad to the East Peak of Mount Tam. Until World War II, Mill Valley remained a quiet, sleepy town with a population of under 4,000, but that began to change in the 1950s when its population began to grow with the increasing suburbanization of the San Francisco Bay area. During the 1960s, it became a music center, the hometown of such musical luminaries as Jefferson Airplane, David Crosby, Country Joe McDonald, Maria Muldaur, Santana, and Sly Stone. Gary Snyder, Richard Brautigan, and other literary lights also hung their hats here.

Today, Mill Valley still plays the role of Marin's cultural and intellectual center—a center where you're as likely to brush shoulders with a CEO or celebrity as a '60s leftover hippie. You might even catch snatches of conversations in which folks are discussing their visits to $200-an-hour "transcendental channelers." To get the flavor of the town, go to **Lytton Square** at Miller and Throckmorton avenues and hang out at the converted railroad depot (which now houses 50 stores) for a while, then take **Cascade Drive,** which curves and twists up around Mount Tamalpais past beautiful homes that will make you envious if you're not very careful.

Lodging & Dining at Mount Tamalpais (Mill Valley)

Herb Caen described the **Mountain Home Inn,** 810 Panoramic Hwy., Mill Valley, CA 94941 (☎ 415/381-9000), as a miniature Ahwahnee, and indeed it is a marvelously rustic hideaway in a magnificent natural setting near the summit of Mount Tamalpais with views of the Bay and East Bay to Mount Diablo. There are 10 rooms, each furnished in a comfortable rustic style. Some have balconies, some have fireplaces, and some have

Jacuzzis, but all have Bay views from the bathtub. Facilities include a **dining room** (open Tuesday through Sunday from 11:30am to 3:30pm and 5:30 to 9:30pm), lounge, and a broad deck with great views. TVs are available on request in advance.

Rates: $141–$249 double.

MUIR & STINSON BEACHES

If you drive the Shoreline Highway or Route 1, the first beach you come to will be **Muir Beach,** which is part of the Golden Gate National Recreation Area. It's a quiet cove beach that is not as crowded as Stinson farther north. Monarch butterflies winter here in a small grove of trees. A short distance north of Muir Beach, stop and take the short trail to the Muir Beach Overlook, which has, as you can imagine, a magnificent view that is certainly not for the faint of heart.

En route to Muir Beach you will pass by another famous Marin landmark, **Green Gulch Farm,** which is the source of the fresh organic vegetables that are cooked and served at Greens Restaurant at Fort Mason in San Francisco. It's also the home of the Zen Center founded by Shunryu Suzuki Roshi. Today the hayloft serves as the zendo. The **Zen Center,** 1601 Shoreline Hwy., Sausalito, CA 94965 (☎ 415/383-3134), purchased the property from George Wheelright in 1967. George, who was the coinventor of the Polaroid process, had bought the ranch in 1945 and lived there with his society wife Hope Livermore, who had previously hung out with such glitterati as Scott Fitzgerald and his crowd. Today the center offers retreats and a series of workshops on Zen, the way of tea, organic gardening, and the environment. Weekend workshops cost $225 to $250, the higher price for private accommodations. Guests can also stay overnight on personal retreats for $75 single, $110 double (including three meals); practice retreats (in which you participate in the zendo program) are $35 and $55, respectively. On Sunday mornings visitors can also participate in a program that begins with meditation instruction and ends with a dharma talk and lunch.

From Muir Beach the drive along the Shoreline Highway is nothing short of spectacular. On the left the ocean crashes to the shore, and to the right the peaks of Mount Tam loom. As you begin to twist and turn along this magnificent, curvaceous road, you will surely begin to wonder where it will all end. Then suddenly there below stretches **Stinson Beach** and the small village of the same name behind it. **Stinson Beach State Park,** Rt. 1, P.O. Box 548 (☎ 415/868-0942), is 3 miles long, more lively than Muir, and very popular with San Franciscans who come to swim, surf, windsurf, and relax either on the main beach in front of town or at the nude Red Rock Beach at its southern end. Stinson is easily accessible today, although you may wonder where you're going as the road winds and twists along the coast before dropping down into the small village. Before the bridge opened and the road was cut, visitors used to have to take a ferry to Sausalito, a train to Mill Valley, then either hike or take the stage over Mount Tamalpais. There are a few stores, galleries, and cafes to hang in for a while. The state park beach is accessible, but the frontage at the very private, very locked, and very wealthy community called Seadrift is not.

If you want to enjoy some incredible views, then take a 6-mile hike that starts behind the Casa del Mar at the **Matt Davis Trail.** The trail crosses **Eskoot Creek** into a Douglas fir forest that is strewn in spring with blue-eyed grass and ground orchids. Another bridge takes you farther uphill to **Table Rock,** which affords terrific ocean views. At the junction of the **Coastal Trail,** continue east crossing grassy hills filled with California poppies in spring to the Pantoll Ranger Station where you access the **Steep Ravine Trail,** which drops down through a fern-lined redwood forest and links up with the **Dipsea Trail,** which circles back to Stinson Beach.

Just north of Stinson Beach there is a turnoff to the left leading down to **Bolinas.** It's unmarked, and that's the way the 2,000 residents prefer it at this '60s backwater, which has not been tarted up in any way for tourists. In the early 19th century it took 5 hours by schooner to reach this small port, which has the Pacific Ocean on one side and the Bolinas lagoon on the other, only 12 miles north of San Francisco. Originally part of the 9,000-acre Rancho Baulenes, which had been granted to Rafael Garcia, it became a lumber port when Gregorio Briones, his brother-in law, leased the lumber rights in 1849. Back then Bolinas was frequented by a rough and ready crowd of lumbermen who sloshed down whiskey at the local saloon after a day's work cutting down the redwoods while the lagoon was filled with schooners that took the lumber south to San Francisco.

Today the main street curves along the lagoon to a small beach. Houses stand on stilts at the water's edge. It's a small, tight-nit community where the residents have resisted any attempts at development ever since a disastrous oil spill in 1971 that destroyed a great deal of marine life along the Marin Coast. They have defeated proposals to install a sewer system, which would inevitably have invited more development; they subscribe to alternative energy; they operate their own alternative school. And so Bolinas has retained its reputation as a haven for hippies, poets, and artists who have included at one time or another Joanne Kyger, Lawrence Ferlinghetti, Aram Saroyan, Duncan McNaughton, Tom Clark, and many others.

If you remember the '60s with sweet nostalgia, then you'll relish the casual, laid-back atmosphere of the place and be content watching the sun sink over the lagoon and the fishing boats bob at the wharf. If you want to experience more of the historical and cultural scene, then pop into the **Bolinas Museum for the Art and History of Coastal Marin,** 48 Wharf Rd. (☎ 415/868-0330), which traces the town's history from Native American settlement to art colony.

Hours: Fri–Sun 1–5pm. *Admission:* Free.

For a real taste of the past, though, go in to the **Bolinas Bakery & Cafe,** 20 Wharf Rd. (☎ 415/868-0211), to sample some of their baked goods made with organic flour. The cafe also serves hearty soups, salads, deli, and microbrews. For another dose of nostalgia stop in also at **Smiley's Schooner Saloon,** 41 Wharf Rd. (☎ 415/868-1311), which is nearby.

Bolinas is also a mecca for bird-watchers, who will want to visit the **Point Reyes Bird Observatory,** located about 3 miles north of Bolinas along Mesa Road on the ocean (☎ 415/868-1221). It operates a banding station, which visitors can observe in action. Bird-watchers also head for the **Audubon Canyon Ranch** (☎ 415/868-9244), which is located on the eastern side of Route 1 overlooking the Bolinas Lagoon, where colonies of egrets and herons nest.

Finally, Bolinas is known for its entertainment options, musical and otherwise, which take place on weekends in the local saloon or at the **Community Center.** For information call ☎ 415/868-2128.

Lodging & Dining at Muir & Stinson Beaches

The Pelican Inn, 10 Pacific Way, Muir Beach, CA 94965 (☎ 415/383-6000), is full of character and extraordinarily reminiscent of a Tudor-style English country pub. It stands among pine and elder surrounded by gardens of honeysuckle and jasmine. Step inside to the paneled and low-beamed bar, equipped, of course, with a dart board and enhanced by an inglenook fireplace decorated with horse brasses. The rooms are also suitably furnished with full or half-canopy beds, Oriental rugs, and English antiques. A decanter of sherry and fresh flowers add extra flair. In the mornings a full English breakfast is served. The **dining room** specializes in such English traditions as bangers and mash, cottage pie, prime rib, beef Wellington, and rack of lamb. Prices range from $15 to $23 for main dishes at dinner. In summer it's lovely to dine on the outdoor patio with outdoor fireplace.

Rates (incl. breakfast): $150–$175 double. *Dining Hours:* Tues–Fri 11:30am–3pm and 6–9pm, Sat–Sun 11:30am–3:30pm and 5:30–9pm.

What makes **Casa del Mar,** 37 Belvedere Ave, P.O. Box 238, Stinson Beach, CA 94970 (☎ 415/868-2124), so alluring are the gardens and the Mediterranean spirit of the place. Guests ramble through the terraced gardens, which are filled with all kinds of magnificent shrubs and flowers—jacaranda, passion flowers, banana trees, cacti—past the fish pond up to the peach-colored inn. Inside they find a serene Mediterranean villa with tiled floors and walls washed in pastels and decorated with bright paintings by local artists. There are four rooms, two with ocean views and two with mountain views. They all have private baths with handsome, shell-shaped sinks and brass fittings. Best of all, though, they have their own private balconies, and of course bouquets of fresh flowers from the garden. Guests can relax on the rattan sofas in front of the adobe-style fireplace in the living room or grab one of the many books and retire to the window seat. Great breakfasts, consisting of such items as blueberry and poppyseed coffee cake, Mexican egg and sausage casserole with a spicy hot chili salsa, and fresh fruit, are served.

Rates (incl. breakfast): $135–$235 double.

Dining Only at Stinson Beach

The Stinson Beach Grill (☎ 415/868-2002) is a favorite spot for oysters, steamers, and other bounty of the sea. Try the local oysters on the half shell, or have them with Anaheim chili pesto or Cajun style. You can follow this treat with one of the pasta dishes like the penne with whiskey fennel sausage, a steak, or one of the southwestern dishes including burritos and tacos. Prices range from $8 to $18. It's a casual, sunny place.

Hours: Mon–Fri 11:30am–9pm, Sat–Sun 10am–9:30pm. Closed Tues–Wed in winter.

The **Parkside Cafe,** 43 Arenal (☎ 415/868-1272), is the place to go for breakfast, where a dozen omelets are offered. Italian specialties are the order of the evening, when such dishes as saltimbocca a la romana and veal pizzaiola and marsala are available, along with a full complement of pastas. Prices range from $8 to $15.

Hours: Mon–Fri 7:30am–2pm, Sat–Sun 8am–2pm; Thurs–Mon 5–9:30pm.

Mount Tam, Muir & Stinson Beaches
Special & Recreational Activities

Beaches: Stinson Beach is undoubtedly the best swimming beach in the area, complete with facilities and lifeguards from Memorial Day to Labor Day. There's good board- and windsurfing too.

Biking: Mountain bikes were tested on Mount Tam in the early '70s, making it the launching pad for this very popular sport; today they are allowed only on fire roads and only at maximum speeds of 15 mph. The closest places for rentals are in San Rafael: **Start to Finish,** 1820 Fourth St. (☎ 415/459-3990), or **Mike's Bike Center,** 1601 Fourth St. (☎ 415/454-3747).

Bird-watching: The canyons, redwood groves, forests, and open grasslands of Mount Tam shelter many different species—among them sapsuckers, sparrows, swifts, quail, hawks, and woodpeckers of varying types.

Camping: The camping at **Pantoll,** the only campground in Mount Tamalpais State Park, is on a first-come first-served basis. There are also a few sites and 10 rustic cabins overlooking the ocean at Steep Ravine, and these can be reserved. For information call ☎ 415/388-2070.

Canoeing/Kayaking: You can reserve a kayak at **Ocean Kayak Rentals**, 3605 Hwy. 1, Stinson Beach (☎ 415/868-2739), and also from **Off the Beach Boats**, 15 Calle del Mar, Stinson Beach (☎ 415/868-9445).

Hiking: There are hundreds of miles of interconnected trails crisscrossing Mount Tamalpais, Muir Woods, and adjacent lands. If you want to hike independently, you should purchase *Tamalpais Trails* by Barry Spitz.

Or you can join group hikes offered either by the **Sierra Club**, 85 2nd St., 2nd floor, San Francisco (☎ 415/977-5500). Costs for backpacking trips range from $395 to $650. They also offer bicycle trips.

Or you can contact the **Mount Tamalpais Interpretive Association** in San Rafael, CA 94912 (☎ 415/258-2410). Rangers also lead 5- to 7-mile walks at Muir Woods during the summer on Saturdays, Sundays, and alternate Wednesdays.

At Muir Woods a moderate trail to look for is the **Fern Creek Loop**, which travels Fern Creek Trail to Alice Eastwood Camp and returns via the Bootjack Trail (3 miles).

On Mount Tam several easy to moderate trails start at the Pantoll Ranger Station. The **Matt Davis Trail** goes down to Stinson Beach (about 3½ miles); the **Old Mine Trail** is a short and easy one-half-mile trip to a grassy outcrop. There's also a short three-quarter-mile trail from the East Peak parking lot that provides some magnificent views.

Horseback Riding: The closest option for horseback riding is at Point Reyes National Seashore. Contact **Five Brooks Stables**, 8001 State Rd. 1, Olema, CA 94950 (☎ 415/663-1570). See details under Point Reyes Activities, below.

Surfing: Boards and wet suits can be rented at **Live Water Surf Shop**, 3450 Shoreline Hwy., Stinson Beach, CA (☎ 415/868-0333).

FROM MILL VALLEY TO SAN ANSELMO

From Mill Valley a string of bedroom communities stretches north along the spine of Marin County. **Larkspur** started out as a logging town but is most famous for the outdoor dances that were held there from 1913 to 1963. Sponsored by the Firemen's Association, they took place in a redwood grove by a creek that was lit by Chinese lanterns hanging from the trees and was enclosed by a rose-covered fence. At the time they were considered the romantic venue of the era. Today Larkspur is a commuter town accessible by ferry from San Francisco with a pleasant downtown area that includes historic **Magnolia Avenue,** which is a good street for a strolling and browsing.

The more appealing towns of the region—**Kentfield, Ross,** and **San Anselmo**—lie in Ross Valley. San Anselmo has an Eastern air and is famous for having more than 130 antique dealers, cafes, and restaurants galore, as well as the beautifully situated San Francisco Theological Seminary, a Presbyterian graduate school.

Nearby **Samuel Taylor State Park** lies in the San Geronimo Valley. Paper Mill Creek, which runs through the park, was where Taylor started the West Coast's first paper mill in 1856.

Dining in the Area

Larkspur

The **Lark Creek Inn,** 234 Magnolia Ave. (☎ 415/924-7766), has won many accolades from the press for its robust, flavorful American cuisine prepared by chef-owner Bradley Ogden. The beautiful surroundings are an added bonus. The historic inn is set in a grove of redwoods and has a creek running through the garden by the patio. The menu changes daily, so you can be certain that the fare will be super fresh. It will also be simply prepared to bring out the natural flavors. On a recent menu you could begin with a fabulous Dungeness crab stew flavored with scallions, sunchokes, cauliflower, mushrooms, and black truffles, or a Castroville artichoke accompanied by an olive-pepper salad. Follow with a selection from eight or so main dishes—a pan-roasted salmon with caramelized onion and contrasting green apple jus, or a lemon tarragon roasted chicken bursting with flavor and accompanied by the best mashed potatoes anywhere. Prices range from $14 to $25. The cellar offers more than 200 selections.

Hours: Mon–Fri 11:30am–1:45pm, Sun 10am–2pm; Mon–Fri 5:30–9:15pm, Sat 5–9:45pm, and Sun 5–8:45pm.

Greenbrae

At elegant **Joe LoCoco's,** 300 Drakes Landing Rd. (☎ 415/925-0808), classic Northern Italian cuisine is the order of the day. Pasta dishes are carefully prepared with such spicy sauces as puttanesca or amatriciana. Other favorites are the mesquite grilled dishes—rack of lamb with rosemary sauce, prawns wrapped in pancetta—plus such dishes as saltimbocca alla romano, which is superb. Prices range from $10 to $19.

Hours: Mon–Fri 11am–2:30pm; Mon–Thurs 5–9pm, Fri–Sat 5:30–10pm, Sun 5–9pm.

FROM SAN RAFAEL TO NOVATO

San Rafael is the county seat and, in fact, the oldest city in the county. Here in December 1817 **Mission San Rafael Arcangel,** the 20th

Mission, was founded by Father Vicente de Sarria as a sunnier, healthier place to where many of the Indians who were falling sick and dying at Mission Dolores could be transferred. The original was a simple building with star-shaped windows and a set of bells hanging from a wooden frame out front. It was never fully completed to form a full quadrangle and in fact was abandoned in 1842 and razed in 1870 although it was used by Captain Fremont as an adequate shelter in 1846. Today **St. Raphael's Catholic Church** stands on the site while a replica of the mission stands nearby. Since no one knows what the interior looked like, the interior is modern.

Other buildings of note in San Rafael include the **Falkirk Mansion** (☎ 415/485-3228), an 1888 Victorian mansion that functions as an art and cultural center; **Dominican College,** 50 Acacia Ave. (☎ 415/457-4440), which stages the Marin Shakespeare Festival in its wooded Forest Meadows Amphitheater; and **San Quentin Prison,** which was established in 1852.

To most of us, though, it's downtown **Fourth Street** that has a nostalgic place in our memories as the backdrop for George Lucas' *American Graffiti*. Fans of Frank Lloyd Wright will also want to visit his **Marin County Civic Center,** 3031 Civic Center Dr. (☎ 415/499-6646), which is home to **Marin County Farmers Market,** one of the top markets of its kind in the nation. For information call ☎ 415/456-FARM (3276).

If you're interested in the historic aspects of the town, then stop by the **Chamber of Commerce** at 817 Mission Ave. and pick up their walking tour map/brochure. Bird-watchers will want to visit the **Shoreline Park,** from which there is a view of the Marin Islands National Wildlife Sanctuary, home to a heron and great heron colony. To the east of the city on Point San Pedro is **McNear's Beach,** which is a county park with swimming pool, tennis courts, picnic area, and beach.

Just to the south of McNear's lies **China Camp State Park,** named after the Chinese immigrants who were smuggled past the immigration station at Alcatraz to this cove. When the North Pacific Coast Railroad was being built in the 1870s, more than 1,000 Chinese lived here and fished for shrimp. Later during the economic recession of the 1870s and 1880s and the resultant anti-Chinese riots, the size of the Chinese population increased to 3,000, many of whom had fled here from San Francisco. They too fished for shrimp until fixed nets were banned in the bay in 1910. Most of the old encampment was destroyed in 1913, but you can still see traces of the Chinese village and enjoy biking, hiking, fishing, swimming, and windsurfing here in a place that has fewer fogbound days than most other spots.

Farther north up Highway 101, **Novato** is virtually a new city, having been incorporated in 1960. The old town that was here before grew up along the creek, its economy based on the orchard and poultry business, which gave it a distinctly Western feel. These industries were wiped out by the Depression, and the developers soon began building tract housing and condominiums for commuters to San Francisco. One historic landmark remains, though: **Rancho Olompali,** which was one of the few land grants made to an Indian. It was granted to Camillo Ynitia who was the son of the last chief of the Olompali Indians. The original adobe building still stands 3½ miles north of Novato in **Olompali State Historic Park,** 8901 Redwood Hwy., at Highway 101.

Novato also incorporates the historic community of **Ignacio.** At nearby Black Point at the mouth of the Petaluma River, the **Renaissance Pleasure Faire** is held every year for 6 weeks from the end of August until early October. It is a living history festival that replicates an Elizabethan fair complete with musicians, jugglers, puppeteers, troubadours, monks, friars, cooks, and craftspeople who don Elizabethan dress and hold medieval court—thousands of them all celebrating a summer holy day.

The rest of the county between Novato and Tomales Bay and Sonoma consists of thousands of acres of ranchlands cut by numerous creeks. Many of the ranches are operated by Swiss-Italian clans. Large herds of Jerseys and Holsteins graze in the fields, and little else disturbs this area of the county's rural life.

Lodging & Dining in San Rafael

The **Panama Hotel,** 4 Bayview St., San Rafael, CA 94901 (☎ 415/457-3993, fax 415/457-4260), is a mixture of old and new. It consists of two 1910 homes that are connected by a garden patio, which gives the place a distinct tropical air. The 15 rooms are decorated individually, but most have canopy beds and clawfoot tubs in the bathrooms. Some, like Ken's Safari Room, have more atmosphere than others; it boasts a bed draped with mosquito netting, travel souvenirs, and ceiling fan. The Bordello room has French doors leading onto a tiny, vine-covered balcony. All have TV, telephone, and kitchenette. Six of the 15 rooms have shared baths. Room service is also available. A continental breakfast is included. The hotel has a restaurant.

Rates (incl. breakfast): $55 double with shared bath, $85–$135 double with a private bath.

THE POINT REYES PENINSULA

If you return from Bolinas to Route 1 and travel north, you'll pass through the Olema Valley, which is the location for several historic dairy ranches: Rancho Baulines–Wilkins, the Randall Ranch—which was staunchly operated by Sarah Randall after her husband's death, making her one of the few female ranchers in California—and several others. At the northern end of the valley sit the towns of **Olema** and **Point Reyes Station,** gateways to Point Reyes National Seashore.

For the record, Olema, a tiny town with a population of 125, just happened to be at the epicenter of the earthquake that struck San Francisco in 1906. Located at the junction of Sir Francis Drake Boulevard and the Shoreline Highway, the town had its heyday in the 1860s and '70s, when it functioned as an important transportation hub with biweekly stagecoach service to San Rafael and weekly steamer service to San Francisco. It fell into obscurity when the railroad passed it by. Today it's a quiet town with an attractive inn and a handful of stores.

A few miles farther up Route 1, Point Reyes Station is so named because this is where the North Pacific Coast Railroad built a depot in the 1870s. It was a stop on the railroad line that ran from Sausalito to Tomales, where freight trains were loaded with shellfish. Today it's only 3 blocks long with a population of 675 and is most famous for its unique noon and 6pm siren, which instead of a whistle is a long moo, an appropriate enough choice for a town at the heart of beef and dairy ranching country. The whistle, by the way, was donated by the George Lucas studio in nearby Nicasio.

While you're in Point Reyes, you might enjoy browsing some of the stores on Main Street, such as the **Black Mountain Weavers** (☎ 415/663-9130), which offers a full range of handwoven clothing, handknit sweaters, quilts, yarn, and painted silk garments, or dining at one of several restaurants, the best being the **Station House Cafe,** described in the dining section below.

Just north of Olema, turn left to reach the **Bear Valley Visitor Center** (☎ 415/663-1092), the headquarters of the 71,000-acre **Point Reyes National Seashore.** The center features displays about the ecology and geology of the peninsula, plus detailed information about the seashore. Additional visitor centers are found at **Drakes Beach** (☎ 415/669-1250) and also at the **Point Reyes Lighthouse** (☎ 415/669-1534). For additional information write to the Superintendent, Point Reyes National Seashore, Point Reyes Station, CA 94956. If you plan to do extensive hiking and camping, always check with the rangers about weather and conditions. Be prepared for fog, wind, and cold at any time of year. Hazards to watch out for include high tides that can suddenly cut you off while walking on the beach (always consult tide tables), heavy surf and rip currents, crumbling cliffs, plus deer ticks and poison oak.

The peninsula is a study in motion—especially geological motion—because it lies at the junction of two great tectonic plates. The peninsula rides high on the eastern edge of the Pacific plate, which creeps northwestward about 2 inches a year. The slower moving North American plate travels westward. In Olema Valley near the park headquarters, the two plates grind together along the San Andreas fault, and occasionally the pressure becomes so great between the two that the underlying rocks break and the surface moves, as it did in 1906 when it literally leaped 20 feet northwestward. If you want to get a clearer idea of what this means, then walk the 0.7-mile **Earthquake Trail** near the visitor center. Along the way, you'll see a fence with a 16-foot break in it, which was caused by the great quake.

Originally the peninsula was home to the Miwok Indians, who were the natives that greeted Sir Francis Drake as if he were a god when he came ashore in 1579 from the *Golden Hind*. It is believed that Sir Francis careened his ship for 6 weeks at Drakes Estero in what is now called Drakes Bay. Here the Indians crowned him with a feather headdress, and Drake, for his part, claimed the land for his Queen by planting a stake with a brass plate proclaiming it as *New Albion*. This brass plate was recovered only in 1937 in Greenbrae, south of San Rafael on the other side of the county. Nevertheless, it has been authenticated and is kept in the Bancroft Library at the University of California at Berkeley. Today, near the Bear Valley Visitor Center, you can visit **Kule Loklo** (☎ 415/663-1092), a replica of a coast Miwok Indian Village, complete with dwellings and a sweat lodge. Hours are the same as park hours, and admission is free.

Drake was followed by others, including Sebastian Rodriguez Cermeno, whose ship the *San Agustin* was wrecked on the coast, and Don Sebastian Vizcaino, who named the rocky headlands *La Punta de los Reyes* in 1603 when he sailed by on the day of the Feast of the Three Kings. Under Mexican rule the peninsula was held by three "Lords" of Point Reyes: James Berry, Rafael Garcia, and Antonio Osio. But after the United States conquest of California, Point Reyes ended up in the hands of Oscar and James Shafter, two lawyers from Vermont who subdivided the property into dozens of dairy ranches.

They fenced the land and provided tenants with buildings, land, and cows, then took in return a certain dollar amount for each cow plus one-fifth of the tenant's total number of cows in the form of calves. The dairy industry is still operating today with ranchers leasing the land back from the National Park Service, so you'll still see beef and dairy cattle roaming the flatlands of Point Reyes.

It's a little over 20 miles to the famous Point Reyes Lighthouse from the Bear Valley Visitor Center. Take Sir Francis Drake Boulevard north along the western shore of Tomales Bay to the sleepy town of **Inverness** (population 1,200), where the pier juts out into the bay and cabins and boathouses hover on stilts above the water. This 12½-mile-long bay is also known as Earthquake Bay because the San Andreas fault runs underneath, cutting across it all the way to Bolinas. At low tide the mud and eel grass attract abundant bird life, particularly herons. As you drive along Inverness Ridge through stands of bishop pines, keep an eye out for turkey vultures and sparrow hawks, also the osprey that are known to nest here.

From Inverness, Sir Francis Drake Boulevard curves around and takes you out along the Point Reyes peninsula, an amazing sight when you see it for the first time. You can't quite grasp that this landscape of magnificent rolling hills, so desolate and so isolated, can exist only 30 miles from the city. And you can't help but marvel at the way the hills roll on as far as the eye can see, on and on into the ocean. The peninsula is a thrilling place, especially brilliant in spring when it's covered with the colors of myriad wild flowers. And it's studded with the calm and comforting herds of cattle at all times of the year.

En route to the lighthouse you'll pass a number of historic ranches dating back to 1836, when Irishman James Berry and Mexican Rafael Garcia were given huge land grants ideal for cattle. You may want to stop in at **Johnson's Oyster Company,** 11171 Sir Francis Drake Blvd. (☎ 415/669-1149), to sample or purchase some of the local oysters. You can visit the incubation area and see the oysters being harvested.

Hours: Tues–Sun 8am–4pm.

At the end of this magnificent drive, the hike down the 300 steps to the **Point Reyes Lighthouse** (☎ 415/669-1534), which stands 290 feet above the surf, is bracing and thrilling. On the rocky platforms below you'll certainly see common murres, as well as sea lions and harbor seals on the offshore rocks. The best time to spot whales from here is December to April when they're en route to Baja or the Bering Sea. While you're here, walk around to the **Sea Lion Overlook.** The lighthouse, which opened in 1870, casts a beam of light that can be seen for 24 nautical miles—an engineering feat for that era.

Hours: Thurs–Mon, weather permitting. *Admission:* Free.

There are plenty of other scenic drives in the park. Instead of turning right to reach the lighthouse, you can turn left off Sir Francis Drake Boulevard to reach the parking lot for **Chimney Rock.** Hike the short trail, which is lined in spring with gold cup, footsteps o'spring, and mission bell. Along the trail you'll find an old **Coast Guard House** overlooking the undulating white cliffs of Drakes Bay, a harbor, and the bluffs of Chimney Rock at the entrance to Drakes Bay.

On the way down or back from either the lighthouse or Chimney Rock, you can also turn off Sir Francis Drake Boulevard to **Drakes Beach,** where you'll be able to walk under the white chalk cliffs and recall that moment in 1579 when Drake landed here. Facilities include a cafe and an information center. Or you can turn off at **Mount Vision Road,** which climbs more than 1,250 feet and provides magnificent panoramic views of the whole peninsula.

Instead of taking Sir Francis Drake Boulevard all the way to the lighthouse, you can also turn right a few miles outside of Inverness and access the 500-acre **Tomales Bay State Park,** which offers picnicking and swimming at Hearts Desire Beach and several other beaches, which are safe for swimming because they're on the bay and not the ocean.

Or you can continue on, taking Pierce Point Road out to the **Historic Pierce Point Ranch.** On the way you might want to stop and take the

Point Reyes National Seashore

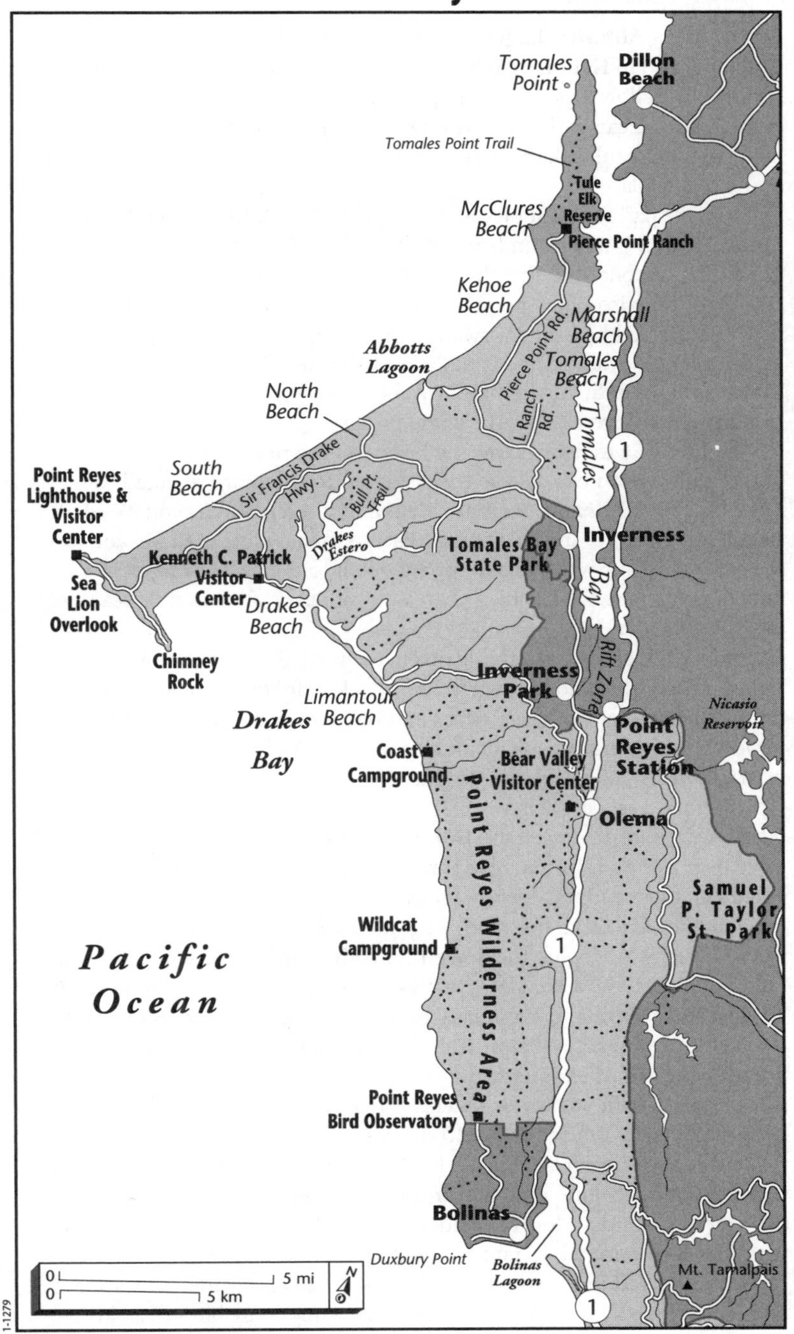

two trails to **Abbotts Lagoon,** which is good for canoeing and bird-watching, and to **Kehoe Beach,** where the surrounding hills are ablaze in spring with yellow lupines, iris, poppies, and tidy tips. At the end of Pierce Point Road you can park and hike down to **McClures Beach,** where you're likely to see the tule elk that roam the Tule Elk Reserve at the northern tip of the peninsula.

From the parking lot at McClures Beach you can also access the **Tomales Point Trail,** a 7-mile roundtrip hike that takes you out to Tomales Bluff and Point. On one side stretches the Pacific Ocean, on the other Tomales Bay. This trail also offers good views of the ocean's Bird Rock. In spring you'll be dazzled by brilliant swathes of golden lupines.

Another enjoyable drive is the trip from Bear Valley Visitor Center to **Limantour Beach.** At the beach, walk west along the spit towards the **Limantour Estero** to view the shorebirds.

The best way to really savor the beauty of the place is to hike as many of the trails as you can. These will lead you to the more remote beaches like **Sculptured Beach, Kelham Beach** and **Arch Rock,** and **Wildcat Beach** and the bays around **Drakes Estero.** At a couple of these, you can see quite dramatic waterfalls dropping down to the beach. The most well known is Alamere Falls, which is on Wildcat Beach about a mile south of the camping area.

Among the short trails that deliver real rewards is the 4½-mile **Bear Valley Trail,** which goes down to Arch Rock. It follows Bear Valley Creek through a forest of Douglas fir, bay, and buckeye trees and crosses Divide Meadow, which is a fine picnicking spot. From Arch Rock you can either return or access a variety of other trails.

One mile east of Olema off Sir Francis Drake Boulevard, mountain bikers will want to travel the **Bolinas Ridge Trail,** which crosses the ridge over rolling hills that give thrilling views and a wonderful sense of openness and freedom. Eleven miles brings you to the Bolinas–Fairfax Road. Before you reach this road, there are two offshoots providing access west to Highway 1 plus the **Jewell** and **Shafter trails,** which go east linking up with the **Cross Marin Bike Path** into 2800-acre **Samuel P. Taylor State Park** and eventually back to Sir Francis Drake Boulevard.

The flora and fauna that inhabit this peninsula are extraordinary. The terrain varies from shore and wetlands to grassland, prairie, and forest sheltering a terrific variety of species. In fact more than 750 plants have been identified and more than 430 species of birds. Each season brings its particular joys. Spring is heralded by the wildflowers and the osprey's cry, winter by the croaking choirs of frogs in November. Winter is the great time for shorebirds. Plovers, sanderlings, curlews, willets, and godwits work the wetlands, while raptors—red-tailed hawks, American kestrels, black shouldered kites, and many others—feed on the abundant rodent population. Spring and fall are the times to see migrating birds of all kinds, though migrants drop in year-round. By March black brants are arriving, and later they are joined by swallows, several varieties of warblers, and pelicans in May.

About 130 species of birds breed on the peninsula, among them, cormorants at Chimney and Arch Rocks, murres at Stormy Stack, Point Resistance, and the rocks below the Lighthouse, and osprey along Inverness Ridge. Genuine nature lovers will want to sign up for one of the workshops offered by **Point Reyes Field Seminars** (☎ 415/663-1200), which cover everything, from tide-pooling and wildflowers to mushrooms and raptors, plus photography and art. Fees range from $32 for day-long seminars to $155 for weekends that include dormitory accommodations.

Other highlights of the area include the **Morgan Horse Ranch,** where the light horses used widely on cattle ranches and in the park system are bred and trained. Currently the ranch operates no formal interpretive programs, but you can visit the ranch and walk a self-guided tour to learn about the characteristics and history of this famous American breed.

After you have explored the Point Reyes Peninsula, you can return to Route 1 and travel north along the eastern shore of Tomales Bay to the town of **Marshall,** home of the Marshall Boatworks and also of **oyster farming.** The latter started in 1875 and continues today. You can stop in at the **Tomales Bay Oyster Company** or the **Hog Island Oyster Company** and select from the many tanks of different kinds of oysters selling for $6 to $8 a dozen. See if you can taste the difference between those that are raised traditionally on a submerged string (at the former) and those raised in net-like bags that sit on the bottom of the bay (at the latter). Or else stop at one of the roadside stands offering barbecued oysters.

The bay is also known for herring, which arrive in shoals in the evening. It's rumored too that great white sharks come into the bay to give birth to their young, although that doesn't seem to deter the surfers who come to Millerton Beach in Tomales Bay State Park.

Four miles north of Marshall, **Tomales** was a boomtown in the 1870s when it functioned as an entrepôt from which boats carried butter and potatoes to San Francisco. The boats were soon replaced by railroad cars, which in turn were closed down in 1930. So Tomales became the ghost town that it is today, with the most frontier-style Victorian buildings in West Marin, some with boardwalks out front.

Lodging & Dining on the Point Reyes Peninsula

Lodging in Olema

The Olema Inn, 10000 Sir Francis Drake Blvd. at Highway 1, Olema, CA 94950 (☎ 415/663-9559), is an historic inn with a lovely alfresco courtyard dining area overlooking the fragrant trellised gardens. The inn originally opened in 1876 and functioned for many years as a stagecoach inn. It has been very nicely restored. The rooms, all upstairs on the second floor, feature Victorian-style oak beds and other similar furnishings.

The **restaurant** offers California Mediterranean cuisine featuring such dishes as fettucine primavera, pork tenderloin with shiitake mushroom cognac cream sauce, grilled tenderloin with a pinot noir sauce, and baked salmon with a sun-dried tomato, lemon, and caper butter. To start, you can always expect to find at least a couple of oyster dishes. Prices range from $13.50 to $19.

Rates: $115–$135 double weekends, $105–$115 midweek. *Dining Hours:* Tues–Sun 11am–3pm and daily 5–9pm.

Roundstone Farm, 9940 Sir Francis Drake Blvd., Olema, CA 94950 (☎ 415/663-1020), stands on 10 acres with views of Mount Wittenberg, the Olema Valley, and Tomales Bay. The property was designed and built as a bed-and-breakfast, which means it has all the comforts and amenities that travelers need. There are five rooms, four with fireplaces. Each is furnished with large armoires and beds that have down comforters and are also well-lit for reading. Fresh flowers and art add decorative accents. It's a pleasure to lounge in the large skylit common room curled up around the wood-burning stove or to relax on the adjacent deck, which overlooks the pond and the pastures where the innkeepers raise their horses. Games and books are available. A full breakfast is served either inside or on the patio.

Rates (incl. breakfast): $135 double weekends, $120 midweek.

Lodging in Port Reyes Station

The **Holly Tree Inn,** 3 Silverhills Rd, P.O. Box 642, Point Reyes Station, CA 94956 (☎ 415/663-1554), stands at the end of a long, tree-lined drive. There are four rooms, all with private baths, and a cottage. They are decorated in Laura Ashley style in different color schemes. The Ivy Room has a spool bed and ruffled curtains in pink and white tones. Mary's Garden Room opens onto a patio and has a private entrance and fireplace, too. The cottage has pine floors, fireplace, stereo, and comfortable furnishings; its bathroom features an old fashioned tub. Guests can relax in the lawn chairs in the front yard and listen to a nearby creek or gather around the brick fireplace in the living room on cold nights. A full breakfast is served.

There are also a couple of cottages for rent that are more separate from the main house. Sea Star, located at the end of a long dock, sits on stilts over the waters of Tomales Bay and is suitable only for two. It has a wood-burning stove, comfortable furnishings, and a fully equipped kitchen and solarium with hot tub. The bedroom has a four-poster bed. The other, Vision, is located among pines with a view of Mount Vision. It has a Franklin fireplace in the living room, which is furnished with wicker and other country pieces. Two outdoor decks invite guests to relax and contemplate the woods. There's also a hot tub. The two bedrooms have pine beds sporting quilts and down comforters.

Rates (incl. breakfast): $130–$155 double; $185 cottage; $240 Sea Star; $210 Vision.

Thirty Nine Cypress, 39 Cypress Rd., P.O. Box 176, Point Reyes Station, CA 94956 (☎ 415/663-1709), a weathered wood building, is set on 3½ acres on a bluff overlooking Tomales Bay with an equally alluring rear vista overlooking the cattle-dotted meadows of a 600-acre ranch. Owner Julia Bartlett is a keen naturalist, and she will gladly share her knowledge of the area. She lives in the adjacent house. The redwood interior is decorated with family antiques including Oriental rugs. There are three rooms plus a cute garden cottage. Two rooms are small, the third more spacious with a view out over the bay. The cottage has a bedroom, partial kitchen equipped with microwave and refrigerator, and a small sitting area with fireplace. Other comforts include a fireplace in the parlor and an eclectic library. Patios and a secluded hot tub face over the bluff. Guests enjoy a full breakfast of fresh local eggs, cheese, and homemade sausage while they look out over the marshland.

Rates (incl. breakfast): $120–$160 double; $160 garden cottage.

Point Reyes Country Inn & Stables, P.O. Box 501, Point Reyes Station, CA 94956 (☎ 415/663-9696), is located on 4 acres. It's an attractive, modern accommodation that has inviting patios sheltered by trellises covered in passion flower vines, a comfortable parlor with fireplace, plus five rooms, each with a private bath. The rooms are eclectically furnished, and all have either private balconies or little private gardens of their own. If you have a horse, you can bring it with you and board it in one of the ten stalls for $15 more.

Rates: $105–$160 double weekends, $75–$150 midweek.

Dining Only in Point Reyes Station

The Station House Cafe, 11180 Main St. (☎ 415/663-1515), seems to be the focal point for local gatherings. The dining room is large, there's a separate bar, and the whole place buzzes with life. The menu is vast and offers breakfast, lunch, and dinner. In the morning, come for the huevos rancheros and omelets; at lunch time, there are fine soups, salads, sandwiches, and dishes like chili and fish and chips to keep you going. At dinner, the atmosphere is more subdued, and the menu will announce a variety of specials. For example, there might be halibut with tarragon vinaigrette or chicken breast with rhubarb chutney in addition to the time-tested favorites, fettucine with local mussels in tomato, garlic, and white wine; meatloaf with garlic mashed potatoes; or turkey and black bean chili with delicious cornbread. Prices at dinner range from $7 to $18.

Hours: Sun–Thurs 8am–9pm, Fri–Sat 8am–10pm. Late supper is served in the bar until 10pm Sun–Thurs, until 11pm Fri–Sat.

Lodging & Dining in Inverness

The **Blackthorne Inn,** 266 Vallejo Ave, P.O. Box 712, Inverness, CA 94937 (☎ 415/663-8621), located in a lovely home crafted from redwood, cedar, and Douglas fir with a turret and an octagonal tower, is a very appealing place. It's set on a quiet side road surrounded by trees and enhanced by pretty gardens. It's like an extra-large treehouse, but a spectacular one that incorporates stained glass windows designed by Julia Morgan and beams that were salvaged from the San Francisco piers. The spine of the house is the spiral staircase that connects the five floors. The most romantic room in the place is the Eagle's Nest at the very top of the staircase. Octagonally shaped, enclosed by glass, and with a private sundeck on top, this tower room lets you imagine that you're sleeping under the stars. The Overlook and the Lupin rooms, both on the third floor, share a bath. The Overlook has two small balconies. On the first floor, Hideaway and Forest View also share a bathroom. The latter has a separate sitting room and a private deck. Both are furnished nicely with wicker pieces, floral fabrics, and modern prints. Guests enjoy the second-floor living room with giant stone fireplace, skylights, and an adjacent 3,500-square-foot deck. A buffet breakfast is served at 9:30am. Facilities include a hot tub on the upper deck.

Rates (incl. breakfast): $110–$205 double.

Manka's Inverness Lodge, 30 Caldendar Way, off Argyll Street, P.O. Box 1110, Inverness, CA 94937 (☎ 415/669-1034), is loaded with atmosphere. It was built as a hunting lodge at the turn of the century, and the trophies still grace the walls of the dark, firelit dining room. There are two rooms in the lodge itself with large decks overlooking Tomales Bay. Among the furnishings you might find a log bed, lamp stands carved into the shape of a wild boar, animal skin rugs, and similar hunting lodge pieces. Other accommodations include two cabins with fireplaces and additional rooms in a redwood annex.

The prime attraction is the **restaurant,** which is known for its game and local fish dishes, which are often grilled in the fireplace. A typical menu might feature wild Canadian pheasant with a Madeira jus accompanied by wild huckleberry jam, or swordfish grilled in the fireplace and served with a sweet red pepper broth, braised spinach, and apple cherry chutney. The highlights among the appetizers might be homemade wild boar sausage served with black pepper polenta and dried fruit mustard, a flavorsome quartet of wild mushrooms—tree oak, yellow foot, black trumpet, and shiitake—or local sweetwaters on the half shell with champagne mignonette. Prices range from $19 to $24.

Rates: $125–$275 double. *Dining Hours:* Thurs–Mon 6–8:30pm; in January Fri–Sat only, and in February Thurs–Sun only.

Dancing Coyote Beach, 12794 Sir Francis Drake Blvd., P.O. Box 98, Inverness, CA 94937 (☎ 415/669-7200), is as the name suggests right down on Tomales Bay. The accommodations are in four very appealing, modern cottages. Acacia, Birch, and Beach are two-story cottages with cathedral ceilings, living rooms, bedrooms, and decks. Skye is a smaller studio with a loft bed and large deck. Each is lit by a skylight and has a galley kitchen, fireplace, and great views of the bay. There's a private beach with barbecue facilities for guests. This is a great value.

Rates: $105–$135 double.

Ten Inverness Way, 1904 Redwood Jungle, P.O. Box 63, Inverness, CA 94937 (☎ 415/669-1648), is located on a quiet street just off Sir Francis Drake Boulevard, a block from Tomales Bay. Enter via the wisteria-covered porch and go up into the very inviting living room, where you can curl up on the sofas in front of the fire and take down a book to read. The rooms, all with private bath, are comfortably furnished with attention paid to such details as good lighting over the bed and a reading lamp placed beside an armchair, as well as a night light, cotton robe, and sewing kit in the bathroom. You'll also find fresh flowers, perhaps a small bouquet of sweet williams in a stoneware jar, in each room. The carved beds are covered with country quilts. There's also a suite with private patio and kitchen. A bountiful breakfast is served—buttermilk spice coffeecake, scrambled eggs with cheese and basil, plus fruits and juices. Out back in the garden you'll also find a hot tub in a tiny wooden building. Guests here enjoy the peace and the opportunity to enjoy the quieter pleasures like reading at the end of a day spent hiking and communing with nature.

Rates (incl. breakfast): $135–$175 double.

Tucked away around the corner from Ten Inverness Way is **Hotel Inverness,** 25 Park Ave., next to the Library and the Jack Mason Museum, P.O. Box 780, Inverness, CA 94937 (☎ 415/669-7393), which was established as a hotel in 1906. Tom and Susie Simms, who are the current proprietors, spent 7 years renovating the property themselves. Originally the building had four stories, but today there are only two. The five rooms are all located off the central hallway upstairs, which means that guests have a little more privacy than in most bed-and-breakfasts. Two of the rooms also have private decks. An expanded continental breakfast will be brought to your room. The acre of grounds provides a lawn for picnicking and playing croquet.

Rates (incl. breakfast): $110–$150 double.

Point Reyes Peninsula
Special & Recreational Activities

Beaches: Five beaches on the Point Reyes Peninsula are accessible by car (although they may require a short hike from the parking lot): **Limantour, Drakes, South Point Reyes, North Point Reyes,** and **McClure's.** Although you can swim at your own risk at Limantour and Drakes Beach, most of the beaches here are reserved for walking and tide-pooling because the water is too cold and the wind and currents much too strong for swimming. The first four beaches are large and sandy. McClures is a small, lovely beach at the mouth of a narrow ravine and is closed off at each end by rocky bluffs. Hike-in beaches include Wildcat, Kelham, Sculptured, and Santa Maria beaches. Sculptured Beach is just that—sandstone that has been sculpted by the wind and water into caves, tunnels, and amphitheaters.

The Tomales Bay beaches are the best and safest for swimming and great for clamming. The most popular is **Heart's Desire** in Tomales Bay State Park. Other bay beaches include **Indian, Pebble, Shell,** and **Marshall Beaches.**

Biking: For bikes contact **Trailhead Rentals** in Olema (☎ 415/663-1958). The Bolinas Ridge Trail is popular with mountain-bikers and links to the Cross Marin Trail, another good bike route.

Bird-watching: At **Point Reyes Bird Observatory,** 4990 Shoreline Hwy., Stinson Beach (☎ 415/868-1221 or 415/868-0655), 3 miles north of Bolinas. A year-round netting and banding program is in operation daily from April to Thanksgiving, and on Wednesday, Saturday, and Sunday in winter. Visitors are welcome. It's best to go early in the day if you can.

The other major birder's mecca is the **Audubon Canyon Ranch,** 49000 Shoreline Hwy. (☎ 415/868-9244), where in-season visitors can observe from above great blue herons and egrets nesting on the tops of trees above the Bolinas lagoon or Olema marsh. Here you will see signs posted that read: "Quiet Birds Nesting." All kinds of woodland, shore, and water birds can be viewed here around the Bolinas lagoon. The Ranch is open from mid-March through mid-July Sat–Sun and holidays 10am–4pm.

Point Reyes is the state's premier birding spot, boasting some 430 recorded species. The best times are spring and fall, although there are plenty of species year-round. The ridge offers several different habitats, and practically any trail you pick will be rewarding, even the short loop trails near the visitor center. The best spot for viewing shore and water birds is at Drakes Estero. Take the road to Limantour Beach, then walk west along the spit for a view of the marshes and herons, grebes, loons, terns, ducks, egrets, and many more. Osprey are known to nest along the Inverness Ridge. Other regularly sighted species include cormorants, red-shouldered hawks, black oystercatchers, black turnstones, Greater and Lesser scaups, common murres, great horned owls, and many more. A lot of so-called vagrants are also spotted here—birds that have been blown off course or strayed from their normal routes.

Tomales Point is great for viewing raptors and seabirds, including those that inhabit Bird Rock—brown and American white pelicans, black oystercatchers, terns, cormorants. Ashy storm-petrels nest here too, but don't expect to see them. Tomales Bay State Park also attracts plenty of waterbirds as well as forest birds and is known for spotted owls. Abbott's Lagoon and the trails to Kehoe and McClures Beach are also great birding spots.

For additional information ask at **Bear Valley Visitor Center** (☎ 415/663-1093).

Camping: There are four hike-in campgrounds. **Coast** and **Wildcat** are both on the coast, the latter above the beach of the same name. **Sky Camp** and **Glen Camp** are in the woods and protected from the damp fogs. Permits are required, and you're limited to 4 nights. Call the **Bear Valley Visitor Center** for details (☎ 415/663-1093).

There are also sites in **Samuel P. Taylor State Park** (☎ 415/488-9897).

Hiking: Trail highlights, such as the Bear Valley Trail to Arch Rock, the Estero Trail, and Tomales Point Trail, are described above.

Horseback Riding: Five Brooks Stables, 8001 State Rd. 1, Olema (☎ 415/663-1570), offers the following trail rides: 1 hour ($20), 2 hours ($35), half day ($60), and all day ($85). Overnight rides cost $100 per horse per day, including camping gear and guide.

State Parks: Tomales Bay State Park offers picnicking and swimming. Samuel P. Taylor State Park has regular camp sites plus equestrian sites.

Whale Watching: The Point Reyes Lighthouse is a favorite spot to watch for whales.

The Napa Valley

Distance in Miles: Napa, 55; Oakville & Rutherford, 68; Yountville, 70; St. Helena, 73; Calistoga, 81

Estimated Driving Times: 1¼ hours to Napa at the beginning of the Napa Valley, another 40 minutes on to Calistoga at its end

---

Driving: From San Francisco you can reach the Napa Valley either via the Bay Bridge and Highway 80, which you follow to Vallejo, where you turn onto Route 29, which goes into the town of Napa. Or you can take the Golden Gate Bridge and Highway 101 to Highway 37; turn onto Highway 121, which you follow as it becomes Highway 12/121 and finally merges into Highway 29 at the town of Napa.

Further Information: For information on the entire Napa Valley wine-producing region, contact the **Napa Valley Conference and Visitors' Bureau,** 1310 Napa Town Center, Napa, CA 94559 (☎ 707/226-7459).

For information on individual towns, you can contact the **Napa Chamber of Commerce,** 1556 First St., Napa, CA 94559 (☎ 707/226-7455); the **Yountville Chamber of Commerce,** P.O. Box 2064, 6516 Yount St., Yountville, CA 94599 (☎ 707/944-0904); the **St. Helena Chamber of Commerce,** P.O. Box 124, 1010A Main St., St. Helena, CA 94574 (☎ 707/963-4456); and the **Calistoga Chamber of Commerce,** 1458 Lincoln Ave. #9, Calistoga, CA 94515 (☎ 707/942-6333).

Napa is celebrated for wine, wine, wine, and food, food, food, and a very sensual hedonistic experience it is indeed. Robert Louis Stevenson seems to have realized this when he wrote in *The Silverado Squatters,* "Those lodes and pockets of earth, more precious than the precious ores, that yield inimitable fragrance and soft fire, those virtuous bonanzas, where the soil has sublimated under sun and stars to something finer, and the wine is bottled poetry: these still lie undiscovered." Even though there is increasing commercialization and huge numbers of visitors to the region—especially on weekends—it's still a beautiful place to visit. More dramatic than Sonoma, the contours of the land, the physical beauty of the

Events & Festivals to Plan Your Trip Around

February/March: The **Mustard Festival** is celebrated throughout February and March. A variety of events—world championships of mustard, mustard parades, mustard tastings, mustard fun runs, and more—are scheduled on weekends at various locales. Call ☎ 707/259-9020 for information.

June: The **Napa Valley Wine Auction** at Meadowood is a star-studded vintner's charity event that extends over 3 days. Tickets cost astronomical prices—more than $500—and allow the holder to bid on wines and attend a series of events. Call ☎ 707/963-5246 for information.

July: The **Napa County Fair** is like any other county fair with lots of entertainment and street food. Napa, though, also has sprint car racing on their dirt track, which draws big crowds. The fair is held at the Calistoga Fairgrounds. Call ☎ 707/942-5111 for information.

July/August: The **Robert Mondavi Summer Music Festival** kicks off traditionally on July 4 with a performance by the Preservation Hall Jazz Band. Past artists have ranged from Judy Collins to Johnny Mathis. Call ☎ 707/963-9617 for information.

September: The **Napa River Festival** includes a concert given by the Napa Symphony on a barge at the Third Street bridge in the town of Napa. Art, entertainment, food, and crafts add to the celebration. Folks watch the concert from their boats, too.

October: The **TransAmerica PGA Senior Gold Tournament** is held at the Silverado Country Club. Call ☎ 707/257-0200 for information.

November/December: The **Festival of Lights** in Yountville, when the village is lit by millions of little white lights, is quite a sight. Call ☎ 707/944-0904 for more information.

vineyards and wineries, and the quality of the light all contribute to the pleasures of being in the Napa Valley.

Soil, climate, and exposure to the elements have all combined to make the Napa Valley perfect for wine cultivation. The first wineries were developed in the late 1800s by such pioneers as Charles Krug, who established the first commercial winery of any size at Napa in 1861. He employed and trained many other wine makers who went on to develop wineries of their own, men like Jacob Beringer and Karl Wente, whose names are still familiar in the valley today.

Jacob Schram founded the first hillside winery in 1862, a few miles south of Calistoga at the end of Schramsberg Road. Robert Louis Stevenson thought highly enough of Schram's wines to devote a whole chapter to the winery in *The Silverado Squatters*, which he researched in 1880 when he brought his bride Fannie Osbourne to what is now Robert Louis Stevenson State Park on Highway 29, about 7½ miles northeast of Calistoga. Back then, there was a silver mine in the area and a small town with about 1,500 inhabitants.

Yountville is named after another pioneer, George Calvert Yount, who was born in North Carolina and traveled west via Missouri to California. He built an adobe house near the current intersection of Cook Road and Yount Mill Road in 1837, as well as a grist and saw mill several years later. He received the 12,000-acre Caymus land grant, one of the first grants made by the Mexicans in 1836, and planted his first vineyard in 1838 just north of Napa. Today his grave can be found at Lincoln and Jackson streets in Yountville.

The Inglenook vineyard was planted at Rutherford in the early 1870s and was later taken over by sea captain Gustav Niebaum, who established the vineyard as the benchmark for quality in the valley. The earliest winery buildings were those of Inglenook, Greystone (later Christian Brothers, and now part of the Culinary Institute of America), Chateau Chevalier, Chateau Montelena—all designed in the French style—and Beringer, which was modeled on a Rhenish property.

Frederick and Jacob Beringer, brothers from Mainz Germany, founded their winery in 1876, and it has never ceased operations, not even during Prohibition. The Beringer brothers dug long, underground wine tunnels to maintain the temperature at a constant 58 degrees. Other early comers included Spring Mountain Winery and Trefethen (originally called Eshcol).

These enthusiastic beginnings, though, were cut off during Prohibition, when many wineries were forced to close, although some survived on the production of grapes and the making of sacramental wine, which was still allowed. Mondavi, in fact, thrived. Beaulieu and Wente Brothers produced medicinal and sacred wines. After Prohibition ended in 1933, large cooperative wineries continued to produce unexceptional jug wines with little concern for quality—the dreadful, generic sauterne and chablis.

Slowly, though, some vintners began to pay attention to making quality wines under varietal designations, something that Frank Schoonmaker, a wine maker himself and one of the first writers to champion California wines, had encouraged Beaulieu, Inglenook, Krug, and Martini to do. Still, it took more than 30 years before Napa became a true wine region. In the 1950s there were still only a couple dozen wineries; today there are more than 200—and 35,000 acres of vines. Back then, one or two people attempted to make quality wines that were properly barrel aged—vintners like Andre Tchelistcheff at Beaulieu and Myron Nightingale at Cresta Blanc and later at Beringer.

The first major breakthrough came in 1966 when the Mondavi brothers, who owned the Charles Krug winery, had a huge disagreement, which

Napa Valley

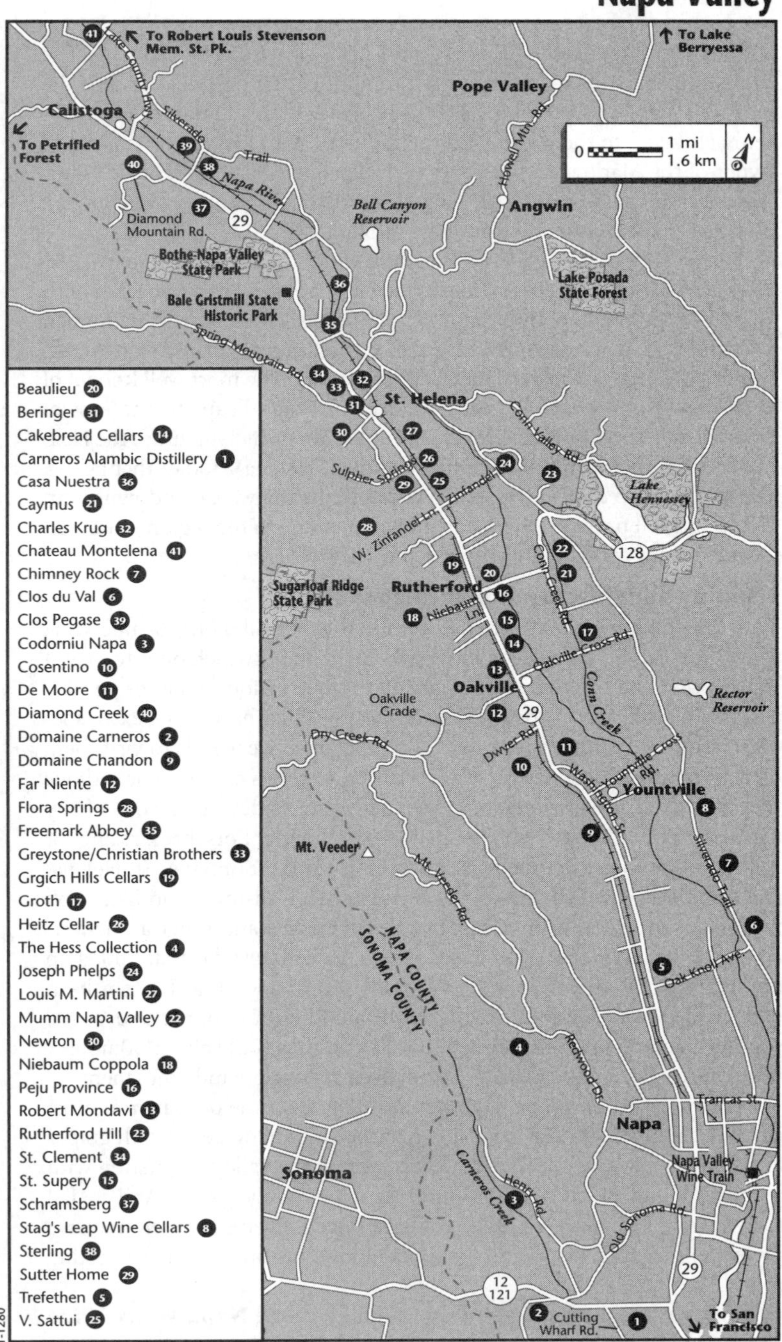

To Robert Louis Stevenson Mem. St. Pk.
To Lake Berryessa
Pope Valley
Calistoga
To Petrified Forest
Lake County Hwy.
Silverado Trail
Howell Mtn. Rd.
1 mi
1.6 km
Napa River
Diamond Mountain Rd.
Bell Canyon Reservoir
Angwin
Bothe-Napa Valley State Park
Bale Gristmill State Historic Park
Lake Posada State Forest
Spring Mountain Rd.
St. Helena
Conn Valley Rd.
Sulpher Springs
Zinfandel
W. Zinfandel Ln.
Lake Hennessey
128
Conn Creek Rd.
Sugarloaf Ridge State Park
Rutherford
Niebaum Ln.
Oakville Cross Rd.
Oakville
Conn Creek
Rector Reservoir
Oakville Grade
29
Dry Creek Rd.
Dwyer Rd.
Yountville Cross Rd.
Washington St.
Yountville
Mt. Veeder
Mt. Veeder Rd.
Silverado Trail
Napa County
Sonoma County
Oak Knoll Ave.
Redwood Dr.
Trancas St.
Napa
Sonoma
Napa Valley Wine Train
Carneros Creek
Henry Rd.
Old Sonoma Rd.
12
121
Cutting Wharf Rd.
To San Francisco
Beaulieu 20
Beringer 31
Cakebread Cellars 14
Carneros Alambic Distillery 1
Casa Nuestra 36
Caymus 21
Charles Krug 32
Chateau Montelena 41
Chimney Rock 7
Clos du Val 6
Clos Pegase 39
Codorniu Napa 3
Cosentino 10
De Moore 11
Diamond Creek 40
Domaine Carneros 2
Domaine Chandon 9
Far Niente 12
Flora Springs 28
Freemark Abbey 35
Greystone/Christian Brothers 33
Grgich Hills Cellars 19
Groth 17
Heitz Cellar 26
The Hess Collection 4
Joseph Phelps 24
Louis M. Martini 27
Mumm Napa Valley 22
Newton 30
Niebaum Coppola 18
Peju Province 16
Robert Mondavi 13
Rutherford Hill 23
St. Clement 34
St. Supery 15
Schramsberg 37
Stag's Leap Wine Cellars 8
Sterling 38
Sutter Home 29
Trefethen 5
V. Sattui 25
1-1280

resulted in Robert leaving Krug to start his own winery in Oakville. The rival Mondavis traveled the country promoting their products, and by the early '70s Napa was becoming a "hot" property with all kinds of entrepreneurs attracted to the region and the industry, men like Bruce Markham, owner of the Markham Winery in St. Helena, and Jack Cakebread. They came despite the obstacles that ranged from drought to taxes and complex laws that made marketing extremely difficult.

The real breakthrough though for the wines themselves came in 1976 when a Chateau Montelena Chardonnay and a Stag's Leap Cabernet both topped their French counterparts in a blind tasting in Paris. The French were stunned. By the early '80s the region was internationally recognized. The Napa Valley now has 10 official appellations. The most well known of these are—from south to north—Carneros, Stag's Leap (to the east of Yountville), Oakville, Rutherford, Mount Veeder (which includes the Hess Collection), and Spring Mountain (west of St. Helena). Today, thanks to a measure approved by voters in 1990 that limits the way a landowner can divide and sell property, the future of winemaking in the region is assured for the benefit of all—winegrowers and visitors.

Planning Your Weekends in the Napa Valley

With 200-plus wineries to choose from in this 30-mile-long, 5-mile-wide valley, you can quickly become overwhelmed about which ones to visit. I suggest that you limit your wine tasting to three or four wineries per day as a maximum. The list below selects about 40 that have some extra special reason for visiting, and it would take 10 or so weekends to visit them all at a leisurely pace. After a while, visiting wineries can become tedious unless you're a real aficionado, so you may want to devote one day of any weekend to another activity like ballooning, biking, horseback riding, or hiking. Don't forget the interesting stores in Napa, Yountville, St. Helena, and Calistoga. Then there is the enjoyment of a Calistoga mud bath. You will also want to drop in to some of the museums and other attractions along the way. Whatever you choose to do, given the traffic that builds up on Highway 29 on weekends, you're advised to anchor at the northern end of the valley on 1 weekend, in the middle on another, and at the southern end on another. While the valley is short (only about 30 miles), negotiating traffic will take away from your relaxation and enjoyment.

As far as seasons go, Napa is wonderful at any time of year. You must come at least once for the harvest, when the vines hang heavy with grapes and there is a festive air everywhere. In spring the valley is bursting with a yellow cloud of mustard. In summer it positively glows. And in fall the vines are brilliant with rusts, golds, and reds. Even in winter you have the benefit of open vistas and far fewer elbows jostling you in the tasting rooms.

On your first weekend you may want to take the **Napa Valley Wine Train,** 1275 McKinstry St., Napa (☎ 707/253-2111), which runs from Napa north to St. Helena in a 36-mile round-trip that takes 3 hours. The train began operating in 1989 along the old Southern Pacific tracks and has caused a great deal of controversy—indeed opposition—from many valley residents, who feel that the train is another tourist intrusion that is turning their historic towns into trashy tinseltowns. For this reason, for a long time the train was not allowed to stop at any of the wineries, and your experience was limited to sitting back and enjoying the passing view (but what a view!) and dining on an elegant lunch, dinner, or brunch accompanied by fine California wines. Along the way, diners would glimpse Trefethen, Domaine Chandon, Robert Mondavi, Cakebread Cellars, Niebaum Coppola, and other wineries without stopping. Now, Monday through Friday, passengers can stop at Grgich Hills Cellars winery for a private, hour-long tour for an additional $4. More stops are planned in the future, too. Reservations are a necessity.

The dining cars are comfortable, with plush swivel chairs, spacious tables, and attractive table settings. The food is well prepared, with such dishes as chicken breast marinated in herbs and white wine and served with wild mushrooms and brandy sauce, or filet mignon with a cabernet and Roquefort sauce, or poached salmon in a saffron sauce. On the lunch-time train only, you can also just ride the train ($25) and sample the wines in the wine-tasting car and the fare in the deli car. The fixed-price brunch or lunch is $63; dinner is $69.50 (prices include the train fare).

Visiting the Wineries

It would take a couple of months or more to visit all the wineries in the valley at a leisurely pace. Below, you will find a list of about 40 wineries notable for something other than their wines—architecture, art, gardens, tours, historic buildings, special events, and more. Most are open daily 10am to 5pm (some only until 4pm), and most charge anywhere from $3 to $7 for tasting. If you really want to take a tour of a particular winery, call ahead to ascertain the time and frequency of tours so you won't be disappointed.

The wineries are listed starting from Napa at the southern end of the valley and ending in Calistoga at the northern end. The ideal number to visit in 1 day is three to four.

For additional information and a free map of the wineries, write or call the **Napa Valley Vintners Association,** Box 141, St. Helena, CA 94574 (☎ 800/982-1371).

In Napa

Carneros Alambic Distillery, 1250 Cuttings Wharf Rd., Napa, CA 94559 (☎ 707/253-9055), is a maker of brandy, so this place makes a pleasant change from the usual winery. The tour explains the art of brandy making.

Chimney Rock, 5350 Silverado Trail, Napa, CA 94558 (☎ 707/257-2641), is open daily for tours and tastings. It has a hospitality center where food and wine seminars and other events are held. Tours and tastings are conducted daily.

Clos du Val, 5330 Silverado Trail, Napa, CA 94558 (☎ 707/259-2200), was founded in 1972 by John Goelet and Bernard Portet. Check out the cartoons in the tasting room after the informative tour. Tours and tastings are conducted daily.

Codorniu Napa, 1345 Henry Rd., Napa, CA 94559 (☎ 707/224-1668), is located in an eye-catching complex with sloping outer walls and dramatic sail-like windows. Both the terrace and visitor center afford great views of the surrounding countryside. A walkway stretches across the production facility enabling visitors to see the whole production process going on down below. There's also a museum and art gallery. Tours and tastings are conducted daily.

Domaine Carneros, 1240 Duhig Rd., Napa, CA 94581 (☎ 707/257-0101). From Route 121 you can't miss Domaine Carneros, located on a hillside in a dramatic, 18th-century–style chateau fronted by a marble staircase. It's modeled on the Château de la Marquetterie, an estate owned by the Taittinger family, who were the chief founders of this winery producing sparkling wines. The interior is decked out in Louis XVI style. Guests can sit in the tasting room and enjoy a glass of wine to the accompaniment of classical music while taking in the glorious view. Tours and tastings are conducted daily.

Hakusan Sake Gardens, 1 Executive Way, Napa, CA 94558 (☎ 707/258-6160), offers daily sake tasting plus a video about its production. The sake is produced from rice grown in the Sacramento Valley.

The Hess Collection, 4411 Redwood Rd., P.O. Box 4140, Napa, CA 94558 (☎ 707/255-1144), is as famous for its art collection—more than 100 works by Francis Bacon, Robert Motherwell, Frank Stella, and other modern artists—as for its wine. The original building dates to 1903 and was the Christian Brothers' first winery.

Stag's Leap Wine Cellars, 5766 Silverado Trail, Napa, CA 94558 (☎ 707/944-2020), was started in 1970 by University of Chicago political scientist Warren Winiarski, who really put California wines on the map when his cabernet knocked out the French wines at a competition. Open daily for tours and tastings.

Trefethen, 11160 Oak Knoll Ave., Napa CA 94558 (☎ 707/255 7700), is the second-oldest wooden winery in the valley. The redwood building was built in 1886. Originally the Eshcol Winery, the Trefethens changed the name when they purchased it in 1968. Tours by appointment; open daily.

In Yountville

Cosentino, 7415 St. Helena Hwy., Yountville, CA 94599 (☎ 707/944-1220). Go for the wines. Tastings are offered daily.

Domaine Chandon, 1 California Dr., Yountville, CA 94599 (☎ 707/944-2280), offers an excellent tour and also has such extras as a museum and restaurant. It was established in 1973 by Moët Hennessy of France. The buildings are attractively designed and landscaped with ponds and waterfowl. There are also some very appealing picnic grounds. Tours and tastings are conducted daily in summer, Wednesday through Sunday only in winter. There are also a variety of musical performances scheduled, sometimes weekdays, other times weekends. Call for information.

In Oakville

De Moor, 7481 St. Helena Hwy., Oakville, CA 94562 (☎ 707/944-2565), is remarkable for its geodesic tasting room. There's a pleasant picnic area. However, no tours are offered.

Far Niente, 1 Acacia Drive, Oakville, CA (☎ 707/944-2861), was built in 1885 and is on the National Register of Historic Places. The building has been beautifully restored by classic car collector Gil Nickel. Tastings are offered daily.

Groth, 750 Oakville Cross Rd., Oakville, CA 94562 (☎ 707/944-0290), is a striking complex designed by Robert Gianelli in the Mission style, complete with bell tower. Tastings are offered daily.

Robert Mondavi, 7801 St. Helena Hwy., Oakville, CA 94562 (☎ 707/259-9463), offers a whole range of tours from 1 to 4 hours in length, and they are certainly among the best, if not *the* best, in the valley. One of them allows you to improve your nose by sampling more than 20 fragrances associated with wine. They start in the vineyard and tour through the winemaking facilities, barrel room, and the tasting room. Mondavi is located in a traditional Mission-style building with Spanish tower and archway. Paintings adorn the Harvest Room; music festivals are held in the courtyard; and sculptures are dotted around the property. In 1979 the vintners joined with Baron Philippe de Rothschild to produce the now famous Opus One. During the summer wine and food seminars are also given, and there's a summer long program of music.

In Rutherford

Beaulieu, 1960 St. Helena Hwy., Rutherford, CA 94573 (☎ 707/967-5231), was founded by French chemist Georges de Latour, who once observed that "the quickest road to ruin is slow horses, fast women, and wineries." Nevertheless, in 1900 he purchased 120 acres north of the famous historic Niebaum (formerly Inglenook) winery. Initially he had gone to the gold fields and begun manufacturing baking powder from cream of tartar, which had introduced him to the wine business. The crude form of tartar (argols) is deposited in wine tanks, so he found himself visiting the wineries to secure argols for his factories at Healdsburg, Fresno, and Rutherford. Soon he was in the wine business employing Andre Tchelistcheff, who began making the vineyard's signature cabernets and chardonnays. Tours and tastings are conducted daily. Picnicking is possible.

Cakebread Cellars, 8300 St. Helena Hwy., Rutherford, CA 94573 (☎ 707/963-5221), was begun in 1973 by Jack and Dolores Cakebread, who still operate it as a family winery. The redwood buildings constructed in 1980 are striking; so too are the gardens. The winery produces fine cabernets. Tastings are offered daily.

Caymus, 8700 Conn Creek Rd., Rutherford, CA 94573 (☎ 707/963-4204), produces a quintessential cabernet sauvignon. It was established in 1972 and is synonymous with Napa. The production facility offers little in the way of charm or facilities and is open by appointment only. In addition to the great cabernets, try the zinfandel, which is only available at the winery. Tours are by appointment only; tastings are conducted daily.

Grgich Hills Cellars, 1829 Hwy. 29, Rutherford, CA (☎ 707/963-2784), is owned by the innovative Mike Grgich, who is from Croatia. He produces great chardonnays, plus some fine cabernets and zinfandels. The tour is informative.

Mumm Napa Valley, 8445 Silverado Trail, Rutherford, CA 94573 (☎ 707/942-3434), is the American arm of the famous French company in partnership with Seagram. Daily tours and tastings are conducted.

Niebaum Coppola, 1991 St. Helena Hwy., Rutherford, CA 94573 (☎ 707/963-9099), is the legendary Gothic stone and wood Inglenook winery that was built in 1886, complete with handsome cellars. It was founded by Gustave Ferdinand Niebaum, a Finnish fur trader from Helsinki, who arrived via Alaska. He gave up fur trading and bought 1,000 acres in 1879. He read everything he could about viticulture in five languages and set about producing great wines, which he believed were made in the vineyards not in the cellar. When Heublein put up the landmark winery for sale in 1995, Francis Ford Coppola bought it for $10 million and joined it to the 1,560 acres of the original Inglenook estate that he already owned. The grand staircase and immense reception hall give a fairy-tale quality to the entire place. Coppola has turned toward making this a center for celebrating food, wine, and the movies. There's a museum filled with movie memorabilia—costumes from Dracula, Don Corleone's desk and chair, the boat from *Apocalpyse Now*—a multimedia presentation that tells the story of the winery, plus food and wine. Tours and tastings are conducted daily.

Peju Province, 8466 St. Helena Hwy., Rutherford, CA 94573 (☎ 707/963-3600), is notable for the architecture designed by Calvin Straub and also for the sculpture found throughout the gardens. There's a self-guided tour. Tastings are conducted daily.

Rutherford Hill, 200 Rutherford Hill Rd., P O. Box 388, Rutherford, CA 94573 (☎ 707/963-7194), has fantastic views of the valley from its eastern hillside perch just beyond the Auberge du Soleil. This is the place to have a picnic, either under shady oaks or surrounded by an olive grove. Tours and tastings are conducted daily.

St. Supery, 8440 St. Helena Hwy., Rutherford, CA 94573 (☎ 707/963-4507), offers a good self-guided tour complete with essence boxes that you can smell. The Queen Anne Victorian winery has been restored to appear as it did in the 1880s and converted into a small museum of Napa Valley history. The gardens are lovely, and there's an attractive picnic area too. Daily tastings are available.

In St. Helena

Beringer, 2000 Main St., St. Helena, CA 94574 (☎ 707/963-7115), was founded in 1876 by the Beringer brothers, Jacob and Frederick. The tasting rooms are housed in the Rhine House, which was Frederick's mansion, a dramatic building dating to 1883 and modeled after the Beringer ancestral home in Mainz, Germany. The house is richly ornamented with turrets and towers, and the interiors feature stained glass windows; floors inlaid with oak, mahogany, and walnut; and carved white oak mantels and staircases. Before establishing the winery, Jacob had been the cellarmaster at Krug. The caves were chiseled by Chinese laborers. It's a large, imposing place with notable gardens. No picnicking is allowed. Expect crowds. The 45-minute tours are filled with history and take you through the caves. Tastings are available daily.

Casa Nuestra, 3451 Silverado Trail North, St. Helena, 94574 (☎ 707/963-5783), is one of the few wineries that has developed some fine-tasting Loire Valley–style chenin blancs. The winery is open weekends only for tastings. Bucolic picnicking spots are available.

Flora Springs, 1978 W. Zinfandel Lane, St. Helena, CA 94574 (☎ 707/963-5711), is in the western hills of the valley, a small, family-operated business that prides itself on farming organically. The bulk of the grapes are shipped to other winemakers. Tastings are offered daily.

Freemark Abbey, 3022 St. Helena Hwy., St. Helena, CA 94574 (☎ 707/963-9694), was started by a woman in 1886, but the current winery was begun only in 1967. It possesses an elegant tasting room furnished with rugs, antiques, and a stone fireplace. Tours and tastings are conducted daily in summer, Thursday through Sunday only in winter.

Greystone/Christian Brothers, 2555 Main St., St. Helena, CA 94574 (☎ 707/967-1100), was started by the Christian Brothers, who funded schools around the world, and was the largest stone winery in the valley. It was sold to Heublein in the 1970s and is now the location of the western branch of the Culinary Institute of America (which is based in Hyde Park, New York). Culinary professionals come here to hone their skills. Visitors can visit the corkscrew room that displays some very fancy corkscrews, originally collected by Brother Timothy, cellarmaster for Christian Brothers, as well as the DeBaun Food and Wine Museum, which contains a grape press, corker, stone olive mill, and other culinary equipment plus displays devoted to the evolution of North American cuisine. The restaurant is described in the dining section, below. Tours and tastings are conducted daily.

Heitz Cellar, 436 St. Helena Hwy. S., St. Helena, CA 94574 (☎ 707/963-3542), is located in an old stone winery built in 1898 by Anton Rossini. A small, family-operated winery, it produces one of the most expensive cabernets going, the famous Martha's Vineyard. Tastings are offered daily.

Charles Krug, 28000 Main St., St. Helena, CA 94574 (☎ 707/963-5057), which was founded in 1861, was the Napa Valley's first winery, and it was here that many early vintners, including Jacob Beringer, served their apprenticeships. Krug died in 1902, and the winery languished until it was reopened by Cesare Mondavi in 1943. You can loll around on the 2-acre lawn and see the handsome Victorian carriage house. It's also known for its August Moon Concerts, Shakespeare Festival, and other special events. Tours are conducted daily, except Wednesday. Tastings are offered daily. Picnic areas are available.

Louis M. Martini, 254 St. Helena Hwy. S., St. Helena, CA 94574 (☎ 707/963-2736), is only of interest because it's one of the earlier wineries in the valley. Tastings are offered daily.

Newton, 2555 Madrona Ave., St. Helena, CA 94574 (☎ 707/963-9000), is a terraced, hillside vineyard with many Chinese accents, via Peter Newton's wife Su Hua. Enter via the Chinese-style gate, and wander among the thousands of roses in gardens that cover 5 acres. Tastings are offered daily.

Joseph Phelps, 200 Taplin Rd., St. Helena, CA 94573 (☎ 707/963-2745), offers dramatic views from its hilltop location. Reserve one of the three outdoor tables for a picnic. There are daily tours and tastings.

St. Clement, 2867 St. Helena Hwy. N., St. Helena, CA 94574 (☎ 707/967-3033), was one of the early wineries in the valley. The Rosenbaum House, a beautiful Victorian residence, has been restored and contains a small tasting room. Tastings are offered daily.

V. Sattui, 1111 White Lane, St. Helena, CA 94574 (☎ 707/963-7774), was originally founded in San Francisco in the 1880s. It opened here in the 1970s and attracts crowds to its shaded picnic area, where deli items are sold—cheeses, meats, salads, and more. This has caused some controversy lately on account of the crowds, but it didn't when they started doing it in the '70s to raise money for the maintenance of the winery. Tastings are offered daily.

Sutter Home, 277 St. Helena Hwy. S., St. Helena, CA 94574 (☎ 707/963-3104), is the valley's oldest wooden winery. Today it's worth visiting for the splendid gardens alone, which display hundreds of varieties of roses, plus lilies, camellias, begonias, and dwarf Japanese maples, all set around an 1884 Victorian residence. The visitor center features displays about regional history and also contains the tasting room and a gourmet store. Tours and tastings are available daily.

In Calistoga

Chateau Montelena, 1429 Tubbs Lane, Calistoga, CA 94515 (☎ 707/942-5105), is housed in a dramatic, French-style chateau built in 1882. This is the winery whose chardonnay knocked the French off their pinnacle at the blind tastings in Paris in 1976. At the base of the chateau lies Jade Lake, which is ornamented with bridges and red-lacquered pavilions and can be reserved for picnicking (call months in advance). The pathways in the gardens are lined with daffodils, roses, calendulas, dogwood, irises, and poppies. Tours are by appointment; tastings are offered daily.

Clos Pegase, 1060 Dunaweal Lane, Calistoga, CA 94515 (☎ 707/942-4981), was designed in a radical, dramatic style by Michael Graves and dedicated to the mythical Pegasus, the winged horse who stamped out the first vineyard. Book publisher and art collector owner Jan Shrem wanted to integrate wine and art, which is why the whole complex—from courtyard to tasting room and caves—is filled with paintings and sculptures. It was opened in 1986. Tours and tastings are conducted daily. Picnicking facilities are available.

Diamond Creek, 1500 Diamond Mountain Rd., Calistoga, CA 94515 (☎ 707/942-6926), produces some intense cabernets. It's open by invitation only 4 days per year.

Schramsberg, Schramsberg Rd., Calistoga, CA 94515 (☎ 707/942-4558), is the winery that Robert Louis Stevenson visited and described in *The Silverado Squatters*. It's the valley's oldest hillside winery and features extensive caves and lovely gardens. Among other famous visitors were Ambrose Bierce and Lillie Coit (of the tower fame). Open by appointment only for tours. No tastings.

Sterling, 111 Dunaweal Lane, Calistoga, CA 94515 (☎ 707/942-3359), is where you can take an aerial tram to the hilltop buildings for a panoramic view of the valley. The stark, white complex, complete with bell tower, has a Greek monastic—yet modern—quality to it. There's a pleasant picnic area. There's a self-guided tour; tastings are conducted daily.

NAPA

The town of Napa is just like any other modern town really, and I would recommend that you stay in one of the smaller villages outside. However, there are some fetching bed-and-breakfasts in Napa itself. It is a riverfront town and does have an old town area, which you can either explore on your own or on a walking tour given by **Napa County Landmarks,** 1026 First St. (☎ 707/255-1836).

Also shoppers will want to stop at the Napa Factory Stores, Freeway Drive at Highway 29 and First Street (☎ 707/226-9876), which houses about 50 discount stores—from Ann Taylor and Liz Claiborne to Cole Haan and Dansk.

Lodging & Dining in Napa

Churchill Manor, Brown St., Napa, CA 94559 (☎ 707/253-7733), is as splendid as it sounds. The house was built for a banker in 1889 who obviously relished the Second Empire style—steep mansard roof, grand front portico supported by several Corinthian columns, and the sweeping side veranda. Although it is in downtown Napa, it stands surrounded by an acre of gardens, lawns, roses, and trees. Inside there are 10 rooms, all with telephones. The largest and most decorated room is Edward's, which offers an antique French bed and triple-mirrored armoire. Armchairs are placed in front of the fireplace, and there's even room for another two tapestry chairs and table. A Renaissance Revival armoire dominates Benjamin's room, which is decorated in deep emerald and furnished with oak pieces. Rates include a full breakfast with made-to-order omelets and similar dishes. This is served in the mosaic marble-tiled sun room or outside on the veranda. Wine and cheese are served in the evening. Tandem bicycles and croquet sets are available, and for those who wish to play the ivories, there's a grand piano in the parlor. The TV/VCR resides in the game room.

Rates (incl. breakfast): $85–$155 double.

What make the **Country Garden Inn,** 1815 Silverado Trail, Napa, CA 94558 (☎ 707/255-1197, fax 707/255-3112), are the rose garden, the aviary housing exotic birds, and the efforts that the English hosts put into the cuisine. This 1850s house, which originally served as a stage stop on the Silverado Route, is surrounded by lovely gardens and offers comfortable rooms furnished with Irish or English pine four-posters and similar furnishings. Rooms in the Rose House have fireplaces, Jacuzzis, and private terraces overlooking the 1½-acre gardens. The champagne breakfasts will start the day right; afternoon tea will be accompanied by cookies and rich chocolate cake, and in the early evening tasty toast and cheese hors d'oeuvres will restore you at the end of the day's activities. The dessert wine before you retire will ensure a sweet, deep sleep.

Rates (incl. breakfast): $145–$215 double weekends, $135–$195 midweek.

Cross Roads Inn, 6380 Silverado Trail, Napa, CA 94558 (☎ 707/944-0646), is set on 23 acres overlooking the Napa Valley. The four rooms are individually decorated and offer Jacuzzi spas and wine bars among the amenities. A full breakfast featuring such dishes as quiche, whole wheat pancakes, or ham-and-asparagus-filled puff pastry with a tarragon sauce will be served in your room or on your private deck.

Rates (incl. breakfast): $210–$235 double.

The **Napa Inn,** 1137 Warren St., Napa, CA 94559 (☎ 707/257-1444, fax 707/257-0251), is located in a downtown Queen Anne Victorian built in 1899. It offers four rooms and two suites. The Oak Room has an appealing window seat overlooking the garden, while the Tower Room features a large bay window and room enough to accommodate a four-poster. The Cheesy Suite has a fireplace and solarium-style sitting room, while the Grand Suite occupies the entire top floor of the inn and has a bathroom tucked away in the turret. Furnishings are pretty and comfortable in all the rooms. You might find an iron bed combined with armoire and wingback or Eastlake-style chairs. Guests have use of the comfortable parlor, which has a fireplace and plenty of books to read. A full breakfast is served at a lace-covered table.

Rates (incl. breakfast): $130–$200 double.

Silverado Country Club, 1600 Atlas Peak Rd., Napa, CA 94558 (☎ 707/257-0200), is where people come to enjoy the two 18-hole golf courses and other amenities of this 1,200-acre resort. The 280 suites are in single-story buildings scattered around the property. They are modern with all the comforts and amenities you might want—sitting room with fireplace, couch, and armchair; dining area; kitchen with oven, microwave, and full-size refrigerator; and bedroom with modern furnishings, TV, telephone, and a sliding door out to a small patio.

The **Royal Oak** and the **Vintner's Court** dining rooms are both located in the southern-style plantation building at the center of the resort. The first specializes in steaks and other charcoal-grilled dishes; the second produces a menu that reveals Pacific Rim influences and on Friday nights offers a popular seafood buffet. There are also three or four outdoor dining areas.

Facilities include 8 swimming pools, a tennis complex with 20 courts (court fees are $13 per person), and two 18-hole golf courses (greens fees are $110).

Rates: $205–$265 one-bedroom suite; from $375 two-bedroom suite. Packages are available.

The **Oak Knoll Inn,** 2200 E. Oak Knoll Ave., Napa, CA 94558 (☎ 707/255-2200), just off the Silverado Trail between Napa and Yountville, has lovely views of the vineyards, Stag's Leap Mountain, and Atlas Peak. It's set far enough away from all the hubbub to make for a romantic hideaway. The inn is located in several pretty, stone buildings screened by a wall of cypresses. It's also a very alluring place with its grass-surrounded pool, wisteria-covered arbor, and riverstone fireplace where a welcoming fire roars on cold days. From the deck there's a beautiful view of the valley. Each room has a king-size brass bed, sitting area furnished with plush modern sofas and armchairs, fireplace, and private bath. In some an elegantly rustic ambience is provided by the riverstone walls and redwood ceilings. Breakfast is a lavish affair; wine and cheese are served in the evenings.

Rates (incl. breakfast): $235–$325 double.

YOUNTVILLE

Yountville is a pretty stone town. At the center of it stands the old stone Groezinger winery, which has been converted into a shopping complex called **Vintage 1870** and shelters about 40 specialty shops.

Lodging in Yountville

Maison Fleurie, 6529 Yount St., Yountville, CA 94599 (☎ 707/944-2056), is located in an attractive vine-covered building. The rooms are decorated largely in country French style with assorted antiques and country pieces, including painted armoires. Rooms in the main house are smaller than those in adjoining buildings. There's a nicely landscaped small pool, a separate hot tub area, and a sundeck from which there are views of the vineyards and hills. The price includes a full breakfast plus wine and hors d'oeuvres in the evening.

Rates (incl. breakfast): $120–$210.

Burgundy House, 6711 Washington St., P. O. Box 3156, Yountville, CA 94599 (☎ 707/944-0889), is in the center of the main street of Yountville. It has great appeal primarily because it is so French-looking and also manages to create a sense of seclusion. Built in the early 1890s from local fieldstone and river rock, the building was used variously as a distillery, winery, warehouse, and store before being converted into an inn. The walls are 22 inches thick—supported by hand-hewn posts and lintels and reinforce the sense of privacy. Each of the six rooms is attractively furnished with antique country pieces and has a private bath. Breakfast is served in the atmospheric distillery or outside in the gardens, which create a very private ambience.

Rates (incl. breakfast): $145 double.

Even though **La Residence,** 4066 St. Helena Highway N., Napa, CA 94558 (☎ 707/253-0337, fax 707/253-0382), is on the main highway just north of Napa yet almost in Yountville, it still has a restful ambience because the 2-acre property is shielded by oaks and pines. The grounds, crisscrossed by flower-lined brick pathways, contain a modern shingle building and an older historic one; there is a fountain playing out front. The 20 rooms all have private bath, phone, fireplace, and patio or veranda. Each is uniquely furnished with antiques and reproductions, fine designer fabrics and linens, and wall-to-wall carpeting. Most have four-poster beds. Breakfast is served in the dining room, which is decked out with polished wood floors covered by Oriental rugs, windows swagged with draperies, and a piano, in addition to the linen-covered tables. Wine and hors d'oeuvres are served in the evenings. The pool area is attractively landscaped so that guests feel quite secluded.

Rates (incl. breakfast): $175–$245 double.

Dining Only in Yountville

The French Laundry, 6640 Washington St. (at Creek), Yountville (☎ 707/944-2380), is an enchanting place set in an unmarked, old stone building that has served variously as a laundry and a bordello. Enter through the small courtyard filled with roses in summer into the small, bi-level dining room with beamed ceiling. It's the domain of chef Thomas Keller, formerly of Cafe Rakel in New York and Checkers in Los Angeles, who recently received a James Beard Award. People seek the restaurant out because of his outstanding menu, which changes nightly. You'll enjoy a $59 five-course prix-fixe menu, or you can opt for a more elaborate $75 nine-course tasting menu. For the former, there will be at least four choices for each course. For example, you might begin with a richly flavored Dungeness crab salad with barrel-aged Tamara-ginger vinaigrette, garden mâche, plum radishes, and curry infused oil, or a puree of white bean soup enriched with a ravioli of white beans and mascarpone cheese. The fish course might be herb-roasted monkfish tail with a grain mustard sauce, or Maine jumbo scallops with melted green leeks and smoked salmon salad in a preserved lemon beurre blanc. Meat courses might include a pan-roasted squab with seared foulard duck foie gras with a compote of French butter pears and Acacia honey-braised Belgian endive, or a rib eye of Sonoma lamb with black truffles, a puree of sweet potatoes, and black truffle sauce. Cheese and dessert choices would follow with such luscious endings as the warm Valrhona chocolate truffle cake with burnt sugar ice cream, or the warm lemon gratin with winter citrus salad and Temple orange sauce. There's also a five-course vegetarian menu featuring such dishes as ragout of Mendocino County yellow chanterelle mushrooms with fall vegetables and black truffle vinaigrette.

Hours: Fri–Sun noon–1:30pm; daily 5:30–9:30pm.

Domaine Chandon, California Drive at Highway 29, Yountville (☎ 707/944-2892), is another legendary dining room in the Napa Valley that is consistently rated by locals as the one place that really deserves its reputation. The dining room has a cave-like air, while the patio is an ideal lunching place in summer. The menu changes seasonally, and you should note that the winter version tends to be less extensive than at other times of the year. You'll dine luxuriously here, though, in any season. The menu will offer caviar to start if you wish, or a more modest pig's-feet salad with haricots verts and shallot parsley vinaigrette, plus 10 or so other appetizers. There will be several seafood dishes, like the mesquite-grilled salmon with brussels sprout leaves, bacon, potatoes, pearl onions, and pinot meunier jus, or the caramelized scallops with a sweet pea sauce, vanilla white corn, and crispy onion rings; plus several meat dishes, like the venison tournedos with a sweet potato napoleon, shiitake mushrooms, and huckleberry-merlot sauce, or the Napa Valley Carneros rack of lamb served with potato goat cheese gratin, sunburst squash, and thyme jus. Prices range from $26 to $38. Finish off with one of the superb desserts—a Valrhona chocolate soufflé with Frangelico sabayon or the tarte au citron with orange sauce. The service is excellent. Note that there is a dress code: No bicycle gear or tank tops at lunch; no jeans or T-shirts at dinner.

Hours: May–Oct daily 11:30am–2:30pm; all year Wed–Sun 6–9:30pm. Closed first 3 weeks of January.

Mustards Grill, 7399 Hwy. 29, Yountville (☎ 707/944-2424), is a lively, casual place that serves a broad and well-prepared grill menu. It's a lot of fun, the decor bold with black and white floor tiles, brilliantly colored original art, and dramatic flower arrangements placed on the bar. You'll find everything from hamburgers and vegetable muffaletta to a center cut filet mignon with three salsas and Yukon gold potatoes, and smoked Peking duck with 100-almond–onion sauce. Prices range from $7.50 to $25. There's more than a dozen selections of wine by the glass, plus a variety of teas and coffees.

Hours: Daily 11:30am–8:30pm.

Anestis' Grill and Rotisserie, 6518 Washington St., Yountville (☎ 707/944-1500), is a color-washed, light, and airy dining room. The menu offers up some fine rotisserie items including a delicious leg of lamb marinated and flavored with a variety of Napa Valley spices, and duckling prepared with a different sauce daily. In addition there are several mesquite-grilled dishes like the pesto chicken, and a mixed grill plus lamb chops served with a cabernet sauce. Pastas round out the menu, and there is always a fish of the day. Prices range from $13 to $20.

Hours: Daily 11:30am–3pm and 5–10pm.

Bistro Don Giovanni, 4110 St. Helena Hwy. (☎ 707/224-3300), is a large, bustling, joyful dining room. Tables are set on terra-cotta tiles and combined with French cafe chairs. There's an open kitchen and long, light oak bar. The menu focuses on pasta and risotto dishes, although there are some grilled dishes like grilled pork chop and seared filet of salmon with tomato white wine and chive sauce. Among the pastas try the linguini *alla tommaso* made with broccoli, garlic, lemon zest, arbol chilis, and pecorino cheese; or try farfalle with asparagus, porcini and wild mushrooms, pecorino cheese, and truffle oil. Burgers and other sandwiches are also available. To start, have the grilled portabella mushroom with sautéed greens, onion rings, and balsamic jus. Prices range from $12 to $17.

Hours: Daily 11am–10pm.

The Diner, 6476 Washington St., Yountville (☎ 707/944-2626), is the place to go for breakfast. It's a counter-and-booth luncheonette, but the breakfast dishes are legendary—chorizo-and-jalapeño–filled burrito, German potato pancakes with sausages and applesauce made from local Gravensteins. There's huevos rancheros, too, and many other egg and pancake combinations. Be prepared for long lines on weekends.

Hours: Tues–Sun 8am–3pm and 5:30–9pm.

OAKVILLE & RUTHERFORD

Oakville and Rutherford are more crossroads at the center of the valley than towns. They're more notable as a growing area for cabernet than anything else. Besides the many famous vineyards located there, Oakville is also known for the **Oakville Grocery,** 7856 St. Helena Hwy. (☎ 707/944-8802), where you can pick up all the ingredients—salads, breads, cheeses, and wine—for a swell picnic.

Lodging & Dining in Rutherford

Auberge du Soleil, 180 Rutherford Hill Rd., Rutherford, CA 94573 (☎ 707/963-1211, fax 707/963-8764), has to be one of the most romantic places in the valley. A complex of terra-cotta–washed adobe buildings, it's set high up in the hills overlooking the vineyards. It seems that everywhere you look you will be seeing something of great beauty, either a sculpture or a garden flower or just the view from the terrace. The interior is refreshingly southwestern in style. The accommodations, either in the main house or in cottages terraced into the hillside, all have a full range of amenities—fireplaces, bathtub and shower, honor bar, stereo, CD, video, voice mail, and private terrace.

The **dining room** also has a southwestern mood with it cedar columns, adobe fireplaces, and French doors that lead out to a terrace with a splendid view. The cuisine is luxurious California. If you really want to indulge, start with a dish like the seven sparkling sins, which brings lobster, kumamoto (a Japanese fish), quail egg, American caviar, foie gras, American river sturgeon, and smoked salmon. You will also find more modest dishes, such as beef carpaccio with roasted pepper-caper relish and lemon oil, and a soup of the evening. Main courses range from pistachio-crusted salmon with pancetta, cannelini beans, and fumé blanc butter, to black-pepper–glazed tenderloin with braised fennel sauce, and a sweet potato latke, or the lamb rack with cabernet sauvignon essence. Prices range from $26 to $35. Nothing beats the coconut chocolate crème brûlée with caramelized banana sauce to complete a wonderful dining experience. Come also to watch the sunset from the bar, which has a refreshing snack menu.

Facilities include a deck-surrounded pool, spa and massage services, exercise room, and three tennis courts. Services include 24-hour room service, valet, and daily newspaper. Children under 16 are discouraged.

Rates: Aug–Nov, $335 double in main house weekends, $285 midweek; from $400 cottage. Apr–Jul, $310 double weekends; $260 midweek; from $380 cottage. Dec–Mar, $260 double weekends; $185 midweek, from $310 cottage. *Dining Hours:* Daily 11:30am–2:30pm; Sun–Thurs 6–9:30pm; Fri–Sat 5:30–9:30pm.

Rancho Caymus Inn, 1140 Rutherford Rd., P.O. Box 78, Rutherford, CA 94573 (☎ 707/963-1777, fax 707/963-5387), was designed in a South

American style. The split-level suites are arranged around a central garden courtyard. Each has high beamed ceilings, wet bar/refrigerator, and balcony. Decorations consist of rugs, cushions, and wall hangings from Latin America and heavy, hand-carved modern furnishings. Many have beehive adobe fireplaces. Some rooms also have Jacuzzi bathrooms decorated with stained glass, plus kitchenettes. All have TV, telephone, and air-conditioning.

Rates: $135–$165 double, suites from $255.

ST. HELENA

St. Helena is an historic town with an attractive main street that is lined today with elegant Victorian buildings, still occupied by some old-fashioned stores as well as some more modern, streamlined emporiums. The town was founded in 1853 by Englishman J.H. Still, who opened a general store and offered land for free to those who would set up businesses. Today you can browse in the many stores, which include several galleries and antique stores. If you're looking for the latest in bed, bath, and table settings, stop in at **Vanderbilt & Co.,** 1429 Main St. (☎ 707/963-1010). Real dedicated shoppers will also want to check out the outlets—**Joan & David, Donna Karan, Coach,** and more—on Highway 29, 2 miles north of St. Helena.

Lovers of Robert Louis Stevenson will find a surprisingly vast collection of first editions, manuscripts, photographs, letters, and other memorabilia at the **Silverado Museum,** 1490 Library Lane (☎ 707/963-3757). The core of the collection was amassed by John Henry Nash, Chairman of the Board of J. Walter Thompson, who retired to St. Helena and funded the museum. Among the treasures in the 8,000-item collection is his desk, his lead soldiers, Stevenson's own copy of *An Inland Voyage* (his first book), and the copy of *A Child's Garden of Verses,* which he presented to his wife.

Hours: Tues–Sun noon–4pm. *Admission:* Free.

The town also has another museum, the **Napa Valley Museum,** 473 Main St. (☎ 707/963-7411), which displays a permanent collection of artifacts relating to local Indian and pioneer history, plus temporary exhibits that might be anything from a photography show of notable people in the Napa Valley to a collection of fossils from around the world. A new home for the museum is currently being built in Yountville, and it is expected to open late in February 1998 at 55 Presidents Circle (☎ 707/944-0500).

Hours: Mon–Fri 9am–4pm, Sat–Sun 11am–3pm. *Admission:* $2 donation.

Before winemaking became the predominant industry in the valley, wheat was a staple crop. Few traces of this era remain except for the **Old Bale Mill** (☎ 707/963-2236), on Highway 29 about 3 miles north of

St. Helena, which was built in 1846. It's open daily from 10am to 5pm, and visitors can see how the mill with its 36-foot water wheel works. Call for times of mill demonstrations.

Four miles north of St. Helena, 1,916-acre **Bothe–Napa Valley State Park** (☎ 707/942-4575) offers respite from the travails of Highway 29. Here you can hike, just sit by the stream and recover some equilibrium, or swim in the pool in summer. There are also 50 campsites available.

Admission: $5 per vehicle.

Before you go to the park, head to **The Model Bakery,** 1357 Main St. (☎ 707/963-8192), for breads, sandwiches, fruit tarts, and cookies or to pick up a sandwich and pastry at the cantinetta at Tra Vigne, which is described in the Lodging & Dining section below.

Lodging in St. Helena

Bartels Ranch and Country Inn, 1200 Conn Valley Rd., St. Helena, CA 94574 (☎ 707/963-4001, fax 707/963-5100), is an exceptional place to stay because of the bubbly personality of host Jami Bartels, who makes sure that her guests have every comfort in their rooms and indeed throughout their whole vacation. The sprawling, single-story house is set on 60 acres on a bluff off the Silverado Trail and makes for a quiet retreat away from all the bustle of Highway 29, yet only 6 minutes from St. Helena. There are only four rooms. The Brass Monarch Room has a brass bed, the Blue Valley Room a canopied bed. The super large Heart of the Valley Suite invites guests to loll in front of the stone fireplace and enjoy the spa tub along with all the other comforts: down comforter, fluffy bathrobes, fine linens, masses of pillows, bubblebath, and candlelight, all of which are found in the other rooms, too. Guests will find plenty of entertainment—chess sets, a library, billiards, table tennis, and assorted movies in the game room, which is much more comfortable than most. In addition, there's a comfortable living room where folks like to sit in front of the fire, listen to a pianist play, or just look at the collections Jami displays from her world travels. A full breakfast is served anytime until noon, so you can really relax if you need to. Wine and hors d'oeuvres are offered in the evening, tea and coffee all day.

Rates (incl. breakfast): $165–$325 double.

The **Ink House B & B,** 1575 St. Helena Hwy., St. Helena, CA 94574 (☎ 707/963-3890), is set back from the road. It is named after Theron H. Ink, who built it in 1884. A veranda wraps around the Italianate Victorian, which has a cupola that is furnished as a sitting room with white wicker and that offers a bird's-eye view of the Napa Valley vineyards. There are seven rooms, each distinctly furnished. A French mahogany bed, crowned with a half canopy, and a massive carved armoire are the centerpieces of the French Room. Other rooms have Eastlake or iron beds and appropriate furnishings. On the first floor there are two parlors where guests can relax, enjoying the grand piano in one and the fireplace and pump organ in the other. An expanded continental breakfast is served. Bicycles are available as are TVs and VCRs. There's a pool table, too.

Rates (incl. breakfast): $155–$175 double.

Meadowood, 900 Meadowood Lane, St. Helena, CA 94574 (☎ 707/963-3646, fax 707/963-3532), is one of *the* places to stay in Napa. It's where many of the wine movers and shakers stay and where the very prestigious annual Napa Valley wine auction is held. Pass through the manned gate into the 250 wooded acres. You'll pass the tennis courts and swimming pool and reach the main lodge and nearby restaurants. Accommodations are located in several attractive, gabled buildings set into the hillsides, making for great privacy. The interiors are light, airy, and spacious. They're furnished in a simple manner with antique reproductions including Shaker benches and Windsor chairs. All have honor bars, coffeemakers, toasters, and private porches; most have fireplaces.

The **Restaurant** and **Grill** are located in the Clubhouse and Conference Center. The Grill has a terrace overlooking the golf course. The Restaurant has steeply pitched ceilings, chairs covered in French fabric, inspiring floral bouquets, and equally inspiring cuisine.

The Restaurant menu changes daily, so depending on the season you might find among the eight or so appetizers a peppered venison carpaccio served with crispy apples and rosemary oil, pan-seared scallops with figs and foie gras vinaigrette, or smoked quail with wild rice and scallion salad and a walnut vinaigrette. Even a dish as simple as pumpkin soup will be made extra special by the addition of roasted chestnuts and black truffles. The entrees will include an equal number of meat and fresh fish dishes. For example, there might be grilled Pacific halibut with flageolet beans, cipolline onions, and chanterelle mushrooms, or delicious honey-glazed pork loin with soft polenta, caramelized apple, and grain mustard. Prices range from $19 to $26, or you can opt for the $48 four-course tasting menu. Each of the five desserts will be exquisite; the list might include, say, a chestnut soufflé with Frangelico sauce or Merryvale Antigua muscat crème brûlée served with cranberry-orange relish.

The Grill menu ranges from an 8-ounce cheeseburger, to braised lamb shank with wild mushrooms in a red wine reduction, to mahimahi served with grilled bok choy, bean salad, and a roast garlic vinaigrette. You'll find several spa selections, too. Prices range from $9 to $19. If you can't make lunch or dinner here, then come for brunch.

Facilities include eight tennis courts, a nine-hole golf course, swimming pool, and two exquisitely maintained croquet lawns laid down in front of a very English-looking lodge. Bicycles are available, and the grounds are crisscrossed by hiking trails. The health spa offers facials, massages, and body treatments as well as fitness classes. Services include valet, daily newspaper, concierge, and video rentals.

St. Helena

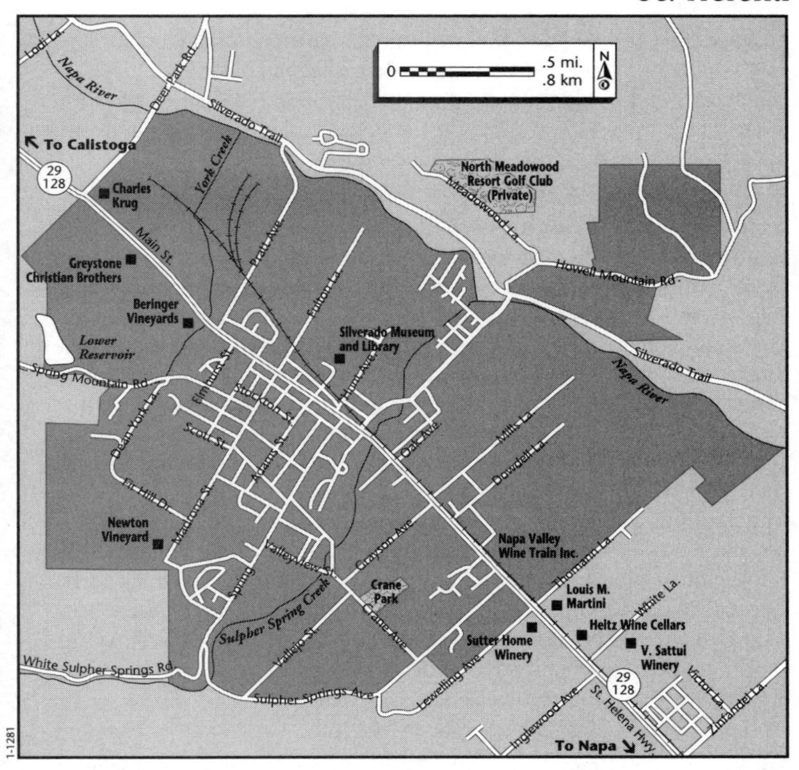

Rates: Jul–mid-Nov, $350–$475 double weekends, $330–$455 midweek; Apr–Jun and mid-Nov–Mar $330–$455 weekends, $290–$405 midweek; $580–$2,000 one- to four-bedroom suites.

Dining Only in St. Helena

Brava Terrace, 3010 Hwy. 29 (☎ 707/963-9300), has several inviting dining rooms, including one with a stone fireplace, but in summer the most magical place is the large outdoor deck, where tables are shaded by market umbrellas (it can be enclosed in inclement weather). The cuisine is comforting and flavorful, ranging from burgers and sandwiches to daily pastas, fish, and risotto. In addition there are such dishes as roasted breast of chicken with pancetta and thyme au jus, or grilled pepper-crusted salmon with mustard sauce. Prices range from $9 to $19.

Hours: May–Nov daily noon–9pm; Dec–Apr Thurs–Tues noon–9pm.

Terra, 1345 Railroad Ave. (☎ 707/963-8931), offers one of St. Helena's best dining experiences. The dining room has a simple decor: terra-cotta tiled floors and walls decorated with art. The cuisine is lusty and original Asian-accented Mediterranean created by chef Hiro Sone, who hails from Los Angeles's Spago. To start, there's a spicy bread and garlic soup with poached egg, or a tataki of tuna with ponzu vinaigrette, daikon sprouts, and wasabi. For your main course, try the grilled lamb with artichokes in an anchovy and black olive sauce, or the salmon in red Thai curry sauce. Prices range from $17 to $23. On the dessert menu, try the innovative banana tarte tatin with rum raisin ice cream.

Hours: Sun–Mon & Wed–Thurs 6–9pm, Fri–Sat 6–10pm (closed Tues).

Almost next door, is **Showley's,** 1327 Railroad Ave. (☎ 707/963-1200), another restaurant to visit for a memorable meal. It's located in an old family home and offers a series of dining rooms accented with watercolors. Table settings are enhanced by gilded fresh fruit and artichokes. The menu changes seasonally. In winter you're likely to find among the starters several recommendable choices: the portobello mushrooms with layered potatoes, red pepper, and zucchini with pesto and red pepper puree; the grilled Japanese eggplant with caramelized onions, capers, pesto, and confit of sun-dried tomatoes; or the *chile en nogada,* which is a pasilla chile stuffed with pork tenderloin, pine nuts, and chutney and served with a walnut crème fraîche. Among the main courses are a tasty sea bass with a green olive tapenade, a delicious tenderloin of pork coated with whole grain mustard and served with garlic sauce, and charred duck breast marinated with balsamic vinegar and served with ollalieberry sauce. Pastas are also available. Prices range from $14 to $19. For dessert try the chocolate phyllo pastry layered with Valrhona pastry cream. On Friday nights dinner is accompanied by a gentle jazz trio.

Hours: Tues–Sun 11:30am–3pm and 6–9pm.

Tra Vigne, 1050 Charter Oak Ave. (☎ 707/963-4444), is one of the most popular and appealing dining rooms in St. Helena. Located right on the main highway, it's set back from the road and enclosed, so it remains sheltered from the noise. The main restaurant is dramatic in proportion with high ceilings, grand bar, and partially open kitchen. The outdoor balcony overlooks a courtyard with several fountains plus shade trees and plantings in terra-cotta tubs set between wrought-iron chairs and tables. This is where patrons of the cantinetta bring their salads and sandwiches to sit out and dine in one of the most pleasant dining spots in the valley.

In the dining room, the menu offers a full range of antipasti and pasta dishes. For example, you might find a deep-flavored polenta *arrosta con funghi,* which is oven-roasted polenta with wild mushrooms and balsamic game sauce; or *spiedini di mozzarella,* consisting of fresh mozzarella and sweet roasted peppers on skewers with basil oil and balsamic vinegar. Among the pastas try the risotto of the day or a dish like *ceppo con salsicce e spinaci,* which is made with sausage, spinach, potatoes, sun-dried tomatoes, and pecorino cheese. For a second course, pizzas are available, plus some delicious grilled dishes like the Sonoma rabbit with Teleme-layered potatoes, oven-dried tomatoes, and mustard sauce; or a pan-roasted salmon with fennel-whipped potatoes, blood-orange fondue, and grilled radicchio. Prices range from $9 to $18.

The cantinetta (☎ 707/963-8888) offers a short menu of sandwiches, pastas, pizzas, salads, and desserts.

Hours: Restaurant, Sun–Thurs 11:30am–9:30pm, Fri–Sat 11:30am–10pm; Cantinetta, daily 11am–6pm.

Trilogy, 1234 Main St. (☎ 707/963-5507), is a tiny, country-style restaurant with only 12 tables. The room is attractively adorned with prints on the walls and tables set with linens, salmon-colored napkins, and bentwood chairs for seating. It offers a three-course prix-fixe menu for $28. Among the first courses, you might find smoked salmon rillettes with shaved fennel and red onion salad, or grilled quail with warm lentil frissée salad. This would be followed by either a soup or salad. The third course would offer six or so choices ranging from seared venison with sun-dried cherry sauce, roasted top sirloin of veal with hedgehog mushroom sauce, grilled salmon with black bean vegetable chili and cilantro pesto, or perhaps seared sea scallops with vegetable julienne and saffron sauce. Whatever is on the menu will be well flavored and nicely presented. The wine list is excellent.

Hours: Tues–Fri noon–2pm; Tues–Sat 6pm–closing.

The *Wine Spectator* and the C.I.A.'s **Greystone Dining Room,** 2555 Main St. (☎ 707/967-1100), located in the historic Christian Brothers winery, has soaring ceilings, lots of brilliantly colored (mustard and blue) tilework, metal sculptures, and a series of circular open kitchens where you can watch the Mediterranean cuisine being prepared. Here you can secure tapas from Spain, antipasti from Italy, meze from the eastern Mediterranean, and other innovative dishes to start—for example a roulade of housemade mozzarella, pesto, and sun-dried tomatoes with tapenade crouton, or ***pissaladière,*** which is a hot dish of onions, olives, and anchovy paste on flat bread. Among the six or so main courses there might be a tagine of salmon with preserved lemons, cracked olives, caperberries, and couscous; or hanger steak with garlic roasted potatoes, grilled fennel, and wild mushrooms. Finish off your meal with Valrhona chocolate cake with ruby port sauce or a sorbet sampler. Prices range from $14 to $18.

Hours: Wed–Mon 11:30am–3pm and 5:30–9pm.

CALISTOGA

Sam Brannan, the famous journalist who ran through the streets of San Francisco announcing the Gold Rush, was the founder of Calistoga. He established it as a mining supply town for the northern mines, and in fact you can see the original store he built at the corner of Wapoo Avenue and Grant Street, where it's said he made $50,000 in 1 year. He is, it is said, also responsible for the town's name. Because the area had mineral springs, supposedly Sam intended to name it Saratoga after the New York resort, but at a celebratory dinner where he planned to make the announcement, he got so drunk that in his address he mispronounced it "Calistoga of Sarifornia" and the name stuck. He did actually manage to build several cottages and plant palm trees in preparation for his grand resort. One of them remains standing at 1311 Washington St. and now serves as a bed-and-breakfast.

His vision for Calistoga as a resort was largely appropriate, for even today it's known for its mineral springs and mud baths, and that's what draws people here. Calistoga is not a tarted up place. It has a funky, Western feel to it with its covered sidewalks, much more so than other towns in the valley.

While you're in town, browse the stores along Lincoln Avenue. Some are located in the Calistoga Railroad Depot. Drop in, too, to the **Sharpsteen Museum,** 1311 Washington St. (☎ 707/942-5911), to view the dioramas and three-dimensional models that evoke in scaled-down detail what Calistoga was like in the 1860s. There's also a room devoted to the man who created the museum, Mr. Sharpsteen, a 20-plus-year veteran animator, director, and producer for Walt Disney Studios. On the premises you can see one of the cottages that was original to Brannan's resort.

Hours: Summer daily 10am–4pm; winter noon–4pm. *Admission:* Free.

If you haven't been to Yellowstone, then wander out to **Old Faithful Geyser,** 1299 Tubbs Lane (☎ 707/942-6463), which tosses boiling hot water 60 feet into the air approximately every hour. Besides the main attraction, there is also a seismograph computer installed by the Carnegie Institute that monitors the geyser and attempts to correlate its activities to earthquakes. You can take a self-guided tour, which will give you further insight into the geothermal activity you see before you.

Hours: Daily 9am–5pm. *Admission:* $5 adults, $2 children 6–12.

Another nearby attraction is the **Petrified Forest** (☎ 707/942-6667). Here you can walk a quarter-mile loop passing 10 or so exhibits that relate how the trees became petrified three million years ago when they were buried under volcanic ash from an eruption by Mount St. Helena. Some of the trees are giant redwoods more than 100 feet tall. There's a geological display explaining the local geology plus an array of fossils in the small museum. Fossils and petrified wood are for sale in the gift shop.

Hours: Daily 10am–4:30pm (until 5:30pm in summer). *Admission:* $3 adults, $1 children 4–11.

In **Robert Louis Stevenson State Park,** 7 miles north of Calistoga on Highway 29 (☎ 707/942-4575), you can hike the 5-mile trail to the summit of Mount St. Helena, from which you can see Mount Shasta, Lassen Peak, and the entire Napa Valley on a good day. The trail actually passes the site of Stevenson's cabin, but no traces of it remain today.

Before you go, pick up picnic supplies at **Palisades Market,** 1506 Lincoln Ave. (☎ 707/942-9549). You'll find all kinds of deli goods, salads, and breads; it's this end of the valley's answer to the Oakville Grocery.

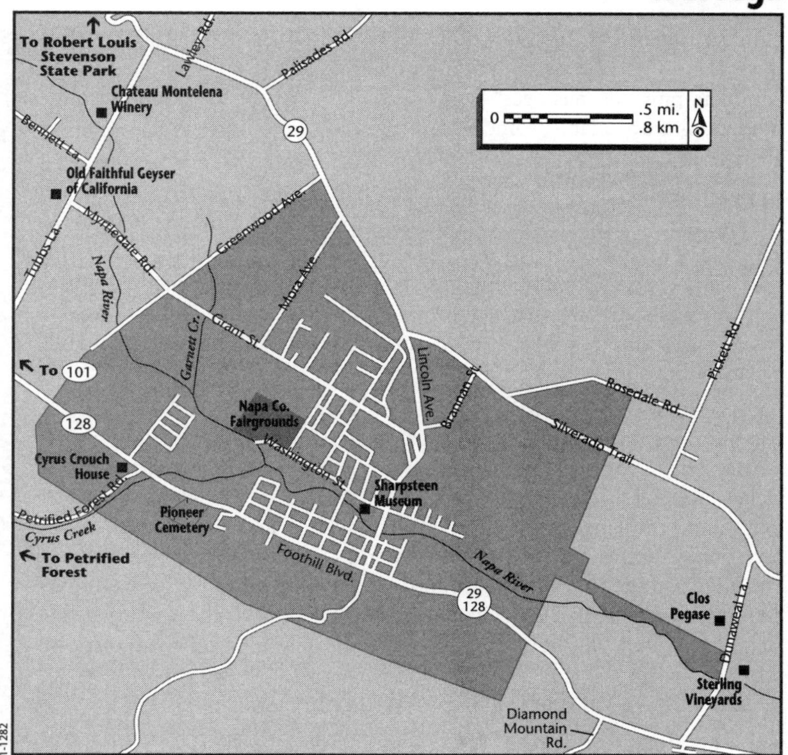

Taking a Mud Bath

If you want to experience a mud bath, by all means do so. Be prepared either to love it or hate it. Some people find it relaxing and rejuvenating; others find it gross and repulsive. Regardless of which spa you choose, the process is pretty much the same. You lie atop this pool of mud while an assistant ladles the stuff on top of you until you are completely covered. Here you remain sweating with your head supported by a pillow for about 20 minutes. After being helped out of the mud, you shower and soak in a mineral bath, then go into a steam room before being swaddled in a blanket and deposited on a bench for a massage.

As far as facilities go, the most modern is the **Lavender Hill Spa,** 1015 Foothill Blvd. (☎ 707/942-4495), which offers a tranquil, prettily landscaped setting complete with private bath houses for couples. It's slightly different from other facilities in that it drains and sterilizes the mud bath between each person's treatment, enabling the management to control the heat more easily, and that makes the bath more comfortable and relaxing. The spa also offers massages, reflexology, and aromatherapy. It has no overnight accommodations. The charge for a mud bath is $48, $72 with a half-hour massage, and $125 with 1-hour massage and mini-facial.

Golden Haven Hot Springs, 1713 Lake St. (☎ 707/942-6793), is also more luxurious than most, offering private mud baths for couples and a complete range of massages, facials, and other body treatments. Accommodations are available, some with Jacuzzi. The prices are similar to those charged at Lavender Hill or Dr. Wilkinson's.

Indian Springs, 1712 Lincoln Ave. (☎ 707/942-4913), is the only spa in the area that possesses a geyser rather than a well or spring. In addition to a full range of mud bath treatments, facials, and massages, it also offers the use of an outdoor Olympic-size mineral pool that is kept at a temperature of 102°F. It also has overnight accommodations starting at $150 on weekends for a studio. The prices are similar to those charged at Lavender Hill or Dr. Wilkinson's.

Dr. Wilkinson's Hot Springs, 1507 Lincoln Ave. (☎ 707/942-4102), has been operating for 50 years, ever since the doctor came to town as a young chiropractor. The place offers a full range of treatments—facials, acupressure face lifts, salt glow scrubs, terra thalasso body treatments, and cerofango treatments, which consist of an application of mud, clay, botanicals, and parafin. Massages and mineral baths are given, too. Facilities include indoor and outdoor pools, and you can stay overnight in rooms with color TV, coffeemaker, and telephone. For a mud bath, facial mask, and half-hour massage expect to pay $79 ($50 without the massage).

Rates: $69–$129 double. Special packages are available.

Calistoga Spa Hot Spring, 1006 Washington St. (☎ 707/942-6269), has four outdoor mineral pools; has mud, mineral, and steam baths; and offers a range of massages. Aerobics classes and exercise equipment are available as well. The 57 rooms have kitchenettes, TV, and telephone. Prices are similar to those at Lavender Hill or Dr. Wilkinson's.

Body wraps and facials, plus a variety of massages and whirlpool baths containing fang mud, herbal bath crystals, seaweed cucumber gel, or milk and whey can be enjoyed at **Mountain View Spa,** 1457 Lincoln Ave. (☎ 707/942-5789), one of the town's most modern facilities. Reservations are necessary. Prices are similar to those charged at Lavender Hill or Dr. Wilkinson's.

Lodging & Dining in Calistoga

The **Brannan Cottage Inn,** 109 Wapoo Ave., Calistoga, CA 94515 (☎ 707/942-4200), is the only building left from Sam Brannan's original resort cottages. It was built in the 1860s and has some eye-catching architectural features—gingerbread gables, five front arches, and a wraparound porch. It's on a small lot on the edge of downtown. Still, the grounds are attractive, and tables are set out for alfresco dining. There are six rooms, all with private bath. They are furnished with white wicker and pine pieces while the windows are hung with lace curtains. Each room has a clock/radio and a small refrigerator. A buffet-style breakfast is served either in the game room or outdoors on the brick terrace in the garden. There's also a comfortable parlor with fireplace where wine is served in the evening.

Rates (incl. breakfast): $170 double.

The Wine Country Inn, 1152 Lodi Lane, St. Helena, CA 94574 (☎ 707/963-7077, fax 707/963-9018), is located in a modern stone building with a Frenchified turret that adds some interest to the exterior. The setting overlooking vineyards is pleasant enough, and many of the 25 rooms have small private balconies with trellises that take advantage of the views. Furnishings consist of iron or brass beds covered with quilts, combined with pine dressers and other pieces. Some rooms have woodburning stoves or fireplaces; none have TVs. The outdoor pool is well landscaped, and from it guests can enjoy valley and winery views. A continental buffet breakfast is served in the rustic dining room.

Rates (incl. breakfast): $140–$234 double (highest-priced room has fireplace, balcony, wet bar, stereo, and vineyard view).

Quail Mountain B & B, 4455 N. St. Helena Hwy., Calistoga, CA 94515 (☎ 707/942-0316), is tucked away up in the hills, off Highway 29. It's a modern house on 26 acres. To reach it, you drive past the orchard and vineyard and up a hill planted with madrona, manzanita, and oak trees. There are only three guest rooms. Each has a private deck and is comfortably furnished in an unassuming way. Guests can relax in the solarium, where they can also take breakfast. In winter, guests usually prefer to have breakfast in front of the fire in the formal dining room.

Rates (incl. breakfast): $110–$140 double.

Dining Only in Calistoga

Catahoula, 1457 Lincoln Ave. (☎ 707/942-2275), is a fun place to go just to see the abstract metal sculptures on the walls and the graphic portraits of the Catahoula Cur, Louisiana's state dog. The food is innovative and great tasting, too. Some dishes are inspired by Louisiana, where the chef is from, but much of the menu consists of California cuisine. For a rich and fulfilling appetizer choose the gumbo ya ya; other innovative appetizers include the andouille sausage combined with onion marmalade and mozzarella pie. To follow, there might be whole fried catfish with melon meunière and Mardi Gras slaw, oxtails braised in red wine with pappardelle and horseradish cream, or pan-roasted quail with corn and black-eyed pea relish and potato onion pie. Prices range from $11 to $21.

Hours: Mon and Wed–Friday noon–2:30pm, Sat–Sun noon–3:30pm; Sun–Mon, Wed–Thurs 5:30–10pm, Fri–Sat 5:30–10:30pm. Closed Tues.

At **Wappo Bar & Bistro,** 1226-B Washington St. (☎ 707/942-4712), the nicest place to dine is out in the courtyard by the fountain under the honeysuckle and grape arbor. The interior with its plain, copper-topped tables is also perfectly pleasant. The cuisine is eclectic with distinct contributions from South America, France, Italy, and other countries. Start with the grilled goat cheese with greens, a startling rendition of this humble dish; or the Portuguese fritters—made with either black-eyed peas and shrimp or salt cod and potatoes—served with pepper sauce and garlic mayonnaise. For a main course, you might enjoy Ecuadorean braised pork with chile and beer served with stuffed potato pancake and hominy, coq au vin made with red wine and prunes, and osso bucco gremolata with white wine and porcini mushroom sauce. If the black-bottom coconut cream pie is on the menu, don't miss it. Prices range from $12 to $17.

Hours: Wed–Mon 11am–2:30pm and 5:30–9:30pm.

All Seasons Cafe, 1400 Lincoln Ave. (☎ 707/942-9111), is a sunny corner bistro in town and has been the domain of chef Mark Dierkhising for more than 25 years. He has been turning out inventive, intensely flavored food worthy of the ingredients to the satisfaction of locals for that long. Dishes show all kinds of influences—Pacific Rim, Southwestern, and Mediterranean—and are designed to complement the many wines that are available by the glass. You might find grilled tenderloin of beef served with potato gratin and sauced with a sweet onion and balsamic reduction, or Sonoma duck breast with herb polenta topped with a rich duck glaze, summer peaches, basil, and toasted almond. Pastas and pizzas are also offered. Stop in, too, at the wine shop.

Hours: Thurs–Tues 11am–3pm and 5:30–10pm.

Napa Valley
Special & Recreational Activities

Aerial Tours: Bridgeford Flying Service, Napa County Airport, on Highway 12/29 just south of the town of Napa (☎ 707/224-0887), offers scenic tours of the valley. Costs range from $40 per person for a local tour to $135 for a Napa & Golden Gate tour.

Ballooning: There are several choices in Yountville. **Adventures Aloft at Vintage 1870** (☎ 707/ 944-4408) has been operating for more than 20 years; **Balloon Aviation** (☎ 707/944-4400) has also been in business a long time; another one of the top companies is **Napa Valley Balloons** (☎ 707/944-0228), which launches from Domaine Chandon.

In the town of Napa, you can also contact **Bonaventura Balloon Company** (☎ 707/944-2822), founded by musician, teacher, historian, and designer Joyce Bowen, who describes ballooning as "meditation" and whose company specializes in small groups of four to six people. Although the time aloft is usually only about 1 hour, allow 3 hours total for travel and post-flight breakfast.

In Calistoga, try **Once in a Lifetime,** 1546 Lincoln Ave. (☎ 707/942-6541).

Biking: In Napa, you might try **Bicycle Trax,** 796 Soscol Ave. (☎ 707/258-8729), where hybrid rentals are $20 a day; **Napa Valley Cyclery,** 4080 Byway East (☎ 707/253-3380), rents road tourers for $22 a day and hybrids for $28 and also has tandems and trailers. The best riding around Napa is along the Silverado Highway. Avoid Highway 29.

For rentals in Calistoga go to **Getaway Adventures,** 117 Lincoln Ave. (☎ 707/942-0332), which rents for $25 a day and also offers half- and full-day tours ($49 and $79, respectively) that visit assorted Napa and Sonoma destinations; you could also try **Palisades Mountain Sport,** 1330 B. Gerrard (☎ 707/942-9687); rates are $15 for 4 hours, $25 for 8 hours.

In St. Helena, try **St. Helena Cyclery,** 1156 Main St. (☎ 707/963-7736), which rents bikes for $25 a day and is well situated closer to the center of the valley.

Boating: Lake Hennessey Recreational Area, Sage Canyon Road (☎ 707/257-9529), has a boat ramp, fishing, picnicking, and hiking facilities open in the summer only. **Lake Berryessa,** east of Rutherford, is another center for water sports, camping, and picnicking. For information call ☎ 707/996-2111.

Camping: In addition to Lake Berryessa, mentioned under "Boating" above, **Bothe–Napa Valley State Park,** 3801 St. Helena Hwy. N., Calistoga, CA 94515 (☎ 707/942-4575), has 50 sites. Reservations are recommended.

Cruising: The sternwheeler **City of Napa** sallies forth on the river for a 3½-hour Saturday night dinner cruise with dancing to Dixieland jazz, and a 3-hour Sunday morning brunch cruise. It leaves from the Napa Valley Marina at 1200 Milton Rd. in Napa. For more information contact **Napa Riverboat Co.,** 1400 Duhig Rd. (☎ 707/226-2628).

Golf: The course to play is at the **Chardonnay Golf Club,** 2555 Jameson Canyon Rd., off Highway 12/29 south of the town of Napa (☎707/257-8950), which costs $80 weekends and $60 weekdays; or the **Napa Municipal Course** at Kennedy Park, Napa–Vallejo Highway, 2295 Streblow Rd. (☎ 707/255-4333), which is a quarter of the price and rated equally.

There are also two courses at the **Silverado Country Club,** 16000 Atlas Peak Rd., Napa (☎ 707/257-0200), for members and guests only.

Hiking: Climb to the top of Mount St. Helena in **Robert Louis Stevenson State Park,** 3801 Hwy. 29 (☎ 707/942-4575), which is located about 7 miles north of Calistoga.

Horseback Riding: Wild Horse Valley Ranch, Wild Horse Valley Rd., Napa (☎ 707/224-0727), offers a 2-hour trail ride for $40, plus pony rides for children under 8.

Soaring: Calistoga Gliders Inc., 1546 Lincoln Ave., Calistoga (☎ 707/942-5000), flies within a 5- to 8-mile radius of Calistoga. Make a reservation if you don't want to be disappointed. A 20-minute ride for one will cost $69, for two $110; or $99 for 30 minutes for one, $149 for two. The best time to go is after a rainstorm when the air is really clear.

Spas: See "Taking A Mud Bath" in the Calistoga section above for details.

State Parks: Bothe–Napa Valley State Park, 3801 Hwy. 29, north of St. Helena (☎ 707/942-4575), is a 1,916-acre park with camping, hiking, and swimming facilities; **Robert Louis Stevenson State Park,** 3801 Hwy. 29, north of Calistoga (☎ 707/942-4575).

Swimming: There's swimming in Bothe–Napa Valley State Park.

Tennis: Many of the more elaborate resorts, including Meadowood and Silverado, have excellent tennis facilities that are open only to their guests. For courts available at local high schools as well as others that might be open to the public, call the local chambers of commerce.

Sonoma County

Distances in Miles: Sonoma, 70; Santa Rosa, 58; Sebastopol, 60; Healdsburg, 75; Bodega Bay, 68; Jenner, 80; Fort Ross, 92; Sea Ranch, 112

Estimated Driving Times: 1½ hours to Sonoma; 1¼ hours to Santa Rosa; 1¼ hours to Sebastopol; 1¾ hours to Healdsburg; 1¼ hours to Bodega Bay; 1¾ hours to Jenner; 2 hours to Fort Ross; 2¼ hours to Sea Ranch

Driving: For the towns of the Sonoma Valley, take Highway 101 north to its junction with Highway 37 in Novato. After a few miles, you'll turn onto Highway 121 north, which you follow to its junction with Highway 12. Instead of continuing east onto Highway 12/121 to Napa, take Highway 12 into the town of Sonoma.

If you are going directly to Santa Rosa or the Russian River Valley, take Highway 101 all the way into Santa Rosa, following it on into Healdsburg.

Highway 1 meanders along the coast and is obviously the most scenic route to most of the destinations along the coast of Sonoma County.

The most direct route to coastal locations, though, is Highway 101 north to the Cotati, which is just south of Rohnert Park. From there, you get onto Highway 116 to Sebastopol, where you can get onto the Bodega Highway. Eventually, it connects with Highway 1, which goes on up the coast from Bodega Bay.

If your destination on the coast is above Bodega Bay, you may save time by continuing on Highway 116 through Guerneville and following it down the Russian River to connect with Highway 1 just south of Jenner for points north.

Further Information: For information on Sonoma County, especially about its wine-producing regions, contact the **Sonoma County Wine & Visitors Center,** 5000 Roberts Lake Rd., Rohnert Park, CA 94928 (☎ 707/586-3795); or you could contact the **Sonoma Valley Visitors Bureau,** 453 First St. E., Sonoma, CA 95476 (☎ 707/996-1090).

For information about Santa Rosa, contact the **Greater Santa Rosa Conference & Visitors Bureau,** 637 First St., Santa Rosa, CA 95404 (☎ 707/577-8674).

For information on Sebastopol, contact the **Sebastopol Area Chamber of Commerce,** 265 S. Main St., Sebastopol, CA 95473 (☎ 707/823-3032). For Forestville, contact the **Forestville Chamber of Commerce,** P.O. Box 546, Forestville, CA 95436 (☎ 707/887-2246).

For information on the Russian River Valley, contact the **Russian River Chamber of Commerce,** 16200 First St., Guerneville, CA 95446 (☎ 707/869-9000); or the **Healdsburg Area Chamber of Commerce,** 217 Healdsburg Ave., Healdsburg, CA 95448 (☎ 800/648-9922 or 707/433-6935).

For information on Coastal Sonoma, contact the **Bodega Bay Chamber of Commerce,** 850 Hwy. 1, Bodega Bay, CA 94923 (☎ 707/875-3422); or the **Gualala/Sea Ranch Coastal Chamber of Commerce,** P.O. Box 338, Gualala, CA 95445 (☎ 800/778-LALA [800/778-5252]).

"The chosen spot of all this Earth" is how the horticulturist Luther Burbank described Sonoma County. Even today, 120 years later, it's hard to argue with that statement. The county is still blessed with a magnificent rugged coastline abundant with fish, fast-flowing streams and rivers, rolling hills and meadows, and rich soil—blessings that have served its residents well. The premier product of Sonoma may be wine, but the county is also famous for many agricultural products, including the luscious Sonoma lamb, ducks from Reichardt farms, and a great variety of dairy (like Laura Chenel goat cheese) and fruit products (including the famous blackberries from Kozlowski's Farms and Gravenstein apples from Sebastopol), plus oysters from Tomales Bay, and salmon caught by the Bodega Bay fishing fleet. Increasingly too, the county is becoming known for its olive oils, flavored vinegars, mustards, salsas, and more.

One way to view and sample this agricultural bounty is to attend the **Sonoma County Farmers Market,** which is held every Saturday from June to October in Santa Rosa. The other is to visit the farms themselves. If you want to do this, secure a copy of the **Sonoma County Farm Trails Map,** which shows the locations of more than 100 farms that are open to the public (20 farms with mini-tours, 21 apple ranches, 22 pumpkin farms, 23 Christmas tree farms, and 24 specialty nurseries). You can pick it up at any of the farmstands or visitor information centers, or write to Sonoma County Farm Trails, P.O. Box 6032, Santa Rosa, CA 95401.

Needless to say, such a rich land affords many splendors for visitors in search of good food, good wine, bountiful and beautiful gardens, dramatic forest and ocean landscapes—in short, many wonderful weekends.

History

And Sonoma is not short on history, either, having spawned many dramatic personalities and events. Amazingly, six different flags have flown over the county—those of Spain, England, Imperial Russia, Mexico, the

Sonoma County

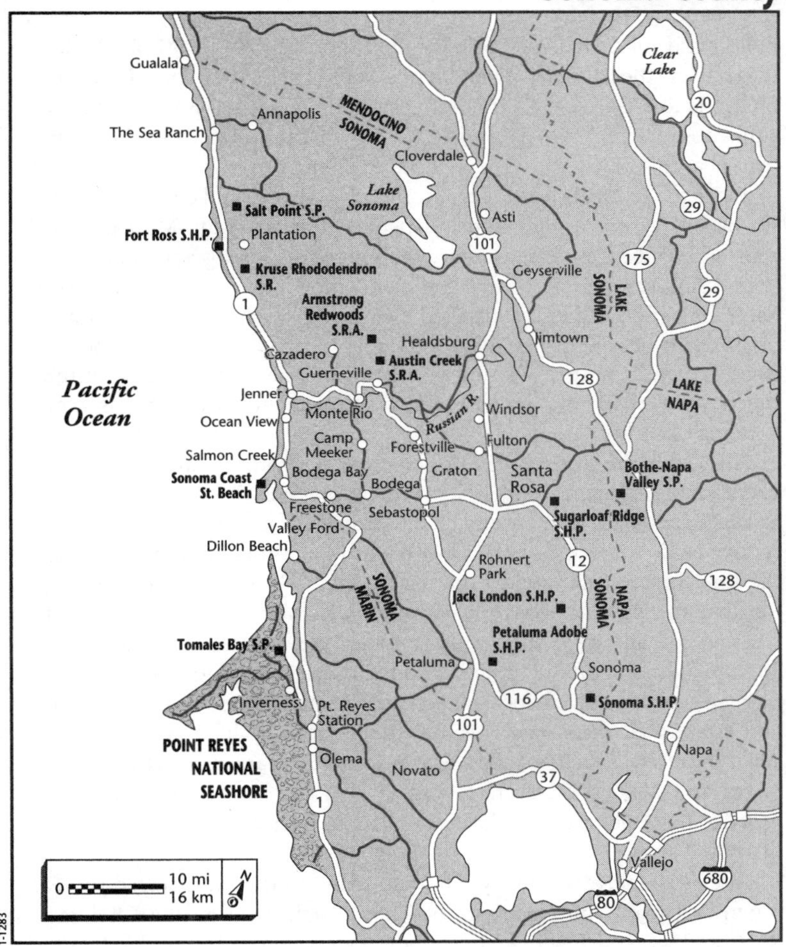

Bear Flag of the Republic of California, and, finally, that of the United States. Before the arrival of the Spanish in the early 1800s, the land was inhabited by the Miwok, Wappo, and Pomo Indians, who fished the rivers and streams and hunted in the forests. After the Spanish conquered Mexico in 1521, they claimed Alta California and sent many explorers north to chart the coastline. Later, in 1579, Sir Francis Drake claimed the region for Elizabeth I when he landed at Drake's Bay in Marin County.

Meanwhile, the Russians, who were searching for a source of supplies for their settlements in Alaska, settled at Ross (an archaic name for Russia) on the Sonoma County coastline and established a fort there in 1812, much to the consternation of the Californios (Mexican rancheros) and the Yankee traders in the region. The group consisted of 95 Russians and 80 Aleuts who built the commander's quarters, a chapel, and seven other buildings behind a redwood palisade. In addition there were 50-plus buildings outside the palisade. When they had exhausted the supply of seal and otter, the Russians sold their holdings to John Sutter in 1841 for a paltry sum, most of which was never paid. Today you can still visit Fort Ross and marvel at this lonely, but very civilized Russian outpost.

Once the Russians left, the real contest for who should control California began. When Mexico won independence from Spain, Mexican citizens and soldiers were rewarded with enormous land grants, none less than 4,500 acres. Here on these ranchos they lived graciously in their haciendas while vaqueros controlled their herds. The hide and tallow trade made them rich, and they lived well, able to purchase such luxuries as rugs, carved furniture, silk and lace garments, and jewelry. One of the rancheros was General Vallejo, who controlled much of what is now Sonoma County.

Although the region was under Mexican control, many Yankees had gained influence. Some, like Captain Stephen Smith, had married Spanish-speaking women and taken Mexican citizenship in order to receive land grants. Others had moved into California from the east after the first wagon train crossed the Sierras in 1841. They began agitating for land and power. Friction was common between the Californios and the Yankees, and in 1846 a group of Americans arrested General Vallejo and took him to Fort Sutter, designed their own flag incorporating a five-pointed star and a grizzly bear, which they erected in the plaza of Sonoma, and established their own government declaring California a republic. Their "republic" lasted but a few days because the war between the United States and Mexico intervened, and the whole of Alta California was ceded to the Americans. California became the 31st state to join the Union in 1850.

After the gold rush, many who had come to the West stayed on. A rough and ready hunting camp had been established on the Petaluma River, and soon the first town in Sonoma county grew up around it. Farmers moved into the area and cultivated hops, grapes, prunes, apples, eggs, and dairy products, but it wasn't until the building of the railroad in 1870 that the county was opened to the lucrative markets of the Bay area. The meat and dairy industries thrived, but the hops and grape industries, forerunners of today's wine industry, suffered severe setbacks during Prohibition and the Depression. It wasn't until the 1970s that the grape and wine industry revived. The hops industry never recovered.

World War II transformed the county and the state. The Golden Gate Bridge had opened up all of the counties north of San Francisco, and the war effort brought thousands to California to man the defense industries. Thousands of soldiers were stationed around Santa Rosa; the shipyards at Sausalito and Vallejo attracted workers from the South and Midwest; and many, if not all, of these new residents stayed in their newfound paradise.

Planning Your Weekends in Sonoma County

You'll need several weekends to fully explore Sonoma County, and for this reason I have divided the county up into four distinct areas: Sonoma and the Sonoma Valley; the Russian River Valley (looping from Santa Rosa via Sebastopol, Occidental, Monte Rio, Guerneville, and Forestville to Healdsburg); Healdsburg, Lake Sonoma, and the Dry Creek, Alexander and Knights valleys; and coastal Sonoma. Of course, you can devise many different wine-tasting weekends, built either around such special events as the Russian River Barrel Tasting or around particular wines—chardonnays one weekend, gewürztraminers another, sparkling wines still another, and zinfandels on yet another.

Wine Legends, Tasting & Touring

Today there are approximately 185 wineries, 36,000 acres of grapes, and 10 appellations in Sonoma County, providing ample opportunities for a variety of pleasurable touring and tasting weekends. For me, touring and tasting in Sonoma County is more down to earth, less pretentious, and less crowded and frantic than Napa, where so many of the vineyards are owned by giant corporations (Seagram, Disney, Coca-Cola and others). Although large corporations like Suntory, Hiram Walker, and Chevron have purchased Sonoma wineries, there are still many that are family-owned and that offer a more intimate, low-key atmosphere and experience. The most familiar names associated with the region are Sebastiani, Gundlach Bundschu, and Ravenswood in Sonoma; Arrowood, Glen Ellen, Kenwood, and Chateau St. Jean farther up the Sonoma Valley; Matanzas Creek out along Warm Springs Road and Bennett Valley Road; plus the names associated with the Russian River and the Dry Creek valleys, from Davis Bynum to Dry Creek and Ferrari–Carano.

Sonoma was, in fact, the birthplace of the California wine industry. The Franciscans at the Sonoma Mission planted the first vines at what is now the Sebastiani winery on 4th Street East in the town of Sonoma, but the key pioneer was Agoston Haraszthy, a Hungarian count whose sons married General Vallejo's daughters and who founded Buena Vista. Haraszthy traveled to Europe, collecting rootstock and cuttings and experimenting with different grapes and techniques. From 1857 to 1858 he erected an impressive villa and established the first commercial winery at Buena Vista. The first vintage was celebrated at a masked ball in October 1864 at his villa on Castle Road.

By 1875, only a decade later, Sonoma was the largest producer of wine in the state. It continued to develop until its decline during Prohibition and the Depression. Not until the mid-1970s did the true rebirth and redevelopment of Sonoma as a prominent wine region begin, when Chateau St. Jean, De Loach, Jordan, and Matanzas Creek were established. Another boom followed in the 1980s. Much of this in hindsight can be attributed to the marketing efforts of the Glen Ellen winery, which promoted chardonnays for under $5 a bottle, an approach that almost singlehandedly, it seemed, primed and prepared the American palate for finer wines.

The California wine business differs from that of France. As you might expect, it's looser and somewhat freer in its application of rules and regulations. In France the variety of grapes one is allowed to grow in a particular region is closely regulated. For example, only chardonnay and pinot noir can be grown and used in Burgundy, and if a winemaker uses grapes from outside the region, he can only call the result a "table wine." In California such strict rules do not apply, though the county is still divided into six distinct appellations. They are, in order of grape acreage Alexander Valley (8,437 acres), Russian River (8,375), Sonoma Valley (5,900), Dry Creek Valley (5,500), Chalk Hill (1,600), Green Valley (1,000), and Knights Valley (1,000).

The **Alexander Valley** stretches north along the east bank of the Russian River from Healdsburg to Cloverdale. It incorporates a variety of soils and microclimates, enabling it to produce exceptional grapes—chardonnay, sauvignon blanc, cabernet sauvignon, merlot, and zinfandel. There are few wineries to visit in the area (Murphy–Goode is one example), but the drive through the Alexander and Knights valleys to the northern end of the Napa Valley is very scenic.

The **Sonoma Valley** stretches north of Sonoma along the Valley of the Moon. Kenwood, Glen Ellen, and Matanzas are the celebrated names here.

The **Russian River** appellation stretches southwest of Healdsburg and is noted for producing chardonnay and pinot noir, plus more sparkling wine than anywhere else in the state. The river and the fog there make it a cool growing area. The Russian River Valley has come a long way from its early days in the 1920s and '30s, when it was known for its hops and prunes. This is a prime touring and tasting area.

The **Dry Creek Valley** extends northwest of Healdsburg along the west bank of the river to Lake Sonoma. The warm hillsides at the northern end are planted with zinfandel, petite sirah, cabernet sauvignon, merlot, and sauvignon. Chardonnay and gewürztraminer are grown in the south. This is another prime touring and tasting area.

Chalk Hill, which is adjacent to the Russian River appellation, derives its name from its white, volcanic soil, which looks like chalk. It is warmer and hillier than the adjacent areas. Chardonnay is the primary grape grown.

The **Green Valley** is centered on Forestville and is known more for its fruit orchards, although chardonnay and pinot noir are also grown here.

Knights Valley extends east between the Alexander Valley and the Mayacamas Mountains, which separate Sonoma from Napa County. Grapes have been grown here since the late 1800s. Because it is not exposed to any ocean influences, this is the warmest area in the Sonoma region. The soil is rocky and few grapes are produced here, but the cabernet sauvignon is quite good.

Events & Festivals to Plan Your Trip Around

Sonoma/Sonoma Valley & Santa Rosa

May: The **Luther Burbank Rose Parade & Festival** in downtown Santa Rosa brings out a medley of marching bands, floats, and fire trucks, all celebrating the beauty of the rose. In addition there's dancing, food and wine, an antique show, and other festivities. For information call ☎ 707/577-ROSE (707/577-7673).

All Summer Long: The **Sonoma County Wine & Food Tasting Series** continues in downtown Sonoma, where there is music as well as food; some events are held in Jliard Park. For information call ☎ 707/576-0162.

July: The **Kenwood Pillow Fights** start with a parade that proceeds to Plaza Park, where the pillow fights take place between individuals and teams. Each fighter sits atop a pole and tries to dislodge the other using pillows until they fall into a mud pit. The fights go on most of the day until the winners are determined. In addition there is music, food, wine, pony rides, and other entertainments. For information call ☎ 707/833-2440.

The **Sonoma County Showcase and Wine Auction** is a 4-day event of wine tastings, barrel auctions, and other private celebrations topped off by an auction of rare and collectible vintages. For information call ☎ 707/586-3797.

The **Sonoma County Fair** is a 13-day celebration of the bounty of the county. Arts and crafts, a flower show, a rodeo, horse races, and a carnival are all part of the event that takes place in the Santa Rosa Fairgrounds.

August/September: The **Scottish Gathering and Games** in Santa Rosa is when some of the stalwart young descendants of Scottish pioneers try tossing the caber and throwing the hammer like their ancestors and join in other Scottish frolics—Highland flings, piping and drumming, and much, much more. Call ☎ 707/577-8674 for information.

September/October: The **Vintage Festival** is a major celebration for Sonoma. On the first day, the grapes are blessed at the Mission. The Festival also includes a reenactment of the marriages between the sons of Count Agoston Haraszthy and the daughters of General Vallejo, the raising of the Bear Flag on the plaza, plus wine tasting, an arts and crafts festival, and other entertainments. For more information call ☎ 707/938-1578.

continues

continued

October: At the **Sonoma County Harvest Fair**, held each year at the Sonoma County Fairgrounds in Santa Rosa, medals are awarded to the best wines produced from the county's grapes. Celebrations also focus on all the other bounties produced in the county. For information call ☎ 707/545-4203.

Sebastopol & the Russian River Valley

March: At the **Russian River Barrel Tasting**, about 50 wineries showcase wines still in the barrel along with foods that enhance them. Each year the participating wineries are listed in a brochure that is available by February 1. For information write or call: Russian River Barrel Tasting, P.O. Box 46, Healdsburg, CA 95448 (☎ 800/723 6336). Usually the first weekend in March.

April: The **Sebastopol Apple Blossom Festival** celebrates the region's prime fruit with a parade, arts and crafts contests, flower show, plenty of good musical entertainment, and a micro-brew and wine tent. Call ☎ 707/823-3032 for more information.

June/July: It's certainly uplifting to view the **Hot Air Balloon Classic** in Windsor. It starts early in the morning (4 or 5am), but it's inspirational to watch the sunrise and the 40 or 50 balloons, all different shapes and colors, filling up in preparation for the race, which involves some challenge or obstacle that has to be met. The event generates a carnival atmosphere, and there are plenty of other activities and festivities to enjoy. For additional information call ☎ 707/577-8674.

July: A unique festival that takes place in Sebastopol each July is the **Teriyaki Chicken Barbecue and Japanese Bon Dancing Festival.** It's held at the Enmanji Temple (☎ 707/823-2252), which is just south of town.

August: The **Gravenstein Apple Fair** is celebrated in an oak grove in Sebastopol. It's a real country event with farm demonstrations, agricultural machinery displays and competitions, farm animals, and a special kids' play area. For information call ☎ 707/824-2060.

Coastal Sonoma

April: At the **Fisherman's Festival** at Bodega Bay, the fishing fleet, decked out in banners and ribbons, is blessed. The festivities include a boat parade, bathtub races (in which boats fashioned from air-filled milk cartons, styrofoam, or similar material race around a buoy), a lamb and oyster barbecue, plus music, an arts and crafts fair, and more. For information call ☎ 707/875-3422.

June: The **Festival of the Arts at Duncans Mill** celebrates summer with an arts and crafts festival and more. For information call ☎ 707/824-8404.

You won't want to miss the **Taste of Bodega Bay** salmon feast. Pick up tickets at the chamber of commerce for a taste of the season. Call ☎ 707/875-3422 for information.

September: The **Bodega Bay Sandcastle-Building Competition** at Doran Beach brings out some inspirational sand architects. It coincides with coast cleanup day—something that has to be done before the fun starts.

The **Taste of Bodega Bay** crab cioppino dinner is another fun event. Pick up tickets for this delicious feast at the chamber of commerce. Call ☎ 707/875-3422 for information.

In addition to these appellations, the **Carneros** region is shared with Napa and produces great pinot noirs and chardonnays.

EXPLORING THE SONOMA VALLEY

If you want to see this area in one weekend, the ideal way to do so is to spend some time in Sonoma exploring the stores, attractions, and wineries there, and then drive over to Glen Ellen and Jack London State Park before entering the Valley of the Moon and exploring the wineries along Highway 12, which will eventually lead you to Santa Rosa.

SONOMA VALLEY WINERIES

Most of these wineries are open for tours or tastings daily from 10am to 4:30pm. Unlike the wineries in Napa, most wineries here do not charge for tastings. If you really want to take a tour of a particular winery, call ahead to ascertain the time and frequency of tours so you won't be disappointed. The wineries in this section are located in a relatively compact area along the Sonoma Highway, from the town of Sonoma in the south to Santa Rosa in the north; they're listed below in alphabetical order. You shouldn't plan to visit more than three or four wineries in one day.

The **Sonoma County Convention & Vistors Bureau,** 5000 Roberts Lake Road, Suite A, Rohnert Park, CA 94928 (☎ 800/326-7666 or 707/586-8100), publishes a useful guide to the Sonoma wine country.

Arrowood, 14347 Sonoma Hwy., Glen Ellen, CA 95442 (☎ 707/938-5170), is a small property without the hoopla of many of its neighbors. Tours and tastings are offered daily by appointment only at 2pm.

Benziger, 1883 London Ranch Rd., Glen Ellen, CA 95442 (☎ 707/935-4046), is one of the prettiest wineries in the valley. Their tours take visitors out into the actual vineyards aboard a tractor-pulled trolley. The winery is located up the hill from Glen Ellen on the slopes of Jack London State Park. It's a delightful place to visit and still retains a family air, thanks to the old home and gardens at the center of the property. Step under the wisteria-draped gate and pass over the hump-backed bridge to the tasting room. The wine label museum is also well worth seeing. You can see the original art that was created by 60-plus contemporary artists for the labels of the Imagery Series of wines. The vineyard's first wines were made in 1981, and its Chardonnay and Sauvignon Blanc won the Sonoma sweepstakes in 1992. There's also a picnic area.

Buena Vista, 18000 Old Winery Rd., Sonoma, CA 95476 (☎ 707/938-1266), is the state's oldest premium winery, dating back to 1857. Guided and self-guided tours are available. Pleasant picnic area, too.

Chateau St. Jean, 8555 Sonoma Hwy., Kenwood, CA 95452 (☎ 707/833-4134), is a very pleasant vineyard to visit. It has an alluring Spanish courtyard with central fountain and attractive gardens and picnic area. There's a self-guided tour.

Gundlach–Bundschu, 2000 Denmark St., Sonoma, CA 95476 (☎ 707/938-5277). Although Jacob Gundlach planted his first vines in 1885, the property wasn't restored and formally opened as a winery until the early 1970s. One of the buildings has a dramatic 120-foot long mural depicting the contributions that the Mexicans have made to the wine industry. There's a small picnic area in front of original stone winery and a self-guided tour.

Gloria Ferrer Champagne Caves, 23555 Hwy. 121, Sonoma, CA 95476 (☎ 707/996-7256), offers a guided tour that explains the *méthode champenoise* and also visits the production area and the caves, depending on the season. The tasting room is spacious and airy, and you can sit down and enjoy a full glass of wine for a charge. There's also a pleasant terrace that visitors may use if they buy a bottle of wine.

Kenwood, 9592 Sonoma Hwy., Kenwood, CA 95452 (☎ 707/833-5891), is an inviting, woodsy winery that makes terrific chardonnays, sauvignon blancs, zinfandels, and cabernets. The chardonnays are made from the grapes that come from the Beltane Ranch vineyard, which can be seen on the eastern side of the valley, set well back from the road. Tastings are available daily, but tours are by appointment only. The tasting room is a lively place and offers a lot of merchandise plus music in the background.

Kunde Estate, 10155 Sonoma Hwy., Kenwood, CA 95452 (☎ 707/833-5501), offers a picnic area but tours by appointment only. Tastings are available daily.

Sonoma Valley Wineries

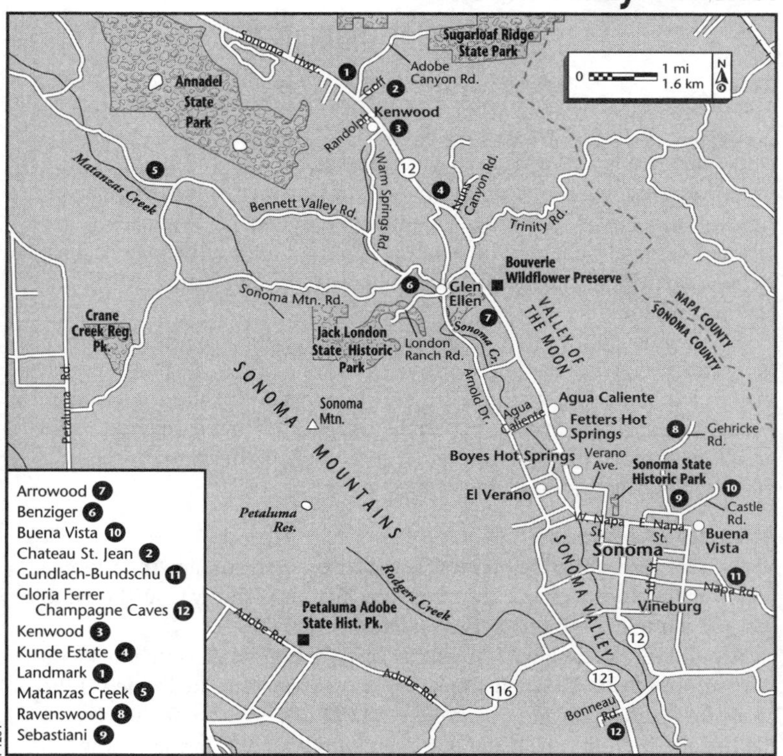

Landmark, 101 Adobe Canyon Rd., Kenwood, CA 95452 (☎ 707/833-0053 or 707/833-1144), is a lovely vineyard to visit. The tiled terrace affords a magnificent view of Sugarloaf Mountain, and in winter the tasting room is warmed by a fire. There's also a pondside picnic area. Tours are by appointment only.

Matanzas Creek, 6097 Bennett Valley Rd., Santa Rosa, CA 95404 (☎ 707/528-6464), which is slightly off the beaten track, makes great merlots, and this is the primary reason to visit. Sculptures add character to the property, and there are two picnic tables set under trees affording inspiring views of Bennett Valley. The company also harvests and sells lavender.

Ravenswood, 18701 Gehricke Rd., Sonoma, CA 95476 (☎ 707/938-1960), has a picnic area. Tours are offered by appointment only.

Sebastiani, 389 Fourth St. E., Sonoma, CA 95476 (☎ 707/938-5532), was the original Mission vineyard, which was purchased by Sebastiani in the last decade of the 19th century. Originally Samuele Sebastiani sold his wine from door to door. Today the vineyard offers a good, informative tour; visitors can also see several hundred barrel-head carvings, including those made by Earle Brown. A picnic area is available.

THE TOWN OF SONOMA

The plaza is the heart of Sonoma. At eight acres, it's the biggest plaza in California. At the center of the square stands a monument to the rebels who, impatient with the Mexican government's law against foreigners (read Americans) owning property, raised the Bear Flag on this spot on June 14, 1846, and declared California a republic independent of Mexico. They arrested General Vallejo, who acted as a very cool and hospitable host offering them wine and victuals before he was transported to Sutter's Fort for imprisonment.

The flag flew until July 7, when the Mexican capital of Alta California, Monterey, was seized by the Americans. When this news reached Sonoma, the United States flag was raised by Lt. Joseph Revere, and the republic ended. Vallejo was returned to Sonoma in August but found that his rancho had been stripped of its horses, cattle, and other commodities by the Bear Flaggers and Capt. John C. Frémont.

Attractions in Sonoma

Visitors may recognize the building at the center of the square, the Sonoma City Hall, because it played the role of the Tuscany County Courthouse in the popular television series, *Falcon Crest.*

Around the plaza stand many other historic buildings, which make up the **Sonoma State Historic Park,** whose headquarters are located at the corner of Spain Street and 3rd Street West (☎ 707/938-1519). To view all the historic buildings near the plaza, pick up a map from the visitor bureau in the center of the plaza and follow the chamber of commerce walking tour.

The most important historic structure in the park is the **Mission St. Francisco Solano,** at the corner of Spain Street and 1st Street East. It was the 21st mission and was established on July 4, 1823, by Father José Altimira. The original no longer stands; the present plain and simple building was built in the 1840s to serve as Sonoma's parish church.

Mission Solano had a somewhat stormy history. Father Altimira had hatched a plan for this new mission to replace San Francisco's Mission Dolores and to subjugate Mission San Rafael. Although he had cleared the plan with Governor Arguillo, neither one of them had secured permission from ecclesiastical authorities. A dispute naturally followed and was resolved by the church allowing Altimira to establish the mission in Sonoma without touching either Mission Dolores or San Rafael.

When the mission was completed, Padre Altimira operated it with an iron fist and mistreated the neophytes to such an extent that an angry band set fire to the buildings and drove Altimira away. Father Buenaventura Fortuni, who arrived in 1826, restored order and operated Mission Solano successfully until its secularization in 1834, when General Vallejo, who had been sent north to observe the Russians at Fort Ross, took over. From then on it served primarily as a parish church for another 50 years

Town of Sonoma

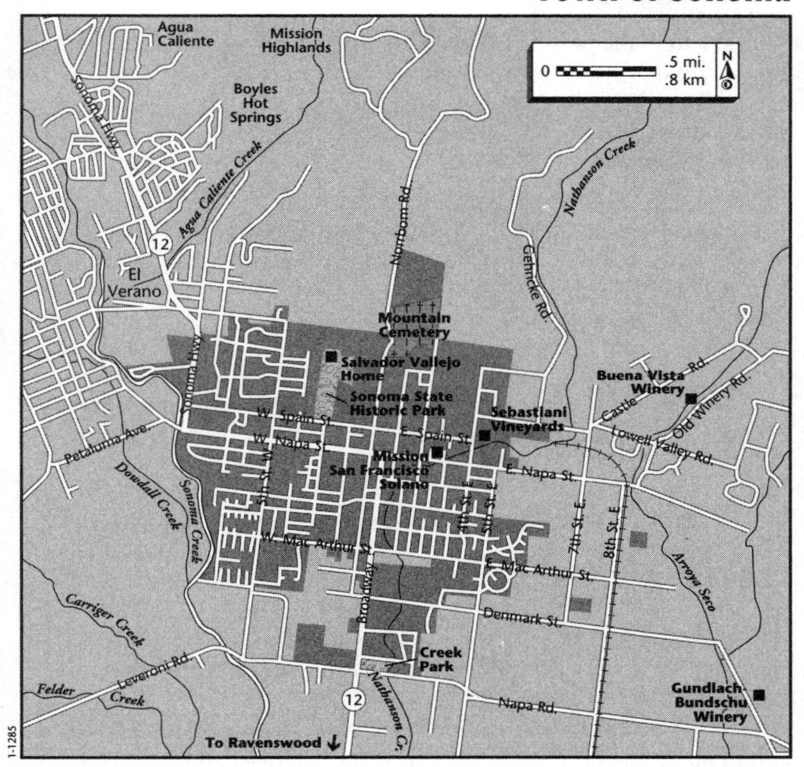

or so before it fell into disrepair and was sold for use as a winery and hay barn.

Today it has been restored. Stroll the arcade that runs along the front of the monastery building and view the single bell remaining from the original group that hung in front of the mission. Grapes are still blessed here every September or October on the first day of the Vintage Festival.

Other buildings in the historic park include the **Sonoma Barracks,** or Presidio, built in 1836 by General Vallejo. The Bear Flaggers used it as their headquarters during the revolt of 1846. Next to the barracks is the **Toscano Hotel.** Originally used as a library and retail store when it was constructed in the 1850s, it later served as a hotel at the turn of the century, often functioning as the first home to many Italian immigrants.

Next door, only the servants' quarters remain standing of the **Casa Grande,** General Vallejo's first house, in which his 11 children were born. In 1846 Vallejo was the most powerful man in Northern California (he owned 175,000 acres), and his house was the most imposing and well-furnished residence on the plaza. It was the center of social and diplomatic life in the region, and it was here, too, that General Vallejo, his brother Salvador, and his brother-in-law Jacob Leese were seized by the Bear Flaggers.

Also part of the park, the **Blue Wing Inn,** 133 E. Spain St., was built around 1840 to house travelers and immigrants and was operated as a hotel during the Gold Rush by a couple of retired seamen. Among its famous guests were John C. Frémont, future president Ulysses S. Grant, Kit Carson, and many others. Today it houses a series of gift shops.

Hours: Daily 10am–5pm. *Admission:* $2 adults, $1 children 6–12.

You might also want to see the **Vallejo Swiss Chalet,** 18 W. Spain St., which was built in 1852 by Don Salvador Vallejo. It was occupied by several pioneers including Dr. Victor Faure, who made the wines from the Vallejo family vineyards. Later it was used as a hotel and restaurant.

There are a variety of stores, restaurants, and hotels also located around the square and on side streets leading into the square, and they are certainly worth extensive browsing. Among them are the **Sonoma Cheese Factory,** 2 W. Spain St. (☎ 707/996-1000); **Vella Cheese Company,** 315 2nd St. East (☎ 707/938-3232); **Handworks,** 452 1st Street West (☎ 707/996-2255), which sells crafts by local artisans; **Legends,** 483 1st St. West (☎ 707/939-8100), which has some fine crafts; **Galerie Chevrier,** which sells works by regional painters and sculptors; **Zimbabwe Shona Sculpture** (☎ 707/938-2200), which displays and sells some magnificent sculpture from Zimbabwe; and the **Wine Exchange,** 452 1st St. East (☎ 707/938-1794). Just off the plaza, another place to try some local brew and enjoy a good breakfast is the **Feed Store Grill & Brewing Company,** 509 1st St. West (☎ 707/938-2122).

Not far from the square on West Spain Street, **General Vallejo's second home** sits in a verdant valley, a huge pomelo tree in the front courtyard. Built between 1851 and 1853 from a prefabricated Carpenter-Gothic frame shipped around the Horn, it was originally the heart of his 66,000 acre rancho and was named *Lachryma Montis* (Tears of the Mountain) after the nearby springs. The interior retains the original features and furnishings—marble fireplaces, crystal chandeliers, lace curtains, and a rosewood concert grand piano. Here, General Vallejo's 11 children grew up, and he and his wife continued to live here for more than 35 years. Although he lost most of his lands and was even forced to sell off the vineyard here, he remained generous to the end and remarkably unembittered. During his last years, he spent most of his time reading and writing a five-volume *History of California.* He died in 1890, aged 82, and is buried in the cemetery on the hill overlooking Sonoma. The house remained in the family until 1932, when it was given to the state.

Hours: Daily 10am–5pm. *Admission:* $2 (ncludes Sonoma Historic Park).

Sonoma possesses several viticultural landmarks. Foremost among them is the **Buena Vista Winery,** 18000 Old Winery Rd., which was the birthplace in 1857 of the California wine industry. Buena Vista was founded by Col. Agoston Haraszthy, who scoured Europe to obtain cuttings for his vines and supervised their planting as well as the construction of the caves.

Details for tours and tastings are given in the wineries section, below. You can also visit the **site of Count Haraszthy's villa,** which was located on Castle Road near the winery, though the villa itself is no longer standing.

Another wine-related landmark is the **Sebastiani Vineyard and Winery,** 394 4th St. East, at Spain Street. Here the Franciscan fathers planted the first vineyard in 1825 and produced sacramental wine until the secularization, when General Vallejo continued to produce wines. The vineyard was taken over in the 1890s by Samuele and Elvira Sebastiani, who had immigrated from Italy. You can take a tour or taste their wine (details given in the wineries section above).

Another historic building in Sonoma that is worth viewing is **Temelec Hall,** 20750 Arnold Ave. (about three miles out of Sonoma), a striking construction with square cupola, widow's walk, and two-story veranda on three sides. It was built in 1858 for Capt. Granville P. Swift, who came west in 1843, prospered during the gold rush, and participated in the Bear Flag Revolt. The house may well have been designed to surpass that of General Vallejo. It's not available for touring, unfortunately.

Lodging & Dining in Sonoma

Even though the **Sonoma Chalet**, 18935 Fifth St. W., Sonoma, CA 95476 (☎ 707/938-3129), is only three-quarters of a mile from the plaza, it has a very rustic air. It's surrounded by 3 acres of 100-year-old eucalyptus trees and rambling flower gardens and overlooks a 200-acre ranch where cattle graze. Guest rooms are located either in cottages or in the charming Swiss-style chalet that was built in the 1940s. In the chalet, you'll find a comfortable, old-fashioned living room featuring hand-painted murals, plus several guest rooms and the kitchen where breakfast is prepared. The two first-floor rooms share a bath. Each is decorated with antiques with an eye towards comfort as well as aesthetics. The upstairs suite has a sitting room and woodstove. The only drawback to staying on the first floor arises if the suite upstairs is occupied, for there is little soundproofing between floors. The three cottages are captivating. The Honeymoon cottage has a small wood stove, private bath with clawfoot tub, and a loft sleeping area. Each cottage is furnished with antiques, including quilts and other collectibles, and each is painted in bold colors. Additional rustic touches are crowing cocks, ducks, and a few geese. Breakfast is usually served outside on the deck with a view of the fields, in the country kitchen, or else brought to your cottage. It will include fresh fruit and juice, pastries, and cereal.

Rates (incl. breakfast): Apr–Oct, $95–$145 double; Nov–Mar, $85–$135.

The **El Dorado**, 405 First St. West, Sonoma, CA 95476 (☎ 707/996-3030, fax 707/996-3148), has a very convenient downtown location, along with some appealing features, such as a pool and a courtyard furnished with tables and market umbrellas—a perfect place for breakfast.

The 27 rooms are rather plainly decorated in a vaguely modern style. The ambience is provided by the Mexican tile floors and the French doors that lead out onto small terraces overlooking either the town square or the hotel's courtyard. Facilities also include **Piatti,** a restaurant serving specialties from the wood-burning oven and rotisserie.

Rates (incl. breakfast): Summer, $145–$155 double weekends and holidays, $115–$125 midweek; winter, $110–$120 and $95–$100, respectively.

The landmark salmon pink **Sonoma Mission Inn,** 18140 Hwy. 12, P.O. Box 1447, Sonoma, CA 95476 (☎ 707/938-9000), is set on eight acres, graced with eucalyptus and plane trees, just outside Sonoma. It bustles with life, receiving a steady stream of stressed-out people seeking relaxation at its European-style spa, which does in fact possess an artesian mineral water well. The building was constructed in 1927 and replicates a California mission complete with arcade and bell tower. The tiled lobby with a massive fireplace establishes the Mediterranean ambience. The 170 accommodations are decorated in a light and airy Plantation style with louvered shutters, ceiling fans, pine furnishings, floral fabrics, and terracotta lamps. Some have fireplaces and terraces. Standard amenities include TV, telephone, minibar, iron and ironing board, hair dryers, and bath robes.

Off the tiled lobby, the **Grille** is the premier dining room. It is light and airy with its pink walls, bleached wood, and rush-seated chairs. The dinner menu here will offer about nine or so dishes, some of which have their cholesterol and fat content spelled out. Among the appetizers, Sonoma foie gras might share a place with maple-glazed Sonoma quail served in a lemon rosemary citronette. Among the main dishes, there might be an oak stave–roasted salmon with French lentils, hickory smoked bacon, and sherry butter; or a succulent grilled rack of lamb with stewed white beans and escarole. There will always be a vegetable dish of some sort and also a pasta dish. Prices range from $17 to $26. The wine list offers more than 200 selections. The bistro-style **Cafe,** at the northern end of the resort, offers pizza, ribs, and other California and Italian favorites, plus bountiful American breakfasts.

The spa offers 50-plus treatments, from seaweed and mud wraps to facials and aromatherapy massages, which range in cost from $35 to $134. There are also weight and exercise equipment facilities plus a full range of exercise classes as well as individual consultations. Additional facilities include two tennis courts and two pools that are now filled with naturally hot artesian water, which was discovered in 1993 and had originally made Boyes Hot Springs, the original name of the springs as well as the name of the Sonoma suburb, famous before the artesian well ran dry. Services include room service, valet parking, turndown, and concierge.

Rates: $125–$390 double, $300–$650 suite.

Dining Only in Sonoma

In addition to Piatti at the El Dorado and the Sonoma Mission Inn Grille, both described under "Lodging in Sonoma" above, there are two other especially recommendable restaurants in Sonoma.

Della Santina's, 133 East Napa St., Sonoma (☎ 707/935-0576), is a tiny restaurant that locals frequent for its excellent, modestly priced Italian cuisine, especially the spit-roasted meats. You can start with salad, soup, or one of the nine or so pasta dishes. The cannelloni Florentine made with chicken, veal, and ricotta is a rich, flavorsome dish, so too is the *ravioli alla Lucchese,* which is veal-and-spinach–filled pasta in a meat and porcini mushroom sauce. There are at least half a dozen roast dishes, including a well-seasoned spit-roasted chicken with fresh herbs, a delicious herb-filled loin of pork, and spit-roasted Petaluma duck. The best deal is the $19.95-per-person special dinner for two or more, which provides salad, pasta, and a choice of three roasts. There are also a few fish dishes, including a fresh catch of the day. Prices range from $9 to $14.

Hours: Daily 11am–9:30pm (dinner from 4pm).

Babette's, 464 First St., Sonoma (☎ 707/939-8921), is set back down a little brick alley and offers a restaurant and separate wine bar, which is a funky, comfortable place where you can relax on sofas or armchairs and really sit back and savor the wine. The dining room is quiet and understated. It's the dining experience that people come for, notably the $45 five-course prix-fixe dinner served Thursday to Saturday evenings. It's a veritable feast that might begin with Dungeness crab "purse" with radishes and lime, and follow with a choice of ruby crescent potato soup infused with black truffle essence or a ragout of artichoke hearts and shiitake mushrooms with roasted garlic-balsamic vinaigrette. For the fish course, there might be poached striped bass with braised endive and thyme beurre blanc, which can be followed by the tournedos of beef loin with potato gratin and oxtail daube. To finish the meal, there will be several cheeses like a wonderful Montbriac, and for an additional $6 you can select one of the five delicious desserts, including a warm bittersweet chocolate tart with sun-dried cherry sauce, which would be my choice even though it takes 30 minutes and requires ordering in advance. For each course, the menu offers three choices, one of which is vegetarian. If you wish, you can add the $29 wine-pairing package and enjoy a wine selected for each course. Also, the first course and second courses will usually offer a splurge item for an additional charge—like Beluga caviar or sautéed Sonoma foie gras medallions with caramelized quince.

The wine bar/cafe menu offers a selection of snacks to accompany wine—mussels, oysters, paté de foie gras, and smoked salmon—plus soups, salads, sandwiches, and such simple entrees as cassoulet and penne with capers, olives, and roasted fennel-tomato sauce. Nightly specials are available after 6pm.

Hours: Summer, Tues–Sat 6–10pm; winter, Thurs–Sat 6–10pm. Wine bar/cafe: Daily noon–9 or 10pm.

KENWOOD, GLEN ELLEN & THE VALLEY OF THE MOON

North and West of Sonoma, stretches the Tuscan-looking **Valley of the Moon,** 17 miles long and barely 5 miles wide, between the Mayacamas to the east and Sonoma Mountains to the west. It's a gentle, heartwarming landscape, and it's worth stopping to linger a while at one of the vineyards or hostelries here or in the village of Glen Ellen. This is a prime grape-growing region, and in fact it supports about 13,000 acres of vineyards. The valley's name came courtesy of the local Indians, who observed that the moon appears to rise several times behind the hills lining the valley.

On the western edge of the valley rises Sonoma Mountain, where Jack London and his wife Charmian resided on their ranch. Today, it's the site of **Jack London State Park,** London Ranch Road (☎ 707/938-5216), an 800-acre park located a short distance from the village of Glen Ellen. London lived here on his ranch from 1905 until his death at the age of 40 in 1916. He settled here because, as he wrote in *Valley of the Moon,* "I ride over my beautiful ranch. Between my legs is a beautiful horse. The air is wine. The grapes on a score of rolling hills are red with autumn flame. Across Sonoma Mountain, wisps of sea fog are stealing. The afternoon sun smolders in the drowsy sky. I have everything to make me glad I am alive." His wife, Charmian continued to live here until her death in 1955, and today you can tour the House of Happy Walls, which she built in 1919 in memory of her husband.

London fans will love the exhibits, which capture the essence of his wild, roisterous life from his early days as the prince of oyster catchers to Alaskan prospector and voyager to the South Seas. Charmian was a sterling character, too, traveling alongside him on many a risky adventure.

From the museum you can wander over to the ruins of the couple's dream home, Wolf House, which was destroyed by fire just after its completion. The plans called for 26 rooms, 9 fireplaces, an 18,000-volume library, a manuscript vault, study, "stag party" room, and an atrium reflecting pool. All that remains are the stone walls and ghostlike brick chimneys. Nearby is London's grave site. West of the parking lot for the museum house, there's another parking area that gives access to London's cottage and some agricultural buildings, and also to the dam, lake, and bathhouse that London built. The park also has some bike and horse trails.

Hours: Daily 10am–5pm. *Admission:* $5 per car, $4 per car for seniors 60 and over.

At the base of the mountain, **Glen Ellen** has some delightful bed-and-breakfasts and also some enchanting dining.

Back in the Valley, Kenwood is a famous Sonoma name recognized for its winery and restaurant. It also boasts **Sugarloaf Ridge State Park,** Adobe Canyon Road (☎ 707/833-5712), which offers camping, horseback riding, and other activities. You can, for example, hike to the summit of Bald Mountain, which grants panoramic views of the area.

Lodging in Kenwood & Glen Ellen

The **Kenwood Inn & Spa,** 10400 Sonoma Hwy., Kenwood, CA 95452 (☎ 707/833-1293), is a wonderful retreat that will transport you to the Tuscan countryside. It's located only a 15-minute drive from the Sonoma plaza. Step through the portico into a lovely flagstone courtyard with pool and fountain surrounded by rose gardens. From here go through the wisteria-covered archway to reach the reception in the main building, easily recognizable by its ivy-encrusted exterior. There are some accommodations in this main building, but most are located in several burned-ocher adobe-style buildings arranged around the beautifully landscaped courtyard. The rooms are each spectacularly decorated and comfortably equipped. All 12 are suites. Each has private bath, fireplace, and balcony, and each is, it seems, more beautifully decorated than the next. My favorite has a burled maple bed as a focal point, set on honey-colored and cream carpets. A burgundy-and-gold down comforter covers the bed along with several cushions. Two large and comfortable off-white chairs are placed in front of the fireplace, and all is set against walls that are painted in an antiqued cream color. The bathroom has terra-cotta tile walls and marble-top sink with brass fittings.

The spa offers a full range of massage, skin care, and body treatments. Non-guests are welcome to use the spa, too.

Rates: Summer, $330–$400 double weekends, $275–$315 midweek; winter, $290–$330 and $245–$285, respectively.

To reach the **Beltane Ranch,** P.O. Box 395, 11775 Sonoma Hwy. (Highway 12), Glen Ellen, CA 95442 (☎ 707/996-6501), you turn off the main highway past fenced fields to a house on the slopes of the Mayacamas Mountains. It's surely among the most casual and relaxed places to stay in the area, where you can settle into a hammock and watch the big harvest moon pass over the valley. The double-porch house was built in 1892 by Thomas Bell for San Francisco "madam" Mary Ellen Pleasant (aka Mammy Pleasant), and it has retained some of its original elements including the rippled-glass panes in the windows. There are five rooms, all with private bath and private entrance. Rooms on the second floor have access to a veranda. They are comfortably furnished with antiques and eclectic pieces, many of which have been restored by the owner herself. There's a tennis court for guests to use and also trails on the property. The gardens, too, are a lovely spectacle.

Rates: $120–$155 double.

The **Glenelly Inn,** 5131 Warm Springs Rd., Glen Ellen, CA 95442 (☎ 707/996-6720), is located on a quiet side street. It was built as a small resort in 1916. The small stick-style house, where the current mother-and-daughter owners Ingrid and Kristi Hallamore reside, contains two suites with garden entrances and covered decks. Six other accommodations are in a second building with a double veranda. The rooms are brightly decorated, named after local wineries, and feature such luxuries as down comforters, thick bath towels, and good reading lights. Each is furnished differently. St. Francis has a white iron and brass bed; Grand Cru has an eye-catching treddle-base sink in the bathroom; St. Jean features a pine four-poster; while Glen Ellen has a whimsical hat collection among the decor. In front of these accommodations through a trellis entryway, there's a very alluring outdoor spa, surrounded by dozens of flower beds, shrubs, and other trees. Guests are pampered by both Kristi and Ingrid. Ingrid, who studied hotel management in her native Norway, is the premier gardener today, while Kristi combines her love of art and cooking in this innkeeping endeavor. A bountiful breakfast is served in the Common Room, which is enhanced by a cobblestone fireplace and handpainted murals created by a former owner; dishes will feature herbs, figs, apples, and plums in season from the garden. Guests might enjoy lemon French toast accompanied by turkey sausage, or a sausage and spinach frittata accompanied by fresh fruit juices, cereal, and pastries. Local cheeses and other delicacies are also served in the afternoon.

Rates (incl. breakfast): $105–$150 double.

In quiet Glen Ellen, the **Gaige House Inn,** 13540 Arnold Dr., Glen Ellen, CA 95422 (☎ 707/935-0237, fax 707/935-6411), is a handsome Victorian landmark with lovely rooms, pretty gardens, a spectacular back garden focused around a large outdoor pool, and a relaxed but formal air. The 1½-acre grounds are bordered by the Calabezas Creek and the wooded hills of the Coastal Range. The house was built around 1890. The nine rooms feature fine antiques and ultra-comfortable decor, as well as such fine details as reading lights with adjustable rheostats and original art in almost every room. Oversized towels, fluffy bathrobes, and English toiletries are found in the bathrooms, which often have clawfoot tubs. All have telephones; fireplaces and TVs are available in some rooms. The most spectacular room is the Gaige Suite, which has a four-poster canopied king bed, large whirlpool tub in the bathroom, and a wraparound balcony overlooking the garden and hills. The floor is covered in thick, wall-to-wall carpeting, and among the furnishings are large rattan peacock chairs. The garden rooms are the most private with outside entrances; they are also closest to the pool. They are furnished in various styles. You might find an iron bed and wicker furnishings or a four-poster combined with a handsome armoire. Breakfast is cooked by a professional chef and served at individual tables in four different seatings. Tea, soft drinks, and cookies are available all day long.

Rates (incl. breakfast): $155–$205 double, $255 suite weekends; $135–$185 double, $235 suite midweek.

Dining Only in Kenwood

The **Kenwood Restaurant**, 9900 Hwy. 12 (☎ 707/833-6326), offers some of the best dining in the wine country. On warm days, it's pleasant to dine outside, but on cooler days the simple oak and brick dining room with its long bar backed by painted vine is a good foil for the food. Start with the duck pâté accompanied by a Cumberland sauce and crudités, or with the baked portabella mushroom with goat cheese, tomato coulis, and garden vegetable. Among the dozen or so main courses, you'll always find a vegetarian dish and pasta of the day, plus such dishes as roast rack of lamb with bordelaise sauce or a Bodega Bay bouillabaisse. Sandwiches are also available. Prices range from $9 to $25.

Hours: Wed–Sun 11:30am–9pm.

SANTA ROSA

At the northern end of the valley, Santa Rosa was once part of a huge Mexican land grant held by Dona Maria Carrillo, mother-in-law of General Vallejo. It was incorporated in 1867 and is today the county seat. Although you may not want to spend a lot of time in Santa Rosa, unless you're searching for evening entertainment, there are a couple of attractions worth visiting.

Attractions in Santa Rosa

The **Luther Burbank Home and Gardens,** on Santa Rosa Avenue at Sonoma Avenue (☎ 707/524-5445), is Santa Rosa's prime attraction. Burbank, of course, was the great horticulturalist who introduced more than 800 new varieties of plants to the world, including the well-known Burbank potato, elephant garlic, and Shasta daisy. He arrived here in 1875 from Lancaster, Massachusetts, and stayed here until his death in 1926. In 1885 he purchased several acres in Sebastopol where he operated an experimental farm, but it wasn't until he published his catalog in 1893 that he became famous. Today you can tour his home and the grounds, including the rose gardens; "demonstration beds" containing lilies, dahlias, zinnias, asters, and various vegetables; as well as the drought-tolerant garden, the Victorian garden (lilacs and saucer magnolias), and the greenhouse. Stop into the gift shop, too, located in the carriage house. Obviously, the best seasons to visit are spring and summer when the gardens are in full bloom.

Hours: Gardens daily 8am–5pm; home Apr to mid-Oct, Wed–Sun 10am–3:30pm. *Admission:* Gardens are free; house is $3 adults, free for children under 12.

A garden of a different sort than Luther Burbank's can be found at 5000 Medica Rd. It took 20 years for Yugoslav artist John Medica to create this remarkable 20th-century **folk art landscape** of castles and other stonework.

Across the street from the Burbank garden, adjacent to Juilliard Park, is the **Ripley Museum,** 492 Sonoma Ave. (☎ 707/524-5233), which is fashioned from just one redwood tree and houses displays elucidating Robert Ripley's life—this museum is far more interesting than any of the zillions that carry his name.

Hours: Apr–Oct, Wed–Sun 10am–4pm. *Admission:* $1.50 adults, 75¢ children 7–18.

Another native son of Santa Rosa is Charles Schulz, the creator of Snoopy. He donated the money to build the **Redwood Empire Ice Arena,** 1667 W. Steele Lane (☎ 707/546-7147), which just happens to have a lot of that dog's memorabilia in the gallery/museum located at the complex.

History enthusiasts might also want to visit the **Sonoma County Museum,** 425 Seventh St. (☎ 707/579-1500), which chronicles the history of the county and offers changing exhibits.

Hours: Wed–Sun 11am–4pm. *Admission:* $2 adults, $1 children 12–18.

If you wish to enjoy some evening entertainment, the **Burbank Center for the Arts** is home to the Santa Rosa Symphony and other local groups like the Baroque Sinfonia plus visiting headline entertainers and ensembles. If you want to find out what's playing during your stay, call ☎ 707/546-3600.

Lodging in Santa Rosa

Although the **Fountaingrove Inn,** 101 Fountaingrove Pkwy., Santa Rosa, CA 95403 (☎ 707/578-6101), attracts a business crowd and is located on a well-traveled route, it does have more style than most similar conference facilities and also offers something more. The buildings, made of native redwood, oak, and stone, were designed low to retain the view of the landmark Round Barn above, which is all that remains from the utopian community that was established here in 1875. The 85 rooms are elegant but spare, in almost a Japanese style. They contain custom-designed wooden furnishings, polished brass accents, dried flower arrangements, and mirrored walls. Special amenities include stereo TV, separate dressing alcove, double closet, and work space with modem jack in each room. Services include complimentary daily newspaper, and laundry/valet, plus room service.

The restaurant **Equus** (☎ 707/578-0149), which features the spectacular Gallery of Sonoma County Wines listing 300 selections, is patronized by locals as well as visitors. At dinner a fine appetizer with which to begin is the duck antipasti, a sampler of Sonoma duck, including pâté de foie gras, barbecue leg, confit salad, and slices of breast. Main courses offer a full range of local specialties like Petaluma chicken roasted and served with a juniper-berry sauce, Pacific salmon coated in potatoes and served atop a sweet onion medley with Chenel's goat cheese and baby spinach, and always Sonoma lamb made in seasonal style. Prices range from $18 to $22. Every Friday there's a special local winemaker featured, and on most nights there's piano entertainment in the lounge. Etched glass, redwood carvings, and the dramatic equine murals set the tone.

Facilities include pool, waterfall, and spa.

Rates: Mar–Nov, $159 double; other times, $89 double. Special packages are available. ***Dining Hours:*** Mon–Sat 5:30–9:30pm, Sun 10am–2pm and 5–9pm.

Although **The Gables,** 4257 Petaluma Hill Rd., Santa Rosa, CA 95404 (☎ 707/585-7777), has a Santa Rosa address, it is set out of town overlooking fields. The High Victorian Gothic Revival farmhouse was built in 1877 and retains many of the original architectural elements—12-foot ceilings, 3 Italian-marble fireplaces, a sleek mahogany spiral staircase, and, most notably, the 15 gables crowning the keyhole-shaped windows, which give the house its name. There are 7 rooms available, plus the romantic and secluded William and Mary's Cottage. Each room is decorated in a different color scheme and furnished with individual country pieces. The Sunrise Room sports peach and ivory shades and a French antique armoire; the Sunset Room has a queen-size brass bed and oak armoire set against a deep forest green and rose color scheme. A king-size four-poster is the focal point of the Garden View Suite, which is decked out in striking raspberry and mint colors. Even the smallest room is large enough to accommodate a king-size pencil four-poster and burled maple dresser. The cottage has a wood stove, kitchenette, double whirlpool tub, queen-size bed, and loft bedroom. A full breakfast is served in the dining room. The sitting room has a marble fireplace, piano, and also an interesting art piece made from tiny framed quilts from the trousseau of the original owner. Guests can also enjoy the large deck overlooking the meadows at the back of the house.

Rates: $120–$160 double, $200 cottage.

Having easy access to one of the county's great restaurants—John Ash & Co., which is located next door—is certainly one reason to stay at the **Vintners Inn,** 4350 Barnes Rd., Santa Rosa, CA 95403 (☎ 800/421-2584 or 707/575-7350, fax 707/575-1426), but it's not the only one. This inn is modern but still has plenty of ambience. Looking out across several vineyards, the red-tile–roofed buildings, which shelter the accommodations, are set around a central plaza that is landscaped with a fountain and flower-lined tile walkways. The 44 rooms are extra large, furnished with European pine furnishings and decorated in French country style with modern armoires and similar pieces. All of the rooms have refrigerators, color TVs, modem/phone jacks, and oval bathtubs/showers with brass and porcelain fixtures. Most have fireplaces, and all have private balconies or patios. A continental breakfast is served in the Commons Building, which also contains a library. Guests can also enjoy a private spa and sundeck edged with trellis. Services include a concierge.

Rates (incl. breakfast): $158–$215 double weekends; $138–$195 midweek (higher prices are for rooms with both fireplace and balcony/patio).

Dining Only in Santa Rosa

In addition to Equus in the Fountaingrove Inn, described under "Lodging" above, Santa Rosa boasts one of the best restaurants in Sonoma County.

The light and airy **John Ash & Co.,** 4330 Barnes Rd. (☎ 707/527-7687), overlooks a vineyard. The dining rooms have cream walls with oak accents and are enhanced by paintings of the Sonoma Valley's natural bounty. My favorite place to dine is in the outdoor dining area. The cuisine is excellent, and the menu changes frequently. To start, you might find Pacific oysters served with a smoked tomato cocktail sauce, or a wonderful warm spinach salad with bacon balsamic vinaigrette and Laura Chenel's goat cheese. There will only be five main courses, supplemented by some extra special dishes. The regular main courses might include a lobster, corn, and roasted-pepper risotto in a corn broth, or sautéed tamarind-glazed chicken. The special might be Sonoma duck served with a whiskey and orange sauce, or the three-peppercorn seared ahi with a zinfandel sauce. Prices range from $15 to $25.

Hours: Tues–Sat 11:30am–2pm, Sun 10:30am–2pm; winter, daily 5:30–8:30pm, summer to 9:30 or 10pm; a cafe menu is served in the afternoon.

Lisa Hemenway's, 714 Village Court (☎ 707/526-5111), is tucked away on a pedestrian alley in Montgomery Village. The dining room is modern and low-key with upholstered banquettes and chairs, all set against cream-colored walls. There are a handful of tables for outdoor dining, too. The cuisine is always surprising and innovative. For example, you might find a grilled chicken breast in a tamarind date sauce, or duck breast with chestnut marsala sauce, or vegetable tamales with ancho honey sauce served over warm black-bean salad with greens. This is also one place where dessert is almost mandatory. Try the caramel-walnut pie served with vanilla-bourbon ice cream, or the warm almond torte and fresh peach compote flavored with muscat. Across the street, **Tote Cuisine** offers cafe fare and takeout.

Hours: Daily 11:30am–2:30pm; Mon–Sat 5:30–9pm, Sun 5–9pm. Tote cuisine: Mon–Sat 10:30am–5 or 6pm, depending on the season.

Sonoma/Sonoma Valley & Santa Rosa
Special & Recreational Activities

Aerial Tours: Aero Schellville, 23982 Arnold Dr., Sonoma (☎ 707/938-2444), offers biplane flights; **Dragonfly Aviation**

(☎ 800/677-9626) and **Let's Fly** (☎ 707/546-9362) both operate from Sonoma County Airport in Santa Rosa and offer aerial tours of the county. The prices for these range from $80 for an aerobatic biplane tour for one person to $195 for a 40-minute tour of the Sonoma and Napa valleys for two.

Ballooning: Air Flambouyant, 250 Pleasant Ave., Santa Rosa (☎ 707/838-8500), has been in business for 22 years, and their balloons are flown by FAA-licensed pilots. They charge $165 per person for their 1-hour flights that are followed by a gourmet champagne picnic brunch. The whole experience, from inflating the balloon to brunch, will last 3 to 4 hours. **Aerostat Adventures,** 2414 Erickson Ct., Santa Rosa (☎ 707/579-0183), offers 1-hour single-hop flights as well as a gourmet champagne brunch.

Bicycling: Rincon Cyclery, 4927 Sonoma Hwy., Santa Rosa (☎ 707/538-0868), rents tandems, mountain bikes, and hybrids by the hour, day, or week and also offers custom tours. Prices are $7 an hour, $25 a day.

In Sonoma, try **Sonoma Valley Cyclery,** 20079 Broadway (☎ 707/935-3377), or the **Good Time Bicycle Company,** 18503 Hwy. 12 (☎707/938-0453). The former rents bikes for $6 an hour, $20 a day; the latter rents for $5 an hour, $25 a day, and will even provide a picnic lunch.

Check out the state parks as well as the Silverado Trail for bike riding.

Camping: There are 50 developed campsites along the Sonoma Creek in **Sugarloaf Ridge State Park,** Adobe Canyon Road (☎ 707/833-5712 or 707/938-1519).

Golf: Bennett Valley Golf Course, 3330 Yulupa Ave., Santa Rosa (☎ 707/528-3673), is an 18-hole, par-72 course. **Sonoma Golf Course,** 17700 Arnold Dr., Boyes Hot Springs (☎ 707/996-0300), is an 18-hole, par-72 course.

Horseback Riding: Sonoma Cattle Company, P.O. Box 877, Glen Ellen, CA 95442 (☎ 707/ 996-8566), leads trail rides in Jack London State Historic Park and Sugarloaf Ridge State Park, meandering past vineyards and through forests. One-hour rides cost $35, two-hour $45. There's also a sunset ride, and you can even arrange private rides. Other special rides include lunch at a winery or a western barbecue.

State Parks: Jack London State Historic Park, 2400 London Ranch Rd., Glen Ellen (☎ 707/938-5216), contains memorabilia of the author plus hiking, biking, and equestrian trails.

Sugarloaf Ridge State Park, 2605 Adobe Canyon Rd., off Hwy. 12, Santa Rosa (☎ 707/833-5712), has camping facilities plus hiking and equestrian trails.

Annadel State Park, 6201 Channel Dr., Santa Rosa (☎ 707/539-3911 or 707/938-1519), offers 35 miles of trails for hiking, mountain biking, and horseback riding. The park is 4,900 acres and covers elevations from 300 to 1,900 feet.

Tennis: Santa Rosa and Rohnert Park have public courts. Call the chambers of commerce for details.

Wine Tasting: See the section on Sonoma Valley wineries, above.

EXPLORING THE RUSSIAN RIVER VALLEY

The Russian River rises north of Cloverdale and flows out into the sea at Jenner. Along the way are several other towns of some interest to weekenders—Geyserville, Healdsburg, Guerneville, Monte Rio, and Duncan Mills. Cloverdale and Guerneville are the largest of these; Healdsburg has the most to recommend it. The river itself provides great recreational opportunities as does the Armstrong Redwoods State Reserve just north of Guerneville. The region is also famous for the products of its orchards and wineries, like the jams, jellies, and sauces manufactured and sold at the famous Kozlowski Farms and the great wines that are produced at such wineries as Davis Bynum, J. Rochioli, Hop Kiln, De Loach, and Korbel.

You can travel the Russian River from south to north or vice versa. If you're traveling south to north, then from Santa Rosa take Highway 12 to Sebastopol. From there, go on to Freestone, via the Boedga Highway, then take the Bohemian Highway north, which follows the old route of the Northwest Pacific Coast Railroad through Occidental to reach the river at Monte Rio. After crossing the river, turn right along Highway 116 into Guerneville, and then branch off along River Road past the Korbel Winery until you reach the Westside Road junction, which will take you along a blissfully beautiful wine route past Davis Bynum, Rochioli, and Hop Kiln vineyards all the way to Healdsburg. Korbel is well worth stopping at for its gardens and tour.

From Healdsburg you can take Route 128 into Geyserville, where you can either continue north along Geyserville Avenue to Asti and Asti Road or on Highway 101, which will lead you into Cloverdale.

Russian River Valley

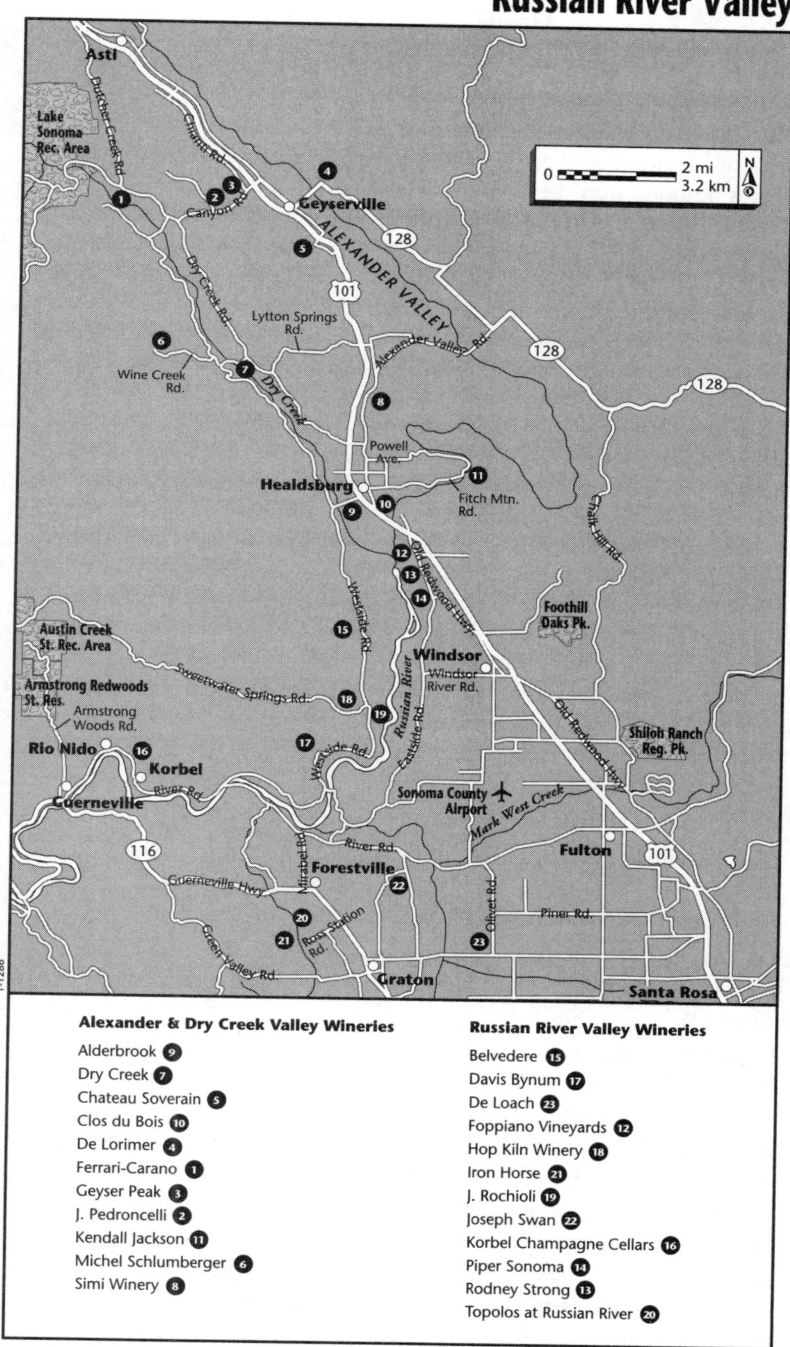

VISITING THE AREA WINERIES

Russian River & Green Valley Wineries

The Russian River is noted for being a cool growing area because of the fog that is introduced by the river and its tributaries. Although you will find several different varietals grown here, the area is most famous for chardonnay, pinot noir, and sparkling wines. More than 8,000 acres are under cultivation for grapes. The adjacent Green Valley, which is centered on Forestville, is more recognized for its fruit orchards (apples, berries, and pears), but grapes are also grown, with chardonnay and pinot noir the main varietals produced. Only about 1,000 acres, though, produce grapes.

One of my favorite wine-touring drives can be taken along Westside Road between Guerneville and Healdsburg. The road winds along a ridge, giving glorious views out over vineyards across to the Mayacamas Mountains beyond. Along this stretch of Westside Road, from south to north, are found some very appealing wineries starting with Davis Bynum, J. Rochioli, Hop Kiln, Belvedere, and Alderbrook. Westside Road turns right into Healdsburg, but if you like, you can continue north on West Dry Creek Road, which will bring you directly to—or to the side roads that lead to—the following wineries: Dry Creek, Michel Schlumberger, Ferrari–Carano, and J. Pedroncelli.

Here are a select few of my favorite wineries in the Russian River and Green Valleys. Most are open daily from 10am to 4:30 or 5pm. Exceptions are noted. There is often no charge for wine-tasting.

Belvedere, 4035 Westside Rd., Healdsburg, CA 95448 (☎ 707/433-8236, ext. 40), offers a pretty garden setting for picnics.

Davis Bynum, 8075 Westside Rd., Healdsburg, CA 95448 (☎ 800/826-1073 or 707/433-2611), is a well-landscaped winery with an air of rustic charm. A picnic area is available.

De Loach, 1791 Olivet Rd., Santa Rosa, CA 95401 (☎ 707/526-9111), another Green Valley winery, has a lawn for picnicking overlooking the vineyards.

Foppiano Vineyards, 12707 Old Redwood Hwy., P.O. Box 606, Healdsburg, CA 95448 (☎ 707/433-7272), is still a family-owned vineyard. It was established in 1896 on 200 acres.

Hop Kiln Winery, 6050 Westside Rd., Healdsburg, CA 95448 (☎ 707/433-6491), has a striking appearance because the buildings were originally used for processing hops for beer. Enjoy a picnic overlooking the pond, and also check out the gallery of local art.

Iron Horse, 9786 Ross Station Rd., Sebastopol, CA (☎ 707/887-2913), in the Green Valley, has appealing flower and herb gardens and contemporary sculptures as additional attractions. It's located 10 miles west of Santa Rosa and only 12 miles from the ocean. It makes a delicate chardonnay.

Joseph Swan, 2916 Laguna Rd., Forestville, CA 95436 (☎ 707/573-3747), is a small winery in the Green Valley. Some of its wines are only available here. Open weekends and holidays only.

Korbel Champagne Cellars, 13250 River Rd., Guerneville, CA 95446 (☎ 707/887-2294), produces brandy as well as champagne. Tours of the lovely gardens are also given.

Piper Sonoma, 11447 Old Redwood Hwy., Healdsburg, CA 95448 (☎ 707/433-8843), produces fine sparkling wines.

J. Rochioli, 6192 Westside Rd., Healdsburg, CA 95448 (☎ 707/433-2305), produces great pinot noirs. It was officially founded in 1976, but the land has been farmed by the current owners' ancestors since the 1930s.

Rodney Strong, 11455 Old Redwood Hwy., Healdsburg, CA 95448 (☎ 800/678-4763 or 707/431-1533), has had a checkered history. When its stock was sold on Wall Street under the "Windsor Vineyards" name, it soared, but the original owners were forced to sell in the slump of the '70s when their liquidity was stretched to breaking point. The buildings include an interesting pyramidal structure. There's also a picnic lawn frequently used for concerts.

Topolos at Russian River, 5700 Gravenstein Hwy. N., P.O. Box 358, Forestville, CA 95436 (☎ 800/TOP-OLOS [800/867-6567] or 707/887-1575), is a family-owned winery where you can also enjoy outdoor dining at the restaurant.

Alexander & Dry Creek Valley Wineries

Here are a select few of my favorite wineries in the Alexander and Dry Creek Valleys. Most are open daily from 10am to 4:30 or 5pm. Exceptions are noted. There is often no charge for wine-tasting.

Alderbrook, 2306 Magnolia Dr., Healdsburg, CA 95448 (☎ 800/405-5987 or 707/433-5987), located in the Dry Creek Valley, offers a welcoming veranda to sit upon and enjoy a glass of wine.

Chateau Souverain, 400 Souverain Rd., P.O. Box 528, Geyserville, CA 95441 (☎ 707/433-3141), is a dramatic, French-style winery in the Alexander Valley that is known for its cafe and restaurant (described under "Dining in the Healdsburg Area" below).

Clos du Bois, 19410 Geyserville Ave., P.O. Box 940, Geyserville, CA 95441 (☎ 800/222-3189 or 707/857-3100), has a typical, standing-only tasting room and a small picnic area. Great wine, too.

De Lorimer, 2001 Hwy. 128, P.O. Box 487, Geyserville, CA 95441 (☎ 800/546-7718 or 707/857-2000), is open weekends only.

Dry Creek, 3770 Lambert Bridge Rd., P.O. Box T, Healdsburg, CA 95448 (☎ 707/433-1000), has become, since its founding in 1972, a premium producer of classically styled wines. There's a lawn for picnics. An annual open house is held on the first weekend in June.

Ferrari–Carano, 8761 Dry Creek Rd., P.O. Box 1549, Healdsburg, CA 95448 (☎ 707/433-6700), is located in a striking Tuscan-style villa and has extensive lovely gardens and a handsome barrel cellar.

Geyser Peak, 22281 Chianti Rd., Geyserville, CA 95441 (☎ 800/255-9463 or 707/857-9400), has a covered picnic area overlooking the Alexander Valley.

Kendall Jackson, 337 Healdsburg Ave., Healdsburg, CA 95448 (☎ 707/433-7102), has a tasting room in town featuring all of the wines produced by this company, which has vineyards throughout the area.

Michel Schlumberger, 4155 Wine Creek Rd., Healdsburg, CA 95448 (☎ 800/447-3060 or 707/433-7427), is set on a hillside estate overlooking the Dry Creek Valley. Tours are given at 11am or 2pm. You must call ahead for reservations.

J. Pedroncelli, 1220 Canyon Rd., Geyserville, CA 95441 (☎ 800/836-3894 or 707/857-3531), has been operating continuously since 1904, although the current family-owners took over in 1927. Visitors enjoy the bocci court and the art displays as well as the wines.

Simi Winery, 16275 Healdsburg Ave., Healdsburg, CA 95448 (☎ 707/433-6981), is one of the oldest vineyards in the region, having been founded in 1876. It offers daily hour-long tours of the cellars and also has picnic facilities.

SEBASTOPOL

Sebastopol is at the heart of Gravenstein Country, an area that is a delight to view in spring, when the area is a sea of pink and white blossoms. The town is known for its antique stores and also for a unique festival held each July, the Teriyaki Chicken Barbecue and Japanese Bon Dancing Festival at the Enmanji Temple (☎ 707/823-2252) south of town. Most of the **antique stores** are located along Highway 116 West, which for some reason is confusingly called Gravenstein Highway South.

FREESTONE

In the 1800s the Freestone Valley was where Russian farmers cultivated wheat, the name *Freestone* deriving from the "free stones" that were given away at a local quarry. When the railroad between Sausalito and Cazadero opened, Freestone became a hub for the railroad and lumbermen.

It is worth visiting today to experience an enzyme bath, a form of heat therapy developed in Japan that relaxes, soothes, and energizes the body, mind, and spirit. This can be enjoyed at **Osmosis,** 209 Bohemian Hwy. (☎ 707/823-8231). The heat of the bath, composed of antiseptic cedar fiber, rice bran, and more than 600 active enzymes, is generated by fermentation. Many prefer this style of bath because they consider it more hygienic than the mud baths at Calistoga. It's a tranquil place. Your experience will begin with a cup of special tea taken in a quiet room overlooking a Japanese garden. The bath will take 20 minutes and will be followed by a shower. You can then either lay back under a blanket wrap, listening to a Metamusic tape, or enjoy a 75-minute massage, which would be my recommendation. The whole process takes about 2½ hours. It is given in a private outdoor wooden pavilion, where you can hear birds singing and the sound of the wind. The pavilion is reached via a bonsai and bamboo garden.

Hours: Daily 9am–9pm. *Cost:* $120, $55 if you opt for the blanket wrap instead of the massage.

From Freestone you can travel the Freestone–Valley Ford Road to **Valley Ford,** a tiny town (population 126) at the heart of a ranching and potato-growing area. The greatest excitement generated in the town was when the "event" artist Christo's famous fence swept through town on its way out to the coast in 1976. There's a grocery store, a cafe, a historic bar/restaurant, an art gallery, a bed-and-breakfast, and a llama ranch. From Valley Ford, you can loop back to the town of Bodega via Highway 1 and complete the loop by returning to Freestone via the Bodega Highway.

OCCIDENTAL

Occidental was put on the map by a narrow-gauge railroad, which was laid in 1876 to transport Douglas fir, redwood, charcoal, and wine to Sausalito and San Francisco, and tourists from San Francisco to Occidental. The town was dominated by two landholders, William "Dutch Bill" Howard and Melvin C. "Boss" Meeker, both of whom developed the area, building summer cabins and homes after the forests had been logged out. By the 1870s the town had its own post office, school, and church as well as two hotels. In the 1880s Italian immigrants arrived, introducing zinfandel grapes into the region. Today it's a striking small town with an excellent inn.

Lodging in Occidental

Superb accommodations are found at the **Inn at Occidental,** 3657 Church St., Occidental, CA 95465 (☎ 707/874-1047, fax 707/874-1078), which is set back above the town. New Englander Jack Bullard has carefully restored this 1870s clapboard and brick Victorian, making it a very comfortable and charming place to stay. Rooms are elegantly and aesthetically furnished, which is not surprising since one of Jack's professions has been selecting art for corporations. There are eight rooms (including two suites), all with private bath, telephone, and connections for cable TV.

Each room is painted to accent the original art that hangs on the walls, and each also features a personal collection of some sort. For example, the Tiffany Suite is painted in a rich periwinkle picked up from the series of woodblock prints that decorate the walls and is named after the silver collection on display; Battenburg lace and a brilliant antique quilt decorate the canopied, mahogany Charleston bed, and there is a brick hearth with comfortable wicker chairs set in front of it. The Cut Glass Room has French doors leading to a private garden, patio, and hot tub; it's furnished with a California king bed and also displays antique English and Irish cut-glass jars dating from the 1860s. The Ivory Suite contains a collection of netsuke (Japanese carved figures that hold tobacco pouches), while the Sandwich Glass Suite celebrates the craftsmanship of the glass makers from Jack's home state of Massachusetts. A Jacuzzi spa and fireplace are added luxuries in the Quilt Suite, which is furnished with a queen pine bed, plush lounge chairs, and a sunny yellow palette. Jack's been a passionate collector for almost all of his life, and his other collections are found throughout the inn—green majolica in the dining room, glass marbles in the Marble Room, pattern glass sugar bowls in the Sugar Suite, and umbrella pattern glass in the Leaf Umbrella Room. The living room is super comfortable, furnished as it is with traditional sofas, needlepoint chairs, antique Oriental rugs, eye-catching decorative lamps, and always arrangements of fresh flowers.

Guests are drawn to the cushioned wicker sofas and rockers on the porch, which is brightened by potted plants of all shades and flags billowing in the breeze; the courtyard with fountain is another inviting place to linger among the gardens. Jack also delights in cooking, and breakfast and afternoon teas at the inn reflect this passion. At breakfast, guests will find a selection of fresh fruit and homemade granola followed by such appetizing dishes as orange-thyme pancakes or French toast with jam.

Rates (incl. breakfast): $105–$205 double.

A Secluded Inn Between Occidental & Guerneville

Huckleberry Springs Inn and Spa, 8105 Old Beedle Rd., P.O. Box 400, Monte Rio, CA 95462 (☎ 707/865-2683), requires some effort to reach, as it is tucked away in the redwoods up a narrow dirt road. It's a very secluded, romantic place set on 56 acres that have not been formally landscaped, largely because the native fauna have not allowed it. The small garden in front of the dining room is in fact a test garden to see what the animals will and will not eat. Accommodations are in four separate, skylit cottages, each of which is decorated differently and comes equipped with VCR, stereo, small TV, coffeemaker, and private bath with hair dryer. A full breakfast is served each morning in the dining room.

The **solarium dining room** is in the main house and also offers four-course dinners on weekend nights (weekdays by arrangement) for $30 per person. Menus change daily, but they feature three entrees and soup, salad, and dessert. For example, the meal might begin with chilled butternut-squash soup, follow with a green salad with tomatoes and gorgonzola, then proceed with a choice of grilled salmon with ginger-lime-cilantro butter, or lime-coriander Cornish game hens with tomatillo sauce. It might finish with raspberry-kiwi clafouti.

In summer the outdoor pool is open. Otherwise the landscaped Japanese spa is available year-round. A special massage cottage is another lure. Here you can enjoy a 75-minute massage ($60) to salve all your pains. Reservations are required five days in advance.

Rates (incl. breakfast): $155 double. Closed Dec 15–Mar 1.

GUERNEVILLE

Guerneville still has a '60s hippies feel and is known for hosting the Russian River Jazz Festival, featuring such artists as Dr. John, Eddie Palmieri, Charles Brown, and Hiroshima. North of Guerneville, there are two prime recreation areas, **Armstrong Redwoods State Reserve** and **Austin Creek State Recreation Area,** both especially good for horseback riding.

Note that if you continue east from Guerneville along Route 116, instead of turning onto River Road, you'll reach **Forestville,** which is home to **Kozlowski Farms,** 5566 Gravenstein Highway (Highway 116) (☎ 707/887-1587), where you can sample the jams, mustards, dressings, and apples and berries in season. From Guerneville, you can also follow the course of the river west along Highway 116 to its mouth at Jenner, which is discussed in the next section, "Coastal Sonoma."

Lodging in Guerneville

The Applewood Inn, 13555 Hwy. 116, Guerneville, CA 95446 (☎ 707/869-9093, fax 707/869-9170), is a lovely three-story, Mediterranean-style inn with a lot of elegance and character. There are 16 rooms and 7 suites, each finely decorated with quality furnishings and fabrics but not finished in an overly precious manner. The rooms are handsomely appointed. One is furnished with an antique walnut bed and has French doors opening onto the fountained courtyard and garden. Other rooms feature such furnishings as Louis XV country pine pieces or a cherry sleigh bed. The most romantic rooms are the suites in the piccola casa with bedside fireplaces, double showers or whirlpools, plus balconies. All rooms have TV, telephone, and private bath.

The **restaurant** is pleasant. Potted ferns and wrought iron and wicker chairs set the ambience.

Rates: Apr–Nov, $135–$260 double; Dec–Mar, $100–$200.

HEALDSBURG & NORTH

Healdsburg is surrounded by three major wine valleys—the Russian River, Dry Creek, and Alexander valleys—and provides a useful gateway for exploring these regions. The town, in turn, is built around a small and elegant **plaza,** where music fills the air every Sunday afternoon throughout the summer as different groups entertain in the gazebo; it's also a place where you can sit on the grass and people-watch the day away. Healdsburg is a small, attractive town with much to recommend it.

Within a few blocks of the plaza, you can sample the wines of eight wineries, all of which are described in the wineries section above. **Clos du Bois** on Fitch Street south of the plaza, **Windsor Vineyards** on Center Street, and **Kendall–Jackson** on Healdsburg Avenue have tasting rooms in town, and **Simi** and **Alderbrook** are really close by.

You'll also want to browse the stores that are found around the plaza. Wine lovers who have the time will want to peruse the titles at the **Wine Library** in the local library at Center and Piper streets.

History buffs will want to drop into the **Healdsburg Museum,** 221 Matheson St. (☎ 707/431-3325), to see what is currently on display.

Hours: Wed–Sat noon–5pm. *Admission:* Free.

There are also several places in town to pick up the ingredients for a picnic, such as the **Center Street Deli,** located on Center Street, near the Plaza.

Just south of Healdsburg is **Windsor,** a small, pleasant town, where the annual Hot Air Balloon Classic takes place in July.

Northeast of Healdsburg, **Geyserville** is the gateway to the Alexander and Dry Creek valleys, where more than 20 wineries beckon visitors. There is also a good bed-and-breakfast and a restaurant there.

Farther north up Highway 101, **Cloverdale** is the gateway to Lake Sonoma and its recreational opportunities and also to Mendocino County's wine country, which is centered on Ukiah and environs and discussed in the next chapter.

Lake Sonoma is a 2,700-acre lake where folks go to fish, water ski, and participate in other water sports. The Visitor Center (☎ 707/433-9483) is open year-round. There's also a fish hatchery where salmon and steelhead spawn. You'll find more about the recreational opportunities here in the Activities section, below.

Lodging in Healdsburg & Geyserville

Pass through the elegant gate along the wooded drive and you'll come to **Madrona Manor,** 101 Westside Rd., P.O. Box 818, Healdsburg, CA 95448 (☎ 707/433-4231, fax 707/433-0703). A National Historic Landmark, the 1881 mansion stands on 8 acres and possesses striking architectural features—steep dormer roof and ornate bracketing and bay windows. There are 20 very spacious rooms and suites, all with high ceilings and each individually decorated with authentic antiques. Eighteen of them have fireplaces, 8 have a balcony or deck. Nine are located in the mansion; those on the first floor contain the antique furniture of the original owner. One room has an extraordinarily beautiful bed and dresser ornamented with a carved sun and inlay work. For an extra-romantic weekend select the suite with fireplace, large private deck, and marble bath with Jacuzzi in the mansion, or opt for the most secluded accommodation of all, the Garden Cottage, which has its own private gardens and deck and is furnished with rattan furniture and warmed by a fire on cool nights. Eight rooms are in the gem of a carriage house, including Suite 400, which is decorated in a French contemporary style. Here in elegant surroundings you can relax in the Jacuzzi and watch the flames flickering in the fireplace. Two rooms are in the Meadowood Complex, one an Oriental-style suite, the other having a fetching bed with a preacher's pulpit headboard.

The public areas include an inviting music room, which has a rosewood piano and Eastlake furnishings set around the fireplace. Each of the living rooms has the luxury of Oriental rugs. The grounds are beautifully landscaped and dotted with sculpture and fountains. The pool is handsomely designed adjacent to a citrus orchard and gardens. Sliced meats, imported cheeses, fresh juice, and local fruits are found on the buffet breakfast table and can be enjoyed on the balcony or in one of the dining rooms.

The **restaurant,** consisting of three dining rooms, is a celebratory place. The reputation of the kitchen is first-rate, and in fact some people stay here for this reason. Only four or five entrees will be offered on the menu. A sample four-course prix-fixe menu ($45) might start with white corn bisque garnished with portobello mushroom timbale, and continue with a selection of crostini—rock shrimp salsa, a green olive tapenade, black olive tapenade, and goat cheese, cherries, and prosciutto, and a salad made with arugula and mache with pine nuts and reggiano parmigiano in a walnut balsamic vinaigrette. A quail with rosemary wine sauce might follow, and the whole meal would finish with a luscious three-citrus crème brûlée featuring orange, lemon, and lime. The à la carte menu will feature only four or five main courses, ranging from Pacific salmon served with curry-coriander compound butter, to a Sonoma lamb medley combining oven-roasted leg, rack chop, and tenderloin seasoned with fresh herbs and garlic. Prices range from $23 to $25.

Rates (incl. breakfast): $180–$205 double in the mansion or Meadowood Complex, $150–$180 in the Carriage House, $220 Garden Cottage, $250 for Suite #400.

The **Raford House Inn,** 10630 Wohler Rd., Healdsburg, CA 95448 (☎ 800-887-9503 or 707/887-9573, fax 707/887-9597), is beautifully situated on a knoll overlooking vineyards at the southern end of the Russian River Valley. From the front porch you can gaze out across this lovely vista and the well-tended gardens, which attract hummingbirds, orioles, and swallows with their many varieties of roses and other flowers. The house, which was built in the 1880s by Raford W. Peterson, is now a Sonoma County Historical Landmark and sits on 4 acres, all that is left of Peterson's original 1,300. There are five rooms, all distinctively furnished and all with private bath, plus a suite consisting of two spacious rooms with a bathroom between. None have TV or phone. The most secluded room is appropriately called the Bridal Room. It has a private entrance and porch overlooking the vineyards, plus a woodburning fireplace and separate sitting area. One book-lined wall adds warmth to the room. The Blue Room also overlooks the vineyards and boasts a handsome four-poster. A full breakfast with hot entree is served on the porch in mild weather. Hors d'oeuvres and local wines are served in the evening, and sherry and chocolate to end the day.

Rates (incl. breakfast): $120–$155 double, $210 suite weekends; $100–$135 double, $190 suite midweek.

Belle de Jour Inn, 16276 Healdsburg Ave., Healdsburg, CA 95448 (☎ 707/431-9777, fax 707/431-7412), is set on a hilltop on 6 acres looking out over rolling hills. Breakfast is served in the kitchen of the original farmhouse, a single-story Italianate dating to 1873. The accommodations are in cottages, all equipped with air-conditioning, individual heat, a Vermont Castings fireplace, refrigerators, and hair dryers, and enhanced by such touches as bathrobes and fresh flowers. The most luxurious is the Carriage House Suite, which has a king canopy bed, fireplace, CD and tape player, and a private bath with whirlpool tub for two. The Atelier is also appealing with its high-vaulted ceilings, queen canopy bed, and Vermont Castings fireplace. It too has a whirlpool tub and shower.

Rates: $145–$205 double, $255 Carriage House Suite.

The **Camellia Inn,** 211 North St., Healdsburg, CA 95448 (☎ 707/433-8182, fax 707/433-8130), is located in a handsome Italianate Victorian built in 1869 on a quiet street two blocks from the town plaza. There are nine guest rooms, each furnished with a mixture of antiques and reproductions. Some have gas fireplaces. In Royalty, a massive tiger-maple half-tester bed from Scotland is coupled with an antique armoire. In Caprice, a canopy bed is combined with wicker furnishings. A brass bed dominates Memento, which also has a clawfoot tub in the bathroom. Tiffany has a whirlpool tub for two in a bathroom, which features stained glass windows. Breakfast is served in a dining room, warmed on cold days by a fire. Oriental rugs cover the hardwood floors, beds are often canopy style, and some rooms have gas fireplaces and whirlpool tubs for two. The double parlors feature twin marble fireplaces and serve as comfortable gathering places. The grounds are a delight, too, with their many varieties of camellias, while the outdoor pool is another draw. Complimentary refreshments are served poolside or in the parlor in the afternoons.

Rates (incl. breakfast): $80–$145 double.

Grape Leaf Inn, 539 Johnson St., Healdsburg, CA 95448 (☎ 707/433-8140), is located in a Queen Anne Victorian, which stands on a street just off Dry Creek Road on the edge of town. There are seven rooms, each decorated in a warm, comfortable manner. Rooms on the first floor have high ceilings and more Victorian styling, while second-floor rooms have whirlpool tubs and stained glass windows as extra-special features. Each is decorated in a different color palette, from burgundy to lilac. Furnishings include iron and brass beds and a range of oak pieces and armoires. A full breakfast with egg dishes and homebaked breads is served at a lace-covered table; in the evening guests are offered local wines and cheeses, sometimes presented on Saturday evenings by the vintners themselves. The living room and parlor are both comfortable retreats.

Rates (incl. breakfast): $95–$160 double.

The **Haydon Street Inn,** 321 Haydon St., Healdsburg, CA 95448 (☎ 707/433-5228), occupies a 1912 Victorian Craftsman home with pretty gardens front and back. It's within walking distance of the town plaza. There are six rooms in the main house, the most luxurious and spacious is the Victorian Cottage. The Rose Room contains a bed with a draped coronet canopy and can accommodate three people; in the Coco Room you'll find an iron and brass bed. The Pine Room offers an inviting pencil poster bed dressed with a Battenburg lace canopy, plus a pine chest and handmade country rugs on the hardwood floors. The Victorian room has a fine wicker bed and rocker. Both of these rooms have double whirlpool tubs. The most appealing room of all, the Turret Suite, is tucked under the eaves and has a tub placed in front of the fireplace.

Rates: $105–$175 double.

The **Hope–Merrill House** and the **Hope–Bosworth House,** 21253 and 21238 Geyserville Ave., Geyserville, CA 95441 (☎ 707/857-3356), are located across the street from each other and operated by the same owners. The first is an Eastlake Victorian built between 1870 and 1885. Among the interior features are the original wainscoting. The rooms are comfortably decorated, though not in lavish Victorian style. Some of the eight rooms (all with private bath) have fireplaces; the Carpenter Gothic room has a whirlpool bath. The second house is a Queen Anne Victorian with four rooms, all with private bath. The heated pool is a nice feature at the Hope–Merrill House.

Rates: $105–$150 double.

Dining Only in Healdsburg & Geyserville

In addition to the restaurant at Madrona Manor, in Healdsburg, these two restaurants are also good choices.

Bistro Ralph, 109 Plaza St., Healdsburg (☎ 707/433-1380), is a casual place but offers great food. Several of the appetizers are great-tasting, like the Szechuan pepper calamari with a lemon, ginger-soy dipping sauce, or the chicken livers with caramelized onion, balsamic vinegar, and pancetta. The menu for main courses is limited, featuring eight dishes that will include pasta and risotto plus meat and fish. You might find filet mignon with huckleberry sauce, or Liberty duck breast with pomegranate reduction and basil polenta, or a grilled swordfish with caramelized fennel and a béarnaise sauce. Prices range from $12.50 to $19.

Hours: Mon–Fri 11:30am–2:30pm; daily 5:30–closing (depends on the dinner traffic).

The Chateau Souverain Cafe at the Winery, 400 Souverain Rd., Geyserville (☎ 707/433-3141), is a good place to enjoy lunch or dinner at moderate prices in an attractive setting at one of the most imposing wineries in the valley. Luncheon fare ranges from roasted Sonoma chicken in natural gravy to an open-face roastbeef sandwich with horseradish butter. Prices range from $10 to $13. At dinner you'll find five or so entrees, such as grilled salmon and red curry butter, or New York strip steak with roasted garlic and cabernet butter. Prices range from $14 to $18

Hours: Fri–Sun noon–2:30pm and 5:30–8pm.

Russian River Valley
Special & Recreational Activities

Ballooning: Once in a Lifetime in Windsor (☎ 707/578-0580) offers daily flights complete with champagne brunch.

Bicycling: Rentals are available in Healdsburg at **Healdsburg Spoke Folk Cyclery**, 249 Center St. (☎ 707/433-7171). Also, in Guerneville at **Mike's Bike Rental** (☎ 707/869-1106).

Boating: Lake Sonoma, north of Healdsburg is the major boating center. Call **Lake Sonoma Marina** (☎ 707/433-2200) about rentals. For additional information contact the **Visitors Center at Lake Sonoma** (☎ 707/433-9483).

Canoeing: Rent canoes at **Burke's Russian River Canoe Trips,** River Road, 1 mile north of Forestville (☎ 707/887-1222), or contact **Trowbridge Canoe Trips**, 20 Healdsburg Ave., Healdsburg (☎ 707/433-7247). Rentals are also offered at Healdsburg Memorial Beach.

Golf: Windsor Golf Club, 6555 Skylane Blvd., Windsor (☎ 707/838-7888), is an 18-hole championship course.

Hiking: There are trails at **Armstrong Redwoods State Reserve** (☎ 707/869-2015) in Guerneville, and also at **Lake Sonoma** (☎ 707/433-9483).

Horseback Riding: Armstrong Woods Pack Station, 17000 Armstrong Woods Rd., Guerneville (☎ 707/579-1520), offers 1-, 1½- and 2½-day rides plus pack trips. Prices start at $40.

State Parks: Two miles north of Guerneville, **Armstrong Redwoods State Reserve** (☎ 707/869-2015 or 707/865-239) is a 500-acre redwood grove offering several hiking trails and also horseback riding. Adjoining is the **Austin Creek State Recreation Area.** The two parks share information numbers.

Swimming: You can swim in the Russian River at **Healdsburg Memorial Beach** (☎ 707/433-1623), and at **Monte Rio Beach** and **Johnson's Beach,** both in Guerneville. There are also swimming beaches at Lake Sonoma Recreation Area.

Tennis: Call the chamber of commerce at ☎ 707/433-6935 for information about courts at local high schools.

Wine Tasting: See the wineries section, above.

EXPLORING COASTAL SONOMA

Although Sonoma is synonymous with great wine, dairy, and other agricultural produce, it is also famous for its splendid coastline stretching from Bodega Bay to Gualala. It's blessed with miles and miles of beaches and many attractive small towns.

BODEGA BAY

A 300-boat fishing fleet operates from the little town of Bodega Bay, and the blessing of this fleet is one of the highlights of the year. Browse the galleries and antique and other stores in this appealing oceanfront town. On an inlet with a narrow strait giving access to the ocean, it's named after Lt. Juan Francisco de la Bodega y Cuadra, who discovered it in 1775. Later in 1811 it was briefly settled by the Russians, who called it Port Roumiantzoff. In 1843 Capt. Stephen Smith claimed Rancho Bodega, and he and his family established the fishing industry that still thrives here.

The coastal town, though, was originally named *Bay* and founded by Firman Camelot in the late 1800s. In the mid–19th century, it was a thriving port whose main cargo was the famous Bodega Red potato, grown on surrounding farms. About 4 miles inland lies Bodega, the site of California's first sawmill, built by Captain Smith.

Today, you can browse the **antique stores and art galleries** and visit the **Potter School House** and **St. Teresa's Church** in this tiny town, which is most famous for being the location Alfred Hitchcock selected for his film *The Birds.* Those who appreciate historic cemeteries will also want to stroll through the **cemetery** between Highway 1 and the town, where some of the tombstones date back to the mid-1800s.

All along the coast are great lookout points for **whale watching,** and the Bodega Headlands are one such. Here, too, naturalists can enjoy sighting such coastal birds as plovers, willets, curlews, godwits, and many other species. In fact, adjacent to Doran Beach, there's a huge bird sanctuary.

The **Sonoma Coast State Beach** (☎ 707/875-3483), stretching for 10 miles from Bodega Bay to Jenner, is spectacular. Although the ocean is too cold for swimming, sports enthusiasts can surf; fish from the shore at Salmon's Creek, Wrights, and Goat Rock beaches; and dive for abalone; or go windsurfing or kayaking. The beaches are great for walking, beachcombing, tide-pooling, and picnicking. The names of the beaches give an inkling of the pursuits they provide, from Salmon Creek to Arch Rock and Shell Beach. The first, by the way, is backed by glorious dunes.

Lodging in Bodega Bay

Inn at the Tides, 800 Hwy. 1, P.O. Box 640, Bodega Bay, CA 94923 (☎ 800/541-7788 or 707/875-2751), offers fine facilities, plus modern, functional accommodations, most with views of the bay. The accommodations are located in 15 or so lodges terraced into the hillside above the harbor. Some of the 86 accommodations have wood-burning fireplaces. All possess such amenities as refrigerator, TV, coffeemaker, hair dryer, bathrobes, and sitting area furnished with a sofa hide-a-bed, and all can accommodate as many as four persons. Guests can enjoy cocktails in the lounge overlooking the harbor before dining in the **Bay View Restaurant,** which features regular monthly "Dinner with the Winemaker" events.

The menu here changes weekly but will always feature local seafood, game, meats, and fresh ingredients. Just to give you some idea of what to expect, among the appetizers there might be smoked pheasant with a stoneground mustard sauce, or delicious portobello mushrooms with cavatelli, lemon, garlic, and shallots. For the main course there might be such dishes as sautéed scallops with gnocchi and portobello mushrooms, pork medallions with a hazelnut crust and marsala sauce, or tournedos of beef with crabmeat, Madeira, and béarnaise. Prices range from $15 to $26. The Friday five-course wine dinners are an excellent value at $54.50.

The inn's facilities include an indoor/outdoor pool, sauna and whirlpool, and a Laundromat. You can also get a massage.

Rates: $ 155–$210 double weekends, $135–$180 midweek; $20 extra person. *Dining Hours:* Sun and Wed–Fri 5–10pm, Sat 5–11pm.

Dining Only in Bodega Bay

In addition to the restaurant at Inn at the Tides, you might also try these two places.

Lucas Wharf, 595 Hwy. 1 (☎ 707/875-3522), is one place to go to sample fresh seafood while you look out at the ocean. Prices range from $12 to $18 for such dishes as sole piccata made with capers and lemon, red snapper with marinara sauce, deep-fried scallops or oysters, and several steak and seafood combinations. In season you can also enjoy fresh crab and salmon. The wine list features a dozen choices.

Hours: Summer, Sun–Thurs 11am–9:30pm, Fri–Sat 11am–10pm; winter, 11:30am–9pm and 11:30am–9:30pm, respectively.

There's also an outdoor **bar/deli** that offers fish-and-chips, and a wholesale fish market featuring fish taken right off the fishing boats.

Hours: Summer, daily 9am–7pm; winter, daily 9:30am–5:30pm.

Tide's Wharf Restaurant, 835 Hwy. 1, P.O. Box 518, Bodega Bay (☎ 707/875-3652), is the other place in town overlooking the water where you can secure grilled snapper, oysters, or petrale sole with eggs and hash browns for breakfast. Traditional lunch favorites include such sandwiches as the crab or shrimp plus fried calamari, pan-fried mahimahi, or deep-fried or steamed clams. At dinner similar items are priced from $12 (for pasta primavera) to $33 (for surf-and-turf), including chowder or salad.

Hours: Daily 7:30am–10pm.

JENNER TO SALT POINT

At **Jenner** the Russian River flows into the sea, and here at Goat Rock Beach lives a colony of more than 200 spotted harbor seals. Behind the beach in the river's estuary, Penny Island is home to a variety of seabirds as well as river otters. The town has a couple of lodgings but little else. At Jenner, if you like, you can branch away from the coast along Route 116, which follows the Russian River to Guerneville and beyond. Before you reach Guerneville, you can take the Bohemian Highway south to Monte Rio, Occidental, and Freestone, then follow the Bodega Highway into Sebastopol and Santa Rosa (all discussed elsewhere in this chapter).

Back on Route 1, from Jenner the road continues along the coast another 12 miles to the dramatically situated **Fort Ross State Historic Park.** It was founded by Russians under the command of Ivan Alexander Kuskof in 1812 as a base from which to hunt and harvest sea otter, which the Spanish didn't want, and also as a settlement to supply the Russian fur-trading posts in Alaska with food and other items.

To those who hunted and fished along the coast, it was a cultural haven, not just a trapping entrepot, as evidenced by the contents of the **Rotchev House,** occupied by the last manager of the compound, who possessed a fine library, a cellar of French wines, a piano, and musical scores by Mozart and other composers. At the **visitor center** (☎ 707/847-3286), you can view some of the samovars and elaborate table service that the Russians used, which will give you some idea of the kind of life that they led here in the wilderness.

From the visitor center, walk down through the woods to the dramatically located compound, which shelters behind its 14-foot-high stockade, warehouses, workshops, and also the first Russian Orthodox church ever built on American soil outside Alaska. Originally it contained 59 buildings—the commandant's residence, barracks, warehouses, workshops, and a jail among them. The Russians paid a small fee to the Spanish for the privilege of hunting otters, and the two nations lived together harmoniously until the Spanish, observing how the Russians thrived, demanded that they abandon the settlement, which they did in 1841. The sea otter population had been virtually exterminated, and although the Russians tried to support the settlement through farming and shipbuilding, they failed. It was bought by Johann August Sutter for a mere $30,000, but only $2,000 was actually paid on the note. Sutter dismantled the place and shipped everything to New Helvetia (Sacramento)—1,700 cattle, 940 horses and mules, 9,000 sheep, and all of the equipment and machinery.

Hours: Daily 10am–4:30pm. *Admission:* $5 per vehicle.

Kruse Rhododendron State Reserve (☎ 707/847-3221) lies 2 miles north of Fort Ross and is best visited in April or May when the native rhododendrons are blooming in this 317-acre reserve. Some stand as high as 30 feet under a canopy of fir and redwoods.

About 6 miles farther north, **Salt Point State Park** (☎ 707/847-3221) affords some thrilling ocean vistas and is also a favorite spot for abalone diving and surf fishing. The 6,000-acre park has 6 miles of shoreline and stretches inland to elevations above 1,000 feet. One of its unique features is the pygmy forest.

Lodging in the Area

Murphy's Jenner Inn, 10400 Hwy. 1, P.O. Box 69, Jenner, CA 95405 (☎ 800/732-2377 or 707/865-2377), is right on the landward side of Highway 1, with views across the road to the ocean. Comfy accommodations are provided in several buildings and cottages, two of which are on the waterfront side of the highway and offer great views of ocean and estuary. The two rooms and a suite in the River House share a hot tub that has been trellised for privacy, while the Rose Cottages share a grassy yard with access to the water. The Rosewater Cottage is the largest of the cottages and has a living room with stone fireplace, chintz-covered couch, large windows, and a deck with water views; the bedroom has a modern four-poster. On the landward side there are two buildings containing six rooms in total, plus two cottages. The Mill Cottage has an Eastlake bed and a living room with brick fireplace, plus full kitchen, balcony, and a private hot tub. In the Jenner House, Captain Will Jenner's room features a beamed ceiling and a bedroom with a canopy bed, plus a living room with fireplace; there's also a full kitchen. Most of the rooms have decks; they are furnished in an informal, country-rustic or contemporary style. Guests gather in the parlor around the wood stove in the evenings and enjoy aperitifs; breakfast is served here, too.

Rates (incl. breakfast): $85–$150 double, $130–$195 cottage.

Timber Cove Inn, 21780 N. Coast Hwy. 1, Jenner, CA 95450 (☎ 707/847-3231), stands on a promontory 3 miles north of Fort Ross surrounded by 26 acres. It's a massive timber building that has definite Japanese accents, including a stone-lined Japanese pond right outside the lobby. The 47 rooms, crafted out of redwood, lack TV and telephone. Among the distinctive furnishings are photographs of the surrounding coastline shot by Ansel Adams, large decorative pieces of driftwood, and wildflower bouquets. Some of the rooms have sunken, tiled tubs; about half also have fireplaces. The most luxurious is number 19, which has an ocean view from a solarium; a sitting room with stone fireplace, sauna and Jacuzzi; and a deck in front of the solarium. Number 9 has a hot tub on the balcony. The less expensive rooms overlook the pond.

The **dining room** affords splendid ocean views and features such seafood dishes as salmon with a mint and basil salsa, and a mixed grill combining salmon, tuna, swordfish, clams, prawns with champagne, basil, and sun-dried tomatoes. These are supplemented by well-prepared meat dishes—chicken breast with shiitake mushrooms and a roasted red pepper sauce, and filet mignon with Madeira wine truffle sauce, for example. Prices range from $17 to $26.

Rates: $120–$370 double weekends, $88–$290 midweek.

Timberhill Ranch, 35755 Hauser Bridge Rd., Cazadero, CA 95421 (☎ 707/847-3258), located near Fort Ross, is set on 80 wooded acres on a ridge 1½ miles from the ocean. It retains a rustic, remote air, but provides guests with privacy in 15 cottages. Each cedar cottage features a fireplace, private deck, and minibar. They are not furnished extravagantly (quite the contrary in fact), but they are enhanced by such extra-special touches as fresh flower bouquets and a selection of books and magazines, plus the greatest luxury of all as far as I am concerned: quiet (no telephone and no TV). The beds are covered with quilts, floors with basic wall-to-wall carpeting; armchairs and other furnishings are not distinguished. A continental breakfast is delivered to your door. The main lodge is furnished with antiques and offers such comforts as plush sofas set around the fieldstone fireplace and plenty of books.

It also contains the **restaurant,** which offers superb cuisine and wines. The menu is limited so as to ensure the finest dining experience, and it changes daily. A six-course dinner might begin with a salmon mousse baked en croûte with a delicate dill and pistachio sauce, continue with a redolent smoked tomato bisque and a salad of seasonal greens, tomatoes, artichoke hearts, and olives served with a raspberry vinaigrette. After a refreshing fruit sorbet, it would proceed with any one of five or so entrees featuring local ingredients—honey-glazed roast rack of lamb with mint jus, or roasted Reichardt Farms duckling with a red wine and currant chutney glaze, or seared ahi tuna with a rice vinegar and wasabi cream reduction—and finish with a dessert like the delicious chocolate pots-de-crème. Facilities include two tennis courts, and a large outdoor pool set against a woodsy backdrop. Trails lead off from the property into the surrounding redwood forest or down to the sea.

Rates (incl. breakfast and six-course dinner): $385 double weekends, $350 midweek.

Dining Only in Jenner

In addition to the dining rooms at the Timber Cover Inn and Timberhill Ranch, there is another recommendable restaurant in Jenner.

River's End, Hwy. 1 (☎ 707/865-2484), seems to jut out over the ocean. It's a basic, typical oceanfront restaurant with a solarium and gray chairs set at tables that are covered with rose-colored tablecloths. The cuisine reflects several ethnic influences—French, Asian, and German. There's a classic roasted duck with oranges and Grand Marnier; baby pheasant roasted with juniper berries and filled with dates, figs, and water chestnuts, served with pineapple wine kraut; chicken curry with peach chutney, and several seafood dishes. Prices range from $13 to $25.

Hours: Summer, daily 11am–9:30pm; Apr–May and Oct–Nov, Wed–Sun only; Feb–Mar, Fri–Sun only; closed otherwise, except between Christmas and New Year.

SEA RANCH AND GUALALA

From Salt Point, it's only 14 or so miles to **Sea Ranch,** the controversial development designed by Joseph Esherick. En route you'll pass Stewart's Point, once one of the major lumber shipping points along the coast. At Sea Ranch, although the architecture blends into the environment well, a controversy erupted over beach access. It was eventually resolved by the provision of six public-access trails. The development also features a restaurant, lodge, and golf course.

Five miles father north, the town of **Gualala** is the center for a variety of adventure activities on the Gualala River.

Lodging & Dining in Sea Ranch & Gualala

Sea Ranch Lodge, Hwy. 1, 2 miles from Stewart's Point, P.O. Box 44, Sea Ranch, CA 95497 (☎ 707/785-2371), occupies an envious natural setting on a bluff above the Pacific and is located in the artfully designed, if controversial, Sea Ranch second-home development. The emphasis is on quiet enjoyment of the natural environment, encouraged by the absence of TV and telephone. The interior of the accommodations are rustic in style. Some have fireplaces, hot tubs, and ocean views; others may have only one of these features. Guests enjoy relaxing in the Fireside Room with its comfortable rustic furnishings, Native American blankets, stone fireplace, and ocean vistas.

Points dining room offers decent cuisine and a representative California wine list. It offers a $30 four-course prix-fixe dinner, which might feature blackened halibut with roasted red pepper aïoli, or confit of duck with wild mushroom risotto. Otherwise, the regular menu lists such dishes as grilled salmon with a blood orange beurre blanc, and pork loin with an oriental glaze served with shiitake mushrooms, baby bok choy, and sweet yellow and red bell peppers. Prices range from $21 to $24.

Facilities include pool, tennis courts, and an 18-hole golf course designed by Robert Muir Graves.

Rates: $135–$200 double.

Old Milano Hotel, 38300 Hwy. 1, Gualala, CA 95445 (☎ 707/884-3256), is my favorite hostelry along this stretch of the coastline. It's thoroughly romantic inside and out. It was built in 1905 by the Luccinetti family on a bluff overlooking the ocean. The 3-acre lawns and gardens sweep down towards the ocean, and you can sit on the Adirondack chairs and reflect on an inspirational view of Cathedral Rock and pounding surf. Inside, one dining room is warmed by a stone fireplace and lit by several floor lamps sporting fringed lampshades; the other also has a wood-manteled fireplace. The six rooms (none with private bath) are all furnished differently with antiques. Room 4, which has a cozy wooden-slatted ceiling, contains a sleigh bed and an oak armoire. Room 6 has an iron bed and Victorian-style sofa set against a floral design wallpaper. The Master Suite (with private bath and living room) contains an Empire-style velvet couch, large armoire, and several lamps with fringed lampshades, all set against a riot of patterned wallpapers. The shell collection table in the sitting area is unique. The Vine Cottage is located in the gardens and features a sleeping alcove with private bath and a wood stove. Some of the furnishings in the rooms look well used, but they provide an authentic, old-fashioned atmosphere. Quiet is ensured because the rooms also lack telephone and TV. My favorite spot on the property is in the hot tub, which is placed next to a ravine with a direct view of Cathedral Rock—a great place to relax on a moonlit night. The back garden is filled with all kinds of flowers including large calla lilies. A full breakfast is served either in your room, on the patio, or by the fire in the wine parlor.

The **dining rooms** are very atmospheric and are known for fine cuisine. Start with baked brie served with roasted whole garlic, or the Pacific mussels and clams steamed in chardonnay, fresh garlic, and herbs. The menu will likely feature eight or so entrees ranging from a breast of Peking duck served with blood orange and cranberry chutney, to herb-marinated tiger prawns grilled and served with a saffron-lime sauce, or tenderloin of pork served with quince and Old Milano apple-tree chutney. Prices range from $19 to $26.

Rates (incl. breakfast): $90–$145 double, $175 suite.

St. Orres, Rte. 1, P.O. Box 523, Gaulala, CA 95445 (☎ 707/884-3303), is a fairy-tale place, even though it is not located on the ocean side of Route 1. The most eye-catching building on the 42-acre property is the inspired wooden, Russian-style building, which houses the lobby, dining room, and some guest rooms. It is crowned at each end with an onion dome and enhanced by leaded stained glass windows. The most appealing accommodations are in very private cottages at the edge of the redwood forest, seven of which have exclusive use of a spa with hot tub, sauna, and sun deck. The most luxurious of these rustic accommodations is Pine Haven, a multidomed building containing two bedrooms, two decks, two bathrooms, a stone fireplace in the sitting area, and a wet bar. Blue Iris features a wood stove; Sequoia has a fireplace and an inviting window seat, plus an elevated bedroom with skylight. More modest cabins are like Fern Canyon, which has two decks but only a double bedroom, and a bathroom with shower only. Some have ocean views. The eight rooms in the hotel are small, rustic, and share three baths, which are painted in shockingly brilliant pink, lemon, and lime. Two of these rooms have ocean views through stained glass French doors that open onto a balcony.

The **dining room** (☎ 707/884-3335) is well-known for its dishes made from game from local farms. For example, there might be Sonoma County quail marinated in tequila and garlic, grilled and served with yam and green onion pancakes, quail wontons, and blood-orange jalapeño pepper glaze; Karlonas Ranch pheasant breast stuffed under the skin with leeks, andouille sausage, and pistachio nuts and served with Madeira sauce and wild mushrooms; or roast wild boar hind stuffed with dates and walnut and served with apple-ginger chutney from the orchards of St. Orres. The $30 price includes three courses.

Rates (including full breakfast): $70–$85 double, $95–$200 cottage.

The **Breakers Inn,** Hwy. 1, P.O. Box 389, Gualala, CA 95445 (☎ 707/884-3200, fax 707/884-3400), is located on the ocean side of the highway at the mouth of the Gualala River. Although it's a modern roadside accommodation and has no grounds to speak of, the Cape Cod–style inn offers 27 rooms, most with full or partial ocean views. They are luxuriously appointed with fireplaces (Duraflame logs), Jacuzzi tubs (some for two), wet bars, TVs, telephones, coffeemakers, and private decks. Some have refrigerators. The furnishings are upholstered with good-quality fabrics. The three least expensive rooms have standard baths.

Rates: $125–$285 double weekends, $105–$195 midweek.

Coastal Sonoma
Special & Recreational Activities

Beaches: Sonoma Coast State Beach stretches 10 miles along the coast from Bodega Bay's Salmon Creek Beach to Goat Rock in Jenner, which is a favorite hangout for sea lions. **Salt Point State Park** (☎ 707/847-3221) also has access to the beach.

Biking: Adventure Rents in Gualala (☎ 707/884-4386) rents bikes for use on roads and trails starting at $15 for 2 hours, up to $100 for a week. Helmets and water bottles are included, and discounts are granted if you rent more than one bike. It's located behind the Gualala Hotel.

Camping: Sonoma Coast State Beach offers 98 sites at **Bodega Dunes Campground** (☎ 707/875-3483) and 30 sites at **Wright's**

Beach Campground (☎ 707/875-3483). There are two campgrounds with a total of 110 sites plus 30 hike-in/bike-in sites in **Salt Point State Park**, Coast Highway 1, Jenner (☎ 707/865-2391 or 707/847-3221).

Canoeing/Kayaking: The Gualala River, which marks the border between Sonoma and Mendocino counties, is backed by 29,000 acres of forest and provides a quiet wilderness experience (no power boats or jet skis are allowed) for both activities. On any river trip you might be lucky enough to glimpse blue heron, osprey, and brown pelicans as well as otters. **Adventure Rents** in Gualala (☎ 707/884-4386) has canoes that hold two to five persons, single and double kayaks, plus self-bailing sea kayaks for rent, and they will provide free instruction to beginners. Prices begin at $15 for a single kayak for 2 hours, rising to $70 for an overnight sea kayak trip. This outfit also sponsors river cleanups each year in the spring and fall, offers popular spectacular moonlight flotillas on or near full moon nights during the summer, and hosts a riverfest in the early fall with music, boat regatta, and more.

Gualala Kayak, 39175 South Hwy. 1, Gualala (☎ 707/884-4705), also rents kayaks starting at $20 for 2 hours for a single, rising to $50 for a sea kayak for a full day.

Fishing: Salmon season runs from February to September; abalone season from April to November (except for July); crab from mid-November to June.

Bodega Bay is the major sport fishing center of the region. The **Bodega Bay Sport Fishing Center,** 1500 Bay Flat Rd. (☎ 707/875-3344), offers open boat fishing trips for a variety of fishing experiences—light tackle rock cod, albacore tuna, salmon trolling and mooching, halibut, shark, and combinations like rock cod, salmon, and Dungeness crab. Prices start at $40. Both the Russian River and the Gualala River offer steelhead fishing.

Golf: Great oceanfront golf can be enjoyed at **Bodega Harbour Golf Links,** 21301 Heron Dr., Bodega Bay (☎ 707/875-3538). Designed by Robert Trent Jones, it is an 18-hole, par-70 course overlooking the ocean with the last 3 holes played across fresh water marshes. Weekend fees are $75.

Sea Ranch Golf, Sea Ranch (☎ 707/785-2468), is an 18-hole, par-72 links-style course designed by Robert Muir Graves.

Hiking: Chanslor Ranch, 26660 Hwy. 1, Bodega Bay (☎ 707/875-2721), offers several guided nature hikes across the wetlands and along Salmon Creek. More than 200 species of birds inhabit the ranch along with other wildlife.

Salt Point State Park (☎ 707/847-3221 or 707/865-2391) covers 6,000 acres, including six miles of coastline. Numerous hiking trails explore beach, hills, and forest.

There are 5 miles of trails at **Kruse Rhododendron Reserve** including a short loop trail.

A 10-mile trail leads along the bluffs at **Sea Ranch.**

Horseback Riding: Chanslor Horse Stables, 26660 Hwy. 1, Bodega Bay (☎ 707/875-2721), offers a variety of rides for beginners to experts that explore the beach, coastal dunes, wetlands, and the hills around Bodega Bay. The 1½-hour beach ride costs $40. The minimum age is 8. There are a petting zoo and pony rides for the tots.

Roth Ranch Trail Rides, 37100 Old Stage Rd., Gualala (☎ 707/884-3124), offers 3- and 5-hour trail rides along logging trails to the Gualala River. The price is $60 and $75, respectively. They will also arrange shorter rides for beginners.

State Parks: Salt Point State Park (☎ 707/847-3221 or 707/865-2391) is on the coast and offers camping, hiking, and diving in the underwater marine reserve.

Whale Watching: From January to April the **Bodega Bay Sport Fishing Center** offers whale-watching trips aboard the *Jaws.* The cost is $25 for adults, $20 for children 12 and under.

You can also spot whales from the coastal headlands at Bodega Head, Fort Ross, and Gualala Point.

Mendocino County

Distances in Miles: Point Arena, Ukiah, 120; Mendocino, 160

Estimated Driving Times: 2½ hours to Ukiah, 3½ hours to Mendocino

Driving: To reach Elk/Mendocino take Highway 101 to Cloverdale, then Highway 128, which meanders 65 miles through the Anderson Valley, to Highway 1 just south of Mendocino. Or you can continue on Highway 101 to Willits and take Highway 20 for 33 miles to Highway 1, 1 mile south of Fort Bragg. The most scenic—but much longer—route is to travel north along Highway 1, but this is only practical for a meandering vacation, not a weekend.

Further Information: For more on Mendocino county, call or write the **Fort Bragg/Mendocino Coast Chamber of Commerce,** 332 N. Main St., P.O. Box 1141, Fort Bragg, CA 95437 (☎ 707/961-6300); there's also an **Anderson Valley Chamber of Commerce,** P.O. Box 275, Boonville, CA 95415 (☎ 707/895-2379).

Mendocino County has much to offer visitors besides the awesome coastline and the appealing, if tourist-conscious, town of Mendocino itself. Just up the road from Mendocino is Fort Bragg, a much more earthy town, which is worth visiting for the botanical gardens, the skunk train, and several food manufacturing outlets. Inland, the lesser known Anderson Valley is a lovely place to go wine-touring. The tasting rooms are quieter, the crowds much much fewer than in the valleys to the south, and some of the wines are outstanding, especially the pinot noirs at Navarro Vineyards and the sparkling wines at Roederer. Nearby Ukiah has two worthwhile stopping places, too, the Grace Hudson Museum & Sun House and Vichy Springs, where you can take the waters and enjoy a fully relaxing mineral bath.

Events & Festivals to Plan Your Trip Around

March: The **Whale Festival** in Mendocino focuses on these marvelous creatures, plus local wines and much more in the galleries and shops.

May: Usually the first weekend in May, the **Historic House Tour** enables visitors to see the interiors of about 10 or so historic homes. Purchase your tickets at the Kelley House Museum in Mendocino (☎ 707/937-5791), and return there at the end of your tour for dessert and tea or coffee.

July: The renowned **Mendocino Music Festival** brings 2 weeks of classical, jazz, and pop to the canvas tent on the Ford House grounds across from the Mendocino Hotel. For information call ☎ 707/937-2044.

December: During the **Mendocino Christmas Festival,** which is usually the first 2 weeks of December, a variety of entertainments are offered—candlelight tours of inns, a singalong Messiah at an historic church, a Christmas tree lighting ceremony, a breakfast with Santa, and Christmas shows at the local theaters. For more information call ☎ 707/961-6300.

INLAND MENDOCINO

The Anderson Valley is the western half of Mendocino County's wine country; its major town is Boonville, which has a nice bed-and-breakfast.

To the east of the Anderson Valley on the Russian River is the much larger Ukiah and the charming small town of Hopland to its south. You can anchor at either one of these towns for a weekend and visit both the Anderson Valley and the Mendocino wineries along the Russian River.

THE ANDERSON VALLEY & BOONVILLE

The 25-mile-long and 2-mile-wide Anderson Valley stretches between the Pacific just south of Mendocino and Ukiah. It's much quieter and far less commercial than either Napa or Sonoma. Just to give you some idea of the relative sizes here, the largest winery in the valley, Roederer, produces only 60,000 cases of wine annually, but most of the wineries here produce under 5,000 cases. Winery touring here is like it used to be 20 years ago in Napa Valley. You can visit the wineries and not be jostled about. Tasting

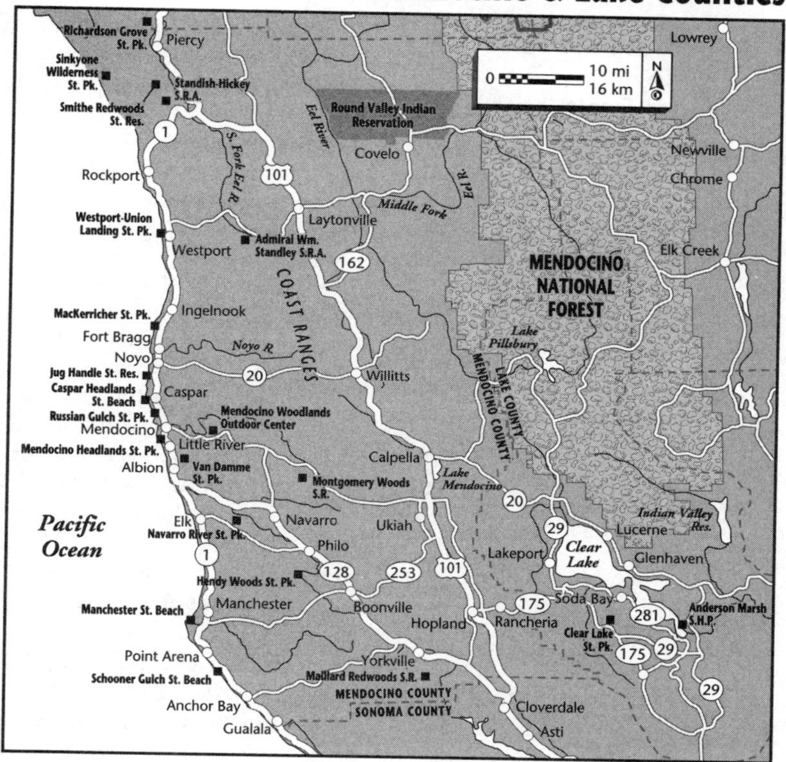

rooms are not filled to the roof with all kinds of ancillary items like T-shirts, hats, and glasses with logos. You can enjoy a conversation with the winemaker about his favorites for the year and so on.

Between Philo and Navarro along Route 128, there are about a dozen producers and about 1,000 acres planted with vines. The Valley has only been recognized as an official appellation since 1983, but already it's producing wines of a distinctive character. And the wineries are so welcoming and easy to visit. The best varietals produced here are richly flavored pinot noir and gewürztraminer, plus sparkling wines.

The major wineries are:

Greenwood Ridge, 5501 Hwy. 128, Philo, CA 95466 (☎ 707/895-2002).

Husch, 4400 Hwy. 128, Philo, CA 95466 (☎ 707/895-3216).

Kendall–Jackson, 5500 Hwy. 128, Philo (☎ 707/895-3009).

Lazy Creek, 4610 Hwy. 128, P.O. Box 176, Philo, CA 95466 (☎ 707/895-3623).

Navarro Vineyards, 5601 Hwy. 128, P.O. Box 47, Philo, CA 95466 (☎ 707/895-3686).

Pepperwood Springs, P.O. Box 2, Philo, CA 95466 (☎ 707/895-2920).
Roederer Estate, 4501 Hwy. 128, Philo, CA 95466 (☎ 707/895-2288).
Scharffenberger Cellars, 7000 Hwy. 128, P.O. Box 365, Philo, CA 95466 (☎ 707/895-2065).

Most tasting rooms are open from 10 or 11am to 5 or 6pm. The Husch tasting room is a charmer, a small wooden building with shingled roof and rose trellis above the door; the Navarro version is light and airy and has a deck overlooking the vineyards. Roederer is the most important grape grower in the region and has built an exquisite redwood winery.

While you're in the Valley, keep an ear out for the local patois called Boontling, which supposedly developed because the Valley has historically been so cut off from most of the world. In this local lingo, *bahl gorms* means good food, *buckey walter* means pay phone, to *pike* is to walk, and to *harp* is to talk. And if you order a *horn of zeese,* you'll be blessed with a cup of coffee!

At the southern end of the Valley is **Boonville,** a small town with a decent inn and restaurant. While you're here, **Boont Berry Farm,** Hwy. 128, Boonville (☎ 707/895-2759), is the place to stop and pick up some natural food and some great-tasting sandwiches and salads. There's also a brewery in town worth stopping at to taste the microbrew. It's the **Anderson Valley Brewing Company and Buckhorn Saloon** (☎ 707/895-2337), right in downtown Boonville (believe me, you can't miss it).

Lodging & Dining in Boonville

The **Boonville Hotel & Restaurant,** Highway 128 at Lambert Lane, P.O. Box 326, Boonville, CA 95415 (☎ 707/895-2210), is a refreshingly modern hotel in a historic building. It's a study in wheat, taupe, and oatmeal, with bleached oak floors and furnishings, set off by South American–style rugs. The eight rooms, each with a private bath, contain modern "craft" beds fashioned out of wood or metal. Some have balconies, and a couple are suites with a sitting area.

The light and airy **dining room** enhanced by splendid flower arrangements has a notable reputation. The limited menu changes daily and features local produce and wines. You might find chicken breast and scallions in mole and lime cream on soft polenta, or a prawn brochette with mango, chile, and mint salsa, plus an unusual pizza, like one made with gorgonzola, tomatoes, glazed onions, and thyme. Prices range from $12 to $20.

Rates: $80–$160 double. Open weekends only in winter, closes for 2 weeks in January.

UKIAH

In **Ukiah,** take some time to stroll the downtown and take the measure of the place. It has some fine historic buildings and several stores worth browsing, like **Habitat,** 110 S. School St. (☎ 707/462-3920), which has great table and other interior decorations. Stop in, too, for some coffee and pastry or pie at **Schat's Courthouse Bakery–Cafe,** 113 W. Perkins St. (☎ 707/462-1670).

If you'd like to do some wine tasting, stop in at **Jepson,** 10400 S. Hwy. 101 (☎ 707/468-8936), known for chardonnay and sparkling chardonnay, or at **Parducci Wine Cellars,** 501 Parducci Rd. (☎ 707/462-WINE [707/462-9463]), which is the oldest winery in Mendocino County (founded in 1932).

There are two major attractions in Ukiah, and the first is the **Grace Hudson Museum & Sun House,** 431 S. Main St. (☎ 707/467-2836). The Sun House, which was built beween 1911 and 1912, is a Craftsman-style redwood building that was the home of Grace Carpenter Hudson, who was an artist, and her husband, who was an ethnologist and authority on Indians (especially the Pomo Indians). It was designed by George Wilcox with a lot of assistance from the couple themselves. Inside, you can see Grace Hudson's studio, the dining room with a sideboard custom-designed for the space, and hanging lamps that were designed by Grace herself. The interior reflects the philosophy and approach of the practitioners of the Craftsman style, which emphasized simplicity, the use of natural materials to harmonize indoors and outdoors, and the elimination of purely decorative ornament. It's a wonderful place to experience.

In the adjoining museum, you can see samples of Grace's work—many sympathetic portraits of Pomo Indians—that she painted between the 1890s and 1930s. The Pomo basket collection is also extraordinary and includes some that are so intricately and ingeniously woven that they can even hold water. There are also interesting exhibits of historical photographs, clothing, and household objects that tell the story of the Indians and the white settlers of the West.

Hours: Wed–Sat 10am–4:30pm, Sun noon–4:30pm. *Admission:* $2 (suggested donation).

The other reason to come to Ukiah is to take the waters at **Vichy Springs Resort.** This marvelous mineral spring was discovered by Frank Marble in 1848, and a resort was established here by William Day in the 1850s. It had more than 100 cottages, a dance hall, a gazebo, and tennis courts. Many famous visitors trekked to the springs. You can, in fact, see photographs of Mark Twain sitting by the springs and such other figures as Jack London, Robert Louis Stevenson, and Teddy Roosevelt. It's one of the oldest and one of the few continuously operating mineral springs in California. The warm, effervescent waters bubble from miles below the ground and contain restorative minerals, including sodium, potassium, calcium, magnesium, iron sulfate, bicarbonate, carbon dioxide, and silica. They are located a distance from the accommodations across Grizzly Creek.

In spring the place is particularly sweet with the scent of lilacs and wisteria, which grow profusely near the spa. At the spa you can bathe or swim in the waters and also enjoy Swedish massage. The water from the spring is bottled at a new plant and is available at the spa and at several hotels in the area. The owners hope to expand the business so we can all drink the waters that resemble those more famous ones in Vichy, France, which Julius Caesar savored. Even if you don't opt to stay here (and you should—see the details below), you can enjoy taking the waters for a day for a $30 charge.

Lodging in Ukiah

If you're stressed out, then you must stay at the **Vichy Springs Resort,** 2605 Vichy Springs Rd., Ukiah, CA 95482 (☎ 707/462-9515), and spend your whole weekend bathing in the springs, swimming in the mineral pool, hiking or mountain-biking the trails, and then indulging in massages and facials and whatever else you feel will help your body and mind relax. It's a wonderful haven and not outrageously expensive, which makes it even more alluring. Over the years, the resort had fallen into disrepair, but enthusiastic owners and world travelers Gilbert and Marjorie Ashoff have set about restoring it without turning it into an excessively decorated and polished place, which is another good reason to come here. And so it remains quiet, restful, and small.

It sits on 700 acres of wooded hills. There are only a dozen rooms, all with private bath, in a long, low redwood building, plus two delightful cottages, a one- and a two-bedroom with fully equipped kitchen. All face out to a grassy area beyond which a little footbridge leads to the spa. Here you will find the grotto where the water bubbles up out of the ground. You can scoop it up with the ladle that is there and drink it, before "uncorking" 1 of the 15 indoor and outdoor tubs to enjoy a soothing, relaxing bath. There's also a large mineral pool, a hot tub, and a massage facility where you can secure a Swedish massage (1 hour $60, 1½ hours $80), and hand and foot reflexology treatment combined with facial ($60 and $80, respectively, including full massage as well).

From the baths you can stroll along the creek up to the falls and hike or bike any of the other trails that run through the woods. A full breakfast is served in an attractive dining room.

Rates (incl. breakfast): $140 double, $180 cottage.

HOPLAND

Hopland is an appealing small town. Its name derives from the days, between the 1860s and 1940s, when hops flourished here, before they were replaced by prunes, walnuts, pears, and, as anyone can see today, grapes. In Hopland itself, there are a couple of attractions to visit.

The **Mendocino Brewing Company,** also known as the Hopland Brewery, 13351 Hwy. 101 S. (☎ 707/744-1361 or 707/744-1015), is one. Famous for its Red Tail Ale, this was California's first brewpub. Stop in the tavern and enjoy an ale or a stout in the outdoor garden with trellised hops or inside in the dining room adjacent to the bar. If you like, you can accompany it with some typical pub fare—chicken wings, burgers, and the like—and a game of darts in between courses.

Hours: Sun–Thurs 11am–10pm, Fri 11am–midnight, and Sat 11am–2am.

The **Fetzer Visitor Center and Tasting Cellar,** 13500 Hwy. 101 (☎ 707/744-1737), across the street from Mendocino Brewing, is the other. Fetzer is a leader in organic viticulture. In addition to wine tastings, it sells kitchenware and prepared oils, vinegars, sauces, and other food items. There's also a separate crafts gallery.

Hours: Daily 10am–5pm.

McDowell Valley Vineyards, 3811 Hwy. 175 (☎ 707/744-1053), is notable for its Fumé Blanc, and for using solar power in its production. The winery is open by appointment only, but there is a **tasting room** in Hopland at 13411 S. Hwy. 101 (☎ 707/744-1516).

Hours: Daily 10am–5pm.

Dunnewood Vineyards also has a tasting room in Hopland.

If your passions are cooking and/or gardening, you'll also want to visit the **Fetzer Food and Wine Center,** P.O. Box 611, Hopland, CA 95449 (☎ 800/846-8637), located at the historic Valley Oaks Ranch. Here you can stroll around the 7-acre organic garden, in which the more than 1,000 varieties of fruits, vegetables, herbs, and edible flowers are labeled. It's a fantastic culinary garden. You can also learn about food and food preparation from researchers who work on the ranch. A variety of classes are given in gardening, cooking, food and wine-pairing, and making herbal medicines by expert chefs and others. Go in just to see the fabulous demonstration kitchens. Guided tours are given. Call ahead for schedules.

Lodging & Dining in Hopland

The **Thatcher Inn,** Highway 101, Hopland, CA 95449 (☎ 707/744-1890), sits down on the main street. Easily identifiable by its turrets and dormers, it was built as a stage stop in 1890. All 20 rooms are on the second and third floors and have telephones. Each is furnished with iron and brass beds combined with armoires, oak dressers, and chairs set on wall-to-wall carpets in either a rose or pale-blue palette. Bathrooms are extra large. On the first floor, there's a lounge/bar decked out in Victorian style, a dining room, and a very handsome paneled library with fireplace and book-filled cherry bookcases where you can sink into a wingchair or sofa and read. The hotel has an outdoor pool.

The **dining room,** which also offers outdoor dining on a lovely patio with fountain, features an Italian menu.

Rates: $110–$165 double.

Inland Mendocino County
Special & Recreational Activities

Biking: Denny Bicycles in Ukiah (☎ 707/446-4117) rents bicycles. You can ride by the vineyards on quiet backcountry roads without too much hassle.

Camping: Hendy Woods State Park (☎ 707/937-5804), located half a mile off Highway 28 on the Philo–Greenwood Road, has 90 sites along the Navarro River.

White-water Rafting: Riverbend Adventures in Hopland (☎ 707/744-1874) offers trips on the Russian and Eel Rivers.

THE MENDOCINO COAST

POINT ARENA TO LITTLE RIVER

Driving north from Point Arena you will pass through the small communities of, first, **Elk** and **Manchester,** then **Albion** and **Little River** en route to Mendocino, all of which were once tiny ports. In the early 1900s in fact this whole coast from Gualala to Fort Bragg and Rockport was called the Doghole Coast, where even the tiniest coastal indentation served as a port. At each of these "dogholes," all kinds of contraptions were operated to get the cargo to and from the schooners. They ranged from fancy trapeze wires to greased chutes. Back then this was the quickest—if the most dangerous—route to San Francisco. It would take 2 days by stage. Today, you can do it in a considerably shorter time and with many fewer hazards.

A few miles north of Gualala in Mendocino County, **Point Arena** itself is a small, unassuming town with a municipal pier.

You might wish to stop in at **Bookends** (☎ 707/882-2287) for coffee and snacks, plus books, videos, and CDs. It's open daily from 7am to 6:30pm.

Browse the other few gift and craft stores before taking Iversen Road down to the Pier to view the boating and docking action and perhaps to enjoy a cocktail at the **Galley Bar** (☎ 707/882-2189).

From Highway 1, Lighthouse Road will take you down to the **Point Arena Lighthouse** (☎ 707/882-2777), which affords great views of the sweep of Manchester State Beach to the north and Schooner Gulch Beach to the south. The lighthouse was built in 1870 after 10 ships were wrecked in just one night on the rocky promontory on which it stands. Back then when a ship ran aground, the residents would go down to the beach and light huge fires in the hopes that some of the sailors would jump overboard and swim towards the light. It's amazing to realize that the original lighthouse, which stood here so many miles north of San Francisco, was destroyed by the 1906 earthquake; it was replaced by the present structure in 1908. Its French Fresnel lens was 6 feet in diameter, weighed more than 2 tons, and was rotated by a clockwork mechanism that had to be cranked every 4 hours by the "wickies" (lighthouse keepers); it was visible from 20 miles. In 1977 it was superseded by an automatic beacon.

Hours: Daily 11am–2:30pm. *Admission:* $2.50 adults, 50¢ children.

Lodging & Dining from Pt. Arena to Little River

The following accommodations are listed from south to north along the coast from Point Arena to Little River, which is just south of Mendocino.

The **Coast Guard House Historic Inn** at Arena Cove, Point Arena, CA 95648 (☎ 800/524-9320 or 707/882-2442, fax 707/882-3233), stands on a hill above Arena Cove offering lovely ocean views. A Cape Cod–style building, it was constructed originally in 1901 as a lifesaving station where lifeboats were stored. Today, the inn has been furnished in Arts and Crafts style. There are seven rooms, plus a secluded cottage up the hill above the inn that has a fireplace, two-person spa, and a patio. Each of the rooms is decorated differently with works by local artists and craftspeople as well as mementos of the inn's maritime history. The Surfmen Cove has a deep, Japanese-style bathtub, woodburning stove, and a sitting area. Flag has a nautical air provided by the captain's bed tucked into an alcove with windows on three sides providing a view of the pier. A couple of rooms share a bath, and one has a tub in the room. The gardens and hot tub are ideal for relaxing; so too is the seating around the parlor fireplace.

Rates: $105–$185 double.

Harbor House Inn by the Sea, 5600 S. Hwy. 1, P.O. Box 369, Elk, CA 95432 (☎ 707/877-3203), is perched on 3 acres on the cliffs above the ocean on the outskirts of Elk. This venerable, redwood-shingled house makes for a quiet retreat. Attractive wooden benches line the winding wildflower-edged path that leads down to the private beach. Accommodations are in the main house or in adjacent cottages, some having decks with lovely views of the ocean and rocky shoreline. All have private bath, but none have a TV or phone. A favorite room is the Lookout, which has a quilt-covered iron bed and its own private deck.

The main building was built in 1916 by Goodyear Redwood Lumber Company as an executive residence, and the common rooms have a comfortable air reminiscent of an earlier, more gracious era. The living room has a large fireplace, warm and solid redwood wall and ceiling paneling, and Oriental rugs on the floors. No credit cards are accepted.

A four-course **dinner** is included in the rates, and it will be a fine meal indeed, featuring local produce and fish, as well as home-grown vegetables.

Rates (incl. breakfast and dinner): $80–$140 per person.

The **Greenwood Pier Inn,** 5928 Hwy. 1, P.O. Box 336, Elk, CA 95432 (☎ 707/877-9997 or 707/877-3423, fax 707/877-3439), combines a number of buildings and elements—a Garden Shop, Country Store, and cafe, plus several houses containing accommodations that are set on the bluffs overlooking the ocean coves. The accommodations include the Sea Castle, which is entered via a Greek Revival portico and contains two trilevel rooms, each of which has a tub with ocean view, glass fireplace, and private deck. The Cliffhouse is the most luxurious accommodation—a redwood cabin perched on the edge of the cliffs with a fireplace and an extra-large deck. The other favored accommodations are the Garden Cottage, which has a good view from upstairs, and the Ocean Suite, which shares a Jacuzzi with the room next door. Other rooms have typical facilities plus wood-burning stoves or similar. Some have ocean views; the cliff-top hot tub can be enjoyed by all. What adds to the charm of the accommodations are the many decorative touches provided by owner, artist, and gardener Kendrick Petty: collages, tile, and marble work. The country store offers books, tapes, and local arts and crafts, while the garden shop, which is surrounded by all kinds of plants and flowers, sells decorative items as well as flora.

The colorful **cafe** is open for breakfast and lunch and also for dinner on weekends. A continental breakfast will be delivered to your room.

Rates (incl. breakfast): $120–$235 double.

The Albion River Inn, 3790 North Hwy. 1, P.O. Box 100, Albion, CA 95410 (☎ 800/479-7944 or 707/937-1919), is a modern complex of accommodations strung along the top of the cliffs with great views of the ocean, and the sunset in particular. Only 20 rooms are available, all of which are comfortably and individually decorated with sleek, modern furnishings. Down comforters grace the beds, wingbacks flank the fireplace, and there's also a well-lit desk. The most luxuriously equipped are the cottages containing Jacuzzis, fireplaces, and decks; but if you don't care about Jacuzzis, the other rooms, each with a fireplace, are equally appealing and less expensive. A full breakfast is served to guests, and it will be above average, featuring such dishes as crêpes filled with raspberry-tapioca custard served hot with a marmalade cream sauce and fresh mint chiffonade.

The **restaurant** is excellent and rightly famous for its seafood. It, too, has a view of the river and the ocean. On Friday and Saturday nights there's sophisticated piano entertainment. The menu changes frequently, but if the grilled prawn appetizer is on the menu, order it. The prawns are sauced with a heavenly blend of green chilies, pineapple, and rum. The seafood chowder is also rich and flavorsome with a touch of sherry. The main dishes will lean towards fish, featuring such dishes as Chilean sea bass topped with sun-dried tomato aïoli, or mahimahi basted with Mongolian barbecue glaze and topped with a spicy peanut-butter sauce, or sautéed halibut with baby artichoke hearts and wild mushrooms in a Madeira cream sauce. There will be a steak and probably a local Sonoma rabbit dish, too. Prices range from $14 to $19. Desserts are very tempting, the most alluring being the caramelized coconut banana served with warm rum-caramel sauce, French vanilla ice cream and chocolate sauce, or the chocolate decadence terrine, a cake that is layered with ganache and served with espresso-flavored crème anglaise and chocolate sauce.

Rates (incl. breakfast): $170–$190 standard double, $235–$260 double with Jacuzzi. *Dining Hours:* Sun–Thurs 5:30pm–closing, Fri–Sat 5pm–closing.

Glendeven, 8221 N. Hwy. 1, Little River, CA 95456 (☎ 707/937-0083, fax 707/937-6108), set back from the road on the east side of Highway 1, about 1½ miles south of Mendocino, is an 1867 farmhouse standing on 2½ acres of well-tended grounds. It offers a range of different, finely decorated accommodations. There are three rooms and two suites in the farmhouse itself. A favorite is the Garret with its sloping ceilings, dormer windows, and Louis XVI bed. Bayview is larger and possesses a sitting area with fireplace. The Eastlin Suite has a sitting room with fireplace and French doors that lead out to the terrace. The King's Room has a porch and a magnificent antique walnut bed. Four delightful rooms are located in the annex, Stevenscroft. Here each room has a corner fireplace or similar. The Briar Rose has a balcony overlooking the gardens, a sky-lit bathroom, and inviting country French decor. The Barnhouse Suite, in a converted 19th-century barn, has two floors containing two bedrooms, 1 and a half baths, and living and dining rooms; it's warmed by a cast-iron stove and also has a deck. There's a very comfortable lounge for the guests to use, with such enhancements as a fireplace and a baby grand piano. A brick patio also overlooks the secluded garden. A fine breakfast of fresh fruit and juice, breads, and egg dishes will start your day; in the evening guests can relax and enjoy a glass of wine.

Rates (including breakfast): $110–$170 double, $210 barnhouse suite weekends, holidays and Aug; $100–$150 and $195 midweek, respectively.

Heritage House, 5200 N. Hwy. 1, Little River, CA 95456 (☎ 800/235-5885 or 707/937-5885), has been here for many years, and it has a somewhat old-fashioned, stuffy air, but the location is magnificent and celebrated for being the backdrop for the movie *Same Time Next Year.* It sits atop the cliff on 37 wooded acres. There are three rooms in the main farmhouse built in 1877. Salem, for example, has an 18th-century four-poster among the furnishings. The atmosphere is quiet, with no television or phone in the rooms. The 60-plus cottages are located in clusters around the grassy grounds. The most expensive are the suites in Carousel, all of which have exceptional ocean views plus such amenities as double Jacuzzis and showers, fireplaces, wet bars, and private decks. Nearly all the rooms have either a fireplace or a Franklin stove, but the furnishings are not extraordinary.

Rates include a full breakfast and dinner for two people, who are expected to dress at dinner, in the **dining room,** which has a dramatic coved ceiling and striking floral mural. The well-balanced menu will offer a broad array of appetizers, ranging from soups and salads to charred rare beef carpaccio with fried capers and Asiago cheese. There will also be about a dozen or so main dishes, including such choices as grilled breast of free-range chicken with a ginger-peach glaze, medallions of veal with whole-grain mustard cream sauce, or seared sea scallops and sun-dried cherry-crusted leg of venison. At breakfast guests help themselves to the buffet spread of fruits and breads before ordering from an extensive menu that includes traditional breakfast egg dishes and omelets, plus a dish like seared filet of red snapper with herbed hollandaise. There's a nursery and garden store on the property.

Rates (incl. breakfast and dinner): $200–$360 double; discounted late Oct to mid-Apr, $172–$305 midweek.

Dining Only from Point Arena to Little River

Pangaea Restaurant, Point Arena (☎ 707/882-3001), is a colorful place that has a stylishly modern Italian ambience and features paintings and other works by local artists. The menu is as fresh as the unexpected style of this restaurant and changes weekly, offering a very limited number of dishes made with organic seasonal ingredients. Among the appetizers my favorite would be the crab cakes with ginger and scallions served with a sauce made from coconut milk, Thai green curry, and lemon grass. Main courses might include a rabbit tagine, braised and stewed in Moroccan spices, harrissa, and mint with dried currants, figs, and eggplant; or braised lamb shanks with wild mushrooms served on Gorgonzola polenta; or a swordfish marinated, grilled, and served on a black-bean–scallion cake with rice and a pomegranate mojo de ajo. There will usually be a pasta dish and also a burger or other sandwich. Prices range from $9 to $17.

Hours: Wed–Thurs and Sun 5:30–7:30pm, Fri–Sat 5:30–8:30pm.

Ledford House, 3000 N. Hwy. 1, Albion (☎ 707/937-0282), occupies a fine location on the bluffs. It's light, airy, and casual, offering a short, well-prepared menu that includes some hearty bistro dishes. Among the appetizers my favorites are the vine-ripened tomatoes, caramelized onions, and Gorgonzola cheese baked in a peppered pâtê brisée tart, and the salmon and corn cakes with tamarind chipotle sauce. The menu changes monthly, but you will always find six or so main courses ranging from a rack of lamb with a rich cabernet sauce to a light and elegant rice timbale filled with roasted eggplant, tomatoes, shiitake mushrooms, pine nuts, basil, and garlic on a golden tomato coulis. The remainder of the dishes will be fish, poultry, or beef. The bistro dishes like garlic-roasted chicken with rosemary and peppers, or the cassoulet are favorites, too, as is the pasta of the evening. Prices range from $12.50 to $21.

Hours: Wed–Sun 5–9pm.

Little River Restaurant, 7750 N. Hwy. 1, Little River (☎ 707/937-4945), is a tiny restaurant (only seven tables) operated by chef-owner Jeri Barrett. Tables are set simply with rose-colored tablecloths. The menu is limited but broad enough so that you will certainly find a dish to satisfy your mood and taste. For example, there might be Pacific red snapper sautéed with lemon-dill butter and shallots, or filet mignon stuffed with prosciutto and served with a marsala butter sauce. Prices range from $17 to $22 and include soup, salad, and bread.

Hours: Summer, daily seatings at 6 and 8:30pm; winter, Fri–Tues seatings only.

MENDOCINO

Famous as the stand-in New England location for the TV show *Murder She Wrote,* Mendocino played the role remarkably well, which is not surprising, since it was in fact originally settled by lumbermen from New England. So beautiful and striking is the setting that several movies have been filmed here, including *Same Time Next Year* and *Summer of '42.* Today, even though it is very popular and caters quite obviously to the tourist, Mendocino has managed to retain its charm despite commercialization.

The beautiful shorefront **Mendocino Headlands State Park** has played a vital role in keeping the village as natural as possible. Go for a hike along the 3 miles of trails in this park, and you will be rewarded with views of sea arches, grottoes, and panoramic vistas. In spring marvel at the wildflowers, and at any time of year watch the many birds, including the black oystercatchers that live here. The headlands are a great place to have a picnic. You can also get down to the beach from behind the Presbyterian Church on Main Street. The interpretive center and museum for the park is located in **Ford House,** on Main Street (☎ 707/937-5397), an historic home built in 1854. Here you will find displays on local ecology and nature, art, history, and Pomo Indian culture. Check here also for nature and history walks that are given.

Hours: Daily 10am–5pm. *Admission:* Free.

Mendocino had been virtually abandoned in the 1930s, and it wasn't until the 1950s that it was rediscovered by artists enchanted by its isolation and rugged beauty. It remains an artists' haven today; in fact you're likely to come across a class of budding artists with their easels set up *en plein air* painting seascapes, cottage gardens, or the historic houses to their hearts' content.

It wasn't always so genteel. William Kasten, who was shipwrecked here in 1850, built the first cabin overlooking the bay, but it was logging that brought the town prosperity, and lumbering still plays an important role in the local economy. A salvager, Jerome B. Ford, had reported the lumber potential of the region to Harry Meiggs of Meiggs Wharf fame in San Francisco, who sent a crew aboard the *Ontario* to set up the first lumber mill in 1852. By 1865 the town's population had grown to 700, consisting of several different ethnic communities—the Chinese, who operated laundries; the Scandinavians and New Englanders, who were mostly lumbermen; and the Portuguese, who logged, fished, and farmed. From 1852 on, nearly every creek had a mill operating, and the coast was filled with schooner traffic. Little River, in fact, became a shipbuilding town to service the lumber industry. The life was rough and the trip to and from San Francisco perilous. Many a ship was wrecked along the rocky shoreline. In November 1865 ten schooners were caught in a sudden storm.

As the century progressed, the smaller mills were abandoned, leaving the larger mills at the mouth of the rivers until later when the railroad and the truck replaced the water-borne trade. If you want to know what the early days were like, drop into the Ford House museum, which also houses the visitor center for Marin Headlands State Park and is described above, and look at the photographs of laboring men hauling lumber and ferrying it out to schooners for the trip south to boomtown San Francisco. When they weren't working, the sailors and lumbermen were entertaining themselves at one of the 8 hotels, 17 saloons, and more than a dozen bordellos. That was when the population was at its highest level, 3,500. Today there are only 1,000 full-time residents of Mendocino.

If you want to learn more about the pioneering families who founded the town, then stop in at the **Kelley House Museum,** 45007 Albion St. (☎ 707/937-5791). The house was built by William H. Kelley in 1861. He had arrived in Mendocino in 1850, having come originally from Prince Edward Island, Canada, via Maine and Bermuda. He was a ship's carpenter but went on to own a variety of successful businesses—sawmills, saloons, general stores, and livery stables—in a very short time. He and his wife, Eliza, raised four children here. The house now houses a library and historical archive and a room with exhibits relating to the early pioneer buildings and families of Mendocino. Stroll out into the gardens, too. Volunteers also lead walking tours; call for a reservation.

Hours: Jun–Sept, daily 1–4pm; Oct–May, Fri–Mon 1–4pm. *Admission:* $1 for adults, free for children.

You'd expect an art colony to have an arts center, and it does, the **Mendocino Arts Center,** 45200 Little Lake Rd., P.O. Box 765 (☎ 707/937-5818). See what's on in the three galleries, stroll the gardens, and shop in the store for arts and crafts. While you're here, pick up its monthly magazine, *Art and Entertainment,* which lists upcoming events in the region. The center also offers weekend workshops in textiles, ceramics, and fine arts. It is open daily 10am to 5pm.

For those who enjoy shopping, there are plenty of cute boutiques and galleries, selling everything from books and soaps to art and clothes. Among them are: **The Highlight Gallery,** 45052 Main St. (☎ 707/937-3132); **Old Gold,** 6 Albion St. (☎ 707/937-5005), which offers beautifully crafted contemporary and vintage jewelry; **Gallery Bookshop** at Main and Kasten streets (☎ 707/937-2665); **Gallery One,** Highway 1 and Main Street (☎ 707/937-5154); **Mendocino Chocolate Co.** (☎ 707/937-1107), where you can sample truffles and chocolates before purchasing from a selection that includes some brilliantly colored edible sea shells; **Deja-Vu the Mendocino Hat Co.** (☎ 707/937-4120), for all kinds of great hats from Stetsons to Panamas; **Mendocino Jams and Preserves** (☎ 707/937-1037), which sells delicious jams, preserves, sauces, and condiments; **Artists Coop** (☎ 707/937-2217), which features the works of local artists whom you can observe working in the upstairs studio/gallery.

Sybarites will want to treat themselves to sauna and hot tub soaks or deep massages at **Sweetwater Gardens,** 955 Ukiah St. (☎ 707/937-4140). It's open Monday to Thursday 2–10pm, Friday to Sunday noon–11pm.

Lodging & Dining in Mendocino

Although the **Stanford Inn by the Sea,** N. Hwy. 1 and Comptche Ukiah Rd., P.O. Box 487, Mendocino, CA 95460 (☎ 800/331 8884 or 707/937-5615, fax 707/937 0305), is a sizable, modern place with 23 rooms and 4 suites. It has much to recommend it, particularly the warmth of hospitality and quality of service provided by Joan and Jeff Stanford, and the views out across the gardens to the sea. A quarter of a mile south of Mendocino, it has a rustic feel and possesses attractively landscaped grounds, which give an air of spaciousness to the property. In fact, one part of the property is given over to fields where llamas and horses graze under old apple trees; another section is given over to an organic garden where all kinds of vegetables and flowers are grown—the source of the splendid bouquets that you'll find in your room. The rooms are furnished comfortably with a mixture of antiques and comfortable sofas placed in front of wood-burning fireplaces. All have private baths, telephones, TVs, VCRs, and CD players. Other facilities include sauna, spa, and a large solarium pool furnished with tropical plants like bougainvillea and hibiscus. The Big River estuary runs just behind the property, and canoes, kayaks, and mountain bikes are available (the latter are free). The champagne buffet breakfast—with breads, fruit, cereal, and egg dishes—is served in an airy dining room. Afternoon tea and evening snacks are also served.

Rates (incl. breakfast): $185–$235 double, $220–$350 suite.

The **Joshua Grindle Inn,** 44800 Little Lake Rd., P.O. Box 647, Mendocino, CA 95460 (☎ 707/937-4143), is a classic Mendocino home set on the edge of town on 2 acres, built originally for the town banker, Joshua Grindle, in 1879; its position on the crest of a hill ensures distant ocean views, at least from the second-floor guest rooms. The spacious gardens are studded with a variety of shrubs (rhododendron in particular) and are suffused with a relaxed, easy air. There are five rooms in the main house, two in the Cottage, and three in the Watertower. The furnishings consist of comfortable antiques; some rooms have wood-burning fireplaces. Each room is decorated differently. In the main house the Library evokes New England with its four-poster bed, hand-painted tile fireplace (illustrating Aesop's Fables) with pine mantel, and floor-to-ceiling bookcase. The most expensive room is the spacious Master, which has a sitting area with a fireplace and the additional luxury of a whirlpool tub and separate shower. The cottages, with their beamed ceilings, wood stoves, and Early American furnishings are very inviting; so too are the Watertower rooms, which feature country pine furnishings and Vermont Casting fireplaces. Guests enjoy relaxing in front of the fireplace in the parlor, which also has an antique pump organ as a conversation piece. Breakfasts are generous repasts of fruit, muffins, pastries, and cereal, plus quiche or frittata, eaten at an antique, pine harvest table.

Rates (incl. breakfast): $105–$185 double weekends, $100–$165 midweek.

In town, the **MacCallum House,** Albion St., P.O. Box 206, Mendocino CA 95460 (☎ 707/937-0289), is part of the legend of Mendocino, having been the home of Daisy Kelley and Alexander MacCallum. Daisy, the daughter of William Kelley, a founder of the town, arrived in 1852, and she herself was a prominent figure until her death in 1953 at the age of 94. The gabled Victorian house was built in 1882 as a wedding gift to Daisy. It stands in town surrounded by gardens. The interiors are alluring, atmospheric, and well furnished with quality antiques, many of which are original to the house and belonged to the MacCallum family. There are six accommodations in the main house, two with ocean views. Other accommodations are in cottages—the Gazebo was the original children's playhouse; the Carriage House features a canopied king bed and is warmed in winter by a Franklin stove; the Water Tower has an ocean view. The most luxurious accommodations are the suites in the restored barn, most of which have romantic stone fireplaces.

The **MacCallum House Restaurant** (☎ 707/937-5763) has similar warmth and style. Like the house, it has riverstone fireplaces, three-quarter wainscoting, and slatted wood ceilings. The cuisine uses local—often organic—ingredients. Start with the Pacific rim oysters with apple cider mignonette. Among the featured main courses, you'll always find a seasonal vegetarian dish like the butternut squash risotto with wild mushrooms, sage oil, and braised balsamic chard. There will also be a couple of fish dishes, like the grilled salmon filet with apple Calvados sauce. Other specialties might include a pan-seared Reichardt duck served with Mendocino wild huckleberry sauce. Prices range from $15 to $17.

The Gray Whale Bar is a convivial place for a drink and snack where you can sit on hump-back Victorian-style sofas.

Rates: $110–$200 double. *Dining Hours:* Summer, daily 5:30–9pm; winter, Fri–Tues 5:30–9pm. Closed for 6 weeks from Jan–mid-February.

The **Agate Cove Inn,** 11201 N. Lansing St., Mendocino, CA 95460 (☎ 707/937-0551), has a splendid setting overlooking the ocean, well away from the downtown village bustle. It also has lovely gardens enclosed by the original candlestick fence and a brick patio where you can relax. The main house was built in the 1860s. Except for 2 rooms, the 10 accommodations are located in cottages with an eclectic mix of furnishings including milk-painted, four-poster beds with canopies. They're pleasant, though, and have small TVs. Some, like Moonstone, have inviting window seats, and several have Franklin stoves. All have private decks. There's a comfortable parlor with a brick fireplace and a wonderful open kitchen where herbs hang from the beams to dry along with a major basket collection. Here, overlooking the ocean, a fine full breakfast (eggs Benedict, omelets, etc.) is served.

Rates (incl. breakfast): $109–$165 farmhouse rooms and single cottages, $185–$260 duplex cottages.

The **John Dougherty House,** 571 Ukiah St., P.O. Box 817, Mendocino, CA 95460 (☎ 707/937-5266), is easily recognizable by the water tower at one end of this simple gabled house. It stands right in town on the street. The Main House, built in 1867, possesses a parlor furnished with period pieces, including wing chairs and Windsors that are placed around the brick hearth. There are six rooms. The Captain's Room has a great view of the ocean from its own large veranda furnished with Adirondack chairs and wood-burning stove; the cozy Water Tower Room has just enough room for the four-poster bed and the wood-burning stove. Three of the accommodations are two-room suites located in cottages at the bottom of the back garden. They have either wood-burning stoves or fireplaces. A full breakfast, consisting of quiche, frittata, or something similar, plus fresh fruits and granola, is served in front of the fire in the keeping room.

Rates (incl. breakfast): $125–$195 double.

The **Whitegate Inn,** 499 Howard St., P.O. Box 150, Mendocino, CA 95460 (☎ 707/937-4892), is on the corner of a street in town. A white center-gable house with bay windows, it has been restored and lavishly furnished. Inlaid tables, Chinese rugs, a button ottoman, and a 17th-century grandfather clock are just a few of the antique pieces found in the parlor. Windows are swagged with tasseled drapes. The back deck, ornamented with plantings and a gazebo, has elegant wrought-iron furnishings, too. There are five rooms plus a cottage. The French Rose room contains a carved bed made up with lace-trimmed linens, Victorian chairs, and the added comforts of a wood-burning fireplace, cable TV, refrigerator, and private bathroom. Three other rooms also have fireplaces. The Garden Room has a brass bed; Daisy's has a clawfoot tub in the bathroom. The Cottage and the French Rose Room are similarly equipped, but the latter is located in the back. A full breakfast is served each morning, wine and hors d'oeuvres in the evening. Added comforts include a refrigerator that is stocked with complimentary sparkling mineral waters.

Rates (incl. breakfast): $129–$199 double.

The **Mendocino Hotel and Garden Suites,** 45080 Main St., P.O. Box 587, Mendocino, CA 95460 (☎ 800/548-0513 or 707/937-0511, fax 707/937-5763), is right in the heart of town. It's one of those typical, old Western hotels with first-floor porch and a balcony that has been modernized to provide the comforts 20th-century visitors expect. It was built in 1878, and when you enter the lobby/reception room, you'll feel as though you have stepped into a Victorian tableau, filled as it is with large antique furnishings, heavy Oriental rugs, and an oak reception desk salvaged from a Kansas bank. The rooms in the main hotel are small and furnished with Victorian reproductions; 24 have sinks in the room with baths across the hall. The most appealing accommodations are the garden suites, which are located behind the hotel itself and are reached by pathways lined with flower beds. These rooms have either a fireplace or balcony, and a separate parlor. All the rooms have TV and telephone and are furnished with reproductions, including wing chairs and armoires.

The hotel also has a **restaurant** and lounge with mahogany fittings, and a cafe and bar featuring a trellis. Room service is available. Breakfast, lunch, and dinner are served daily with main courses priced from $15 to $20.

Rates: $65–$90 double with shared bath, $85–$190 double with private bath; $160–$235 suite.

Captain's Cove Inn, 44781 Main St., Mendocino, CA 95460 (☎ 800/780-7905), overlooks Big River Cove from its windows, decks, and gardens. It's located in a weathered sea captain's home that was built in 1861. The five rooms have private baths and outside entrances plus such features as a TV and a wood-burning stove or fireplace. They are furnished in a mixture of modern and country styles. Beds are covered with modern quilts. You might find a couple of wicker chairs in front of the fireplace and such decorative accents as dried flower wreaths. The house has a comfortable sitting room furnished with some nautical regalia, including a table fashioned from a ship's wheel; there's also a hot tub and access to a private beach from the backyard. A full breakfast is served.

Rates (incl. breakfast): $183–$215 double weekends, $165–$183 midweek.

A short ride south of town, **Rachel's Inn,** 8200 N. Hwy. 1, P.O. Box 134, Mendocino, CA 95460 (☎ 707/937-0088), is a refreshing change from antique-filled, Laura Ashley bed-and-breakfasts. And it's also extra special because of owner Rachel herself, who has been—and still is—one of the region's fiercest defenders of the environment. She helped organize the fight against offshore oil drilling that would have marred this beautiful coastline for current and future generations. Her inn, located about 2 miles south of and on the west side of Highway 1, sits on an acre of land adjacent to a state park. There's even beach access from a trail behind the house. The Main House, which was built in the 1860s, has the grace, elegance, and high-ceilinged rooms of the period. It contains the dining room and five guest rooms. The Parlor Suite has a private sitting room with a fireplace and piano, a comfortably furnished bedroom with queen bed, and an ocean view. My favorite is the Garden Room, with a private entrance off the garden plus a fireplace. Across the brick patio from the Main House, the Barn features a central sitting room with a fireplace and four guest rooms. Each one is spacious and furnished in a contemporary traditional manner. The South Room is one of the best-equipped wheelchair accessible rooms you'll find anywhere; it also has a fireplace. The most luxurious is the Upper Suite, which has a large sitting room with private balcony, fireplace, wet bar, and refrigerator. Breakfasts are extraordinary, consisting of fresh fruit and great breads plus a flavor-filled hot dish like huevos rancheros or fruit-filled pancakes.

Rates (incl. breakfast): $120–$200 double weekends, $100–$180 midweek.

Set back from the road, the **Mendocino Village Inn,** 44860 Main St., P.O. Box 626, Mendocino, CA 95460 (☎ 800/882-7029 or 707/937-0246), is a gabled Victorian with steep dormers and windows decorated with finials. It was built in 1882 for a doctor and lumber baron and later became the residence of Emmy Lou Packard, a painter and local conservationist. The furnishings blend Victorian, country, and family heirlooms. There are 13 rooms in the house. The first- and second-floor rooms have private baths, the third-floor attic rooms share a bath on the second floor. Some of the rooms have a private entrance, including number 11, which also offers a wood-burning stove, a bathtub set under a skylight, and access to a small private garden. The water-tower suite is the most secluded and romantic room. It also has a wood-burning stove and a private deck. The bountiful breakfasts consist of cornmeal pancakes, herb omelets, and similar dishes accompanied by fresh fruit and baked goodies.

Rates (incl. breakfast): $85 double with shared bath, $105–$160 double with private bath; $185 suite.

Dining Only in Mendocino

Cafe Beaujolais, 961 Ukiah St. (☎ 707/937-5614), is the topnotch dining spot in town. It's country comfortable with polished wood tables. The menu is limited, but everything will be well seasoned and expertly prepared. The dishes will always be innovative, too. Start with, say, the warm duck leg confit salad in cranberry vinaigrette with persimmons, toasted almonds, and blue cheese on spinach and frisé. Among the five main courses might be Yucatecan–Thai crab cakes served with avocado salsa, achiote-roasted tomato sauce, coconut rice, and black beans; or roasted chicken with Calvados sauce and sautéed apples. Prices range from $16 to $19. Desserts are worth saving room for, especially the wild huckleberry pie served with vanilla ice cream, or the trio of chocolate nougatines.

Hours: Daily 5:45–10pm. Closed during Dec.

955 Ukiah Street, between Howard and Evergreen (☎ 707/937-1955), is a casual, comfortable restaurant that occupies the former studio of artist Emmy Lou Packard, who was so active in the preservation of historic Mendocino. The room is split-level, the walls decorated with local art, and the tables covered with white linen. The menu features a range of dishes from pasta—canneloni and five-cheese ravioli with a sauce of mushrooms, tomato, and red onion, for example—to swordfish in red chili-tomatillo sauce, or crispy duck in a sauce of ginger, apples, and calvados. Prices range from $8 (for pasta dishes) to $19. For dessert, try the bread pudding with huckleberry compote, a local favorite.

Hours: Summer, Wed–Sun 6pm–closing; winter, Thurs–Sun 6pm–closing.

FORT BRAGG

This old logging town, 10 miles north of Mendocino, is much less artsy-fartsy than its more picturesque neighbor, but it has a lot of flavor to it.

Along Main Street, you'll find some stores to browse like **For the Shell of It,** 344 N. Main St. (☎ 707/961-0461), where almost everything is crafted from shells or has a nautical theme; the **Hot Pepper Jelly Company,** 330 N. Main St. (☎ 707/961-1422), which sells great jams and jellies as well as red and jalapeño pepper jellies, chutneys, and other food products; the **Mendocino Chocolate Company,** 542 N. Main St. (☎ 707/964-8800); **Northcoast Artists,** 362 N. Main St. (☎ 707/964-8266), which is an artists' cooperative displaying jewelry, ceramics, paintings, prints, photography, weavings, and woodwork, and where on the first Friday of each month between 6 and 9pm visitors are welcome to attend a reception; and **Windsong,** 324 N. Main St. (☎ 707/964-2050), which sells gift items including kites and candles.

Fort Bragg is also the home of the **Mendocino Coast Botanical Gardens,** 18220 N. Hwy. 1, Fort Bragg, CA 95437 (☎ 707/964-4352), 47 acres of coastal gardens crisscrossed by meandering paths where you can picnic or stroll. The signature plants in the gardens are hybrid rhododendrons. There are also collections of heathers, succulents, fuchsias, roses, dahlias, and camellias all sheltered by groves of pine, cypress, and eucalyptus. Walk down to the cliff house and enjoy the inspiring view.

Hours: Mar–Oct, daily 9am–5pm; Nov–Feb, 9am–4pm. *Admission:* $5 adults, $4 seniors, $3 children.

The **Skunk Train** (☎ 707/964-6371)—so called because the old gas engine powering it led people to say, "You can smell 'em before you can see 'em"—also operates from Fort Bragg along an old logging railroad established in 1885. Today the trains travel 40 miles from Fort Bragg to Willits, crossing many trestles and bridges, traveling through tunnels, and following the course of Pudding Creek and the Noyo River through the redwoods. The railroad was established in 1885 to haul logs to the mill. Passenger service was started in 1904 using steam engines that were discontinued in 1925 when the "skunk" rail cars using gas engines were inaugurated. Today, several engines operate on the track—the old Baldwin Steam engine, a 1925 MS-100; a 1935 MS-300; and a diesel-powered no. 64, for those of you who are real railroad buffs. Passengers can either take a full-day roundtrip from either Willits or Fort Bragg or else take a 3-hour excursion to the midway point of Northspur and back again. At Northspur, you can relax in a beer garden.

Fares: Round-trips, $26 adults, $12 children 5–11; half-day or one-way, $21 and $10, respectively.

The town's fishing fleet operates out of Noyo Harbor, the place to head for whale watching and fishing charters.

Lodging & Dining in Fort Bragg

The Grey Whale Inn, 615 N. Main St., Fort Bragg, CA 95437 (☎ 800/382-7244 or 707/964-0640, fax 707/964-4408), occupies a classical revival redwood building that originally served as a hospital, which explains the wide halls and doorways. It has now been converted into a comfortable inn by John and Colette Bailey, who have furnished the 14 rooms, all with TV and telephone, with inviting and colorful country decor. Some rooms are exceptionally equipped, like the Campbell, a corner room equipped with TV/VCR, fridge, microwave, and gas fireplace, or the Penthouse Sunrise room, which has a private deck, double Jacuzzi, and wicker furnishings. The other penthouse room has a great ocean view and private covered deck. Other rooms are nicely decorated with French country or rustic pieces. Quilts, featuring log cabin, wedding ring, rainbow fan, and many other familiar designs, brighten the walls of nearly every room. A buffet breakfast is included.

Rates (incl. breakfast): $94–$175 double.

The Pudding Creek Inn, 700 and 710 N. Main St., Fort Bragg, CA 95437 (☎ 800/227-9529 or 707/964-9529, fax 707/961-0282), occupies two Victorian homes that are linked by a shared courtyard with fountain, plants, and seating. There are four rooms in the main house, including Grandma's Attic, which is furnished with a brass bed covered with a wedding ring quilt; Pot Pourri, which is decorated with wicker pieces; and the Spinning Room, which has a spinning wheel among its decorative accents. The rooms in the 710 building are a little larger and somewhat more stylish than those in the Main House. The Count's Room, for example, has a king-size brass bed with partial canopy, fireplace, and a decent selection of antique pieces. Guests have use of a parlor where they can read or play games, and also of TV and recreation rooms. A buffet breakfast is served. Phone, fax, and laundry service are available.

Rates (incl. breakfast): $90–$140 double.

Dining Only in Fort Bragg

The Restaurant, 418 N. Main St. (☎ 707/964-9800), is a hospitable place where you will likely make some local friends. It's located in a storefront on Main Street and is decorated with the works of local artists. At dinner the menu lists about eight entrees, which are served with soup or salad. Try the sesame-crusted chicken breast with ginger soy sauce, or the sautéed halibut with green peppercorn aïoli sauce. Prices for main courses range from $16.75 to $20. Light meals, like grilled polenta with mozzarella, mushroom and a tomato-herb sauce (all priced under $10) are also available. My favorite among the desserts is the warm caramel apple crêpes. On weekends, you might discover a small local jazz combo playing.

Hours: Thurs–Fri 11:30am–2pm, Sun 10am–1pm; Thurs–Tues 5–9pm.

If you're a beer lover and also want to meet some of the locals, then head for the bar at **North Coast Brewing Company,** 444 N. Main St. (☎ 707/964-3400). It produces five flavorful beers year-round—Red Seal, Scrimshaw Pilsner, Old No. 38 Stout, Old Rasputin Russian Imperial Stout, and Blue Star Wheat beer—plus several seasonal beers, including Christmas Ale and Oktoberfest Ale. All five of the annual beers have won medals at the World Beer Championships in Chicago. These beers can be enjoyed at the bar/restaurant, which occupies a building that has been variously a mortuary, a church, and a college before being converted to a brew pub complete with large copper storage tanks. The menu offers a good range of dishes to accompany the beer (or local wines), from wild mushroom ravioli and charbroiled snapper with lemon-dill sauce, to barbecue chicken and pork loin baked in a banana leaf and served with chipotle chile sauce. Prices range from $10 to $17. Burgers, sandwiches, and dishes like chili, fish and chips, and nachos are also available.

Hours: Tues–Sun noon–9pm.

Mendocino Coast
Special & Recreational Activities

Beaches: You can reach the beaches below the headlands in Mendocino as well as the beach where the Big River flows out into the ocean.

Biking: There are paved trails in **Van Damme State Park** (3 miles south of Mendocino) and **Russian Gulch State Park** (☎ 800/444-7275), 2 miles north of Mendocino, for regular bikes. Highway 1 is a National Bike Route but is heavily trafficked in summer, when you're better off traveling the backroads.

There are also plenty of mountain-biking opportunities along logging roads and trails. In Mendocino, **Catch a Canoe & Bicycles Too,** Highway 1 and Comptche–Ukiah Road (☎ 707/937-0273), rents good mountain bikes.

In Fort Bragg, **Ocean Trail Bikes and Rental,** 1260 N. Main St. (☎ 707/964-1260), rents bikes for $25 a day and will point you towards the bike trail that runs along the ocean. **North Coast Divers Supply,** 19275 S. Harbor Dr. (☎ 800/961-1143 or 707/961-1143), also rents mountain bikes.

Camping: There's camping in the dunes at **Manchester State Beach.** Three miles south of Mendocino, **Van Damme State Park** (☎ 707/937-5804) has 74 sites. **Russian Gulch State Park** (☎ 800/444-7275), 2 miles north of Mendocino, has 30 sites. **MacKerricher State Park** (☎ 707/937-5804), 3 miles north of Fort Bragg, has 143 sites plus a few hike-in camps. **Hendy Woods State Park,** Philo–Greenwood Road (☎ 707/937-5804), offers 92 sites in 2 campgrounds. You can also camp in sight of the ocean at **Westport Union Landing State Beach** (☎ 707/937-5804), about 2 miles north of Westport. The beach is good for surf fishing, abalone picking, and tide-pooling. There are 130 primitive camping sites available.

Canoeing/Kayaking: Catch a Canoe & Bicycles Too, Highway 1 and Comptche–Ukiah Road (☎ 707/937-0273), rents canoes, sea cycles, kayaks, and a locally designed redwood canoe with outrigger, which prevents rollover. You can take these craft on the Big River's 8-mile-long tidal estuary watching for herons, osprey, and ducks plus harbor seals and other wildlife.

Lost Coast Adventures at North Coast Divers Supply, 19275 S. Harbor Dr., Fort Bragg (☎ 800/961-1143), operates sea kayaking tours in Van Damme State Park. Tours are $40 for adults, $20 for children 8 to 12.

Fishing: Fort Bragg is the sport fishing center. Party boats leave from **Noyo's Fishing Center,** 3245 N. Harbor, Noyo (☎ 707/964-7609).

Golf: There's only one course in the area, and that's the 9-holer at the **Little River Inn,** 7751 Hwy. 1 (☎ 707/937-5667). Greens fees for non-guests are $20 for 9 holes, $30 for 18 holes.

Hiking: The old logging haul road in MacKerricher State Park follows the coastline, but there are plenty of other nature and hiking trails. See the list of state parks below.

Horseback Riding: Trail rides along the beach and custom 3-hour, 4-hour, or all-day rides are offered by appointment at **Lari Shea's Ricochet Ridge Ranch**, 24201 N. Hwy. 1, Fort Bragg (☎ 707/964-7669). Serious riders, though, may want to take one of her weekend or longer vacations, which offer fast riding on fine Arab or Arab-Orlov horses through redwood forests, over coastal bluffs, and along the beach. Picnic lunches, good inn accommodations, and candlelight dinners and evening musical entertainment are included in the price of longer vacations (camping or motel accommodations on weekends). It all amounts to a fantasy come true for many equestrians. Prices range from $495 to $1,750. The owner, Lea, takes great care to carefully match horse to rider and caters to beginners as well as ultra-serious equestrians.

Scuba: If you want to participate in a half-day non-certification introduction to scuba diving, during which you go out with an instructor, learn about the sport and equipment, and do some diving, then contact **Sub Surface Progression**, 18600 N. Hwy. 1, Fort Bragg (☎ 707/964-3793). It will cost $100. The outfit rents equipment to certified individuals and also operates a 6-week certification course. Guaranteed best diving months are August, September, and early October.

State Parks: 5 miles south of Point Arena, **Schooner Gulch State Park** (☎ 707/937-5804) is a small, 70-acre beach and headland park that is little visited. Go to walk on the beach, beachcomb, surf fish or just watch the sunset.

Manchester State Beach sweeps dramatically north of Point Arena Lighthouse providing 5 miles of sandy beach for great beachcombing (especially for driftwood), surf fishing, and birding. There are also 45 not very private, primitive campsites available in the dunes behind the beach.

Van Damme State Park, 3 miles south of Mendocino (☎ 707/937-5804), is a favorite place for abalone picking. It also has biking, hiking, and nature trails traversing its 2,160 acres.

Mendocino Headlands State Park has a visitor center (☎ 707/937-5397) in Ford House on Main Street in Mendocino. It's bracing and invigorating to stand atop these bluffs looking out along the sculptured coastline crafted into archways and other brilliant rock formations. In spring the headlands are painted in myriad hues by numerous wildflowers; while in summer wild berries can be gathered along the trails. A trail behind the Mendocino Presbyterian Church takes you to a staircase that leads down to the beach—a beachcomber's delight with its bird life and driftwood.

Two miles north of Mendocino, **Russian Gulch State Park's** (☎ 800/444-7275) most famous feature is the Punch Bowl, a collapsed sea cave where the ocean pounds and whirls. The 1,300-acre park also has hiking, biking, and equestrian trails. Hike the 3-mile Waterfall Loop Trail to a 36-foot cascade.

At 764-acre **Jug Handle State Reserve,** 1 mile north of Caspar (☎ 707/937-5804), the most fascinating feature is the trail that leads up the so-called ecological staircase, a series of ridge-terraces that were pushed up from the sea. Each ridge represents 100,000 years and supports a different variety of flora and fauna starting with coastal prairie and ending with a unique pygmy forest.

Three miles north of Fort Bragg, **Mackerricher State Park** (☎ 707/937-5804) has 1,600 acres that include an 8-mile beach; 7 miles of old logging trails for hiking, biking, and horseback riding; and two freshwater ponds, one of which is stocked with trout. Walk to Laguna Point to view the colony of harbor seals. Good whale watching, too.

Hendy Woods State Park, located one-half mile off Highway 28 on the Philo–Greenwood Road (☎ 707/937-5804), is a small 690-acre park in the Anderson Valley that stretches along the Navarro River, where visitors can fish for steelhead, swim, and canoe or kayak in the spring.

Standish–Hickey State Recreation Area (☎ 707/925-6482) stretches along the banks of the South Fork of the Eel River. This 1,000-plus-acre park, 1 mile north of Leggett on Highway 101, offers 162 campsites in 3 separate campgrounds, fishing, swimming, and 9 miles of hiking trails, some quite steep. The park also contains the Miles Standish Tree, a 225-foot redwood.

Sinkyone Wilderness State Park (☎ 707/946-2311), on the border of Mendocino and Humboldt counties, possesses a fantastic, rocky coastline where the cliffs sweep down to the ocean. It's very remote and most accessible from Redway via County Road 435.

Whale Watching: The best times for whale watching are from December to March. Boats operate from Noyo Harbor. Contact **Anchor Charters** in Fort Bragg (☎ 707/964-4550). Trips last 2 hours and cost $20 per person.

The Redwood Empire— Humboldt County & Eureka

Distances in Miles: Garberville, 200; Scotia/Ferndale, 265; Eureka, 276; Arcata, 286

Estimated Driving Times: 3¼ hours to Garberville, 4¼ hours to Scotia and Ferndale, 4½ hours to Eureka, 4¾ hours to Arcata

Driving: Highway 101 from San Francisco leads directly up to Humboldt County, all the way to Crescent City at the top of Redwood National Park.

Further Information: For information on the entire area, contact the **Redwood Empire Association,** 2801 Leavenworth, San Francisco, CA 94133 (☎ 415/543-8337).

Local organizations include the following: the **Garberville/Redway Chamber of Commerce,** P.O. Box 445, Garberville, CA 95542 (☎ 707/923-2613); **Avenue of the Giants,** P.O. Box 1000, Miranda, CA 95553 (☎707/923-2555); **Shelter Cove Information Bureau,** 412 Machi Rd., Shelter Cove, CA 95589 (☎ 707/986-7069).

Ferndale Chamber of Commerce, P.O. Box 325, Ferndale, CA 95536 (☎ 707/786-4477).

Eureka/Humboldt County Convention & Visitors Bureau, 1034 2nd Street, Eureka, CA 5501 (☎ 800/346-3482 or 707/443-5097, in CA 800/338-7352); **Eureka Chamber of Commerce,** 2112 Broadway, Eureka, CA 95501 (☎ 800/356-6381 or 707/442-3738); **Arcata Chamber of Commerce,** 1062 G St., Arcata, CA 95521 (☎ 707/822-3619); **Trinidad Chamber of Commerce,** P.O. Box 356, Trinidad, CA 95570 (☎ 707/441-9827); **Willow Creek Chamber of Commerce,** P.O. Box 704, Willow Creek, CA 95573 (☎ 916/629-2693); **Six Rivers National Forest,** 1330 Bayshore Way, Eureka, CA 95501 (☎707/442-1721).

This is the region to visit to encounter the great trees that Steinbeck called "ambassadors from another time." Here you can walk under the cool canopy of majestic redwoods on a forest floor made brilliant with moss, ferns,

Events & Festivals to Plan Your Trip Around

March: The 3-day **Redwood Coast Dixieland Jazz Festival** in Eureka kicks off with "A Taste of Main" and follows with Dixieland bands appearing at six or so different venues. Call ☎ 707/445-3378 for information.

April: The **Rhododendron Festival & Parade** in Eureka is filled with spring color as floats gilded with rhododendron blooms file by. The 6-day festival also includes a golf tournament, art shows, concerts, and more. Call ☎ 707/442-3738 for information.

May: The **Avenue of the Giants Marathon and 10K Run** are held in Humboldt Redwoods State Park. The events are sponsored by the Six Rivers Running Club. For information call ☎ 707/443-1226, or write P.O. Box 214, Arcata, CA 95521.

The **Tour of the Unknown Coast Bicycle Race** is run from Ferndale to Petrolia. For information call ☎ 800/995-8356 (or 707/822-3757).

The Portuguese **Holy Ghost Festival** in Ferndale, which takes place 6 weeks after Easter, commemorates a historic incident when Portugal was saved from famine by a little girl who touched the reigning Queen as she was about to attend mass. Right after that the mass ships appeared in the harbor loaded with food. To celebrate this event the local Portuguese community choose the Holy Ghost Queens, who represent the Queen and the child, and parade behind them in ethnic costume from Ferndale's Portuguese Hall to the Roman Catholic church where a mass is celebrated. For more information call ☎ 707/786-9640.

The **Great Arcata to Ferndale Cross County Kinetic Sculpture Race** is a 3-day, 38-mile race of human-powered vehicles over land and water. Call ☎ 707/725-3851 for information. It's held on Memorial Day weekend.

June: During the **Arcata Bay Oyster Festival,** you can go to Arcata Plaza and taste the way they're prepared at more than 30 restaurants in the region. Call ☎ 707/826-9043 for more information.

The Scandinavian-inspired **Midsummer Festival** in Ferndale is a weekend celebrating the summer solstice with music and dancing, Scandinavian foods, and Viking revelry. It culminates on Sunday with a parade of people in ethnic costumes and a flag ceremony. For information call ☎ 707/786-4477.

The **Trinidad Fish Festival** is a big day when everything in the town, including the lighthouse and the Humboldt

continues

continued

University Marine Lab, is open to everyone. Fish is the food order of the day, and there's also a large crafts show to browse afterwards. Call the Trinidad Chamber of Commerce for information at ☎ 707/677-0591.

July: The **Fortuna Rodeo** is a week-long celebration with street entertainment. It starts with the chili cook-off and culminates in the weekend rodeo at Rohner Park. For information call ☎ 707/725-3716.

August: The **Mad River Festival** is a month-long festival of comedy, music, storytelling, puppetry, and vaudeville performed by the Dell'Arte Players Co. in Blue Lake. Call ☎ 707/668-5663 for information.

The **Reggae on the River Festival** attracts more than 10,000 people to the banks of the Eel River in Piercy (9 miles south of Garberville) to hear top reggae and African artists. Past performers have included Jimmy Cliff, Hugh Masekela, The Wailers, Baaba Maal, Lucky Dube, and David Lindley. It's so popular you need to purchase tickets when they go on sale in early April. For information, write to The Mateel, P.O. Box 1910, Redway, CA 95560.

September: At the **Professional California Cowboys Rodeo Association Championship Rodeo** in Fortuna, the top 15 cowboys in each event, from saddle to bareback to team roping and more, compete in the championships.

December: At the **Lighted Tractor Parade and Truckers Christmas Convoy** in Eureka, more than 150 big rigs parade through town decked out in brilliant lights carrying logs that have been decorated to look like candy canes. Call the radio station that sponsors the event for information (☎ 707/442-5744).

sorrel, and trillium by visiting either Humboldt State Park and the Avenue of the Giants, or Redwood National and State Parks some miles farther north.

The coastal redwood grows only in the humid coastal climate of a narrow, 500-mile strip stretching from the southwestern corner of Oregon to approximately 150 miles south of San Francisco. The magnificent specimens that grow here on 160,000 acres protected by the National and State park services are all that remain of what was once a huge redwood forest that extended over about 2 million acres. These amazing trees are in fact some of the oldest life forms on our planet and exhibit some remarkable natural characteristics. They require the thick summer fogs and abundant winter rains of the region. They are slow to burn and resistant to fungal

The Redwood Empire

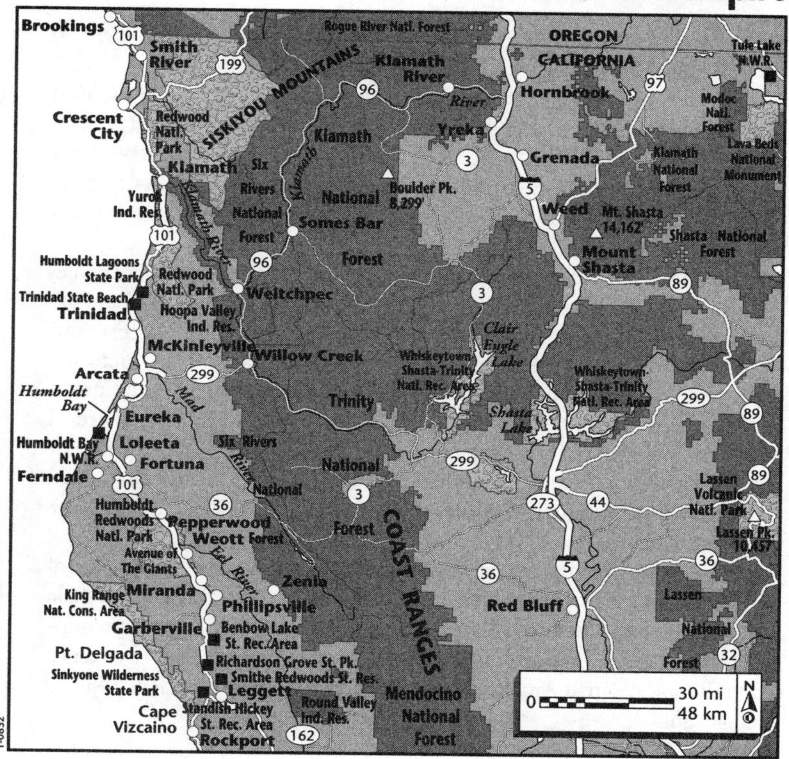

and other decay (and to most insects) primarily because their bark grows extremely thick (as much as 1 foot) and is high in tannic acid. They are also able to regenerate, sprouting new growth in the event of an injury. Consequently, they survive for anywhere from 500 to 700 years, with the oldest on record having lived to the ripe age of 2,200 years.

Sadly they were, and still are, not as resistant to the insatiable appetites of the lumber and construction industries, which have destroyed in a few decades what had taken centuries to grow. In fact, so many of the old-growth redwoods have been cut that a group was formed to save them from extinction by establishing and protecting Memorial Groves. Most trees that are cut average 250 feet in height, 12 feet in diameter and are 1,000 years old.

In the early logging days—when men used axes—it might take two men a full week working from dawn to dusk to bring down one tree. The trees were bucked into short lengths, debarked, and moved downhill using a jackscrew to a skid trail, where they were moved out with the help of ox teams. By the turn of the century, the forests had been decimated. The Save the Redwoods League was formed in 1918 when more than a third of the redwood area had already been logged. Thanks to their efforts, some of these marvelous trees have been preserved for posterity, but even so about 85% of the old-growth forest has been destroyed.

In addition to the trees, there's also plenty to enjoy. You'll find beaches and the bounty of the ocean—oysters in particular. After lumber, fishing is still one of the prime industries, and along the coast there are several fishing fleets operating from such ports as Shelter Cove, Eureka, and Trinidad. North of Humboldt Bay, the Klamath River is famous for salmon.

And the towns themselves offer the visitor much as well. Ferndale, which was built upon the wealth of the dairy industry, is a National Historic Landmark jam-packed with all kinds of Victorian commercial and residential buildings. The Old Town of Eureka is also an historic Victorian enclave in which to wander. Eureka, of course, has the magnificent Carson House, one of the most splendidly ornate Victorians found anywhere. If you're more interested in engaging in an active weekend, then Humboldt State University in Arcata offers some excellent and very reasonably priced weekend trips through its **Center Activities** program (☎ 707/826-3357 for information).

If you prefer to get out in nature on your own, there are plenty of opportunities for bird-watching, fishing, white-water rafting and whale watching. And for those of you who want to watch one of the most whimsical events in the nation, visit the region on Memorial Day weekend, when the 3-day Great Arcata to Ferndale Cross-County Kinetic Sculpture Race is run.

THE AVENUE OF THE GIANTS & THE LOST COAST

The **Avenue of the Giants** is one of the most scenic routes in the West, running for 31 miles and cutting through 51,000-acre Humboldt Redwoods State Park along the banks of the Eel River. The Avenue, which parallels Highway 101, starts around Phillipsville and ends just south of Scotia. As you drive along the shady roads, you'll be driving through some of the last remaining coastal redwoods. Along the route there are, sadly, several typical tourist sites like the Chimney Tree, the One Log House, Shrine Drive-Thru Tree, Immortal Tree, and Eternal Tree house. Ignore these unless you enjoy such phenomena, and get off the beaten path along the more than 100 miles of mostly short-loop hiking, mountain biking, and equestrian trails in **Humboldt Redwoods State Park,** P.O. Box 100, Weott, CA 95571 (☎ 707/946-2409).

There are more than 100 memorial groves within the park. The first of these, Franklin K. Lane Grove, lies just north of Phillipsville at the southern entrance to the park. The road courses along through Miranda past the Stephens Grove and through Myers Flat to Williams Grove and the Garden Club of America Grove.

You'll want to stop at the **Visitor Center and Park Headquarters** (☎ 707/946-2409), about 2 miles south of Weott. This center has displays about the redwoods, as well as the ecology, flora, and fauna in the park; it also supplies information about trails, camping, and other activities. In summer the rangers present special programs and activities.

As you drive this route, you'll see signs for several towns, but most are merely names on signposts; most of these towns were washed away by the devastating floods of 1955 and 1964 as were hundreds of redwoods. A sign on the road testifies to these events, marking the spot where the river rose to a height of 33 feet.

About 1.2 miles north of Weott at the Federation Grove, you can see the fireplace structure complete with four sheltered fireplaces that was designed by Julia Morgan, the architect of many California buildings, most notably Hearst Castle. About half a mile farther on is Canfield Grove. And a little beyond that, the Dyerville Loop Road leads to the Founder's Tree in the grove of the same name. It is 346 feet tall and dedicated to the founders of the Save the Redwoods League. The Founder's Grove also contains the Dyerville Giant, which fell in 1991; you can see the root ball that measured 38 feet across.

From here, the Avenue of the Giants continues north to Scotia. Mattole Road cuts off west along Bull Creek through the Rockefeller Forest—which is the largest old-growth redwood forest in existence—to the Big Tree Area, where you'll find the champion coast redwood, so named by the American Forestry Association, and the Flat Iron Tree, which is so named because of the unusual shape of its base.

At the end of the Avenue of the Giants in **Scotia,** you can visit the mill at the **Pacific Lumber Company,** which also owns the whole town—hospital, stores, post office, hotel, school, shipping facilities, lumber products factory, and employee housing. It's one of the few true company towns left in the nation. On this self-guided tour you will see massive logs being stripped of their bark by high-pressure jets of water and then being cut into 20-foot lengths of timber, a noisy and highly charged process indeed. Scanners then determine what cuts will produce the most lumber from these 20-foot logs. Any waste is used to make flooring or molding, and any additional waste is then burned to generate electricity. The mill is open Monday through Friday from 7:30am to 2pm. (This is the company, by the way, that has generated so much controversy recently by its plan to cut the trees at Headwaters Grove southeast of Eureka.)

West of the Humboldt Redwoods State Park lies the remote **King Range National Conservation Area,** Bureau of Land Management (☎ 707/825-2300), which stretches 35 miles along the coast and up to 6 miles inland. It contains 540,000 acres of timbered mountains fringed by shoreline. Within its confines stands the highest mountain directly on the west coast, King Mountain, which rises to 4,087 feet. This coastal region is referred to as the Lost Coast, where waves crash against the rugged coastline and cliffs leaving only small, covelike beaches to discover. It's accessible by one road only and so, except for Shelter Cove, little has been developed.

Here in this remote region you can climb **Horse Mountain** for one of the most spectacular views in the whole county and also enjoy hiking, fishing, and camping. A road leads west from Highway 101 at Redway through **Briceland** (stop in at the winery) and Whitehorn for 26 miles to **Shelter Cove.** Here in this small community with a sheltered harbor, you can walk on a black-sand beach; go fishing for salmon, rock fish, lingcod and abalone; and hike the many trails, some of which lead to the small, abandoned **Punta Gorda Lighthouse.** There are a few facilities at the Cove including grocery, deli, and other community services.

Nearby you can also explore the 7,312-acre **Sinkyone Wilderness State Park** across the border in Mendocino county. The visitor center is located at Needle Rock and provides permits for the hike-in campsites. To reach Shelter Cove take the Garberville/Redway exit from Highway 101. Note that the 26-mile drive along this steep and curving road will take 45 minutes.

Avenue of the Giants Area Lodging & Dining

The **Benbow Inn,** 445 Lake Benbow Drive, Garberville, CA 95542 (☎ 707/923 2124, fax 707/923-2122), is a splendid Tudor-style inn designed by Albert Farr for the Benbow family in 1926. Many famous figures from earlier eras have passed through the portals of this inn into the large lobby lounge—Herbert Hoover, Eleanor Roosevelt, Charles Laughton, and Spencer Tracy to name a few. Cherry wainscoted hallways lead to the rooms, which have been strikingly furnished, many with four-poster beds. All have air-conditioning, telephone, and private bath. Nice extra touches include sherry, coffee, tea, and a basket of mysteries for your reading pleasure in each room. The loveliest rooms are perhaps the four in the main building, which are furnished in country antique style. Three have wood-burning fireplaces; one has a Jacuzzi, too. Afternoon tea (mulled wine when the weather is chilly) and hors d'oeuvres are also served daily.

The **dining room** offers fine California cuisine—a variety of pastas plus such dishes as pork tenderloin roasted with lavender and mint with a maple miso sauce, fresh trout grilled with a nut-seed crust and served with an apple-hazelnut glaze, or Petaluma chicken with lemon and herbs. Prices for main courses range from $13 to $24. Among the appetizers both the artichoke and sweet pepper tart and the whole roasted sweet onion with Black Forest ham, aged Jack cheese, and walnut balsamic vinaigrette are winners. In summer the outdoor terrace is particularly inviting.

For sports enthusiasts, Benbow lake is right around the corner for hiking and swimming, and so is the Benbow Valley Golf Course; bicycles are available. The inn also has a library of more than 250 films for guest

Avenue of the Giants

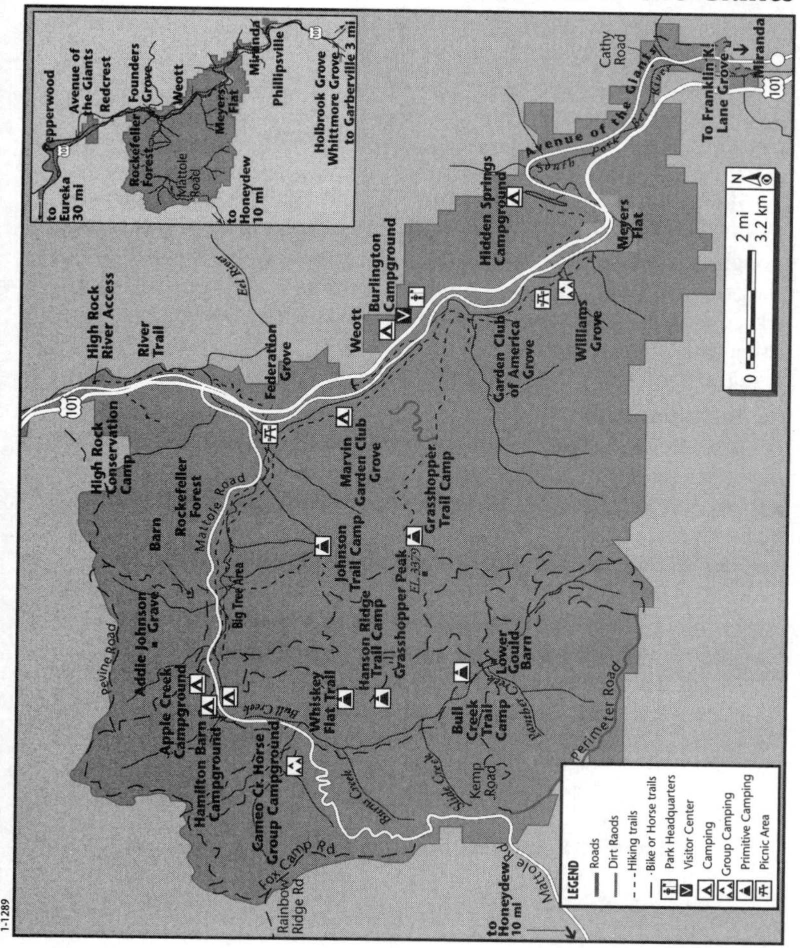

screenings. The gardens are inspirational, with narcissus and tulips in spring and roses, lilies, and marigolds in summer.

Rates: $125–$225 double, the higher prices for the rooms in the main building with a terrace and/or a fireplace.

Bell Glen Bed & Breakfast, 70400 Hwy. 101, Leggett, CA 95585 (☎ 707/925-6425), stands on 10 acres with a riverfront beach. Gene and Sandra Barnett have spruced up the cottages of this old resort, furnishing them in country style with four-poster beds and a floral look. They've also added such extra touches as fresh flowers, potpourri, coffee, tea, wine, and bubble bath. Some of the cottages have tubs for two; one even has a private Jacuzzi for two in its deck overlooking the river. There are no TVs or phones. A breakfast basket containing muffins, fresh fruit, cheese, juice, and coffee and tea are delivered to your room the night before. Guests enjoy the swimming hole, which actually contains warmed river water. The Bistro, which was originally a stage stop, now contains a candlelit dining room (open weekends only) and a rathskeller that has been decorated with the national flags of the many visitors who have stopped in.

Rates (incl. breakfast): $105–$150 double.

The **Shelter Cove Beachcomber Inn,** 7272 Shelter Cove Rd., Whitehorn, CA 95489 (☎ 707/986-7733), offers five housekeeping units. One is large enough to sleep six. It has two bunk beds, plus a double sofa bed in the living room, full kitchen, wood stove, and bathroom. Another unit is similarly equipped and can sleep four. The remainder have only minikitchens with a toaster, microwave, and refrigerator.

Rates: Summer, $55–$95 double; winter, $55–$85.

The Lighthouse (☎ 707/923-4143) is a unique one-room accommodation providing a 360-degree view of the mountain and ocean setting from the decks that surround the tower. Added luxuries include a Jacuzzi and fireplace, plus a tiny galley kitchen equipped with small refrigerator and microwave.

Rates: $185 for the lighthouse room.

Avenue of the Giants/Lost Coast
Special & Recreational Activities

Camping: Benbow Lake State Recreation Area (☎ 707/946-2311) has a 76-site campground open from April 1 to November 1. There are three camping facilities in the park.

Humboldt Redwoods State Park (☎ 707/946-2409) has camping at 247 serviced sites in 3 campgrounds. The largest is Hidden Springs in Myers Flat with 155 sites; Burlington is next to Park Headquarters and has 56 sites; Albee Creek is west of the Avenue of the Giants on Mattole Road and has 38 sites. Only Burlington is open year-round. Additional primitive campsites for hikers, bikers, and horse riders are also available. Burlington sites can be reserved by calling **MISTIX** (☎ 800/444-7275).

King Range Conservation Area (☎ 707/822-7648) offers 48 sites in 5 campgrounds—Wailaki, Tolkan, Nadelos, Horse Mountain, and Mouth of the Mattole. The last, located 5 miles west of Petrolia, is the best camping area from which to spot seabirds, and other sea creatures—sea lions, harbor seals, and sea otters.

At **Sinkyone Wilderness State Park** there are 31 hike-in sites near streams at the northern end of the park in protected areas with access to beaches. Usal Beach at the southern end has 16 drive-in sites.

Canoeing: You can rent a canoe at Benbow Lake, which is a good place for beginners to practice their skills.

Cross-Country Skiing: There are trails at **Horse Mountain** in Six Rivers National Forest near Willow Creek. Call ☎ 916/629-2118 for snow conditions, though.

Fishing: In Humboldt State Park, fishing for salmon and steelhead in the Eel River is mainly a fall sport. There's ocean fishing from Shelter Cover and also fine fishing in the Marrole River in the King Range Conservation Area. Fishing conditions are unpredictable, so call the California **Department of Fish and Game**'s north coast river information number (☎ 707/442-4502).

Hiking: Hiking opportunities abound in all the area's state parks, which are listed below. One of the most spectacular trails, the Lost Coast Trail, winds along the coast in the King Range National Conservation area past the abandoned Punta Gorda lighthouse.

Mountain Biking: In Humboldt Redwoods State Park, the best roads are found in the Bull Creek area about 10 miles northwest of the Visitor Center. Here the old park fire roads can be used, like the Bull Creek Fire Road. Ask at the Visitor Center for more information.

State Parks: Smith Redwoods Richardson Grove State Park (☎ 707/247-3318), 8 miles south of Garberville, offers hiking (10 miles of trails), fishing for steelhead and trout, swimming, and camping at 169 sites in 1,000 acres of park land.

The Avenue of the Giants runs through **Humboldt Redwoods State Park** (☎ 707/946-2409). It contains about 10,000 acres of old-growth redwoods within its 51,000 acres; in fact, this park contains more than 10% of the state's old-growth redwoods. There are miles and miles of trails to hike, good mountain biking, horseback riding, and fishing and swimming in the Eel River.

Grizzly Creek Redwoods State Park, 18 miles east of Highway101 on Highway36 (☎ 707/777-3683), is a small 390-acre park that is little visited. It has groves of redwoods, 6 short hiking trails, picnicking areas, and a 30-site campground that is close to the highway.

Swimming: The best area swimming spots are in the Eel River at Humboldt Redwoods State Park and Richardson Grove State Park.

Whale Watching: These great creatures are often sighted from Shelter Cove.

ALONG THE NORTHERN COAST FROM FERNDALE TO TRINIDAD

FERNDALE

Ferndale is a charming Victorian town (some might find it too charming) that has been designated a State Historical Landmark. It also hosts one of the weirder and more whimsical events in California, the annual world champion **kinetic sculpture race.** This race was begun by sculptor Hobart Brown who "improved" his son's tricycle, transforming it into a piece of brilliant art, and then raced it against another metal sculptor in 1969. Ever since, this bizarre, fun race has been run by vehicles that must roll and float in order to complete the course. Most of the vehicles still incorporate bicycles. The race starts at Arcata Plaza, but it is the second day, when participants must cross the bay, and the third day, when they must cross the Eel River, that the most dramatic and hilarious upsets can be seen. The first vehicle, by the way, is not necessarily the winner because a complex set of rules applies. To see some of the ingenious contraptions that have competed in this challenging and entertaining race, stop in at the **Kinetic Sculpture Race Museum** at 580 Main St. in Ferndale.

Main street is one long National Historic treasure lined with storefronts in all kinds of Victorian styles including Eastlake, Stick, Mission Revival, and Italianate. Today, thanks to the effort of a local resident who bought up the Main Street properties in the '60s to preserve them, storefronts are now occupied by artisans and traditional tradespeople as well as galleries and antique and jewelry stores. Among my favorite stores for browsing are: **Ferndale Books** at 405 Main St. and **Dave's Saddlery** at 491 Main St., where you can watch saddles and tack being hand tooled.

Also on Main Street stands the **Ferndale Repertory Theatre,** occupying a former cinema, built in 1920. The company offers year-round theater. For information call ☎ 707/725-BEST (707-725-2378).

Don't just stay on Main Street, though, if you want to view fine **Victorian architecture,** because there's plenty here on the side streets of what was once called "cream city." The ample Victorian residences, or butterfat palaces as they're sometimes called, stand today as a testament to the wealth that was amassed by the dairy farmers who built them. Drive along the side streets to view such homes as the lovely 1883 Eastlake at 1249 Ambrosini Lane; the Putnam House, a Foursquare and Italianate beauty at 1027 Van Ness; or the 10 examples on Berding Street. The chamber has a sheet that will take you on a driving tour past more than 60 of these remarkable Victorian buildings.

One block off Main Street, the **Ferndale Museum** on Shaw Street displays a collection of farm, dairy, and blacksmith equipment as well as other artifacts from the area. There's even an old seismograph that is still used.

Hours: Summer, Tues–Sat 11am–4pm, Sun 1–4pm; winter, Wed–Sat 11am–4pm and Sun 1–4pm.

Lodging in Ferndale

The **Shaw House Bed & Breakfast,** 703 Main St., Ferndale, CA 95536 (☎ 707/786-9958), occupies a striking Carpenter Gothic building set well back from the street behind lovely gardens filled with huge rhododendrons and other shrubs. It is in fact the town's oldest residence, built by the town's founder, Seth Louis Shaw, for his bride in about 1854. A lovely accommodation, it offers five rooms. The interior throughout is decorated with personal style, charm, and great comfort. The rooms are filled with collections of baskets, old prints, Chinese and Japanese antiques, and other treasures. The Shaw Room contains the builder's original honeymoon bed; the Honeymoon Suite has an impressive domed coffered ceiling, a bathroom with clawfoot tub and shower, and a private balcony. Some smaller rooms are tucked under the gables. There are two comfortable parlors and a library. Guests can also enjoy lounging on the two front verandas or on the deck overlooking Frances Creek.

Rates: $85–$145 double.

The Gingerbread Mansion Inn, 400 Berding St., P.O. Box 40, Ferndale, CA 95536 (☎ 707/786-4000, fax 707/786-4381), on a quiet side street, is a visually striking cream and pink Queen Anne–Eastlake Victorian complete with witch's-cap turret and plenty of gingerbread ornamentation. It was built in 1899 for a doctor. The gardens are carefully tended and contain artistically pruned shrubs, a very decorous palm tree and fountain, plus fuchsia, camellia, and other flowers that attract hummingbirds and others. There are five rooms and suites available, all decorated differently and all with private baths, some with old-fashioned tubs. The most luxurious is the third-floor Empire suite, which has a private entrance and contains a large tub in front of a fireplace plus a sitting area with another fireplace. The Fountain suite features a bonnet-canopied Queen bed; twin clawfoot tubs for that relaxing, romantic bubble bath; and a fainting couch to complete the scene. Even the most modest rooms are decorated in eye-catching colors and exhibit special features. The Lilac room, for example, has a clawfoot tub located under a brilliant stained glass window. In the morning guests can enjoy coffee or tea delivered to their room plus a breakfast of pastries and fresh fruit. Afternoon tea is served, and at night there's turndown service with chocolates. Guests gather in the evenings to read or play games in the four comfortable parlors. Bicycles are available.

Rates (incl. breakfast): $160–$190 double, $250–$370 suite.

LOLEETA

Dairying is what created this small town's wealth, and today it's still an important industry in the region, as you can see when you visit the **Loleta Cheese Factory** (☎ 707/733-5470) to sample 14 varieties of locally made cheeses (flavored Monterey jacks and cheddars) and also to see the cheese-making process.

Also in Loleta, bird-watchers and naturalists will want to visit the **Humboldt Bay National Wildlife Refuge**, 1020 Ranch Rd., Loleta, CA 95551 (☎ 707/733-5406). The bay is one of the major stopping points for birds along the Pacific Flyway and the winter habitat of thousands of ducks, geese, swans, and shorebirds. More than 200 species regularly feed, rest, or nest on the bay or in the marshes and willow groves of this 22,000-acre refuge. The wetlands here provide an essential habitat for several endangered species including the peregrine falcon, brown pelican, Aleutian Canada goose, American bald eagle, western snowy plover, and others. Thousands of black brant are attracted by the eel grass beds. The refuge lacks the facilities for extensive public use but welcomes people who are genuinely interested in wildlife and ecology. The peak viewing season for waterbirds and raptors is September to March, for brant from March to late April. There are two interpretive trails to follow.

EUREKA

Eureka, the county seat and largest city in Humboldt County, is located at the center of beautiful Humboldt Bay, which makes for plenty of waterfront fishing and other activity. This bay was "rediscovered" in 1849 by Dr. Josiah Gregg, who had traveled west from the Trinity mines looking for a supply route alternative to the Sacramento Valley, which was often flooded and impassable. Both Eureka and Arcata were established during the Gold Rush to serve as transportation and supply centers for the mines that were being worked around Willow Creek, Orleans, and Weitchpec along the Klamath, Trinity, and Salmon rivers. Equipment and miners were brought into the Humboldt Bay ports and lumber shipped out south to San Francisco. By 1856 there were 9 sawmills operating in Eureka, producing 2 million feet of lumber every month, and the Bay was jammed with 140 lumber schooners. The mines were soon exhausted, but both towns continued to thrive on lumber, dairying, and fishing. Today, in fact, the county's main industry is still lumber and forest products, and commercial forests cover about 74% of the county's land area.

The earlier lumber barons displayed their newfound wealth by building elaborate Victorian mansions, and this is what gives the town its great appeal today. Elegant Victorians line the residential streets and also the 13 blocks of the Old Town commercial section. The most famous and most photographed Victorian in the West, the **Carson Mansion,** which was built around 1884, stands at 143 M St. It's astonishingly beautiful even though it mixes many different styles—Queen Anne, Italianate, and Eastlake—and uses many different materials—redwood, white mahogany, onyx, and stained glass. It was designed by Newsom and Newsom, the architectural duo responsible for so many of California's painted ladies, for lumber baron William Carson. It took 2 years and 100 men to build and was supposedly constructed to keep Carson's men employed during the depression of the early 1880s. The exterior is flamboyant indeed, decorated with fish-scale and other pattern shingles, vertical strips, and such ornamental details as decorative gables and balconies and several towers. Today it is a private men's club, and, sadly, unless you go as a guest of a club member you will not be able to view the interior. If you do, you will see among other features dramatic horseshoe arches in the upper hall and fantastic ornamental detail throughout.

Across the street stands another gem, the **Pink Lady,** at 202 M St., which Carson had built for his son Milton around 1889 as a wedding present. It was also designed by the Newsom brothers in both Queen Anne and Eastlake styles.

Passionate architecture buffs will want to visit other Victorians, too—the **Queen Anne** at 904 G St., an **Italianate** example at 828 G St., and the **Second Empire-style home** at 933 I St. The **Chamber of Commerce** at 2112 Broadway (☎ 707/442-3738) publishes a pamphlet listing more than 30 Victorians around town if you're interested. You can also sign up there for the **Victorian Home Driving Tour,** which visits more than 125 Victorians in the region.

Even if you're not interested in architecture, take the time to stroll around **Old Town.** The handsome, characterful buildings house stores that are substantial and well worth browsing. Among my favorites are the **Authentic Indian Art & Gift Shop** operated by the Northern California Indian Development Council, 241 F St. (☎707/445-8451), which sells arts, crafts, and jewelry fashioned by Yurok, Karuk, Sioux, Hupa, Hopi, and Zuni; **Many Hands Gallery,** 438 2nd St. (☎707/445-0455), which sells crafts from around the world; **Clipper Trading Company,** 438 2nd St. (☎ 707/445-4700), which specializes in seascapes by local artists plus ship's models crafted by local artisans; **Eureka Books,** 426 2nd St. (☎707/444-9593); the **Irish Shop,** 2nd and E sts. (☎ 707/443-8343); the **Old Town Art Gallery,** 233 F St. (☎707/445-2315), a cooperative featuring paintings, photography, ceramics, and sculpture; and the **Book Legger,** 402 2nd St. (☎707/445-1344).

There is a very active arts community in the County. Both Eureka and Arcata have a substantial number of murals. Go to the chambers of commerce to pick up walking tours of these colorful community projects.

In town, several attractions provide insights into the history and cultural life of the region. **The Clarke Memorial Museum,** 240 E St. at 3rd

(☎ 707/443-1947), displays furniture, glassware, clothing, and other items relating to the county's 19th-century history. The collection of Indian baskets by Hupa, Yurok, and others is worth seeing.

Hours: Tues–Sat noon–4pm.

The **Humboldt Bay Maritime Museum,** 1410 2nd St. (☎ 707/444-9440), focuses on maritime history—mostly shipwrecks, lumber schooners, and fishing boats—and displays a variety of photographs and maritime artifacts associated with the development of the local fishing industry, which began as early as 1851 when salmon fisheries operated along the Eel River. Within 7 years 2,000 barrels of cured fish and 50,000 pounds of smoked salmon were being processed and shipped out of the Bay. The Bay was also a major whaling area with stations at Fields Landing and farther north at Trinidad, where the station operated from 1923 to 1929.

Fort Humboldt State Historic Park, 3431 Fort Ave. (☎ 707/445-6567), also dates back to this bustling era. It was established in 1853 as the northernmost military outpost on the coast to protect settlers against Indian attacks. For the most part, the routine at Fort Humboldt was monotonous, and many soldiers took to drink, as did Ulysses S. Grant, who served as an Army captain here for 5 months in 1853–54. The commander, Colonel Buchanan, demanded that Grant either resign from the Army or be tried for drunkenness. Grant chose to resign, returning to his family in Missouri.

Although there was no outright war with the Indians, the settlers were never satisfied with the military's efforts to control them, and in 1863 Governor Leland Stanford put a Colonel Black in charge of six companies of volunteers with express orders to control the Indians. Black's troops took these orders very seriously, killing many without cause. Soon the Indians sued for peace and signed the Hupa Treaty in August 1864, which guaranteed them the Hupa Valley. Today you can drive out to the reservation and visit the tribal museum if you wish to know more.

The Fort was abandoned in 1870. Only the hospital building survived, and it is used as a museum today. Slowly, the other 19 or so buildings are being reconstructed. Besides the museum, there's also a self-guided outdoor logging display. The equipment on display helps to trace the history of the lumber industry from the early days when oxen hauled the logs out of the forest. Oxen were replaced by the steam donkey, an 1882 invention that dragged the logs over skid roads. It, too, was eventually superseded by the railroad in 1914, when the Northwestern Pacific Railroad opened between San Francisco and Eureka. The steam engines are fired up twice a month.

Hours: Daily 9am–4pm.

The Blue Ox Millworks Historical Park, at the foot of X Street (☎ 707/444-3437), will interest those who are fascinated by machinery and industrial processes in general, who appreciate fine craftsmanship, or who need custom woodwork for an architectural restoration. On the self-guided tour you can observe craftsmen creating rosettes on a lathe or forging antique door hinges using machinery dating from between 1852 and 1940, see logging machinery from the misery whip to the Caterpillar, and come to understand the logging life when small towns were virtually pulled by oxen and steam donkeys from one logging site to the next on sleds or skids. The tour will take an hour.

Hours: Mon–Sat 9am–5pm, Sun 11am–4pm. *Admission:* $5 adults.

Today fishing is still an important industry in the region. Humboldt Bay, Trinidad Bay, and Shelter Cove all have commercial fishing fleets. Visitors can watch the fishing fleet land its catch at **Woolly Island Marina,** reached via the Samoa Bridge Exit off Highway 101. The **Cafe Marina** (☎ 707/443-2233) makes a nice spot for an outdoor luncheon, and from here you have a good view of the egret rookery in the cypress grove on Indian Island.

Humboldt and Arcata Bays produce more than 80% of the oysters grown in California. About 10 million oysters are harvested annually, so if you're an oyster lover this is one place to sample them. For a look at the local oyster industry and to pick up some of these precious crustaceans, visit the **Coast Oyster Company** at the foot of A street. It offers free tours by reservation (☎ 707/442-2947).

In summer it's great to get out onto the water aboard the ***M V Madaket*** (☎ 707/499-0810), which leaves from the foot of C Street for a 1¼ hour cruise of the bay accompanied by an informative commentary.

Hours: Apr–Sept, daily cruises at 1, 2:30, 4, and 5:30pm. *Admission:* $8.50 adults, $7.50 youths and seniors, $5.50 children 6–11, free for children under 6.

Lodging & Dining Eureka

If you seek a genuine historical experience plus warm, engaging hospitality and a marvelous breakfast the next morning, then stay at **An Elegant Victorian Mansion,** 14th and C sts., Eureka, CA 95501 (☎ 707/444-3144). This has to be one of the most carefully and authentically decorated Eastlake Victorian cottages in the entire country, notwithstanding all the inns in such Victorian enclaves as Cape May, New Jersey, and Pacific Grove, California. The reason for this is retired forester and schoolteacher Doug Vieyra's passion for history and for the Victorian era in particular. Both he and his wife Lily (an inspired needlewoman and chef) have gone to great lengths to research and find the fabrics and wallpapers that grace the walls and windows of the downstairs rooms. Each room is a riot of patterns—geometric and figurative, mythological and animal—and colors—brilliant blues, golds, jades, and reds.

The house was built in 1888 for Mayor William Clark and stands on a quiet residential street. A balustraded stairway leads up to the front porch, which is supported by lavishly turned pillars. Here you may be greeted by the butler in morning dress—surprise enough—but you may be further astonished once you step inside the foyer. The ceiling sports a brilliantly patterned turquoise and ochre wallpaper; the staircase newel post supports a sculptured oil lamp; heavy velvet and fringed valances and drapes hang in the parlor doorways. Similar drama follows in the parlors and dining room, which are decked out with tasseled and fringed drapes, Eastlake sofas, Victorian needlepointed chairs, gilt pictures suspended from picture rails; they are finished off with such favorite Victorian elements as busts, ferns, pheasant and peacock trophies, and a working Victrola. Doug even provides the music for silent movies and early talkies from the era and goes so far as to keep a sock/silk scarf at the ready to place into the Victrola's trumpet, which he happily explains is the source of the phrase "put a sock in it."

The three guest rooms themselves (one with private bath) are not as lavishly decorated as the public rooms, but each is different and contains family heirlooms of interest. The Van Gogh room contains Lily's mother's bedroom suite plus Van Gogh prints, while the Lily Langtry room features an oak four-poster and memorabilia from the great actress, who stayed here as a guest of the Mayor when she performed locally. Country French furnishings await in the Governor's Room.

At breakfast the table is lavishly set with lace, china, and crystal. Lily, who was born in Belgium, is a trained chef, so breakfast is a treat of croissants, breads, pastries, fruits, and egg dishes that might include omelets, eggs Benedict, and creamed eggs in salmon with puff pastry. Instead of afternoon tea, typical Victorian treats—ice-cream sodas and lemonade—are served in the lovely gardens blessed with a palm tree, roses galore, and a lawn that is manicured enough for croquet. Exceptional facilities and service for an inn of this size include a sauna, Swedish massage, laundry service, and complimentary bicycles. The entire inn is non-smoking.

Rates (incl. breakfast): $145–$175 double.

At **Hotel Carter, Carter House, and Bell Cottage,** 301 L St., Eureka, CA 95501 (☎ 800/404-1390 or 707/445-1390, fax 707/444-8062 or 707/444-8067), Mark and Christi Carter are the human dynamos behind these three separate domains, which make up one larger establishment. The largest, Hotel Carter, contains the restaurant and the most elaborate rooms, at least in terms of their facilities (Jacuzzis and VCRs, for example). This commercial building has been given an airy appearance with interiors painted in peach and white and furnished with bleached pine. There are 19 rooms and 11 suites in the hotel, all large and furnished with pine four-posters. The suites have VCRs, whirlpool spas, and fireplaces. The front suites have distant views of the waterfront from the whirpool tubs.

Across the street stands the Carter House, a replica of an 1884 San Francisco Victorian designed by Joseph Newsom, which Mark Carter built himself in 1982 according to the original blueprints. It has seven rooms, most with views of the harbor and all tastefully decorated with antiques, including one room containing a dramatic corkscrew four-poster. They are made more comfortable by those special extras like down comforters, flannel robes, an honor bar, and fresh flowers. Oriental carpets lie on the parlor floors, and contemporary local art graces the walls. There's also a stocked kitchen for guest use.

The third component of this hostelry is Bell Cottage, another single-floor Victorian that contains three suites with Jacuzzi, fireplaces, and a large, common fully stocked kitchen.

In the morning guests head for the Hotel Carter dining room, where breakfast begins with fresh squeezed juice and a selection from the muffins and fresh fruits that are on display. Eggs Benedict made with Black Forest ham will follow, then an apple-almond phyllo tart. In the evening guests gather around the lobby fireplace for complimentary wine and hors d'oeuvres.

At night **Restaurant 301** is the place to dine in Eureka. The cuisine is fine, using local fresh fish plus herbs, greens, and edible flowers from the hotel's own gardens. Start with the local oysters barbecued with Smokey Jim's BBQ sauce, and follow with another local fish like the grilled rock cod marinated in soy, sake, lime juice, garlic, ginger, and sesame seed, or the heartier and very flavorful duck breast with seasonal fruit in a port wine sauce. Other fine-tasting dishes include pork tenderloin with chutney and applesauce, and chicken breast stuffed with mushrooms and tarragon crème. Finish off with chocolate torte or the delicious bread pudding with caramelized brandy and Benedictine. Main course prices range from $14 to $19. The wine list is extensive, and Mark is building a top-class cellar.

Rates (incl. breakfast): Hotel Carter, $135–$155 double, $195–$260 suite; Carter House, $165–$285 double; Bell Cottage $155–$205. *Dining Hours* (Restaurant 301): Daily 7:30am–10am; Sun–Thurs 6–9pm, Fri–Sat 6–9:30pm.

The **Eureka Inn,** 7th and F streets (☎ 707/442-6441), is a downtown hotel that was built in Tudor style in 1922. It has an old-fashioned air, and the 105 rooms tend to display a somewhat old-fashioned decor, but the hotel has such facilities as dining rooms and heated pool and sauna. A National Historic landmark, the inn has played a major role in the social life of the community—Sir Winston Churchill as well as Presidents Hoover, Ford, and Reagan stayed here—and you can feel a sense of history in the lobby with its redwood beams, brass-hooded fireplace, and leather club chairs and sofas.

The **Rib Room** is the main restaurant. It features a classic California cuisine offering such dishes as roasted rack of lamb in a mustard crust served with pinot noir sauce and grilled salmon with lemon-herb butter. Prices range from $18 to $25. There's also a cafe for breakfast and lunch and two bars—the Rathskeller pub and the Palm Lounge. The inn is also renowned for its Christmas celebrations, which begin when the

20-plus-foot-tall tree goes up a week before Thanksgiving and continues through the New Year with musical entertainments and other events.

Rates: $98–$158 double.

Dining Only in Eureka

At **Sea Grill,** 316 E St. (☎ 707/443-71870), fish lovers appreciate the amazing variety of fresh fish available—salmon, halibut, mahimahi, lingcod, red snapper, shellfish—and the range of preparations offered—from sautéed, grilled, and broiled to poached and pan fried. A favorite dish is the cod Louisiana made with Cajun spices, tomatoes, green peppers, and mushrooms. The chowders are powerfully flavored, too, and if you don't want fish then the Harris ranch steaks are worth tasting (the same ones served in the justifiably renowned Harris's in San Francisco). Prices range from $12 for fish and chips to $17 for a fisherman's combination of scallops, shrimp, calamari, oyster, sole, and cod.

Hours: Tues–Fri 11am–3pm and 5–9pm, Sat and Mon 5–9pm only.

Ramone's, 209 E St. (☎ 707/445-2923), is great for breakfast and lunch. It's a bakery, so the pastries and breads—Danish, croissants, muffins—are great to get you started in the mornings. At lunch there are good-tasting soups, sandwiches, and salads priced from $3 to $5.

Hours: Mon–Sat 7am–6pm, Sun 7am–5pm.

Lazio's, 327 Second St. (☎ 707/443-9717), is one of those good old-time fish restaurants, and it's been in business for more than 50 years. Among the signature dishes are the Humboldt Bay shore plate, a medley of snapper, prawns, scallops, salmon, halibut, and oysters; and the Skin Diver, a generous sampling of crab, shrimp, and cocktail sauce to taste. My favorite, though, is the broiled salmon. Prices range from $12 to $35.

Hours: Mon–Fri 11am–3pm, Sat–Sun noon–3pm. Summer, also daily 3–11pm; winter, daily 3–9pm.

Tomasso's, 216 E St., Eureka (☎ 707/445-0100), is the place to go if you're a garlic and oil lover, for they know how to use these ingredients here on their specialty, tomato pies—which is another way of saying pizza. The original favorites are still on the menu: a whole-wheat pizza, a calzone made with fresh spinach, mozzarella, and garlic in a whole-wheat crust; and an intensely cheesy spinach pie called Spinzone. Today, there are many more exotic pizzas to try, like the Polynesian bursting with the flavors of Canadian bacon, pineapple, mushrooms, pepper, and onions. Pasta dishes, including a fine cannelloni made with chicken, cheese, and spices, baked in a white wine cream sauce with marinated artichoke hearts and mushrooms, are also available. Prices range from $8 for a small pizza to $21 for a large, and from $10 to $15 for pastas.

Hours: Mon–Sat 11:30am–9pm, Sun 5–8:30pm.

Lost Coast Brewery, 617 4th St. (☎ 707/445-4480), has 10 microbrews on tap that can be enjoyed with buffalo wings, burgers, tacos, and fish-and-chips.

Hours: Daily 11am–midnight.

SAMOA

While you're in Eureka, take a trip to nearby **Samoa** and visit the last authentic logging camp cookhouse in the West, dating back to 1885. Food was a vital commodity in any logging operation. Many a lumberman would leave and move to another camp if he wasn't satisfied with the cooking and quality of the food. Here at the Samoa Cookhouse you can get a good idea of the role the cookhouse played in any logging camp. Now, anyone can eat here; see "Dining Only in Samoa, " below, for all the details.

Dining Only in Samoa

Samoa Cookhouse, Cookhouse Rd., 445 W. Washington St. (☎ 707/442-1659), is the last surviving cookhouse in the West. It serves the traditional hearty lumber camp meals family style at tables spread with red-checked oil cloths. Portions are large, and you can request additional helpings. It's strictly meat-and-potatoes cuisine, but the price includes soup, salad, main course, and dessert. A different dish is offered each day—fried chicken, roast beef, or pork chops. Afterwards, stop into the museum, which displays memorabilia from the early days of logging when 500-plus men were fed three meals a day here for a mere 30 to 40 cents each. Prices begin at $10.95 for a complete meal.

Hours: Mon–Sat 6am–3:30pm and 5–9pm; Sun 6am–9pm.

ARCATA

Ten miles north of Eureka, **Arcata** is a college town that also has its fair share of Victorians. If you want to see them, pick up the walking tour pamphlet at the Chamber of Commerce. A couple of landmark buildings face the plaza that is the center of the town—the old brick and stone Jacoby's Storehouse (1857), which houses several stores and restaurants, and the Hotel Arcata (1915).

Other attractions in Arcata include the **Humboldt State University Natural History Museum,** 1315 G St. (☎ 707/826-4479), which is perhaps most famous for its collection of 2,000 fossil specimens collected from all over the world. Other exhibits focus on the contemporary natural history of Northern California. Among these are several interactive computer displays on whales, bird songs, and dinosaurs; there are also "discovery boxes" to investigate your sense of smell, the nature of reptiles, and other subjects. It's great if you have kids in tow.

Hours: Tues–Sat 10am–4pm.

The **University,** which is renowned for its science and environmental programs, offers some excellent adventure weekends and instructional courses that are extremely reasonably priced. Activities include backpacking, rock climbing, downhill and Nordic skiing, fishing, canoeing, river and sea kayaking, windsurfing, sailing, and more. Prices start as low as $25 for weekend backpacking trips. The center rents every conceivable type of equipment—canoes, kayaks, etc., plus camping and backpacking gear. For information contact **Center Activities,** University Center, Humboldt State University, Arcata, CA 95521 (☎ 707/826-3357).

The **Arcata Marsh and Wildlife Sanctuary** at the foot of I street (☎ 707/826-2359) is part of an ingenious experiment and an example of how blighted industrial and landfill sites can be reclaimed and converted into places of recreation and beauty. The series of marshes that exist here fostering abundant bird, plant, and animal life are actually part of a natural process that recycles waste and waste water before returning it to the bay. The experiment was undertaken in the late '70s to demonstrate the effectiveness of wetlands for treating wastewater. It succeeded, and Arcata won an Innovations in Government Award from the Ford Foundation/ Harvard University Kennedy School of Government. Because of the project's success, representatives from other municipalities come frequently to see the facility and to learn about the process. The 154-acre sanctuary has an interpretive center (open from 1 to 5pm daily), 4½ miles of trails, and offers free guided nature walks on Saturday mornings and afternoons. This is a major bird-watching area. Ducks and many other waterfowl—mallards, teal, grebes, and coots—breed here; osprey, herons, grebes, and egrets feed here; and thousands of shore birds can be seen foraging on the mud flats of Humboldt Bay—sandpipers, godwits, willets, plovers, and many more. Just north of the interpretive center you may also see black-crowned night herons roosting in the willows around the reclaimed log pond. The oxidation ponds are where you're most likely to spot a rare species along with scaup, Northern shovelers, and many other ducks. The best time for bird-watching is during the spring and fall migrations.

A few miles outside Arcata on Route 299 is Blue Lake, famous for the **Dell'Arte School of Physical Theatre,** 131 H St. (☎ 707/668-5663), which trains students in the arts of mask, mime, movement, theater, clowning, and commedia. The school's international touring company, the Dell'Arte Players (☎ 707/668-5664), puts on the month-long Mad River Festival (see "Special Events to Plan Your Trip Around," above).

Up the coast from Eureka, the next town along Highway 101 is McKinleyville, which provides access to the **Azalea State Reserve.** This reserve is at its best in spring. McKinleyville also boasts at its downtown mall a very tall totem pole (160 feet in fact) made from a 500-year-old redwood.

Lodging in Arcata

Cat's Cradle Bed & Breakfast, 815 Park Place, Arcata, CA 95521 (☎ 707/822-CATS [707/822-2287]), is located on the side of a redwood-covered hill overlooking Arcata, not far from Humboldt University and a municipal park. It is a quiet place, with some unusual features for a bed-and-breakfast, notably the 18 × 40 indoor pool and a special meditation room in the garden. There are three rooms (one with private bath) and one suite, each furnished differently. The Star Trek room features memorabilia from the space show; the Alice room offers a maple four-poster plus an Alice in Wonderland collection. They share a bath. The Nostalgia Suite accommodates five, although it has only a tiny bedroom plus kitchenette, dining area, and living room with a sectional couch. A full breakfast of waffles, French toast, or frittata, plus cereals and fruits will be served. The terraced gardens with their fountains are a delight. So too is the spa-tub. There's also a library and plenty of reading material throughout the house.

Rates: $65–$75 double; $110 suite.

Dining in Arcata

The **Abruzzi Plaza Grill,** in the basement of Jacoby Storehouse, 791 8th St. (☎ 707/826-2345), consists of two dining rooms—the Abruzzi on the first floor, which is more formal, and the Plaza grill, which offers more casual atmosphere and fare. The menu in the first offers a great variety of pasta dishes, including a fine fettuccine carbonara made with garlic and butter and tossed with pancetta, mushrooms, Parmesan, and cream. Other specialties might be chicken Frascati, which is a chicken breast with hearts of artichoke, mushrooms, pancetta, garlic, fresh rosemary and Frascati wine. Calzones, salads, and small pizzas are also available. Prices range from $8 to $18.

Hours: Mon–Fri 1130am–1:30pm; Sun–Thurs 5–8:30pm, Fri–Sat 5–9pm.

TRINIDAD

The next coastal town, **Trinidad,** about 20 miles north of Eureka, has its own fishing fleet, a memorial lighthouse to visit, a beautiful state beach, and a trail around Trinidad Head, which is a fine whale-watching spot. The drive from Trinidad to Moonstone Beach, south of the state beach, provides some memorable ocean views. Just for the record, Trinidad is one of the oldest towns established in Northern California having been founded in 1850 as an important port for supplying the mines in Klamath, Trinity, and along the Salmon River.

Just north of Trinidad lies **Patrick's Point State Park** (☎ 707/488-2041). Besides the large sweeping beach and hiking trails, this park also has a unique cultural facility, the Sumeg Village, a reconstruction that was created to preserve and maintain the traditions of the local Yurok people. It is used by the tribe today. Follow the self-guided walking tour into replicas of dwellings and sweat houses used for purification rituals. There is also a brush dance pit, which is used for ceremonial and healing dances (please do not enter this sacred place though).

Lodging in Trinidad

From the grounds and deck of the **Lost Whale Inn,** 3452 Patrick's Point Dr., Trinidad, CA 95570 (☎ 800/677-7859 or 707/677-3425, fax 707/677 0284), there are views of the ocean through the pines. This Cape Cod–style inn is ideally situated for visiting the coast and Redwood National Park, only 16 miles away in Orick. Set on 4 acres, the house is modern, comfortable, light, and airy thanks to picture windows and skylights. Quilts grace the beds in the rooms, which are also lit by skylights. Guests can enjoy relaxing in the large sitting room with its polished wood floors, wood-burning stove, assortment of books, and floor-to-ceiling windows, or out on the very large deck. Breakfasts featuring main dishes like casseroles, frittatas, and cobblers are a great way to start the day, while the afternoon tea of wine, sherry, pastries, and fruit provides a convivial welcome home. Facilities include a hot tub. A trail leads down through alder and wildflowers to the cove beach where tide pools, sea stacks, seals, and sea lions await. Children are welcome—there's even an enclosed play area and playhouse waiting for them.

Rates: May–October and major holidays, $130–$160; Nov–April, $110–$140.

Trinidad Bay B & B, 560 Edwards St., P.O. Box 849, Trinidad, CA 95570 (☎ 707/677-0840), overlooks the Bay and offers two suites and two rooms, all with private bath. The Mauve Suite is the most luxurious. It has a private entrance, a king-size bed, and two rockers standing in front of the fireplace. The Blue Bay View suite has a telescope for whale watching. Breakfast will be brought to both of these accommodations so you can enjoy it in privacy. The other two rooms have knotty pine walls, dormer windows (one with an inviting window seat), and queen beds. Breakfast consists of homemade breads, muffins, baked fruits, and fresh local cheeses. The inn is closed during December and January. It's only about 15 minutes from Redwood National Park.

Rates: $135–$175.

Dining in Trinidad

Larrupin Cafe, 1658 Patrick's Point Dr. (☎ 707/677-0230), has a delightful atmosphere that has been created by the judicious display of artifacts from Indonesia and Africa, bounteous bouquets of fresh flowers, and contemporary paintings by California artists. The room glows, and the food is equal to it. Specialties include items that have been barbecued over mesquite, such as tuna and halibut that are then served with a mustard-flavored dill sauce, or Cornish game hen that has been glazed with orange and brandy. Prices range from $12 to $21.

Hours: Wed–Sun 5pm–closing.

FARTHER AFIELD

Route 299 from Arcata also provides easy access to the **Six Rivers National Forest, Trinity River,** and **Trinity National Forest,** a playground for adventure enthusiasts with a major recreational center at **Willow Creek,** where outfitters organize white-water rafting, kayaking, and canoe trips on the Trinity, Klamath, Smith, and Salmon rivers. Obviously, spring is the time for thrill seekers who want to experience class IV and V waters; summer is calmer.

From Willow Creek Route 96 courses north through the **Six Rivers and Klamath National Forest** leading to another recreational center at **Somes Bar.**

Route 96 also cuts through the **Hupa Valley Indian Reservation,** which is the largest Indian reservation in California. Stop in at the **Tribal Museum** (☎ 916/625-4110) in the shopping center on the reservation to view redwood dugout canoes, ceremonial regalia, and other artifacts crafted and used by the Native Americans. The buckskin dresses decorated with bear grass, abalone shell, and pine nuts are remarkable, and so, too, are the amazing variety of baskets made for gathering fruits and nuts, cleaning huckleberries, cooking and storing, and carrying babies.

Another way to gain insight into the Hupa culture is to take the **Native American River Tour** operated by Aurora River Adventures in Willow Creek (☎ 800/562-8475 or 916/629-3843), which includes a visit to the tribal museum, lunch, and an informative cruise along the river. The price is $90 for adults, $50 for children 7–11.

Ferndale to Trinidad
Special & Recreational Activities

Beaches: Clam Beach, 14 miles north of Eureka, is great for beachcombing and clamming. **Trinidad State Beach** (☎ 707/677-3570 or 707/445-6547), a small, cove-like beach with a rock arch at one end, is one of the more beautiful beaches along this stretch of coastline. You'll have to climb down from the bluffs above. **Humboldt Lagoons State Park,** 31 miles north of Eureka on Highway 101 (☎ 707/488-2171) has 7 miles of beaches.

Bicycling: Hum Boats, foot of F Street, Eureka (☎ 707/444-3048), rents bicycles at $18 for half a day and $24 for a full day.

Pro Sport Center, 508 Myrtle Ave., Eureka (☎ 707/443-6328), rents bikes for $20 a day.

Mountain-biking trips are also organized by **Access to Adventure**, 92520 Hwy. 96, Somes Bar, CA 95560 (☎ 916/469-3322).

Bird-watching: See the descriptions of Arcata Marsh and Wildlife Sanctuary and Humboldt Bay National Wildlife Refuge above. Note, too, that puffins breed at Elk Head at Trinidad State Beach, which also attracts several other species including northern flickers. For the latest **information on local bird sightings**, call ☎ 707/822-5666 or 707/826-7031; these numbers also provide information on local Audubon Society events and field trips.

Camping: See "State Parks," below. Also, there are several National Forest campgrounds in Six Rivers National Forest. Four are near **Orleans and Somes Bar** (☎ 916/627-3291), three near **Willow Creek** (☎ 916/629-2118), and three at **Mad River and Ruth Lake** (☎ 916/574-6233).

Canoeing/Kayaking: Hum-Boats, 3rd and A streets, Eureka (☎ 707/443-5157), or dockside at the foot of F Street (☎ 707/444-3048), rents sailboats, canoes, kayaks, row boats, and motor boats by the hour and by the day. Canoes are $15 an hour or $35 a day; kayaks are $10 to $20 an hour or $30 to $45 a day. There are discounts for long-term use, and the company also offers a variety of instructional classes and group tours. Canoes and kayaks can also be rented at **Center Activities** at Humboldt State University (☎ 707/826-3357).

Guided canoe trips are given by **Laughing Heart Adventures,** 3003 Hwy. 96, Willow Creek, CA 95573 (☎ 916/629-3516), on the Trinity, Klamath, and Eel rivers and at Stone Lagoon. Half-day trips start at $35 per person; full-day trips, including lunch, begin at $55 per person. They rent canoes and kayaks, too.

Cross-Country Skiing: There are cross-country ski trails at **Horse Mountain Winter Sports Area** off Highway 299 on Titlow Road.

Fishing: Larry's Guide Service, 3380 Utah St., Eureka (☎ 707/444-0250, or 916/596-347 in summer), offers fall and winter fishing trips to the Klamath River and coastal waters with the main trophies being rainbow trout, steelhead, and salmon. Fall provides an unforgettable fly-fishing experience in September and October, when the river is filled with salmon and steelhead, with bonus sights including redwoods, maples, and wildlife. Regular trips are 7 hours long and cost $125 per person. The outfit also offers instructional trips (maximum three persons) for $85 per person.

Several charter boats operate out of Trinidad Harbor. Steelhead and salmon fishing trips are also offered by **Access to Adventure,** 92520 Hwy. 96, Somes Bar (☎ 916/469-3322), and

Klamath River Outfitters, 3 Sandy Bar Rd., Somes Bar (☎ 916/469-3349).

Golf: There are several 18-hole golf courses in the area; two of the best are **Eureka Golf Course,** 4750 Fairway Dr., Eureka (☎ 707/443-4808); and **Beau Pre Golf Club,** 1777 Norton Rd., McKinleyville (☎ 707/839-2342).

Hiking: See "State Parks," below.

Horseback Riding: Access to Adventure, 92520 Hwy. 96, Somes Bar (☎ 916/469-3322), has a variety of trail rides and saddle and paddle packages.

Scuba Diving: Pro Sport Center, 508 Myrtle Ave., Eureka (☎ 707/443-6328), rents equipment and grants certification. It also rents abalone diving equipment.

State Parks: Twenty-five miles north of Eureka, **Patrick's Point State Park** (☎ 707/667-3570) is particularly appealing because it provides access to a 2-mile beach, while the point itself is a good place from which to watch for whales. There's a 2-mile hiking trail along the bluffs, plus 123 campsites, and a Sumeg village described in the attractions section above.

Humboldt Lagoons State Park, 31 miles north of Eureka (☎ 707/488-5435 or 707/488-2171), contains 4 lagoons, 2 of which—Stone Lagoon and Big Lagoon—burst their perimeters in stormy seasons overflowing into the ocean. The third lagoon is a freshwater marsh. This park affords opportunities for fishing, boating, bird-watching, and windsurfing, plus primitive camping at 25 sites. It has 7 miles of beaches and also shelters wild elk.

The 300-acre **Samoa Dunes Recreational Area,** across the bay (take Highway 255 to New Navy Base Road and turn left), is great for bird-watching, hiking, surfing, fishing, and picnicking. It's open to all-terrain vehicles.

Six miles north of Orick (45 miles north of Eureka), **Prairie Creek Redwoods State Park** (☎ 707/445-6547) possesses 14,000 acres of redwoods and a remarkable beach fern canyon. The 30-foot deep canyon is thickly carpeted with ferns. There are 75 miles of hiking and mountain-biking trails in the park plus abundant wildlife, including herds of Roosevelt elk. Camping is available.

Swimming: Contact chambers of commerce for information about community pools. It's too cold and too dangerous to swim at the coastal beaches, though good swimming holes can be found in some rivers.

Tennis: Call **County Parks Administration** (☎ 707/445-7651) for courts that are open to the public.

Whale Watching: Great vantage points include Wedding Bluff in Patrick's Point State Park and Trinidad Head.

White-water Rafting: A variety of packages is offered by **Aurora River Adventures** in Willow Creek (☎ 800/562-8475 or 916/629-3843) on several rivers: the Trinity, Klamath, Smith, Salmon, Eel, and Sacramento. Besides their regular programs, they operate rafting excursions combined with horseback riding or mountain biking. Trips range from half a day to 6 days and are priced from $39 to $75 a day. Accommodations are not included, although camping and meals can be for an additional $20 a person per night.

Other outfitters include **Electric Rafting Co.,** Arcata, (☎ 707/826-2861), with prices from $40 for a half day; and Bigfoot Outdoor Co, P.O. Box 729, Willow Creek, CA 95573 (☎ 916/629-2263), which offers half- to 3-day trips starting at $40 for adults.

At Somes Bar, **Access to Adventure** (☎ 916/469-3322) is based at Marble Mountain Ranch, where there are 11 housekeeping cabins and campgrounds plus other facilities. They offer a variety of rafting trips from beginner to advanced, which can be combined with fishing, mountain biking, and horseback riding. Half-day raft trips begin at $50, day trips at $105. A 3-night saddle, paddle, and peddle package is $305.

Klamath River Outfitters, 3 Sandy Bar Rd., Somes Bar (☎ 916/469-3349), also offers rafting trips.

Windsurfing: Center Activities at Humboldt State University (☎ 707/826-3357) rents equipment.

GETAWAYS TO THE EAST: SACRAMENTO, THE GOLD COUNTRY, LAKE TAHOE & THE HIGH SIERRAS

Sacramento & Vicinity

Distances in Miles: Sacramento, 85; Stockton, 84

Estimated Driving Times: 1½ hours to Sacramento; 1½ hours to Stockton

Driving: The easiest route to Sacramento from San Francisco is to take the Bay Bridge (Highway 580) to Highway 80, which leads directly into Sacramento.

Stockton is about 50 miles south of Sacramento on Highway 5 or California 99. If you wish to go directly to Stockton, it might be best to take Highway 580 to Highway 5 and approach Stockton from the south.

Further Information: For information about Sacramento, call or visit the **Sacramento Convention & Visitors Bureau**, 1421 K St., Old Sacramento, CA 95814 (☎ 916/264-7777 or 916/442-7644), or the **Folsom Chamber of Commerce**, 200 Wool St., Folsom, CA 95630 (☎ 916/985-2698).

SACRAMENTO

When gold was discovered in California in 1848, it was found along the American River on Capt. John Sutter's land about 30 miles east of Sacramento, and it was to Sutter's Fort that the news of the gold discovery was first brought. From that point on, Sacramento became a boomtown supplying the needs of the mining towns that developed in a long strand from Coloma south to Amador City, Sutter's Creek, and Placerville; north to Grass Valley and Nevada City; and of all the other camps that lined the rivers, ravines, ridges, and sandbars of the Sierra Foothills. This is what Old Sacramento is all about.

The link between old and new Sacramento is still there in the city's current role as a transhipment hub for the agricultural bounty of the great Central Valley. New Sacramento, though, is also about politics and about

Events & Festivals to Plan Your Trip Around

March: In 1853 J.L.L.F. Warren introduced the camellia from the East Coast. It became the official flower of Sacramento and is the reason for the annual **Camellia Festival.** For information call the exhibition center (☎ 916/264 5181).

April: The **Festival de la Familia** is a great open-air celebration featuring food, crafts, and music from more than 25 Latin countries. It's held in Old Sacramento. For information call ☎ 916/552-5252, ext. 4127.

The **Stockton Asparagus Festival** features arts, crafts, four stages for entertainment, a "fun run," and an abundance of asparagus and asparagus-inspired cuisine, including an asparagus recipe contest. For information call ☎ 209/943-1987 or 209/477-8103.

May: On Memorial Day weekend the **Sacramento Jazz Jubilee** features bands from all over the world and attracts more than a quarter of a million people. For information call the Jazz Society (☎ 916/372-5277).

July: At the **Folsom Rodeo,** professional cowboys ride for the grand prize. At the Dan Russell Arena in Folsom (☎ 916/985-2698).

August/September: The **California State Fair** has been celebrated in Sacramento since 1859. There's food, entertainment, carnival rides, and nightly fireworks.

December: The **California International Marathon** begins in Folsom and finishes at the State Capitol in Sacramento. For information call ☎ 916/983-4622.

being the capital city of a state that has a greater gross national product than most countries. It's a gracious city with broad, tree-lined streets and makes for a rewarding weekend jaunt.

Seeing the City Highlights

Start your weekend explorations at **Old Town Sacramento.** Because Sacramento was so close to the mines, it became a thriving, bustling, and rowdy supply center that grew up along the riverfront. Some of this flavor can be recaptured as you stroll the boardwalks and look at the old restored western buildings, but it takes a lot of imagination because the area is dominated by stores selling trinkets and T-shirts.

For me, one of the best places to dream and cast your mind back to those times is aboard the **Riverboat Delta King,** 1000 Front St. (☎ 916/444-5464), a paddlewheeler that has been converted into a hotel and is anchored at the dock in Old Town. If you can't stay aboard, then have dinner here (both these options are discussed further in "Lodging & Dining in Sacramento," below), or take one of the paddlewheelers that operate from Sacramento—***The Spirit of Sacramento,*** 110 L St. (☎ 916/552-2933), or the ***River City Queen,*** which is operated by Capital City Cruises, 1401 Garden Hwy. no. 125 (☎ 916/921-1111).

Other historic landmarks in Old Sacramento include the **Big Four Building** at I Street, between Front and Second streets (☎ 916/324-0539), which contains a reconstruction of the 1855 Huntington, Hopkins & Co. hardware store filled with tools of all sorts, household items, and handmade wooden toys and other goods that would have been sold at the time. The building is named after the four founders of the Transcontinental Railroad—Leland Stanford, Mark Hopkins, Collis P. Huntington, and Charles Crocker—who first discussed their dream of the railroad at a meeting above this hardware store. A **monument** to the brilliant engineer who conceived the plan for the railroad, Theodore Judah, also stands at 2nd and L streets.

Hours: Daily 10am–4pm.

The **B.F. Hastings Building,** at the corner of 2nd and J streets (☎ 916/445-4209), was originally occupied by several companies including Hastings Bank, Wells Fargo, and the Alta Telegraph Company, an agent for the Central Overland Pony Express while it was in operation. From here the first rider set out for an eastward journey on April 4, 1860. Today the building houses a reconstructed Supreme Court, plus Pony Express and Wells Fargo offices and other communications exhibits.

Hours: Daily 10am–4pm. *Admission:* Free.

At 925 Front St., the **Old Eagle Theatre** (☎ 916/446-6761) was the first building constructed as a theater in California in 1849. Performances are still given here today in a reconstruction, completed in 1974. At 2nd and J streets, a monument memorializes the brief glory days of the **Pony Express** when 80 riders were able to complete the 1,966-mile run from Sacramento to St. Joseph, Missouri, in 10 days, until they were put out of business by Western Union's telegraph in 1861.

Military buffs will also want to visit the **California Military Museum,** 1119 Second St. (☎ 916/442-2883), to view the more than 30,000 military collectibles—documents, medals, and other memorabilia housed here.

Hours: Tues–Sun 10am–4pm. *Admission:* $2.50 adults, $2 seniors, $1 children.

At 101 I St., **The Discovery Museum** (☎ 916/264-7057) is a combination history and science museum. It focuses on local history exhibits including a display of gold specimens, plus interactive science exhibits and demonstrations. There's also a planetarium.

Hours: Summer, Tues–Sun 10am–5pm; winter, Wed–Fri noon–5pm, Sat–Sun 10am–5pm. *Admission:* $4 adults, $2.50 children 6–17.

Downtown Sacramento

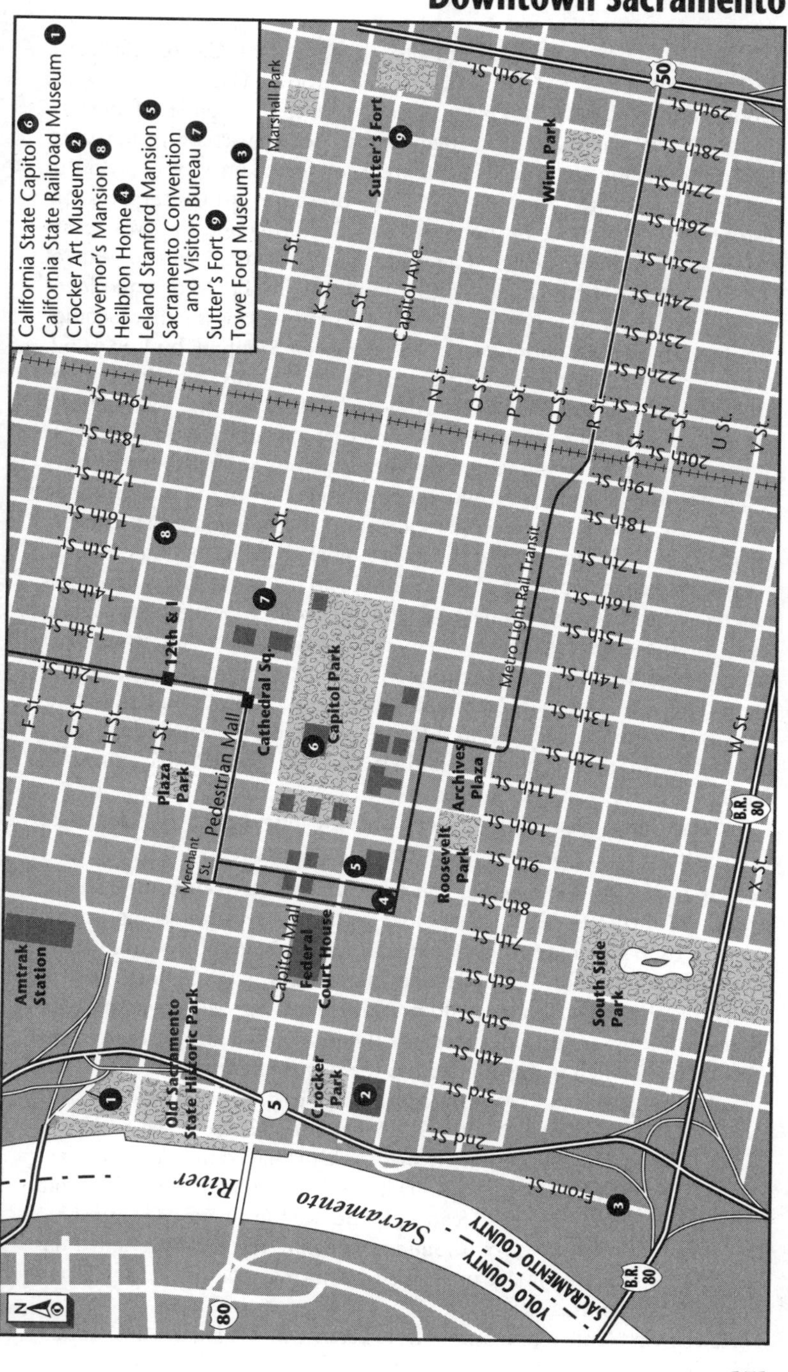

The best attraction in Old Sacramento, though, is the **California State Railroad Museum,** 111 I St. (☎ 916/448-4466), a fascinating museum dedicated to explaining and helping visitors grasp the wonder of an engineering marvel, the Transcontinental Railroad, which was completed when the Central Pacific and Union Pacific were connected on May 10, 1869, at Promontory Point, Utah. The museum preserves and interprets the history and significance of the railroad in California and the West. Start your visit by seeing *Evidence of a Dream,* which summarizes 160 years of railroad history. The highlights of the museum are the 21 restored locomotives, which positively glisten. At the entrance stands the first locomotive that ran on the Central Pacific, the *Governor Stanford,* built in 1862. You'll also see the Virginia and Truckee Railroad's *Empire,* built in 1873 for the (then) huge sum of $8,000. Take time to climb aboard and walk through the collection of railroad cars: a sleeping car, post office, and dining car (where you can view the varied dinnerware from several different lines and the menus that offered multicourse dinners for only $1), all from the *Gold Coast;* as well as passenger cars from the *Sonoma* and *Governor Stanford.* In addition to these, there are more than 40 exhibits to view, many detailing the building of the railroad and the tremendous hardships suffered by the 10,000 Chinese who made up 90% of the construction team. On the second floor there's a great toy train exhibit plus an outdoor balcony, from which you can get a good view of the railroad turntable and the Sacramento River. The admission price also allows you to visit the Passenger Station outside. Train rides are offered on weekends during the summer aboard the Sacramento Southern Railroad. Call ☎ 916/552-5252, ext. 7245, for fares and schedules.

Hours: Daily 10am–5pm, except major winter holidays. *Admission:* $5.50 adults, $2.25 children 6–12, free for children under 5.

Not far from Old Sacramento, the **Crocker Art Museum,** 3rd and O streets (☎ 916/264-5423), is another gem that is worth seeing for the glorious 1873 Italianate building alone. It was the state-of-the-art home of E.B. Crocker, brother of Charles, and featured a bowling alley, skating rink, billiard room, elaborate ballroom, and library, as well as gallery space for his paintings collection. It became the first public art museum in the West in 1885 when it was donated to the city by Margaret Crocker. The collection ranges from European to Californian art. It's particularly strong on 19th-century German painting. Crocker also collected many contemporary California artists, and their works are displayed in a separate California Gallery—Charles C. Nahl, Thomas Hill, William Keith, William Hahn and Norton Bush are all featured. The two most famous paintings in the museum are two by Nahl: *Sunday Morning in the Mines* and *Fandango,* a romanticized image of Spanish California. Another gallery shows California artists since 1945.

Hours: Wed–Sun 10am–5pm, Thurs 10am–9pm. *Admission:* $5 adults, $2.25 children 7–17, free for children under 6.

From Old Sacramento you can walk through the modern Downtown Plaza to the **Wells Fargo History Museum,** at 400 Capitol Mall (☎ 916/440-4161). Back in the mid-1800s the wagon train and the stage were the only viable overland modes of transportation. Wells Fargo was the major stage company, and millions of dollars were carried aboard the coaches of this world-famous company. The museum has hundreds of items on display, including old photographs depicting the role that the company played in the West since 1852. See the restored Concord coach and gold exhibits too.

Hours: Mon–Fri 9am–5pm. *Admission:* Free.

During the heady days of the Gold Rush fortunes were being made by supplying the miners with equipment and supplies; a stroll along the streets of the city, especially from 7th to 16th streets between E and I, will reveal the many fine Victorian homes that were built with such fortunes. Don't miss the **Leland Stanford Mansion** at 8th and N streets (☎ 916/324-0539) or the **Heilbron home** at 740 O St. Tours are given of the former, which was designed by Seth Babson in 1857 and acquired by Leland Stanford in 1861 (call for information regarding when tours are given; admission is free). The latter is home to a cultural center, **La Raza/Galeria,** celebrating the art and life of Chicano/Latino and Native American peoples (it's open Mon–Fri 10am–6pm, Sat 11am–5pm).

Sacramento was made the capital of California in 1854. The **California State Capitol,** 10th Street between L and R streets (☎ 916/324-0333), has been restored to its early glory complete with marble mosaic floors, crystal chandeliers, and monumental staircases and sculptures. The dome is extraordinarily beautiful. The desks in the Senate and Assembly chambers were crafted by Johann Breuner, who came to California in search of gold and turned to importing and manufacturing furniture instead. Here you can attend the sessions of the Assembly and Senate and tour the basement **museum,** where offices have been restored to their 1906 appearance. Free tours of the capitol are conducted daily.

Hours: Daily 9am–4pm. *Admission:* Free.

A few blocks away from the Capitol, the **Governor's Mansion,** 1526 H St. (☎ 916/323-3047), was home to 13 of California's governors until Ronald Reagan decided that he wanted to live in more modern quarters. Built in 1877, this splendid Second Empire Italianate mansion was the former home of merchant Albert Gallatin, the manager/partner of Huntington, Hopkins & Co. He sold it in 1888 to Joseph Steffens, father of muckraker journalist Lincoln Steffens, who grew up there. It was made the official governor's residence in 1903. It, too, is a splendid mansion containing 15 rooms filled with Oriental rugs, marble fireplaces, chandeliers, and ormolu mirrors—the accumulated stuff of the state's first families. Note the portraits of its residents, especially the most recent holders of the office.

Hours: Daily 10am–4pm. *Admission:* $3 adults, $1.50 children, free for children under 5.

Today at **Sutter's Fort,** 2701 L St. (☎ 916/445-4422), you can take a tour using an audio wand and see the original copper and blacksmith's shops, bakery, prison, and living quarters and imagine what it must have been like just before the news of the gold discovery.

John Augustus Sutter had received a 48,000-acre land grant from Governor Alvarado of Mexico when he landed here on the banks of the Sacramento River in 1839. Alvarado wanted Sutter to keep an eye on his uncle and political rival, General Vallejo. To avoid debtor's prison after a business enterprise failed, Sutter had left his wife and four children in his native Switzerland in 1834 and journeyed more than 20,000 miles via New York, St. Louis, Hawaii, and Alaska until he arrived here and set about building the settlement New Helvetia. Because he needed a steady supply of lumber, he contracted in August 1847 with James Marshall, a young carpenter from New Jersey, to build a sawmill on the American River, 30 miles east of the fort. Here, Marshall discovered traces of gold on January 24, 1848.

On that day San Francisco had a population of 460, and Sacramento 150. They were the largest communities in the area. A year later, they were five times their size. The news spread, and gold fever gripped first the coastal towns, then the eastern states, and finally the whole world. When the news reached this fort, it was initially turned upside down and became the place for all kinds of trading and other activities. As gold fever spread, Sutter's men deserted the fort, leaving crops to rot in the fields and cattle to be butchered by marauding miners. As early as 1849, Sutter sold all his holdings for only $40,000 and continued to lose money through poor judgment and bad luck. He died impoverished in 1860 in Washington, DC. Sacramento's waterfront, meanwhile, was turning into a bustling supply center for the miners and became a boomtown.

Special living-history programs are given during the summer. Only the central two-story oak and adobe building is original; the outer walls are reconstructions.

Hours: Daily 10am–5pm. *Admission:* $2.50 adults, $1.25 children 6–18, free for children under 6.

Next door to Sutter's Fort, the **California State Indian Museum,** 2618 K St. (☎ 916/324-0971), features displays on aspects of Indian life, including the life of the Nisenan, a branch of the Maidu, who were the first to inhabit the Sacramento Valley. There's also an exhibit focusing on Ishi, the last Yahi Indian, who was discovered in 1911 and subsequently studied by anthropologists.

Hours: Daily 10am–5pm. *Admission:* $3 adults, $1.50 children 6–17, free for those under 6.

Some Nearby Sights

Vintage car enthusiasts will want to stop in at the **California Towe Ford Museum,** 2200 Front St. (☎ 916/442-6802), which displays more than

175 vintage Fords—Model As, Edsels, and Thunderbirds—documenting Ford's genius from the turn of the century into the '50s. It's great to be able to get close to these beauties and to even sit behind the wheel of one or two of them. There are even a few competitors' vehicles on display, too, notably Jerry Brown's '74 blue Plymouth Satellite and Alexander Haig's armored Cadillac.

Hours: Daily 10am–6pm. *Admission:* $5 adults, $4.50 seniors, $2.50 children 14–18, $1 children 5–13, free for those under 5.

A final place to soak up some of the city's history is at the **Sacramento City Cemetery,** 10th and Broadway (☎ 916/264-5621, or 916/448-0811 for tours), where so many of the city's pioneers are buried: John Augustus Sutter, Judge E.B. Crocker, Mark Hopkins, William Hamilton, the son of Alexander Hamilton, several governors, and the first mayor of the city, to name a few.

Hours: Daily 8am–4:30pm. Guided tours are given on most weekends.

Instead of spending your whole weekend in the city, you may want to pass a day at some nearby attractions. Shoppers will want to head 20 minutes east of town to **Folsom,** which is famous for its 50-plus **factory outlets** (Nike, Geoffrey Beene, Fieldcrest Cannon, and so on) and a plaza featuring more than 200 **antiques dealers.** The former are located at 13000 Folsom Blvd. (☎ 916/985-0313), the latter at 11395 Folsom Blvd., Rancho Cordova, off Highway 50, between Sunrise and Hazel (☎ 916/852-8517). Here also you may want to visit the **Gekkeikan Sake tasting room** and plant at 1136 Sibley St. (☎ 916/985-3111), which also features a Japanese garden and koi pond. Admission and tasting are free.

Lodging & Dining in Sacramento

Abigail's, 2120 G St., Sacramento, CA 95816 (☎ 800/858-1568 or 916/441-5007, fax 916/441-0621), is located in a lovely 1912 Colonial Revival mansion conveniently close to downtown Sacramento. The five guest rooms all have private baths and sitting areas and are furnished with fine, but not pretentious, antiques. Additional in-room amenities include telephone, radio, terrycloth bathrobes, magazines, and beverages. Aunt Rose's room has a queen-size brass bed and an inviting bathroom with whirlpool tub. Margaret's room has a canopy bed with leaf-cutout wrought-iron head- and footboard set against a white and gold decor. Among the furnishings are a dashing chaise lounge and a comfortable wing chair with a floor lamp beside it for easy reading. Uncle Albert's is designed along more masculine lines and decorated with a burgundy pin stripe, paisley print, and hunting regalia; for comfort it boasts a large wing chair, while the bathroom's shower has a built-in bench for comfortable bathing. Anne's room features a cornstalk four-poster with satin skirt, desk, loveseat, and soft window treatments. The L-shaped "solarium" is the brightest room in the house and boasts its own private balcony. It's furnished in lovely wicker furnishings and canopy bed.

A full breakfast—fresh juice, spicy pears, and French toast or quiche—is served each morning, with tea and cookies served each afternoon. Guests are welcome to use the living room and parlor, both of which are very comfortably furnished with clusters of armchairs and Oriental rugs plus attractive ceramic and china displays. The sitting room has a piano and games, including chess, for guests' use. An added bonus is the outdoor hot tub and the garden patio. Phone and television available on request.

Rates (incl. breakfast): $105–$165 double.

On a broad, tree-lined street, **Amber House,** 1315 22nd St., Sacramento, CA 95816 (☎ 916/444-8085, fax 916/447-1548), is a lovely place to stay. The main house is a 1905 Craftsman-style home, which features stained glass windows and beautiful woodwork. To the right of the entrance there's an inviting living room. Burnished coach lamps hang above the mantel; Oriental rugs grace the redwood floors; beams support the ceiling; and underneath are set several comfortable couches and armchairs. All rooms have telephone, clock-radio/cassette player, and cable TV. Some have VCR and a Jacuzzi for two.

Five rooms are in the main house. Each is named after a poet and furnished in appropriate style. The Lord Byron has an Italian marble–tiled bath with large oval Jacuzzi for two and an iron canopy bed with sheer drapes. The Chaucer bathroom contains an antique washstand, while the room is furnished with oak antiques and lit by a stained glass window. Four rooms are located in the adjacent Spanish Revival home built in 1913. Each of the beautifully decorated and comfortable rooms here is named after an artist. The Degas boasts a lace-trimmed, four-poster canopy bed. The Van Gogh has a white wicker bed plus a heart-shaped Jacuzzi in a brilliant solarium bathroom.

A full breakfast is served in the dining room or in your room on request. Guests also receive coffee or tea plus the newspaper in the early morning; wine, champagne, and hors d'oeuvres in the evening; and a chocolate chip cookie at turndown.

Rates (incl. breakfast): $159–229 double weekends, slightly less midweek.

The **Delta King Riverboat,** 1000 Front St., Old Sacramento, CA 95814 (☎ 916/444-5464), is anchored on the waterfront. Step up the gangplank onto this historic polished wood sternwheeler. It has 44 staterooms and suites, all equipped with cable TV and telephone. The rooms are paneled in mahogany and furnished with queen-size brass beds and wicker chairs and include a private deck area. Rates include a continental breakfast buffet served in the Pilothouse Restaurant, which is also open for lunch and dinner. There are also a saloon and lounge and theater with live entertainment.

Rates (incl. breakfast): $109–$159 double.

Hartley House, 700 22nd St., Sacramento, CA 95816 (☎ 916/447-7829), is another handsome downtown Victorian that was built in 1906.

Handsome architectural features of the interior are the inlaid-wood floors, leaded and stained glass windows, and original brass gas lamps that have been converted to electricity. It offers five guest rooms with private bath, TV, and telephone. The Dover has an attractive coved ceiling and is furnished with a brass bed, desk, rocker, and a bathroom with clawfoot tub. A high-back, cottage-style Victorian bed is the centerpiece of the Stratford room. Other rooms are very stylishly decorated in oak pieces. The parlor with stained glass window accents and brick fireplace is a welcoming retreat for guests. A full breakfast, which might be Belgian waffles or eggs Benedict, plus tea and coffee is served at an oak table in the dining room.

Rates (incl. breakfast): $115–$165 double.

Dining Only in Sacramento

At **Biba,** 2801 Capitol Ave. (☎ 916/455-2422), the menu promises about an equal number of pasta and specialty dishes. Among the former might be an orecchiette fully flavored with broccoli rabe, garlic, and chili pepper, or fettuccine with wild mushrooms and tomato cream sauce. Specialties might include a filet of beef studded with fresh herbs and garlic, braised rabbit with wine, tomatoes, sage, and white beans, or veal or fish of the day. Prices range from $10 to $20. For dessert, go for the *zuppa a due colori,* which is a rich concoction of double chocolate trifle with dark and white chocolate, Grand Marnier–soaked pound cake, and raspberry puree.

Hours: Mon–Fri 11:30am–2:30pm, Mon–Sat 5:30–9:30pm.

As might be expected, a political crowd hangs out at the **Capitol Grill,** 2730 N St. (☎ 916/736-0744). Polished wood tables and a historic bar set the scene for some good, flavorsome food. At dinner you'll find such hearty dishes as grilled beef tenderloin with portobello mushrooms in a cabernet sauce served with mashed potatoes, or grilled salmon with leeks and parsley in a saffron broth. If you're just looking for a simple burger, you can enjoy it on focaccia with grilled red onions, homemade ketchup, and garlic fries. Prices range from $7 to $20. A favorite appetizer is the smoked chicken and caramelized onion quesadilla with apple and celery root salad.

Hours: Mon–Fri 11am–11pm, Sat 5–11pm, Sun 5–10pm.

Harlow's, 2714 J St. (☎ 916/441-4693), is a casual dining room with a club atmosphere. The eclectic menu offers everything from steamed mussels in a Thai-style red curry to seafood ravioli with tomato and basil cream as first dishes. Main courses are more typically grilled New York steak *marchand de vin,* barbecued chicken, or filet of salmon with lentil ragout and tarragon Dijon aïoli. Prices range from $12 to $19 for main courses.

Hours: Tues–Sat 5:30–10pm. The cigar bar upstairs stays open later.

Across the street from the Capitol Grill, **Paragary's Bar and Oven,** 1401 28th St. (☎ 916/452-3335), is slightly more casual, especially in the cafe with its bentwood chairs set at Formica tables. The menu offers a range of Italian grilled dishes, plus pasta and a dozen specialty pizzas, which range from a rich version made with smoked salmon, capers, red onions, chives and crème fraîche to a more modest arrangement of sun-dried tomatoes, mozzarella, and eggplant, all flavored with garlic and basil. The grilled dishes are very tasty, too. Try the salmon flavored with fennel and niçoise olive-lemon vinaigrette accompanied by olive oil–braised potatoes, or the braised lamb shank with polenta, porcini mushroom sauce, and gremolata. Prices range from $10 to $17.50. The wine list features close to 20 choices by the glass.

Hours: Mon–Thurs 11:30am–11pm, Fri 11:30am–midnight, Sat 5pm–midnight, Sun 5–10pm.

An Inn in Lodi

Sweep into the **Wine and Roses Country Inn,** 2505 W. Turner Rd., Lodi, CA 95242 (☎ 209/334-6988), and you'll find yourself at an elegant small hotel set in 5 acres of lovely gardens. The 10 rooms are elegantly and tastefully furnished with antiques, well-chosen art, and fresh flowers. Each is decorated differently. In Edelweiss, for example, you'll find a brass bed combined with an oak chest, wing chair, and other pieces against a hunter-green background. Memories has a spindle four-poster, while another room has a bed with an elaborate tented effect created above it. Each has a small TV and telephone. Wine is served in the late afternoon in the comfortable sitting room containing a library and a hearth, in front of which guests can curl up to read. Facilities include an inviting restaurant serving fine California and continental cuisine. There's outdoor dining overlooking the gardens, too. Lodi is located south of Sacramento, about 12 miles north of Stockton.

Rates: $125 double weekends, $109 midweek.

A SIDE TRIP TO STOCKTON

Sacramento is also the gateway to the Delta area. Three great rivers, the Sacramento, Mokelumne, and San Joaquin, flow together out into San Francisco Bay, creating a labyrinth of navigable channels dotted with hundreds of islands in the delta area just northwest of **Stockton.** The town is only 23 feet above sea level, and before the many levees were built the spring runoff could turn more than 600 miles of the San Joaquin Valley into a vast inland lake. Stockton itself played a role in the gold rush, supplying the gold mine settlements in the mid-Sierras—Mokelumne Diggings and Tuolumne. In 1850 Bayard Taylor reported on a canvas town with 1,000 inhabitants plus a port with 25 vessels at anchor. This settlement had arisen in 4 months. Supplies were shipped in from San Francisco and carried out on mule trains and wagons.

Its wealth, though, really derived (and still does) from the Delta and the navigable waterways that carry shipping. Stockton's deep water channel is navigable to 85% of the world's shipping traffic, and today the port is filled with large cargo vessels carrying such goods as cotton to Taiwan or almonds to the Russian Republic. The waterways, 50-plus islands, and levees make for a veritable pleasure ground for anglers and boaters, and a wonderful weekend can be spent here in the Delta **houseboating** or anchoring at an inn in nearby Lodi, 12 miles north of Stockton.

Lodi also has a couple of **wineries** worth visiting—**Oak Ridge** at 61000 E. Hwy. 12 (☎ 209/369-4758), and **Phillips Farms Winery & Vineyards,** 4580 W. Hwy. 12 (☎ 209/368-7384), which is also renowned for its fruit market and large pumpkin patch. There are also 10 or more wineries in the area.

Stockton itself also has a museum that is worth visiting, the **Haggin Museum,** Victory Park, 1201 N. Pershing Ave. (☎ 209/462-4116), which has a surprisingly rich, though small, collection of art that includes a dozen Bierstadts and works by such Americans as George Inness and William Keith, and such Europeans as Gauguin, Renoir, and Jean-Léon Gérôme. The collection was amassed by three generations of the Haggin family.

The museum also exhibits examples of the Holt and caterpillar tractors, which were developed in Stockton, and possesses a well-displayed historical collection relating to the San Joaquin Valley and California. Although it may seem a foregone conclusion that the San Joaquin would turn into the food basket of the nation, it wasn't that easy. The valley is vast, and it required vast machinery. The pioneers, therefore, developed such large-scale equipment as the Standish California steam plough, which could plow 15 to 30 acres a day, along with harvesters pulled by 30 horses, and threshing machines. Initially, wheat was king with 60 million bushels being shipped along the Sacramento River, but it was soon replaced by other crops—citrus, nuts, vegetables, and grapes.

Hours: Tues–Sun 1:30–5pm. *Admission:* Free.

The town's **Children's Museum,** 402 W. Weber (☎ 209/465-4386), is the fifth-largest in the nation. It's filled with all kinds of creative play opportunities and games. Kids can do a lot of role-playing at the Hospital, the Grocery Store, and TV Station, to name only a few play areas.

Hours: Tues–Sat 9:30am–5pm, Sun noon–5pm. *Admission:* $4, free for children under 2.

FARTHER AFIELD

From Stockton the Sacramento Valley runs all the way south to Bakersfield. I-5 slices right through it, and Highway 99 travels its length through the modest towns of Modesto, Merced, Fresno, and Hanford/Visalia to Bakersfield, a distance of almost 300 miles. Here in this valley is the garden of California.

When the miners headed out to Gold Country, they crossed this great Central Valley, parched in summer but abundant in winter and spring. Game was abundant—millions of ducks, geese, cranes, antelope, tule elk, and even grizzly bears inhabited the area. Today, of course, there is no trace of this pristine natural life; fruit and nut groves and field after field of strawberries, lettuce, and other vegetables stretch for miles in what has become the great food basket of the nation. It all started in the 1850s when many of the disappointed miners tried farming or ranching in the valley. Even back then the fruits of the valley were garnering praise, if the comments of William Henry Brewer in ***Up and Down California,*** published in 1861, are to be believed. At the California State Fair, he reported seeing apples that measured over 15 inches in circumference, 17-inch round pears, and 7-pound clusters of grapes. Today it's still the nation's food basket, the source of 50% of our food.

Not exactly a tourist haven, its towns are largely ugly and uninspiring, but the valley itself and the orchards and fruits that grow there are awesome and must be seen in all their glory if you really want to grasp what California is and means to this nation. One way to do this is to follow the **Fresno Blossom Trail** in the spring from the end of February to the first 2 weeks in March. It's a 62-mile self-guided tour that takes you past orchards shimmering with the blossoms of almond, plum, apple, orange, lemon, peach, nectarine, and apricot. For information and a map, call the **Fresno Convention & Tourist Bureau,** 808 M St., Fresno, CA 93721 (☎ 209/233-0836).

Sacramento & Vicinity
Special & Recreational Activities

Antiquing: In addition to the huge **Plaza** in Folsom, Sacramento has an **antique row** on 57th Street off H. Go Saturday because some shops are closed Sundays.

Bicycling: The **Jedediah Smith Memorial Bicycle Trail** runs 23 miles, from Old Sacramento to Beal's Point at Folsom. Rentals can be obtained at **River Rat**, 9840 Fair Oaks at Pennsylvania (☎ 916/966-6555).

Boating: See "Houseboating," below.

Fishing: You can fish year-round in the Delta for striped bass, salmon, catfish, and largemouth bass. Marinas listed under "Houseboating," below, also offer fishing boat rentals.

Golf: Here is a selection of public golf courses in Sacramento. **Bartley W. Cavanaugh Golf Course**, 8301 Freeport Blvd. (☎ 916/665-2020), is a links course; **Bing Maloney Golf Course,** 6801 Freeport Blvd. (☎ 916/428-9401), offers 27 holes plus a lighted driving range; **Haggin Oaks Golf Course**, 3645 Fulton Ave. (☎ 916/481-4506), features 36 holes, 3 putting greens, and lighted driving ranges; **William Land Park Golf Course**, 1701 Sutterville Rd. (☎ 916/455-5014), is a 9-holer in William Land Park. **Rancho Murieta Country Club** (☎ 916/354-3400) is home to the PGA Senior Gold Rush golf tournament It's semi-private.

Horseback Riding: Contact **Gibson Ranch** (☎ 916/991-7592).

Houseboating: The thing to do in summer is rent a houseboat and cruise the Delta. For rentals contact **Paradise Point Marina**, 8095 Rio Blanco Rd., Stockton, CA 95209 (☎ 209/952-1000); **Tower Park Marina**, 14900 W. Hwy. 12, Terminous, CA 95242 (☎ 209/369-1041); or **Herman and Helen's Houseboats**, Venice Island Ferry, Stockton, CA 95209 (☎ 209/951-4634). A standard houseboat will have fully equipped kitchen with stove and refrigerator. Luxury models will have microwaves, toasters, and blenders plus air-conditioning. You can usually rent them for 3, 4, or 7 days. Weekend rates in summer will run around $595 (more on holiday weekends) for a boat that sleeps four. You can usually rent boats for skiing and fishing at these marinas as well.

Parks: For an active break, **Discovery Park**, at I-5 and Richards Boulevard (☎ 916/875-7066), at the confluence of the Sacramento and American Rivers, offers good opportunities for biking, walking, and picnicking. **Del Paso Regional Park**, at I-80 and Auburn Boulevard (☎ 916/566-6581), occupies 100 acres and offers hiking and riding trails.

Tennis: For information call the city's tennis program at ☎ 916/566-6435.

Water Sports: About 20 minutes from town, Folsom Lake and Lake Natoma offer kayaking, sailing, windsurfing, and waterskiing.

Whitewater Rafting: There are several possibilities for river rafting on the American and Sacramento Rivers, near Grass Valley and Coloma. Contact **Tributary Whitewater Tours**, 20480 Woodbury Dr., Grass Valley, CA 95949 (☎ 916/346-6812), or **Whitewater Connection**, P.O. Box 270, Coloma, CA 95613-0270 (☎ 916/622-6446, fax 916/622-7192), which offers trips on the North, South, and Middle Forks of the American River and also on the Stanislaus.

The Gold Country North of Sacramento: From Grass Valley & Nevada City to Placerville

Distances in Miles: Nevada City, 161; Grass Valley, 157

Estimated Driving Time: 2¾ hours to Nevada City, 2¾ hours to Grass Valley

⊰o⊱⊰o⊱⊰o⊱⊰o⊱⊰o⊱

Driving: Highway 80 continues from Sacramento directly into Auburn.

Most of the other destinations in this chapter are on Highway 49 between Nevada City on the north and Placerville on the south.

Further Information: You can get information about the Grass Valley and Nevada City area, contact the **Grass Valley/Nevada County Chamber of Commerce,** 248 Mill St., Grass Valley, CA 95945 (☎ 530/273-4667), or the **Nevada City Chamber of Commerce,** 132 Main St., Nevada City, CA 95959 (☎ 530/265-2692).

For information about the Auburn and Placerville area, contact the **Auburn Chamber of Commerce,** 601 Lincoln Way, Auburn, CA 95603 (☎ 530/885-5616); **El Dorado County Chamber of Commerce,** 542 Main St., Placerville, CA 95667 (☎ 530/621-5885); or **Pollock Pines–Camino Chamber of Commerce,** 6532 Pony Express Trail, P.O. Box 95, Pollock Pines, CA 95726 (☎ 530/644-3970).

⊰o⊱⊰o⊱⊰o⊱⊰o⊱⊰o⊱

Between 1848 and 1898 it is estimated that some 125 million ounces of gold were taken from the hills of California. That's $50 billion at current values. Little wonder that the discovery of gold brought a stampede of fortune seekers to this little-known and thinly populated state. As the news of the discovery spread, whole towns were abandoned from Sonoma to Monterey, and soon hordes began arriving via South America and overland to seek their fortunes in these Sierra foothills. For a brief number of years, they scratched and scarred, gashed and pummeled the earth in search of this precious metal. Then they left. But their legacy can still be seen today, written on the landscape and in the layouts of the towns that line

The Northern Gold Country

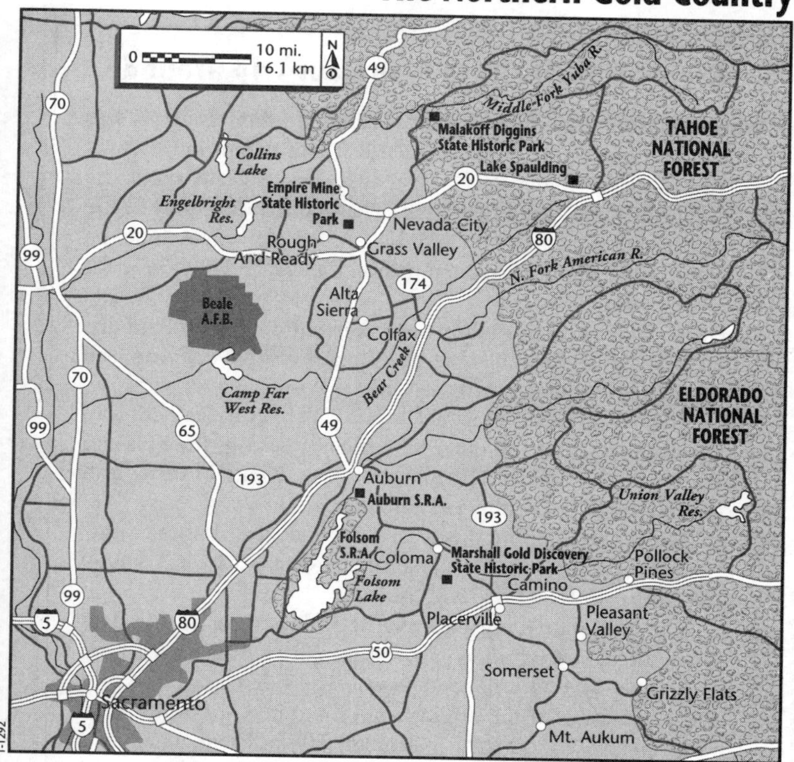

Highway 49 from Grass Valley in the north to Mariposa in the south. This is the area known today as "Gold Country."

In an 1848 letter home, prospector William Swaim described mining as "a dog's life" and went on to say: "A man has to make a jackass of himself packing loads over mountains that God never designed man to climb . . . we see nothing here but hills, mountains, and rocks, . . . no female society, hear no music, except the occasional squeaking of a hoarse fiddle in some lone cabin and the croaking of ravens, the chattering of woodpeckers and the roaring of the Rio de los Plumas." It was, to say the least, not an easy life.

Further, the opportunity for instant riches soon passed as thousands of gold seekers streamed in from all over the continent and the world to these mines in the Sierra foothills. In 1848 the non-Indian population of California was a mere 14,000; by 1852 the state's population was 223,000. First Sacramento was largely deserted, then San Francisco, then Monterey, and so on until it seemed everyone was seeking his fortune in the flimsy mining camps.

As a consequence, prices for even the most basic supplies soared. A boiled egg cost 75 cents, an onion was worth a dollar, boots cost $40 a

Events & Festivals to Plan Your Trip Around

January: Gold Discovery Day is celebrated every January 24 at the Marshall Gold Discovery Park. That's when you can try your hand at gold panning, listen to speakers talk about the Gold Rush, and see movies, too. The 150th anniversary of the discovery will be in 1998, and the celebrations will include the World Gold Panning Championships. Call ☎ 530/622-3470 for information.

April: The **International Teddy Bear Convention,** Miners Foundry, Nevada City, turns out some very special bears every year. Call ☎ 530/265-5804 for information.

June: The **Nevada City Bicycle Classic** is held every Father's Day, when professional and other bike riders challenge the hills and corners of the 35-lap, 1.1-mile city route. Plenty of thrills and spills. Call ☎ 530/265-2692 for information.

Music in the Mountains is a 3-week festival of classical music. For information write P.O. Box 1451, Nevada City, CA 95959 (☎ 800/218-2188 or 530/265-6124).

The **National Pony Express Re-Ride** returns to the days when these intrepid riders carried the mail over the Sierras from St. Joseph, Missouri, to Sacramento. The ride takes place over the 1,966 miles of the original trail route in 4- to 5-mile legs. More than 550 riders participate in the 10-day event, which cuts through Camino–Pollock Pines en route to Sacramento. In even years the riders leave from Sacramento, in odd years from St. Joseph, Missouri. Call ☎ 530/621-5885 for information.

September: The **Draft Horse Classic** features events and competitions that show the pulling ability of such breeds as the Percheron, Belgian, and Clydesdale. For information call ☎ 530/273-6217.

pair, and a steam engine worth $2,000 could be sold for $15,000. And not only goods were sold for inflated prices. In 1849 even a prostitute claimed to have made $50,000. Gold dust was used for currency, with whatever could be held between thumb and finger representing $1, a wine glass full of gold dust representing $100, and a tumbler full representing $1,000. Still the men kept arriving, driven by their dreams of finding wealth in the mountains and rivers and returning home rich. They in turn were followed by the monte dealers, who set up tents and dispensed liquor and debauchery.

Louis Clapp in her *Shirley Letters* reports and describes the lust for gold and how men were moved to follow the latest big strikes and better diggings. In her letters Clapp describes how miners were permitted to stake off 40 feet and how they had to renew their claim every 10 days if they did not begin digging immediately. Each community made its own rules, it seems. Thus thousands of (mostly) men and women went to work using longtoms and riffle boxes, or sinking wells called coyote holes into the bed rock.

Mule trains transported supplies. Passengers traveled aboard the Concord Stagecoach, which was designed in 1850 and came equipped with a thoroughbrace, a kind of shock absorber that enabled the coach to handle the rough roads to the extent that Mark Twain could call it "a veritable cradle upon wheels." In contrast, today you can travel Highway 49 quite comfortably as it snakes its way through the hills and along the ridges, creeks, and rivers that were the focus of so much fevered activity. No traces remain of the early 1850s mining camps that were built of canvas and wood and fell prey to fire; many of the later mines became ghost towns once they were exhausted. Only their haunting names remain to remind us of the men that followed their dreams to such places as Rough and Ready, You Bet, Gouge Eye, and many others. Still, if you travel Highway 49 today through the old mining towns that do remain, you will certainly feel some of the excitement that once charged these towns from Nevada City and Grass Valley in the North through Auburn and Sutter's Creek to Sonora and Mariposa in the south.

THE NORTHERN MINES

GRASS VALLEY

In 1849 Grass Valley was indeed just that when it was named by a group of pioneers who had survived the crossing of the Sierras and woke one morning to find their half-starved cattle grazing cheerfully in the meadows. Later, the first settlers established themselves at Badger Hill and Boston Ravine, both of which later became part of Grass Valley. These settlements were surrounded by rich placer mines (that is, where gold could be dredged or washed out from sand deposits) that were worked in the 1850s—Humbug Flat, Grass Valley Slide, and the Lola Montez diggings, to name only a few. The hardrock Gold Hill Mine was discovered by George Knight in October 1850, and from it, between 1850 and 1857, more than $4 million was taken. It and other similar deep rock mines attracted Cornish miners experienced in the techniques required to build the underground tunnels to extract the ore. They taught the forty-niners how to use drill steel and the single jack and also brought with them such inventions as the Cornish pump for forking the water out of the deeper tunnels. By 1910 Grass Valley was 66% Cornish, which is why today you'll still see so many stores selling the miner's luncheon, a Cornish pasty.

It is reckoned that more than $80-million worth of gold was taken from the mines in this area, although some say $400-million worth was taken out in more than a century of mining. Certainly in the 1850s Grass Valley expanded rapidly and was incorporated as a town in 1855. It suffered many disastrous fires, like one in late 1855 that destroyed 300 wood-frame buildings. The determined residents simply rebuilt the town, this time using brick and stone. Several churches were established.

Some famous names are associated with the town. Philosopher, historian, and noted Harvard professor Josiah Royce was born here in 1855 (a plaque marks the site at the library at 207 Mill St.). **Lola Montez** arrived here in 1854 on the run from the East Coast and a failed marriage. She had been born Maria Gilbert in Ireland in 1818. Beautiful and adventurous, she had seduced society with her Spider Dance, becoming the friend of such figures as George Sand, Alexander Dumas, Victor Hugo, and Franz Liszt. She eventually married one of her aristocratic patrons, the Bavarian Count of Landsfeld. She fled from this marriage to the United States, first to New York, then San Francisco, and finally in 1852 to Grass Valley, where her presence caused quite a stir.

You can see a **replica of the house** she bought and occupied in 1853 at 248 Mill St. (☎ 530/273-4667). Today it serves as the Chamber of Commerce, but it does contain some of Lola's personal effects. From here she used to sashay along the streets with her pet bear on a leash. While she resided here, Lola had a powerful influence on a young, shy 6-year-old who lived in a boarding house a few doors down from Lola's place, at 238 Mill St. Lola taught the little girl to dance and sing, and that same little girl went on to become a great entertainer who earned more than $3 million and became the toast of the nation and of San Francisco in particular. Her name was **Lotta Crabtree.**

Pick up a walking tour map at the Chamber of Commerce and walk around town to capture some of this flavor from yesteryear. Drop into the **Grass Valley Museum** at Mount Saint Mary's Convent on South Church Street (☎ 530/273-5509). The museum is located on the second floor of the convent, which served the community from 1866 to 1927. The nuns came to care for the children whose parents had been killed in mining accidents or by illnesses. On display are a restored music room and doctor's office and a collection of glassware, clothing, and the like.

Hours: Tues–Fri 12:30–3:30pm. *Admission:* Free.

The most evocative historic site on the walking tour is across the street from the convent in **St. Patrick's Cemetery,** where you'll find markers dating back to 1853. At the **Holbrooke Hotel,** 212 W. Main St., built in 1862, the register contains the signatures of four U.S. Presidents. Along the way, you'll discover that Grass Valley had its own **Chinatown** on Bank Street, where more than 1,000 Chinese lived in the 1870s. It was razed in 1938. At 114 Stewart St. a certain Maybelle Foster operated a **bordello** in the 1920s and '30s. Before that, the site served as a wrestling ring where Cornish miners held their bouts. Brothels also occupied 122 and 124 Stewart St. and 110 E. Main St.

If you would like to see the remains of a real gold mine, you might wish to visit the site of the Empire, which yielded an estimated 5.8-million ounces of gold ($960 million based on current prices) between 1850 and 1956 when it closed. Today it is the focal point of the **Empire Mine State Historic Park,** 10791 E. Empire St., Grass Valley (☎ 530/273-8522), just outside Grass Valley. Here in this 777-acre park the story of hardrock mining is told, and visitors can travel 50 feet down a mineshaft. They can also see a scale model of the mine that was more than 11,000 feet deep and had tunnels that ran for some 367 miles underground. The mine was operated by the Bourn family from the 1870s to 1929, when it was bought by the Newmont Mining Corp., which operated it until 1956. The **Bourn Cottage** (1905) has been restored, and the park affords hiking, biking, and picnicking opportunities. The best time to visit is during Living History Days, which take place in September and October.

Hours: May–Labor Day daily 9–6pm; Labor Day–Dec daily 10am–5pm; Jan–Apr daily 10am–5pm; May daily 9am–5pm. *Admission:* $3 for adults, $1 children 6–12.

A mile south of downtown, you can also visit the **North Star Mining Museum and Pelton Wheel,** at Mill Street and McCourtney and Allison Ranch roads (☎ 530/273-4255), which displays a variety of mining equipment including the Cornish pump and a stamp mill for those interested in engineering.

Hours: May–Oct daily 10am–5pm.

A few miles west of Grass Valley, **Rough & Ready** is the town that made history by seceding from the Union on April 7, 1850, because of a mining tax. They rejoined the Union on the 4th of July when Old Glory was raised up the flag pole. Every year, the secession is celebrated on the last Sunday of June. At one time the town had 3,000 residents. It was given Zachary Taylor's nickname *Rough and Ready* by its founder, who served under Taylor and admired him.

If you want to do some gold panning yourself, then take old Highway 20 to Bitney Springs Road, turn right, and go to Pleasant Valley Road; take another right to one of the oldest single-span covered bridges anywhere. It makes a lovely setting, so you won't be too disappointed if your luck doesn't pan out. Or you can go to the Keleher Picnic Area in the Tahoe forest, 2 miles outside the town of Washington. Take Highway 20 east. Dredging for gold requires a state permit.

Lodging in Grass Valley

The **Holbrooke Hotel,** 212 W. Main St., Grass Valley, CA 95945 (☎ 800/933-7077 or 530/273-1353, fax 530/273-0434), is one of those typical

Western-style hotels with a double porch along the front. It was built in 1851 and has hosted many western luminaries—Mark Twain; Bret Harte; Lotta Crabtree; presidents Grant, Garfield, and Cleveland; and Gentleman Jim Corbett among them. The 27 rooms all have private bath and TV. The front rooms with access to the balcony are super large. Some bathrooms have clawfoot tubs. Furnishings are mostly oak pieces combined with brass or carved-oak Victorian beds. They're not fancy at all.

Facilities include a dining room and the Golden Gate Saloon, which has a great back bar. The cuisine in the dining room is good. A complimentary continental breakfast is served. The dining room is open Mon–Sat 11:30–2pm, Sun 10–2pm, daily 5:30–9pm.

Rates (incl. breakfast): $80–$116 double weekends, $70–$96 midweek. Further discounts Jan–March.

Murphy's Inn, 318 Neal St., Grass Valley, CA 95945 (☎ 530/273-6873), was built for Edward Coleman, owner of the North Star and Idaho mines as a wedding gift to his wife. It's an appealing home with a welcoming, wraparound veranda enhanced by hanging baskets of ivy, lovely gardens with fountains and a bird bath, all set behind a low fence. Guests enter to find two comfortable sitting rooms, both with fireplaces. They are furnished in Victorian style with sofas, fringed lamps, gilt mirrors, and other elegant antiques. There are eight rooms, all with private bath. Four have fireplaces. Lace curtains, floral wallpapers, and country furnishings are the hallmarks of each. The most luxurious accommodation is Sara's suite, which is in a separate building and boasts a living room and kitchen in addition to the bedroom. A full breakfast is served. For a quiet moment together, go sit on the sundeck under the sequoia tree in the yard.

Rates (incl. breakfast): $100–$150 double.

Swan–Levine House, 328 S. Church St., Grass Valley, CA 95945 (☎ 530/272-1873), is very much the personal vision and expression of artists/printmakers Peggy Swan and Howard Levine. Throughout the house you will find their prints, mostly colored etchings, monotypes, or lithographs made in the studio that is on the property (they have 3 etching presses and at least 20 litho stones). Peggy and Howard themselves have restored the turreted Victorian, which is set on a bank above the street. The house was built in 1880 by William Campbell, a merchant who later sold it to a doctor who converted it into a small hospital. It's a casual and relaxed, but at the same time a creatively energetic, kind of place. The rooms are eclectically furnished. Quilts cover the beds; the furnishings might be wicker or oak. The original surgery with its octagonal white floor tiles is furnished with wicker and lots of plants. One room has its own entrance and also a small kitchen with refrigerator and microwave. Guests can relax in the library/art gallery, which also features a favorite curiosity, an old jukebox, or in the living room, which has a large bay window and tile fireplace. Breakfasts are not just typical eggs-and-bacon affairs—you're more likely to sample quesadillas with mango, cheese, and onions, or huevos rancheros, or lemon yogurt pancakes, all of which are prepared in a homey, welcoming kitchen that is also filled with artwork.

Rates (incl. breakfast): $75–$90 double.

Dining in Grass Valley

In addition to the dining room at the **Holbrooke Hotel** (see the Lodging reviews above for more information), here are your best dining choices in Grass Valley.

Across the street from the Holbrooke Hotel, the **Main Street Cafe,** 213 W. Main St. (☎ 530/477-6000), is a casual restaurant/saloon with a big old bar and glass-topped tables. Brick walls, posters, and oak booths provide the "look" of the place. The food is continental in style with a distinct Caribbean influence; the menu includes such dishes as coconut rum–battered prawns and pork loin with maple-bourbon sauce, along with such familiar dishes as salmon with champagne and dill. Prices range from $15 to $19.

Hours: Mon–Sat 11:30am–3pm and daily 5–9pm.

Mrs. Dubblebee's Pasties, 251 S. Auburn (☎ 530/272-7700), is the place to go to secure one of the inexpensive Cornish pasties that the Cornish miners introduced to the area. Scones, cookies, soups, and more are also available.

Hours: Mon–Fri 10am–6pm and Sat–Sun 10am–5:30pm.

NEVADA CITY

Four or so miles northeast of Grass Valley, Nevada City is a very appealing town. It's also a very literary and artistic town, if you ask the local bookstore owner about who chooses to live here these days. Residents enjoy the quiet and the slow, easy pace of the town, which is set on a series of small hills covered with sugar maples and backed by pine-covered mountains.

It wasn't always so quiet. James Marshall, who found gold at Coloma, came to Deer Creek in 1848 and also panned successfully for gold. Word spread, with reports of miners who had dug a pound of gold a day from the creek. First known as Deer Creek Dry Diggins and later as Caldwell's Upper Store, the town was incorporated in 1850 as Nevada, which means "snow covered" in Spanish. By then there were 10,000 miners within a 3-mile radius of the spot in the river where Marshall had panned. The town grew rapidly, initially from placer mining. The miners were so eager to strike it rich that they even dug up the streets until an irate local merchant resorted to firing a pistol at some offenders.

The eastern end of Lost Hill was especially rich, and in 1850 miners were extracting as much as a quart of gold (worth $6,000) a day in this area. Supposedly as much as $8 million was taken from here in 2 years. There were dozens of other mines in the area, too. By 1856 Nevada City was the third-largest city in the state with 10,000 residents, which is hard to believe today. Among some of its more famous residents were future-president Herbert Hoover, who worked here as a miner, and at least three U.S. Senators.

Today the whole town has been declared a national historic landmark, and it's a lovely place to wander and get a sense of what it must have been like in the 19th century. Pick up a walking tour map at the Chamber of Commerce and explore. Most of the buildings date to 1864, the year after a major fire had destroyed most of the town. Drop into the **National Hotel** (1856) at 211 Broad St. and look at the memorabilia on display.

Or go into the **Firehouse No. 1 Museum** at 214 Main St. (☎ 530/265-5468), where among other artifacts are relics from the Donner party and a Chinese altar.

Hours: Summer, daily 11am–4pm; winter, Mon 11am–2:30pm, Tues–Sun 11am–4pm. *Admission:* Free.

On Main Street, browse in the galleries and stores. At no. 132 visit the **South Yuba Canal Building** and **Ott's Assay Office** (☎ 530/265-2692). The first is one of the oldest buildings in town, dating to 1855; the second, dating to 1857, is where James Ott assayed samples of ore that set off the silver rush to the Comstock Lode in 1859. Over on Spring Street at no. 325, the **Miner's Foundry Cultural Center** (☎ 530/265-5040) was built in 1856 to make machinery for the mining and lumber industries. This is where the Pelton Water Wheel, useful in deep quartz mining, was invented in 1878. Today it's used as a community center and worth stopping in just to see what's happening in the town.

A good place to stop for lunch in this bookish town is at **Broad Street Books,** 426 Broad St. (☎ 530/265-4204), where you can enjoy sandwiches, soups, breads, and good baked items in a space adjacent to the bookstore or outside.

Hours: Mon–Fri 7am–5pm, Sat 8am–7pm, Sun 8am–5:30pm.

About 28 miles north of Nevada City, along the San Juan Ridge, major hydraulic mining took place. This required a lot of water, so high up in the Sierras that reservoirs were built to supply it to hundreds of mines along the ridge via a system of canals and flumes. One can see remnants of this at **Malakoff Diggins State Historic Park,** 23579 N. Bloomfield Rd. (☎ 530/265-2740), 26 miles northeast of Nevada City. The site was once one of the biggest hydraulic mines in California and the cause of one of the first environmental battles ever fought in the state.

At the center of this 3,000-acre park lies the townsite of North Bloomfield, which had a population of 1,500 in the 1870s when the mine was operating. Gold had first been discovered here in a creek in 1851 by three miners who came from Nevada City. One of them went back to the city for supplies and was followed back by many folks who had seen his golden nuggets and were hoping to get rich, too. The followers, though, did not find any riches, so they named the Creek Humbug. Gold was later rediscovered, and a settlement called Humbug was established, boasting two hotels and two general stores and a population of 500 in 1857 when the town filed for a post office. Because the residents felt the name was too undignified, they renamed the town North Bloomfield.

Today many of the buildings have been restored, and you can visit the general store, the blacksmith shop, the pharmacy, and a few other buildings. By 1860 the surface gold had been exhausted, and most miners had shipped out to the Nevada silver mines. Jules Poquillon, though, purchased all claims at depreciated prices and raised enough capital to begin hydraulic mining to extract gold in 1866. He built dams and ditches to bring the enormous amount of water needed for this kind of mining. Hundreds of Chinese worked on these projects, and there were in fact 2 Chinese townships here. By 1876 the mine was operating with 7 huge water cannons. The population was 750, and the town contained 5 hotels, 8 saloons, 4 stores, and a half dozen other businesses. Whole hillsides were washed away by the enormous force of the water, which was powerful enough to hurl 50-pound boulders 200 feet. The debris and silt generated by the process and the millions of gallons of water used daily in the mine caused flooding in nearby Yuba City and Marysville and navigational problems in the Sacramento River. San Francisco Bay was even filling with silt.

The Sacramento Valley farmers brought suit against the mining company, and in January 1884 Judge Lorenzo Sawyer handed down a decision in their favor. The mine was forced to close because of the expenses of the lawsuit and the cost of meeting the regulations demanded by the judgment. The population of 2,000 dwindled until the town was abandoned and left to decay. Some of the original buildings are still standing and can be toured. There's also a lake for swimming and fishing and many miles of hiking trails through the old mining pit, the townsite area, and along old wagon roads. The park is particularly lovely in spring when wildflowers bloom and in fall when the leaves turn to their autumn colors. Tours and campfire programs are conducted during the summer. A museum features a movie that explains hydraulic mining.

Hours (for museum and visitor center): Summer, daily 10am–5pm; winter, weekends only 10am–4pm. ***Admission:*** $5 per vehicle.

Wine lovers will want to try the wines of Nevada County. In the 1870s there were several wineries and 500 acres planted with vines. Today the **Nevada City Winery** operates only a couple of blocks from where it stood more than a century ago, at 321 Spring St. (☎ 530/265-9463).

Hours: Daily noon to 5pm.

The town also has a brewery, the **Nevada City Brewery** at 75 Bost Ave. (☎ 530/265-2446), which is open for tours and tastings.

Hours: May–Dec Fri 3–5pm, Sat 1–5pm.

From either Grass Valley or Nevada City you can drive the Yuba–Donner Scenic Byway, which loops through the towns of Downieville, Sierra City, and Truckee in the Sierras.

Lodging in Nevada City

On a hill overlooking Nevada City, the **Red Castle Inn,** 109 Prospect St., Nevada City, CA 95959 (☎ 530/265-5135), is a stunning Gothic Revival brick mansion—a rare phenomenon in California—that was built in 1860. It makes for an ideal retreat where you can escape such distractions of the modern age as televisions and telephones and enjoy the strains of Mozart instead. Conley and Mary Louis Weaver have been innkeepers for 10 years and know how to make guests feel welcome. They care about history and have lovingly restored and now maintain this home. Inside you will find pine floors, doors with porcelain knobs, and brilliant chandeliers. There are four rooms and three suites, all beautifully decorated. Ceilings are high in the rooms on the main and lower floor. These rooms also have verandas or access to garden areas of their own. Both the Garden Room and the Forest View room have lacy-canopied queen beds. On the second floor are three-room suites with lower ceilings, while the top floor contains the Garret Suite, a charmer with sloping ceilings, windows at floor level, and a great view from the tree-top veranda.

Guests will find plenty of books in the parlor along with comfortable wing chairs and a sofa. An afternoon tea of cucumber sandwiches, scones, cakes, and tarts is served (the tea is brewed in Mary's antique silver teapot). The buffet breakfast is special, too, and will always feature a historic dish, like Indian pudding or Miner's biscuits, plus banana bread, quiche, and more. It can be enjoyed in the gardens, on the veranda, or in your room. The gardens are lovely, combining lily pond, lawns, and terraced flower beds filled with cutting flowers.

Rates (incl. breakfast): $110–$150 double.

Elaine and Chuck Matroni are the welcoming owners of the **Deer Creek Inn,** 116 Nevada St., Nevada City, CA 95959 (☎ 530/265-0363, fax 530/265-0980), which sits on the edge of town on an acre of land alongside Deer Creek. The gardens are well tended and beautiful, with a rose-covered trellis and gorgeous cherry trees that flower in spring. The house, a Queen Anne Victorian, was built in 1860. It has two parlors furnished with eye-catching pieces like an Oriental fish-bowl table and a grand piano. Although the parlors are comfortable—there's a large TV in one—guests drift into the black-and-white-check kitchen where a bountiful breakfast is prepared and served in the dining room or on the veranda.

There are five uniquely furnished rooms, all named after the women who owned the house formerly. Elaine's Room is tucked away on the lower level of the house and features an iron canopy bed decked out in a rose-patterned comforter and lace canopy. It has a private deck with a view of the creek and a large Roman tub with two shower heads. The other romantic room is Sheryl's, which is decorated in peach and gray and contains a king-size bed piled high with pillows. The bathroom has a clawfoot tub and a sink that is set into an antique dresser. To cap it all off there's a large balcony, too. In some of the smaller rooms, like Winifred's, the clawfoot tub is situated in the main room.

Breakfasts are lavish buffets featuring dishes like apple crisp baked pancakes or cheddar and mushroom baked potatoes. In the evenings wine and hors d'oeuvres are served. Guests also appreciate the refrigerator stocked with complimentary beer and soft drinks. And don't miss the porch overlooking the creek.

Rates (incl. breakfast): $100–$150 double.

Flume's End, 317 S. Pine St., Nevada City, CA 05050 (☎ 530/265-9665), seems to hang out over Gold Run Creek overlooking a natural waterfall. It's set on three wooded acres and is run by friendly Steve and Terriane with her golden retriever guide dog, Jamar. There are six comfortable rooms with private baths and inviting decks. Two are equipped with Jacuzzis. The Creekside is closest to the waterfalls and shares a lower-level sitting room with the Garden room. My favorites are the attic, which has a clawfoot tub in the bathroom, and the cottage, which is separate from the main building and has a wood-burning stove and secluded deck looking out over the woods and waterfall. The sitting room has a TV, wet bar, and refrigerator for guest use, and there's also a fun room with piano and other entertainment possibilities. A full breakfast is served.

Rates (incl. breakfast): $85–$145 double.

The **Parsonage,** 427 Broad St., Nevada City, CA 95959 (☎ 530/265-9478), is rightly named because it was in fact the home of the minister for the nearby Methodist Church. It's a handsome Victorian with porch and picket-fenced garden, conveniently located in town. There are six rooms, all with private baths. Each is furnished with an assortment of family heirlooms and antiques. The largest room is the Victorian room, which has a Victorian bed, vanity, and armoire plus a wicker daybed. The Balcony room has, as you would expect, its own balcony and also a gas-log stove. On weekends a full breakfast is graciously served on a table set with linen and china; weekdays it's continental.

Rates (incl. breakfast): $100–$145 double.

The **National Hotel,** 211 Broad St., Nevada City, CA 95959 (☎ 530/265-4551), resonates with the history of the Mother Lode. It was established in 1852 and served as the headquarters of the local telegraph and telephone and also the Wells Fargo Express Company. Period pieces—such as the grand square piano, which was shipped around Cape Horn, and the old clock—enhance the lobby. During the gold rush days, the bar and lounge were crowded with men making all kinds of deals, the medium of exchange being gold dust, which could be traded for 12½-cent tokens. Some of these can be seen in the cabinet on the lobby stairway landing. The back bar came, though, from the Spreckels Mansion on Nob Hill (though the era is right). Early celebrity guests, like Lola Montez and Black Bart, have been replaced with more modern stars like Lindsay Wagner, Ann Baxter, Tim Conway, and Governor Jerry Brown. The building is of brick with a covered balcony on the first floor and an open balcony on the second. There are 43 rooms, 30 with private baths; all have telephones. Some have canopy and four-poster beds.

Converted coal oil lamps hang in the Victorian **dining room,** where a continental menu features steaks and such dishes as chicken marsala and pork loin with apricot brandy sauce. Prices range from $13 to $23. There's an outdoor pool, too.

Rates: $78–$134. *Dining hours:* Daily 7am–9:30pm.

Dining in Nevada City

Try the dining room at the **National Hotel** (see the Lodging reviews above for more information). Otherwise, the best dining is found in Nevada City at the following.

Friar Tuck's, 11 N. Pine St. (☎ 530/265-9093), is an atmospheric spot with its hand-hewn beams and large, wooden bar imported from Liverpool. The restaurant offers a series of dining rooms with high-back oak booths. It's also probably the liveliest place in town. It's known for its cheese fondues, and also for hot-oil fondues in which you cook your own Swiss meatballs, beef, shrimp, scallops, or chicken. In addition there are about a dozen dishes ranging from pan-roasted salmon with a ginger-lime sauce to filet mignon wrapped with bacon, grilled, and served on caramelized shallots with a whiskey sauce. Prices range from $15 to $23.

Hours: Sun–Thurs 5–9pm, Fri–Sat 5–10pm.

Cirino's, 309 Broad St. (☎ 530/265-2246), is a fun, casual place with red gingham-covered tables and a long mahogany saloon bar. Historic photographs add character to the atmosphere. The Italian fare is familiar and heart-warming—linguine with shrimp, veal and chicken parmigiana, veal piccata, and spaghetti bolognese. Prices range from $9 to $15.

Hours: Daily 11am–4pm; Sun–Thurs 5–9pm, Fri–Sat 5–10pm.

Posh Nosh, 318 Broad St. (☎ 530/265-6064), has an inviting, tree-shaded brick patio plus wine cellar dining. It's a great place for lunch. You can select from 20 or so sandwiches made with sourdough, rye, or whole-wheat bread and filled with everything from Southwest roast beef (with everything from onions, jack cheese, chili, and barbecue sauce, to shrimp topped with creamy dill sauce, melted jack cheese, and sautéed mushrooms). Salads, pastas, vegetarian specialties, and burgers round out the menu. At dinner you'll find three or four daily specials. The week I was there, for example, I enjoyed a fresh salmon with a basil cream sauce, which arrived with potato pancakes and applesauce. These specials will range from $8 to $12, while the main menu ranges from $5 to $10.

Hours: Daily 11:30–4pm; Sun–Thurs 6–9pm, Fri–Sat 6–10pm.

Grass Valley & Nevada City
Special & Recreational Activities

Biking: The Chambers of Commerce publish pamphlets outlining a dozen mountain-biking loops in the Grass Valley/Nevada City area. For rentals try **Samurai Mountain Bikes** in Grass Valley (☎ 530/477-0858).

Camping: **Malakoff Diggins State Park** (☎ 530/265-2740) has 30 campsites open in summer only.

The **Tahoe National Forest** has seven or so campgrounds in Western Nevada County. The headquarters is in Nevada City at Highway 49 and Coyote Street (☎ 530/265-4531).

There's also camping at **Bullard's Bar Reservoir** (☎ 530/692-3200) and at **Rollins Lake** (☎ 530/346-2212), which is off Highway 174 towards Colfax.

Canoeing/Kayaking: **Wolf Creek Wilderness**, 411 Commercial St., Nevada City (☎ 530/265-9653), offers guided trips as well as classes.

Fishing: North and South Forks of the Yuba River are prime fishing areas. You might also try Englebright Lake, west on Highway 20, and Bullard's Bar Reservoir, west on Highway 49.

Gold Panning: This can be done along the Yuba and Bear Rivers and Deer Creek. **Yuba Trek Adventures,** P. O. Box 642, Grass Valley, CA 95945 (☎ 530/292-4377), offers tours plus dredging lessons.

Golfing: Try **Alta Sierra Country Club**, 144 Tammy Way, Grass Valley (☎ 530/273-2010), or the **Nevada County Country Club**, 1040 Main St., Grass Valley (☎ 530/272-6586).

Hiking: There are several trails in Malakoff Diggins State Historic Park and also in Empire Mine State Historic Park. The Tahoe National Forest also has 125 miles of trails. For information on the latter write to Tahoe National Forest, U.S. Forest Service, Coyote Street and Highway 49, Nevada City, CA 95959 (☎ 530/265-4531). The local chambers of commerce also publish a pamphlet describing 16 different nearby trails.

Houseboating: On Englebright Reservoir and Bullard's Bar Reservoir (40 minutes from Nevada City off Highway 49).

Llama Trekking: A company of the same name at 14223 Highland Dr., Grass Valley (☎ 530/273-8105), offers 1-day and longer pack trips.

Skiing: **Sugar Bowl** (☎ 530/426-3651) and **Donner Ski Ranch** (☎ 530/426-3635), both in Norden, and **Soda Springs** in Truckee (☎ 530/426-3663) are only 45 minutes away. The Tahoe resorts are about an hour away. For cross-country, the facilities at Eagle Mountain are only 30 minutes from Nevada City.

Swimming: Try Scotts Flat Lake near Nevada City and Rollins Lake between Grass Valley and Colfax. There's also swimming in Blair Lake in Malakoff Diggins State Park.

Tennis: Public tennis courts are available at some local parks and high schools. Call the chambers of commerce for details.

White-water Rafting: Contact **Tributary Whitewater Tours,** 20480 Woodbury Drive, Grass Valley (☎ 530/346-6812).

AUBURN, COLOMA, PLACERVILLE, CAMINO & POLLUCK PINES

AUBURN

One of the first mining camps in the state, Woods Dry Diggings, stood on the site of what is Auburn. Gold had first been discovered in the Auburn Ravine by Claude Chana in May 1848. Soon prospectors, drawn to the diggings because in 1849 miners could make $1,000 to $1,500 a day from their labors, were pouring in, and camps were being established throughout the area. Moreover, Auburn became a major transportation hub connecting Sacramento and Grass Valley. Like many other mining towns, though, it was destroyed by fire. Afterwards, the townspeople built brick houses with iron doors and window shutters, and these can be seen in Old Town today.

COLOMA

What is left of the town of Coloma lies along the South Fork of the American River. Today it has a population of 175, but in the 1850s the population was a huge 12,000: This is where it all started. On January 24, 1848, James Marshall first spied gold particles in the tailrace of a mill he was building for Capt. John Sutter, setting off a "gold fever" that spread across continents. Although Sutter and Marshall had tried to keep the discovery secret until they had secured the land grant legally, word got out, and by May the news was being reported in San Francisco by Sam Brannan, who paraded the streets waving a bottle containing gold and yelling, "Gold, Gold, Gold from the American River!" Reports reached all across California and abroad to Mexico, South America, Hawaii, and the East Coast, prompting mass emigration to California and to the foothills of Sierra.

The pack-mule trails from Sutter's Fort (now Sacramento) to Coloma were soon being traveled by all kinds of traffic originating from San Francisco, Oregon, and other points. As a result, the Coloma road became the first of California's stage routes. From Coloma the argonauts fanned out, establishing claims throughout the surrounding region along the South, Middle, and North Forks of the American River. These old river bar camps are not traceable today because many were only temporary encampments.

Miners would build their shacks or pitch their tents around a central tent where they could gamble and buy liquor; there was usually an adjoining dance house where you'd find "squawking violins, dark-skinned señoritas puffing cigarettes, and more liquors on sale." (Oftentimes at these dances, the men would tie a handkerchief or bell on their arm to signify that they were playing the role of a woman on the dance floor.) On the main streets tradesmen would operate their businesses out of all kinds of structures—some stone, some canvas, and some wooden. Scores of these camps existed, but not a trace of them remains today, even though it is reckoned that $10-million worth of gold was taken from the Middle Fork of the American River alone.

At Coloma, the miners were lucky to average one ounce of gold after standing all day in icy water, or picking and shoveling in canyons where the temperatures reached 90 to 100 degrees. The placer deposits were soon exhausted, and the town became a quiet agricultural retreat again.

The rhythm of the town today is a lot more sedate than it was back then, but some of the flavor of the Gold Rush town can be experienced at the **Marshall Gold Discovery State Historic Park,** 310 Back St., P.O. Box 265, Coloma, CA 95613 (☎ 530/622-3470). Start here and view the films and the exhibits about the Gold Rush era. Little remains of the town, but if you walk any one of the four trails in the park, you'll get some idea of the history of the place.

The **Discovery Tour** takes you on a half-mile loop. First, you visit a mining exhibit, which shows the equipment needed for the three methods of gold mining—placer, hardrock, and hydraulic—used in the region. Then it's on to two stone Chinese stores, all that remains of a large Chinese settlement in Coloma. From here the tour leads you to the replica of Sutter's Sawmill, where the Gold Rush was sparked. Demonstrations are given of the operation. The trail then leads you down to the river, to the original site of the mill on the South Fork of the American River and the spot where Marshall made his remarkable discovery.

Another trail takes you along Main Street to the school house and back. Each building or site is identified by a plaque and a short history. On **Historic Demonstration Days,** which are held several times a year, Gold Rush–era trades are demonstrated. The tinsmith pounds out lanterns and candlesticks, the blacksmith tends the fire and hammers out horseshoes and hardware, and the gunsmith mends firearms.

You can also hike up the hill to the poignant **statue of John Marshall** looking out over the river valley, pointing in the direction of the spot where he found gold. He is buried here under this monument. Farther down the hill, the cabin he lived in until 1868 has been restored. It's sad to remember that Marshall benefited little from his discovery and in fact was forced to live on a small state pension from 1872 to 1878, when the pension was allowed to lapse after people criticized his drinking habits. Marshall died bitter, lonely, and poor at age 75. Be sure to stop and see the wooden **Emanuel Church,** which was built by Episcopalians and Methodists in 1856. James Marshall's funeral was held here in 1885, and from its front yard there's a fine view of the valley.

While you're here, walk or drive out Cold Springs Road to the **Pioneer Cemetery.** Among the people buried here are members of the Gooch–Monroe family. Nancy Gooch was brought to California as a slave in 1849, secured her freedom during the chaos of the Gold Rush, and did laundry and other chores until she had amassed enough money to purchase the freedom of her son and his wife, Andrew and Sara Ellen, in Missouri. They came to California by covered wagon and together planted orchards, bought land, and prospered. The last of the line, Jim Monroe, died in 1988 at age 99.

Hours (visitor center): Daily 10am–5pm; closed major winter holidays. *Admission:* $5 per vehicle.

Lodging in Coloma

Although the address of the **Coloma Country Inn,** 345 High St., Box 502, Coloma, CA 95613 (☎ 530/622-6919), would suggest its being located in a town, it is in fact idyllically situated on 5 acres surrounded by a 300-acre state park. The main farmhouse, which was built in 1852, has been very charmingly decorated by Cindi Ehrgott with American antiques, quilts, folk art, and crockery. In the hallway, for example, you'll find a coat rack supporting straw and other hats, plus a fringed shawl and a fishing rod and hamper. In the living room, which is often warmed by a wood fire, the floor is covered with an Oriental rug, while bird boxes, Shaker boxes, baskets, and other country pieces add character to the decor.

Each of the five rooms in the house has a different decor. Three have private bathrooms with clawfoot tubs; the other two share a bath. The Rose Room has its own private brick patio and rose garden and is furnished with a high-back Victorian bed and wicker loveseat, among other pieces. The Eastlake Room has a bed and dresser in that style plus a wicker table and cushioned bunk seats, all set against pink walls. Two suites are located in the Carriage House, a lovely building with cupola that was built in 1898. The Geranium Suite, which has a kitchenette, is the most secluded; French doors lead out into a fragrant kitchen garden with a grape arbor. The Cottage Suite has two bedrooms furnished with brass beds plus kitchen and bathroom. The front porch of the main house is a favorite lolling place; guests can also wander down to the pond to use the canoe or watch for green or blue herons and belted kingfishers, or take a basket and go blackberrying in summer.

A full breakfast is served in the dining room or outside under the pergola overlooking the pond. Besides the quality of the accommodations and the warmth of the hospitality, there are other reasons to stay here. Alan Ehrgott is a veteran balloon pilot and offers hot-air balloon flights along the American River Canyon ($165 per person with four-person minimum or a specially priced package at $215 per person). The Ehrgotts offer white-water rafting packages, too. No credit cards are accepted.

Rates: $94 double (shared bath), $109 double (private bath); suites $130 and $180.

Placerville

Placerville, originally known as Old Dry Diggins (because the miners had to cart the soil down to running water to wash out the gold) and then as Hangtown, was established in 1848. The story goes that it was discovered by William Daylor, a rancher who along with a couple of partners and some Indians took out more than $17,000 in one short week's work. By the fall of 1848 the place was swarming with miners and had replaced Coloma as the place to be. By the next year, Old Dry Diggins had a more dubious distinction and a name change.

Not everyone was willing to work for his or her reward, so crime soon became a problem. Miners were being murdered in isolated camps along the American River, while others were only relieved of their gold at knifepoint. In early 1849 three miners were accused of stealing, and a crowd met to decide their punishment when someone shouted "Hang them," so the first known hanging in the Mother Lode took place at the center of town. Today a **plaque** marks the spot where the Hangman's tree stood at 305 Main St. As the town's reputation for lynch law spread, it became known as Hangtown.

By 1854 Hangtown was California's third-largest town (after Sacramento and San Francisco), and the more sober residents wanted to change its morbid name. They chose Placerville, and the town was incorporated as such in 1854, becoming the seat of El Dorado County in 1857. In the 1850s Placerville had thrived as the western terminus of the Overland Trail. After the discovery of the Comstock lode in 1859, the town continued to thrive when the Placerville–Carson Road (Highway 50 today) witnessed the greatest era of freighting and staging ever recorded.

Today, the streets still follow the old contours of the hills, ravines, and pack-mule trails along Hangtown Creek. Visitors can still get a sense of the earlier days by following the walking tour and seeing the historic buildings that stand on Main Street. A copy of the walking tour is available from the El Dorado Chamber of Commerce.

On the corner of Sacramento and Main streets stands the statue of a man named **Snowshoe Thompson,** a legendary figure who, for 13 years from 1855 to 1868, carried mail sacks weighing 60 to 90 pounds across the Sierras every 2 weeks. He hiked more than 8,000 vertical feet up to the Sierra summit and then skied down to Genoa near Carson City in Nevada, where he picked up the mail for the return trip. Once, he carried a printing press over the mountains, section by section; another time he skied coolly through a pack of wolves devouring some prey; and on another occasion he rescued a man who was almost frozen to death in a log cabin. He labored without pay and was only replaced when the railroad was cut through the mountains. He lobbied for a just settlement from the American government but failed and was instead supported by grateful members of the community until his death in 1872.

Among some of the town's other famous citizens was J.M. Studebaker, who made wheelbarrows for the miners from 1853 to 1858 before moving to South Bend, Indiana, to make his wagons and later cars of the same name. A **plaque** marks the site of his shop at 543 Main St. Another famous Gold Rush figure got his start here, too. Mark Hopkins purchased groceries and supplies in Sacramento, then carted them to Hangtown to open a store, and made a fortune.

The **Cary House,** at 300 Main St., stands on the site of the old Eldorado Hotel, where legend has it the "hangtown fry" was invented in 1849. It is said that a prospector who had struck it rich rushed into the saloon and ordered the bartender to cook up the most expensive meal in the house. The cook emerged from the kitchen and announced that the most expensive items on the menu were eggs, bacon, and oysters. And thus the first hangtown fry was created. The Cary House itself holds a lot of legends. The three-story brick hotel was built in 1857 and became the headquarters for the stage lines. Gold bullion en route to the mint in San Francisco was often dumped on the porch. It was also here that Horace Greeley descended from the stagecoach at the end of his hair-raising journey across the Sierras led by the famous stagecoach driver Hank Monk. Greeley addressed a crowd from the hotel's balcony in his campaign for president in 1868.

Much of the history of the area can be gleaned at the **El Dorado County Historical Museum,** 100 Placerville Dr. (☎ 530/621-5865), from its mining displays and replica of a country store. The museum's collection of vehicles includes a wooden wheelbarrow, a Concord stagecoach, a horse-drawn buggy, and a steam engine. In the museum yard, Pelton water wheels and other mining machinery are displayed.

Hours: Wed–Sat 10am–4pm; Sun noon–4pm. *Admission:* Free.

At Hangtown's **Gold Bug Park,** 549 Main St. (☎ 530/622-0832), visitors can take a self-guided audio tour through a restored gold mine. The 61-acre park also offers hiking trails and picnicking facilities.

Hours: June–Sept daily 10am–4pm. *Admission:* $1.

Today's Highway 50 also parallels another road that was built during the mining era, the **Placerville Road,** which was located at a lower elevation than the Carson–Placerville Road and could be kept open year-round. But even before the road was formally opened in the late 1850s, J.B. Crandall's Pioneer Stage Company was operating between Placerville and Genoa, Nevada, a journey that took 24 hours. The first Overland Mail from Salt Lake City to California traveled this route, too, arriving in California at 1pm on July 19, 1858. Once the Comstock Lode was discovered, the road became a major artery for mule trains, wagons, Concord coaches, and those inveterate riders of the west, the Pony Express. The traffic was enormous, and Placerville was at the center of it all, with 320 tons of freight passing through in 1864 and 1865.

Today, if you drive old highway 50 via Camino and Pollock Pines, you'll find markers indicating the remount stops along the **Pony Express Route** and other landmarks. From April 1860 to June 1861, Placerville was a relay stop on the Central Overland Express, and from here the first eastbound rider set out. From July to October 1861, it was the western terminus of the Pony Express. Among the legendary figures of this route were the men who drove the stages as well as the men who plundered them. Among the former was Hank Monk; among the latter was Thomas Poole, who with a band of 14 men stopped a stage in 1869 robbing it of eight sacks of bullion and a treasure chest.

Lodging in Placerville

In Placerville's heyday, **The Cary House,** 300 Main St., Placerville, CA 95667 (☎ 530/622-4271), was the town's finest hotel and the place where the stage stopped, dropping off such famous visitors as Black Bart and Horace Greeley, who addressed a crowd from the balcony here when he was seeking nomination for the presidency in 1868. Although the current building dates to 1915, it is in fact a replica of the original, which was built in 1857. It's loaded with Victorian atmosphere. The lobby features stained glass windows, rich red carpeting, and a Victorian sofa and desk. A grand mahogany staircase leads from the lobby to the rooms, all spacious and pleasantly decorated. They all have private baths and cable TV. Some have a full kitchen or kitchenette, but none have telephones. This is a terrific value.

Rates: $55–$85.

The **Chichester–McKee House,** 800 Spring St., Placerville, CA 95667 (☎ 530/626-1882), is a lovely Victorian-style house that was built for a local lumber magnate in 1892. It's set on a steep, sloping bank and has a rock garden in back and a veranda with swing-seat in front. The building has been lovingly restored, revealing fine fretwork, carved moldings, stained glass, and fireplaces. Heidi the dachshund will greet you and even entertain you by barking out the answers to simple arithmetical problems.

There are three guest rooms. The Carson Room, for example, contains a brass bed set off by a Lone Star quilt; the Yellow Rose room boasts a bed with fishnet canopy and oak furnishings. Each room has a convenient sink; bathrobes are provided for the hallway bathroom, which is shared by all three rooms. A full breakfast is served. There is a comfortable living room plus a library filled with books and games and a couple of old Victrolas. The veranda provides a pleasant place to sit.

Rates (incl. breakfast): $85–$95.

CAMINO & POLLOCK PINES

From Placerville, travel out along Highway 50 to Apple Hill and the towns of **Camino** and **Pollock Pines.** This is **apple and wine country.** There are about 40 or so ranches that sell their apples—along with pies, cider, and other apple products—directly to the public. Obviously, spring (when the trees blossom) and fall (when they're laden with fruit) are the best seasons to come. But you can also visit this area during the winter to select and cut your own Christmas tree. As for the vineyards, most are small and often family owned so that a day of leisurely wine tasting can be a very pleasant, unhurried experience capped off by a gourmet picnic at one of the vineyards along the way. It's far less daunting than the frenzy that reigns in the Napa Valley.

There are several vineyards worth visiting in El Dorado County. **Boeger Winery,** 1709 Carson Rd., north of Highway 50, Placerville, CA 95667 (☎ 530/622-8094), produces a smooth and spicy merlot, a light oak chardonnay, plus zinfandel, barbera, sauvignon blanc, and several other varietals. **Latcham,** 2860 Omo Ranch Rd., P.O. Box 80, Mt. Aukum, CA 95656 (☎ 530/620-6834), produces a rich and creamy chardonnay, a fruity and light oak cabernet, and several other varietals. **Charles B. Mitchell Vineyards,** 8221 Stoney Creek Rd., Somerset, CA 95684 (☎ 530/620-3467), produces a dozen different wines, a classic zinfandel among them. **Sierra Vista,** 4560 Cabernet Way, Placerville, CA 95667 (☎ 530/622-7221), is known for its Rhone-style wines and also for a rich and soft cabernet sauvignon and a fruity chardonnay. Finally, **Windwalker Vineyards,** 7360 Perry Creek Rd., Somerset, CA 95684 (☎ 530/620-4054), is a family vineyard that produces pleasant chardonnays and sauvignon blancs. For more information about the wineries call or write the **El Dorado Winery Association,** P.O. Box 1614, Placerville, CA 95667 (☎ 530/446-6562), which can provide you with a map. Boeger is accessed from Placerville via Highway 50 and Carson Road. The other wineries mentioned above—Windwalker, Charles B. Mitchell, Latcham, and Sierra Vista—are clustered off Mt. Aukum Road (E16), between Mt. Aukum and Pleasant Valley.

Lodging in Camino

The **Camino Hotel,** P. O. Box 1197, 4103 Carson Rd., Camino, CA 95709 (☎ 800/220-7740 or 530/644-7740), is located out of town, up in the Apple Hill region. This old loggers' barracks has been lovingly restored and offers a warm welcome to guests. There are nine rooms (three with private bath), each furnished in warm country style. The Wagon Train Room has two double beds covered with quilts, and such decorative accents as cowboy boots, lassos, and a large lithograph of *Man Moves West*. The Granny Smith Room has such granny items as aprons, tea towels, and potholders hung on a line. All of the rooms have bathrobes.

Upstairs there's a deck with a telescope and an enclosed sitting area, which is also home to a couple of exotic birds and many plants and dried herbs. On the ground floor there's a large parlor with pellet-burning stove where guests can get to know each other. A full breakfast is served.

Rates (incl. breakfast): $75–$105 double.

Dining Only in Pleasant Valley

Zachary Jacques, 1821 Pleasant Valley Rd. (☎ 530/626-8045), is the premier dining room in the Placerville area. The cuisine is well-flavored and not overly embellished. In fall and winter, specialties include several game dishes, such as the loin of wild boar with a sauce made of red wine, junipers, red currant, and chestnuts, or the venison prepared with a cognac and green peppercorn sauce. Sadly, on weekends you won't be able to sample the cassoulet, the other specialty of the house, which is served on Wednesday only. The rest of the menu features such dishes as duck with orange sauce, and a rich and redolent chicken breast stuffed with Auvergne blue cheese and served with a Dijon mustard sauce. Prices range from $16 to $22. This is the place to try a hangtown fry as an appetizer.

Hours: Wed–Sat 5:30–9:30pm; Sun 5–8:30pm.

The **Smith Flat House,** 2021 Smith Flat Rd., a quarter mile from Placerville (☎ 530/621-0667), has a lot of history attached to it. The restaurant occupies a building dating to the 1860s, which stood on what was then the Lake Tahoe wagon road and has served as hotel, restaurant, dance hall, and Pony Express post office. There is even a legendary tunnel in the cellar saloon that ran from Weber Creek to White Rock Canyon, from which $18 million in gold (with gold bringing $18 an ounce) was taken. Today, it still serves as a social center. The menu offers a variety of fare, from steaks to teriyaki chicken and fish specials. Prices range from $11 to $16.

Hours: Mon–Sat 11:30am–2pm; Mon–Thurs 5–9pm, Fri–Sat 5–10, Sun 4:30–9pm.

Dining in Pollock Pines

Weird Harold's, 5631 Pony Express Trail, Pollock Pines (☎ 530/644-5272), is a rustic restaurant that is warmed by a central wood fire in winter. The food is hearty, consisting of good quality steaks and seafood, and a handful of stir-fry dishes. Don't expect anything fancy. The halibut, for example, is served with a tartar sauce or with Cajun spices, and the salmon with a dill or béarnaise sauce. The favorite beef dish is prime rib.

Prices range from $10 to $16. Desserts are equally down-home—cheesecake, ice cream, and chocolate mousse.

Hours: Mon–Thurs 5–9pm, Fri–Sat 5-10pm, Sun 4–9pm.

Auburn, Coloma & Placerville Area
Special & Recreational Activities

Ballooning: Ballooning trips are offered by **Whitewater Connection.** For complete information, see "White-water Rafting," below.

Hiking: There are plenty of trails in the Eldorado National Forest that are accessible during the summer and fall. For information contact **Eldorado National Forest Information Center,** 3070 Camino Heights Dr., Camino, CA 95709 (☎ 530/644-6048).

White-water Rafting: Whitewater Connection, Coloma (☎ 530/622-6446, fax 530/622-7192), offers trips on the North, South, and Middle Forks of the American River and also on the Stanislaus, as well as on some other California rivers.

The Gold Country South of Sacramento: From Amador City to Sonora

Distances in Miles: Amador City/Sutter Creek, 150; Angels Camp, 130; Sonora/Columbia, 140; Groveland, 150; Mariposa, 171

Estimated Driving Times: 2½ hours to Amador City/Sutter Creek; 2¼ hours to Angels Camp; 2¼ hours to Sonora/Columbia; 2½ hours to Groveland; 3 hours to Mariposa

---

Driving: Most of the destinations in this chapter are on or near Highway 49.

From Sacramento, take Highway 16 to its intersection with 49; from there Amador City is just a few miles south, followed by Sutter Creek and Jackson; Volcano and Indian Grinding Rock State Historic Park are both off Highway 88, east of Jackson, while Ione is off Highway 88 to the west of Jackson. Other destinations are south of Jackson.

Angels Camp is near the intersection of Highways 49 and 4. Murphys and Bear Valley are reached by traveling east on Highway 4 off Highway 49. The remaining destinations are on Highway 49 or a short detour from it.

Further Information: Contact the **Amador County Chamber of Commerce,** 125 Peek St., P.O. Box 596, Jackson, CA 95642 (☎ 209/223-0350); the **Columbia Chamber of Commerce,** P.O. Box 1824, Columbia, CA 95310 (☎ 209/536-1672); the **Tuolumne County Visitors Bureau,** P.O. Box 4020, Sonora, CA 95370 (☎ 209/533-4420); or the **Mariposa County Chamber of Commerce,** 5158 Hwy. 140, P.O. Box 425, Mariposa, CA 95338 (☎ 209/966-2456).

The so-called Southern Mother Lode towns are rich in history and offer many opportunities for great weekends. If you wish, you can try your hand at gold-panning, and there are plenty of other attractions and activities to keep you busy.

Events & Festivals to Plan Your Trip Around

May: At the **Calaveras County Fair & International Jumping Frog Jubilee,** held during the third weekend in May, there are daily frog jumps, carnival rides, rodeo and horse events, and other good old-fashioned entertainment. For information write P.O. Box 96, Angels Camp, CA 95222 (☎ 209/736-2561).

Visit several of the mines that brought forth so much wealth and also some of the atmospheric ghost towns like Mokelumne Hill and Volcano in Amador County, and Hornitos, west of Mariposa in the southern reaches of Gold Country. Mokelumne Hill and Hornitos really do have a sad, authentic sense of having been abandoned.

In this area, too, is one of the best preserved Gold Rush towns in the state, Columbia, where you can really imagine what life was like back in the old mining days. Jamestown is another place to capture the old days when the railroad was king and those old steam engines were featured in such legendary movies as *High Noon* and *Union Pacific.*

If history and gold dust are not your bag, there are other possibilities to pursue. Amador County is, in fact, securing quite a reputation for its wines—zinfandels in particular—and you can enjoy tasting them at the small, often family-owned wineries along the back roads of the county.

As for sports, there's white-water rafting on the South and North Forks of the American River and skiing at Bear Valley. If you're looking for some unusual sports, come to Angels Camp when the frog-jumping contests are held and think back on Mark Twain and Bret Harte, who started their early careers right here in Calavaras County.

EXPLORING AMADOR COUNTY

The boundaries of Amador County are set in the north by the Cosumnes River and in the south by the Mokelumne River, both famous mining sites for the forty-niners.

Amador City began as a mining center in 1848, but the placers were not very rich, and the town really was put on the map by quartz mining and, in particular, by the opening of the Bonanza quartz mine in 1869. This mine yielded $40,000 during the first month's crushing, a production that continued until the 1880s. Today the town is little more than a few buildings at the side of the road, most prominent of which is the Amador Hotel.

Three miles south of Amador City, **Sutter Creek** is an attractive town where you can enjoy browsing the stores along the main street, which still

The Southern Gold Country

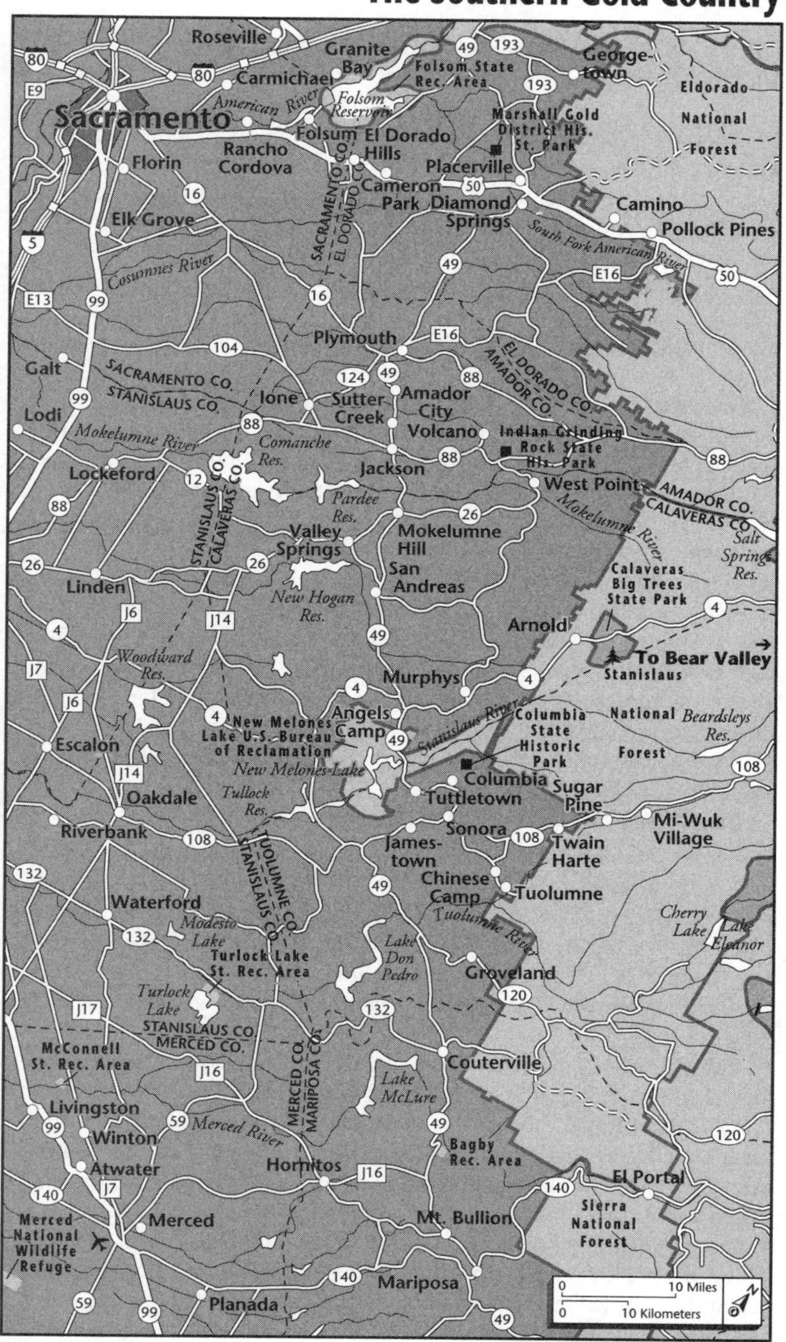

sports a couple of short, wooden arcades. It was named after John Sutter, who first arrived in the region in 1846. Although the Old Eureka Mine was opened in 1852, profitable mining really began with the discovery of the Central Eureka Mine in 1869. This mine has produced more than $17 million over the years and was still operating after Word War II. Leland Stanford had an interest in the Lincoln Mine, which was located between Amador City and Sutter Creek. He had acquired it as payment for a customer's debt; his sale of this share launched him on his way to millionaire status. Take some time to browse the shops on Main and to dart down Eureka Street. Among my favorite galleries on Main is the **Fine Eye,** 71 Main St. (☎ 209/267-0571), which has some very appealing modern arts-and-crafts pieces.

Jackson is the county seat of Amador County, named after a miner named José María Amador. Much history remains in the old buildings that line Main and Court streets today. The National Hotel (detailed in the "Lodging & Dining" section below) has been restored and certainly retains much of its old flavor. Note, too, the Serbian Orthodox **Church of St. Sava,** which stands at one end of town.

The **Amador County Museum,** 225 Church St. (☎ 209/223-6386), has exhibits on gold mining and the history of the county. The most interesting exhibit is the working scale model of the Kennedy Mine. It took the man who built it 9 years to complete and includes the mine's stamping and tailing rooms. It's put into operation on weekends only for 15 minutes and is accompanied by an audio tape. The museum also has an Indian room, a costume room, and other rooms filled with county artifacts and everyday objects.

Hours: Wed–Sun 10am–4pm. *Admission:* By donation.

Gold was first discovered outside of town, along the Mokelumne River, in the spring of 1848 by Capt. Charles Weber, the founder of the city of Stockton. He was followed by Col. J.D. Stevenson, who arrived with some 100 of his men who had been mustered out of the military; the Colonel was responsible for drawing up one of the first mining-law codes. By the 1870s it was all over. The thousands who had come had departed, and not always the richer.

Either Amador City, Sutter Creek, or Jackson can provide a useful base for exploring other nearby attractions in the county.

At **Daffodil Hill,** about 3 miles before the town of Volcano at the junction of Shakeridge Road and Ram's Horn Grade (☎ 209/223-0608), more than 400,000 daffodils bloom each spring. Many people visit the 6-acre gardens and take a picnic along to celebrate the rites of spring. Supposedly, the first bulbs were planted in memory of a pioneer mother who died in 1857, and the tradition of planting continued from year to year until it made for the astonishing display you see today.

Hours: Open only from mid-March for about 4 weeks during daylight hours. *Admission:* Free.

Off Route 88, you can visit the town of **Volcano,** located at the bottom of a deep gash in the mountains. Today there are only a few stores to browse, but back in mining days Volcano had a population of 5,000 and was at the center of a very rich hydraulic mining area. Some historic buildings remain standing, including the stone brewery, the Masonic temple, and the three-story balconied **St. George Hotel,** Main Street (☎ 209/296-4458), which is the most interesting place (it's detailed in the "Dining Only" section below).

Between Pine Grove and Volcano, **Indian Grinding Rock State Historical Park** (☎ 209/296-7488) gives you some idea of what the landscape was like before the arrival of the forty-niners, when the Miwok Indians wintered in the area. Here you can see the rocks they used to grind their staple, acorns, into meal. In one large limestone outcrop you can see more than a thousand mortar cups (or *chaw's*) that have been made in the rock surface. Note the petroglyphs, too. Near the grinding rock stands a roundhouse, where important ceremonies were performed and still are by various tribes today. Elsewhere in the park there are teepee-shaped barkhouses. At the **Chaw'se Regional Museum,** also in the park, you can see traditional Miwok crafts demonstrated.

Hours: Park and museum Mon–Fri 11am–3pm, Sat–Sun 10am–4pm. *Admission:* $5 per vehicle (includes the museum).

There are also 20 or so **wineries** in Amador County, which is famous for producing robust zinfandels. The majority of the vineyards are located along the Shenandoah Valley near Plymouth, with one or two set off in the Jackson Valley around Ione. The wineries are small, often family-owned, enterprises and very relaxing to visit. Here are some of the more interesting, all around Plymouth: **Amador Foothill,** 12500 Steiner Rd., Plymouth (☎ 209/245-6307), which produces fine red and white zinfandels, plus sangiovese and a crisp and dry sauvignon blanc (open weekends noon to 5pm); **Shenandoah,** 12300 Steiner Rd., Plymouth (☎ 209/245-4455), which offers a pleasant floral and spicy sauvignon blanc (open daily 10am to 5pm); **Renwood,** 12225 Steiner Rd., Plymouth (☎ 209/245-6013), which makes a classic and peppery zinfandel (open daily 11am to 4:30pm); **Montevina,** 20680 Shenandoah School Rd., Plymouth (☎ 209/245-6942), which produces a berry-flavored and spicy zinfandel and other varietals and offers an attractive trellised patio for picnicking (open daily 11am to 4pm).

A few miles south of Jackson, along Highway 49, you'll come to a turnoff to **Mokelumne Hill,** which is, at least for me, one of the most hauntingly atmospheric spots in the Gold Country, where you can really get a sense of what it must have been like during the mining years. The main street runs along a ridge, and on it stand several stone and brick buildings, some with characteristic false fronts and traditional iron shutters. There's also an old hotel/saloon and the Odd Fellows Hall, which was formerly the Wells Fargo office. It's hard to imagine that this town was the Calaveras

County seat from 1852 to 1866 and the leading town in the Mother Lode at that time, but it was. Everyone arrived "up on the hill," and the miners came into town to buy, trade, file legal papers, exchange gold, and seek entertainment. Back then, French Hill overlooked the town, so-called because it was worked by a group of French miners who were so successful that they were envied by the Americans, who on one occasion went so far as to attack them under a pretext that they had raised the French flag.

Lodging & Dining in Amador County

Amador City

The **Imperial Hotel,** Main St., P.O. Box 195, Amador City, CA 95601 (☎ 800/242-5594 or 209/267-9172), has much to recommend it. It's located in an extremely quiet, almost nonexistent, town; possesses the finest dining room and most convivial historic bar in the area; and also offers attractive guest rooms. An old brick building which has been a hotel since 1879, the Imperial has been restored by innkeepers Bruce Sherrill and Dale Martin, who have furnished the six rooms upstairs in fine and comfortable style with such unexpected conveniences as heated towel bars and hair dryers. Each is decorated differently. One might have a wicker bed combined with garden print fabrics; another might be decked out with a hand-painted bed and art deco appointments. At the back of the hotel, there's a delightful stone patio enhanced by gardens, fountain, and statuary. It's lovely to have breakfast here. Another nice extra guests appreciate is room service to rooms, balcony, or patio.

The **Oasis Bar** sports a magnificently carved bar, and it's certainly a place to mingle with the locals and other visitors. The food in the adjacent **dining room** is fresh, well-prepared, and graciously served. The menu changes seasonally, but you might find such appetizers as roasted garlic and brie served with lavosh (unleavened bread), which can be followed by a delicious grilled pork loin on sour cherry zinfandel sauce, or equally enticing molasses-glazed salmon on mixed greens with a black-mustard dressing. Entrees include soup or tossed salad and are priced from $16 to $22. Desserts, which change weekly, are also luscious. Try the blackberry-lemon cheesecake covered with lemon and blackberry curd and served with blackberry sauce. The wine list concentrates on wines from Amador and El Dorado counties with an occasional nod to Napa.

Rates (incl. breakfast): $90–$105 double weekends, $75–$85 midweek. *Dining Hours:* Daily 5–9pm.

Sutter Creek

The Foxes, 77 Main St. (Highway 49), P.O. 159, Sutter Creek, CA 95685 (☎ 209/267-5882), is right on the main street but protected from it by an attractive garden. The house was originally built in 1857; it now offers seven rooms, all with private bath and all exquisitely furnished and maintained. The Garden Room is most appealing, with a private entrance, two comfortable chairs in front of the wood-burning fireplace, a half-canopy bed, and a bay window overlooking the gardens. The Fox Den is another charmer, with a library for book lovers. The Anniversary Room contains a large, ornately carved armoire as well as a clawfoot tub in the bathroom. The Honeymoon Suite also has a private entrance, a brick fireplace, and an old-fashioned tub and toilet in the bathroom. Some rooms have TV. A full breakfast is served on silver service and delivered either to your room or the gazebo, weather permitting; guests can choose when it will be served and what they desire from a menu. It's an elegant place, air-conditioned too.

Rates (incl. breakfast): $125–$165 double weekends, $110–$150 midweek.

The Sutter Creek Inn, 75 Main St. (Highway 49), P.O. Box 385, Sutter Creek, CA 95685 (☎ 209/267-5606, fax 209/267-9287), has a more rumpled, relaxed air and a lot of charm thanks to innkeeper Jane Way. It's also on the main street, but well shielded by shrubs and gardens. The house dates back to 1859. The 18 rooms, all with private bath and air-conditioning, offer great variety. Only 3 are in the main house, the rest tucked away in the back off brick pathways shaded by trellised grape arbors. The Tool Shed, for example, contains a swinging bed (it can be stabilized) and a fireplace. The Library Room is filled with shelves of books, while the Garden Cottage boasts a queen canopy bed. Ten rooms, in fact, have fireplaces, and 4 contain swinging beds.

The living room is inviting with its library, piles of magazines, piano, and games. In summer, guests can enjoy lounging in the hammocks and lawn furniture set out in the gardens. Breakfast is served at 9am in the comfortable old kitchen. Handwriting analysis, reflexology, and professional massages are available by appointment.

Rates (incl. breakfast): $105–$150 double weekends, $75–$165 midweek.

The **Picturerock Inn,** 55 Eureka St., Sutter Creek, CA (☎ 209/267-5500), is set on a quiet street only 1½ blocks from Main Street, making for a pleasant and quiet retreat. It occupies a 1914 Craftsman-style home with a front stone porch overlooking a small garden. The interior spaces are handsomely proportioned and crafted from redwood and rosewood, with striking wainscoting, beams, and staircase. The innkeepers have furnished the inn with their collections of oil and watercolor paintings, and also such nostalgic objects as the carousel horse that is displayed in the front parlor. The six rooms, all with private bath, are attractively furnished with iron or pencil poster beds covered with quilts and trimmed with lace, plus armoires and colorful rugs. A full breakfast is served.

Rates (incl. breakfast): $100–$110 double weekends, $85 midweek.

Grey Gables, 161 Hanford St., P.O. Box 1687, Sutter Creek, CA 95685 (☎ 209/267-1039), is located on the main road. It offers eight very attractively decorated rooms that are named after poets. My favorite is the

Browning Room, which is decorated in lavender and teal and furnished with a brass bed and country pine pieces; its bathroom features a clawfoot tub. The other rooms are decorated in a range of palettes and feature everything from Renaissance Revival beds and classic French-style beds combined with armoires. All are carpeted and all have a fireplace. Afternoon tea is served as well as a full breakfast. The fountain and the wisteria and other vines and flowers that grow in the small backyard make it an inviting place to linger.

Rates (incl. breakfast): $115–$145 weekends, $95–$125 midweek.

The **Gold Quartz Inn,** 15 Bryson Dr., Sutter Creek, CA 95685 (☎ 800/752-8738 or 209/267-9155, fax 209/267-9170), is outside town off the highway. It's a modern building designed with some Victorian elements, such as the shingled tower and wraparound porch. The guest rooms have been furnished with mostly Queen Anne reproductions, decorated with floral wallpapers and gilt-framed pictures, and equipped with such modern amenities as private bath, cable TV with HBO, air-conditioning, and telephone. The inn often hosts small business meetings and seminars. A full breakfast is served as well as afternoon tea. There's also a VCR in the parlor and a video library.

Rates (incl. breakfast): $100–$160 double weekends, $90–$135 midweek.

Ione

The Heirloom, 214 Shakeley Lane, P.O. Box 322, Ione, CA 95640 (☎ 209/274-4468), is at the end of a quiet lane and makes for a lovely, romantic retreat. The house was built around 1863 and stands at the center of some lovely gardens. Guests enter into a comfortably furnished living room filled with antiques, books, games, and a piano. Each of the four rooms in the main house is attractively decorated and furnished. My favorite is Springtime, primarily because it has a large, furnished balcony where in spring you can appreciate the scent and the vision of the wisteria and magnolia in the backyard. The room is graced with watercolors by local artists plus Audubon prints, and it has the additional comfort of a wing chair with a floor lamp for reading. Summer contains a handsome Eastlake walnut bed. Autumn, which is the smallest, offers an antique brass bed. It, too, has a semi-private balcony overlooking the garden. Winter has a fireplace and a colonial four-poster covered with a burgundy and blue handmade quilt. If you're seeking privacy, you'll love the rooms in the adobe Cottage, which is fashioned out of hand-hewn cedar, redwood, and pine. The aroma from the wood-burning stoves and the moonlight creeping in through the skylights make for the romance of these two rooms. One room is decked out in Early American style with an antique quilt on the wall; the other is furnished in Early California with a distinct Spanish flavor. A full breakfast is served, as well as afternoon refreshments, either in the delightful gardens, on the porches, in your room, or in the dining room.

Rates (incl. breakfast): $80–$110 double.

Jackson

National Hotel, 2 Water St., Jackson, CA 95642 (☎ 209/223-0500), is another classic Western hostelry built in 1862. It has retained the old-fashioned, Victorian atmosphere. There's an atmospheric saloon, complete with large carved-oak bar, where a piano sing-along takes place on weekends. Upstairs the 30 rooms, all with private bath, are decorated in simple Victorian style. They have no TV or phone. Note too that breakfast is not included, though there is a discount off Sunday brunch with a Saturday-night stay.

The inn's restaurant, **Louisiana House** (☎ 209/223-3448), serves a typical American menu. To start, try the ravioli with red pepper sauce. Main courses include everything from orange roughy meunière to veal with an Amador county zinfandel-raspberry sauce and shiitake mushrooms. Prices range from $14 to $20.

Rates: $55 double (Sat only, $75, including a $20 discount off dinner in the restaurant and $10 off Sun brunch). *Dining Hours:* Fri 5:30–9:30pm, Sat 5:30–10pm, Sun 10–2pm and 5:30–8:30pm.

The **Court Street Inn,** 215 Court St., Jackson, CA 95642 (☎ 209/223-0416, fax 209/223-5429), is set 2 blocks from Main Street in a home that was built in 1870. There are eight rooms to choose from, each decorated in different colors. The decorative theme of the Peiser Room is the rose, with cabbage rose wallpaper, rose-patterned linen, and a rose-topped wicker canopy bed. Added interest is provided by the ruby-colored converted oil lamp and the old shoeshine stand. The Banker Room is much plainer with its pine furnishings and mint green and peach color scheme; it has a small deck. Lilac and ivy predominate in the Blair Suite, which has a sitting room, a whirlpool tub, and a wood-burning stove. The tin ceilings in the parlor and dining room are striking. The parlor has comfortable leather-studded seating and two conversation pieces—an old gramophone and a player piano. A full breakfast is served in the attractive dining room. Complimentary late afternoon refreshments are also served.

Rates (incl. breakfast): $105–$145 double.

Dining Only in Amador County

Sutter Creek

At **Zinfandels,** 1 Hanford St. (☎ 209/267-5008), the decor draws upon the local wineries for inspiration. Walls feature photographs of the wineries and their wine makers. Even the color scheme of burgundy and green underlines the theme. Small wood tables are set with runners in a vintage style. To start, try the crisp polenta topped with mushrooms, garlic, shallots, and smoked bacon—the best anywhere. The menu changes weekly, but it will likely feature three or so pasta or risotto dishes, like the Drunkard's Pasta (fettucine with whiskey-fennel sausage, portobella mushrooms, Kalamata olives, garlic, shallots, red wine, crushed red chilies, pine nuts and tomato puree). Among the entrees there might be fresh fish sauced with citrus ginger beurre blanc, or chicken breast topped with caramelized onions and melted Gorgonzola cheese. Prices range from $13 to $14. The chef formerly worked at Greens, the famous vegetarian restaurant in San Francisco, so he will always happily prepare a special vegetarian dish. For dessert there are good fruit cobblers made with pears or cranberries, plus such items as chocolate pecan pie. The extensive wine list features about 60% local wines.

Hours: Tues–Sun 5:30–9:30pm.

Ron and Nancy's Palace Restaurant & Saloon, 76 Main St. (☎ 209/267-1355), has a saloon bar up front, where the locals gather to chat and sometimes to enjoy sing-alongs. The restaurant in the back is decked out in garish Victorian style. The menu offers a typical array of steak, veal, and chicken dishes but also such choices as sautéed halibut with garlic, capers, lemon, and dry vermouth. This is a casual, comfortable place. Prices range from $12 to $18.

Hours: Daily 11:30am–3pm and 5–9pm.

Jackson

The **Upstairs Restaurant,** 164 Main St. (☎ 209/223-3342), offers some of the town's finest cuisine in an atmosphere of romance created by candlelight, fresh white tablecloths, and large bouquets of fresh flowers. The menu is innovative and broad, offering everything from simple pasta (fettucine Alfredo) and seafood (trout sautéed with lemons, capers,and roasted pine-nut sauce) to poultry (duck grilled with blackberry-ginger sauce) and meat dishes (pork tenderloin with apple and walnut compote). Prices range from $11 to $19.

Hours: Tues–Sun 11:30am–2:30pm and 5:30–9pm.

Volcano

Drop in to the bar or enjoy a meal at the **St. George Hotel,** Main Street (☎ 209/296-4458). There's only one entree offered each night, and it will be something straightforward like roast pork, roast lamb, or prime rib, plus soup, salad, dessert, and coffee. The price ranges from $12 to $17, depending on the main course being offered that day.

Hours: Wed–Thurs and Sun 7pm dinner seating; Fri–Sat 8pm dinner seating.

Amador County
Special & Recreational Activities

Camping: Indian Grinding Rock State Historic Park (☎ 209/296-7488), which is described in more detail above, has 23 year-round family camping sites. There are also several bark huts that can accommodate six. Call for reservations.

Fishing: Good fishing is available on the Mokelumne River and Lakes Amador and Comanche.

Wine Tasting: See the Amador County wineries listed above.

EXPLORING THE ROUTE FROM ANGELS CAMP TO JAMESTOWN

Angels Camp was named after Henry Angel, a storekeeper who founded the town in 1849 when it was already a lively mining community of 4,000. The area's placer deposits, which could be recovered through panning, were soon exhausted, but rumor has it that a certain Bennegar Rasberry fired his rifle into the ground, splitting a stone that revealed gold inside. Indeed, there was still gold under the ground, but it required blasting and significant digging.

Thus, quartz mining began in Angels Camp with the opening of a string of mines along Main Street: the Sultana, the Angels, the Lightner, the Stickle, and—the most famous of all—the Utica Mine, which was sold for practically nothing and later yielded millions. The town became a frenzy of noise and action. Handcars containing ore traveled along tracks to the roaring stamp mills. The estimated gold recovered from the five mines between 1886 and 1910 was close to $20 million, and according to production records more than $100 million was taken from Angels Camp and vicinity.

At the town hotel, Mark Twain first heard the story of the famous Celebrated Jumping Frog of Calaveras County, which was supposedly told to him by the bartender, Ben Coon. Today, an annual festival is still held in commemoration of this hilarious story, and you can watch the "frog jockeys" cajole, curse, and try all kinds of wild antics to get their frogs to make that leap. The current world record is held by Rosie the Ribiter, who jumped 21 feet 5¾ inches in 1986! Other denizens of the town included the notorious bandits Black Bart and Joaquin Murieta.

Several buildings remain standing today from the late 1850s. Pick up a **walking tour map** at the Chamber of Commerce and explore this small town, where the hills are honeycombed with mining tunnels and so steep that often the front door of a home is located on one street and the back door on another. During its heyday, Angels Camp was a very international community—Cornishmen, Italians, Chinese, Mexicans, and Serbs all rubbed shoulders together. If you want to get a sense of the people who lived here, then wander through the several cemeteries—the Protestant and Catholic ones dating to 1855, the Serbian one established in 1910.

From Highway 49, you can detour east along Route 4 to **Murphys.** Some people have identified Murphys as the location of Bret Harte's Wingdam, which appeared in several of his stories, but most literary historians believe that Harte's places are fictional amalgams of many different places. Murphys is an old mining town that was first established in 1848 by two brothers Daniel and John Murphy, who operated a trading post here. By fall 1849 there were 50 tents, several lean-tos, 2 block houses, and a government of sorts that the miners had organized. John Murphy used the local Indians in his mining operations, and with their help left for San Jose with 6 mules and all they could carry in December 1849. He never returned.

By 1852, the camp's population was 3,000, and it had become a rough, tough place filled with miners from all over the world, who drilled and blasted out solid bedrock to bring water to the mines, who fought each other and dispensed justice in a courtroom tent where gambling, drinking, and billiards were carried on at the same time as a trial. It's reckoned that as much as $20-million worth of gold was taken out from the Murphys area. Pick up a **walking tour map** at the Chamber of Commerce and wander down Main Street, which is shaded by cottonwoods and sycamores, to view some of the more than 70 historic buildings dating back to the second half of the 19th century.

One mile north of Murphys, just off Highway 4, **Mercer Caverns,** (☎ 209/728-2101) offers visitors the chance to see a variety of natural crystalline formations—stalagmites, stalactites, columns, helictites, curtains, flowstone, and more on a tour through a series of 10 rooms more than 160 feet underground.

Hours: Memorial Day–Sept daily 9am– 5pm; Oct–May weekends only 11am–4pm. *Admission:* $5 adults, $2.50 children 5–11.

Calaveras County also has some wineries of its own, mostly concentrated around Murphys. The most well-known label is probably **Stevenot,** 2690 San Domingo Rd., Murphys (☎ 209/728-3436). It's about 3 miles from town.

Hours: Daily 10am–5pm.

Continue along Route 4, and you'll climb some 20 miles up the foothills to **Calaveras Big Trees State Park** (☎ 209/795-2334), which is surrounded by the Stanislaus Forest. This grove of sequoias was supposedly discovered by John Bidwell in 1841 and later rediscovered by A.T. Dowd, a bear hunter from Murphys who was stunned by his discovery of a tree 100 feet in circumference. Today the 6,000-acre park offers camping, hiking, fishing, and picnicking.

Admission: $5 per car.

Continue on Route 4, and you'll eventually reach **Bear Valley** ski center.

Retrace your route, turning south before you reach the junction of Highway 49, and drive to **Moaning Cavern** (☎ 209/736-2708), which has stalagmites and stalactites reaching heights of 14 feet. Visitors descend to the large gallery via a 100-foot spiral staircase or, if they choose, by rappelling 180 feet down dressed in loaned coveralls, gloves, and hardhats and using loaned equipment. The more adventurous can continue down deeper with professional guides using lighted helmets and ropes.

Hours: Summer, daily 9am–6pm; winter, daily 10am–5pm. *Admission:* $6.75 adults, $3.50 children.

Continue south along the same road, and you come eventually to **Columbia State Historic Park,** P.O. box 151, Columbia, CA 95310 (☎ 209/532-4301), where the whole town has been preserved and still functions as a town. Gold was first discovered in Columbia in March 1850 by Dr. Thaddeus Hildreth and his brother George. Extracting the gold, though, proved a problem because there was not enough water, so a ditch was built to Five Mile Creek. Families settled as early as 1851, and soon the town was thriving with a population of 5,000 and more than 150 businesses. It was incorporated in May 1854 but almost destroyed by fire in the same year. A second fire in 1857 destroyed all the wooden buildings again. Fireproof buildings replaced the old ones, and these sturdy brick buildings remained even after the miners had left in the 1870s, which explains why the town (and the park) exists today. The best time to come is during the Columbia Diggin's, a 4-day living history program in June when you can really get the flavor of those early mining days.

Anchor at one of the restored hotels, then step out to stroll the tree-shaded streets lined with false-front Western buildings now occupied by shops, restaurants, and living-history attractions. Twenty-seven brick buildings and the stone jail, all built between 1854 and 1860, have been restored; some other buildings are replicas. Each bears a plaque that tells its history. While you're here, drop in at the **Gouglass** or **St. Charles** saloons, catch a performance at the restored **Fallon Theater,** which is adjacent to the evocative **Fallon Hotel** (detailed in "Lodging & Dining" below), take a stagecoach ride, watch the blacksmith, and browse the specialty shops. Don't miss the **Wells Fargo building** and the scales that weighed out $55 million in gold. At the **barber shop** you can view the miners' baths in the rear of the store, all part of a barber's service back then. Wagons can be seen at the **Livery Stable;** behind the stable, the **ice house** is where huge blocks of ice taken from the Sierra lakes in winter were stored until August or later. The park is open daily year-round, during the summer 10am to 6pm, during winter 10am to 5pm.

Next stop after Columbia along Highway 49 is **Sonora,** which still has much charm and many historical buildings dating from the 1850s. Walk the side streets to get the flavor. It was founded by some Mexican miners who were soon followed by a group of white settlers in spring of 1849. By fall 1849 the town's residents numbered 5,000. The most famous mine in the area is the Big Bonanza, located on Piety Hill. It was first worked by Chileans and then later by three partners in the 1870s who struck solid gold and shipped $160,000 out in one day to San Francisco. A week later they took another half million and then another million before they sold the property.

Don't miss the striking **"Red Church,"** a wooden, Gothic Revival Episcopalian Church at Snell and Wyckhoff streets, which has been painted red to suggest that it is built of masonry. Also notice the **Street–Morgan Mansion,** 23 W. Snell St., across the street, a rambling Victorian with porches and witch's cap turret.

The **Tuolumne County Museum,** 158 W. Bradford Ave. (☎ 209/532-1317), is located in the old county jail and displays paintings, photographs, and artifacts that reveal local history.

Hours: Mon–Fri 9am–4:30pm; weekends (summer only) 10am–3:30pm. *Admission:* Free.

Just strolling the streets will bring you to many striking buildings, like the **cast-iron building** at 64 S. Washington St.; the domed **Bradford Building,** 42 S. Washington St.; the Italianate **County Courthouse,** 41 W. Yaney Ave.; and the **home of lumber magnate Fred Bradford,** 56 W. Dodge St., with a steamboat-style porch and tower. Folks who are fascinated by grave markers will want to visit one or two of the six or so cemeteries—the **Hebrew Cemetery** at Yaney Avenue at Oak Street, the **Masonic Cemetery** on Cemetery Lane, and the **Old City Cemetery** at the end of West Jackson Street.

From town, the Sonora–Mono Highway (Highway 108) follows the old stagecoach road that used to go from Sonora to Bodie on the other side of the Sierras. Skiers will want to follow this route out to **Dodge Ridge** (☎ 209/965-3474) in the Pinecrest Recreation Area.

Jamestown, 4 miles southwest of Sonora, was named after Colonel George James, a lawyer from San Francisco. It's Gold Rush claim to fame is that first gold found in Tuolumne County (a 75-pound gold nugget) was found 1 mile southwest of Jamestown in August 1848; a second discovery was made at Jackass Gulch, so named because a miner found the nuggets while he was looking for a lost jackass. Soon afterwards, settlements sprang up at Jamestown and Sonora. Jamestown is a historic place with several restored Western hotels and has been the location for several well-known films, including *High Noon, Dodge City, Union Pacific,* and *Butch Cassidy* *and the Sundance Kid.* Today, stroll along Main Street and browse in the many antique and other stores.

Jamestown was also home base for the Sierra Railroad, which opened in 1897, and that heritage is celebrated at **Railtown State Historic Park,** located at the end of Fifth Avenue (☎ 209/984-3953). From here, not only can you ride old steam trains, but you can also visit the roundhouse where the steam engines are rebuilt and maintained. The "Mother Lode Cannonball" leaves Railtown on hour-long journeys every Saturday and Sunday.

Hours: Daily 9:30–4:30. *Closed:* Major winter holidays. *Admission:* Free. *Train Schedule:* Sat–Sun at 10:30am, noon, 1:30pm, and 3pm. *Fare:* $6 adults, $3 children 3–12. The train doesn't operate from Jan–Apr.

Fans of Mark Twain may want to visit **Jackass Hill,** about 7 miles west of Sonora, which was stampeded in 1851 and '52 by miners who wanted to make their pile in the rich, small-pocket mines that yielded as much as $10,000 from 100 square feet. It was named after the braying of the mules in the pack trains. Mark Twain stopped here as a guest of William Gillis in 1864–65, and a replica of the cabin he stayed in stands on the hill about a mile from Tuttletown.

Ten miles south of Sonora, **Chinese Camp** is thought to have been the home of 5,000 Chinese miners. It was the site of the second big tong war in California. It all began at Two Mile Bar on the Stanlislaus River, when members of the Sam Yap Tong were working near members of the Yan Wo Tong, and a large boulder rolled from one claim to another. Insults were traded. On September 26, 1856, 900 Yan Wo confronted 1,200 Sam Yap. Four were killed and 4 wounded before American officers of the law came and arrested 250 rioters.

Lodging & Dining from Angels Camp to Jamestown

Murphys

The front porch of the **Dunbar House,** 271 Jones St., P.O. Box 1375, Murphys, CA 95247 (☎ 209/728-2897), with its hanging flower baskets and wicker furnishings, draws people to this charming inn. It's on a quiet street in town. The building dates to 1880, when it was built for the bride of Willis Dunbar, a state assemblyman and owner of Murphys' Dunbar Lumber Company. The rooms are top-quality, furnished with antiques as well as such comforts as a wood stove, down comforter, plenty of pillows, appealing art, and nice amenities including hair dryer, makeup mirror, and good reading lights. Each room also has telephone, TV/VCR, and a refrigerator stocked with mineral water and a complimentary bottle of local wine. There are two rooms and two suites. The Cedar Suite has a lovely sun porch and is decorated with hand-crocheted pieces by innkeeper Barbara's mother; it also has a whirlpool bath, hot towel rail, and a stereo system for guests' listening pleasure. Each room has a special feature of its own—a clawfoot tub and real water closet or antique French screen. A full breakfast is served either in the pretty garden, or in front of the fire in the dining room or in your room. Appetizers and wine are served in the evening.

Rates (incl. breakfast): $125–$165 double.

The **Redbud Inn,** 402 Main St., Murphys, CA 95247 (☎ 800/827-8533 or 209/728-8533), stands on the town's main thoroughfare. Although it lacks any gardens, the building and the quality of the 12 rooms are fine. Each room is decorated differently and has a private bath. Most have fireplaces or wood stoves, balconies, or window seats. The Carousel Room features carousel horses on the wall borders and is furnished with a four-poster bed; Wedgewood's bathroom boasts an antique cherry bed and rose marble corner sink; Blue Doris is decked out in gingham, chintz, and white wicker. A full breakfast is included, as well as wine and appetizers in the evenings.

Rates (incl. breakfast): $100–$165 double.

Columbia State Historic Park

The **City Hotel,** Main Street, P.O. Box 1879, Columbia State Historic Park, CA 95310 (☎ 209/532-1479, fax 209/532-7027), has been providing hospitality for over 130 years and continues to do so today in an atmosphere that recalls the Gold Rush days. The parlor-lobby is decorated with sofas and heavy Victorian mirrors and other traditional pieces of Victoriana. Each of the 10 rooms contains handsome, high-back Victorian "cottage-style" beds set on Oriental rugs and combined with metal-topped dressers and similar pieces. The rooms contain sink and toilet, but the bathroom is down the hall. Facilities include a **restaurant** plus the saloon with an original cherry wood bar that was shipped around Cape Horn from New England. A buffet breakfast is served.

Rates (incl. breakfast): $80–$105 double. *Dining Hours:* Tues–Sun 5–8:30pm and Sun 11am–2pm.

The brick **Fallon Hotel,** Washington St., P.O. Box 1870, Columbia State Historic Park, CA 95310 (☎ 209/532-1470), is just one of the town's many authentic buildings. This double-porched building was built in 1857, and today it has been restored and furnished with Victoriana—chintz wallpapers, heavy gilt-framed pictures and elaborate shades on sculpted lamps—to reflect 1890s styles. The rooms are similarly furnished with high-back oak beds. Bathrooms are down the hall.

Rates (incl. breakfast): $65–$100 double (higher prices for balcony).

Sonora

The **Ryan House,** 153 S. Shepherd St., Sonora, CA 95370 (☎ 800/831-4897 or 209/533-3445), located in town on a quiet street, is named after an Irish pioneer family who came to Sonora during the gold rush and started this house as a two-room home in 1855. Obviously, the house has been expanded since and now incorporates four guest rooms. Each is furnished in Victorian country style. The Mae Kelly Library Room contains a hand-carved oak bed made up with a Williamsburg coverlet; the Lavender Room has a brass four-poster covered with a quilt; while the Garden View Suite offers a parlor with gas log stove and a queen-size bed. Nancy and Guy Hoffman provide a full breakfast featuring such items as sourdough waffles, French toast, and other baked goodies.

Rates (incl. breakfast): $95–$160 double.

Barretta Gardens Inn, 700 S. Barretta St., Sonora, CA 95370 (☎ 209/532-6039, fax 209/532-8257), is set on a quiet, steep street about a mile from downtown. This Victorian building with three porches stands surrounded by terraced gardens of fragrant shrubs and trees. The inn offers five appealing rooms. The most elegant, the Christy Room, is on the first floor and has a queen bed set under an original crystal chandelier; it also has a floor-to-ceiling mirror and a bathroom with twin sinks. Both Gennylee and Angelina, on the second floor, are attractively decorated. But the most lavish room here is Krystal, which has a whirlpool tub for two, stained glass accents, and views from the dormer over the Sonora hills.

A full breakfast—quiche or crêpes, plus fruit and baked items—is served in the formal dining room. Guests also enjoy the warmth of the fire in the living room in the winter and the solarium filled with plants in the summer. There's also an additional parlor upstairs.

Rates (incl. breakfast): $100–$110 double.

Two blocks from downtown up on a hill, **Lulu Belle's,** 85 Gold St., Sonora, CA 95370 (☎ 209/533-3455), is located in a 110-year-old Victorian with wraparound porch complete with porch swing. There are five accommodations, all with private bath and private entrance. Sweet Lorraine features two four-poster canopied beds and a sitting area, plus balcony. The Parlor Suite is decked out in red velvet and crystal; it has a brass bed and an adjoining parlor, which is furnished with mostly mahogany pieces. The Calico Room is the most rustic. A full breakfast is served in your room, the dining room, or the garden. Sometimes guests gather in the music room to sing around the piano, but usually they cozy around the fireplace or relax in the gardens.

Rates (incl. breakfast): $95–$105 double.

Serenity, 15305 Bear Cub Dr., Sonora, CA 95370 (☎ 800 426-1441 or 209/533-1441), has been aptly named, for it is located outside Sonora on 6 acres among pines and oaks, providing a quiet retreat for guests. The house, which was built by innkeeper Fred Hoover, is large and possesses a welcoming wraparound porch on the first floor. The four rooms are large and nicely decorated and maintained. All have a private bathroom and sitting area. Each is decorated in different colors—rose and hunter green or green and yellow. My favorite is the Violets-are-Blue Room, which has sponge-painted walls, a white iron bed made up with lace-trimmed linens, and two wingback chairs placed in front of the fireplace.

The living room, library, and dining room are all extremely comfortable and furnished with antique reproductions. In winter the living room is warmed by a fire in the hearth. There's also an upstairs reading and game area. Breakfast is served at the long Georgian table and will include such dishes as mushroom crust quiche, as well as date cake and fresh fruit or similar fare. From the dining room you can step out onto a wooden deck, which is furnished with tables with umbrellas if you wish to take your breakfast outside.

Rates (incl. breakfast): $95–$135 double.

Jamestown

The **Jamestown Hotel,** Main St., P.O. Box 539, Jamestown, CA 95327 (☎ 209/984-3902, fax 209/984-4149), is located in a classic Western building with double porches decorated with flower-filled tubs. Each of the eight rooms has a private bath with brass fittings. Each is furnished slightly differently, most with white, black, or creme iron beds, which are matched with wicker or oak pieces set against floral wallpapers and windows covered with lace curtains. Calamity Jane is the prettiest room, decked out in rose carpeting and furnished with two loveseats. Most of the rooms have old-fashioned bathtubs, and some have pull-chain toilets.

The bar is handsome and atmospheric. There is also a **restaurant** that serves typical favorites like duck à l'orange, scallops with garlic sauce, prime rib, and pepper steak priced from $15 to $17. Breakfast is included in the rates. There's a deck for alfresco dining outback.

Rates (incl. breakfast): $75–$105 double. *Dining Hours:* Mon–Sat 11:30am–2:30pm and 5–9pm; Sun 10am–3pm and 4:30–9pm. Closed Tues–Wed during winter.

The **National Hotel,** 77 Main St., P.O. Box 502, Jamestown, CA 95327 (☎ 800/894-3446 or 209/984-3446, fax 209/984-5620), is a classic Western-style hotel complete with an authentic redwood saloon bar and upstairs rooms that are unpretentiously decorated in appropriate style with quilt-covered brass beds and oak or pine furnishings. There are 11 rooms, 5 with private baths. The hotel was established in 1859 at the height of the local Gold Rush. Step into the saloon and look at the old photographs from the 1890s showing the bartender and his rough-and-ready clientele.

The same menu is served in both the **restaurant** and saloon. It leans towards Italian, with such dishes as veal piccata and marsala, but is supplemented by such items as pork loin with a green peppercorn and brandy sauce, fresh fish, and steaks. Prices range from $11 to $18. The dining room with its displays of Western pioneer dress and oak wainscoting has an appealing atmosphere.

Rates (incl. breakfast): $75–$90 double. *Dining Hours:* Mon–Sat 11:30am–5pm, Sun 10am–4pm; Mon–Thurs 5–9pm, Fri–Sat 5–10pm, Sun 4–9pm.

Dining Only in Jamestown

At **Smoke Cafe,** 18191 Main St. (☎ 209/984-3733), metal palm trees decorate the bar, Mexican tiles line the floor, and an adobe-style front all point to the kind of cuisine prepared at this popular cafe. But it has a lot more than the usual combination plates of enchiladas, tacos, fajitas, and burritos. Among the specials, you might find a pan-fried snapper with tomatoes, capers, onions, and spices; or tacos with shredded pork achiote and onion-lime jalapeño salsa; or vegetable enchiladas filled with grilled vegetables and smoked cheddar cheese served with roasted tomatillo sauce. Prices range from $9 to $14.

Hours: Tues–Sat 5–10pm, Sun 4–10pm.

Classic statuary and shrubs add appropriate panache to **Michelangelo,** 18228 Main St. (☎ 209/984-4830). This local favorite offers a menu featuring a variety of Northern Italian dishes ranging from *paglia fiena,* made with fettuccine, white sauce, peas, pancetta, mushrooms, and cheese, to grilled chicken and veal with lemon-and-caper sauce. Prices range from $8 to $14. Several different pizzas are also available, including a tart and tasty one made with apple, chicken, sausage, and Gorgonzola.

Hours: Wed–Mon 5–9pm.

Angels Camp to Jamestown
Special & Recreational Activities

Biking: The cross-country ski center at **Bear Valley** is converted into a mountain bike center in summer. Rentals are under $30. For information call ☎ 209/753-2834. See "Skiing" below for more information about Bear Valley.

Camping: There are several National Forest campgrounds in the Stanislaus National Forest. **Pinecrest** has 200 sites near Pinecrest Lake open from April to mid-October; **Meadowview** has 100 sites open in summer only. Both are located about 30 miles east of Sonora on Highway 108.

Smaller campgrounds are found another 20 miles farther east at **Boulder Flat, Brightman, Dardanelle,** and **Eureka Valley.** For reservations call the **National Forest Reservation System** (☎ 800/280-2267).

Canoeing/Kayaking: Bear Valley operates trips and a canoeing/kayaking school on the lakes and reservoirs in the area. For information call ☎ 209/753-2834. See "Skiing" below for more information about Bear Valley.

Gold Panning/Prospecting: Between Angels Camp and Murphys, **Jensen's Pick & Shovel Ranch,** 4977 Parrotts Ferry Rd., Vallecito (☎ 209/736-0287), provides gold-prospecting trips to their mining claims. On these trips you'll learn how to pan, sluice, and dredge (the last only if you secure a permit beforehand). If you find up to an ounce of gold, it's yours; but if you find more, the haul is split. The charge is $25 an hour, $30 for 2 hours to a maximum of $80 a day. This is one way to find out how tough and tedious gold prospecting really is.

Gold Prospecting Expeditions, 18170 Main St., Jamestown (☎ 209/984-4653), offers a variety of prospecting trips—panning, dredging, electronic prospecting—as well as a 3-day course, which will, they say, help you narrow down a river to the 15-inch section that will most likely deliver the gold. You keep whatever you find. Prices start at $10 for a half hour of panning to $100 for day trips.

Hiking: For information on the hiking trails in the Stanislaus National Forest, write **Stanlislaus National Forest,** 19777 Greenley Rd., Sonora, CA 95370 (☎ 209/532-3671).

Horseback Riding: The **Columbia Stable,** Columbia (☎ 209/532-0663), operates short rides (maximum 4 hours) into the surrounding woods and meadows, where you can explore the landscape that was molded by hydraulic mining. Rides begin at $7 for a 15-minute pony ride to $75 for 4-hour trek.

Two pack stations are authorized to offer pack trips in the Stanlislaus Forest: **Aspen Meadow Pack Station,** Pinecrest (☎ 209/965-3402), and **Kennedy Meadow Pack Station,** Sonora (☎ 209/965-3900).

Houseboating: Rent a houseboat from **Lake Don Pedro Marina** (☎ 209/852-2369), about 30 miles west of Sonora on Lake Don Pedro.

Skiing: Located between Lake Tahoe and Yosemite off Highway 4 in the Stanislaus National Forest, Bear Valley (☎ 209/753-2301), has more than 60 trails and offers varied terrain spread over 1,280 acres. It's 30% beginner, 40% intermediate, and 30% advanced skiing trails. Lift rates are reasonable. There are also more than 30 cross-country ski trails with several trailside huts and other facilities. Ice skating, too. For information on skiing, contact **Bear Valley Cross Country,** P.O. Box 5128, Bear Valley, Ca 95223 (☎ 209/753-2834).

Dodge Ridge, Pinecrest (☎ 209/965-3474), offers downhill skiing as well as 11 kilometers of groomed cross-country trails.

White-water Rafting: Half-day and other trips on the American River are offered by **Oars,** Angels Camp (☎ 209/736-4677, fax 209/736-2902). The charge is $80.

Sierra Mac River Trips, Sonora (☎ 209/532-1327), arranges trips on the Tuolumne and the North Fork of the American River. Day trips start at $180.

Ahwahnee Whitewater, Columbia (☎ 209/533-1401), also operates trips on several rivers including the Tuolumne, Merced, and Stanislaus. Day trips begin at $120.

Also contact the **American River Touring Association,** 2400 Loma Rd., Goveland, CA 95321 (☎ 209/962-7873), for information.

CONTINUING ON TO MARIPOSA FROM JAMESTOWN

Continue down Highway 49 to Highway 120, which will take you to **Groveland,** high up in the Sierra foothills, only 23 miles from Yosemite. A thriving small town, it has an authentic frontier air with its wooden sidewalks and such establishments as the **Iron Door Saloon,** 18761 Main St., at Highway 120 (☎ 209/962-8904), which was established in 1852. Step through the iron doors and look at the historic photographs while you drink down the specialty of the house, a Woo Woo.

Originally named First Garrote, because of its lynch-happy justice, Groveland was at the center of a mining camp called Savage's Diggings, which yielded about $25-million worth of gold. These hillsides along the Tuolumne River were staked, and there were also several stamp mills and deep shaft mines. In the 1870s and '80s tourism to Yosemite began having an impact on Groveland's economy, and the town continued to thrive until the late 1920s, serving as the headquarters for the building of the Hetch Hetchy Dam, which was completed in 1925. The Depression reduced it to a virtual ghost town. It's a wild, twisting, and turning road back down to Highway 49.

Back on Highway 49, visitors can continue down to **Mount Bullion.** The name has nothing to do with bullion in the mercantile sense. It is derived from the nickname given to Sen. Thomas H. Benton, John Frémont's father-in-law.

Thirteen miles west of Mount Bullion, visitors can take a detour to **Hornitos,** a ghost town consisting of a cluster of buildings around a small plaza. It was settled originally by Mexicans. The name *Hornitos* is thought to refer either to the Mexican stone tombs that are shaped like ovens or to the bake ovens used by Mexican women. This eerie ghost town is also associated with the bandit Joaquin Murieta, who is said to have taken refuge here. The story goes that he embarked on a life of crime after seeing a friend lynched for an alleged theft. Murieta's career ended when the California Rangers caught up with him in 1856 at Coalinga. One of them pickled his head and put it on public display.

It's hard to believe that these few buildings were part of an incorporated town in 1870. Today it stands unspoiled by any modern infiltration, an eerie, haunted place of stone and adobe. Surreal almost. You can still make out the stone **jail,** one wall of the **Ghirardelli building,** the original store of the famous pioneer-merchant now associated with San Francisco and chocolate.

Return to Highway 49 and continue south to **Mariposa.** Named after a butterfly for some reason, Mariposa is the county seat and has been since 1851. Among the town's old buildings worth seeing are the Greek Revival **courthouse** (1854), complete with a tower housing a clock that dates to 1866. The oldest court of law in California, it heard many landmark mining cases, and much of U.S. mining law is based on decisions that were made here.

There's also an interesting **California State Mining and Mineral Museum** in Mariposa (☎ 209/742-7625), where you can view leaf gold, wire gold, and gold nuggets and operate a scale model of a five-stamp quartz mill.

Hours: Summer Wed–Mon 10am–6pm; winter Wed–Sun 10am–4pm. *Admission:* $4 adults, $3 seniors and children 14–18.

While you're visiting any of these towns, you may want to experience **panning for gold.** You can do so by signing up with an outfit that provides such experiences, such as **Matelot Gold Mining Company,** P.O. Box 28, Columbia, CA 95310 (☎ 209/532-9693), or do it independently in such wilderness places as the Stanlislaus National Forest as long as you do not use any motorized equipment. Ask at the Ranger District Office for further information, and then settle down beside a river or stream and start panning. If it's real gold, it will sink to the bottom of the pan. If it's a golden color but floats on the top, then it's not. Don't under any circumstances trespass on private property.

Lodging & Dining in the Area

Groveland

The **Groveland Hotel,** 18767 Main St., P.O. Box 481, Groveland CA 95321 (☎ 209/962-4000, fax 209/962-6674), is right on the main street that winds through this small town, but since Groveland is located at 3,000 feet and because the town has such a pleasant air, you don't feel hemmed in at all. The original adobe building was built in 1849; the second 1914 wood-frame building was added to accommodate workers building the Hetch Hetchy Dam. Grover and Peggy Mosley have restored the inn carefully. There are 14 rooms and 3 suites. Although the rooms are small, they have been attractively furnished with European armoires and carved walnut or iron-and-brass beds made up with down comforters and sometimes embellished with tented fabric treatments. Lace or fabric swags grace the windows, floral design wallpapers pattern the walls. The suites have fireplaces and spa tubs. The front porches have ample wicker seating for guests, who also enjoy using the parlor with its books, games, TV, and fireplace, not to mention the whirlpool spa on the back porch. A continental breakfast is served daily.

Regional and fresh cuisine is served in the **dining room,** where the lincrusta wall covering gives it a distinct period feeling. The fare might consist of crab cake in cilantro-and-caper sauce or fresh salmon en croûte in a fruit puree. Breast of chicken is served with a fresh fruit salsa, while the rib steak might be prepared with shiitake and porcini mushrooms and a wild mushroom sauce. Prices range from $13 to $18. In summer, the flower-filled flagstone courtyard is delightful for lunch.

The hotel is also only 23 miles from Yosemite. Guests may also use the golf, tennis, and swimming facilities at the nearby Pine Mountain Lake Country Club.

Rates (incl. breakfast): $105–$120 double; $185 suite. *Dining Hours:* Daily 6–9pm; closed Mon in winter.

Mariposa

The Mariposa Hotel-Inn, 5029 Hwy. 140, P.O. Box 745, Mariposa CA 95338 (☎ 209/966-4676), is right on Main Street in a false-front Western building that dates to 1901. Up the narrow stairs of this old stage stop, guests will find six large rooms decorated with floral-motif wallpapers. Each room is furnished differently. Floors are carpeted. The two largest rooms have TV and access to the veranda. Marguerite's has a clawfoot tub and pedestal sink in the bathroom. Breakfast can be enjoyed on a back patio.

Rates (incl. breakfast): $85–$99 double.

Lake Tahoe

Distances in Miles: South Lake Tahoe, 200; Squaw Valley/Northstar, 196

Estimated Driving Times: 4 hours to South Lake Tahoe; 4 hours to Squaw Valley/Northstar

---

Driving: To Squaw Valley and northern Lake Tahoe, take I-80 East to Highway 89 South along the western shore of the lake.

To southern Lake Tahoe take I-80 to Sacramento and U.S. 50 to Highway 89 North.

Further Information: If you would like to receive information about the entire Lake Tahoe area, write or call the **Lake Tahoe Visitors Authority,** P.O. Box 16299, South Lake Tahoe, CA 96151 (☎ 530/544-5050).

For South Lake Tahoe, try the **South Lake Tahoe Chamber of Commerce,** 3066 Lake Tahoe Blvd., South Lake Tahoe, CA 96150 (☎ 530/541-5255).

For North Lake Tahoe/Squaw Valley area, contact the **Tahoe North Visitors & Convention Bureau,** P.O. Box 5578, Tahoe City, CA 96145 (☎ 530/583-3494); **North Lake Tahoe Chamber of Commerce,** 245 N. Lake Blvd., Tahoe City (☎ 530/581-6900); or the **Incline Village/Crystal Bay Chamber of Commerce,** 969 Tahoe Blvd., Incline Village, NV 89451 (☎ 702/831-4440).

Mark Twain described it as "the fairest picture the whole earth affords," and still today the first sighting of Lake Tahoe will surely thrill you. It's such an intense, turquoise blue, and it's so high up in the mountains that you can't quite grasp where you are—6,225 feet above sea level and surrounded by mountains that rise from 8,000 to 11,000 feet. It's the largest alpine lake in North America, being 22 miles long and 12 miles wide, and the second deepest after Crater Lake in Orgeon. A spectacular location for a wonderful weekend and one that affords endless opportunities for all kinds of activities, whatever the season. Imagine skiing down a snow-covered slope overlooking that azure lake. Little wonder they call one of the resorts Heavenly Valley.

Events & Festivals to Plan Your Trip Around

February and March: Snowfest is one of the biggest winter carnivals in the west, lasting 10 days. It includes a torchlight parade, polar bear swim, snow-sculpture contest, ski races, fireworks display, food events, and many other zany competitions like the "Dress Up Your Dog" contest. Events take place in Tahoe City, Truckee, and Incline Village. For information call ☎ 530/583-7625.

Mid-June to Early October: The **Valhalla Summer Music Festival,** held at the Tallac Historic Site celebrates the arts with a series of concerts featuring jazz and bluegrass bands, plus special concerts like the Fiesta Latina with Leo Buscaglia and Friends. There are also art displays and workshops. For information call the Tahoe Tallac Association (☎ 530/542-4166).

This incredible basin, which offers such myriad thrills today, was formed about 25 million years ago when the mountain ranges to the east and west were lifted up along two parallel north-south faults and the basin itself sank, gradually filling with water over the years. Today 63 tributaries flow into the lake, and only one flows out, the Truckee River from Tahoe City eastward into Pyramid Lake. During the Ice Age, less than a million years ago, glaciers formed in the surrounding mountains and scooped out the U-shaped valleys that are Cascade Lake, Fallen Leaf Lake, and Emerald Bay. In some places, the lake is 1,645 feet deep, which means that there's a huge amount of water in the lake, so much that it could cover a flat area the size of California to a depth of 14 inches. The water is so clear that in some places objects—a white dinner plate, for example—can be seen 75 feet beneath the surface.

While you're exploring the region, look out, especially in spring, for such plants as the lupine, mariposa lily, Indian paintbrush, mule's ears, yarrow, and buttercup. Fir and pine—white fir, lodgepole, jeffrey, and sugar pine (in D.H. Bliss State Park)—line the rims of the basin along with quaking aspen and some other deciduous trees. Along the sandy shoreline you'll find sagebrush and manzanita. Nearly 150 species of birds inhabit the Lake area. You'll surely hear the Steller's jay, and more than likely see the mountain chickadee, Oregon junco, white-headed woodpecker, and red-shafted flicker.

The Lake has attracted summer visitors for thousands of years to its fragrant, pine-scented shores. The first inhabitants were the Washo, who migrated each summer from the Carson Valley in search of cooler temperatures and abundant fish and game. They settled the area between Taylor Creek and Camp Richardson. The first non-Native American to set eyes on the lake was John Frémont who arrived in 1844, but it was not until the 1850s that the southern shore became the route to the Comstock silver mines in Nevada.

Once the transcontinental railroad was laid in 1869, Lake Tahoe became a favorite retreat for the wealthy from San Francisco, Sacramento, and Virginia City. The most famous of the resorts was Yank Clement's Tallac Point House, which once stood west of today's Kiva Picnic Area. A later owner, Lucky Baldwin, expanded the resort, adding a hotel and casino. The arrival of the auto ended the opulent era, and Lucky's daughter demolished the resort in 1916. At the 150-acre Tallac Historic Site you can see architectural traces of this era in the sample buildings featured from the Baldwin, Pope, and Heller Estates.

On the northwestern side, Tahoe City was the first town established on the lake in 1864. A lumbering town, it too became a place that attracted the elite of the period to such resorts as A.J. Bayley's Grand Central Hotel, which opened in 1871. It had room for 160 guests and offered panoramic views of the lake and mountains as well as such facilities as a billiard parlor, bowling alley, and saloon. Visitors arrived aboard the proprietor's own Tahoe-Truckee Flyer. Many legendary figures visited the Grand Central, Lillie Langtry and Gen. Ulysses S. Grant among them. In 1895 fire swept through the hotel leveling it.

On the eastern side of the lake, the equivalent attraction was the Glen Brook House. Virtually no traces of this great era at the lake survive, and today, although Tahoe City is more attractive than South Lake Tahoe, it consists largely of a highway lined with modern stores and small shopping malls.

DRIVING AROUND THE LAKE

You can drive around the 72-mile shoreline from any point. The whole drive will take anywhere from 2½ hours to much longer, depending on how often you choose to stop along the way. Let's assume you're starting in **South Lake Tahoe.** The south shore of the lake has been completely developed and is just one long strip of motels, hotels, fast-food outlets, and strip malls capped off at the eastern end at Stateline by high-rise casinos. It's ugly, and you're best to leave here as soon as possible.

For a bird's-eye view of the lake, take the signposted road to Heavenly Valley, and take the **Heavenly Valley Tram** from the top of Ski Run Boulevard (☎ 530/541-1330) to the summit, 2,000 feet above the lake. If you like, you can enjoy a drink or meal at the Monument Park Restaurant atop the mountain.

Tram Hours: Daily 10am–9pm. *Admission:* $11.

Return to Lake Tahoe Boulevard and go west.

Before you leave South Lake Tahoe, you may want to stop at the **Lake Tahoe Historical Society and Museum,** 3058 Hwy. 50, South Lake

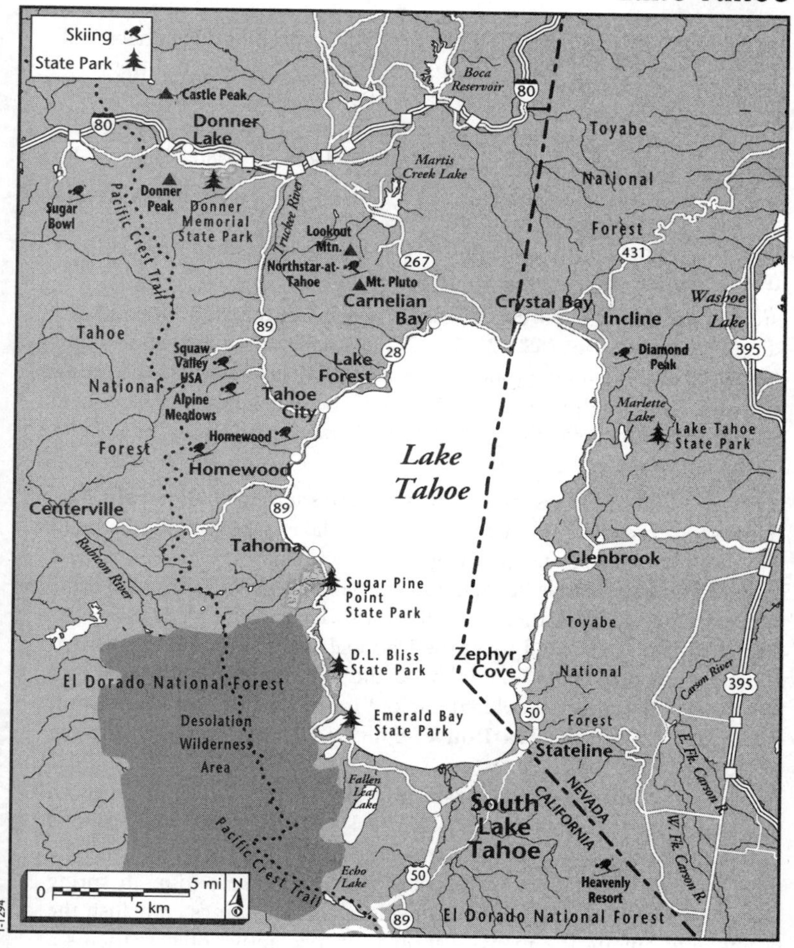

Tahoe (☎ 530/541-5458), if you're a genuine history buff and really interested in the area. Inside you'll find displays of Washoe Indian baskets, logging tools, steamer models, and historic photographs.

Hours: Summer, daily 11am–4pm; winter, weekends only noon–4pm. *Admission:* Free.

Continue along Lake Tahoe Boulevard to its junction with Highway 89, or Emerald Bay Road, and take that north. The first place you'll come to is **Camp Richardson,** where you can stop for a picnic down on Pope Beach.

The next stop will be the **Tallac Historic Site** (☎ 530/541-5227), where you can visit several restored, rustic mansions that were built around the lake in the late 19th and early 20th centuries. A museum is located in one of them, the Baldwin House, which was built in 1921 by Dextra Baldwin, a granddaughter of Lucky Baldwin. Here you can see some Washo exhibits as well as art displays in the nearby guest cabins. From here walk or bike around to the Pope House, Honeymoon Cottage, and the boathouses. The Pope House was built in 1894 by George Tallan and was purchased by George Pope in 1923. Today it serves as an interpretive center. The extravagant Valhalla was built in 1924 by Walter Heller, who entertained summer guests here for about 20 years. Special events are now held here, such as the Summer Festival of the Arts.

Hours: Summer (late June–mid-Sept), 10am–4pm; Memorial Day–late June weekends only 11am–3pm. *Admission:* Free.

Drive on to the **U.S. Forest Service Visitor Center,** 870 Emerald Bay Rd., South Lake Tahoe (☎ 530/573-2600), to pick up information about the region and the hiking trails and other activities offered. At the center there are nature trails to walk and also the Stream Profile Chamber where you can view kokanee salmon making their way upstream in the fall.

Hours: Mon–Fri 8am–4:30pm.

From here the road loops around the southern shoreline of **Emerald Bay.** Here you can really see how aquamarine the lake is. Stop at the Emerald Bay Lookout, which is just past Eagle Creek and Falls. If you want to, you can hike the quarter mile down the steep trail to Eagle Falls from the Eagle Falls parking area and then continue on to Eagle Lake. Permits are required and can be picked up at the National Forest Visitor Center mentioned in the preceding paragraph. At the lookout you look down into this incredibly turquoise-colored bay out to the small **Fannette Island,** where you can spy the **Tea House,** built by Mrs. Lora Knight atop the island, where she hosted guests.

She also constructed **Vikingsholm** (☎ 530/525-7277), a 38-room replica of a Scandinavian Castle dating back to 1929, which was designed to blend into the wooded landscape. During the summer, you can hike the 1½ miles down to this whimsical place and take a tour. In spring wildflowers grow on the sod roof. Inside, dragon carvings embellish the beams, and among the many Scandinavian decorative objects there's a traditional Finnish grandfather clock, with a base shaped in human form and the face designed to look like a human visage.

Hours: July 1–Labor Day 10am–4pm. *Admission:* $5 adults, $1.50 children 6–17.

The shoreline around the Bay is in **Emerald Bay State Park** (☎ 530/988-0205), which adjoins **D.H. Bliss State Park** (☎ 530/525-7277). There are two campgrounds in this park, including one located on the lakefront. One popular trail leads you to see the **Old Lighthouse.** Another is the Rubicon leading out to **Emerald Point** for a fabulous view of the Bay.

Hours: Most of these parks are open daily 6am–10pm during the summer, with more restricted hours other times of the year. *Admission:* Usually $6 per car.

Continue north along Highway 89, past the community of Meeks Bay, until you reach **Sugar Pine Point State Park** (☎ 530/525-7143). Visit the interpretive center and the **Ehrman Mansion** (☎ 530/525-7982), plus the original log cabin of Indian fighter General Phipps. The Queen Anne–style mansion was designed by Bliss and Faville for Isaias Hellman in 1902. The name Ehrman comes from Sidney Ehrman, who was the husband of Hellman's daughter. The stone building with circular turrets and three porches is grand indeed. The interior features bespeak wealth too—leaded glass windows, a 30-foot-long oak dining table, handpainted Dutch tiles around the fireplaces, and Oriental carpets on the slate floors. There were several other buildings on the estate including an astonishing $60,000 children's house and a building for a private generator.

Hours: June 15–Labor Day daily 11am–4pm. *Admission:* $2 adults, $1 children 6–12.

From here continue along Highway 89 through the communities of Tahoma and Moana Beach to **Homewood,** where in summer you can ride the **cable car** at Homewood Ski Area.

About 6 miles on, just before you enter Tahoe City, Highway 89 veers off along the Truckee River for 5 miles to the famous ski resort at **Squaw Valley,** site of the 1960 Winter Olympics. Take a detour and ride the **Squaw Valley Cable Car** (☎ 530/583-6985) summer or winter for the incredible vista from the top.

Hours: Daily 8am–4pm. *Admission:* $14 adults, $5 children 12 and under.

From Squaw Valley return to Highway 28 and take it around the northern rim of the lake via **Carnelian Bay** and **Tahoe Vista,** all the way to the **Kings Beach State Recreation Area** (☎ 530/546-7248).

From Kings Beach, Highway 267 leads north to **Northstar, Truckee,** and **Donner State Park,** which has a museum and monument memorializing the tragedy of the 1846 Donner Party. The monument stands on a 22-foot-high pedestal, which was the depth of the snowfall that trapped this emigrant group in the winter of 1846–47.

The 89 members of the Donner party joined a wagon train and set out in April 1846 from Springfield, Illinois. At South Pass in Wyoming, they left the main wagon train, electing to follow the recommendation of explorer Lansford Hastings to take a 350-mile shortcut via Fort Bridger. The way led through the Wasatch Mountains, across the Great Salt Lakes Desert, a desolate route that, in fact, caused them to fall 3 weeks behind the wagon train they had left. In late October they rested in Truckee Meadows (Reno) before attempting to make the difficult mountain crossing that lay ahead. This delay proved fatal, for winter came early that year to the Sierras, and at Donner Lake the party became snowbound. They settled in for the winter, but food was scarce and they were soon close to starving.

Ten men and five women left the camp to seek help. Five days out, Stanton, the only one who knew the route, became exhausted and snowblind and died. The others became lost, and four more died; the rest ate their bodies. The two Native Americans in the party who refused to eat human flesh were shot and eaten. One month later, two men and all five women arrived at Sutter's Fort. They had survived on one deer and the bodies of those who had died. Several rescue parties went to save what remained of the party at Donner Lake. They too had succumbed to cannibalism. Only 47 survived from the original 89.

Return to Highway 28, and at Brockway you'll cross the stateline into Crystal Bay, Nevada. Continue along Highway 28 about three miles to **Incline Village.** From the village you can take a side trip up the **Mount Rose Highway** for a spectacular view of the whole Tahoe basin. Just east of Incline Village there's the **Ponderosa Ranch** (☎ 702/831-0691), where the popular TV series *Bonanza* was filmed. Visit the Cartwright ranch and the children's petting farm, see gunfight shows, take a haywagon ride, and hang for a while in the tourist-oriented mock-up of a Western town.

Hours: Apr–Oct daily 9:30am–5pm. *Admission:* $8.50 adults, $5.50 children 5–11.

From here the road continues due south along the lake past Rocky and Sand Points to **Sand Harbor Beach,** which is located in the **Nevada Lake Tahoe State Park** (☎ 702/831-0494). Continue on Highway 28 to **Spooner Lake State Park** (☎ 702/831-0494) and take a walk around Spooner Lake.

Highway 28 then links up with I-50 about 12½ miles from Incline Village. Take I-50 south through the exclusive community of **Glenbrook,** famous for its golf course. A little farther south you'll pass through the Cave Rock tunnel. **Cave Rock** was a holy place to the Washoe Indians, who placed their dead in the cold waters below the rock.

Farther along is **Zephyr Cove,** with a charming old lodge, beach, and tour boats, about 4½ miles from the casinos at Stateline and neighboring South Lake Tahoe, where your drive began.

SEEING THE LAKE FROM A BOAT

Another way to experience the lake is to take a cruise on it. Cruise boats leave from several locations around the perimeter. Most offer cruises to Emerald Bay, as well as sunset dinner cruises, in glass-bottom boats. Following are the details for several options.

The big paddlewheeler ***The Tahoe Queen*** (☎ 530/541-3364), operates year-round for day cruises, leaving daily from a dock at the end of Ski Run Boulevard in South Lake Tahoe.

Hours: Summer and Fall, cruises at 11am, 1:30 and 3:55pm, with a dinner cruise at 7pm; winter and spring, 12:30pm. *Fares:* Day cruise, $14 adults, $5 for children 11 and under; dinner cruise, $18 adults, $9.50 children.

Smaller cruise boats, like the ***Sun Runner II,*** which is operated by North Shore Cruises, Inc., leave from Tahoe City. *Sun Runner II* offers a full-moon jazz cruise in addition to the regular cruises.

Fares: $18 adults, $9 children for the Emerald Bay cruise; $15 adults, $7.50 children for the sunset and other cruises.

Perhaps the most luxurious paddlewheeler is the ***Ms Dixie II*** (☎ 702/588-3508), which leaves from Zephyr Cove. It offers a breakfast cruise, a champagne brunch cruise, and a Dinner & Dancing cruise.

Hours: Departures daily noon and 7pm. *Fares:* Brunch cruises, $16 adults, $5 children 12 and under; dinner cruises, $38 adults only.

For a bracing experience take one of the sailing cruises. **Woodwind,** P.O. Box 1375, Zephyr Cove, NV 89448 (☎ 702/588-3000), is a three-hulled sailing ship that can carry 30 passengers. There are an enclosed cabin, wide decks, bathroom, and full bar on board. It operates from April 1 to October 31.

Fares: $16 adults, $8 children 2–12 for 1-day cruises, $22 adults for champagne sunset cruises.

Three cruises a day are also offered aboard the ***Ketch Tahoe,*** behind Timber Cove Lodge, 3411 Lake Tahoe Blvd., Hwy. 50 (☎ 530/544-5150), a 41-foot vessel with full facilities. Beverages and appetizers are served on each cruise, plus champagne on the sunset cruise.

Hours: Departures at noon, afternoon, and sunset. *Fares:* $45 per person for noon and afternoon cruises; $50 per person for dinner cruise.

SEEING THE LAKE FROM ABOVE

The other perspective from which to view the lake is from above while soaring silently in a glider. For information write to **SOAR,** P.O. Box 1764, Minden, NV 89423 (☎ 702/782-7627). Flights operate year-round, leaving daily from Douglas County Airport, about 20 minutes from South Lake Tahoe. For ballooning opportunities see the Activities section below.

Fares: $100–$140 for two.

SOUTH LAKE TAHOE

Lodging & Dining

For those who want to combine skiing or summer watersports with gambling, then **Caesars,** 55 Hwy. 50, P.O. Box 5800, Lake Tahoe, Nevada 89449 (☎ 800/648-3353 or 702/588-3515), is the place to stay. It's as far from a quiet, romantic retreat as you can get, attracting large convention groups and other crowds of "entertainment" seekers. The rooms are spacious and predictably furnished; most have the requisite Roman tub. In addition to the casino and the top-of-the-line entertainment offered, there are several restaurants—Empress Court for Chinese, Primavera for Italian, and the Broiler Room for steak and Cajun specialties. More downhome fare is featured at the new Planet Hollywood and Cafe Roma. Facilities include an indoor swimming pool designed like a lagoon, with waterfalls and rock islands; plus racquetball court, outdoor tennis courts, and a fitness center with Universal weight machines. Facials, body wraps, and massages are also offered at the spa.

Rates: $155–$235 double weekends, $125–$185 midweek.

Harrah's Casino Hotel, U.S. 50, P.O. Box 8, Stateline, NV 89449 (☎ 800/648-3773 or 702/588-6611), is the other contender for top casino title. It's flashy and glitzy, and the 540 rooms are extra large and also feature two bathrooms equipped with TV and telephone. The furnishings are plush, if not exactly tony. They do offer every possible convenience though—bedside remote control TV and room lights, focused bedside reading lights, blackout drapes, computerized minibar, and double sound-proofed walls. There are seven dining rooms serving everything from deli sandwiches to top-rated cuisine. The Summit on the 16th floor affords panoramic views; Friday's Station specializes in steaks and seafood; Cafe Andreotti turns out decent Italian cuisine; Asia offers cuisines inspired by the several different Asian cultures—Thai, Chinese, and Japanese. Buffets are also served on the 16th floor in the Forest Buffet. Facilities include a glass-domed swimming pool, fitness center with Universal weight machines, and sundeck plus massage and whirlpool.

Rates: Summer $189–$249 double; $239–$299 suite weekends; winter $159–$219 and $299–$269, respectively. Always ask about their excellent packages.

Even though it's right next door, the pace is less frenetic at **Embassy Suites,** 4130 Lake Tahoe Blvd., South Lake Tahoe, CA 96150 (☎ 530/544-5400, fax 530/544-4900). The 400 suites are very comfortable and have all the added convenience of home—separate living room with sofa bed, armchair, remote control TV, coffeemakers, minibar, microwave oven, and well-lit working/dining table. The bedroom also has a TV, and the bathroom features the usual amenities. The whole is decorated in modern style. Guests receive a complimentary breakfast and are invited to attend a manager's reception in the evening. There's a dining room offering American cusine plus a sport's bar. Facilities include an indoor pool, whirlpool, sauna, fitness center, and outdoor sundeck.

Rates (incl. breakfast): $179–$249 suite.

Christiana Inn, 3819 Saddle Rd., P.O. Box 18298, South Lake Tahoe, CA 96151 (☎ 530/544-7337, fax 530/544-5342), is situated only 50 yards from the main chairlift to Heavenly Valley. It's an alpine-style accommodation with plenty of atmosphere. There are only two rooms and four suites.

The suites are very inviting with their wood-burning fireplaces. Suite Six is the most luxurious, its stained glass enhancing the first-floor living room, which also has a bathroom with whirlpool tub; the second floor contains a bedroom with wood-burning fireplace and sitting area. Suite Four has a loft area with platform bed and overhead mirrors. The regular rooms are furnished with brass beds and have small dining nooks. Facilities include a lounge and dining room, both with fireplaces. The parking is a bonus, too, because it can be horrendous at the ski hill.

Rates: Summer, $60–$70 double, $95–$135 suite; winter, $85–$95 and $155–$185, respectively.

On the southern shores of the lake away from the commercialized strip adjacent to the Tallac Historic Site, **Camp Richardson,** 1900 Jameson Rd., P.O. Box 9028, South Lake Tahoe, CA 96158 (☎ 530/541-1801), is a well-used historic resort offering a variety of accommodations. It's right down on the lake and has its own marina plus a waterfront restaurant, the **Beacon Bar & Grill** (☎ 530/541-0630), where you can actually sit on a bench at the base of a pine tree. The majority of the accommodations—38 in fact—are rustic, well-kept cabins, although there are a few basic hotel rooms in the lodge, a beach condo, plus tent and RV campgrounds. There are no TVs or phones in the accommodations, and maid service is only available for an additional charge. The cabins sleep anywhere from two to eight people. Furnishings are country plain. Seventeen of the cabins are rented year round, and all of these have either a wood stove or fireplace. The lodge has a large beamed sitting/game room with stone fireplace. Additional facilities and services include bike rental, horseback riding, tennis court, beach, and cross-country skiing.

Rates: Summer-only cabins, $545–645 per week; year-round cabins, summer $800–$1145 per week; lodge rooms, $84–$94 per night summer weekends, $64–$74 summer midweek, $69 winter.

Dining Only

Nepheles, 1169 Ski Run Blvd. (☎ 530/544-8130), well-situated en route to Heavenly Valley, is a pretty restaurant where the California cuisine is infused with inspiration from the East and other traditions. Among the seasonal specials you might find such game dishes as broiled elk with a black currant–merlot sauce and chipotle chiles, or wild boar chops stuffed with prunes and cabbage and served with an orange-apricot brandy sauce, or venison sautéed with Stilton cheese in a zinfandel demi-glacé sauce. The fish dishes will be prepared more lightly, like the swordfish marinated in tropical fruit juices and topped with a mango chutney. Among the favorites on the regular menu is the roast duck with wild blueberry–thyme–pinot noir sauce, tropical grilled prawns in an ancho chili-citrus marinade finished with a Caribbean rum, papaya, and banana salsa, and the steaks served with Gorgonzola cheese, walnut butter, and black peppercorn–shallot sauce. Prices range from $14 to 20.

Hours: Daily 5–10pm.

Scusa, 1142 Ski Run Blvd. (☎ 530/542-0100), is an ideal spot to fall into en route to or from Heavenly Valley. Although there's not a romantic dining scene, the food is very well prepared. All the traditional Italian favorites are on the menu, including chicken saltimbocca and scampi made with a flavorsome garlic herb butter enhanced by fresh basil and roasted peppers, along with linguini with clams and a classic lasagna made with Italian sausage as well as ground beef. Prices range from $10 to $17.

Hours: Daily 5–9:45pm.

South Lake Tahoe
Special & Recreational Activities

Ballooning: Rise early for an inspiring ride above the lake. **Lake Tahoe Balloons,** 2244 Inverness, South Lake Tahoe (☎ 530/544-1221), has champagne balloon flights that float over the Carson Valley at 10,000 to 12,000 feet for 1 to 1½ hours. After your flight, you're treated to champagne brunch at Caesars Cafe Roma.

Bicycling: Ride the Pope–Baldwin bike path, which takes you through Camp Richardson to Pope and Baldwin Beaches and through the Tallac Historic Site to Fallen Leaf Lake.

Anderson's Bike Rental, Highway 89 at 13th Street (☎ 530/541-0500), has mountain and other bikes.

Boating: On the eastern shore, **Zephyr Cove Resort Marina** (☎ 702/588-3833) rents pedal boats, canoes, kayaks, and power boats. Fees range from $14 to $18 per hour for the self-powered boats; small fishing boats start at $25; and larger more powerful power boats start at $54 per hour and go up from there.

Paradise Watercraft at Camp Richardson (☎ 530/541-7272) rents kayaks and power boats; **Lakeview Sports,** 3131 Hwy. 50 (☎ 530/544-8888), rents speedboats.

Camping: On the lakefront, **Camp Richardson** (☎ 530/541-1801) is a private campground that has 333 sites. Fees range from $16 to $22 per night.

The U.S. Forest Service operates a campground at **Fallen Leaf Lake** (☎ 530/573-2600 or 530/544-5994) with 205 sites (water and flush toilets, but no showers). Fees are $12 per night.

There's a State Park campground at **Eagle Point** (☎ 530/541-3030). They are open summer only and cost $14 per night.

Cruises: See "Seeing the Lake from a Boat," above for information on cruises on the following: *Tahoe Queen* (☎ 530/541-3364), which is based in South Lake Tahoe; *Ms Dixie II* (☎ 702/588-3508) and Woodwind sailing cruises (☎ 702/588-3000), both of which are based in Zephyr Cove, Nevada, on the eastern shore.

Fishing: The season is open year-round. Because the water is so clear, it's not an easy fishing ground, and you're best to fish when the surface is rippled rather than calm. Rainbow and brown trout and kokanee salmon are fished, but the premier fishing in Lake Tahoe is for Mackinaw or lake trout, which regularly weigh in from 3 to as much as 10 pounds. Occasionally, a 20-pounder is reeled in (the lake record is a 37-pounder caught in 1973).

Blue Ribbon Fishing Charters, South Lake Tahoe (☎ 530/541-8801), offers open boat charters from Tahoe Keys Marina for half and full days. Bait tackle and beverages are provided along with 1-day licenses, for about $75 for 5 hours.

Tahoe Sportfishing, Ski Run Marina, 900 Ski Run Blvd., South Lake Tahoe (☎ 530/541-5448), offers 4-, 5-, and 7-hour trips with fares starting at $70.

Gambling: The casino action is at the California/Nevada state line at **Caesars Tahoe,** 55 Hwy. 50, Lake Tahoe (☎ 800/648-3353 or 702/588-3515); **Harrah's Casino,** U.S. 50, Stateline (☎ 800/427-7247 or 702/588-6611); **Harvey's,** Hwy. 50, Stateline (☎ 800/427-8397 or 702/588-2411); **Horizon Casino,** Hwy. 50, Lake Tahoe (☎ 800/648-3322 or 702/588-6211). Both Caesars and Harrah's are described fully under South Lake Tahoe "Lodging & Dining" above.

Golf: Edgewood Golf Course, Lake Parkway, Lake Tahoe (☎ 702/588-3566), right down on the lake, is the championship course in the region and hosts an annual celebrity pro am. Expect to pay at least $150 for greens fees.

Hiking: See "Driving Around the Lake" above for some short, easy trail suggestions along the route, including the trail to Vikingsholm and the nature trails in Sugar Pine Point State Park. You might also be interested to try the Rubicon Trail to Emerald Point. The most strenuous trail leads to Eagle Falls.

Horseback Riding: A variety of rides and pack trips are given by **Camp Richardson Corral,** Emerald Bay Road at Fallen Leaf Road, South Lake Tahoe (☎ 530/541-3113). You can select a brisk morning ride to a bacon, egg, and hotcake breakfast or a late afternoon ride to a steak barbecue ($30 and $35, respectively). All inclusive pack trips start at $350 for 2 days and 1 night. Also 1- and 2-hour and half-day trail rides are available starting at $22.

Or try **Sunset Ranch,** Highway 50, South Lake Tahoe (☎ 530/541-9001), which offers similar trips at similar prices.

Inline Skating: Rentals are available at **Lakeview Sports,** 3131 Hwy. 50, South Lake Tahoe (☎ 530/544-0183).

Jet Skiing: Rentals are available at **Lakeview Sports,** 3131 Hwy. 50, South Lake Tahoe (☎ 530/544-0183).

Skiing: There are 14 downhill and 15 cross-country areas around the lake. The region's largest ski resort is **Heavenly Valley,** P.O. Box 2180, Stateline, NV 89449 (☎ 702/588-4584), which straddles 4,800 acres of terrain and is accessible from California and Nevada. The vertical drop is 3,500 feet, which is the steepest in the area. The terrain is 20% beginner, 45% intermediate, and 35% advanced. There are 25 lifts, including a 50-passenger aerial tram. The easier terrain is on the California side at Heavenly West. The Nevada slopes are less crowded but steeper. Parking is a nightmare, but the view from the top of the 10,000-plus-foot summit is dazzling. To get there, take Ski Run Boulevard from Highway 50 in South Lake Tahoe.

Kirkwood, P.O. Box 1, Kirkwood, CA 95646, off Highway 88 (☎ 209/258-6000), is famous for the amount of snow it receives—76 feet in 1995! The terrain is only 15% beginner, 50% intermediate, and 35% advanced. There are 11 lifts, including 3 triple chairs.

Snowmobiling: Try the **Zephyr Cove Snowmobile Center** on the Nevada side of the lake (☎ 702/882-0788) for rentals.

TAHOE CITY & THE WESTERN SHORE

Lodging & Dining

Meeks Bay Resort, 7901 Hwy. 89, P.O. Box 411, Tahoma, CA 96142 (☎ 530/525-7242) (summer), and P.O. Box 70248, Reno, NV 89570 (☎ 702/829-1997) (winter), offers a variety of cabins and condominiums to visitors. They range from a small, lakefront studio with fireplace, efficiency kitchen with small stove/sink/refrigerator unit, and private bathroom, which rents for $85 a night, to the Kehlet Mansion, which is located on a secluded point and has seven bedrooms, three bathrooms, and large kitchen and living room with a fireplace, plus a deck out over the water. This last rents for $3,000 a week. All, except the studio, rent by the week in midsummer, but they can be rented nightly from mid-June to June 30 and from Labor Day to September 25. The property also has a campground and marina.

Rates: Cabins and condos, $650–$1250 weekly; $95–$155 daily; for the mansion, $3,000 weekly $550 daily.

Swiss Lakewood Restaurant & Lodge, 5055 W. Lake Blvd., P.O. Box 205, Homewood, CA 96141 (☎ 530/525-5211), is primarily known for its dining room, but it also has some appealing housekeeping cabins, which have wall-to-wall carpeting in the living room, cable TV, private bath, and fully equipped kitchens.

The **dining room** glows with an Alpine atmosphere. The cuisine is Swiss, with a definite tilt towards the Italian region. Cheese fondue or raclette are among the specialties, as well as fondue bourguignonne, which is only served in winter. For a treat try the ***escalopes de Chevreuil,*** which are escalopes of venison glazed with chestnuts and a balsamic vinegar-lingonberry sauce. For an appetizer, the ***viande de Grison*** (Swiss dried beef) arrives with tiny pickles, marinated artichoke hearts, and baby corn. Desserts are traditional favorites, like peach Melba and Grand Marnier soufflé or cherries Jubilee. Prices range from $18.50 to $26.

Rates: Cabins, $105 double; motel rooms, $75. *Dining Hours:* Tues–Sun 5:30–closing (usually around 9:30pm).

Chaney House, 4725 W. Lake Blvd., P.O. Box 7852, Tahoe City, CA 96145 (☎ 530/525-7333, fax 530/525-4413), is one of my favorite accommodations on the western shore. It's the beautiful stone home of Gary and Lori Chaney. Tucked among pine trees, it was built in the 1920s by skilled Italian stonemasons, who installed the magnificent stone fireplace that reaches to the top of the cathedral ceiling in the living room. The fireplace is flanked by two windows that provide views of the lake. The living room is beautifully, but comfortably, furnished with art objects and sculptures. There are four rooms. Jeanine's Room has a brass queen bed dressed with pink quilt and lace dust ruffles set against stone and pine walls; Russell's Suite has a lake view, is paneled in pine, and features a bed with a red and green quilt plus book-filled shelves; the Master Suite is the largest; while the most appealing is the one-bedroom apartment over the garage, which has a kitchen as well as a bedroom. A delicious breakfast is served on the patio overlooking the lake, and evening refreshments are offered around the fireplace. The breakfast will be a buffet spread featuring such eye-openers as Swahili pie (a Swedish pancake soaked in honey with fresh fruit) or Eldorado eggs (made with sausage, peppers, onions, and tomato on biscuits with cheese). Extra benefits include a private beach and pier across the street, and bike and paddleboat rental. Note there is a dog and cat in residence.

Rates (incl. breakfast): $120–$160 double.

Sunnyside Restaurant & Lodge, 1850 W. Lake Blvd., P.O. Box 5969, Tahoe City, CA 95730 (☎ 530/583-7200), is on the east, lakefront side of the road. It's a typical pine lodge with riverstone fireplaces and modern, uninspiring decor, but it has the advantage of sitting right out on the water so that guests can sit on the wooden deck and look out over the sailboats and azure-blue water to the mountains beyond. There are 23 attractive rooms, all with full or partial views of the lake as well as small decks. They are furnished with bleached pine pieces and have TV and telephone. Some have rock fireplaces. The bar is warmed in winter by a fire in the fieldstone fireplace, which is presided over by a bison trophy. There's a restaurant, which has a special seafood bar and also offers some Hawaiian-inspired dishes.

Rates: Winter, $135–$145 double weekends; $110–$120 midweek. Fall $120–$130 weekends; $95–$105 midweek. Summer, $165–$180 at all times.

Chinquapin Resort, 3600 N. Lake Blvd., P.O. Box 1923, Tahoe City, CA 96145 (☎ 530/583-6991, fax 530/583-0937), is located three miles east of Tahoe City right down on the shoreline. Here on 95 acres, which include 1 whole mile of shoreline, you will find 172 townhouses and condominiums, about a third of which are rented to visitors. They range from 950-square-foot one-bedrooms to 2,800-square-foot four-bedrooms. All have fireplaces, washer-dryer, TV, telephone, and full kitchen; some have saunas. Daily maid service is not included in the rates but can be requested for $25 an hour.

Facilities are excellent—a pool, seven tennis courts, beaches with floating docks offshore, and a pier.

Rates: Mid-June–mid-July and Labor Day–Oct 1, one-bedroom $150–$220; two-bedroom $180–$230; three-bedroom $220–$360; four-bedroom $230–$430 (higher rates are for lakefront units). In July and August there's a 1-week minimum, starting at $900. In winter rates are discounted about 8%.

The **Resort at Squaw Creek,** 400 Squaw Creek Rd., P.O. Box 3333, Olympic Valley, CA 96146 (☎ 800/327-3353 or 530/583-6300, fax 530/581-6632), delivers the very best to guests—comfortable rooms, fine food in the restaurants, and terrific sports and other facilities. Beautifully situated on 626 acres at 6,200 feet above sea level, the resort affords great views of the High Sierra. The buildings have been designed to blend into the environment and to allow the outside to enter into the interior public spaces. There are 405 accommodations with extra-fine amenities, including granite vanity counters in the bathrooms, spacious study and sitting areas, minibars, two phones with speakers, and remote control TV. Extra touches include hair dryers, ironing boards, and bathrobes. Sixty rooms have fireplaces.

There are three major restaurants plus a pub-sports bar and outdoor dining facilities. **Cascades** is the all-day dining room, which usually has a Friday night seafood buffet. **Glissandi** looks out onto the mountains and offers continental cuisine. My favorite is **Ristorante Montagna,** which delivers spicy, flavorsome pastas and pizzas, plus slow-roasted rotisserie dishes. It has a marvelous atmosphere created by Italian folk and opera music plus faux marble tables. **Sweet Potatoes,** a patisserie and gourmet gift shop, is the place to stop for breakfast.

The sports facilities are superb. In summer the 18-hole championship golf course designed by Robert Trent Jones, Jr., challenges golf aficionados in beautiful mountain, forest, and wetland surroundings. The water sports facilities are laid out in garden style with a free-form swimming pool, beach pool, plunge pool, water slide, and dramatic 250-foot waterfall. The fitness center is well equipped with weight-training equipment, redwood saunas, massage rooms, and aerobics studio. There are eight tennis courts. In winter it's strictly ski-in and ski-out to the slopes, with the most luxurious item of all, an on-site ski lift. There's ice skating and cross-country skiing, too.

Rates: Winter, $285–$310 double; spring, $245–$270; summer, $265–$290; fall, $235–$250. Suites from $400, $360, $380, and $350, respectively.

Dining Only

The aromas at **Tahoe House,** 625 W. Lake Blvd., Tahoe City (☎ 530/583-1377), will excite you even before you reach the table, for en route to the dining room you'll pass through the bakery where sacher torte, carrot cake, tiramisu, and almond-chocolate dipped nectarines are displayed. In the dining room the specialties are Swiss and Italian. On the menu you'll find such items as grilled bratwurst served with red cabbage and spaetzli, or grilled venison with a mushroom-merlot sauce, along with veal marsala and capellini con vongole. Prices range from $12 to $19. There are always daily specials, too.

Hours: Daily 5–10pm; bakery 6am–10pm.

Wolfdale's, 640 N. Lake Blvd., Tahoe City (☎ 530/583-5700), is on the lakefront and has a captivating, trellissed outdoor dining area. Inside there's a small bar and a dining room where light pine Windsor chairs are set at cloth-covered tables. The menu is very limited but will always include a vegetarian dish, like spaghetti squash pancake with grilled vegetable skewers and saifun noodles. Seafood might be represented by a ragout of scallops, lobster, king crab, and prawns with corn, potatoes, saffron, crostini and rouille, a worthy feast indeed. In addition, there might be roast quails stuffed with wild rice or grilled veal chop with a wild mushroom demi-glace. For dessert the sorbets are full flavored; chocoholics will love the chocolate sac, filled with dark chocolate mousse embellished with blackberries and raspberries.

Hours: Wed–Mon 6–9:30 pm.

Although **Jake's on the Lake,** 780 N. Lake Blvd., Tahoe City (☎ 530/583-0188), is located in a small mall, it does have views of the lake. The menu is broad, featuring a range of seafood, pasta, and meats sometimes prepared in a traditional way and sometimes with an Oriental flavor. For example, there's ginger chicken slathered with a sauce made with ginger, roasted red peppers, olive oil, and soy sauce; and a classic rack of lamb roasted with herb Dijon mustard and served with a mint mango chutney butter. There are always daily seafood specials, too, and such delicious fish dishes as rainbow trout with a lemon beurre blanc. The majority of the appetizers are seafood specialties—sashimi of ahi, macadamia nut–coated calamari served with a spicy pineapple relish. Sandwiches and salads are available, too. Sandwiches are $7.95, main course prices from $14 to $21.

Hours: Sun–Thurs 11:30am–10pm, Fri–Sat 11:30am–10:30pm.

Sunsets on the Beach, 7320 N. Lake Blvd., Tahoe Vista (☎ 530/546-3640), located right down on the lake, is a regional dining favorite. The menu offers a broad variety of choices, including Italian pastas and such items as pork tenderloin marinated in sesame, ginger, and soy and served with Thai peanut sauce and grilled pineapple. Prices range from $11 for the vegetarian dish to $29 for a 2-pound lobster split, wood-grilled, and brushed with tomato-basil butter. Innovative pizzas are also available, including one made with barbecue sauce, tomato, roasted corn, onion, cilantro, and smoked mozzarella. To start, try the wood-grilled polenta and wild mushroom gratin made with fontina, Gorgonzola, and tomato marinara.

Hours: Mon–Sat 11am–2:30pm; Sun 9am–2pm; daily 5pm–closing.

An old Tyrolean-Bavarian atmosphere prevails at **Pfeifer House,** 760 River Rd., (☎ 530/583-3102), which is a favorite local dining spot that has been operating since 1939. The specialties include such traditional dishes as sauerbraten, Wiener schnitzel, Swiss bratwurst, and Kasseler rippchen (smoked pork loin), priced from $15 to $20. Finish your meal with Bavarian apple strudel.

Hours: Wed–Mon 5–10pm.

Christy Hill, 115 Grove St., Tahoe City (☎ 530/583-8551), is a comfortable, elegant restaurant where you can secure a very fine meal. The cuisine is modern California with some distinct Pacific Rim and southwestern overtones. For example, you might want to start your meal with the Anaheim chili relleno stuffed with house-smoked chicken and Sonoma pepper jack cheese, or the raw oysters with fresh salsa. Among the entrees you're likely to find a chicken breast that has been blackened with three peppers and is served with a New Mexico chili-roasted red pepper and orange sauce, or pork medallions sautéed with caper and shiitake mushrooms in a lemon-garlic demi-sauce, or a richly flavored salmon pan-seared with cracked pepper and ginger and served in a cabernet demi-sauce. Prices range from $18 to $24.

Hours: Tues–Sun 5:30–9:30pm.

Tahoe City/West Shore
Special & Recreational Activities

Biking: Bikes can be rented at many places. **Cyclepaths,** 1785 W. Lake Blvd., Tahoe Park in Sunnyside (☎ 530/581-1171), also offers guided cycle tours; **Porter's Ski and Sport,** 501 N. Lake Blvd., Tahoe City (☎ 530/583-2314); **Tahoe Gear,** 5095 W. Lake Blvd., Homewood (☎ 530/525-5233); and **TSR Mountain Bike Rentals,** 185 River Rd., Tahoe City (☎ 530/583-0123).

Fifteen miles of paved bike pathways extend from Tahoe City in three directions. The network connects Sugar Pine Point State Park on the south, Alpine Meadows on the northwest, and Dollar Point on the northeast.

Boating: Boat rentals are available all around the lakeshore. **High & Dry,** Homewood Marina, Hwy. 89 (☎ 530/525-5966), rents pedal boats, jet skis, and power boats; **High Sierra Water Ski School,** 1850 W. Lake Blvd., Sunnyside (☎ 530/583-7417), and Homewood Marina (☎ 530/525-1214) rent power and sail boats; **Sunnyside Marina,** Hwy. 89, Sunnyside (☎ 530/583-7201), offers power boats and jet skis.

Lighthouse Water Sports Center, 700 N. Lake Blvd., Tahoe City (☎ 530/583-6000), rents both power boats and jet skis.

Bungee Jumping: For this daredevil sport go to **Squaw Valley Bungee** (☎ 530/583-6985 or 530/583-4000) at the Squaw Valley USA ski resort, which is located off Highway 89 northeast of Tahoe City.

Camping: There's good camping in **D.L. Bliss** (☎ 530/525-7277), **Eagle Point** (☎ 530/525-7277), and **General Creek** (☎ 530/525-7982) state parks. The first has 168 sites, the second 100 sites, and the third 175 sites. General Creek is the only one that is open year-round. All three parks are located along Highway 89 between South Lake Tahoe and Tahoma.

Canoeing/Kayaking: For rentals try **Tahoe Paddle & Oar** in Tahoe City (☎ 530/581-3029), which rents both. Canoes can also be rented from **Tahoe Water Adventures,** Grove Street, Tahoe City (☎ 530/583-3325).

Cross-Country Skiing: The largest and most specialized cross-country skiing area has got to be **Royal Gorge Cross Country Ski Resort,** Soda Springs (☎ 530/426-3871), which offers 88 trails, with 328 kilometers (204 miles) of groomed track at a 7,000-foot elevation. Along the trails there are 10 warming huts and 4 trailside cafes, plus Wilderness lodge (35 rooms with a French restaurant) at the center of the track system and Rainbow Lodge (32 rooms with a European/Italian restaurant) at the west end of the track system. There's also a 22-kilometer (17.4-mile) inn-to-inn trail between the two lodges. Special weekend programs are available. Track fees are $21.50 for adults, $10.50 for children 7–12.

Squaw Valley Tahoe Nordic Ski Center, Highway 28, near Dollar Point Shell in Tahoe City (☎ 530/583-9858 or

530/583-0484), has 65 kilometers (40.4 miles) of groomed trails overlooking Lake Tahoe. It offers three warming huts and is close to Tahoe City for lodging choices. Fees are $15 for adults, $7 for children 7–12.

Eagle Mountain Nordic, 15250 Ventura Blvd., No.710, Sherman Oak (☎ 530/389-2254), is at a base elevation of 5,800 feet, 20 miles west of Donner Summit. It offers 75 kilometers (46.6 miles) of groomed trails and is popular with families. Day passes are $16 for adults, $10 for children 7 to 12.

Northstar-at-Tahoe in Truckee (☎ 530/562-1010) has 65 kilometers (40.4 miles) of groomed trails.

Squaw Creek (☎ 530/583-6300) has 400 acres of cross-country skiing. Track fees are $14 for adults, $12 for children.

There are also more than 8 miles of trails in **Sugar Pine Point State Park,** south of Tahoma on Highway 89 (☎ 530/525-7982).

Fishing: There are many fishing charter operations. Try **Mac-A-Tac Charters,** North Tahoe Marina, 7360 N. Lake Blvd., Tahoe Vista (☎ 530/546-2500); **Kingfish Guides Service,** 5180 Hwy. 89, Homewood (☎ 530/525-5360); or **Mickey's Big Mack Charters,** Sierra Boat Co., Carnelian Bay (☎ 530/583-4602). Five-hour trips are around $70 per person from any of these outfitters.

Golf: Among the best and most challenging courses in the area are the following: **Northstar Golf Course,** Basque Drive off Northstar Drive (☎ 530/562-2490), an 18-hole, par-72 course, has numerous water hazards and a beautiful back 9 in the woods. Greens fees are $67 in high season, $45 at other times.

The **Squaw Creek Golf Course** at the Resort at Squaw Creek in Squaw Valley (☎ 530/583-6300), is an 18-hole, par-71 course (the most expensive in the area) designed in links style by Robert Trent Jones, Jr.

Finally, the **Tahoe Donner Golf Course,** off old Highway 40 in Truckee (☎ 530/587-9440), is another championship 18-hole, par-72 course and a good value.

There's also a course at Incline Village.

Hiking: On the western shore, there are several easy trails—the three-quarter-mile nature trail in **Sugar Pine Point State Park,** for example, and the trail down to Vikingsholm in Emerald Bay State Park.

In **D.L. Bliss State Park,** the Rubicon Trail, which follows the shoreline to the mouth of Emerald Bay and then from there to Vikingsholm, is moderately difficult. It's 3.1 miles to Emerald Point and 4.4 miles to Vikingsholm, making for a round-trip total of about 9 miles. From the **Eagle Falls Picnic Area,** you can take the short, 2-mile round-trip hike to Eagle Lake, crossing Eagle Falls after about one-third mile on a steel footbridge.

If you want a longer hike, continue on to the Velmas, Dicks, and Fontanillis lakes.

For a real thrill, take the tram up at **Squaw Valley** and hike down to Shirley Lake. Or, of course, you can hike from the valley trailhead at the end of Squaw Peak Road next to the tram building along Squaw Creek to Shirley Lake. Follow the creek. It will take you about 3 hours.

More ambitious hikers will want to walk part of the **Tahoe Rim Trail.** In this northwestern region there's a trailhead off Highway 89 in Tahoe City, located across from the Fairway Community Center on Fairway Drive. This 18½-mile trail leads to Brockway Summit, affording panoramic views of the mountains, the Truckee River Canyon, and Lake Tahoe. Twelve miles along the trail is Watson Lake, where you can stop to camp or picnic.

Horseback Riding: Contact **Alpine Meadows Stables,** Alpine Meadows (☎ 530/583-4266); **Northstar Stables,** 950 Lake Blvd., Northstar (☎ 530/562-1230); and **Squaw Valley Stables,** 1525 Squaw Valley Rd., Squaw Valley (☎ 530/583-7433). All are open snow and weather conditions permitting.

Ice Skating: Try the Olympic Pavillion at Squaw Valley USA Resort (☎ 530/583-6985).

Jet Skiing: The following rent jet skis: **High & Dry** in Homewood Marina (☎ 530/525-5966); **Lakeside Boat & Sail** in Kings Beach (☎ 530/546-5889); **Lighthouse Water Sports Center,** 950 N. Lake Blvd., Tahoe City (☎ 530/583-6000); **Sunnyside Marina** in Sunnyside (☎ 530/583-7201); and the **Tahoe Boat Co.** in Tahoe City (☎ 530/583-5567). In addition try **Tahoe Water Adventures,** 120 Grove St., Tahoe City (☎ 530/583-3325).

Mountain Biking: Some of the best is at **Northstar-at-Tahoe,** Truckee (☎ 530/562-1010), which has more than 100 miles of trails, plus two transport chair lifts, technical and slalom courses, as well as a mountain bike school and rentals.

At **Squaw Valley USA** (☎ 530/583-6985), you can ride the cable car to the top and cycle down. Tours and packages are available.

Parasailing: If you've never done it, then this is your chance. Go to **Lake Tahoe Parasailing,** Tahoe City (☎ 530/583-7245), or **West Lake Parasail,** Sunnyside (☎ 530/583-6103). Prices average $50 to $60, depending on how long you wish to stay up.

Skiing: Tahoe is California's premier skiing area, and there are many resorts to choose from on the northwest side of the lake. **Ski Homewood,** 5145 Westlake Blvd., Homewood (☎ 530/525-2992), is a favorite family skiing resort, with kids 8 and under skiing free. The base elevation is 6,230 feet. It has 57 trails, a vertical drop of 1,650 feet, and 9 lifts including 1 quad chair, 2 triple chairs, and 2 double chairs that can handle 8,500 skiers per hour. Prices are $36 for an all-day adult lift ticket, $12 for youth 9 to 13.

Squaw Valley USA (☎ 800/545-4350 or 530/583-6985) is the fashionable place to ski. It's spread over 6 separate mountain peaks, which are serviced by 33 lifts, including a 150-passenger cable car, a super gondola, and 3 high-speed quads. The terrain is rated 25% beginner, 45% intermediate, and 30% advanced with plenty of chutes, gullies, and steep powder bowls. Lift tickets are $47. Skating and swimming are available also.

Sugar Bowl, Norden (☎ 530/426-3651), which is the closest resort to Sacramento and San Francisco, has an old-world atmosphere. It's currently being expanded and improved. The base lodge is at a 6,883-foot elevation. Lift tickets are $41 for adults, $12 for children 5 to 12.

Alpine Meadows, Tahoe City (☎ 800/441 4423 or 530/583-4232), has more than 100 trails covering 2 mountains. It's rated 25% beginner, 40% intermediate, and 35% expert. It's at a 7,000-foot elevation and has a vertical drop of 1,800 feet. The lifts include 2 high-speed quads, 2 triple chairs, 7 double chairs, and a surface lift. At this elevation, skiing can begin as early as Halloween and extend as late as July. Lift tickets are $47 for adults, $20 for children 7–12, and $8 for children 6 and under.

Northstar-at-Tahoe, Truckee (☎ 800/466-6784 or 530/562-1010), has 60 runs, 11 lifts, including a 6-passenger express gondola, and 4 express quad chairs. Lift tickets are $46 for adults, $20 for children 5 to 12. The resort is popular with families because it really does satisfy skiers of all levels.

Snowboarding: Snowboard parks and halfpipes are located at Squaw Valley USA and Ski Homewood. Diamond Peak also has a park, and the sport is also allowed at Northstar-at-Tahoe and Sugar Bowl.

State Parks: There are three state parks on the western shore: **Sugar Pine Point, D.L. Bliss,** and **Emerald Bay.** For information about the parks, guided hikes, and seasonal activities write to **California State Parks,** Sierra District, P.O. Box D, Tahoma, CA 96142.

Swimming: If you stay at one of the many lodgings at **Northstar-at-Tahoe,** you can use the junior Olympic pool in the recreation center. For reservations call ☎ 800/466-6784. Swimming is also available at **Squaw Valley USA** year-round.

Tennis: If you stay at one of the many lodgings at **Northstar-at-Tahoe,** you can play on the 10 courts at the recreation center there. Courts are also available at **Squaw Valley USA.** For high school and other tennis facilities, call the **Tahoe North Visitors & Convention Bureau** (☎ 800/824-6348 or 530/583-3495).

Waterskiing: A popular lake recreation. Go to **High Sierra Water Ski School** in Sunnyside (☎ 530/583-7417) or **Lighthouse Water Sports Center** in Tahoe City (☎ 530/583-7417).

White-Water Rafting: Adventure companies operate on the Truckee and other rivers. One is **Tahoe Whitewater Tours,** 2630 River Rd., Tahoe City (☎ 530/581-2441), which offers trips on five Sierra rivers as well as sea-kayaking trips in Emerald Bay. The latter include luncheon stops on Fannette Island.

Tahoe Vista, Kings Beach, Incline Village & East Shore

Special & Recreational Activities

Biking: Bikes can be rented at many places: **Porter's Ski and Sport** in Incline Village (☎ 702/831-3500); **Tahoe Bike & Ski** in Kings Beach (☎ 530/546-7437). The Lakeshore drive bike path starts at Gateway Park on Highway 28 and passes Crystal Bay on its 2½-mile route along the shore.

Boating: Boat rentals are available all around the lakeshore. Try **Lakeside Boat & Sail** in Kings Beach (☎ 530/546-5889); **North Tahoe Marina** in Tahoe Vista (☎ 530/546-8248); and **Tahoe Paddle & Oar** in Kings Beach (☎ 530/581-3029).

Camping: There are at least 34 campgrounds in the lake region. Most are operated by the U.S. Forest Service or California State Parks and are on the California side of Lake Tahoe. The largest on the east shore is the private campground at **Zephyr Cove** (☎ 702/588-6644), which has 170 sites. One of the most appealing is the Sandy Beach camp, another private campground with 44 sites and full facilities. Zephyr Cove is open year round.

Canoeing/Kayaking: Try **Tahoe Paddle & Oar** (☎ 530/581-3029), which rents canoes and kayaks for $10 to $25 per hour or $60 & up per day. Rentals are available at North Tahoe Beach Center in Kings Beach at 7860 N. Lake Blvd.

Fishing: Call **Mac-a-Tac,** Tahoe City Marina, Tahoe Vista ☎ 530/546-2500.

Golf: Seek out the **Incline Village Championship Course,** 955 Fairway Blvd., off Northwood Boulevard (☎ 702/832-1144), an 18-hole, par-72 course designed by Robert Trent Jones, Jr. Greens fees are $115 in high season, $90 otherwise.

The **Incline Executive Course,** Golfers Pass, off Mt. Rose Highway (☎ 702/832-1150), is a much shorter 18-hole, par-58 course and costs half the price of the Incline Village course, namely $50 in high season, $40 otherwise.

Hiking: There's an easy day hike from Spooner Lake Picnic area on the east side of Highway 28. It leads 10 miles round-trip to Marlette Lake.

Horseback Riding: Daily1- and 2-hour trail rides, plus breakfast, lunch, and dinner rides are arranged by **Zephyr Cove Resort Stables,** Zephyr Cove (☎ 702/588-5664). Prices start at $22.

Jet Skiing: Rentals at **Lakeside Boat & Sail** in Kings Beach (☎ 530/546-5889). In addition, try **Tahoe Aquatic Center,** also in Kings Beach (☎ 530/546-2419).

Mountain Biking: Varied terrain, appropriate to every level of ability, can be found in **North Tahoe Regional Park** in Tahoe Vista (☎ 530/546-7248).

Parasailing: For the fun of it contact **North Shore Parasailing** in Kings Beach (☎ 530/546-5098).

Skiing: A good intermediate resort, **Diamond Peak,** 1210 Ski Way, Incline Village (☎ 702/832-1177 or 702/831-3249), also has a snowboard park and cross-country skiing.

Snowmobiling: Rentals are available at **High Sierra** in Kings Beach (☎ 530/546-9909).

Swimming: An indoor pool can be used at **Incline Village Recreation Center** (☎ 702/832-1310).

Tennis: There are two courts at **Incline Village High School** on Village Boulevard; 7 courts are available by reservation only at **Ivgid Courts,** behind the Hyatt Lake Tahoe (☎ 702/832-1236). **Lakeside Tennis Club** (☎ 702/831-5258), on Highway 28, has 13 courts.

Waterskiing: For instruction plus, go to **Goldcrest Water Ski School** in Kings Beach (☎ 530/546-7412), or try **Skier's Paradise** in Tahoe Vista (☎ 702/546-8522).

The High Sierra: Yosemite & Sequoia

Distances in Miles: Yosemite Valley in Yosemite National Park, 214; Giant Forest in Sequoia National Park, 279

Estimated Driving Times: 4 hours to the Yosemite Valley in Yosemite National Park; 5½ hours to the Giant Forest in Sequoia National Park

Driving: Yosemite can be reached via Highway 140 from Merced (the best route in winter because it's the least mountainous), which leads to the **Arch Rock Entrance,** where most visitors enter the park since it's the closest entrance to the Yosemite Valley. Highway 120 from Manteca leads to the **Big Oak Flat Entrance,** which is near the Tuolumne and Merced Groves of giant sequoias. Highway 41 from Fresno, which you're less likely to take, leads to the **South Entrance,** near the Mariposa Grove. For weather/road conditions call ☎ 209/565-3351.

For Sequoia National Park, take Highway 99 South to either Highway 180 from Fresno into Kings Canyon or Highway 198 via Visalia. For road and weather information call ☎ 209/565-3351.

Further Information: For information on Yosemite, contact the **National Park Service,** P.O. Box 577, Yosemite, CA 95389 (☎ 209/372-0200); or the **Yosemite Association,** P.O. Box 230, El Portal, CA 95318 (☎ 209/379-2646).

For information about Sequoia or Kings Canyon, contact the Superintendent, **Sequoia and Kings Canyon National Parks,** Three Rivers, CA 93271 (☎ 209/565-3134).

The first sight of the sawtooth ridge of the Sierras is thrilling. These mountains are the glory of eastern California, stretching 400 miles, a chain of ridges and canyons, each carrying a river that has chiseled and carved and pummeled and smoothed the rock to create what you see today.

"Climb the mountains and get their good tidings. Nature's peace will flow into you as sunshine flows into the trees. The winds will blow their own freshness into you and the storms their energy, while cares will drop off like autumn leaves." So wrote John Muir at the turn of the century. Thanks to him and the other early conservationists we can enjoy these mountains today and experience the beauty of nature by visiting these three national parks and hiking on backcountry trails to the alpine beauties above.

YOSEMITE NATIONAL PARK

No matter how many photographs you may have seen of Yosemite and no matter how many tour buses may be drawn up along the main road through the canyon, nothing can prepare you for the grandeur of the place—the immense presence of the rocks and the mystery of the millions of years that it took to carve out this magnificent space in nature. The best time to visit the park is in the off-season, from October to April, when visitors are fewer. Spring is when the waterfalls for which the park is known are at their radiant best, but at any season Yosemite still shines in all its magnificence.

History

Glacier Point is perhaps where you can see most clearly how this magnificent terrain was created. Fifty million years ago, there was a broad, shallow valley here cut by the meandering Merced River. Ten to five million years ago the Sierra Nevada rose on each side, while the Merced River continued to cut the canyon. The Ice Age arrived, and glaciers filled the valley, widening and carving it into a U-shape until about 10,000 years ago, when the temperatures rose and the last glacier melted. There was left behind a deep lake that was eventually filled with silt and became the valley floor.

The early dwellers in the valley were the Miwok Ahwahneechee and the Mono Lake Paiute, who gathered every summer in Tuolumne meadows to trade with each other. Of these early dwellers John Muir wrote in *My First Summer in the Sierra* (1911): "Indians walk softly and hurt the landscape hardly more than the birds and squirrels, and their brush and bark huts last hardly longer than those of woodrats, while their enduring monuments, excepting those wrought on the forests by the fires they made to improve their hunting grounds, vanish in a few centuries." Although this may be stretching it a little far, in essence it's true of the Indian way of life, which emphasizes the harmony of nature and the sagacious use of everything in nature. Today, you can see for yourself; west of the Visitor Center, you can visit an Indian village to observe how the local Indians lived.

The first Europeans to see the valley were fur trappers like Joseph R. Walker, who came through in 1833, and others who followed in the 1840s. The valley, though, was not formally discovered until the Mariposa Battalion entered it on March 27, 1851, in pursuit of some Indians they wanted to relocate away from the mining camps in the Sierra foothills. Members of the battalion named the valley Yosemite, thinking that this was the name used by the local Indians. In fact, the Indians called the valley Ahwahnee. Shortly thereafter, in 1855, the first tourists arrived.

The first step in securing the valley for public use was taken in 1864, when the 48.6 square miles that included the valley and the Mariposa Grove were granted to California to hold for public use for all time. The subsequent history and development of Yosemite as a national park involved several famous characters, some of whom are buried in the Pioneer Cemetery, near the main visitor center.

Galen Clark (1814–1910) was appointed the first guardian of the Yosemite by the Governor of California. When he came to the park at age 42, he was dying, but he went on to live to be 96. A New England miner, he homesteaded 160 acres in Wawona, and his cabin became a regular overnight stop for park visitors. A great nature lover and mountaineer, he lobbied to secure Yosemite, and when the grant was made in 1866, he was made "Guardian of Yosemite," playing the role of superintendent of sorts by repairing trails, roads, and bridges and maintaining the park in general.

James Hutchings (1820–1902) was the second guardian. He commissioned Thomas Ayres to make the first sketches of the valley that encouraged people to visit, and he also opened one of the early hotels. Both of these men are buried in the Pioneer Cemetery. Stephen Mather, who had complained about conditions at Yosemite, helped establish the National Park Service and became its first director.

The most famous of them all, though, was John Muir. Muir was born in Dunbar, Scotland, in 1838 and came to the United States in 1848. He attended the University of Wisconsin but dropped out to take a 1,000-mile hike south to Florida before coming via Panama to San Francisco, where legend has it he asked a stranger to direct him out of town. The stranger asked him where he wanted to go, and Muir replied, "To any-place that is wild." The stranger pointed east, so Muir took the Oakland ferry, crossed the great Central Valley, and arrived in Yosemite in 1868.

In 1874 the first road into the valley was built, and the chapel, which still stands, was built in 1879. By this time, entrepreneurs and land speculators were already establishing a presence in Yosemite. In the 1870s, even though Muir had worked as a shepherd, he was not thrilled to find the Tuolumne Meadows overrun with sheep, and he began a vigorous campaign in conjunction with Robert Underwood Johnson of *Century* magazine to establish the wilderness around the valley as a national park. Yellowstone had already been established in 1872, so there was a precedent. Johnson lobbied Washington; Muir wrote and lectured. In 1890 Yosemite became a national park.

Muir went on to found and become the first president of the Sierra Club and pushed for the park to be placed under Federal administration, which it was in 1906. He continued to fight for conservation, giving his all to save Hetch Hetchy Valley, but he failed. The O'Shaughnessy Dam was built on the Tuolumne River, and the valley was turned into a reservoir, which now provides San Francisco with water. Some say that the loss of this beautiful valley broke his heart. He died December 24, 1914. Two years later the National Park Service was established.

Meanwhile, Yosemite was fast becoming a tourist sight. In 1899 the Curry Camping Company had been established, and in 1900 the first automobile entered the park. From then on roads and trails were cut through the park, and lodgings and other facilities established to cater to visitors, which today come close to four million per year.

Flora & Fauna

Just for the record, about 250 species of birds, 78 species of mammals, and 1,400 species of flowering plants reside in the park.

While you're there, you will certainly see numerous squirrels and chipmunks as well as mule deer. If you're lucky, you may also see a coyote trotting along the roadside as I did shortly after entering the park. About 300 American black bears (often brown or caramel in color) are also park inhabitants and might be seen anywhere in the park from April to December, when they go into hibernation. Be sure to follow all the instructions about food storage at your cabin, campsite, or car trunk in order to minimize your chance of suffering bear damage. California bighorn sheep have been reintroduced to the area, and there is now a self-sustaining herd. You might see them along Route 120 but usually only on the stretch outside the park.

Bird life is also abundant. You will likely see or hear acorn woodpeckers, great horned owls, Steller's jays, red-winged blackbirds, warblers, belted kingfishers, mountain chickadees, and several species of nuthatch. Among the most thrilling is the peregrine falcon, which swoops on its prey in midair and dives at speeds of 100 miles an hour. It's an endangered species, and there are only a handful of pairs living in the park. You're most likely to spy them around El Capitan or Half Dome.

In spring, the meadows and woodlands are mosaics of wildflowers—black-eyed susans, cow parsnips, lupines, goldenrods, wild iris, shooting stars, and many more.

There are three groves of giant sequoias in the park: the Mariposa Grove, near the southern entrance (Route 41); the Tuolumne Grove, near Crane Flat off the Tioga Road; and the Merced Grove, off the Big Oak Flat Road between Crane Flat and the Big Oak Flat entrance.

Yosemite National Park

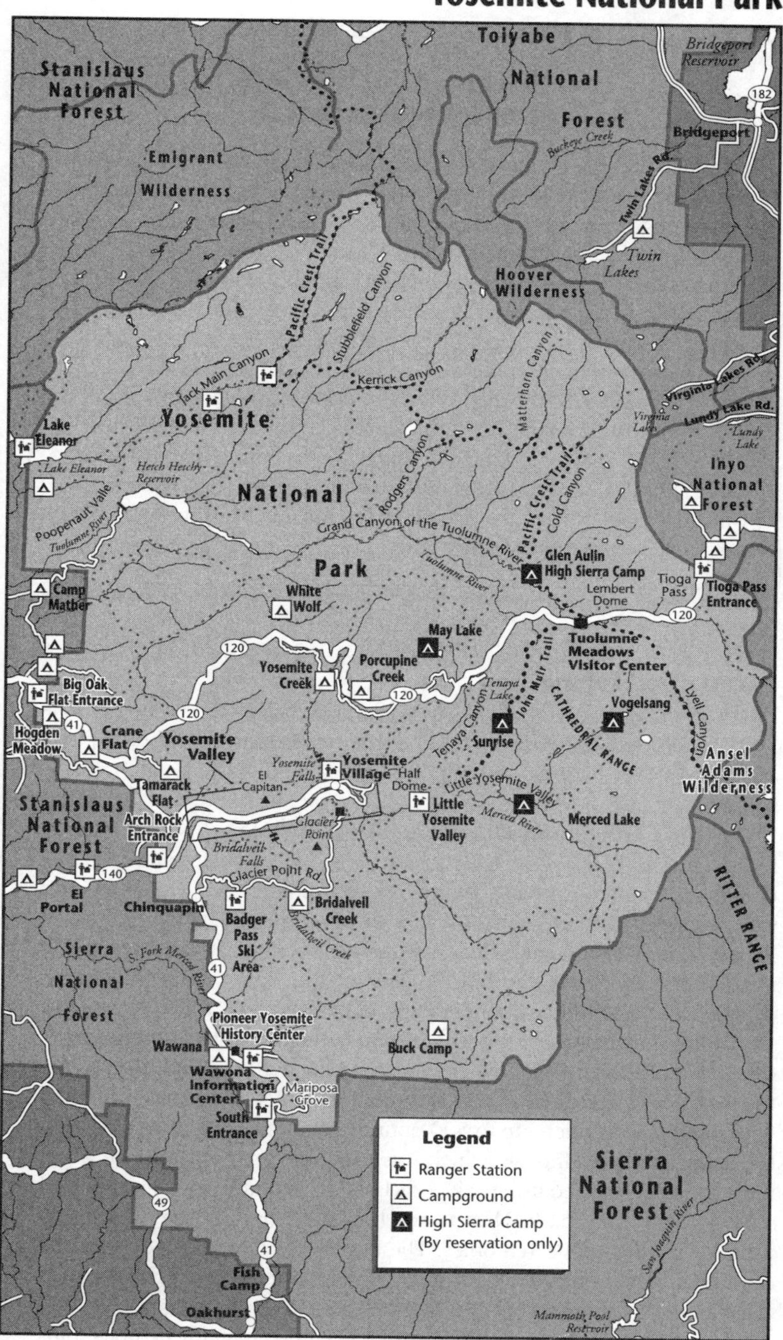

The 1997 Floods in Yosemite: A Temporary Disruption

Although the recent spring floods had a major impact on Yosemite—especially in the Valley—and although they have led to some major replanning in the park, overall the effect on visitors will be short term. Yosemite opened again in mid-March 1997. And though fewer campsites and fewer rooms were available (about 300 fewer campsites, for example), it is anticipated that additional sites and accommodations will be rebuilt and/or repaired and that new facilities will be built in other parts of the Valley. Some of these should be finished by 1998, so the disruption should be temporary and (hopefully) minimal. For the latest information, call either the 24-hour hotline (☎ 209/372-0200) or speak to an information officer (☎ 209/372-0265) during traditional office hours (be prepared to wait), or else look at the Yosemite section of the National Park Service's Web site: **<www.nps.gov>**.

Essential Park Information

Entry Fees: Entrance to the park is $20 per vehicle. An annual pass is $40. A Golden Eagle Pass is $50 and grants access to all national parks and many other national monuments and sites, including national seashores.

Visitor Centers and Other Facilities: The Main Visitor Center is located in the center of the Valley. Stop here to secure maps and information about the park, special activities, weather conditions, what roads and trails are open, and answers to whatever other questions you may have. Pick up a copy of *Yosemite Guide*, the newspaper that lists what's going on in the park. Also take the time to look at the exhibits—especially the Indian baskets—and to see the orientation video.

Behind the visitor center is the **Indian Village**, a re-creation of a typical Ahwahneechee village, where you can take a self-guided tour. Along the way, you will see the *chuckah*, a pine bough–covered structure lined with wormwood, where up to 500 pounds of acorns could be stored; and the *ahangi*, or roundhouse, which was used for ceremonial dancing and prayer and constructed using oak posts lashed with grapevines and shingled with incense cedar bark. Next to the last is the sweathouse, which was used for purification ceremonies. The Miwok dwellings called *u mu cha* are built in a cylindrical shape using pine and cedar poles, which are lashed together with wild vines.

Next door at the **Yosemite Museum** you'll find changing exhibits, plus a permanent exhibit of the cultural artifacts of the local Miwok and Paiute people. Often demonstrations of weaving, beadwork, and other arts are given. Check a Yosemite schedule for information, as hours change frequently.

A short distance west of this whole complex is the **Pioneer Cemetery,** where many early pioneers associated with the park are laid to rest.

To the east of the Visitor Center the **Ansel Adams Gallery** displays and sells the prints by the photographer, who is as synonymous with the park as John Muir.

There are three additional smaller information stations in the park. **Big Oak Flat** is open daily from May 1. **Wawona Information Station** is open daily. **Tuolumne Meadows** is open from late May or early June through September.

For recorded information 24 hours a day call ☎ 209/372-0200.

Planning Your Weekends

You'll need to spend several weekends in the park to explore its many pleasures. The best time to visit is between October and April, when there are fewer people. Still, if you can't plan to come at those times, don't be deterred. Although summer is busy—70% of the four million annual visitors arrive then—it's only really busy in the Valley, and that's a very small section of this 1,200-square-mile park. You can enter the park from the West via Highway 120, over Big Oak Flats, or via Highway 140, via Merced. Both will deposit you at the entrance to the 7-mile long, 1-mile wide Valley.

On a **first weekend** you may want to drive or cycle (bicycles can be rented summer only at Curry Village, year-round at Yosemite Lodge), or, easiest of all, take the free shuttle bus through the valley along the one-way loop road to various vista points. Take a couple of short hikes from the parking lots along the way, notably to the base of Yosemite Falls (half an hour) from the Lower Yosemite Fall parking lot; to the base of Bridalveil Falls (half an hour) from the Bridalveil Falls parking area; and to the base of Vernal Fall (1 hour), a steeper trail than the other two that leaves from the Happy Isles Nature Center. For great views of Half Dome reflected in Mirror Lake, take the 1-mile trail to this lake; which will take a half hour. You can return or continue around the lake (3 miles, 2 hours).

On the **second day,** weather permitting, take one of the more challenging hikes. For example, take the bus out to Glacier Point, and hike down from the point along the **Four Mile Trail.** It will take about 2½ to 3 hours. Or you can take a 3-hour, 6-mile climb to the **top of Vernal Fall,** accessed in summer from Happy Isles via the **Mist Trail.** Or you can devote the whole day to hiking either to the **top of Yosemite Falls** (7 miles, 6 to 8 hours) leaving from the Sunnyside Campground parking lot, or to the **top of Nevada Fall** (7 to 8 miles, 6 to 8 hours), accessible from the Happy Isles Nature Center via the **Mist or John Muir Trails.** The best day hike, though, is the 8½ mile, 6-hour hike down to the valley via the **Panorama Trail,** a route that takes you around the tops of three waterfalls and affords great views of the valley all the way down. Or take the **Pohono Trail** from Glacier Point, a 13-mile trail that also leads down to the Valley and will take 6 to 8 hours. Take the hiker's bus from the Valley to Glacier Point.

On **another weekend** you may want to climb to the **top of Half Dome** via the John Muir or Mist Trails to Little Yosemite Valley, where you can camp if you have a backcountry permit and then ascend to the summit using the cables strung along the shoulder of the backside of the dome. It's tough but worth it for the view. It's 17 very strenuous miles and will take 10 to 12 hours round-trip. For additional hiking suggestions, see "Hiking" in the activities section below.

On still **another weekend** choose one of the options listed under activities below. Sign up for **rock climbing** instruction or a **horse pack trip,** and really enjoy the challenge and the park the way it should be seen. Alternatively, take a **camera walk** or an **art class** at the Art Activity Center and really look at the scenery.

On **another weekend** you might spend the first day in the park and the second day on an excursion along the Tioga Road to **Lee Vining** and **Bodie,** an authentic ghost town that is only a few miles north on Highway 395. Or take Highway 41 past Fish Camp and the Sugar Pine Railroad to **Oakhurst** and **Bass Lake.**

Everyone should also make an effort to **visit in the winter** when the snow and sun make the whole place brilliant, there are fewer people, and the wildlife is easier to see. There are plenty of activities to pursue then, too—cross-country skiing, snowshoeing, and skating to begin with. There are Snowcat tours to the top of the ridges as well.

Also, note that Yosemite hosts a variety of **special events** throughout the year ranging from the Yosemite Vintner's Holidays, when California vintners present their wines, and the Chef's Holidays, when chefs perform their own magic.

Seeing the Park

The Yosemite Valley

A road loops through the valley in a counter-clockwise direction. You can drive or, better yet, take the shuttle bus, which operates every 6 to 8 minutes in summer and every 12 to 15 minutes at other times past the following vista points:

Bridalveil Falls never dries up. It drops 620 feet, and in the afternoons you'll often see rainbows forming in the spray. The name was probably inspired by the breezes that cause the mist to swirl around the falls.

Ribbon Falls has a short life span—they're dried up by July, but when they are in full flow, they drop an amazing 1,612 feet.

El Capitan rises 3,600 feet above the valley floor and takes 5 to 8 days to climb.

Three Brothers is so called because of the parallel rock fractures that were formed in the rock as it solidified millions of years ago.

Christmas in Yosemite: The Bracebridge Dinner

The Bracebridge Dinner is a famous traditional Christmas pageant that is held in the grand dining room of the Ahwahnee. It consists of Christmas carols, medieval music, and other entertainment, including a jester/juggler named the Lord of Misrule and his bear. The ceremony is adapted from descriptions in Washington Irving's *Sketchbook of a Christmas Day* set at Squire Bracebridge's Old English Manor in 1718. Chimes and trumpets announce the arrival of the Squire and his family, and each course is presented on fantastically elaborate litters to accompaniment of the Bracebridge Singers. There's the procession for the Fish, the Peacock Pie, the Boar's Head, the Baron of Beef, the Pudding, and the Wassail. The seven-course menus vary from year to year. A typical recent one featured roast chestnut soup, cold poached lobster tail with remoulade and three caviars, grilled stuffed quail, roast tenderloin of beef with candied shallot sauce, plum pudding, and wassail. Only 1,675 guests can be accommodated at the 5 dinner seatings on December 22, Christmas Eve, and Christmas Day. Because the event draws as many as 60,000 requests for seats, places are allocated by lottery. Applications can be obtained by writing to **Yosemite Concessions Service Corporation,** 5410 E. Home Ave., Fresno, CA 93727. They must be submitted between December 1 and January 15 for the following year's dinner. Each dinner costs about $200, including tax and tip, but excluding wine.

Upper Yosemite Falls is the upper portion of the tallest waterfall in the park; it drops 1,430 feet.

The appealing **chapel,** with witch's cap and belfry, was designed by Charles Geddes and built in 1879.

If you park and take a walk on to the **Sentinel Bridge,** there's a great view of Half Dome with the Merced River in the foreground.

Half Dome, at the eastern end of the Valley, is a magnificent piece of granite rising to an elevation of 8,842 feet (4,733 feet above the valley floor). Although the granite is 87 million years old, it is in fact the youngest plutonic rock in the Valley. It may be hard to believe, but it is thought that the other half of the dome was ground away by a glacier. Legend has it that Nangas, one of the bird and animal people, went to Mono Lake, married an Indian woman named Tesaiyac, and brought her back to Yosemite. On their journey she was carrying a cradle and a basket on her back. At the site of Mirror Lake they are said to have quarreled, she wanting to return home and he refusing to let her go. She ran away. He ran after her. First, she threw the basket at him, which became Basket Dome. Then she threw the cradle, which became the Royal Arches. Because they had brought anger to the Valley, they were both turned into stone: he into North Dome and she into Half Dome. She cried, and her tears of regret formed Mirror Lake.

Glacier Point rises 3,214 feet above the Valley, providing one of its most dramatic views.

North Dome is the second-highest granite formation in the park, after Half Dome, rising 3,526 feet above the valley floor. Following the legend related above, some say that **Washington Column** is Nangas's walking stick.

Yosemite Falls is the tallest waterfall in North America, dropping from a ledge 2,425 feet above the valley. The upper fall drops 1,430 feet to the middle cascade; the middle cascade 675 feet to the lower fall; there, it makes a final drop of 320 feet to the valley floor. The falls is at its fullest in late May, but it's hardly detectable by August.

Cathedral Spires, two shafts that have withstood erosion, stand 1,936 and 2,147 feet above the valley floor.

At **Valley View,** El Capitan stands on the left, Cathedral Rocks on the right, and there are glorious views all around the valley.

South of the Valley

If you enter the park via the Southern entrance (Route 41), you may want to turn off before you reach the entrance to the Valley and take the road out to **Glacier Point,** one of the most spectacular overlooks anywhere in the world. You will be looking down from the rim of the Valley 3,214 feet to the valley floor, and you'll be able to see several of the park landmarks including Yosemite Falls, Royal Arches, and Half Dome. Here at this point you can see how the valley was formed. Originally, the Merced River meandered through rolling hills. Then the rise of the Sierras forced the river to cut deeper, V-shaped valleys. Just before the Ice Age, further uplift caused the river to chisel a steep-walled gorge. Then the glaciers came grinding along the original river valleys, quarrying sheer cliffs and turning sloping tributaries into waterfalls. After the last glacier melted, Lake Yosemite was formed, flooding the whole valley, but eventually the Merced and the other streams filled the lake with sand and silt until today it is the level valley floor.

The Point is 30 miles (1 hour) from the Valley. Several trails leave from here—the 4-mile Trail, the Panorama, the Mist, and the Pohono trails. Hang gliding is also a popular sport that is practiced at Glacier Point, and it's also an excellent location for star gazing. Note that Glacier Point can only be reached on skis or snowshoes in winter.

The historical center of the park lies in the Southwest Corner at **Wawona,** the name the Indians gave to the giant sequoias. Here in this corner of the park, visitors can see the **Pioneer Yosemite History Center** and **Mariposa Grove** of giant sequoias. The former is a collection of buildings associated with people and events that shaped the national park from the artist Chris Jorgensen's cabin to a ranger's cabin. It's more interesting in summer months when it offers a living-history program. The Mariposa Grove is about a 1¼-hour drive (36 miles) from the Valley. From the parking lot trailhead, you can hike three-quarters of a mile to view the **Grizzly Giant.**

The **Grove Museum** is about 2 miles down the trail, the **Fallen Tunnel Tree** about 2½ miles, and **Wawona Point** 3 miles. You can take a 1-hour tram tour of the grove in summer; there's also a free shuttle that operates from the beginning of spring through the fall from Wawona, and this will avoid any parking delays.

North of the Valley

At **Crane Flat/Big Oak Flat,** 16 miles from the Valley on Highway 120, you can see another grove of sequoias—the **Tuolumne Grove.** From the grove parking area you can hike the 2-mile roundtrip (2 hours) to the grove and then walk the self-guided nature trail in the grove, which will add half an hour to your visit. Weekend nature walks are offered every Saturday (more often in May and June).

The beautiful **High Country** is what Muir worked so hard to save. It is only accessible by car in summer, when the Tioga Pass is open. The best way to explore the scenery is on foot or on horseback, but a drive along the 45-mile Tioga Road will take you through a 4,000-foot change in elevation and afford fine vistas of forests, lakes, and mountains. You can stop at **Tenaya Lake** for a picnic and then continue to **Tuolumne Meadows,** a sub-alpine meadow at an elevation of 8,600 feet. There you'll be surrounded by peaks and domes—the heart of the high country. Here, the temperature in summer is about 15 to 20 degrees cooler than the valley.

Hetch Hetchy Reservoir is located in the northwest corner of the park and is one of its least visited areas. In this area you can access several lakes and falls—Laurel Lake, Lake Vernon, and Rancheria falls. Because it's at a relatively low 3,900 feet, it is good for spring and fall hiking.

Guided Tours

For people who prefer to leave their car behind, there are seven guided tours offered. The most enchanting is the **Moonlight Tour,** which is given on full moon nights and a few nights before, from May through October. Others go to the Valley Floor, Glacier Point, and Mariposa Grove. Prices range from $17 to $45 for a tour that combines Mariposa and Glacier Point.

Lodging & Dining in the Park

Note: All of the lodgings and camps in the park are operated by the same concession. You can make reservations up to 366 days in advance, and you're well advised to do so. The best time to call and make reservations is on Saturday or Sunday. Due to flood damage from the New Year's flood of 1997, lodging possibilities will be strained a bit further until 1998, but rebuilding should restore most of the campsites soon.

The **Ahwahnee Hotel** (☎ 209/252-4848) is the premier hotel in the park, located in the Valley about a mile east of the Village with views of Half Dome, Glacier Point, and Yosemite Falls. A national historic landmark, it was opened in 1927 and named after the native word for Yosemite Valley, which means "place of the gaping mouth." The story goes that Lady Astor visited the park in the 1920s checking into a hotel called the Sentinel. Moments later she checked out. The park director at the time was determined to correct the lack of good accommodations in the park and commissioned the construction of the Ahwahnee.

The building designed by architect Gilbert Stanley Underwood is a massive, six-story structure faced with native granite and concrete that has been stained to look like redwood. Inside, the public rooms are dramatic and elegant. The Great Lounge, 77 feet long, 51 feet wide, and 24 feet high, is flanked at each end by huge, walk-in fireplaces. The windows reach from floor to ceiling, each with a top panel of original stained glass featuring Indian designs. A priceless collection of kilims and other rugs grace the walls because at the time of construction, there was not enough time to commission local Native American rugs. Other handsome public rooms include the mural room decked out in French style with copper-hooded fireplace, dark paneling, and a mural of Yosemite's flora and fauna painted by Robert Boardman Howard, as well as the Solarium, which affords a superb view of Glacier Point and is filled with ferns and plants set around a local Jasper fountain. The entrance lobby contains watercolor paintings by Gunnar Widforss, its mural painted by Jeannette Dyer Spencer, who also created the designs for the stained glass in the Great Lounge.

There are only 123 rooms, which means that, in order to secure a room, you must reserve a year in advance. Rooms are furnished with large, hand-hewn beds covered with hand-blocked bedspreads featuring Native American designs and such decorative accents as stenciling and serigraphs of either one of the hotel's Indian baskets or a fragment of a handwoven kilim. The nicest accommodations are in the seven cottages on the grounds, which were, by the way, landscaped by Frederick Law Olmsted.

The **dining room** (☎ 209/372-1489) is very dramatic. It has a 24-foot ceiling supported by large sugar pine trestles, granite pillars, and floor-to-ceiling windows providing views of Glacier Point and Yosemite Falls. At night it is lit by wrought iron chandeliers and candles placed on the table in wrought iron holders. The cuisine is certainly the best in the park, though it's not innovative. You'll find poached salmon with tomato coulis, filet mignon béarnaise, prime rib, and perhaps rack of lamb with pineapple-mint chutney. Prices range from $16 to $26. It's open daily for breakfast, lunch, and dinner. Note that a jacket and tie is required for men at dinner.

Additional hotel facilities include a heated pool and two tennis courts. Services available are concierge, bellman, valet parking, turndown, and room service.

Park Lodging & Dining: What to Expect

It will help you make your choice of accommodations if I define the terms used to describe the various types of lodging. Only 38% of park accommodations have private bath. Note, too, that the rates below are discounted between November and March, except on major holidays.

A **tent cabin** is a wood-frame canvas tent on a raised wooden platform with a wood-frame door. It is furnished with iron beds, made up with linen and wool blankets. Daily maid service, towels, and soap are provided. Rest rooms and showers are centrally located. In Yosemite Valley these accommodations have electric lights but no heat or other electrical gismos. Tent cabins in the High Sierra have concrete floors and no electricity at all. Most have wood stoves for heat, though.

A **housekeeping camp unit,** which is only available at Housekeeping Camp, consists of three concrete walls, a concrete floor, and double canvas roof. The fourth wall is a canvas curtain that separates the sleeping area from a covered cooking/dining area, which is screened by a fence and contains a picnic table and electrical outlets. Two fold-down bunks are located in the sleeping area, plus a double bed, mirror, light, and electrical outlets. There's a central showerhouse, rest room, and laundry.

Cabins come with or without bath. They are free-standing and plainly furnished with beds, dresser, propane wall heater, and electric lights. Daily maid service is provided. There are no phones or TVs. If there is no bath in the cabin, you'll find a centrally located bathhouse.

Standard hotel rooms, some with bath, some without, are simply furnished. They lack a TV, but usually have a telephone. The Lodge hotel rooms at Yosemite Lodge are the most modern in the park and are pleasingly furnished and also have patio or balcony. Most of the rooms at Wawona also have access to a veranda. The best equipped rooms are at the Ahwahnee. They feature comfortable furnishings, TVs, refrigerators, bathrobes, hair dryers, and bathroom amenities.

As for **dining,** with the exception of the Wawona Hotel Dining Room and the Ahwahnee Dining Room, the quality of the food in the park is average to poor, especially in winter when fewer places are open. In short, when you emerge from the park, unless you have been able to secure reservations at the establishments mentioned above or prepare your own meals, your first quest once outside the park will be a fine meal.

Rates: $240 double. *Dining Hours:* Daily 7–10:30am, 11:30am–2:30pm, and 5:30–8:30pm.

The **Wawona Hotel** (☎ 209/252-4848) is also a national historic landmark, located about 30 miles from the Valley on Highway 41, near the South Entrance and the Mariposa Grove. In front of the Victorian buildings, there's a large lawn dotted with Adirondack chairs and shaded by tall pines. The hotel's name is derived from an Indian word meaning "big trees." The first hotel on this site was built in 1856 by Galen Clark, who hosted visitors en route to Yosemite. The oldest building at the resort is the Clark Cottage, which dates to 1876. The main building was built in 1879. There are 105 rooms (50 with private bath, 55 without) in several buildings on the property. The Clark Cottage has been refurbished and contains the most modern accommodations of the hotel. Nicer accommodations are also located in the Little White building and the Washburn Cottage. The rooms are furnished in plain style and usually only contain bed, side tables, desk, and chair, with soap and tissues the only amenities in the bathroom. The main building and the annex contain the old-fashioned small, bathless rooms. Note that there are no telephones or TVs in any of the rooms.

The **dining room** (☎ 209/375-6556) is open daily for breakfast, lunch buffet, dinner, and Sunday brunch from Easter through Thanksgiving (on weekends the rest of the year). The room, which has a fireplace, has long paned windows that provide views of the surrounding woods. Beyond the fireplace, there is a piano room where someone is usually entertaining on weekends. The menu offers such classics as duck with cranberry-orange sauce and braised pork stuffed with apples and toasted almonds, as well as steaks and grilled fish. Prices range from $13 to $21. There's a traditional lawn barbecue held every Saturday evening in summer, and the restaurant's outdoor dining area is really lovely then.

Facilities include a 9-hole golf course, an outdoor pool, tennis courts, and stables.

Rates: $100 double with bath, $77 double without bath. Ask about their special packages. *Dining Hours:* Daily 7:30–10:30am, noon–1:30pm, and 5:30–9pm; Sun brunch 7:30am–1:30pm.

Yosemite Lodge (☎ 209/252-4848), which is open all year, is in the Valley about a mile from Yosemite Village. After Ahwahnee and Wawona, it has the most appealing accommodations. There are 226 rooms with balconies or patios, which are referred to as "lodge" rooms. These are the most modern rooms and are decently furnished with bed, desk, chair, and table with two wicker chairs. In addition, there are 64 hotel rooms with bath, 16 without bath; and 100 rustic cabins with bath, 89 without bath. Standard rooms and cabin rooms are plainly decorated and furnished with pine. Deluxe rooms have slightly better, more colorful furnishings. Facilities include an outdoor pool, bike rentals, the amphitheater (where ranger-naturalist programs are presented nightly in summer), a post office, and other stores.

It offers several **dining rooms**—Mountain Room Broiler, which also has an outdoor patio, for steaks as well as fish and fowl (open daily spring to fall and on weekends and holidays in winter); the Four Seasons for California/American food (open year-round for breakfast and dinner); and The Loft for sandwiches and California fare (open for lunch and dinner, spring to fall). There's also a cafeteria serving three meals daily and a sports bar.

Rates: $118 lodge double; $97 standard double; $81 room without bath; $84 cabins with bath; $70 cabins without bath.

Curry Village (☎ 209/372-1445) is also in the Valley, about a mile east of the Village. It was founded in 1899. It is the largest accommodation in the park, and nestled in the shadow of Glacier Point and Half Dome, it is the coolest in summer. It offers a variety of accommodations. There are 18 standard rooms, 103 cabins with private bath, 80 cabins without, and 427 tent cabins sharing centrally located bathroom facilities. Cabins are plainly furnished. Curry Village is open from spring to fall and on weekends and holidays in winter. Facilities include a cafeteria that is open from spring to fall for three meals a day, plus pizza and hamburger decks, and a cocktail lounge. Additional bonuses include outdoor pool; the mountaineering school; outdoor ice rink with skate rentals; bike, raft, and cross-country ski rentals; and an amphitheater where naturalist programs are shown.

Rates: $97 standard rooms; $84 cabins with bath, $70 cabins without bath; $55 tent cabins.

In summer only, **Tuolumne Meadows Lodge** (☎ 209/372-1313) has 69 tent cabins plus a canopy tent beside the Tuolumne River serving breakfast and dinner in summer. Bonuses include the mountaineering school and stables.

Rates: $59 double.

White Wolf Lodge (☎ 209/252-4848), also open in summer only, has 4 cabins with bath and 24 tent cabins. Breakfast and dinner are served in the dining room (☎ 209/372-1316). Make reservations for dinner.

Rates: $77.50 cabins with bath; $54 tent cabins.

Housekeeping Camp has 282 units located along the Merced River. It's located right in the Valley, about a half-mile from Curry Village.

Rates: $48.50 tent cabin.

For details about the **High Sierra Camps,** see "Camping" in the activities section below.

Other dining facilities outside the hotels/lodges are found in the Village. The **Yosemite Village Grill,** which is open all year, serves burgers, chicken strips, sandwiches, and hot dogs. From spring to fall, **Degnan's Deli** serves sandwiches and salads.

Lodging & Dining Near the Park

The Estate by the Elderberries, 48688 Victoria Lane, P.O. Box 577, Oakhurst, CA 93644 (☎ 209/683-6860, fax 209/683-0800), is the place to stay if you want to enjoy a truly wonderful weekend. The accommodations are beautifully designed and decorated, the gardens are enchanting, and the restaurant's cuisine is the best for miles around. It's located about 16 miles outside the park. The accommodations, located in a Mediterranean-style villa (built in 1991) with round turret and terra-cotta tile roof, are approached through lovely gardens with a fountain that is spotlit at night. Enter through the lobby into the exquisite parlor with a large brick fireplace and carved bookcases. A grand piano sits in the circular turret area, Oriental rugs adorn the floors, and every single piece of furniture is upholstered with beautiful fabric.

There are only nine rooms, each individually decorated in superb style. The Saffron Room has a dramatic ebony bed and armoire inlaid with ivory, extravagant art nouveau lamps, black marble fireplace, and yellow and black marble bath, all set against a burnt orange, black, and gold palette. The Rosehip Room contains a polished, Empire-style queen bed inlaid with mother of pearl, an ormolu-ornamented armoire, and an adobe-style fireplace. The Lavender Room is decked out in periwinkle blue and lavender and offers a locally crafted sleigh bed and other furnishings. Other rooms have beautifully coiffed four-posters. All have king-size beds made up with the finest Italian linens and goosedown comforters, authentic antique furnishings and bathrooms featuring hand-painted French tiles. They also have wood-burning fireplaces, TVs, CD systems, and wrought iron balconies. Facilities include an alluringly landscaped pool, gardens, and a tiny chapel.

Erna's Elderberry House (☎ 209/683-6800) is this establishment's elegant dining room. There are, in fact, two rooms—a light and airy tile and stucco space and a more formal room lit by chandeliers with jade carpet and tables covered with rose-colored cloths. The cuisine is expertly prepared and spectacularly presented and served. The six-course prix-fixe menu will leave you feeling that all is perfect with the world. A sample menu might begin with a champagne and elderberry nectar followed by a delicious salmon en croûte accompanied by red pepper pasta and a fragrant raspberry sauce. Cream of spinach soup might follow and then an apple or pear compote before the entrance of the main course. This could be Manchester quail filled with sausage spoonbread and served with huckleberry sauce and an assortment of fresh vegetables. A salad would follow, and the whole meal would finish with a dessert, such as cranberry-walnut cake with pumpkin icing. Three wines are suggested to accompany the appetizer, main course, and dessert for an additional amount, or you can select from the fine wine list. This magnificent repast will cost $68.

Rates: $320–$420 double. *Dining Hours:* Wed–Fri 11:30am–1pm, Sun 11am–1pm; daily 5:30pm–closing; closed Tues in winter.

The **Marriott Tenaya Lodge,** 1122 Hwy. 41, Fish Camp, CA 93623 (☎ 209/683-6555, fax 209/683-8684), is located in a modern, three-story building located just two miles outside the park. The lobby has a Western feel, with its large, fieldstone fireplace, deer trophy, and sitting area decorated with Indian pattern rugs. There are 242 spacious, modern, and comfortable rooms, each equipped with cable TV, clock radio, minibar, and three telephones.

Fine dining is offered in the **Sierra Restaurant.** Dishes range from pastas, such as angel hair with fresh salmon in a basil cream sauce, to meat dishes, such as filet of beef with roasted garlic and tomato demi-glace. Prices range from $14 to $23.

Steaks are the mainstay at Jackalope's Saloon. The Parkside Deli offers sandwiches, pizzas, and a short list of entrees. Facilities include a fitness center, indoor and outdoor pools, and spa.

Rates: Summer, $179–$269 double; fall, $169–$239; winter, $79–$179; spring, $109–$219.

Yosemite Activities

Check the park paper for what's going on. There are a variety of evening programs, including talks, movies, and campfire programs at the campgrounds. **Living History** programs are given at the Pioneer History Center at Wawona Wednesday through Sunday in summer. All kinds of nature walks, talks, and hikes are offered, and the customs of native peoples are demonstrated in the Indian village in summer. A variety of tours is also offered, from the 2-hour tour of the valley floor to the 6-hour tour to Mariposa and Big Trees grove, and the 2-hour moonlight tour given during full moon periods in summer only.

Yosemite
Special & Recreational Activities

Biking: Bikes can be rented at **Yosemite Lodge** year-round and at **Curry Village** in summer only. There are more than 8 miles of bike paths in Yosemite Valley. Note that you must stay on the bike paths and not go off on any other trails. The cost is $20 a day.

Camping: For campground information call ☎ 209/372-4845; for reservations, which may be made 4 months in advance, call **Destinet** (☎ 800/452-8787); international callers should call ☎ 619/452-8787. From June 1 to September 15 there is a 7-day camping limit in the Valley and a 14-day limit outside. For the remaining months and the calendar year there is a 30-day limit. Reservations may be made up to eight weeks in advance at some of the campgrounds; otherwise it's first come first served.

There are 16 campgrounds in the park; 6 are in the Valley, the rest are anywhere from 17 to 55 miles away. All Valley campgrounds require reservations, except for Sunnyside Walk-In, but there are only 35 sites there. Reservations are also required at **Hodgdon Meadow** and **Crane Flat,** the two largest campsites outside the Valley. Fees range from $7 to $15 per site.

Wawona, Hodgdon Meadow, and two Valley campgrounds are open year-round; the others are open summer only, with Tuolumne Meadows only open from mid-August through September.

The most sought-after campsites are at the **High Sierra Camps** (☎ 209/454-2002): Glen Aulin (8 tent cabins), at the foot of the White Cascades on the Tuolumne River; May Lake (8 tent cabins), beneath the eastern wall of Mt. Hoffman and on the shore of May Lake; Sunrise (9 tent cabins), on a long narrow shelf above Long Meadow, which is the second highest in elevation and has a remote wilderness atmosphere; Merced Lake (19 tent cabins), the lowest in altitude and also the warmest, offers the peace of Merced Lake and great fishing; Vogelsang (12 tent cabins), the highest and most dramatic of the camps, sits above the timberline near some of the finest fishing lakes in the park.

These camps provide accommodations in dormitory-style four- or six-person tent cabins furnished with beds with mattress and springs, linen, and blankets. Breakfast and dinner are included. The High Sierra camps are open from late June to Labor Day. Reservations are by lottery, and applications are accepted from October 15 to November 30 only, for a lottery held in mid-December. You will be notified at the end of March about the outcome. Contact **High Sierra Desk,** Yosemite Reservations, 5410 E. Home Ave., Fresno, CA 93727, to make an application.

For **backcountry** camping you'll need to reserve a permit. For summer trips reservations can be made by mail only, between March 1 and May 31. Send details, dates, as well as trailheads that you intend to use with alternatives, and mail all the information to the **Wilderness Office,** P.O. Box 577, Yosemite, CA 95389. At other times, pick up your permit a day in advance at the issuing station closest to the trailhead.

Fishing: The season opens the last Saturday in April and extends to mid-November. Special regulations apply on certain stretches of the Merced. Ask at the information center.

Golf: The **Wawona Golf Course** (☎ 209/375-6572) is the oldest mountain course in the state, having opened in 1918. There's also an 18-hole course at the **Ahwahnee Resort and Country**

Club (☎ 209/683-6620), 2 miles west of Oakhurst on Highway 49.

Hiking: Eight hundred miles of trails make hiking the premier activity in the park. Backpacking instruction and trips are offered by the **Yosemite Mountaineering School and Guide Service** (☎ 209/372-1244).

The **Yosemite Association** (☎ 209/379-2646) also offers guided trips. Permits are required for backcountry camping. The 7-day guided hikes leaving from Tuolumne Meadows Lodge, with stay en route at the High Sierra camps, are very popular, quite strenuous, and require reservations. See above also under "Planning Your Weekends" for some suggested short hikes.

One loop that is often overlooked and less used than many others is the **Valley Floor Loop,** which is 13 miles long and will take five to seven hours. It begins about 50 yards behind the chapel.

Horseback Riding: There are three stables in the park that offer everything from pony rides for kids to longer rides, including 4- and 6-day pack trips, which must be booked in advance. Custom trips are available too.

Yosemite Valley Stables (☎ 209/372-1248), offers a 2-hour ride to Mirror Lake, a half-day scenic ride to Vernal and Nevada Falls, and an all-day scenic ride to Glacier Point or Half Dome. It is open from Easter to mid-October.

Wawona Stables (☎ 209/375-6502) offers trips to Meadow Loop, Chilnualna, and Deer Camp. It's open in the summer only.

Tuolumne Meadows Stables (☎ 209/372-1327) offers trips to Tuolumne View, Tuolumne Falls, Waterwheel Falls, and Young Lake. It's open in the summer only.

For information about horseback riding, call the stables or the **High Sierra Reservation** desk (☎ 209/454-2002). Prices range from $40 for a 2-hour ride to $50 for 4-hours and $70 for a full-day trip.

Ice Skating: There's an outdoor rink at **Curry Village** charging $7.50 for adults, $6 for children.

Picnicking: Hotels will provide picnics if ordered in advance. Otherwise, purchase ingredients at park food stores.

Rafting: Rafts for use on the Merced River can be rented at Curry Village.

Rock Climbing: Given the terrain, this is a premier park activity. The **Yosemite Mountaineering School and Guide Service** is one of the best in the nation, offering basic and advanced instruction plus specialty courses. Lessons are given every day from May through September. In summer, the school is at Tuolumne Meadows; in winter, it's at Curry Village. For information call ☎ 209/372-1244.

Skiing: January and February are the best months for skiing. **Badger Pass** is a good place to learn; it has nine trails, one triple-chair, three double-chair, and one surface lift. Weekend all-day lift tickets are $30 for adults, $15 for children 4 to 12. There are also 90 miles of groomed cross-country trails here.

Note, too, that you can ski 350 miles of trails and roads in the park. Overnight trips to **Glacier Point Hut** are exciting. All-day equipment rental is $16.50 for adults, $11.50 for children. For information on the ski schools, call ☎ 209/372-1244. Shuttle buses operate to the ski area.

Snowshoeing: Rangers lead trips in the winter. You can contact the Yosemite Visitor Center on arrival or in advance of your trip.

Swimming: There are pools at Yosemite Lodge, the Ahwahnee Hotel, and Curry Village. There are also swimming holes in the Merced River at the eastern end of the Valley, but you should know that swimming in the river can be dangerous.

SEQUOIA & KINGS CANYON NATIONAL PARKS

Although they lack the spectacular waterfalls of Yosemite, Sequoia and Kings Canyon offer magnificent sequoia groves, an awesome river canyon, brilliant caves, and some spectacular scenery and wildlife. And because the park attracts under two million people, it's a lot less crowded than neighboring Yosemite, providing an opportunity to experience nature at a quieter and much more leisurely pace.

There is only one real road through the park; most of the terrain is accessible by trail only. And what terrain it is! Here you will find the highest mountains in the contiguous United States—including Mount Whitney—30 of the world's remaining sequoia groves, and a canyon that is deeper than the Grand Canyon itself. If you enter the park in fall or early winter, you will find yourself climbing through burnt-ocher foothills into a conifer forest. From here you can hike to the spectacular alpine landscape of mountain peaks, lakes, and sky.

History

The early dwellers in the park were the Monaches, a Paiute group that migrated from around Mono Lake. Other subgroups also occupied the area. The first non-native to enter the park area was Gabriel Moraga who arrived in 1806 and named the river "the River of the Holy Kings" because he discovered it on the day of the Epiphany. Miners and trappers explored the region in the 1850s, and one of them, Hale Tharp, is credited with discovering the Giant Forest in 1858. The first scientific exploration was undertaken in 1864 by a team sent by geologist Josiah Dwight Whitney. By the 1870s loggers were cutting these magnificent trees, even though they were too brittle to use as timber. Instead, would you believe, they were used to make fence posts, pencils, railroad ties, and grape stakes in the vineyards.

A third of them were used up this way until conservationists like John Muir began lobbying on their behalf crying, "As well sell the rain clouds and the snow and the rivers to be cut up and carried away." Muir joined forces with George Stewart, editor of the ***Visalia Delta***, and U.S. Sen. John Miller of California in an attempt to pass legislation that would protect the trees. Finally, on September 25, 1890, Sequoia National Park was established. A week later, it was tripled in size, and General Grant National Park was established to protect the General Grant Grove. More acreage was added later, along with Kern Canyon and Mount Whitney in 1926. In 1940, Kings Canyon was founded, and General Grant merged with it. Mineral King was added to Sequoia National Park in 1978. Today, Sequoia and Kings Canyon are managed jointly.

Flora & Fauna

When John Muir first came upon the Giant Forest, he wrote, "When I entered this sublime wilderness the day was nearly done, the trees with rosy glowing countenances seemed to be hushed and thoughtful, as if waiting in conscious religious dependence on the sun and one naturally walked softly and awestricken among them." And they still inspire us to do so today.

The giant sequoia grows naturally only on the western slopes of the Sierra Nevada, usually between 5,000 and 7,000 feet where there are some 75 groves in total. The tree is the largest living organism on earth. It's not the tallest in the world—that title belongs to the coastal redwood—nor is it the oldest—that honor falls to the California bristlecone, one of which has been estimated as 4,900 years old—but it is undoubtedly the largest. The General Sherman tree stands 275 feet tall, is between 2,300 and 2,700 years old, has a base that is 102 feet in circumference, and possesses one branch that is almost 7 feet in diameter.

The species has certain characteristics that help to ensure its long life. The bark and wood contain chemicals that make it resistant to insects and fungi, while its lack of resin makes it largely impervious to fire. When giant sequoias die, they usually succumb to toppling because they have shallow root systems with no tap root. They differ from the coastal redwood, even though they both belong to the sequoia family. They are shorter, and their trunks and branches much stouter. Everything about them, except height, is bigger—cones, bark thickness, and trunk and limb size. Sequoias live to be 3,200 years old, have bark as thick as 31 inches, trunks as large as 40 feet in diameter, and limbs as much as 8 feet in diameter. The respective comparisons for coastal redwoods are 2,000 years, 12 inches, 22 feet, and 5 feet.

It's hard to believe that these giants grow from tiny seeds that are contained in the chicken-egg–size cones. These cones hang on the tree for up to 20 years until they are opened, preferably by fire, which dries them up and causes them to open and disperse their seed.

Other trees and shrubs that are common in the parks are California black oak and Mariposa manzanita in the foothills, plus several varieties of conifers—incense cedar, sugar pine (identifiable from its huge cones), ponderosa pine, Jeffrey pine, lodgepole pine, and white fir.

According to park officials there are 1,431 species of plants, more than 345 species of animals, and around 170 species of birds living in the park. These include mule deer, black bears, coyotes, pine martens, mountain lions, raccoons, gray foxes, and many more mammals. The rivers are stocked with brown, brook, and other kinds of trout. Each type of terrain—foothills, forest, and alpine—supports a different cast of characters.

The foothills are bursting with flowers and shrubs for a brief two months before the onset of the long, dry summer that arrives in late May, turning everything into dust. They are also home to coyotes, gray foxes, bobcats, and rattlesnakes.

The forest region, between 5,000 and 9,000 feet, supports firs, pines, and the giant sequoia along with abundant bird life and such woodland characters as black bears, mule deer, squirrels, and pine martens.

At the alpine level, above 9,000 feet, only the hardiest survive—a few scrubby trees and such birds as the golden eagle.

Essential Park Information

Entry Fees: A pass good for one week is $10 per vehicle. An annual pass is $20. A Golden Eagle Pass is $50 and grants access to all national parks and many other national monuments and sites, including national seashores.

Visitor Centers & Other Facilities: There are three visitor centers in the park. **Foothills Visitor Center** (☎ 209/565-3134) is 8 miles east of Three Rivers on Highway 198, near the Ash Mountain entrance; **Lodgepole Visitor Center** (☎ 209/565-3782) is inside the park, near the General Sherman Tree; and **Grant Grove Visitor Center** (☎ 209/335-2856), which is on Kings Canyon Highway, right inside Kings Canyon Park, near the Grant Grove.

There are also two ranger stations: **Mineral King** (☎ 209/565-3768), in the southern part of Sequoia, and **Cedar Grove** (☎ 209/565-3793), on the Kings Canyon Highway in Kings Canyon, both of which are open in summer only.

Seeing the Park

First, pick up a copy of the ***Sequoia Park,*** which provides information about what's on in the park.

The **Generals Highway** connects the two parks, making for a pleasant 2-hour (46-mile) drive from Park Headquarters at Ash Mountain to

Sequoia & Kings Canyon National Parks

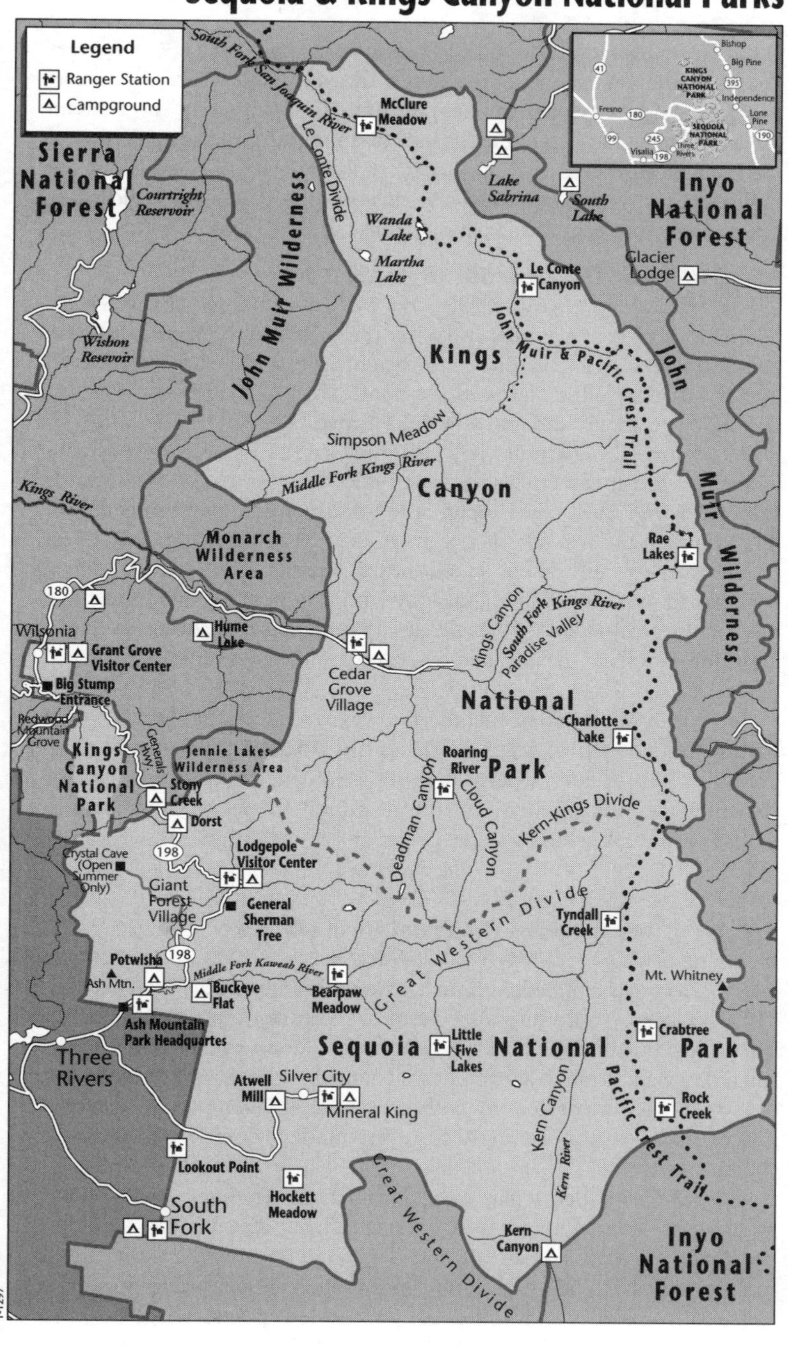

Grant Grove (open year-round). In summer only Highway 180 continues out along the South Fork of the Kings River to Cedar Grove. One other road, which is only open in summer, traces the course of the Kaweah River; and a couple of other roads lead to campgrounds; the remainder of the park is accessible only by hiking trails. The lack of roads and the limitation it places on vehicles make this park a place for true wilderness lovers. Eighty percent of the park is, in fact, only accessible by foot.

Along Highway 198/Generals Highway

If you enter along Highway 198, you will pass through **Three Rivers** (stop and explore the stores) and enter the park at **Ash Mountain Park Headquarters.** Before you reach the headquarters, you can turn off along a road that travels the course of the South Fork of the Kaweah River to South Fork campground and **Garfield Grove.**

Alternatively, a few miles beyond Three Rivers, you can turn off and travel the road that parallels the East Fork of the Kaweah River towards **Mineral King.** This road is open only from June 1 to November 1, and the 25-mile route will take 1½ hours to drive. The name "Mineral King" recalls a time when miners hoped to find another silver lode here. The best way to see this subalpine meadowland is to hike to one of the many lakes in the area—Monarch, Eagle, and Franklin lakes for example. There are a dozen trails in the area and two campgrounds, Atwell Mill and Cold Springs.

From Ash Mountain, Generals Highway leads towards **Giant Forest Village.** As you drive, watch for **Hospital Rock,** 6 miles north of the Fernhill Visitor Center, where you can see some faint, faded pictographs drawn by the Monache Indians and the grinding holes that they used to make acorn meal, which was their staple food, made either into bread or mush.

Before you reach Giant Forest Village, you may want to take the 7-mile road going west that leads to **Crystal Cave (☎** 209/565-3759), a 2½-mile-long marble cave carved by the forceful flow of the sinking Cascade and Yucca creeks coupled with the erosion caused by acidic groundwater. There's a steep, 15-minute hike down to the cave from the parking lot. This is just one of close to 200 caves that are found in the park. Visitors can take a walk through a magnificent chain of underground rooms, some that open from a passageway with only 10-foot ceilings, to magisterial spaces with 40-foot ceilings, or even smaller rooms with 100-foot ceilings.

The cave has a spectacular array of formations. The Junction Room has an array of stalactites and stalagmites, arranged around flowstone and rimstone. The Marble Hall, 150 feet long and 40 feet wide, is the largest room in the cave. The astonishing Dome Room contains a huge variety of formations—slender hollow soda straws, rimstone pools, stalagmites, and stalactites. The Organ Room, which is named after the curtain and flowstone formations that look like pipe organs, also contains rare shield formations. In addition to the regular tour, there is a Wild Tour Route that takes visitors on a more challenging route than the standard one.

Hours: Tours daily 10am–3pm from mid-June–early September (less frequently in May and late September). *Admission:* $5 adult, $2.50 children/seniors. Tickets must be purchased in advance at Lodgepole or Foothills Visitor Center.

Return to Generals Highway and take the road (open summer only) through the Giant Forest to Crescent Meadow (about an hour's drive). En route you'll pass the **Auto Log,** upon which you can drive if you wish; **Moro Rock;** and **Tunnel Log,** which you can drive through. The short climb up the granite dome called Moro Rock via 400 steps (30 minutes total) is worth doing for the view from the top across the Great Western Divide to such peaks as Mount Kaweah, which is close to 14,000 feet high. At the end of the road, you can enjoy a picnic in **Crescent Meadow,** or hike the mile-long trail around the meadow. Another trail from Crescent Meadow leads to **Tharp's Log,** a log cabin built from a fallen sequoia by Hale Tharp, the first non-Native American settler in the region. You can also access the **High Sierra Trail,** which leads 71 miles to Mount Whitney, the highest mountain in the Sierras.

Retrace your route back to Generals Highway and continue north into Giant Forest Village and then on to the short turnoff to the **General Sherman Tree,** a huge specimen that is considered the largest living tree in the world because of its volume (52,500 cubic feet in 1975 with about 40 cubic feet added each year). To give you an idea of how big this actually is, this tree alone could produce 119 miles of 1-by-12s, which would stretch from the park to the Pacific Ocean or to Bakersfield. The trunk alone, it is reckoned, would fill 2,770 half-ton pickup trucks. The tree, it is estimated, is between 2,300 and 2,700 years old, soars to 274.9 feet, and has a circumference of 102.6 feet. Take the time to sit on the benches provided and contemplate this natural wonder and then take the 2-mile **Congress Trail** around the grove past the 246-foot tall Washington tree.

Grant Grove

From here, the highway continues about 4 miles to the **Lodgepole Visitor Center,** which has some interesting displays about the sequoias. There's also a market, deli, and ice-cream parlor here.

From here, the road veers west past Lost Grove to **Stony Creek** and on to **Grant Grove.** About 2 miles before you reach Grant Grove Village, you can see the damage caused by early logging if you take the **Big Stump Trail,** which leads through an area that was clear-cut in the 1880s. You'll see stumps like that of the Mark Twain, which is all that remains of a 1,700-year old tree that took two men 13 days to cut down in 1891.

When you reach Grant Grove itself, you can see several remarkable trees. The **General Grant** (267 feet tall, 107 feet in girth, 40 feet in diameter, and 1,800 to 2,000 years old) weighs more than 700 large cars and could be used to construct more than 40 average-size five-room houses. It was designated the Nation's Christmas Tree by Pres. Calvin Coolidge, and at Christmastime special celebrations are given at the tree. The **Robert E. Lee** is 254 feet tall. You'll also pass a huge stump of a tree that took 9 days to cut in 1875, so that a section could be shipped off to the Centennial Exhibition in Philadelphia, and the **Fallen Monarch** tree, where the cavalry who guarded the park at the turn of the century stabled their 32 horses.

A short road (closed in winter) leads out from Grant Grove to **Panoramic Point,** where you can take a quarter-mile trail to a 7,250-foot high ridge for a fine view of **Hume Lake,** the main unit of Kings Canyon National Park just beyond, and a range of peaks, from Mt. Goddard in Kings Canyon to Eagle Scout Peak in Sequoia Park. Hume Lake was built as a mill pond supplying water to a flume that carried lumber to the planing mill at Sanger, 54 miles below. Today you can fish, swim, camp and rent boats at the lake. To reach the lake, take Highway 180 8 miles north of Grant Grove to Hume Lake Road, then travel about another 3 miles.

Along Kings Canyon Highway

From Grant Grove, Highway 180 (usually open only from May 1 to November 1) will take you another 30 miles into the main unit of **Kings Canyon National Park,** past some of the most dramatic scenery anywhere along the Middle and South Forks of the Kings River, and all the way to Cedar Grove.

This 8-mile long canyon is what you're here to see, and it's what the park is named for. The road twists and turns along the rim of the canyon before dropping down into the valley, where the river thrashes along. If you want an atmospheric drink, stop along the way and go into the remote **Kings Canyon Lodge,** where you'll see black and brown bear skins on the ceiling and plenty of trophies behind the bar—cougar, gray fox, deer, and more.

After the road reaches the valley, it travels another 6 miles through the canyon, where the walls of the valley rise as much as 1 mile—as high as a 500-plus story building—above the river. It's an amazing experience.

About 10 miles before you reach Cedar Grove, you'll pass the entrance to **Boyden Cave** (☎ 209/736-2708), a smaller version of Crystal Cave, complete with Chime room and draperies of stalagmites and stalactites.

Hours: Summer, daily 10am–5pm. *Admission:* $6 adults, $3 children 6–12. Cave tours take about 45 minutes.

Cedar Grove provides access to the **High Country,** where the peaks rise from 11,000 to 14,495 feet, the tallest being Mount Whitney, which is the highest peak in the 48 contiguous states. Cedar Grove landmarks include **Grand Sentinel** and **North Dome,** both granite domes, the first rising 3,500 feet and the second 3,700 feet above the river. You can also see **Roaring River Falls** and **Zumwalt Meadow,** which is named after the railroad magnate D.K. Zumwalt, who was moved to buy the land in 1889.

One mile east of Cedar Grove Village, there's a great view of the canyon from **Canyon Viewpoint.** A mile or so farther on, a trail leads from a parking area to **Knapp's Cabin,** used by Santa Barbara magnate George Knapp, who sponsored elaborate fishing expeditions into the area. From the Roaring River Falls parking area, about 3 miles east of the village, an easy hike of one-fifth mile (30 minutes) leads to **Roaring River Falls** or to **Zumwalt Meadow.** For a real experience, drive the one-way dirt road called the **Motor Nature Trail** (about 3½ miles east of the village), which winds along the river. **Grand Sentinel** can best be seen from the viewpoint/turnoff of the same name, about 5 miles east of Cedar Grove Village.

The deepest part of the canyon—8,000 feet from ridge to river—lies outside the park in the Sierra National Forest, where the Middle and South forks of the Kings River flow together. It is only accessible on foot from a trail that runs from **Yucca Point,** 15 miles northeast of Grant Grove on Highway 180.

Lodging & Dining in the Parks

Lodging and dining facilities are found at Giant Forest and Lodgepole in Sequoia, and at Grant Grove and Cedar Grove in Kings Canyon. For all reservations call **Guest Services Inc.,** P.O. Box 789, Three Rivers, CA 93271 (☎ 209/561-3314). Don't expect luxury or palatable food. It's strictly down-home style. Note that rates are reduced slightly from early October to late April. Note that a new lodge is under construction, but it won't be completed until the end of 1999.

At **Giant Forest Lodge** you can either stay in one of the motel-style rooms or in one of 103 cabins, 64 with bath, 39 without electricity or water. Don't expect luxury. The motel rooms are pretty standard and decorated in old-fashioned style. The cabins are rustic and show signs of age and wear, including peeling paint, stained bedspreads, and the like. But they are relatively comfortable. Those without water or electricity have kerosene lamps and oil or propane heat. The lodge is open from May through October only.

Giant Forest Lodge **dining room** offers the only adequate fare in the parks. It has a continental menu featuring pasta, and such dishes as chicken in Dijon mustard sauce, steak with pepper sauce, prime rib, and crab-stuffed shrimp Monterey. Prices range from $15 to $20. The dining room is open from mid-May through mid-October.

Rates: $75–$95 motel room; $36–$75 cabin.

Bearpaw Meadow Camp is on the High Sierra Trail, about 11 miles from Giant Forest. It has six tent cabins similar to those described in the Yosemite "Lodging & Dining" section above. The camp is open from mid-June to mid-September only.

Rates: $125 tent cabin.

Stony Creek Lodge is 15 miles north of Giant Forest and has 11 motel-style accommodations with private bath. The lodge is open from late May to September only. Facilities include a coffee shop.

Rates: $82.50 double.

Grant Grove Lodge has 9 cabins with bath, 19 without bath, and 24 rustic housekeeping cabins featuring patios with wood-burning cook stoves. These are open year-round. Facilities include a coffee shop.

Rates: $75 cabin with bath, $36–$45 cabin without bath (the higher price is for the housekeeping cabins).

Cedar Grove Lodge has 18 motel-style accommodations with shower. It overlooks the Kings River. The Village also has a cafeteria open in summer only.

Rates: $94.50 double.

Lodging & Dining Outside the Park

Montecito–Sequoia Lodge, on Generals Highway 9 miles south of Grant Grove in the Sequoia National Forest (☎ 800/227-9900 or 209/565-3388), is a comfortable, rustic lodge offering low-key, down-home, camp-style hospitality. From the lodge deck there are glorious views across the tops of pines to the Sierras. It has no pretensions to fashion and attracts families, seniors, and groups as well as eco-tourists. The accommodations, which are in four lodges, are furnished in a plain, old-fashioned way, but they do have private baths, electric blankets, and often appealing wilderness views. Maid service is not provided. There are also eight rustic cabins without bath, but they are insulated and equipped with electricity and wood-burning stoves. They are carpeted and basically furnished but lack running water.

Meals are served in the **dining room** with its large stone fireplace or out on the redwood deck overlooking a marvelous vista. Dinners are buffet-style, featuring two entrees (one vegetarian) plus vegetables, salads, and desserts. Beverages, snacks, and cereals are available 24 hours a day; people enjoy socializing before dinner over vegetables and dips. Facilities include a whirlpool spa, a small outdoor heated pool, tennis, stables, an archery and rifle range, and an arts-and-crafts studio/shop. Other activities are also offered—canoeing, square dancing, cross-country skiing (35km [21.7 miles] of groomed and backcountry trails), children's programs, volleyball, ice skating on Lake Homavalo, and ping-pong. For information write to 1485 Redwood Drive, Los Altos, CA 94024. Note too that day skiers are welcome to ski and partake of meals.

Rates (incl. breakfast and dinner): $79 per person double-occupancy in the lodge-$59 per person in cabin. Rates also include activities with instruction—except for horseback riding and waterskiing, for which you pay extra.

Sequoia/Kings Canyon Activities

Check the park paper for talks, films, guided nature and history walks, and evening campfire programs. The **Sequoia Natural History Association** also operates weekend field seminars on topics that range from bird life to outdoor photography. Contact them at Ash Mountain, P.O. Box 10, Three Rivers, CA 93271 (☎ 209/565-3758). Or check with one of the **visitor centers:** Grant Grove (☎ 209/335-2856); Giant Forest–Lodgepole (☎ 209/565-3782); or Foothills Visitor Center (☎ 209/565-3134).

Sequoia/Kings Canyon Special & Recreational Activities

Camping: There are 1,200 sites in about 14 campgrounds in the parks. The annual limit for camping is 30 days (14 days in summer). Fees range from $6 to $13 per night. For camping reservations call **Destinet** (☎ 800/365-2267); they accept reservation requests 4 months in advance.

Lodgepole Campground in Sequoia NP, which has 260 sites, is the only campground that requires reservations, and then only in summer.

The other large campsites are **Dorst,** 12 miles north of Giant Forest Village (218 sites); **Azalea** (118 sites) and **Sunset** (184 sites), both near Grant Grove; and **Moraine** (120 sites), **Sheep Creek** (111 sites), and **Sentinel** (83 sites), all in the Cedar Grove area. None of the remaining campgrounds has more than 45 sites.

Permits are required for backcountry camping. Reserve a permit via mail. Letters must be postmarked after March 1 and must reach the office at least 14 days before your planned trip. Write to **Wilderness Permit Reservations,** Sequoia and Kings Canyon National Parks, Three Rivers, CA 93271. Only a few permits are granted on a daily basis in the park, so it is best to reserve ahead.

Fishing: From April to November you can fish for trout in the Kaweah and Kings rivers as well as in several lakes. Anyone over 16 years of age needs a California fishing license.

Hiking: There are more than 800 miles of marked trails accessed from 25 trailheads. In fact, 80 percent of the park is only accessible by foot, which is what makes this place so special.

Two easy nature walks are the **Hazelwood Nature Trail** in Giant Forest, a 1-mile loop that will take about an hour, and the **Cold Springs Nature Trail** at Mineral King, along the East Fork of the Kaweah River, a quarter-mile, 45-minute walk.

Other easy trails include the 2-mile **Congress Trail** in Giant Forest, which loops through the grove and will take anywhere from 1 to 3 hours; the **Crescent Meadow Loop,** which is 1.8 miles and will take 2 to 3 hours. Several trails start here at Crescent Meadow, including the High Sierra Trail, which runs 71 miles to the summit of Mt. Whitney.

From Lodgepole and Wolverton in Giant Forest Village, several trails access the High Sierra. One of the most popular is the **Lakes Trail,** which starts at the Wolverton parking area and leads to several lakes, including Heather Lake (4.6 miles), Emerald Lake (5.7 miles), and Pear Lake (6.7 miles). It's strenuous, rising 2,300 feet in altitude. There's camping at both Emerald and Pear lakes. About 4½ miles north of the village you can access the **Tokopah Falls Trail,** a 1⅓-mile trail, along the Marble Fork of the Kaweah River, which dead-ends below the granite cliffs and waterfall of Tokopah Canyon.

Mineral King is for ambitious hikers. You'll need to spend 1 or 2 days acclimating yourself to the altitude before attempting any of the hikes, all of which are steep. In summer, rangers lead daily hikes here. The **Eagle Lake Trail,** which leaves from the Eagle–Mosquito parking lot, is 6.8 miles round trip. It's steep (the lake is at 10,000 feet, and the trail starts at around 7,500 feet). Other trails lead to White Chief Canyon.

In Kings Canyon National Park, Cedar Grove is the gateway to the High Country. For a good day hike try the **Paradise Valley Trail** to Mist Falls. It's 8 miles round trip to the falls and will take 4 to 5 hours, but you'll be rewarded with fantastic views of the U-shaped, glacially carved gorge.

From the falls you can continue on to Paradise Valley, which is a much longer hike of 14 miles round trip that will take 6 to 8 hours. The trailhead is at Roads End.

This trail links to the **John Muir Trail,** which ambitious hikers will want to walk part or all of. It runs for 100 miles through the two parks above 9,000-foot elevation.

For a strenuous day hike try the **Don Cecil Trail** to Lookout Peak, which offers terrific high-country views. The trail is accessed about a quarter-mile east of the village.

The **Pine Ridge Trail** and the **Redwood Trail** are also good day hikes, the last is among the least-traveled in the park.

Horseback Riding: Wolverton Pack Station (☎ 209/565-3445) offers rides ranging from 2-hour trips to overnight pack trips. Similar opportunities are available at Mineral King (☎ 209/561-4142); and Cedar Grove (☎ 209/565-3464) pack stations. Reservations recommended and mandated at Mineral King. **Grant Grove Pack Stables** (☎ 209/335-2482) offers day rides only.

Other pack operators include **Bedell Pack Train** in Three Rivers (☎ 209/561-4142); and **Corral Pack Station** in Woodlake (☎ 209/565-3404). They all operate from mid-May through September. Prices vary, but expect to pay around $15 for 1 hour, $25 for 2 hours, $50 for a half-day, and $75 for a full day. Overnight trips, with all expenses included, run $150 to $160 per person.

Skiing: Downhill skiing for beginners and some intermediates is offered at **Wolverton Ski Area** (☎ 209/565-3435), which has two rope tows and a platter lift.

Cross-country skiing is available both at Wolverton Ski Area (☎ 209/335-2314) and also at Grant Grove. There are about 75 miles of marked cross-country trails in the parks connecting Giant Forest, Wolverton, and Lodgepole in Sequoia National Park, and from Grant Grove into Sequoia National Forest. For ski rentals call ☎ 209/565-3435.

Snowshoeing: Naturalist-led walks are usually offered on weekends. Call the visitor centers for details: **Grant Grove** (☎ 209/335-2856); **Lodgepole/Giant Forest** (☎ 209/565-3782); or **Foothills** (☎ 209/565-3134).

Swimming: Swimming is not recommended because the rivers are cold, fast, and dangerous. The lakes in Sequoia are also too cold for swimming.

VISALIA: A STOP EN ROUTE TO SEQUOIA–KINGS CANYON

Visalia is the oldest community between Stockton and Los Angeles and has plenty of Victorian architectural highlights, if you're interested. It also is a convenient place to stop overnight en route to Sequoia National Park, which is about 30 miles away.

While you're here you might visit **Mooney Park** to view the moving statue of a solitary Indian brave on horseback called *The End of the Trail*. It portrays a battle-weary warrior, head dropped onto his chest, spear tip down, seated on an equally tired pony. It was created by James Earle Fraser for the 1915 Panama–Pacific Exposition in San Francisco. Originally made of plaster, it stood here in the park until 1968, but the elements had wrought considerable damage, so after some debate, the original was traded to the National Cowboy Hall of Fame in Oklahoma, and Visalia was given in return the bronze replica you see today.

The **museum** here in the park also contains some fine Indian baskets and a few kachinas, examples of the famous Visalia stock saddle, and of C.V. Witt's cattle brands, plus some beautifully carved model farm wagons created by Norman Rankin when he was in his late '80s.

Hours: Wed–Mon 10am–4pm. *Admission:* $2 adults, $1 children under 11.

Visalia Lodging & Dining

Ben Maddox House, 601 N. Encina St., Visalia, CA 93291 (☎ 800/401-9800 or 209/739-0721), is named after the owner/publisher of the *Visalia Daily Times,* who helped to establish Sequoia National Park. It's a Greek Revival home dating around 1876 with a center portico flanked by two small balconies. The three rooms, all with private bath, are attractively decorated with appropriate period pieces. For example, the front first-floor room has Eastlake-style furnishings set against floral wallpaper and white painted wainscoting; there's a pedestal sink in the bathroom. Another contains a wicker bed and other wicker furnishings, while another boasts a spindle bed.

Breakfast—fresh fruit, cereal, and baked goods—is served in the dining room, which is lined with handsome oak cupboards. Guests can relax on leather couches and admire *The End of the Trail* in nearby Mooney Park. In the back, enclosed for maximum privacy, is a very attractive pool and whirlpool.

Rates (incl. breakfast): $75–$95 double.

The Spalding House, 631 N. Encina St., Visalia, CA 93291 (☎ 209/739-7877, fax 209/625-0902), was built in 1901 by lumberman W.R. Spalding. It has been meticulously restored, and today guests can enjoy several beautiful, public spaces on the first floor—a parlor with Steinway grand and another sitting area with comfortable sofas, TV, and games. The most spectacular rooms, though, are the library, which has damask walls and leaded-glass cases, and the dining room, which is paneled in pine and has some ornate carving. Upstairs there are three suites. The first has a coved ceiling and shelters a wicker bedroom suite and French doors that lead out to what was once a bird aviary (now it has tiled wet bar). Another has a four-poster and a large armoire in the bedroom, with wicker furnishings in the sitting room. A hearty breakfast of omelets, cheese blintzes, or similar is served. If guests want to relax, there's a swing seat on the front porch and a pretty rose garden in which to sit.

Rates (incl. breakfast): $95 double.

Dining Only in Visalia

The Vintage Press, 216 N. Willis St. (☎ 209/733-3033), is the place to dine in town. Here you can dine in a large, elegant, softly lit room, which has semicircular booths among the seating arrangements. The menu features classic favorites—salmon in a champagne sauce with chives, filet mignon stuffed with mushroom duxelles and a cabernet-shallot sauce—but you'll also find daily specials like a venison with red currant sauce, or the rack of lamb in pistachio crust with rosemary sauce. Prices range from $15 to $29. There's an excellent wine list and plenty of selections by the glass. Adjacent to the dining room is a large bar with piano entertainment.

Hours: Mon–Sat 11:30am–2pm and 6–10:30pm, Sun 10am–2pm and 5–9:30pm.

Michael's on Main, 123 W. Main St. (☎ 209/635-2686), is the other dining spot in town. Here the cuisine is slightly more innovative. For example, there might be blackened ahi tuna served in a jalapeño butter sauce or ravioli stuffed with lobster and ginger and served in a vanilla cream sauce with pink peppercorns, or Petaluma duck in a cherry-plum sauce, or even pork tenderloin with wild mushrooms in a port sauce. Prices range from $15 to $24.

Hours: Mon–Fri 11am–3pm, Mon–Thurs 4:30–9:30pm, Fri–Sat 4:30–10:30pm.

GETAWAYS TO THE SOUTH: MONTEREY BAY, THE MONTEREY PENNINSULA & BIG SUR

Half Moon Bay & Santa Cruz

Distances in Miles: Half Moon Bay, 28; Santa Cruz, 77; San Juan Bautista, 97; Salinas, 106

Estimated Driving Times: 45 minutes to Half Moon Bay; 1¾ hours to Santa Cruz; 2 hours to San Juan Bautista; 2¼ hours to Salinas

Driving: To Half Moon Bay the fastest route is via Highway 92 west from either Highway 280 or Highway 101 out of San Francisco. Alternatively, take Highway 1 to the Highway 92 exit.

To Santa Cruz take Highway 101 south (or Highway 280 to Highway 101 south). Exit to Los Gatos, and take Highway 17 to Santa Cruz. Again, you can also take Highway 1 all the way.

If you are going directly to San Juan Bautista or Salinas, remain on Highway 101. There is a turn-off for San Juan Bautista about half-way between Gilroy and Salinas. From Salinas, you can take Highway 68 on into Monterey.

Further Information: For information on Half Moon Bay, call the **Half Moon Bay Coastside Chamber of Commerce** (☎ 650/726-8380).

For Santa Cruz, it's the **Santa Cruz County Conference and Visitors Council,** 701 Front St., Santa Cruz, CA 95060 (☎ 408/425-1234).

You might also try the **Gilroy Visitors Bureau,** 7780 Monterey, Gilroy, CA 95020 (☎ 408/842-6346); or the **San Juan Bautista Chamber of Commerce**, 402A Third St., San Juan Bautista, CA 95045 (☎ 408/623-2454).

HALF MOON BAY

Even though, or perhaps because, Half Moon Bay is less than an hour from San Francisco, this seaside town has been overlooked by folks speeding south to Santa Cruz and Monterey. As a result, it's managed to restrain

AREA CODE CHANGE ALERT IN 1998

All of the new technologies that have been introduced in the last decade require additional phone numbers, and as a result some area codes are being split, with new area codes being introduced to replace them. The old area code 408 will be split and a new area code of **831** introduced for the following communities covered in this chapter: Santa Cruz, Gilroy, Salinas, Pinnacles, and San Juan Bautista. The new area code will be introduced in July 1998; until February 1999 you will be told that the old 408 number is now in the new 831 area when you dial a number. Thereafter, you must use the new 831 area code.

itself from developing any theme parks or time-share condos. Instead, it's retained a rural air with sandy beaches, fishing harbors, redwood forests, and organic farms. Originally settled by Mexican ranchers and later by Portuguese and Italians who came to fish and farm, it was named first San Benito and later Spanishtown.

The best things to do in Half Moon Bay are the same things the locals do. Walk, hike, bike, or skate the 3-mile **paved beach trail** that winds from Half Moon Bay north to Pillar Point Harbor. Stop occasionally to see if you can spy a school of dolphins or a pod of whales. Go down to Pillar Point Harbor and watch the 350-strong fishing fleet unload its catch at the end of the day.

In Half Moon Bay itself, shop and browse in the stores along Main Street, which sell everything from feed and tackle and camping gear to arts and crafts. Stop in at **Buffalo Shirt Company,** 315 Main St. (☎ 650/726-3194), for casual wear, Indian rugs, and outdoor gear; the **Half Moon Bakery,** 514 Main St. (☎ 650/726-4841), where you can pick up some delicious Portuguese sweet bread; **Cunha's Country Store,** 448 Main St. (☎ 650/726-4071), the town's beloved grocery and general store, another Portuguese heritage site where you can purchase some ingredients to go with the Portuguese bread; **Coastside Books,** 521 Main St. (**☎ 650/726-5889**), for a full range of titles plus children's books and postcards; **Cottage Industries,** 621 Main St. (**☎ 650/712-8078**), for high-quality hand-crafted furniture; and **Coyote Creek,** 641 Main St. (**☎ 650/712-8731**), for western wear, jewelry, and saddlery. Outside of town on Highway 92, the Spanishtown Art Center offers courtyard shopping with a degree of charm.

The region around Half Moon Bay is famous for fresh flowers and organically grown produce. The former have been associated with the region since 1925, and today visitors still flock to the **flower market,** which

Events and Festivals to Plan Your Trip Around

May: The **Chamarita Festival** in Half Moon Bay is also known as the Holy Ghost Festival, a thanksgiving for the salvation of the Azores in the 14th century from a series of devastating disasters, including flood and famine. Celebrated by the Portuguese community on Pentecost Sunday, it includes dances, a parade, and the crowning of the Queen of the festival.

At the **California Indian Market** in San Juan Bautista, traditional peoples gather to dance, sing, and participate in other cultural events; there are also craft exhibits. Call ☎ 408/623-2379 for more information.

July: The **Coastside Country Fair** in Half Moon Bay is similar to a state fair with livestock and other agricultural contests, plus a rodeo and crafts fair.

August: The **Steinbeck Festival** in Salinas gives the residents of the town where he was born and wrote a chance to celebrate their famous native son with tours, films, presentations, and dinners. Call ☎ 408/753-6411 for information.

October: The **Half Moon Bay Art & Pumpkin Festival,** featuring a Great Pumpkin Parade, pie-eating contests, a pumpkin-carving competition, arts and crafts, and all kinds of squash cuisine. The highlight of the event is the Giant Pumpkin Weigh-In, won recently by an 875-pound monster. For more information call the Pumpkin Hotline (☎ 650/726-9652).

is held every third Saturday of the month (outdoors in summer, in La Piazza in winter). If you like, stop in at one of the nurseries along Highway 92 en route to town, such as the **Half Moon Bay Nursery,** 11691 San Mateo Rd. (☎ 650/726-5392), which is the place where all the serious green thumbs in the county go to get their prized perennials. About 3 miles out of town, it's open daily from 9am to 5pm. A few miles out of town there's also the **Obester Winery,** 12341 San Mateo Rd., off Highway 92 (☎ 650/726-9463), which occupies a small wooden shack where you can taste the wines for free. It's open daily from 10am to 5pm.

One of the best places to view and sample organic produce is the **Andreotti Family Farm,** 227 Kelly Ave. (☎ 650/726-9461), off Highway 1. Every Friday, Saturday, and Sunday a member of the Andreotti family opens the heavy door to their weathered old barn at 10am sharp to reveal a cornucopia of strawberries, artichokes, cucumbers, and more. It's a saccharine, old-fashioned outfit that has been in business since 1926.

Hours: Fri–Sun 10am–6pm, year-round.

Another place is down the coast at Pescadero, at **Phipps Ranch,** 2700 Pescadero Rd. (☎ 650/879-0787), where you'll find a huge assortment of fresh, organically grown fruits and vegetables, including an amazing variety of dried beans. Gardeners will enjoy browsing the nursery and gardens. A popular early-summer pastime is picking your own olallieberries and boysenberries in the adjacent fields.

Hours: Daily 10am–7pm; winter, 10am–6pm.

Nature lovers will want to visit the **Fitzgerald Marine Reserve** (☎ 650/728-3584), north of town beyond Pillar Point in Moss Beach. It's a 35-acre tidal reef supporting more than 200 species of marine animals, including starfish, snails, urchins, sponges, sea anemones, and hermit and rock crabs. Tide-pooling can be dangerous in some places along the coast, but here it's not because the shoreline is protected by a rock terrace 50 yards from the beach. Call ahead for tide and tour schedules (the latter usually offered on Saturdays). No dogs are allowed, and rubber-soled shoes are recommended. It's located at the west end of California Avenue off Highway 1 in Moss Beach.

A few miles farther north stands the **Point Montara Lighthouse,** which has been converted into a youth hostel.

South of Half Moon Bay, beyond Bean Hollow Beach, you can also visit **Pigeon Point Lighthouse,** which dates from 1872 and is open for tours on Sundays.

From here it's only a short distance to one of the most dramatic wildlife spectacles anywhere, the 1,500-acre **Año Nuevo State Reserve,** on New Years Creek Road in Pescadero (☎ 650/879-2025), the protected breeding site for the northern elephant seal. Between December and March they come ashore here to give birth to their pups and to mate and return the following year to do the same thing. At one time there were only 50 or so remaining on the earth, but today more than 2,000 come ashore here annually. The bulls are huge, some weighing in at 3 tons, and they engage in brutal battles for females during the mating period. Guided walks are led from December through March; they take 2½ hours and cover 3 miles. At other times you can secure a permit and guide yourself, enjoying the beach, the dunes, and some bird-watching, especially in spring or fall. The reserve is about 20 miles north of Santa Cruz.

Note: Temperatures rarely venture into the 70s in Half Moon Bay, so be sure to pack for cool (and often wet) weather.

Lodging in Half Moon Bay

The **Cypress Inn on Miramar Beach,** 407 Mirada Rd., Half Moon Bay, CA 94019 (☎ 800/83-BEACH [800/832-3224] or 650/726-6002, fax 650/712-0380), is refreshingly free of Victorian charm and is, in fact, as its name indicates, right on the beach. It occupies a modern, well-designed building that has been fetchingly decorated with folk art and furnished with great flair in natural pine and wicker. Each of the 12 rooms offers bed, private balcony, gas fireplace, private bath, and an ocean view, as well as such luxuries as radiant heated terra-cotta–tile floors. Each is decorated individually with a different color palette. Adjacent to the inn are four Beach House rooms equipped with built-in stereo systems and hidden TVs, although they lack the Santa Fe–meets-California decor found in the main house. Best facility of all is the resident massage therapist. Breakfasts are extra special, too, often featuring the house specialty, peaches-and-cream French toast. The inn is 3 miles north of the junction of highways 92 and 1. To reach the inn, take Medio west to the end.

Rates (incl. breakfast): $175–$285 double.

The Mill Rose Inn, 615 Mill St. (1 block west of Main Street), Half Moon Bay, CA 94019 (☎ 650/726-9794, fax 650/726-3031), is a romantic place surrounded by rose- and other flower-filled gardens that are made even more inviting by their wrought-iron furnishings, fountains, and trellisses. Each of the six rooms is individually decorated in daring palettes (peach, crimson, and ivory in the Bordeaux Rose Suite) and combinations that work wonderfully well, although some folks may find them a little overwhelming. Balloon treatments billow at the windows, beds are enhanced with lacey canopies, or else they are made of brass and covered with fine fabrics and sumptuous pillows. The furnishings consist of eclectic antiques ranging from oak tables and chairs to Eastlake dressers. Bathrooms feature hand-painted sinks and sometimes a clawfoot tub. Vaulted ceilings give several of the rooms an extra dash of elegance. The accommodations also offer such amenities as private entrances, fireplaces (except the Baroque Rose room), well-stocked refrigerators, televisions with cable and VCRs, plus access to a Jacuzzi that's tucked inside a frosted-glass gazebo filled with plants. And, of course, there are fresh flowers and also chocolates and turndown service, too. A full breakfast, plus a complimentary *San Francisco Chronicle,* is delivered to your room or to the dining room. Guests enjoy the comforts of the parlor and library, where they can enjoy afternoon wine and desserts. Just off Main Street, it's in a quiet neighborhood.

Rates (incl. breakfast, afternoon tea, wine, and hors d'oeuvres): $215–$295 double weekends, $175–$265 midweek.

Located across from Pillar Point Harbor, **Pillar Point Inn,** 380 Capistrano Rd. (4 miles north of Half Moon Bay on Highway 1, across from the Pillar Point Harbor), Princeton-by-the-Sea, CA 94019 (☎ 800/400-8281 or 650/728-7377, fax 650/728-8345), is a modern establishment that has been designed to resemble a classic Cape Cod inn. Each of the 11 rooms is well equipped with such amenities as gas fireplaces, TV/VCRs, radios, refrigerators, and telephones. Some have steam baths, others have window seats, and all but one have harbor views. Breakfast is served in the airy common room at light oak tables set in front of the fireplace.

Rates (incl. breakfast and afternoon sherry): from $170 double weekends and holidays, from $150 midweek.

The **Old Thyme Inn,** 779 Main St. (south end of Main Street near Filbert Street), Half Moon Bay, CA 94019 (☎ 650/726-1616, fax 650/726-6394), is located at the quiet, southern end of Half Moon Bay's Main Street, in a stately 1899 Victorian. It's run by energetic hosts George and Marcia Dempsey, who tend the herb garden and make the house a welcoming retreat for guests. The seven guest rooms—each named after one of the fragrant herbs in the garden—are decorated with floral wallpapers and bedspreads, trademark teddy bears, and furnished with assorted oak armoires and other antiques. Some, like the Thyme Room, have added luxuries—a double whirlpool tub, fireplace, and queen-size canopy bed. Behind the main house, the Garden Suite, often reserved by honeymooners, features a queen-size four-poster canopy bed, fireplace, double whirlpool tub under a skylight, TV/VCR, and a refrigerator stocked with complimentary beverages. A bountiful breakfast—banana bread, blueberry muffins, frittata, and fresh fruit—is served in the parlor. At night guests gather around the wood stove in the parlor for drinks or relax with one of the many games or books available.

Rates (incl. breakfast and afternoon beverages): $125–$230 double weekends, $100–$175 midweek. No credit cards are accepted, although they can be used to guarantee reservations.

The **Zaballa House,** 324 Main St. (at the north end of town), Half Moon Bay, CA 94019 (☎ 650/726-9123, fax 650/726-3921), occupies the oldest building in Half Moon Bay, a pale-blue, pretty but unpretentious Victorian. The nine guest rooms in the main house are pleasantly decorated with understated wallpaper and country furniture; some have fireplaces, vaulted ceilings, or Jacuzzi tubs, and all have private baths. Three new minisuites have been added behind the main house, each equipped with a kitchenette, double Jacuzzi, fireplace, TV/VCR, and private deck (my favorite is the Casablanca room, which comes with an eponymous video). None have telephones, but guests are welcome to use the phone in the front parlor. Breakfast brings fresh fruit, waffles or similar, apple muffins, and other breads. Late afternoon tea and hors d'oeuvres are served in the front parlor, where guests are encouraged to put their feet up in front of the fire and relax with a good book.

Rates (incl. breakfast): $100–$180 double weekends, $80–$135 midweek; $220–$260 mini-suite weekends, $150–$185 midweek.

Before Karen Herbert and her husband Rick opened **Seal Cove Inn,** 221 Cypress Ave., Moss Beach, CA 94038 (☎ 650/728-7325, fax 650/728-4116), she was the writer and publisher of *Karen Brown's Country Inns Series,* so you can understand why she knows what it takes to create and run a superior bed-and-breakfast like this one—a stately, sophisticated home that harmoniously blends California, New England, and European influences in a spectacular seacoast setting. All 10 rooms have wood-burning fireplaces, country antiques, original watercolors, unobtrusive TV/VCRs, refrigerators stocked with complimentary beverages, and

Half Moon Bay & Vicinity

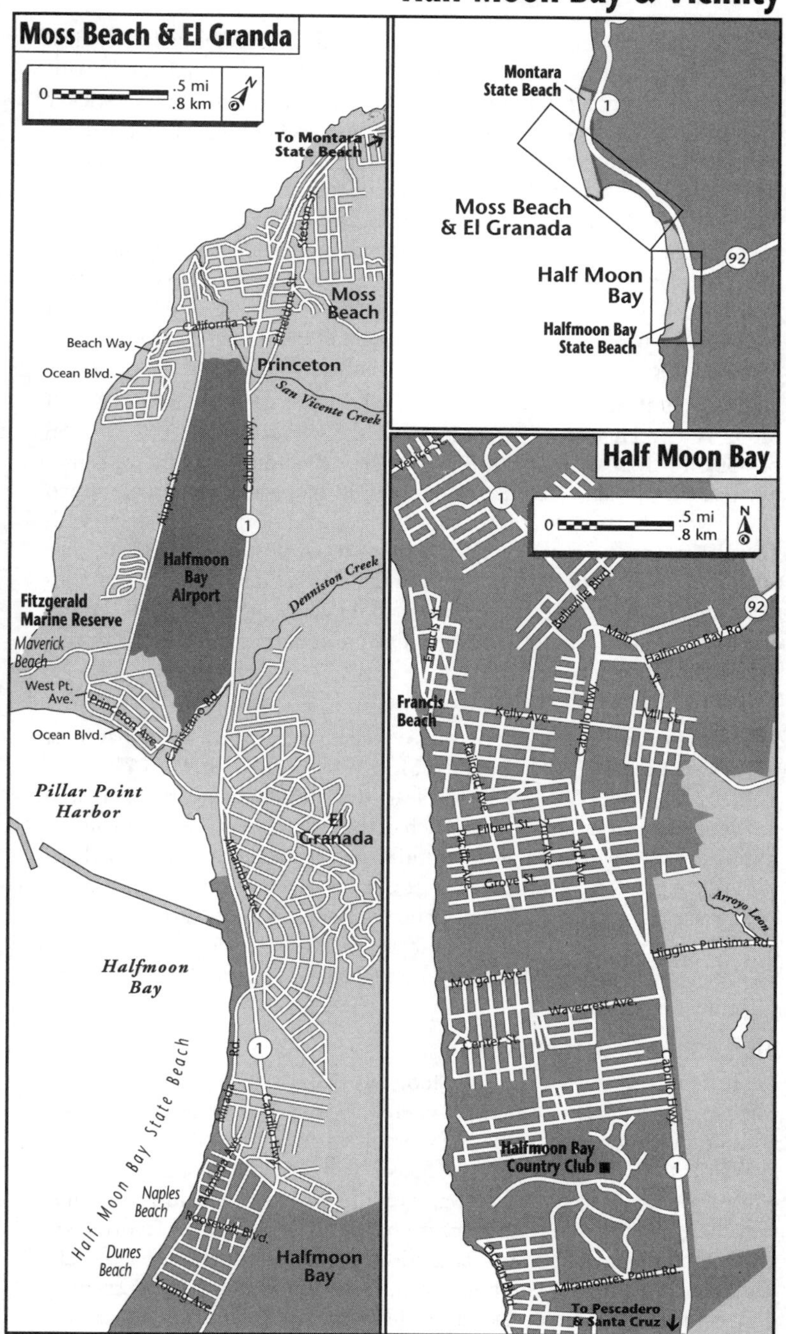

views overlooking the distant cypress trees and a delightful half-acre wildflower garden dotted with birdhouses. Each is furnished differently with cannonball, Jenny Lind, brass, or iron beds matched with pine or wicker and enhanced by decorative prints or paintings elaborating a motif or color palette. The largest and most luxurious room is the Fitzgerald, which contains a canopied king bed and has a Jacuzzi tub and two Juliet-style balconies with marvelous views of park and ocean. In the morning you'll find coffee and a newspaper outside your door, brandy and sherry by the living room fireplace in the evening, and at night chocolates beside your turned-down bed. The ocean is just a short walk away. The inn is 6 miles north of Half Moon Bay off Highway 1; follow signs to Moss Beach Distillery.

Rates (incl. breakfast): $190–$270 double.

The **Beach House Inn,** 4100 N. Cabrillo Hwy. (3 miles north of Half Moon Bay on Highway 1), Half Moon Bay, CA 94109 (☎ 800/315-9366 or 650/712-0220, fax ☎ 650/712-0693), is a modern conference center where each of the 54 rooms is decorated in modern style and equipped with a wood-burning fireplace, king-size bed and sleeper sofa, stereo with CD player, private patio or deck access, *two* color TVs and VCR, *four* telephones with data ports and voice mail, and a kitchenette with microwave and stocked refrigerator. Best of all they have great views of the bay and the harbor. Facilities include a heated pool, ocean-view whirlpool, fitness room, and sauna.

Rates (incl. continental breakfast): $155–$255 double; $295 suite.

Harbor House, 346 Princeton Ave. (3½ miles north of Half Moon Bay, west of Pillar Point Harbor), Half Moon Bay, CA 94019 (☎ 650/728-1572, fax 650/728-8271), is a clean, quiet, moderately priced modern inn with a fine view of the ocean. Each of the six rooms is simple but attractively decorated with natural wood and wicker furnishings, queen-size beds with down comforters, kitchenettes, TV, telephone, and fireplace. And best of all each has a private deck or patio overlooking the ocean. The "penthouse" is a huge, barn-sized studio that is ideal for families or groups.

Rates (incl. continental breakfast): $125–$175 double; $200–$250 penthouse.

Dining Only in Half Moon Bay

Pasta Moon, 315 Main St., Half Moon Bay (☎ 650/726-5125), is a handsome, nouveau-Italian restaurant where the pasta is made on the premises and combined with the freshest of ingredients. You might find such dishes as ravioli stuffed with butternut squash, white truffle oil, and Parmesan with a sage butter sauce, or pappardelle with sweet fennel sausage, tomatoes, and cream. Prices range from $12 to $16.95. Other favorites are the French oak-smoked pork tenderloin served with braised Savoy cabbage and pancetta fruit compote, or the fresh seafood stew. For dessert try the tiramisu, layered marsala-and-espresso-soaked ladyfingers and creamy mascarpone.

Hours: Mon–Fri 11:30am–2:30pm; Sat noon–3pm; Sun 11am–2:30pm; Sun–Thur 5:30–9:30, Fri–Sat 5:30–10pm.

Mezza Luna, 3048 N. Cabrillo Hwy. (Highway 1), Half Moon Bay (☎ 650/712-9223), serves traditional Italian cuisine starting with the *antipasto della casa,* a large platter of marinated grilled vegetables in extra-virgin olive oil and red wine vinegar. Among the entrees are six or so pastas including a tortellini with prosciutto and mushroom in a cream sauce, and linguini with tomato, mussels, clams, calamari, prawns, and shrimp. Other main dishes range from Cornish game hen with rosemary sauce to veal with marsala wine and mushrooms. Prices range from $10 to $15. The dining room is not much to look at.

Hours: Mon–Sat 11:30–3pm; Sun–Thur 5:30–10; Fri–Sat 5:30–10:30pm.

2 Fools Cafe and Market, 408 Main St., Half Moon Bay (☎ 650/712-1222), will deliver healthful dishes, most of them made with organic meats and vegetables. You can secure light, crunchy buttermilk waffles for breakfast, hefty salads and sandwiches for lunch, and entrees ranging from organic meat loaf with shiitake mushroom gravy to buttermilk-roasted free-range chicken for dinner. Prices range from $3.50 to $12.95. Everything can be taken out, and an array of organically grown teas, jellies, wines, olives, and other goods can also be purchased.

Hours: Mon 11am–2pm; Tue–Fri 11am–9pm; Sat 8am–9pm; Sun 8am–8pm.

Barbara's Fish Trap, 281 Capistrano Rd., Princeton (☎ 650/728-7049), hovers above Pillar Point Harbor. It's a traditional down-home fish house serving a variety of fresh fish either deep-fried, broiled, or grilled. The atmosphere is derived from the typical trappings of fishnets, floats, and other seaside baubles. Stick to the garlic prawns, steamed mussels, or fish and chips, or select from the daily fresh catch specials. Prices range from $10 to $15.

Hours: Daily 11am–9:30pm. They do not accept credit cards.

Located in an old stucco distillery on a cliff above the beach, **Moss Beach Distillery,** Beach Street (at Ocean Street), Moss Beach (☎ 650/728-5595), affords a magnificent view of the ocean. Once frequented by silent film stars and city politicians in search of liquor and other pleasures at the adjacent bordello, today it attracts a more sober crowd who come primarily for the sunsets and, secondarily, for such dishes as grilled salmon with smoked-salmon beurre blanc, grilled pork chops with a mustard-shallot sauce, Dungeness crab cakes with roasted chile-corn chowder sauce and Tabasco-scallion aïoli, and bouillabaisse, priced from $17 to $23. The brunch offers such dishes as pear-and-walnut-stuffed French toast and eggs *cangrejo,* an omelet made with crab, wild mushrooms, spinach, and fontina cheese. Brunch is $22.95 and includes the fruit bar, breads, and a drink.

Hours: Mon–Sat noon–10pm (closing hours vary, though); Sun brunch 10am–3pm (closing hours vary).

San Benito House, 356 Main St., Half Moon Bay (☎ 650/726-3425), has enjoyed a long reputation for fine cuisine and service, and although that reputation has faded somewhat recently, the kitchen still turns out some very fine dishes—ravioli stuffed with fennel, fontina, and toasted almonds and served with a rich and creamy leek sauce on a bed of red chard, or an applewood-smoked pork chop served with scallion couscous and chunky applesauce with raisins. Prices range from $11 to $16. For dessert reserve some room for the strawberry and rhubarb wrapped in a crêpe served with crème Anglaise and strawberry sauce.

Hours: Thur–Sun 5:30–9pm.

Super fresh fish and innovative sushi can be found at **Sushi Main Street,** 696 Mill St., Half Moon Bay (☎ 650/726-6336). Try the New Zealand roll (mussels, radish, sprouts, avocado, and teriyaki), the unagi papaya (eel with papaya), and the marinated salmon roll with cream cheese and spinach. The Balinese inspired decor adds a beautifully serene dimension to the dining experience. Prices range from $5 to $10.

Hours: Mon–Sat 11:30am–2:30pm and 5–9pm; Sun 5–9pm.

Down the coast in Pescadero, **Duarte's Tavern,** 202 Stage Rd. (☎ 650/879-0464), is still owned and operated by the fourth generation of the family that built it in 1894, installed a whiskey barrel on the bar, and began selling it for 10 cents a shot. It's famous for its artichoke dishes, including a soup and crab cioppino. You'll also find New York steak, prime rib, plenty of shellfish dishes, and various sandwiches including one filled with linguica. Prices range from $5 to $14. Fruits and vegetables from the gardens behind the restaurant accompany each dish. This is a good breakfast spot for typical egg dishes and omelets. Reservations recommended for dinner.

Hours: Daily for breakfast, lunch, and dinner.

Half Moon Bay
Special & Recreational Activities

Beaches: The 2-mile arc of golden-colored sand that is called **Half Moon Bay State Beach** is divided into four separate beaches—Dunes, Venice, Roosevelt, and Francis. These beaches are great for walking, picnicking, surfing, and fishing. Family camping is available at Francis Beach; group camping near Venice. There's a $4 per vehicle entrance fee for all four beaches. The beaches can also be accessed via Mirada Road. The water's too cold for swimming but you can surf if you want to. For additional information call ☎ 650/726-8820.

When the surf is really frothing, watch the banzai surfers at **Maverick Beach,** located just south of the radar-tracking station past Pillar Point Harbor. To get there, take Westpoint Road to the West Shoreline Access parking lot and follow the trail to the beach (while you're there, keep a lookout for sea lions basking on the offshore rocks).

The best beaches though are south of Half Moon Bay at **Pescadero** (across from the Marsh reserve) and **Bean Hollow,** which is about 3 miles farther south.

Biking: Bicycles can be rented from the **Bicyclery,** 432 Main St. (☎ 650/726-6000), in downtown Half Moon Bay. Prices range from $6 an hour to $24 a day.

Bird-watching: Adjacent to the West Shoreline Access parking lot, **Pillar Point Marsh** welcomes fresh- and salt-water visitors including great blue herons, snowy egrets, and red-winged blackbirds.

Sixteen miles south of Half Moon Bay on Highway 1 (at the turnoff to Pescadero), the **Pescadero Marsh Natural Preserve** (☎ 650/879-0832) is one of the few remaining natural marshes on the central California coast, incorporating creeks, ponds, sand dunes, a salt marsh, and tidal flats. On the Pacific flyway, it's a resting stop for nearly 200 bird species, including great blue herons that nest in the row of eucalyptus trees on the northern boundary. Expect to see all kinds of waterfowl—sandpipers, cormorant, Northern shoveler, willet, black turnstone, and many more. The mile-long Sequoia Audubon Trail crosses the marsh and is accessible from the parking lot at Pescadero State Beach on Highway 1 (the trail starts below the Pescadero Creek Bridge). Docents lead tours every Saturday at 10:30am and every Sunday at 1pm, weather permitting. Best time is spring or fall although you can see wading birds and raptors year round.

Canoeing/Kayaking: On weekends from May to October for $90 you can take a 7-hour sea-kayaking class at **California Canoe & Kayak,** 214 Princeton Ave. at the Half Moon Bay Yacht Club (☎ 650/728-1803), near Pillar Point Harbor. Rentals and winter classes are also offered.

Fishing: A day's fishing will cost anywhere from $40 to $60 (including tackle), depending on the catch (lingcod, rockfish, or salmon). Try **Captain John's Fishing Trips** (☎ 650/726-2913) or **Huck Finn Sportfishing** (☎ 800/572-2934 or 650/726-7133). Both leave from Pillar Point Harbor. Some of the lingcod fishing trips go to the Farallon Islands.

Golf: At the south end of Half Moon Bay, **Half Moon Bay Golf Links,** 2000 Fairway Dr., adjacent to the Half Moon Bay Lodge (☎ 650/726-6384) was designed by Arnold Palmer. This ocean-side 18-hole course has been rated among the top 100 in the country. Green fees range from $50 to $100. Make reservations as far in advance as possible.

Horseback Riding: Guided or unguided rides along the beach are given by **Sea Horse Ranch** (a.k.a. Friendly Acres Horse Ranch) for about $35. It's open daily from 8am to 6pm and located on Highway 1, 1 mile north of Half Moon Bay (☎ 650/726-2362 or 650/726-8550).

State Parks & Nature Reserves: The most spectacular reserves are the **Año Nuevo Reserve,** where the elephant seals breed, and the **Pescadero Marsh Reserve,** plus the state beaches.

Southeast of Pescadero, **Portola State Park,** Alpine Road, off Highway 35 (☎ 650/948-9098), is a small park with 50 campsites and 14 miles of trails.

Between Pescadero and Bean Hollow, about 3 miles from the shore, 3,200-acre **Butano State Park** (☎ 650/879-2040) offers trails that wind through redwoods and overlook Año Nuevo island. It offers 40 campsites, plus bike- and hike-in camping, about 6 miles south of Pescadero, accessed by Cloverdale Road.

Whale watching: January through March **Captain John** and **Huck Finn Sports,** listed under "Fishing" above, both offer whale-watching trips for about $20 per person (reservations recommended). They travel to the Farallon National Wildlife Refuge, a sanctuary for hundreds of thousands of seabirds including storm petrels, and Brandt's cormorants, as well as seals, sea lions, and other marine life.

SANTA CRUZ

Santa Cruz is one cool town—a surfin' city, a fun city, the birthplace of the wet suit and of health food, and still a city that seeks to be on the cutting edge and yet concerned with community. Behind the boardwalk and seaside resort facade, you'll find a serious community that is concerned with social and other issues. It's a down-to-earth, comfortable place where people are accepted and welcomed into the community. It's a mecca for everyone from the Peninsula, for when they are sweltering, Santa Cruz is cool. In addition to the ocean and Santa Cruz itself, people are drawn to the area by the small town of Capitola and a string of state parks that line the shore and dot the inland mountains behind.

The **Beach Boardwalk,** 400 Beach St. (☎ 408/423-5590), provides visitors with a nostalgic blast from the past. It's one of the few authentic ones left in the nation. Here you can still ride the 1924 wooden Giant

AREA CODE CHANGE ALERT IN 1998

All of the new technologies that have been introduced in the last decade require additional phone numbers, and as a result some area codes are being split, with new area codes being introduced to replace them. The old area code 408 will be split and a new area code of **831** introduced for the following communities covered in this chapter: Santa Cruz, Gilroy, Salinas, Pinnacles, and San Juan Bautista. The new area code will be introduced in July 1998; until February 1999 you will be told that the old 408 number is now in the new 831 area when you dial a number. Thereafter, you must use the new 831 area code.

Dipper roller coaster and also climb aboard the back of a wooden horse on the carousel that swirls around to the accompaniment of a 342-pipe band organ.

Hours: Daily in summer; weekends only in spring and fall. *Admission* (with unlimited rides): $17.95.

The **Municipal Wharf,** at Washington and Beach streets (☎ 408/ 429-3628), juts out into the surf, a favorite with fishermen and others who just come to get out on the ocean and consort with the sea lions below. Stroll down it just for childhood memories' sake. If you want to go deep-sea fishing, many boats leave from here. Cruises and sea kayaking and parasailing outfitters also operate from here.

Santa Cruz was part of the chain of California Missions, but all that remains of the original is the **Neary–Rodriguez Adobe,** which was built in 1824 and was part of the mission complex. The original **mission church** was destroyed by an earthquake in 1857; today you can visit a one-third-size replica. Both are located in the **Santa Cruz Mission State Historic Park,** 144 School St. (☎ 408/425-5849).

Hours: Tues–Sat 10am–4pm; Sun 10am–2pm. *Admission:* $5.

Drive along the East or West Cliff Drive for a transcendent view of the ocean. On West Cliff Drive you'll find the **Surfing Museum** (☎ 408/ 429-3429), which is located in the Mark Abbott memorial lighthouse. Here you'll discover some of the earlier, more primitive boards that people used—a far cry from today's streamlined, curvaceous versions—and the outlandish costumes they wore. Below, you can watch the rubber-suited enthusiasts catching the waves and sweeping into shore on what is referred to as Steamers Lane.

Hours: Thurs–Mon noon–4pm. *Admission:* Free.

At the end of West Cliff Drive, you'll reach **Natural Bridges State Park,** where there are sandstone arches and crumbling cliffs. It has a nice sandy beach backed by dunes covered with purple, pink, and yellow plants. Seek out the eucalyptus grove, one of the few places in which the monarch butterflies choose to winter. The best time to see butterflies is in October.

The University of California at Santa Cruz, which is set on a bluff overlooking the town, is worth a stroll. It also operates the **Long Marine Laboratory and Aquarium,** 100 Shaffer Rd. (☎ 408/459-4308), where you can observe marine scientists at work and also see the creatures with which they work and examine a blue whale skeleton. There's also a good view of the whole bay from here.

Hours: Tues–Sun 1–4pm. *Admission:* $2 adults, free for children 16 and under.

In nearby Felton, railroad buffs will want to ride one of the few narrow-gauge railroads that remain from logging days at the **Roaring Camp & Big Tree Narrow Gauge Railroad** on Graham Hill Road (☎ 408/335-4484). The 100-year-old steam train travels through the redwoods on a narrow track, twisting and turning up into the Santa Cruz Mountains.

Departures: Sat–Sun noon, 1:30, and 3pm in winter; from April additional departures Mon–Fri 11am. *Fare:* $13 adults, $9.50 children 3–12.

A series of state beaches and parks embrace Santa Cruz. Some to the north have already been discussed in the Half Moon Bay section above—San Gregorio, Pomponio, Pescadero, and Bean Hollow state beaches; Portola and Butano state parks.

In addition, there's Big Basin Redwoods, as well as Henry Cowell, Castle Rock, and Forest of Nisene Marks state parks, all offering a full range of recreational activities. **Big Basin Redwoods State Park,** Highway 236, Boulder Creek (☎ 408/338-6132), is the oldest state park in California and really helped launch the campaign to save the redwoods back in the 1920s. It covers 16,000 acres and has 80 miles of hiking trails plus 183 camping sites.

Henry Cowell, Highway 9, Felton (☎ 408/335-4598), is a 4,000-acre park with 15 miles of trails and camping at 112 sites. In winter, the San Lorenzo river is open for salmon and steelhead fishing. For camping information, call ☎ 408/438-2396.

Castle Rock, Highway 35, (☎ 408/867-2952), is a 3,600-acre park along the crest of the Santa Cruz mountains offering backpacker camping only. There are some 32 miles of trails through this largely untouched coastal redwood, fir, and madrone forest.

Forest of Nisene Marks, Aptos Creek Road (☎ 408/335 4598), is largely undeveloped, though there are 30 miles of trails, picnic grounds, and a hike-in campsite. It was once a logging area, and it does have some historic sites from the old logging days.

On the south side, between Santa Cruz and Moss Landing, there are a string of state beaches: Twin Lakes, New Brighton, Seacliff, Manresa, Sunset, and Zmudowski.

Twin Lakes (☎ 408/688-3241), which extends along East Cliff Drive in Santa Cruz, is good for swimming (with lifeguard) and has access to good birding spots at Schwann lagoon.

At **New Brighton Beach** (☎ 408/475-4850), which is in Capitola, there are 100 camping sites on a bluff overlooking Monterey Bay.

Pier fishing is the most popular activity at **Seacliff** (☎ 408/688-3222) in Aptos.

At **Manresa** (☎ 408/724-1266) the prime pastimes are walking, clamming, and surf fishing. To get there, take San Andreas Road, off Highway 1 just south of Aptos.

Sunset has a popular camping facility sheltered behind the dunes with 90 sites. Follow directions to Manresa, but continue on to marked turnoff.

Behind these beaches lies some prime agricultural land, and as you drive from Santa Cruz to the Monterey Peninsula, you'll pass field after field of strawberries, cauliflower, and lettuce. Around **Castroville,** acre after acre of artichokes have made it the artichoke capital of the world (an artichoke festival is held in town in September), while farther inland **Gilroy** is famous for its garlic and the huge garlic festival that is held here every year, when chefs turn out fantastically flavored dishes and all kinds of garlic-related celebrations take place. Before the advent of trucks, **Moss Landing** served as the port for all the produce that came from the Salinas Valley, which was dubbed the salad bowl of the United States. Today it's a mecca for anglers and antique-lovers.

From Moss Landing, the estuary stretches inland and through the wetlands of the **Elkhorn Slough Reserve** (☎ 408/728-2822), which is home for a colony of heron and other waterbirds.

Hours: Wed–Sun 9am–5pm. *Admission:* $2.

Lodging in Santa Cruz & Vicinity

Santa Cruz

The Darling House, 314 W. Cliff Dr., Santa Cruz, CA 95060 (☎ 408/458-1958), has a great oceanfront location. It's a quintessential California-style house designed by William Weeks, with terra-cotta tile roof, beveled-glass windows, and adobe walls. It's a relaxing yet elegant place. On the front porch hangs a hammock. The back gardens are filled with orchids and citrus trees, while several palm trees grace the front lawn. The interior is extremely comfortable, from the sitting room, warmed on cool nights by a fire, to the splendid tiger oak–paneled dining room. The seven rooms have polished wood wainscoting, and each is well furnished with quilts and other carefully chosen pieces and accents, including Tiffany lamps. The most extraordinary room is the Pacific Ocean Room, which has a great ocean view, fireplace, and is furnished in antique oak. It also has private bath; other rooms share. Another striking accommodation is the Chinese Room, which has a silk-draped Chinese carved rosewood canopy bed. An expanded continental breakfast of fresh fruits and breads is served.

Rates (incl. breakfast): $105–$160 double; $235 for the Pacific Ocean Room.

The **Babbling Brook Inn,** 1025 Laurel St., Santa Cruz, CA 95060 (☎ 408/427-2437), is actually on a main street in Santa Cruz, so it's not as country as it sounds. Nevertheless the brook that winds down between the shingled buildings is what makes the place so appealing. Originally a tannery stood here, and before that a gristmill with little else around it. Today's main building was erected in 1909. It is beautifully landscaped with ferns, ivy, and all kinds of flowers—from Easter lilies to polyanthus—growing around the property, which is shaded with pines and redwoods. The 12 rooms, which are all very inviting, are located in different buildings connected by brick pathways. All have TV, telephone, and private bath. Among my favorites is the Toulouse-Lautrec Room, which has its own deck overlooking the brook plus a Jacuzzi in the bathroom. The furnishings include a pine bed made up with a floral quilt standing on a rose-colored carpet. The Van Gogh Room is decorated in beautiful mauve and blue and possesses a fireplace as well as a deck; its half-canopy bed is swathed in lace, and there's a double Jacuzzi in the bathroom. The largest room is the Countess Room, with stained-glass windows, hardwood floors, a fireplace, plus books to read.

The breakfasts are extra special here, too. You might enjoy huevos rancheros and poached pears in raspberry sauce. And best of all, you can take it out on the deck and listen to the sound of the brook bubbling. Wine and cheese are served in the afternoons. It's within walking distance of the beach.

Rates (incl. breakfast): $95–$175 double.

Capitola

The **Inn at Depot Hill,** 250 Monterey Ave., Capitola, CA 95010 (☎ 408/462-3376), is one of the best accommodations—for its size and type—that you will find in Northern California, or for that matter anywhere. It's located in a converted 1901 railroad station only a few blocks from the beach. There are five suites and seven extra-large rooms, each exquisitely evoking a singular time, place, and state of mind. All have color TV with VCR, stereo, fireplace, telephone, and private bath with robes and hair dryers. The owner, Suzanne Lankes, has paid great attention to detail so that every room also features the following thoughtful extras: a private hot tub, two spigots in the showers, dimmers on all the light switches, recessed lighting and spotlights where you need them, a nightlight that can be used as a torch, lights in the closet, a lint remover, make-up remover,

Santa Cruz

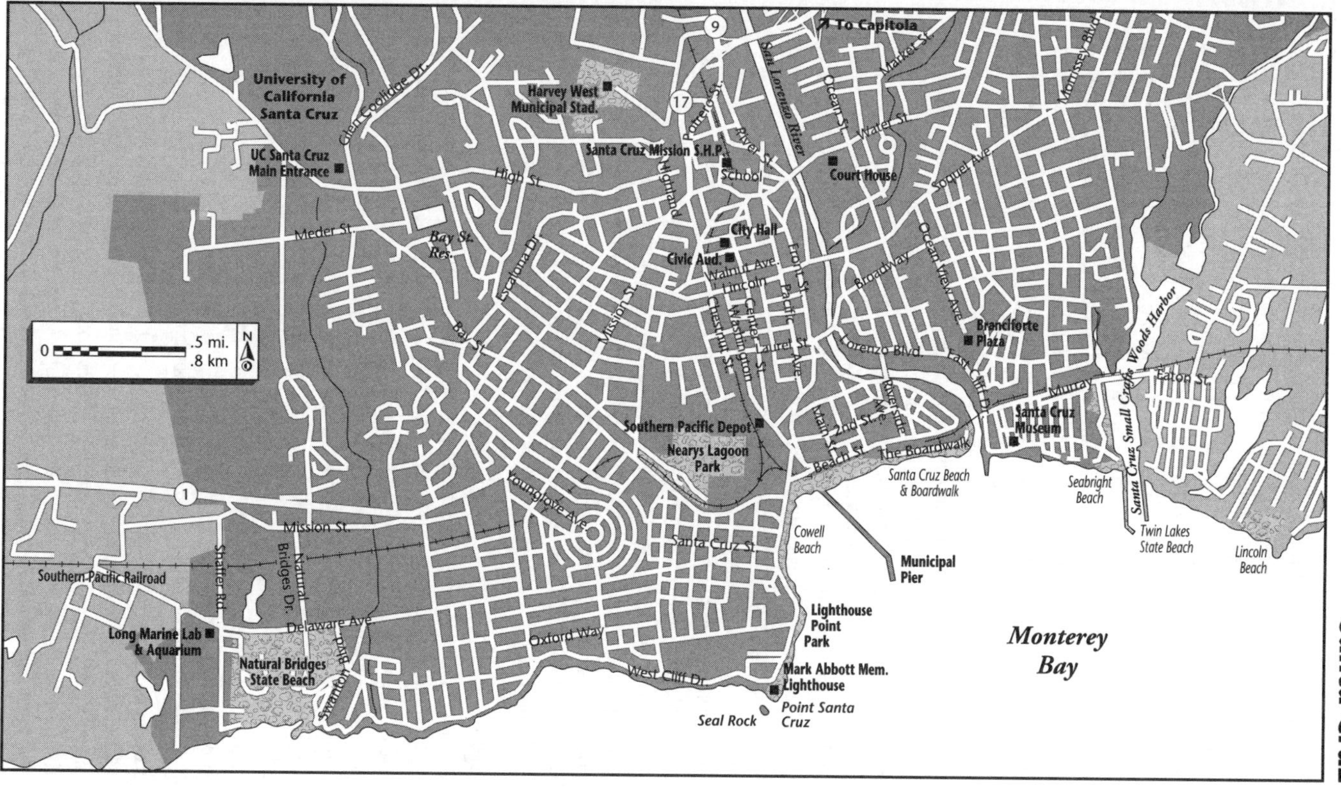

Monterey Bay
Santa Cruz Small Crafts Woods Harbor
Lincoln Beach
Twin Lakes State Beach
Seabright Beach
Santa Cruz Museum
Eaton St.
Murray
Branciforte Plaza
East Cliff Dr.
Ocean View Ave.
Morrissey Blvd.
Soquel Ave.
Broadway
Santa Cruz Beach & Boardwalk
The Boardwalk
Municipal Pier
Riverside Ave.
Lorenzo Blvd.
2nd St.
Main St.
Beach St.
To Capitola
Market St.
Water St.
Court House
Ocean St.
San Lorenzo River
Front St.
Pacific Ave.
Laurel St.
Center St.
Washington
Chestnut St.
Lincoln
Walnut Ave.
City Hall
Civic Aud.
River St.
School
Santa Cruz Mission S.H.P.
Highland
Southern Pacific Depot
Neary's Lagoon Park
Cowell Beach
Lighthouse Point Park
Mark Abbott Mem. Lighthouse
Point Santa Cruz
Seal Rock
Santa Cruz St.
West Cliff Dr.
Oxford Way
Younglove Ave.
Mission St.
Harvey West Municipal Stad.
Escalona Dr.
High St.
Bay St.
Bay St. Res.
Glen Coolidge Dr.
University of California Santa Cruz
UC Santa Cruz Main Entrance
Meder St.
Natural Bridges Dr.
Delaware Ave.
Swanton Blvd.
Natural Bridges State Beach
Shaffer Rd.
Long Marine Lab & Aquarium
Southern Pacific Railroad
.5 mi.
.8 km
0
N

and more in the bathroom, and a needlepointed "Do Not Disturb" sign. Throughout, the finest fabrics and linens have been used as well as the most decorous fixtures. In Sissinghurst the four-poster is covered with an embroidered coverlet, and a loveseat is placed in front of the brick fireplace. Rich, cherry-colored curtains enclose the bed while a hollyhock design is used as the window curtain fabric. The walls have been given a marbleized look. The Delft Suite contains a rich, blue decor that includes a chaise lounge. Handmade Belgian lace drapes the metal bed, and blue tile surrounds the fireplace; specially crafted, half-moon metal tables are at either side of the bed. The Capitola Beach Room is a study in oatmeal, taupe, and cream. The bed is curtained with brocaded fabric; wooden louvers grace the windows. The side tables are glass on sculptured stone bases. The Railroad Baron Suite is a riot of color and flamboyance. A gilded, bull's-eye mirror hangs over the fireplace; button-studded armchairs stand on the burgundy carpet in front of the hearth; and the sitting area is separated by velvet, gold tassel tiebacks. The bed sports a burgundy coverlet, and to cap it off there is a leopard-skin stool at the foot of the bed. The Côte d'Azur Suite takes you there with its terra-cotta tile floor, pillars painted with grape fronds, and pastel palette of peach and jade. Among the furnishings are French-style armchairs with tufted foot rests. In the evening fine hors d'oeuvres are offered—Brie and Monterey Jack cheeses, feta cheese vegetable dip, hot spinach pies, and more. Breakfast is also carefully prepared and bountiful. Behind the inn lies a herringboned brick patio with pond, potted plants, azaleas, and colorful trumpet vines where guests can go to sit on the wooden benches under the rose-covered trellis. Market umbrellas shade the tables and wrought-iron chairs.

Rates (incl. breakfast and hors d'oeuvres): $175–$260 double.

Aptos

Across the street from the Cafe Sparrow, stands the **Bayview Hotel,** 8041 Soquel Dr., Aptos, CA 95003 (☎ 408/688-8654), an 1878 Victorian with a steep mansard roof and wraparound porch. There are 11 attractively furnished rooms on the second and third floors. Each is furnished differently in a comfortable, unpretentious style. Most have iron or cottage-style, high-back Victorian beds combined with wicker or oak furnishings. The third floor rooms have sloping ceilings and also gas fireplaces. Facilities include a dining room. A breakfast of fruit and baked goods will be brought to your room.

Rates (incl. breakfast): $100–$160 double.

Mangels House, 570 Aptos Creek Rd., P.O. Box 302, Aptos, CA 95001 (☎ 408/688-7982), sits on 4 acres in a secluded spot surrounded by trees and shrubs. It was built in the 1880s for Claus Mangels, who was the partner of the sugar magnate, Claus Spreckels. So, as you can imagine, the house is lavishly constructed and ornamented. The sitting room has a large, stone fireplace, grand piano, Oriental rugs, and handsome book-cases. Breakfast is served in the formal dining room, which is lit by brass sconces and features molded wainscoting. The rooms are very large. The Mauve Room has a marble fireplace, white-painted furnishings, and brass reading lamps above the bed. Tim's Room is decorated in a peach palette with wall-to-wall carpeting and a plush loveseat. Nicholas's Room is decorated with artifacts from East Africa. Furnishings throughout the house are eclectic. Guests can sit out in the lovely garden under the rose trellis. A full breakfast is served, as is complimentary sherry in the evenings.

Rates (incl. breakfast): $125–$160 double.

Apple Lane Inn, 6265 Soquel Dr., Aptos, CA 95003 (☎ 408/475-6868), is located up a little lane off the main road. It's a small farmhouse that was built in the 1870s on 3 acres of fields and apple orchards. Wisteria and roses bloom in the garden, which also features a gazebo and brick patio. There are five rooms, all with private bath. Uncle Chester's Room is most appealing, with its redwood wainscoting, pressed-tin ceiling, and massive 18th-century Spanish mahogany four-poster. In the skylit Blossom Room there's a lace canopy bed; while the Pineapple Room has a high pine four-poster. The Wine Cellar Room is very atmospheric with its low, beamed ceiling; it also has a sitting area with TV and a dining area with refrigerator. The parlor is comfortable and has interesting personal collections, including early 19th-century family portraits and a doll collection. A full breakfast with egg dishes is served in the parlor.

Rates (incl. breakfast): $105–$160 double.

Dining Only in Santa Cruz & Vicinity

Santa Cruz

Casablanca, 101 Main St. (☎ 408/426-9063), offers views of the beach and pier from the rattan upholstered chairs. The cuisine is fresh and California style. Start with the piquant calamari in lime sauce or the roasted Anaheim chilies filled with herbed chevre and served with tomatillo salsa. Among 10 or so entrees, you might find a cilantro-marinated chicken breast served with sun-dried tomato pesto, a rack of lamb with raspberry-black truffle jus, or local swordfish with mango salsa. Prices range from $15 to $23. Finish off with cheesecake or the chocolate sundae.

Hours: Sun–Thurs 5–9pm; Fri–Sat 5–10pm; Sun 9:30am–1:30pm.

India Joze, 1001 Center St. (☎ 408/427-3554), as the name suggests, provides fare from India and Southeast Asia, so that you'll find really pungent vindaloo made with either chicken or lamb alongside satay and *nasi goreng,* a Malay wok dish made with calamari, chicken, vegetables, and spices. There are also good soups and some Middle Eastern dishes like felafel or *sis,* a Turkish marinade that can be used for chicken, snapper, or lamb. Prices range from $10 to $16. Desserts are more along the lines of pecan pie and mud pie although there is a very sweet almond rosewater baklava, which can be served warm if you wish.

Hours: Sun–Thurs 5:30–9pm; Fri–Sat 5:30–10pm.

Capitola

At **Shadowbrook,** 1750 Wharf Rd. (☎ 408/475-1511), guests have a long hike to reach the dining rooms, down a wooden staircase beside a brook cascading over rocks, ferns, and shrubs. At the bottom are a series of dining rooms located on several floors overlooking a river at the base of a ravine. The rooms have a '70s look, with lots of wood and somber colors. The food is equally traditional. Appetizers run the gamut from artichoke hearts to prawn cocktail and escargots Provençal. The main specialties are steaks, roasted chicken with herbs, and similar, but every evening the specials add some more innovative flair to the menu. For example, you might find a Cajun-style tenderloin of lamb served with roasted garlic bordelaise, or a grilled salmon with honey-lemon thyme vinaigrette. Prices range from $13 to $22.

Hours: Mon–Thurs 5:30–8:45pm; Fri 5:30–10pm; Sat 4:30–10pm; Sun 10am–2:15pm and 4:40–8:45pm.

Aptos

Cafe Bittersweet, 787 Rio del Mar (☎ 408/662-9799), is located in a historic tavern. It has an elegant bar and a series of dining rooms, several with fireplaces plus one that provides a full view of the open kitchen and wood-fired pizza oven. The cuisine is American bistro with distinct Mediterranean influences. Key specialties include game (peppered venison steaks with sun-dried cherry-pinot noir sauce) and enticing fresh fish (porcini-crusted monkfish with mushroom marsala sauce), plus a simple rib-eye steak served with a rich cabernet-shallot sauce. Prices range from $13 to $24. Desserts are exceptional, too. For example, the tiramisu is made with hazelnut genoise, mascarpone, and white chocolate ganache and served with three sauces (bittersweet chocolate, milk chocolate, and crème anglaise) plus espresso ice cream. Another specialty is the chocolate trio, one of which is a chocolate bread pudding. There's also an outdoor dining area. The wine list is extensive, featuring more than 200 selections.

Hours: Sun and Tues–Thurs 5:30–9pm; Fri–Sat 5:30–10pm.

Cafe Sparrow, 8042 Soquel Dr. (☎ 408/688-6238), has a French country air with its chintz banquettes, dried flowers, cotton-print tablecloths, and bottle-filled wine racks. It's a pretty room with sponge-painted yellow and eggshell-blue walls and a tented ceiling. The dinner menu offers a broad selection of fish and meat dishes. There might be rack of lamb with rich, red wine mint sauce; or sautéed chicken livers with garlic, apples, and bacon and finished with crème fraiche; or calamari with lemon, butter, and capers. Prices range from $10 to $21. The Sunday brunch brings an array of delights, from Frenchman's Hangover, which is two poached eggs in a spicy broth with Italian sausage and potatoes, to crab Benedict on a croissant, which substitutes crab cakes for the usual ham in this egg dish. Prices range from $10 to $15.

Hours: Mon–Sat 11am–2pm; Sun 9am–2pm; daily 5:30–9pm.

Santa Cruz & Vicinity
Special & Recreational Activities

Beaches: See above for details.

Biking: Rent a bike at the **Bicycle Rent and Tour Center,** 131 Center St., Santa Cruz (☎ 408/426-8687), and take yourself for a spin along the cliff walk. Prices start at $7 an hour to a maximum of $25 a day.

Camping: See descriptions of the area's state parks above for information about camping possibilities.

Fishing: Most party boats leave from the Municipal Pier in Santa Cruz, including **Stagnaro's** (☎ 408/423-2010). They leave at 7am and return around 3pm. The weekday charge is $31 for adults, $25 for children under 16, weekends it's $36 and $29, respectively. Equipment can be rented for $13 more, or you can bring your own.

Several outfits operate from the Santa Cruz Harbor at 135 5th Ave. (☎ 408/475-6161). One such company, **Shamrock Charters,** 2210 E. Cliff Dr. (☎ 408/476-2648), charges $30 weekdays and $35 weekends. Reservations are needed for both.

Golf: Pasatiempo Golf Course, 18 Clubhouse Rd. (☎ 408/459-9155), is an 18-hole course playable for $122.

Kayaking: Adventure Sports Unlimited, 303 Potrero St. no. 15 (☎ 408/458-3648), rents kayaks for $25 a day and also offers classes.

Kayak Connections, 413 Lake Ave. no. 4 (☎ 408/479-1121), rents single kayaks starting at $34 a day, with doubles for $40. It also operates a full tour and instructional program. This operator also rents canoes at their store in Moss Landing (☎ 408/724-5692).

Parasailing: Look down on the bay from one of **Pacific Parasail's** contraptions. They're located at 58 Municipal Wharf, Santa Cruz (☎408/423-3545).

Sailing: For sailboat plus kayak and water bike rentals, go to **Venture Quest,** 931 Pacific Ave., Santa Cruz (☎ 408/427-2267). They're located at Building 2 on the wharf.

Scuba Diving: For equipment rentals, go to **Adventure Sports Unlimited,** 303 Potrero St. no. 15 (☎ 408/458-3648).

State Parks: These are described in the area attractions section, above.

Surfing: Equipment can be rented at **Cowells Beach Surf Shop,** 109 Beach St., Santa Cruz (☎ 408/427-2355); and from **Club Ed Surf School,** 5 Isabel Dr., Cowell Beach, (☎ 408/459-9283).

Whale Watching: Most of the fishing outfits operate whale-watching trips in season. **Stagnaro's** (☎ 408/423-2010) also offers whale-watching trips. They leave from the Pier in season, charging $17 for adults and $13 for children. Trips last 3 hours.

Shamrock Charters, 2210 E. Cliff Dr. (☎ 408/476-2648), operates 2½-hour trips for $16 for adults, $12 for children 12 and under.

Wine Tasting: In the mountains behind Santa Cruz there are about 40 wineries that produce mainly for the local market only, many using grapes from outside the area. Although wine has been produced here since the 1800s, it was only recognized as a distinctive appellation in 1981. It encompasses the Santa Cruz mountain range, from Half Moon Bay in the north to Mount Madonna in the south.

Storrs, 303 Potrero St. #35, Santa Cruz (☎ tel 408/458-5030), is one winery that is developing its own varietals and gaining a reputation throughout California and the nation. You can enjoy tastings Friday to Monday from noon to 5pm, tours by appointment.

Bargetto Winery, 3535 N. Main St., Soquel (☎ 408/475-2258), offers regular daily tastings and tours by appointment.

On the western slopes most success has come with chardonnay, pinot noir and on the eastern with cabernet. For more information on wines produced in the Santa Cruz area, contact **Santa Cruz Winegrowers,** P.O. Box 3000, Santa Cruz, CA 95063 (☎ 408/479-9463).

EN ROUTE TO MONTEREY: SAN JUAN BAUTISTA & SALINAS

San Juan Bautista

Located just off Highway 101 between San Jose and Salinas, San Juan Bautista is one of the most atmospheric small towns you'll find anywhere. Helen Hunt Jackson, who began her novel *Ramona* on a visit here in 1883, wrote, "At San Juan there lingers more of an atmosphere of the olden time than is to be found in any other place in California." And it's still true today. The town has a very Spanish-Mexican air and is dominated by a very large and eerily compelling mission.

The **Mission San Juan Bautista,** 408 S. Second St. (☎ 408/623-2127), stands on a ridge occupying the whole west side of a plaza, flanked by several other buildings from the Spanish-Mexican era in

California. It was the 15th mission in California, founded on June 24, 1797, by Father Fermín Lasuén. The present church was begun in 1803 and dedicated in 1812. It has been in continuous use ever since, with the original bells still summoning the largely Spanish-speaking congregation to worship—a fact that may very well account for the spiritual magnetism that you can still feel here today. The glowing reredos and altar were painted by a stranded sailor from Boston, Thomas Doak, who was willing to work for room and board in contrast to the originally commissioned Mexican artist, who demanded 75¢ a day. The mission was run by Father Arroyo, who could preach to the Indians in seven different dialects, and Father Estevan Tapis, who nurtured a famous Indian boys choir—locking them up on Saturday nights in the jail adjacent to the church lest they get drunk and fail to attend the service the next day.

In the museum you can see a hurdy-gurdy, or hand organ, that is said to have saved the mission from a group of Tulare Indians who were bent on destroying it. The padre went out to them with the hand organ, cranked its handle, and instead of attacking the Mission Indians, he began singing, much to the astonishment of the Tulares. They were so captivated that they put aside their weapons and even asked to stay. While you're here, walk through the cemetery at the side of the church, and look out just beyond the walls to the pathway that marks a section of the original Camino Real, which once ran 650 miles from San Diego to San Rafael. It later became a stage road and eventually U.S. Highway 101. Beyond this road were the rodeo grounds. Stand here for a second or two—it's a glorious spot for some active imagination.

Hours: Mar–Oct daily 9:30am–5pm; Nov–Feb daily 9am–4:30pm. *Admission:* $1 adults, 25¢ students.

There are several other buildings around the plaza of some historical interest. Together, they constitute the **San Juan Bautista State Historic Park** (☎ 408/623-4881).

Hours: Daily 10am–4:30pm; closed Christmas and Thanksgiving days. *Admission:* $2 adults, $1 children 6–12.

On the south side is the **Castro House** (1840), which was the home of the Mexican administrator, Maj. Gen. José Castro. It looks much as it did when it was built, except inside it has been furnished in the style of the 1870s, when the Breen family lived here. Patrick and Margaret Breen had been among the survivors in the Donner Party and settled in San Juan Bautista. One of their sons became rich in the Gold Rush, and they were able to purchase the Castro adobe. Their descendants lived here until 1933, when it became part of the Historic Park. You can stroll through the rooms and get some idea of what their daily life was like.

Next door is the **Plaza Hotel,** which was a major stop on the stage line between San Francisco and Los Angeles. The long, single-story adobe building originally served as a barrack until Angelo Zanetta added a second story in 1858 and converted it into a hotel.

On the east side of the plaza the **Zanetta House** was built in 1815 as a dormitory-home for unmarried Indian women. It was purchased by Zanetta, who remodeled it as a residence in 1868.

The **Plaza Stable,** built about 1861, was operated by a succession of men who serviced the seven or so stage lines that ran through San Juan Bautista until the railroad arrived in nearby Hollister in 1876, turning the town into a quiet backwater. Inside, an assortment of carriages and wagons is on display.

After exploring the mission and the plaza, stroll along the main street of the town. There are several historic adobes on the street. The **Juan de Anza Adobe,** at Franklin and 3rd, was a cantina in the 1850s; also take a look at the **Theophile Vache Adobe** in the same block. At the corner of Washington and 3rd, **Tuccoletta Hall** was originally a tavern, then a bakery, and later a general store. Stop in at one of several antiques stores, or else enjoy a Mexican lunch at one of several restaurants.

My favorite place to eat is either **Dona Esther,** 25 Franklin St., at 3rd Street (☎ 408/623-2518), where you're more likely to meet the locals dining on the enclosed patio in the back, or **La Casa Rosa,** 107 3rd St. (☎ 408/623-4563), which also has a small, attractive courtyard.

The major events in town are the **Annual American Indian Spring Market** in May, and the **California All Indian Market** in September, plus a large annual flea market, antiques and collectible show in August.

Salinas

Further along Highway 101 toward Monterey, Salinas is not a very appealing town, but passionate Steinbeck fans may want to go just to visit the house where he wrote and to get a sense of the region and the characters that he wrote about.

The Salinas Valley is flanked to the east by the Gabilan mountains and to the west by the Santa Lucias, which John Steinbeck always associated with danger and foreboding, since that is the direction the night came from. From both sides of the valley, streams flowed out of the canyons into the Salinas River, which once ran 100 miles along an inlet to the sea.

Here in this valley and estuary, the climate and cycle of drought and bounty were almost Biblical in their extremes. Five or 6 wet years were followed by 6 or 7 moderately wet years, and they in turn were followed by several dry years. No matter what, during each cycle, people always forgot the stress and struggle caused by the one before so that during the dry everyone would forget the wet, and during the wet everyone forgot the dry. During the dry cycles, the earth cracked, cows starved to death, and folks hauled water in barrels for drinking or else abandoned the land and sought their livelihood elsewhere.

Today the extremes can be smoothed by modern irrigation and water control systems, but floods do still occur, and the climate is ever present. In spring the grasslands are colored with brilliant wildflowers: lupines, poppies, buttercups, violets, and Indian paintbrushes. In summer the grass turns brown, and the wind blows the dust about. At those times it's easy to imagine yourself into one of Steinbeck's stories, where the climate and geography play major roles.

The city's downtown streets are still lined with Victorian storefronts, and agricultural trucks are as likely to be parked out front as cars. And even though the town was embarrassed by Steinbeck's socialist philosophies, it has begun to appeal to visitors who are interested in this California son. In August there's a **Steinbeck Festival and International Congress,** when fans converge to celebrate and discuss the author and his works in films, lectures, and performances.

Visit the **Steinbeck House,** 132 Central Ave. (☎ 408/424-2735), where Steinbeck was born and wrote several of his novels. Built in 1897, it's a substantial Victorian with several gables and turrets. John was born in the front bedroom (no reception room) on February 27, 1902. When he was 10, he occupied the front upstairs bedroom, and it was here that he wrote *The Red Pony* and *Tortilla Flat*. In *East of Eden* there are several descriptions of both the exterior and interior of the house. Today it is operated as a restaurant by the Salinas Valley Women's Guild. Cannelloni, quiche, and chicken pot pie are the kind of light dishes served. Stop in for lunch or just to pay your respects.

Hours: House is open Mon–Sat 11am–3pm; lunch is served Mon–Fri 11:45am–1:15pm and Sat 11:30am–2:30pm.

The Monterey Peninsula

Distances in Miles: Monterey/Pacific Grove, 118; Carmel, 116; Carmel Valley, 130

Estimated Driving Times: 2 hours to Monterey/Pacific Grove; 2½ hours to Carmel; 3 hours to Carmel Valley

Driving: From San Francisco, you can take Highway 101 south or Highway 280, which connects to Highway 101 at San Jose, and then Highway 101).

To reach Monterrey and Carmel, turn off onto Highway 156 West at Prunedale and turn south onto Highway 1, which you follow into Monterey and on to Carmel.

Another more circuitous route is via Highway 280 or 101, exiting to Los Gatos and then, via Highway 17, to Santa Cruz at the northern rim of Monterey Bay. From there, Highway 1 will lead you south to Monterey. If time is not an issue, take Highway 1 all the way down the coast.

Further Information: For information about Monterey in general, contact the **Monterey County Visitors & Convention Bureau,** P.O. Box 1770, Monterey, CA 93942-1770 (☎ 408/649-1770).

For Pacific Grove there is the **Pacific Grove Chamber of Commerce,** at the corner of Forest and Central avenues (☎ 408/373-3304).

On a map, the Monterey Peninsula juts out like a tiny nodule at the southern end of Monterey Bay, which sweeps down from Santa Cruz all the way around to the towns of Monterey and Pacific Grove. This small, 25-square-mile Peninsula supports three major destinations, all within a few miles of each other—Monterey, Pacific Grove, and Carmel. Its name conjures early Spanish–American history; evokes the wind-gnarled beauty of the Monterey cypress; stimulates visions of grand, sweeping, oceanfront golfing greens; and brings to mind the legendary works of those artists that have been inspired by its landscape—Robert Louis Stevenson, Robinson Jeffers, John

AREA CODE CHANGE ALERT IN 1998

All of the new technologies that have been introduced in the last decade require additional phone numbers, and as a result some area codes are being split, with new area codes being introduced to replace them. The old area code 408 will be split and a new area code of **831** introduced for the following communities covered in this chapter: Monterey, Pacific Grove, Carmel, and the Carmel Valley. The new area code will be introduced in July 1998; until February 1999 you will be told that the old 408 number is now in the new 831 area when you dial a number. Thereafter, you must use the new 831 area code.

Steinbeck, Richard Henry Dana, Gertrude Atherton, Mary Austin, and Edward Weston, to name only a few.

Planning Your Weekends

Several weekends can be spent exploring the Peninsula and the nearby towns and regions. Lively Monterey has much to offer— historic Spanish-Mexican adobes, the wharf, Cannery Row, and the other icons of Steinbeck and the fishing and canning industry that thrived here ever so briefly, plus the amazing Aquarium. Next door, Pacific Grove beckons with quieter charms—small, painted cottages and grand, waterfront Victorians, monarch butterflies by the thousand in the winter, and a great waterfront for cycling or walking. Carmel is famous, period—famous for being an art colony, famous for having a mayor named Clint Eastwood, and famous for being very touristed by fashionable, well-heeled folks. Still, it has a lot to recommend it. There are fine galleries and stores, fine dining, and charming hostelries, two lovely beaches, and the glorious Mission. Nearby, Pebble Beach and the 17-mile Drive give access to inspiring shoreline vistas. To the south lies Point Lobos, the greatest meeting between land and sea, which it is. From the peninsula you can also visit the ranches of Carmel Valley, where they'll tell you it's always sunny.

MONTEREY

Although Monterey is a modern town, it is still the best place to visit to get a sense of what early California was like when it was under Spanish and Mexican rule from 1770 to 1846. The story of Monterey begins with its discovery by Sebastián Vizcaíno and the celebration of mass by Father Antonio de la Ascension on the shore on December 16, 1602. Vizcaíno

The Monterey Peninsula

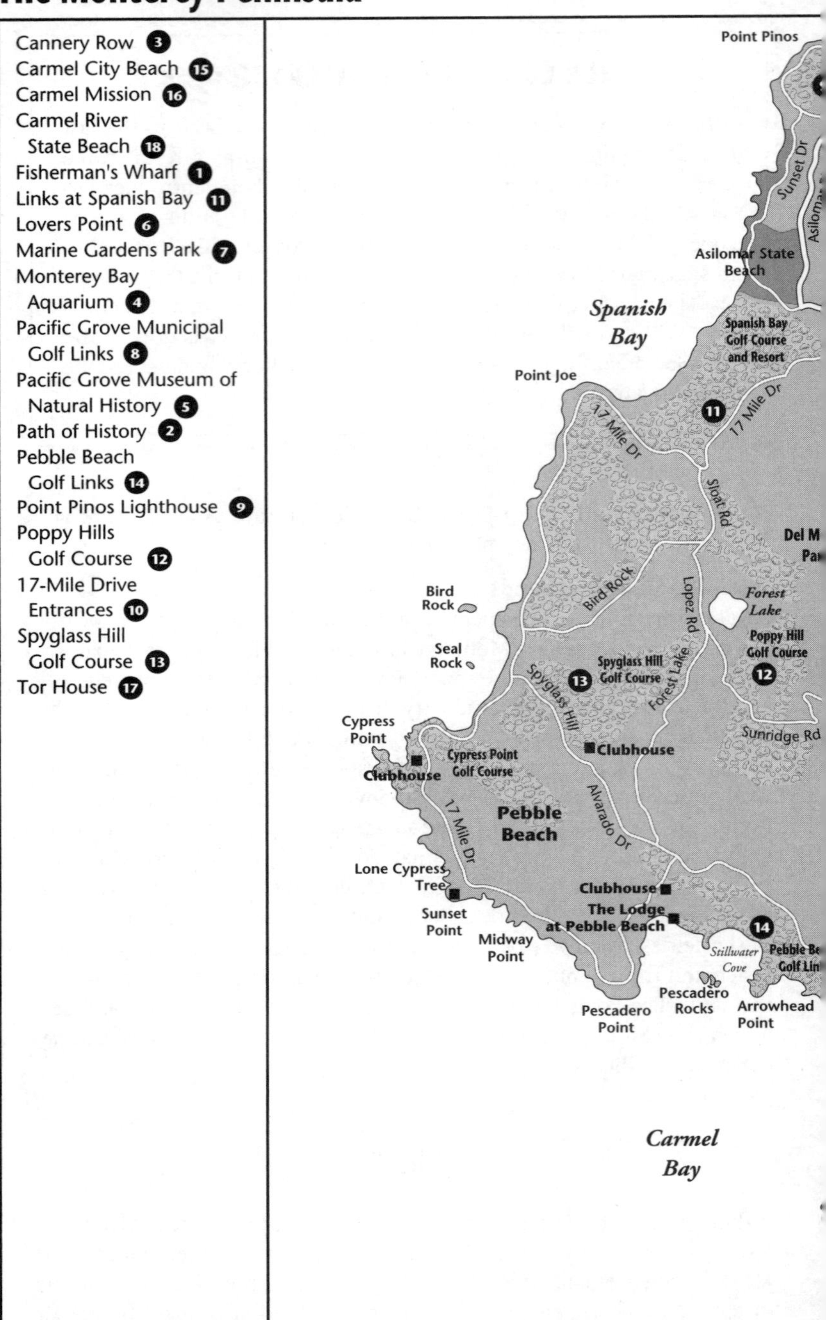

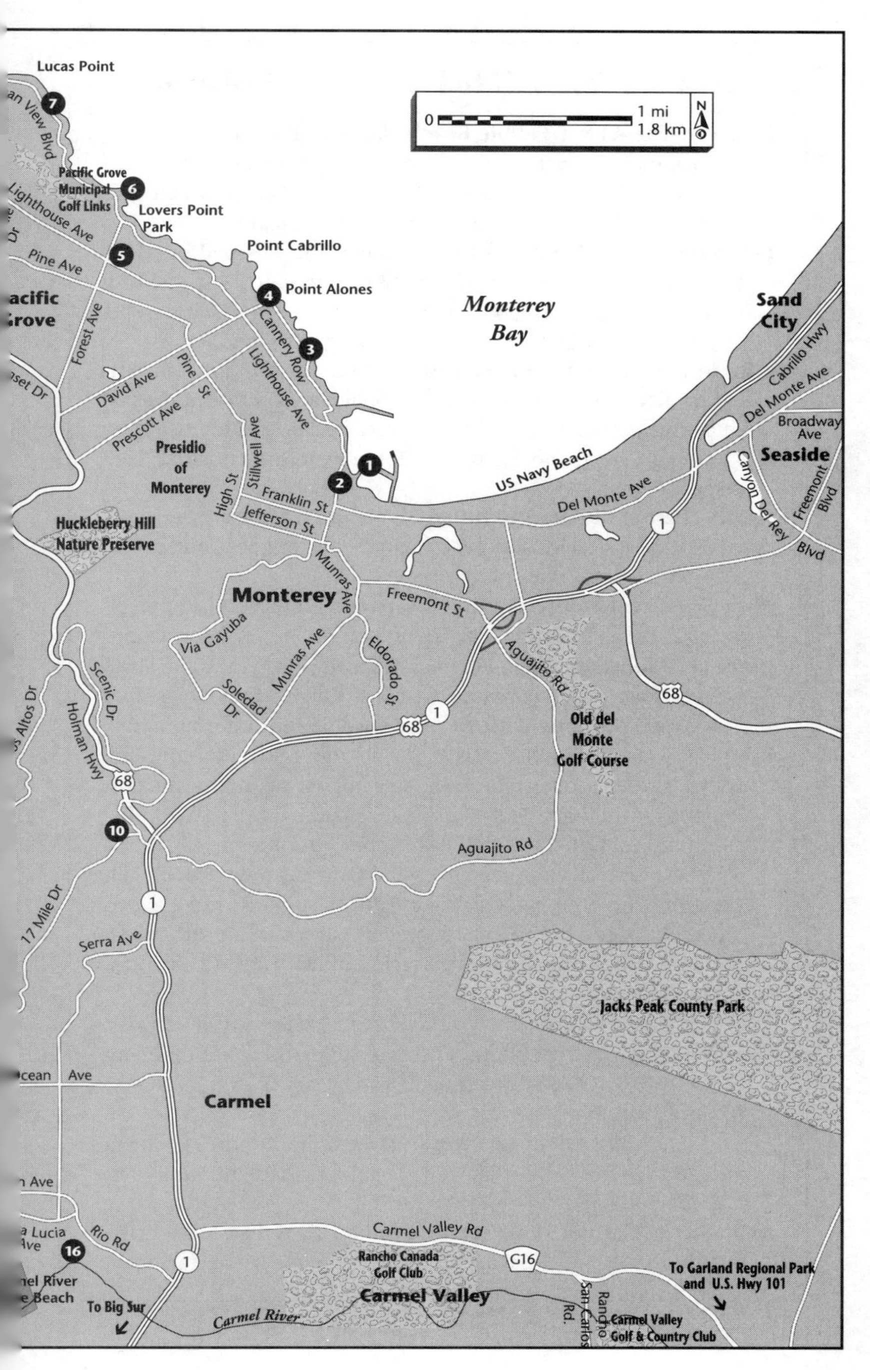

Lucas Point
Pacific Grove Municipal Golf Links
Lovers Point Park
Lighthouse Ave
Pine Ave
Point Cabrillo
Point Alones
Monterey Bay
Sand City
Cabrillo Hwy
Del Monte Ave
Broadway Ave
Seaside
Forest Ave
Cannery Row
Lighthouse Ave
David Ave
Pine St
Prescott Ave
Presidio of Monterey
Stillwell Ave
High St
Franklin St
Jefferson St
US Navy Beach
Del Monte Ave
Canyon Del Rey Blvd
Freemont Blvd
Huckleberry Hill Nature Preserve
Monterey
Munras Ave
Freemont St
Via Gayuba
Eldorado St
Aguajito Rd
Soledad Dr
Munras Ave
Scenic Dr
Holman Hwy
Old del Monte Golf Course
Aguajito Rd
17 Mile Dr
Serra Ave
Jacks Peak County Park
Ave
Carmel
Rio Rd
Carmel Valley Rd
Rancho Canada Golf Club
Carmel Valley
To Garland Regional Park and U.S. Hwy 101
To Big Sur
Carmel River
Rancho San Carlos Rd.
Carmel Valley Golf & Country Club
0
1 mi
1.8 km
N

Events & Festivals to Plan Your Trip Around

January: The **AT&T Pebble Beach National Pro-Am,** a celebrity golf tournament par excellence with the great stars of the PGA Tour, is held in late January each year at the Pebble Beach Golf Links. Call ☎ 408/649-1533 for more information.

February: At the **Masters of Food and Wine Festival,** international chefs and master winemakers gather to host cooking classes, wine tastings, gourmet meals, and other culinary events at the Highland Inn (☎ 408/624-3801) in Carmel.

March: Dixieland Monterey 1997 will be the 17th annual festival, which draws more than 20 national bands performing at 10 different locations. It's held each year in early March. Call the Monterey Chamber of Commerce for more information (☎ 408/649-1770).

April: The **Big Sur International Marathon** is a great ocean-side run with classical musical accompaniment along the course. Call ☎ 408/625-6226 for information.

The **Great Monterey Squid Festival** is for those who appreciate squid in all its forms. Call ☎ 408/649-6547 for information.

June: The **Monterey Blues Festival** keeps the blues tradition alive. Past performers have included Gladys Knight, Etta James, Lou Rawls, and B.B King. Call ☎ 408/394-2652 for information.

July: The **Carmel Bach Festival** is a 23-day festival of concerts, recitals, lectures, open rehearsals, and children's concerts. It's most famous for the Founders' Memorial Concert at the Carmel Mission Basilica. Call ☎ 408/624-2046 for information.

The **Feast of Lanterns** in Pacific Grove is a week-long celebration with a pet parade, dancing in the streets, and a Saturday night pageant with entertainment, barbecue, a boat parade, and fireworks at Pacific Grove Beach. Call ☎ 408/372-7625 for information.

The **Gilroy Garlic Festival** celebrates garlic every which way, as it is used in every culture. There's always lots of entertainment plus close to 100 arts and crafts booths. Call ☎ 408/842-1625 for information.

At the **Moss Landing Antique Street Fair,** hundreds of dealers gather in this fishing village also famous for its antique stores. Call ☎ 408/633-4501 for information.

August: The **Carmel Shakespeare Festival** gives theater-goers the chance to see Shakespeare and the classics under the stars in an old amphitheater. This traditional festival was begun by George Sterling and Mary Austin, among others. Call ☎ 408/622-0100 for information.

September: At the **Santa Rosalia Festival** in Monterey, an outdoor mass is celebrated, and the fleet is blessed. There's a parade, entertainment, arts and crafts, and, of course, Italian food. Call ☎ 408/649-6544 for information.

Top names in jazz perform at the **Monterey Jazz Festival.** There are also exhibits, photography, jazz clinics, seminars, and much more. Call ☎ 408/373-3366 for information.

The **Castroville Artichoke Festival** celebrates (you guessed it) the artichoke; in addition, you can enjoy arts and crafts booths and live entertainment, as well as a 10K run and 4K walk. Call ☎ 408/633-2465 for information.

October: For the **Butterfly Parade and Bazaar** in Pacific Grove, school children parade in butterfly costumes to welcome the Monarchs back to their winter home. Call ☎ 408/646-6540 for information.

named it after the Viceroy of Mexico, Count Monterey. One hundred and fifty years later, a second mass was celebrated under the same oak tree by Father Junípero Serra and Father Juan Crespí, who accompanied Gaspar de Portolá on the expedition that eventually went on to discover San Francisco Bay.

The Presidio of Monterey and the Mission San Carlos Borromeo were both founded in 1770 (the Mission moved to Carmel in 1771). In 1775 Monterey was named the capital of California, and it remained so until on July 7, 1846, when California was proclaimed part of the United States and was formally accepted into the Union in 1850. Even under first Spanish and then Mexican rule, many Americans, especially New Englanders, had settled in Monterey, men like William Edward Petty Hartnell, John Rogers Cooper, and Thomas Oliver Larkin, who arrived in 1832 as a merchant. He was appointed U.S. consul to Mexico.

The town's history is rich indeed and gives a West Coast Spanish twist to the East's Plymouth Rock. Here in the late 1700s the wealthy rancheros, which operated their thriving hide and tallow trade, set the tone of society and daily life. Every Saint's day was celebrated with a Mass and a fiesta. Dancing, parties, and horseback riding were the passions of Alta California society as well as such recreations as bull-and-bear fights. Gala receptions were held for Spanish governors and for other visiting dignitaries, and the rancheros in general lived a lavish way of life.

As more foreigners arrived, the power of the rancheros declined, and by the time the Americans took over in 1846 Walter Colton, who was appointed the first alcalde, could describe Monterey's population as follows: "Here is the reckless Californian, half wild Indian, roving trapper, lawless Mexican, licentious Spaniard, the scolding Englishman, the absconding Frenchman, luckless Irishman, adventurous Russian and discontented Mormon"—a veritable mosaic of immigrants. The Gold Rush shifted the focus away from Monterey, which was thereafter of little commercial importance, except for its whaling industry, which was undertaken largely by the Portuguese.

For many years Monterey remained in essence a Mexican village, with Spanish the prevailing language. When Robert Louis Stevenson visited in 1879, he remarked on the grace and charm of the people in that "world of absolutely mannerless Americans." Ironically, it was the decline of Monterey as an economic and governmental center that helped to preserve so much of Old Monterey.

Behind all the hoopla and tacky tourist activity around the pier and the aquarium, Monterey's Spanish-Mexican soul can still be found. The flavor of the Old Capital is still there behind the obvious tourist trappings and can be traced most clearly by following the gold tiles that mark the "Path of History Walking Tour," a guided tour that lasts 1½ hours, in **Monterey State Historic Park,** 20 Custom House Plaza (☎ 408/649-7118). The tour itself leaves from the **State Park Visitors Center,** Stanton Center, 5 Custom House Plaza, where you can also view a film on the history of Monterey (it's shown free every 20 minutes). If you don't wish to have the guide, you can follow the walking-tour route on your own, going from one adobe building to another, stopping in some of them along the way.

Hours: Guided tours at 10:15am, 12:30pm, and 2:30pm. *Cost:* $2 adults, $1.50 youths 13–18, and $1 children 6–12.

The solid walls of the adobe houses are plastered and whitewashed; from them extend balconies with overhanging roofs of terra-cotta tile. The verandas often look over a patio with a fountain at the center. Roses and jasmine climb the veranda posts and overhang the roofs as they do at the Larkin House, for example. Some houses were originally decorated with colored pebble and shell designs. What follows are some of the highlights along the route of the tour. Several of the houses are open to visitors, but they are operated by different organizations, so their hours vary. Most of the buildings have prominently placed descriptive signs that tell their story, even if they are not open to the public.

Enter Custom House Plaza and find the **Old Pacific House,** which was built in 1835 as a hotel and saloon by James Santiago McKinley. Behind it there was a bull-and-bear-fight arena, in which bears and specially trained bulls fought, with the bear usually winning by ripping out the bull's tongue. The last fight was staged in the 1870s. The farewell dinner for California's last military governor, Gen. Bennett Riley, was held here in

Historic Monterey

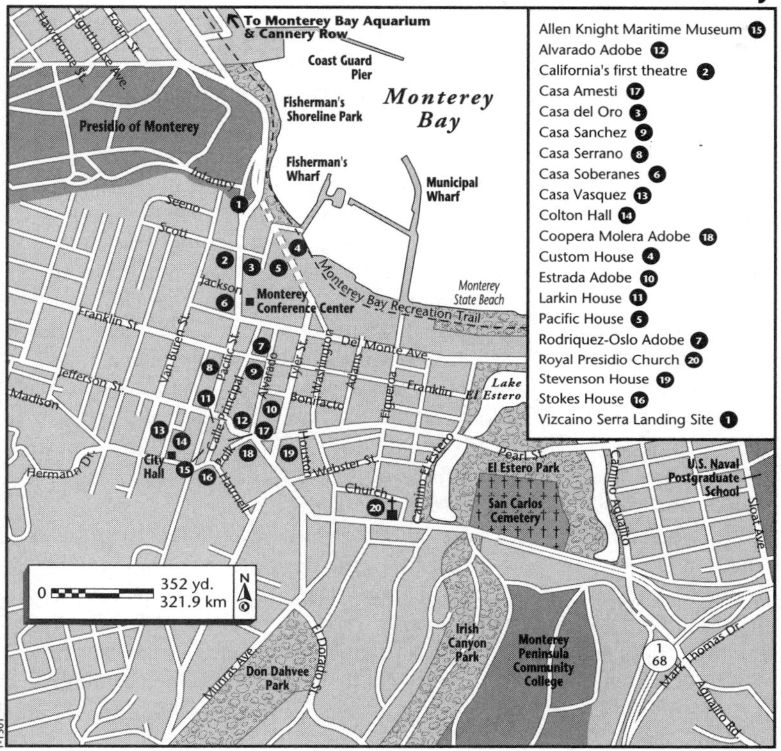

July 1850. When it was sold to David Jacks in 1880, the house became the home of a Presbyterian minister and then much later the Salvation Army Headquarters. Today it's a history museum with displays relating to different periods in California's history.

Hours: Daily 10am–5pm. *Admission:* Free.

The next building you come to is the **Custom House,** Custom House Plaza, between Scott and Decatur streets, which dates from 1827. Under Spanish rule, duties (as much as 25% of the cargo's worth) were collected from traders—many from Boston and New England—who were required to stop first at Monterey before exchanging their manufactured goods for hides and tallow anywhere else.

In the first decades of the 19th century, trade was a mere trickle, and life at the Custom House was largely quiet, except when the pirate Hippolyte de Bouchard landed on the beach in front of the building and sacked the town. Spain had restricted foreign trade, but when Mexico became independent in 1822, she opened Monterey to foreign trade and it flourished. The ranchos delivered hides and tallow to the ports, and then they were taken to New England factories. When foreign ships arrived, celebratory balls were often held here at the Custom House. At one such celebration a particular stir was caused by the Padre's banning of the new dance, the waltz! Under the Mexican regime, the customs duties were used to finance local government expenses, so commandants were tempted to raise tariffs, and they did. At one point tariffs were raised to more than 40% of the cargo's value.

Revenues were large, and for this reason control of the Custom House became a major political prize, so bitter that there were often fierce struggles to secure the office. In one such power struggle, José Castro, two customs officers, plus an army of mostly American trappers, sailors, and other foreigners seized the Presidio in November 1836 and deposed the Governor. Such were the riches of the port of Monterey that Mariano Guadalupe Vallejo tried to have the Custom House relocated to San Francisco.

In the middle of this feuding over the disposal of the revenues between northern and southern Californians, no one noticed the arrival of American warships in the bay in 1846. On July 7, 250 seamen and marines landed on the beach from Commodore John D. Sloat's flagship, the *Savannah,* and hoisted the American flag up over the Custom House.

From here, too, the state's first newspaper, the *Californian,* was published on a makeshift press. After 1847 the importance of the building declined because all other California ports were open, and ships were no longer required to stop first at Monterey. The Custom House was formally closed in 1868, and although it was occupied afterwards, it had slipped into decay by the turn of the century. It's the oldest government building in California. Today, it displays a typical ship's cargo of the 1830s.

Hours: Daily 10am–5pm. *Admission:* Free.

The **first brick house** in Monterey was occupied by a former member of the Donner Party, Gallant Duncan Dickenson, a Virginian who began building the house himself but then took off for the gold fields. The house was completed by his son-in-law, brickmason Amos G. Lawrie. Dickenson eventually became alcalde of Stockton and a delegate to the constitutional convention.

Hours: Daily 10am–4pm. *Admission:* Free.

The **old whaling station** was originally built in 1847 by David Wight, a Scot. He and his family lived here for only a short time, however, before they too left for the gold fields. In 1855 it became a boarding house for Portuguese whalers of the "Old Company." This company of 17 men and 2 boats managed to harvest 800 barrels of oil annually for 3 years. Blubber was rendered in huge kettles on the beach in front of the building (note the iron pot in the back garden, a reminder of those times). The path that leads to the front door is made out of whale vertebrae. A second whaling company was formed, and both harvested between 600 and 1,000 barrels a year, harpooning humpbacks and gray whales. There were, in fact, about 500 to 600 whalers operating between California and Hawaii, but the industry faded quickly. By 1877 only 40 vessels were operating. Only the **garden** is open to the public, daily from 10am to 4pm.

The **Vizcaíno–Serra landing site,** at the corner of Pacific and Artillery, is supposedly where Vizcaíno first landed in 1602 and also where Father Serra came ashore in 1770. On this hilltop stands the **Serra Monument,** a statue of the father standing in a boat. North of this monument, a marker indicates the site of **El Castillo de Monterey,** which was built in 1792. It was captured by Bouchard in 1818 and again by Commodore Thomas Catesby Jones in 1842. The calaboose was used as a jail for several years after the American conquest as a place to sober up drunken Montereños. Farther up the hill is a huge bronze statue of Commodore Sloat who took over California for the U.S. in 1846.

Jack Swan was a Scot who came to Monterey in 1844 and finished building a lodging house and tavern for sailors on Pacific and Scott streets in 1847. One evening in 1850, to please some U.S. army officers who wanted to stage live drama, Swan agreed to build a small stage and to provide benches, whale-oil lamps, and curtains fashioned from blankets. Thus was **California's first theater** launched. After Swan's death in 1896, the building decayed until it was reopened as a theater in 1937. Plays are produced here to this day by the Gold Coast Theatre Company. Call for reservations after 1pm Wednesday to Saturday at ☎ 408/375-4916. Tickets cost $9 for adults, $7 for children 13 to 19 and seniors 60 and over, and $5 for kids 12 and under. Show times are Wednesday to Saturday at 8pm in July and August, and on Friday and Saturday at 8pm the rest of the year.

The **Casa del Oro,** at the corner of Olivier and Scott streets, was built around 1845 by Thomas Larkin, its name derived from the big safe inside that was used as a gold and gold dust depository. During the 1850s it housed a general store run by Joseph Boston and Company. It's still operated as a general store today.

Casa Soberanes, 336 Pacific St., at Del Monte, was built in 1830 by Rafael Estrada, who was a half brother of Gov. Juan Alvarado and nephew of General Vallejo. In 1860 it was sold to Don Feliciano Soberanes and remained in the Soberanes family until 1922. It's a handsome house with cantilevered balcony and lovely garden. Inside there are displays of local and modern Mexican folk art, plus New England–style furnishings and objects from the China trade. The interior can only be seen on the guided tour.

Hours: Tours Mon, Wed and Fri–Sun 10 and 11am. *Admission:* $2.

Casa Serrano is the home of the Monterey History and Art Association. It was built in 1845 by Thomas Larkin and sold to Florencio Serrano, a teacher, merchant, and alcalde of Monterey. It is open weekends only.

Little is known about the **Lara–Soto Adobe** before the 1890s, when it was occupied by Manuel Soto and his Indian wife Felicidad. Afterwards it had a variety of owners. In 1919 artist and curator Josephine Blanch resided here. John Steinbeck lived here briefly in the 1940s. Today it houses professional offices.

Colton Hall, on Pacific Street between Jefferson and Madison, is named after Walter Colton, who arrived as chaplain aboard Commodore Stockton's ship, *Congress,* which had been sent to relieve Sloat in 1846. He became the first American alcalde and commissioned this building in 1848 as a school and meeting hall. The money for construction was provided by taxes on liquor and fines on gamblers, and the labor was supplied by convicts. Here in the upstairs room 48 delegates gathered September 1, 1849, to draft, debate, and finally approve the constitution for the state of California. However, statehood didn't officially happen until September 1850, when John C. Frémont and William C. Gwin were elected senators and Peter Burnett governor. The building is a two-story stone structure designed in New England style with an impressive pediment above the entrance.

Hours: Daily 10am–noon and 1–5pm (until 4pm in winter). *Admission:* Free.

Juan Bautista Alvarado (Governor of Mexican California from 1836 to '42) built **Casa de Alvarado,** 494–498 Alvarado St., in the 1830s for his mistress Raymunda Castillo. Although she had three children by him, she refused to marry him because he drank too much. When she married a widower, Mariano Soberanes, and moved to San Luis Obispo, Alvarado sold the house to Manuel Dutra, a Portuguese trader.

The bandit Tiburcio Vásquez, who terrorized the stage roads in the 1870s, spent his youth at the **Vásquez Adobe,** 546 Dutra St., until he became an outlaw after California was taken over by the U.S. The house was later occupied by his sister.

In 1854 the granite-walled **Old Monterey jail,** on Dutra Street, was built to replace an older adobe building. It was a second home, it seems, to Steinbeck's Big Joe. It continued as the jail until 1956, and it is said that no one ever escaped beyond the thick granite walls.

Hours: Daily 10am–4pm. *Admission:* Free.

The **Larkin House,** 510 Calle Principal, at Jefferson Street, is named after Thomas Oliver Larkin, who arrived in Monterey from Massachusetts in 1832. A merchant who ingratiated himself with everyone, he was eventually appointed United States Consul to California in 1843, when the area was under Mexican rule. He attempted to secure California peacefully for the U.S., but Frémont, Sloat, and Commodore Stockton did it their way. Larkin was an extremely wealthy man with landholdings throughout California. The furnishings in the house and the architectural features of the house attest to that. It's a lovely, two-story adobe and really inaugurated the style that is commonly called Monterey Colonial. It combines New England features, like a hip roof and central hall and staircase, with adobe walls and a second-floor balcony with an overhanging roof. The official proclamation of United States rule of California was spoken from this balcony by Sloat. The interior can only be seen on a guided tour.

Hours: Tours Mon and Wed–Sun at 1, 2, and 3pm. *Admission:* $2.

The **Sherman Quarters,** on Calle Principal, was originally built as a store and warehouse. After the takeover of California by the United States in 1847, William Tecumseh Sherman, then a lieutenant, shared quarters here with Henry Halleck and Edward Ord, all of whom served as generals in the Union Army much later during the Civil War.

At 540 Calle Principal stands **The House of Four Winds,** so called because of the wrought-iron weathervane that stands atop the roof, an oddity when it was first built in 1835 by Thomas Larkin as an early hall of records.

Casa Amesti was built by Jose Amesti, who became one of the city's leading citizens after his arrival in 1822. He served as alcalde in 1844. The house is a fine example of Monterey Colonial and possesses a lovely garden.

Hours: Sat–Sun 2–4pm. *Admission:* Free.

The **Cooper–Molera Complex** was the impressive home of a very successful merchant, John Rogers Cooper, who was born in the English Channel Islands on Alderney and emigrated with his mother to Massachusetts, where his half brother, Thomas O. Larkin, was born in 1802. John arrived in California in 1823 as master and part owner of the merchant ship *Rover.* He subsequently sold the vessel and married the sister of General Vallejo. He began building the house in 1827, and it remained in the family for at least three generations. Cooper also amassed huge land grants along the Big Sur coast. He died in San Francisco in 1872. Today the house contains exhibits, a carriage display, and a visitor center. It also has an historic period garden.

Hours: Tours Tues–Sun at 10 and 11am. *Admission:* $2.

Nearby was the site of Simoneau's Restaurant, where Robert Louis Stevenson came to eat, play chess, and talk with Jules Simoneau or fellow writers like Charles Warren Stoddard. The chessboard, by the way, is on display in the museum at the Old Custom House. When he wasn't enjoying these pastimes, Stevenson was courting (successfully) Fanny Osbourne.

Fanny lived nearby in the **Casa Bonifacio** on Alvarado Street with her sister Nellie Sanchez. Stevenson visited here frequently, and it's said that he began *The Amateur Emigrant,* wrote *The Pavilion on the Links,* and gathered notes for *The Old Pacific Capital* here. The Bonifacio adobe was also known as the "House of the Sherman Rose." In short, as the story goes, William Tecumseh Sherman was courting María Bonifacio, who lived in the house. One day, he unbuttoned a rose from his lapel and planted it in the ground, saying that if it grew, their love would, too. The rose grew into a glorious tree that rambled over the adobe, but Sherman never returned, and María never married. The house, now a private residence, has been moved to a new location, 785 Mesa Road.

When he was in Monterey, Stevenson lived at the **Stevenson House,** 530 Houston St., for 3 months in the fall of 1879 and wrote eloquently in *The Amateur Emigrant* of the community that he found here, including the

Chinese fishermen who had settled at Point Lobos and other coastal points.

Hours: Tours Tues–Sun at 1, 2, and 3pm. *Admission:* $2.

The **Royal Presidio Chapel,** on Church Street, was built in 1795 after an earlier version had burned down. The bas relief on the front facade was carved by Manuel Ruíz in 1794; much of the original remains. It is, in fact, the oldest structure in Monterey and all that is left of the presidio that once stood here and served as California's first capitol.

Before you head off for the other Monterey landmark that speaks to the city's history, Fisherman's Wharf, you may want to drop in to the **Maritime Museum** on Custom House Plaza (☎ 408/373-2469), which displays all kinds of maritime art and artifacts. Among the highlights is a model of the *Savannah* (Commodore Sloat's flagship), as well as several Chinese junks and many photographs of Old Monterey.

Hours: Daily 10am–5pm. *Admission:* $5 adults, $3 youths 13–17, $2 children 6–12.

When viewed from a distance or from the water **Fisherman's Wharf,** 99 Pacific St. (☎ 408/373-0600), still offers a nostalgic glimpse of those days when Chinese, Portuguese, and Italian fishermen trawled for sardines and when Steinbeck was writing about all the characters who worked the ocean and the wharf. If you make the effort to view the pier from the water, you can still imagine it as it was when Steinbeck wrote about it. But you'll at least want to go to the end of the pier and try to ignore the crowds and the honky-tonk. There's still the salt air, the spray, and the memories of sailors who once worked here.

Although it is regarded with nostalgia, in many ways the story of Monterey and its fishing industry—and sardine industry in particular—is a tale of greed and rapacity, an early example of environmental destruction. The Monterey suggested by the "Path of History" tour changed in 1880, when the Hotel de Monte opened and helped turn the town into a resort for the wealthy, attracting such folks as Charles Crocker, Mark Hopkins, Collis P. Huntington, and Leland Stanford—partners in the Central Pacific Railroad and collectively known as the "Big Four"—Andrew Carnegie, Joseph Pulitzer, and others.

For a while tourism dominated the economy, but in 1900 Frank E. Booth established the first cannery to process salmon here. He was later joined in the cannery business by Knute Hovden. But it wasn't until 1915, when Peter Ferrante arrived from Italy and introduced the lapara net—capable of trapping whole schools of fish—that the industry really took off. Back then the wharf was lined with huge kettles of boiling crabs and shuddered with the noise of Chinese girls pounding abalone. The men who worked on and around the wharf came from all over the world—Greeks, Italians, Japanese, Chinese, Portuguese, Spanish, and Mexicans. By 1918 there were nine plants packing 1.4 million cases of sardines.

Other larger, more efficient nets were introduced in the mid-1920s, such as the purse seiner, which could embrace an area as wide as a football field and reach depths of more than 100 feet. By 1935 the catch had reached a peak of 230,000 tons, and by 1945 there were 19 canneries operating alongside 20 reduction plants, which produced ancillary products like fish meal for fertilizers and livestock feed, soap, glycerin, salad oil, and a chemical for tanning leather. There were 100 vessels sailing from the wharf. After the war, the harvest declined to very low levels, except in 1950 when the industry summoned its last breath, taking in 132,000 pounds of sardine.

By 1952 the canneries were folding one after the other. Oddly enough, Steinbeck's novel *Cannery Row* wasn't published until 1945 when the industry was already in decline; by the time the city council got around to changing the name of Ocean View Avenue to Cannery Row in 1953, the canneries had already closed.

Although it's hard to pierce the commercial boosterism and tawdriness of **Cannery Row** itself, between David and Drake avenues (☎408/649-6690), if you have read Steinbeck's novels, you can still find Doc Rickett's lab, Wing Chong's market, and the Lone Star Cafe where Dora Flood and her "girls" hung out. To Steinbeck, Cannery Row was "a poem, a stink, a grating noise, a quality of light, a tone, a habit, a nostalgia, a dream." Today it's far from that, a strip of restaurants, art galleries, hotels, factory outlets, and gift shops. But if you enter into a reverie, you can see that some of the memories are still there in the historic buildings.

Walk the 8-block-long complex, and you can still find some real sites still standing. Chinatown, at China Point, has burned to the ground, but the American Can Company building still stands, now occupied by the American Tin Cannery Factory Outlets. The Aquarium occupies the site of the Hovden Cannery. But 800 Cannery Row still stands, where Ed "Doc" Ricketts collected and studied his sponges, anemones, barnacles, and octopi; today it's a private club, though. Other fictional locations are now occupied by restaurants or stores. Real Steinbeck fans will want to pick up a copy of the self-guided driving tour by Esther Trosow from the **Pacific Grove Chamber of Commerce,** at the corner of Forest and Central avenues (☎ 408/373-3304), or purchase a copy of *Cannery Row, The History of Old Ocean View Avenue* by Michael Kenneth Hemp.

Today the other big draw for tourists is the **Monterey Bay Aquarium,** 886 Cannery Row (☎ 408/648-4888), which attracts 20 million visitors annually. You'll need to wait in line unless you're staying at an accommodation that will allow you to bypass the lines by providing advance tickets, or if you have ordered them in advance (☎ 800/756-3737 in CA only; 408/648-4936 out of state); there is a $3 surchage for ordering advance tickets. At the center of this bustling place is a huge tank containing a swaying kelp forest and sheltering a variety of marine life—sardines, leopard sharks, garibaldis, anchovies, and rockfish among them. The aquarium features more than 100 exhibits housing more than 365,000 specimens of fish, mammals, reptiles, birds, and plants found in Monterey Bay. A variety of habitats have been replicated—deep reefs, shale reefs, sandy sea floor, and wharf. Among the big hits with children is the sea otter feeding, which takes place several times a day, and also the touch-pool area, where they can dip in and stroke the bat rays. Other pools contain starfish, sea urchins, sand dollars, and other creatures of the tide pool.

Needless to say, the excitement here is at a fever pitch and not conducive to a romantic weekend, if that's what you're here for. That can better be found in the new area of the aquarium, the Outer Bay, where you can get a sense of the ocean's depth and silence. Thousands of anchovies cruise around, jelly fish hang on the currents, and yellowfin tuna, barracuda, sunfish, soupfin sharks, and green sea turtles float in the dark silence.

Hours: Summer, daily 9:30am–6pm; the rest of the year, 10am–6pm. Closed Christmas Day. *Admission:* $13.75 adults, $11.75 seniors and youths 13–17, $6 children 3–12.

Lodging in Monterey

The Old Monterey Inn, 500 Martin St., Monterey, CA 93940 (☎ 408/375-8284; fax 408/375-6730), has a warm, wonderful style. The 1929 Tudor house is adorned with ivy and surrounded by an acre of lovely gardens filled with hydrangeas, geraniums, rhododendrons, and roses. The 10 rooms, all with private bath and sitting area, are individually furnished. Books line the walls by the large stone fireplace in the Library Room; English hunting decor sets the tone in the Dovecote Room, which is decorated primarily in pine. Some rooms have private entrances, such as the romantic Chawton Room, which features such decorative accents as a hand-painted rose garland above the bed, as well as cherubs and angels. A full breakfast will start your day, and it is served either in the dining room, the garden, or in your own room. Additional amenities include a concierge.

Rates (incl. breakfast): $180–$250 double.

Hotel Pacific, 300 Pacific St., Monterey, CA 93940 (☎ 800/225-2903 or 408/373-5700, fax 408/373-6921), has a very Spanish air. Guests enter past a fountain and tubs of flowers into a large lobby with terra-cotta tile floor. Rooms are arranged around a series of prettily landscaped terraces with fountains and umbrella-shaded tables. The accommodations are spacious suites with dining areas and minibars and full amenities, including VCRs and even a TV in the bathroom. They are decorated in adobe style and colors of terra-cotta and ocher. Each bedroom is furnished with a heavy, rustic pine bed and side tables fashioned from large tree stumps. The desks are tiled, too. Most have a wood-burning fireplace and a patio or terrace.

Rates (incl. breakfast): $159–$299 double.

Spindrift Inn, 652 Cannery Row, Monterey, CA 93940 (☎ 800/232-4141 or 408/46-8900, fax 408/646-5342), is right down in the center of Cannery Row, occupying an oceanfront location. Rooms here are decorated in traditional style with contemporary comforts. The bed might be a four-poster; the chairs in front of the fireplace French style or more contemporary. There will either be an inviting corner window seat or a balcony. A continental breakfast is delivered to the room.

Rates (incl. breakfast): $149–$389 double.

Tucked up on the hill behind Cannery Row the **Jabberwock,** 598 Laine St., Monterey, CA 93940 (☎ 408/372-4777), is a delightfully whimsical bed and breakfast operated by two warm, hospitable owners, Jim and Barbara Allen. Each room is named after a character from Lewis Carroll's poem, "Jabberwocky," and has a unique look. Borogrove has a Jenny Lind bed, brick fireplace, and a telescope to enhance the already fine view of the bay; it's the most luxurious of the accommodations. My favorite rooms are the two third-floor garrets, the Mimsey and the Wabe, which share a bath and a sitting area. The Mimsey has an appealing window seat where you can loll and gaze out across the bay. An intricately carved bed dominates the Toves, which also has its own garden patio. At the back of the house, the attractive gardens are the source of the fresh flowers in the rooms. Breakfast is served in a comfortable dining room or in your room, and every evening around 5pm, hors d'oeuvres are served on the back veranda.

Rates (incl. breakfast): $115–$200 double.

Dining in Monterey

Great ocean views, elegant decor, and fine food are the hallmarks of **Fresh Cream,** Heritage Harbor, 99 Pacific St. (☎ 408/375-9798). The cuisine is California-inspired French. Start with the most alluring appetizers—either the crab cakes with corn salsa and red bell pepper sauce or the raviolis of lobster. Dinner entrees, which change daily, offer a balance of fish and meat dishes that might include a spiced pan-seared ahi tuna in a pineapple rum sauce; grilled veal loin with wild mushrooms, roasted shallots, and white wine butter sauce; or half a roast duckling with black currant sauce. Prices range from $22 to $30. To finish there are several really rich desserts to choose from—a soufflé with Grand Marnier or the gâteau au chocolat celestine, a flourless dark chocolate torte with a quenelle of vanilla bean ice cream on a raspberry coulis. There's a bar area for aperitifs.

Hours: Daily 6pm–closing (which might be 9pm on a slow night or 10pm on a busy night).

PACIFIC GROVE

Only seconds from the honky-tonk of Cannery Row and Fisherman's Wharf, you can cross into another world offering a jolting contrast to the touristy hustle and bustle. It's quaint and peaceful Pacific Grove.

Founded by Methodists in 1875, the town actually banned the sale of alcohol right up until 1969 and had some severe injunctions against a variety of other behaviors. Gambling, dancing, frivolity on the Sabbath, and even fast buggy driving were all banned, and bathing suits were required "to be provided with double crotches or with skirts of ample size to cover the buttocks." Today it continues to be a quiet resort town that is also famous for attracting some very special natural visitors—thousands of monarch butterflies that choose to stop and rest here every year. By the way, the city's bylaws state that it is "unlawful for any person to molest or interfere with in any way the peaceful occupancy of monarch butterflies on their annual visit to Pacific Grove." (Any such behavior is punishable by a $500 fine.)

In the early days Pacific Grove was a summer retreat consisting of an encampment of tents. Wood-framed tents were erected on 30- by 60-foot lots that sold for only $50. At the end of the summer, the canvas was taken down and the frames left standing until the next summer. Gradually, these accommodations were converted into more permanent homes, and by 1889 there were 1,300 residents and Pacific Grove was incorporated as a city.

Today, gracious Victorian homes, some of them converted into inns, stand peering out across the bay. A road and hiking/biking trail courses around the shoreline to **Lovers Point** (named for the love of Christ, not the love of flesh), and out to the **Punta de los Piños Lighthouse** (☎ 408/648-3116), which was built in 1855 and now houses a museum.

Hours: Sat–Sun 1–4pm. *Admission:* Free.

If you continue along Ocean View Boulevard, its name changes to Sunset Drive just past the lighthouse. You'll pass **Asilomar State Beach** on one side and the **Conference Grounds,** a stone and redwood conference center, which is set among the dunes and pines and was designed by Julia Morgan, on the other. As you drive, hike, or jog, keep an eye out for sea otters, harbor seals, sea lions, whales (between December and March), and a variety of birds—black turnstones, sandpipers of all sorts, brown pelicans, and cormorants, as well as others.

Back in town, stroll the streets and view the pretty painted cottages and gardens that often surround them. The **Pacific Grove Museum of Natural History,** 165 Forest Ave., at Central Avenue (☎ 408/648-3116), is a fine, small museum with a variety of exhibits about the local flora and fauna, including seaweeds, insects, reptiles, and mammals, and extensive displays on monarch butterflies and their habits, migratory and otherwise. The collection of 400-plus mounted birds is outstanding. The museum also has some fine Native American baskets and other artifacts. Stroll out into the garden, too, which shelters some rare and endangered plants.

Hours: Tues–Sun 10am–5pm. *Admission:* Free.

John Steinbeck fans will also want to visit the tiny **John Steinbeck Memorial Museum,** 222 Central Ave. (☎ 408/373-6976), which is in a small cottage. It is filled with memorabilia, photographs, many different editions of his books, and his typewriter.

Hours: Daily 10am–4pm. *Admission:* By donation.

Pacific Grove

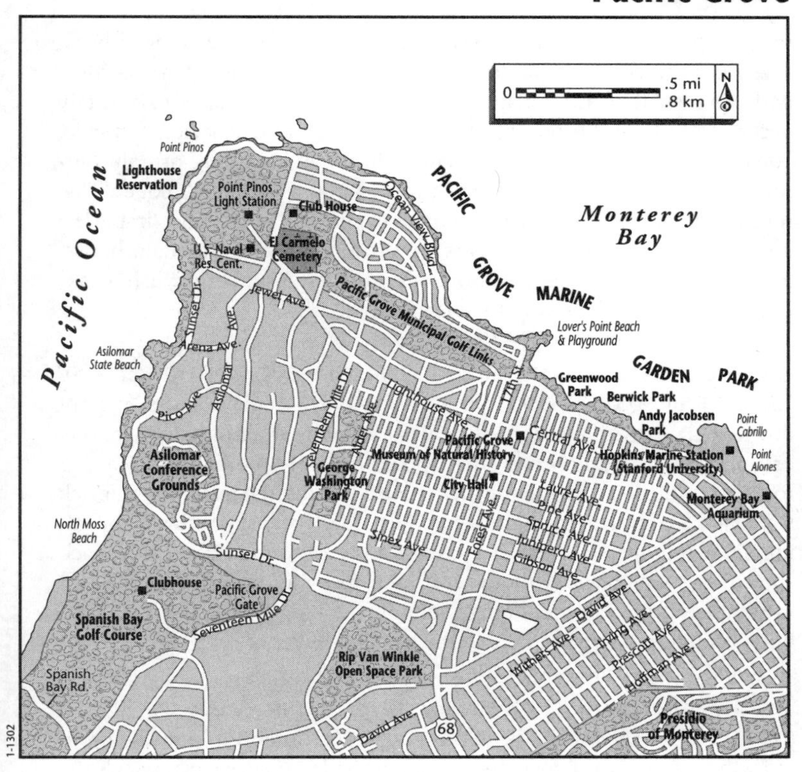

Steinbeck and his family spent many weekends and vacations here in Pacific Grove at the family cottage at 147 11th St., between Lighthouse and Ricketts Row. Here he worked on *The Red Pony, The Pastures of Heaven, Tortilla Flat,* and *Of Mice and Men,* the first draft of which was destroyed by the family dog. Steinbeck also owned a cottage of his own at 425 Eardley Ave., between Spruce and Pine. He occupied it only briefly, while working on *The Sea of Cortez* and *The Forgotten Village* before moving to New York City. Both are private residences, not open to the public.

The **monarch butterflies** begin to arrive in October on their long migration south from Alaska, Canada, and other points north. They rest, their wings folded, in groves of eucalyptus in George Washington Park, at Pine Avenue and Alder Street, unremarkable in every other way. There is also a sanctuary for them at Monarch Grove, Lighthouse Avenue, and Ridge Road. Don't molest or in any way bother them; the town imposes strict fines.

Lodging & Dining in Pacific Grove

The **Seven Gables Inn,** 555 Ocean Blvd., Pacific Grove, CA 93950 (☎ 408/372 4341), which stands at Rocky Point, is the place that you've seen in the credit card ads. It was built in 1886 and does indeed boast seven gables. The sun porches overlook the well-tended gardens filled with English flowers. Today it's a luxurious home that is exquisitely decorated with fine European antiques in an elegant French/Victorian style. You'll find inlaid sideboards and chests in the living room, ormolu mirrors, gilt-framed portraits, and such furnishings as a fainting couch. The rooms are sumptuously decorated with Oriental rugs, fine draperies, armoires, and Victorian armchairs. Seven rooms are in the main house, four are in the guest house, and three are cottages. A suitably stylish breakfast is served as well as afternoon tea at 4pm.

Rates (incl. breakfast): $135–$235 double.

Green Gables Inn, 104 5th St., Pacific Grove, CA 93950 (☎ 800/722-1774 or 408/375-2095, fax 408/375-5437), built in 1888, is right down on the edge of the bay, a short walk from the aquarium. Its signature ornament is the teddy bear, which appears in every room. There are four rooms sharing two baths in the main house. Behind the main house, brick walkways lead past a tiny fountain to the garden rooms, which are appealing. The Sandpiper, for example, has an iron bed covered with a candlewick spread, a gas fireplace, window seat, and rose-pattern wallpaper. A full breakfast is served in the dining room overlooking the Pacific; wine and hors d'oeuvres are served here in the evening. Bikes are available.

Rates (incl. breakfast): $120–$170 double.

The **Martine Inn,** 255 Oceanview Blvd., Pacific Grove, CA 93950 (☎ 408/373-3388, fax 373-3896), occupies a shorefront location. From the windows—with binoculars that are provided—guests can watch the seals, otters, and whales frolicking offshore. There are 17 rooms and 3 suites, all with private bath. Each is furnished with different antique decor. One is furnished in Eastlake style, another in Early American. The Art Deco room contains a French Art Nouveau bedroom set combined with such decorative accents as an ice-glass candelabra and a Coca-Cola mirror. The Parke, which is the most expensive room, has a four-poster with canopy and side curtains, a mid-19th century Chippendale bedroom set, and a clawfoot tub in the bathroom. It also has a magnificent view. Any room might reveal a couple of unusual pieces, such as a kwanyin lamp or a carved, Austrian inlaid table. Some of the rooms have fireplaces, but most of these have only views of the courtyard in the back. Guests enjoy the comforts of the Victorian sitting room. There's also a pool table for guests' use. The breakfast room takes full advantage of the view. Here, you'll have a lavish full breakfast using silver service; in the afternoons guests gather in the same room for wine and hors d'oeuvres.

Rates (incl. breakfast): $145–$250 double.

Gosby House, 643 Lighthouse Ave., Pacific Grove, CA 93950 (☎ 800/527-8828 or 408/375-1287, fax 408/655-9621), is located in town and offers 22 rooms that are individually decorated with chintz wallpapers and Victorian furnishings. The Carriage House rooms have fireplace, deck, and extra-large bathroom with a spa tub. Some rooms in the main house also have tiled fireplaces with wooden mantels.

Rates (incl. breakfast): $95–$160 double.

Asilomar Conference Center, 800 Asilomar Blvd., P.O. Box 537, Pacific Grove, CA 93950 (☎ 408/372-8016), is a complex of buildings occupying 105 acres of pines and dunes with terrific views of the ocean and a boardwalk that leads to the State Beach. It was established as a YWCA retreat in 1913 and designed by the famous architect, Julia Morgan. Today it is operated by a nonprofit group under the auspices of the State Parks. There are 28 lodges with accommodations, many of which have fireplaces. None have TV or phone. Some buildings are older than others. It's hard sometimes to secure individual accommodations because the facility caters mainly to groups, but it represents great value, given the location and that breakfast (taken in the cafeteria) is included.

Facilities include a swimming pool, chapel, and general store. Park rangers are also available to inform guests about the area's ecology and environment.

Rates (incl. breakfast): $81–$91 double; $132 for four people in inn/ cottages.

Dining Only in Pacific Grove

I always find myself returning to **Fandango,** 223 17th St. (☎ 408/ 372-3456), when I'm in Pacific Grove. It's a pretty restaurant with good food, amiable service, and reasonable prices. There's a small patio protected by hedge and trellis for outdoor dining, a couple of small, appealing dining rooms with stone walls and decorative strands of garlic, and then the long main dining room with a fireplace at the end. The menu is broad, eclectic, and will also be supplemented by several specialties of the day. Start with a selection of tapas. Main courses range from delicious pastas, including a spicy puttanesca, to cassoulet and steaks grilled over mesquite with shallot, tarragon, and cognac herbed butter. Several fish dishes will also be available, including both paella and bouillabaise. Prices range from $11 to $22.

Hours: Mon–Sat 11am–2:30pm; Sun 10am–2:30pm; daily 5–9:30pm.

Melac's, 663 Lighthouse Ave. (☎ 408/375-1743), is a traditional French restaurant serving some fine cordon bleu cuisine. Tables are well spaced in the dining room, which, although plain, takes on a romantic, candlelit air at night when the bottles in the wine racks and the brick walls glow. Janet Melac trained in the Cordon Bleu, and her husband, Jacques, acts as sommelier, pairing the fine wines to the cuisine. The menu is limited and changes frequently. To start, try the flavorsome crêpes filled with wild mushrooms and goat cheese, or the jumbo sea scallops with a garlic herb sauce. Among the six or so main courses, the Monterey Bay salmon with a polenta crust is fresh and cooked to retain its moisture and flavor; the rack of lamb is enriched with thyme, rosemary, and a balsamic vinegar that gives it an extra little frisson. Prices range from $20 to $26. The Melacs are related to Jacques Melac, who runs the famous Parisian wine bar of the same name, and you can pick up a bonus card that will secure a free glass of wine at the establishment on the Rue Leon Frot.

Hours: Tues–Fri 11:30am–2pm; Tues–Sat 5:30–9:30pm.

El Cocodrilo, 701 Lighthouse Ave. (☎ 408/655-3311), is not a romantic place to dine because it's noisy and plainly decorated with piñatas, gourds, and similar gaudy trappings, but it's a fun spot for some spicy, reasonably priced Latin fusion cuisine. Start with a seafood chowder or the *Tostaditas Caribena,* filled with lobster. From the dozen or so main courses, select pecan-crusted filet of Pacific snapper, the popular smoked West Indian baby-back ribs, or sautéed prawns diablo in a spicy cashew tomato sauce. There are pasta dishes, too. Prices range from $10.95 to $14.95.

Hours: Wed–Mon 5–10pm.

The Old Bath House, 620 Ocean Blvd. (☎ 408/375-5195), sits where you would expect it to sit, right down by the beach. It's a traditional place serving classic cuisine. Start with the California quail served over organic greens with a balsamic vinaigrette or, if you prefer a richer dish, the tortellini with salmon, dill, and Gorgonzola cream. Follow with one of 10 main-course selections—including duck with sun-dried cherries in a merlot sauce or sautéed Dungeness crab with champagne cream sauce. Prices range from $18 to $29. Sorbets, soufflés, and crêpes are the dessert specialties, of course. The wine card lists 300-plus selections.

Hours: Mon–Fri 5pm–closing; Sat–Sun 4pm–closing (usually 11pm Fri–Sat but depends on the last reservation).

PEBBLE BEACH

Pebble Beach is famous for two things: the 17-Mile Drive around the southern shore of the peninsula and golf. The drive is justifiably famous, with stunning views of the ocean. More than anywhere else, this is a serious golfer's paradise. Each year, one of the most popular professional golf tournaments is held at the Pebble Beach Golf Links, one of five world-class golf courses located on the peninsula. Though the greens fees are pegged at stratospheric levels, visitors to the plush golf resorts here don't seem to mind, and Monterey remains on the must-do list of the well-heeled golfers worldwide, so much so that staying at one of the golf resorts here is just about the only way you'll get to play golf.

When you first enter the **17-Mile Drive,** after having paid your $7 for the privilege, you may wonder why you bothered, as the road seems to travel past endless pines and lavish residences located in the Del Monte Forest. Then suddenly it opens to the shoreline overlooking the Pacific, a

The Golfer's Paradise

The most famous and perhaps the most loved of the five Pebble Beach golf courses is the oceanfront **Pebble Beach Links,** at the Lodge at Pebble Beach (☎ 800/654-9300 or 408/624-3811), where the 18th green hovers above the surf. Opened in 1919, it hosts the annual AT&T National Pro-Am and has hosted several U.S. Opens. It is, in fact, scheduled to host the 100th Open in the year 2000. It was designed by Jack Neville and Douglas Grant and hugs the shoreline. The charge to nonguests is $295 (even guests at the resort pay $235!). But the chance that you'll get to play here unless you're a resort guest is almost nil.

Spyglass Hill Golf Course, Stevenson Drive and Spyglass Hill Road (☎ 800/654-9300 or 408/624-6611), which was designed by Robert Trent Jones, Sr., and named in honor of Robert Louis Stevenson, has some very challenging holes. At the first the green is, in fact, an island in the sand; no. 14 is named Long John Silver for its double dogleg. The course charges guests of the lodge or inn $185, nonguests $220. Reservations for the course must be made a month in advance.

The Links at Spanish Bay was designed by Robert Trent Jones, Jr., Tom Watson, and Frank Sandy Tatum, and opened in 1987. It is also located on the bay and designed around banks of dunes. It's as close to a Scottish links course that you will get. The charge is $160 to guests, $185 to nonguests, with a mandatory $25 cart rental. Reservations can be made up to 60 days in advance; this is the most easily booked of the four major courses.

Poppy Hills, on the 17-Mile Drive (☎ 408/624-3811), is considered by *Golf Digest* to be one of the world's 20 best courses. It was designed by Robert Trent Jones, Jr., in 1986. Fees are $105, with a mandatory $30 cart rental. Reservations may be made 30 days in advance.

The **Del Monte Golf Course,** 1300 Sylvan Rd. (☎ 408/373-2700), which opened in 1897 and is the closest to downtown Monterey, has long, narrow, tree-lined fairways and small, impeccably maintained greens. It charges $83 to nonguests, with a cart rental fee of $18. Resort guests pay $60, plus a cart fee.

joyous sight indeed of ocean waves crashing against rocks and flocks of seabirds.

At **Spanish Bay** you can get onto the beach and enjoy a picnic; this is where Gaspar de Portolá supposedly camped in 1769 while he was searching for Monterey Bay. At the next promontory, **Point Joe,** the ocean churns and roars due to colliding ocean currents and is always turbulent, even on the most windless day.

From here, cruise on along **Fanshell Beach** and pull into the parking lot near **Bird Rock,** from which you'll have a fine view of this rock that is home to sea lions and harbor seals that sprawl on the rocks, and to countless sea birds, including cormorants and gulls of all kinds. Take the 1-mile self-guided nature trail from the parking lot.

Not far away is another marine life shelter, **Seal Rock,** where seals and sea lions loll and sea otters float on their backs in the kelp. **Fanshell Beach** is where the harbor seals come to breed in late March to late May; there's an overlook, but it may be closed during breeding time, as will Cypress Point. Pitch pines and those famous cypresses, which have been twisted and torqued by the wind, abound along this section of the coast culminating at **Cypress Point.** They have been sculpted, hammered, chiseled, and beaten into all kinds of contorted and fantastic shapes. From this point on a clear day you can see all the way to Point Sur lighthouse, a distance of 20 miles. The most famous of all the cypresses, the **Lone Cypress,** stands farther around the coast, as lonesome as ever, clinging to the bare rock of an ocean-sprayed promontory. From here it's a short distance to **Pescadero Point,** which provides glorious views across Carmel Bay and Stillwater Cove.

Lodging & Dining in Pebble Beach

Inn at Spanish Bay, 2700 17-Mile Drive, Pebble Beach, CA 93953 (☎ 800/654-9300 or 408/647-7500, fax 408/648-7899), is larger and more contemporary in style than its companion Lodge at Pebble Beach. The furnishings in the 270 rooms and suites are overstuffed and comfortable; in each room you'll find a fireplace and a patio. Brass and marble enhance the bathrooms. The **Bay Club** offers fine Italian cuisine, while **Roy's at Pebble Beach** is the domain of Roy Yamaguchi, famous for his unique Eurasian cuisine. Three bars are available for evening cocktails—the Clubhouse Bar and Grill, which also serves a broad popular menu, the Lobby Lounge, and Traps, a sports bar.

The golf links are famous. The Tennis Pavilion has eight plexi-paved courts and a stadium court for tournaments. The Spanish Bay Club boasts a heated swimming pool and full fitness facilities. And to cap it all off, a Scottish bagpiper walks the links at the close of day.

Rates: $286–$400 double; from $600 suites.

The Lodge at Pebble Beach, 17-Mile Drive, Pebble Beach, CA 93953 (☎ 800/654-9300 or 408/624-3811), is a full-facility resort that has been operating for more than 75 years. The 161 rooms and suites are tastefully furnished in contemporary style with all the expected amenities—cable TV, minibar, bathrobes, and telephone in the bathroom, as well as a private patio. Some have wood-burning brick fireplaces, too. Services include 24-hour room service and twice-daily maid service.

Facilities include **Club XIX** for fine dining and the **Cypress Room** for seafood grills (it's famous for its Friday evening clambakes). Both of these restaurants have views of Carmel Bay and the 18th green of Pebble Beach Golf Links. The **Gallery** is a casual bar and grill; the **Tap Room** offers pub fare. There's also the Terrace Lounge for cocktails and nightly live entertainment.

The golf links, of course, are premier, certainly the best known and perhaps the best loved on the peninsula. Guests who stay here also have easy access to the other courses—at Spanish Bay, Spyglass Hill, and Del Monte—and also to the Beach and Tennis Club, which offers pool, tennis courts, and state-of-the-art fitness center. A spa is planned for 1998.

Rates: $340–$570 double; from $850 suites.

CARMEL

Writers and artists discovered Carmel and the peninsula earlier than most, drawn by its remoteness and beauty. Robert Louis Stevenson had lived in Monterey in 1879, and some say used Point Lobos as his inspiration for *Treasure Island.* In the 1880s land sold for $20 a lot, but there were few buyers and the village was not shaped until 1903, when James Franklin Devendorf and Frank Powers developed it and succeeded in luring a veritable colony of writers—George Sterling, Ambrose Bierce, Mary Austin, Gertrude Atherton, Jack London, Jimmie Hopper, Nora May French, Upton Sinclair, and Sinclair Lewis. Carmel thus became the Bohemian center of the west and was often referred to as the Nantucket of the West. This Bohemian crowd didn't bother with appearances too much. None of them cared how they dressed, and tolerance prevailed. As someone put it: "One may wear a smock, prate of batik or Ibsen for all ones neighbor cares. One may part his mane in the middle, perch shell-rimmed glasses on his nose and to all intents and purposes he becomes a stone in the literary mosaic of Carmel." Times have changed a little on the streets today. Now the swank and wealthy folks gather to shop, to see and be seen on the streets of the town that did, after all, boast Clint Eastwood as its mayor.

Carmel has become *the* shopping mecca of the peninsula, famous for its many art galleries and other boutiques. In spite of this and in spite of the crowds, it has managed to retain an elegant village air primarily because the local government imposes stringent restrictions—no traffic lights, no parking meters, no neon signs or billboards, and no buildings taller than three stories. Stroll around and visit some of the quality stores downtown. Whatever you do, drop in to the many galleries, which are very inviting and not intimidating at all.

The heart of the gallery district is between San Carlos and Lincoln, between 5th and 6th. Among my favorites are **Malcolm Moran Studios,** on Mission between 5th and 6th; **Richard MacDonald** and **Trotter**

Galleries, both at San Carlos and Sixth; **Carmel Art Association Galleries,** on Dolores between 5th and 6th; **New Masters Gallery,** on Dolores between Ocean and 7th; and **Weston Gallery,** on 6th between Dolores and Lincoln. There are at least 50 more galleries to browse if you're interested. If you have enough energy on Friday nights, from May through September the galleries stay open from 6 to 9pm, and you can follow a self-guided **Carmel Art Walk.** Pick up the map from the **Carmel Business Association,** which is located at San Carlos and 6th (☎ 408/624-2522).

After you've shopped and strolled, drive or walk out to **Carmel City Beach,** an inviting stretch of white sand bordered by dunes and cypress trees and a cliff-top residential street with handsome homes and gardens. From the street above, you can climb down to the beach and enjoy an invigorating walk in search of particularly eye-catching driftwood.

If you continue along Ocean Boulevard, you'll pass several typical Monterey homes including the famous storybook houses with undulating roofs. You'll also come to **Tor House,** 26304 Oceanview Ave. (☎ 408/624-1813), the one-time home of Robinson Jeffers, perched high above the ocean. Standing as it does cheek by jowl with other homes, it's hard to imagine it as the "lonely outpost on the shore where Western civilization ends" that Jeffers conceived for himself.

Robinson Jeffers, whose poetry sings of Monterey and Carmel, arrived in 1914 filling the void that George Sterling had left when he returned to San Francisco. Jeffers abandoned first medicine and then forestry, determined to become a poet. His father, William Hamilton Jeffers, was a Presbyterian minister who had married a much younger woman. Although he was a disciplinarian who educated his son so rigorously that by the age of 12 young Robinson had mastered French, German, Latin, and Greek, the elder Mr. Jeffers also appreciated his son's talents. In fact, on one of Robinson's birthdays, his father gave him two volumes of poetry, one by a conservative traditional poet, the other by Dante Gabriel Rossetti. The last is what moved Robinson to become a poet. In 1913 Robinson married Una Kuster, a passionate woman with a mystical bent, with whom he had had an affair while she was still married. Una had spent the previous year in Europe at her current husband's request, and during this time Jeffers wrote his first volume of poetry, *Flagons and Apples.* On her return, she left her husband, secured a divorce, married Jeffers, and settled with him in Carmel.

Jeffers had always been overwhelmed by the landscape of the Monterey coast. He began building Tor House, which stands on the crest of a hill 50 yards above the ocean. It has walls of granite 4 feet thick. Back then, he planted 2,000 trees on the property and later added the legendary **Hawk Tower.** The last took him 4 years to build, from 1920 to 1924. Each floor offers a lookout to the ocean, from the second via an oriel window, from the third and fourth floors via an open turret. Jeffers selected and rolled the boulders himself to the site. To personalize it further, he cemented

Carmel

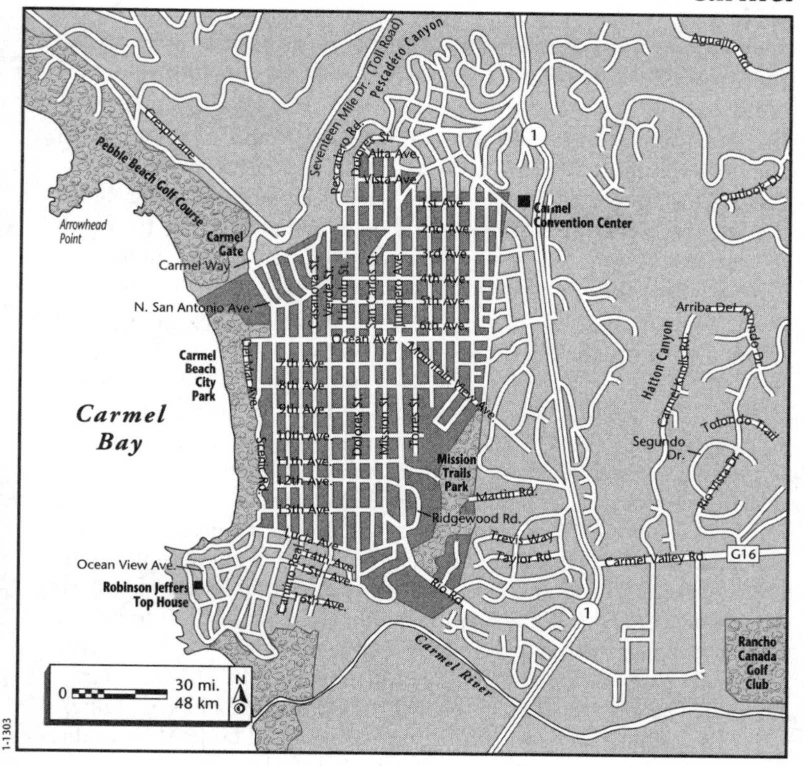

into the walls such found objects as a carved stone head from Angkor, a fragment from Newstead Abbey (Lord Byron's home), and a piece of the Great Wall of China. Other special stones were also placed on the property.

Here he and Una established a routine. After working outside, they would walk along the shore for several miles and then return to sit by the fire. Una would sew while Robinson read aloud to the children, then they would relax alone. Here in his aerie the ocean and the shore inspired and filled his poems as it does in "Hooded Night":

> Before the first man
> Here were the stones, the ocean, the cypresses,
> And the pallid region in the stone-rough dome of fog where
> the moon
> Falls on the west. Here is reality.

Una died in 1950, Robinson in 1962. Both their ashes are buried under a yew tree in the courtyard at Tor House. Although the house still stands in all its solidity, it is now surrounded by other houses—not nearly as remote as it once was when Jeffers wrote his Western idylls here.

Hours: Fri–Sat 10am–3pm. Tours on the hour; reservations required (only six people can be accommodated at one time). *Admission:* $5 adults, $3.50 college students, $1.50 youths 12–17. No children under 12 allowed.

Keep going along Ocean View Boulevard all the way until it curves around **Carmel River State Beach.** This beach is lovely to walk on in the evening. The beach is backed by a bird sanctuary, and the river flows into a lagoon and out onto the beach so that the bird life is abundant. From the beach you can look across Highway 1 to the isolated Carmelite Monastery.

Hours: 7am–10pm (parking lot closes at sunset).

If you return to the shoreline road, eventually you'll reach the **Carmel Mission, San Carlos Borromeo de Carmelo,** 3080 Rio Rd., at Lasuen Drive (☎ 408/624-3600), a singularly beautiful place in the Carmel Valley, only a few thousand feet from the sea. It's the second in the chain of 21 missions that were established in California by the Spanish. Father Junípero Serra is buried here in what became his favorite mission.

Originally located in Monterey at the Presidio, the Mission was moved here in December 1771 by Father Serra, who sought a more suitable location far enough away from the Presidio so that it would be surrounded by good agricultural land and near a large population of local Indians. Although he planned to build a stone building, he did not live to see the magical building that visitors see today, with its star window, bell towers, and lovely gardens. Father Serra died in August 1784 and was buried alongside Father Crespí in the sanctuary of the original adobe building.

Today visitors can view the sarcophagus sculpted by Jo Mora of this tiny man (he was only five-foot-two), who founded 9 of the 21 missions in California and is currently being considered for canonization. At his head stands his lifelong friend Father Crespí. Also on view is the cell where he lived, sparsely furnished with a bed of boards, blanket, table and chair, chest, candlestick, and gourd. In the mortuary chapel of the church stands the statue of the Virgin that traveled with Serra to the founding of the San Diego Mission and later to the dedication of this mission.

Serra was followed by Father Fermín Francisco de Lausén, who, like Father Serra, made his headquarters at Carmel but traveled far and frequently to attend to the business of the missions stretched along the Camino Real. In 1793 he undertook the building of the present stone church. It was built of local sandstone. The tower is of Moorish design and contains four bells. It was dedicated in 1797. Under Father Lausén the Mission thrived, and there were close to 1,000 Indians here, but after secularization in 1834 the mission fell into ruin. Restoration was begun in the 1880s.

As you stand in the mission garden and courtyard, it's hard to imagine what the Mission looked like in 1861, when it was overrun with squirrels, infested with birds, and filled with cattle that wandered about the broken front and around the crumbling columns and walls. Today it is a glorious, serene sanctuary, where you can sit quietly in the large square courtyard and listen to the fountain playing.

Hours: June 1–Aug 31 Mon–Sat 9:30am–7:15pm; Sun 10:30am–7:15pm. Other times of the year Mon–Sat 9:30am–4:15pm; Sun 10:30am–4:15pm. *Admission:* $2 adults, $1 children 5 and over.

From the Mission, drive south on Highway 1 to the **Barnyard,** an appealing shopping complex consisting of several barns. My favorite store here is the bookstore/cafe Thunderbird.

Farther south on Highway 1, **Point Lobos** separates the Bay of Carmel from the Pacific Ocean (see chapter 13 for more on this wonderful reserve). It's an inspirational place that is strongly associated for many of us with Edward Weston, for it was here that he took so many of his memorable photographs of eroded rocks, tide pools, dead pelicans, cypress groves, and shells.

Lodging & Dining in Carmel

About 4 miles south of Carmel, the **Highlands Inn,** Highway 1, P.O. Box 1700, Carmel, CA 93921 (☎ 800/682-4811 or 408/624-3801; fax 408/626-1574), is located on 12 acres, high on the cliffs overlooking Point Lobos, a stunning place. A series of buildings hold 142 rooms and suites cantilevered into the hillside. The furnishings are fine contemporary, almost Japanese in their inspiration. All rooms have such amenities as color TV with VCR and CD player. Most have a deck or balcony and a wood-burning fireplace. All the suites have spa baths, dressing areas, and completely equipped kitchens. The main lodge is airy with vast windows facing the ocean; here, overlooking the inspiring scene, guests can enjoy cocktails and snacks in the Lobos and Sunset Lounges. The central space has two handsome, granite fireplaces; sleek, contemporary furnishings; and also doubles as a gallery exhibiting works by contemporary and historic artists like Edward Weston.

In the **Pacific's Edge** dining room, every table has a splendid ocean view. The food is first-class California cuisine as befits the host of the annual Masters of Food & Wine celebration. You can select the $47 prix fixe, or choose from the à la carte menu, which features 12 or so dishes. There will always be a vegetarian dish, such as the fennel and onion tart with balsamic-scented lentils served with a ragout of winter vegetables, and a special fish dish. In addition, there might be a succulent salmon wrapped in pancetta with wild mushrooms served with butternut squash and pearl onions in thyme jus, or a filet of beef with roasted shallots and portobello mushroom-red wine sauce. Prices range from $22 to $32.

The **California Market** is a more modest restaurant where you can dine around the pot-bellied stove or al fresco on the large, redwood deck. A more modest menu offers such simple, tasty fare as roasted garlic chicken with mashed potatoes, roasted salmon with stir-fry vegetables, and a burger topped with white Vermont cheddar. Prices range from $8 to $15.

Stairs lead down to the kidney-shaped pool that has been terraced into the hillside. Other facilities include three hot tubs, a fitness room, and complimentary bicycles.

Rates (incl. breakfast): $300 double; from $425 suites. ***Dining Hours:*** Pacific's Edge, daily 11:30am–2pm and 6–10pm; California Market, daily 7:30am–10pm.

La Playa, Camino Real and 8th Avenue, P.O. Box 900, Carmel, CA 93921 (☎ 800/ 582-8900 or 408/624-6476, fax 408/624-7966), is a very lovely Spanish-style villa on the fringes of the village and a couple of blocks from the ocean. The gardens are filled with roses, the rooms arranged around an attractively landscaped, grassy courtyard with heated pool. It's traditional and comfortable. The lobby invites with its marble fireplace, Oriental rugs, and plush couches. The rooms continue the Mediterranean theme, featuring hand-carved Spanish-style furnishings; headboards include the hotel's mermaid motif. All have color TVs and minibars. The hotel offers such services as room service and nightly turndown. Some of the rooms have ocean views; the five cottages have full kitchens, garden patios, and wood-burning fireplaces. The **Terrace Grill** looks out over the gardens and also has an outdoor terrace for dining.

Rates (incl. breakfast): $126–$225 double; from $230 suites; from $325 cottages.

The core of the **Mission Ranch,** 26270 Dolores St., Carmel, CA 93923 (☎ 800/538-8221 or 408/624-6436, fax 408/626-4163), is the 1850s farmhouse that looks out across meadows and marsh to the bay. It's a quiet place situated out of town, close to the Mission. There are only 31 rooms, many of which have fireplaces and Jacuzzi tubs. Each is decorated differently in a comfortable, country style with pretty window treatments and plenty of pillows on the beds, along with star quilts or similar. The tiled restaurant with its gingham tablecloths is comfy and casual and made even more so by the blazing fire in the stone hearth on cool nights. There's also a piano bar. Other facilities include six tennis courts.

Rates (incl. breakfast): $100–$155 double.

Cobblestone Inn, Junipero Street, between 7th and 8th avenues, P.O. Box 3185, Carmel, CA 93921 (☎ 800/833-8836 or 408/625-5222), is rightly named. The 24 rooms are arranged around a slate courtyard bordered by English gardens. The welcoming lobby features a huge, stone fireplace and comfortable chairs to rest in. All the rooms also have a stone fireplace, plus queen- or king-size bed and such amenities as telephone, TV, and stocked refrigerator. Breakfast is buffet style—fresh fruit, breads, cereals, and a main course—and is usually enjoyed on the patio or in your own room, if you wish.

Rates (incl. breakfast): $105–$185 double.

The **Cypress Inn,** Lincoln Street and 7th Avenue (☎ 408/624-3871), has lots of style. Guests enter through a tiled courtyard with an outdoor fireplace into a white, Spanish-style building with a Moorish cupola. The rooms are each decorated differently in vibrant colors; some of the beds have half-canopy treatments. In addition to such standard amenities as telephones and color TVs, expect to find a decanter of sherry and a daily newspaper delivered to your room. Guests can relax on the couches and French-style chairs in front of a warm fire in the living room or enjoy a drink in the cocktail lounge. A continental breakfast is served in the sunny breakfast room or in the garden courtyard.

Rates (incl. breakfast): $110–$155 double.

Four blocks from the beach and 3 from town, The **Green Lantern Inn,** Casanova Street and Seventh Avenue, P.O. Box 1114, Carmel-by-the-Sea, CA 93921 (☎ 408/624-4392), is set among pretty gardens around a courtyard. The 19 accommodations are located in two- to four-room cottages. Each room is decorated differently in a country style. The most secluded is the Cypress Suite, which possesses a fireplace and loft with dormer window; amenities include a refrigerator. The Cedar Suite has a nice stone patio to recommend it, while the Spruce Suite is inviting, with its iron canopy queen bed and private porch. A continental breakfast and afternoon tea are served in front of the fire in the dining room or outside in the courtyard.

Rates (incl. breakfast): $100–$199 double weekends, $80–$169 midweek.

The **Sandpiper Inn at the Beach,** 2408 Bay View Ave., Carmel-by-the-Sea, CA 93923 (☎ 408/624-6433; fax 408/624-5964), is eye-catching because of its brilliant gardens. The early California-style house stands a block from Carmel Beach and offers views across the bay. There are 13 standard rooms and 3 cottage rooms. Each is decorated comfortably, often with a floral motif. Some have four-posters, some fireplaces. A buffet breakfast is served so that guests can take their selections to one of the garden patios or to their room. In the evening guests often gather around the stone fireplace in the beamed living room.

Rates (incl. breakfast): $105–$200 double.

At **Vagabond's House Inn,** Dolores Street and 4th Avenue, P.O. Box 2747, Carmel, CA 93921 (☎ 408/624-7738, fax 408/626-1243), a great live oak stands at the center of a flagstone courtyard, which features waterfalls and a veritable jungle of vines, ferns, and flowers. Around it stretches the brick, half-timbered Tudor building. The 11 rooms, plus suites, are decorated in a country fashion. Most have beamed ceilings, floral bedcovers, and assorted furnishings, including some antique reproductions. Some have a fireplace, and some even have a kitchen. The living room is inviting, especially when the fire is lit. It has several collections to examine—British lead toy soldiers, toys from the 1920s and '30s, and copies of Don Blanding's *Vagabond's House,* for which the inn is named. A continental breakfast is served either in your room or in the courtyard. The inn is conveniently located right in town.

Rates (incl. breakfast): $95–$175 double.

Dining Only in Carmel

Anton & Michel, Court of the Fountain, Mission Street, between Ocean and 7th avenues (☎ 408/624-2406), is *the* culinary landmark in Carmel. The dining room is elegantly appointed with fine paintings among the decorative accents, and it looks out onto a splendid courtyard with playing fountain. The cuisine combines classic French and California. To start try the delicious Dungeness crab cakes with cilantro-pesto-aïoli, or the delicate ravioli filled with goat cheese, sun-dried tomato, and shiitake mushroom mousse and served with curry-cream sauce. Among the main courses you'll find Pacific salmon, either poached with an herb-lemon Hollandaise or broiled with gazpacho beurre blanc, and grilled lamb medallions with a fresh mint pesto listed alongside classic medallions of veal in a Madeira sauce. Prices range from $20 to $26. And for dessert, if you're romantically inclined, why not treat yourself and your partner to bananas Foster or crêpes suzette? The wine list is extensive (600-plus selections).

Hours: Daily 11:30am–3pm and 5:30–9:30pm.

Crème Carmel, San Carlos Street and 7th Avenue (☎ 408/624-0444), is fresh and contemporary in tone, which is appropriate for the updated French-California cuisine. Tucked away at the back of a little complex, the restaurant is light and airy, with soaring ceilings and contemporary art pieces. To start, treat yourself to the Sonoma foie gras seared and garnished with glazed onions and puff pastry, or the prawn and goat cheese tart with a jalapeño and shallot sauce. The main course selections, which change frequently, will likely feature eight or so entrees ranging from an exciting vegetarian plate, combining Maui onion pancakes with wild mushrooms and a crêpe with julienne vegetables, to tenderloin of beef with a cabernet sauce, fresh horseradish, and potato cake. Fish and poultry are also represented on the menu. Prices range from $17 to $25. Finish with the divine chocolate soufflé with Chantilly cream or the hazelnut pavé layered with mocha and vanilla-bean ice cream.

Hours: Mon–Fri 11:30am–2:30pm; Mon–Sat 5:30–9pm. Closed for 2 weeks each January.

La Boheme, Dolores Street at 7th Avenue (☎ 408/624-7500), is a warm and inviting restaurant with a very French country atmosphere, complete with French music playing in the background. It offers excellent value by providing a classic $21.75 three-course prix-fixe dinner. You'll start with soup and salad, which will be followed by the main course of the evening (menus are laid out for the month). It might be roast pork lyonnaise (apples, onion, and cream sauce), breast of chicken Martinique (flavored with ginger and shallots), or scampi conquistador (flavored with garlic, cilantro, tomato, and wine). Whatever dish happens to be on the menu for that evening will be nicely prepared and presented. Desserts, which are extra, are French classics like crème caramel and tarte Tatin.

Hours: Daily 5:30–closing. No reservations are taken.

Casanova, 5th Avenue, between San Carlos and Mission streets (☎ 408/625-0501), as its name would suggest, is indeed one of (if not the most) romantic restaurants in Carmel. Inside a pretty, flower-covered cottage with old-fashioned shutters, there are several small, intimate dining rooms with beamed ceilings. The Italian and French regional cuisine is well prepared. The first course is a nice antipasto plate. A second course can be selected from such items as artichoke with a Dijon mustard vinaigrette or cannelloni Florentine made with spinach and ricotta. Main courses vary, from linguine with lobster, prawns, and shellfish in a white wine and lemon cream sauce, to filet mignon with a classic béarnaise. The salmon alsacienne—broiled salmon with mushroom duxelles and mild sauerkraut simmered in gewürtztraminer—is a rare treat. Prices range from $20 to $34 and include the first-course antipasto and choice of second and main course.

Hours: Daily 11:30am–3pm and 5–10pm.

Patisserie Boissiere, Carmel Plaza, Mission Street, between Ocean and 7th avenues (☎ 408/624-5008), is a favored spot for lunch or dinner. It's a pretty room with a tile fireplace and polished wood tables lit by sconces and gilt chandeliers. At lunch you can select from soups and such salads as the snow crab and avocado, then follow with one of the pastas or other specialties—shepherd's pie or delicious, oven-baked salmon with artichoke quarters in lemon-basil butter, for example. At night there are additional specialties added to the menu, always including a fish of the day. Prices at dinner range from $11 to $15.

Hours: Daily 11:30am–4:30pm; Wed–Sun 5:30pm–closing.

CARMEL VALLEY

The Carmel Valley, which is located inland from Carmel along Carmel Valley Road, gets a lot more sunshine than the shoreline. It's a scenic valley of rolling hills dotted with manicured golf courses, horse ranches, and a few wineries. It also has a couple of rather spectacular places to stay.

You might want to hike the trails of **Garland Regional Park,** which is located 8 miles east of Carmel. You could sign up for a trail ride at the **Holman Ranch,** 60 Holman Rd. (☎ 408/659-2640), about 12 miles east of Highway 1. A fine **golf course** is located at the Quail Lodge Resort, which is detailed below. While you're in the valley, you might even want to do a little wine-tasting at **Chateau Julien Winery,** 8940 Carmel Valley Rd. (☎ 408/624-2600), which is open daily.

Lodging & Dining in Carmel Valley

Stonepine, 150 E. Carmel Valley Rd., Carmel Valley, CA 93924 (☎ 408/659-2245), is an exquisite place to stay—a chateau surrounded by 330 acres. From the electronically controlled gate, drive up past the polo field and stables to the French-style building at the top of the hill, which is further enhanced by formal gardens. The villa was built for Henry Potter and Helen Crocker Russell of the San Francisco banking family. The building was designed by Burrell Hoffman, while the four gardens—rose, perennial, fruit, and cutting—were designed by Mrs. Russell herself. Inside, both the public areas and the rooms are grand in the true sense of the word. All of the eight rooms in the villa are suites, the most splendid being the Taittinger Suite, which is decorated in champagne-colored satin. It boasts a wood-burning fireplace, marble Roman bath with Jacuzzi, plus two dressing rooms and a sitting room. The Venetian Suite has a balcony overlooking the pool, a canopied king bed, and a private entrance, all of which make it a perfect romantic hideaway. Four less formal accommodations are located in the Paddock House, where guests have use of a kitchen and dining room. All of the rooms here have Jacuzzi tubs, and all are decorated with fine fabrics and antiques. My favorite is the Russell Suite, decorated in green and burgundy. The most secluded accommodation is the Briar Rose Cottage, which has a porch overlooking its very own rose garden. The centerpiece of the living room is the polished Carmel stone fireplace. Palladian-style French doors lead into the gardens. The cottage also has a dining room, kitchen, two bedrooms, and a TV/entertainment room with its own private bar. A complimentary breakfast is provided.

In the hotel's **dining room,** a four-course prix-fixe menu ($65 for guests, $75 for nonguests who have reserved ahead—minimum of six persons) changes daily. Your meal will begin with a soup, such as curried mussel soup with cilantro, proceed with a salad, and then your choice of three entrees; fish, meat, or poultry. For example, there might be hazelnut-crusted salmon with tomato-ginger sauce, roast rack of pork with Dijon cream sauce, or pan-seared squab with crêpes and basmati rice. A chocolate Grand Marnier cake might bring the whole meal to a close. Lunch is also served.

Facilities include an outdoor pool, tennis court, croquet lawn, archery range, bicycles, weights, and an equestrian center, which offers Western and English trail rides and is equipped with track, dressage areas, and hunter and cross-country jumping courses. Children must be 12 to stay in the chateau rooms; any age is allowed in the Paddock and the Cottage.

Rates: Villa rooms, $350–$800 double; Paddock House rooms, $275–$425; Cottage, $800. *Dining Hours:* Daily noon–3pm; dinner begins with a reception at 6:30pm.

Even though its address is in Carmel, **Quail Lodge Resort & Golf Club,** 8205 Valley Greens Dr., Carmel, CA 93923 (☎ 408/624-1581), is situated about 4 miles east of the town, in the Carmel Valley on 250 acres. It's a traditional, five-star resort. Trellised walkways lead to the 100 rooms, which are decked out in floral fabrics complete with all the expected amenities—bathrobes, coffeemakers, and more. At the center of the complex is a pool with fountains.

A bridge leads across the pool to the traditional fine dining room, **The Covey,** which is known for its classic cuisine. Oysters, smoked salmon, and caviar are the traditional appetizers. In addition to the beef tenderloin with béarnaise and the rack of lamb, there will be eight other choices from a petrale sole with asparagus and lobster nage to a spice-crusted pork tenderloin with fresh fruit chutney. Prices range from $16 to $30. The **Clubhouse** is also open for breakfast and lunch.

Other resort facilities include an 18-hole golf course ($95 greens fees for guests), two outdoor pools, a whirlpool, fitness center, four tennis courts, jogging and hiking trails, plus such services as in-room massages, spa treatments, baby-sitting, and room service.

Rates: Summer, $285–$505 double; winter, $215–$415. *Dining Hours:* The Covey, daily 6:30–9pm.

Carmel Valley Ranch, 1 Old Ranch Rd., Carmel, CA 93923 (☎ 408/625-9500, fax 408/624-2858), is known for its tennis courts and golf course. There are 10 hard and 2 clay courts, plus a fitness center and indoor/outdoor dining area at the clubhouse. Pete Dye designed the 18-hole golf course, whose clubhouse now boasts a lounge and bar, outdoor dining by a fireplace, as well as a pro shop. There are 100 accommodations, all spacious and made even more so in appearance by their cathedral ceilings. The beds are covered with handmade quilts, and original watercolors adorn the walls. Many have a wood-burning fireplace and deck; some have a Jacuzzi. All have two televisions, three telephones, and stocked minibar. Other facilities include an outdoor pool.

Rates: $285–$585 double (the top price is for the luxury spa suite).

Robles del Rio, 200 Punta del Monte, Carmel Valley, CA 93924 (☎ 408/659-3705), occupies a beautiful setting atop a mountain overlooking the valley. Opened in 1928 by Frank Porter, it was one of the first resorts in the valley. Portraits of its early days as a rustic retreat can be seen on the walls of the Cantina along with the luminaries of the era that visited—Arthur Murray, Red Skelton, Doris Day, Alistair Cooke, Merv Griffin, and many more. It's still a distinctly rustic place. There are 33 rooms, some in the main lodge, including the suites, and some cottages with fireplaces. Most are furnished in plain, old-fashioned country style featuring iron beds, all with color TV. Guests enjoy the living room with its large stone fireplace. Facilities include a prettily landscaped outdoor pool and hot tub, tennis court, horseback riding, hiking and jogging trail. There's also a **restaurant** serving French/California cuisine and a cantina.

Rates: $109–$150 standard rooms; from $205 suites; $230–$250 cottages.

Monterey Peninsula
Special & Recreational Activities

Ballooning: View the coast and the mountains from one of the early morning flights operated by **Balloons by the Sea,** 3261 Imjin Rd., Marina (☎ 408/424-0111), which is 10 miles north of Monterey. The cost is $155 per adult, $120 for each child 12 and under. Meet at the Marina airport before being taken to the launch site for a 45- to 50-minute flight that is topped off on your return with a champagne celebration.

Beaches: Monterey State Beach stretches from the wharf; there's a beach in front of Cannery Row that is often used by scuba divers. Beaches extend from Hopkins Marine Laboratory out past Lovers Point, from Point Piños all the way to **Asilomar State Beach,** which is great for the dunes and the tide-pooling. **Carmel** and **Carmel River State Beaches** are both great for walking.

Biking: Rentals can be secured at **Adventures by the Sea,** 299 Cannery Row in Monterey (☎ 408/372-1807), for $6 an hour or $24 a day. This company also has outlets in Pacific Grove at Lovers Point (☎ 408/648-7238), and in Doubletree Plaza behind the Maritime Museum in the Monterey Historic district (☎ 408/648-7235).

Canoeing/Kayaking: Several outfitters operate in the Monterey Bay area. Go to **Monterey Bay Kayak,** 693 Del Monte Ave., Monterey (☎ 408/373-5357), on Del Monte Beach north of Fisherman's Wharf. It offers instruction, plus natural history tours. Prices begin at $25 a day for rentals and $45 for tours led by marine biologists.

Adventures by the Sea, 299 Cannery Row, Monterey (☎ 408/372-1807), also rents kayaks and offers tours. It charges $25 a day for rentals and $45 for a 2- to 3-hour guided tour with a marine biologist or docent from the Monterey Aquarium.

Diving: San Carlos Beach in front of Cannery Row is a well-known diving spot, and you'll see many rubber-suited folks trekking up from the beach to the Row. They're here to explore the massive underwater canyon. Another prime diving spot is at Lover's Point Beach in Pacific Grove.

Fishing: The Bay is still a major fishing ground for cod, salmon, and whatever else is running, and there are plenty of party boats operating. Try **Chris' Fishing Trips,** 48 Fisherman's Wharf, Monterey (☎ 408/375-5951), which operates trips starting at $28 per person, plus $5 for renting a rod and reel.

Sam's Fishing Fleet, 84 Fisherman's Wharf, Monterey (☎ 408/372-0577), has daily departures, at 7:30am weekdays and 6:30am weekends. Prices begin at $28, including equipment costs.

Golf: The Monterey Peninsula is a golfer's dream. There are five major golf courses in Pebble Beach, four of them world-class, including the **Del Monte,** 1300 Sylvan Rd. (☎ 408/373-2436), which is the oldest golf course west of the Mississippi. The other four courses are described in more detail in the Pebble Beach section, above: **Pebble Beach Golf Links,** at the Lodge at Pebble Beach (☎ 800/654-9300 or 408/624-3811); **Spyglass Hill Golf Course,** at Stevenson Drive and Spyglass Hill Road (☎ 800/654-9300 or 408/624-6611); **Poppy Hills,** on 17-Mile Drive (☎ 408/625-1513); and the Links at Spanish Bay, at the Pebble Beach Resort/Inn at Spanish Bay (☎ 408/624-3811).

The Carmel Valley is also home to four good courses: at the **Quail Lodge Resort,** 8205 Valley Greens Dr., (☎ 800/538-9516 or 408/624-1581), and at the **Carmel Valley Ranch,** 1 Old Ranch Rd., (☎ 408/625-9500). Both of these are described in the Lodging & Dining in Carmel Valley section above. Also in the Carmel Valley is **Rancho Canada,** on Carmel Valley Road (☎ 408/625-2035), which has two courses—one championship, the other a shorter course. Fees are $70 and $50, respectively.

A more reasonably priced alternative is the **Pacific Grove Municipal Golf Course,** 77 Asilomar Ave. (☎ 408/648-3177). The back nine holes overlook the sea. With panoramic views and better-than-average maintenance for a public course, it's a reasonable choice if you want to play golf without three-digit greens fees. Greens fees are $26 Monday to Thursday, $32 Friday to Sunday; optional carts are $23.

Hang Gliding: Western Hang Gliders at Marina Beach, Monterey (☎ 408/384-2622), offers the opportunity to really experience hang gliding in a tandem with an instructor for $140. They also offer instruction for beginners ($89), but you won't be flying very high in the sky—only about 10 feet above the beach with an instructor running alongside.

Horseback Riding: Trail rides are led by instructors from the **Pebble Beach Equestrian Center** in Pebble Beach right off Portola Road (☎ 408/624-2756) through the Del Monte forest, along the beach, and over the dunes. Individual riders and private groups only. The cost for a 1¼-hour ride is $45; reservations are necessary.

You'll also find some horseback riding opportunities in the Carmel Valley. Try the **Holman Ranch,** 60 Holman Rd. (☎ 408/659-2640), about 12 miles east of Highway 1; or you might consider staying at **Robles del Rio,** 200 Punta del Monte, Carmel Valley (☎ 408/659-3705), which offers horseback riding.

Scuba Diving/Snorkeling: Try **Twin Otters** in Monterey for trips only for experienced divers with their own equipment and one tank (☎ 408/394-4235). The company specializes in scuba-diving trips along the reefs of Monterey and Carmel bays.

Whale Watching: The whale-watching season lasts from December to March, and several companies offer whale-watching trips from Fisherman's Wharf. Monterey Bay Whale Watch (☎ 408/375-4658) offers trips that last 3 to 3½ hours and are led by marine biologists. Because the trips are longer, you're more likely to spot more whales and dolphins. The biologists narrate and answer any questions. The cost is $23 for adults, $18 for children.

Randy's (☎ 408/372-7440) charges $15 for adults, $10 for children 12 and under for a 2-hour cruise, which departs four to six times daily from December to March.

Monterey Sport Fishing (☎ 408/372-2203) operates trips from December to March and also June to September.

The Big Sur Coast

Distances in Miles: Big Sur, 152; Ventana Wilderness, 150

Estimated Driving Times: 3 hours to Big Sur; 3 hours to Ventana Wilderness

Driving: Follow the directions in the previous chapter to Monterey. From there, take Highway 1 south to Big Sur.

Further Information: For information on Big Sur, contact the **Big Sur Chamber of Commerce**, P.O. Box 87, Big Sur, CA 93920 (☎ 408/667-2100).

For maps of the Big Sur Wilderness contact **U.S. Geological Survey Map Sales,** P.O. Box 25286, Denver, CO 80225 (☎ 303/236-7477). For maps of Ventana Wilderness, contact the **Monterey District,** Los Padres National Forest, 406 S. Mildred, King City, CA 93930 (☎ 408/385-5434).

Slowly is the only way to drive the spectacular stretch of coastline from Carmel to Big Sur. As you do, you can marvel at this place that Henry Miller called "a region where one is always conscious of eloquent silence . . . the face of the earth as the Creator intended it to look." It remains that way today, a remote wilderness place where nature takes precedence and where development is a dirty word. As Gertrude Stein would say, there is no Big Sur there, there is only a state of mind, a clear state of mind that is encouraged and nurtured by the landscape.

THE BIG SUR COAST

Before the road was built in 1937, Big Sur, or El Sur Grande ("the Big South"), as it was called, could only be reached via a narrow wagon trail that was frequently washed out. The journey took 4 days. Today, even

AREA CODE CHANGE ALERT IN 1998

All of the new technologies that have been introduced in the last decade require additional phone numbers, and as a result some area codes are being split, with new area codes being introduced to replace them. The old area code 408 will be split and a new area code of **831** introduced for the following communities covered in this chapter: Big Sur. The new area code will be introduced in July 1998; until February 1999 you will be told that the old 408 number is now in the new 831 area when you dial a number. Thereafter, you must use the new 831 area code.

though the area is still remote you can head south in comfort, thrilling at the awesome vista that greets you around every curve as you soar above the ocean, sometimes only 50 feet above the surf, past coves, bays, and rocky outcroppings on one side and mountain slopes or peaks on the other. Drive it in early morning at sunrise and in the evening at sunset. Even in winter it can be majestic, savage, and primal when the storms strike.

Although it was Point Lobos that landscape artist Francis McComas dubbed "the greatest meeting of land and water in the world," such praise could equally apply to the magnificent coastline to the south. But the region has more than mere physical beauty. The people drawn here have helped make Big Sur more of a state of mind than anything else, a place with a magical, mystical quality. Indeed, there isn't even really a town here, just a Post Office.

In summer, the area is often shrouded in fog, making it even more mysterious and evocative, though if you're visiting for the first and only time, you may not appreciate this climatic feature as much as the local poets, artists, and writers who reside here do. In winter, storms may rage, and sometimes every few years the so-called El Niño visits, usually around Christmas, often causing floods and mudslides that result in washed-out bridges and isolation. At these times, the whole of Big Sur can become cut off from Monterey, as it was in 1995. The best time to visit is in spring and fall after the rains, which usually fall from mid-October to April or May.

Any number of weekends can be tailored to suit your particular enthusiasms. You can opt for a totally sybaritic sojourn at one of the fabulous coastal resorts or a learning experience at Esalen. You can stay in one of the campgrounds at the state parks, or else hike into the wilderness and do some really remote backwoods camping. Or you can stay at one of the resorts or campgrounds and enjoy leisurely hikes to the beaches and drives along Highway 1. After some history of the area and a discussion of

Events & Festivals to Plan Your Trip Around

February: Mardi Gras is celebrated with gusto in Big Sur. You'll find music, entertainment, and craft booths plus the costume ball. For information call ☎ 408/625-5255.

April: Big Sur International Marathon begins 26 miles south of the Carmel River and ends at Highway 1 near Rio Road. The first finishers take 2 hours or less to come in after running this inspiring course. Noncompetitive walks of 7, 10, and 21 miles are also undertaken with as many as 7,000 people participating in the events. For information call ☎ 408/625-6226.

October: The **Big Sur River Run 10K Race** is run through the redwoods and oak groves of Pfeiffer State Park. Call ☎ 408/624-4112 for more information.

the natural environment, including flora and fauna, what follows are some of the highlights that you'll find driving from north to south along Highway 1, from Carmel to San Simeon.

History

Big Sur was first inhabited by several Indian tribes who moved into the region some time between 500 B.C. and A.D. 500. The Ohlone, or Costanoan, were the largest group, numbering about 10,000. They occupied an area stretching from Point Sur to the Golden Gate. The Esselen, numbering between 800 and 1,300, inhabited territory from Point Sur to Big Creek and the shores of the Upper Carmel River and Arroyo Seco. The Salinan, who numbered around 3,000, lived in an area stretching from San Carporforo Creek inland, along the Salinas River Valley to Big Creek. All these tribes were hunters and gatherers, living off the bounty of the region and eating everything from cormorant eggs and sardines to venison and rabbit. Oak trees were vital to their way of life, and each fall the tribes harvested acorns, which they crushed with mortar and pestle to produce a kind of flour that was then leached and eaten. They used reeds for rafts, willow for baskets, and all manner of plant and herb for medical purposes.

The first Europeans to see Big Sur were the navigators Juan Cabrillo and Sebastián Vizcaíno in the mid-16th century. It was not until 1769 that the first European set foot in the area, when Gaspar de Portolá's expedition from San Diego was forced inland by the barrier of the San Carpoforo Canyon. His first expedition entered the Nacimiento River Valley and traveled to the Salinas River, bypassing Big Sur. Although he missed Monterey, which is what he was looking for, Portolá did discover San Francisco Bay. A second Portolá expedition successfully arrived at Carmel Bay on May 24, 1770, and established the Mission at the Carmel River.

In 1822 Mexico won independence from Spain, and later in 1834 the Mission lands were secularized, making way for the great ranchos of the era that followed. In 1834 Juan Bautista Alvarado was granted the 8,949-acre Rancho El Sur; another 8,876 acres named Rancho San José y Sur Chiquito (which included today's Garrapata State Park) was granted to Marcelino Escobar. Neither of these grants was settled by the grantees, and it wasn't until sometime between 1860 and 1900 that a few intrepid homesteaders, anxious to claim the 160-acre homesteads that were offered in the region, arrived in Big Sur itself. These were the Pfeiffers, Posts, Partingtons, Castros, Harlans, and others whose names live on today in such geographical landmarks as Pfeiffer Ridge, Post Summit, Cooper Point, and Partington Cove.

At the turn of the century, there were more people living in Big Sur than there are today. They were sustained by redwood lumbering and the tanbark industry. Still, life was hard. The only trail between homesteads was a wagon trail, and supplies were shipped into the coves along the coast. The homesteaders survived by hunting and raising hogs and cattle, but their lives were difficult, for they were completely isolated. There were no roads or harbors, and even the wagon trail ended where the Ventana Inn is today. Some of these early pioneers shipped bark from Partington Cove as well as limestone from Lime Kiln and Bixby Creeks, but most lived a hard life with occasional trips either to Monterey or south to King City to sell their cattle.

Much later, artists and writers, who had settled in Monterey, discovered Big Sur—Robinson Jeffers, Ansel Adams, and Edward Weston—but it wasn't until 1937, when Highway 1 opened, that the region was really discovered. The road took 18 years to build and cost $10 million, even though the convicts who built it were only paid 75 cents a day. And even after its completion, the people who settled here were mostly artists, writers, musicians, and philosophers who have guarded the region's environment fiercely.

In the 1940s and '50s the legendary residents were Henry Miller and Nicholas Roosevelt. Miller lived in a cabin on Partington Ridge for many years. He invited his friend Emil White to come out to Big Sur and told him to become a painter, which he did. Back then you could live in one of the shacks that had been built for the convict laborers who built the road for as little as $5 to $10 a month. Thus, Big Sur became Miller's American Rive Gauche. He attracted a bohemian crowd of artists, astrologers, and loafers, which made the region the West Coast's Greenwich Village.

There was no center; people just came to find themselves and to work on their chosen art or craft. This questing tradition continued in the '60s and '70s, when Big Sur became synonymous with Esalen and the human potential movement. In the '70s, '80s, and '90s the region has attracted many celebrities from the TV and movie worlds, but development has still been rigorously restricted and the region's environment carefully protected, though there are always potential threats of recreational over development and of offshore drilling lurking in the background.

The Natural Environment

Big Sur is a remarkably ecologically diverse region. Here in this stretch of coastline the ecologies of southern and northern California meet, making for abundant natural life. The coastline is backed by the 100-mile-long Santa Lucia mountains, which rise in many places as if from the ocean floor—as they seem to do at Cone Peak, which soars to a summit of 5,155 feet in less than 3 miles. The mountains rise in east-west folds, crisscrossed by more than 50 rivers that cut canyons and gullies to the sea. Along these many river canyons grow California redwoods; Big Sur is the farthest point south on the coast where they are found. The rest of the terrain is covered mostly by either coastal scrub, meadowlands where cows graze, or dry chaparral at the higher elevations.

Each natural habitat shelters an abundant variety of flora and fauna. Along the coast in spring your eye will be drawn by the brilliance of the blue-purple lupine and wild lilac, the yellow glow of the California poppy, and many more wildflowers. Later there will appear yellow lizard tail, the white trumpet-shaped morning glory, fluffy pink-headed buckwheat, seaside aster, and fuchsia, to name only a few.

Offshore, the land canyons are matched by underwater canyons, which drop to immense depths of 300-plus feet and which nurture and support an abundance of marine life. When you go tide-pooling (and do stop and take the time to do so), you may be lucky enough to observe any of the following: barnacles, mussels, sea stars, sea urchins, clams, limpets, periwinkles, black turban snails, hermit crabs, and purple shore crabs.

Offshore forests of kelp are frequented by otters, seals, and birds (including cormorants, pelicans, oystercatchers, loons, and grebes). On shore you may see a black turnstone patiently turning over stones with its beak in search of food, and if you're lucky willets, sanderlings, plovers, sandpipers, egrets, and great blue herons. The most exciting bird species of all that you might see around the underwater canyons are albatrosses, shearwaters, and storm petrels.

January is the time to spot gray whales en route to Baja along this stretch of coastline; in March and April they return with their babies. Observe them from any one of the points along the coast—Gamboa, Lopez, Partington, or Hurricane. At one time they were so numerous that whalers spotted them from the shore and then put out to sea to hunt them, but by 1888 they had virtually disappeared. Today, though, the whales are once again easy to spot thanks to the recent campaign to save them.

Onshore in the coastal scrub, all kinds of birds can be spotted—jays, thrushes, hummingbirds, warblers, and, of course, California quail. You might also see a variety of hawks, including the red-tailed, golden eagle, American kestrel, turkey vultures, and black-shouldered kite. The latter are most likely to be spotted soaring overhead in winter, a thrilling sight.

As for mammals, there are bobcats, gray fox, coyotes, badgers, deer, black bears, and mountain lions, although the latter are so shy they are rarely seen.

EXPLORING THE COAST FROM POINT LOBOS TO POINT SUR

Three miles south of Carmel the first stop is **Point Lobos State Reserve** (☎ 408/624-4909), a 550-acre beauty spot facing a 700-acre offshore underwater reserve. The original Spanish name, *Punta de Los Lobos Marinos,* means Point of the Sea Wolves, a reference to the sea creatures that lived here. Today people come to scuba dive in Whaler's and Bluefish coves, hike the 12 trails (7 miles total) and to view the birds and wildlife. More than 160 species of birds have been spotted here. Sea lions, harbor seals, and sea otters frolic or loll around near Whalers Cove while cormorants dive for fish, loons cry, and brown pelicans float on their huge wings above. The sea lions return to the region in early to mid-summer, and you'll most likely hear their barking before you see them out on the rocks. Harbor seals are more difficult to see because they are camouflaged by their mottled skins.

For most of us, this landscape has been made familiar by Ansel Adams but even more so by the photographs of the late resident photographer, Edward Weston, who lived in Carmel from 1929 to 1935. He spent much of his time roaming the beaches and coves, taking brilliant black-and-white photographs of the landscape—Monterey cypress, driftwood, eroded rocks, seaweed, skeletons of dead shore birds, shells, and other striking images.

You can follow in his footsteps by visiting **Weston Beach** and exploring the tide pools. The best time for this is in the afternoons from November to March and in the mornings from April to July. As you stand on the rocky shoreline of Whaler's Cove, try to imagine what this area must have been like from 1862 to 1879, when a whaling station and abalone cannery operated here and when Chinese, Japanese, and Portuguese fishermen plied their trade.

At the **Whalers Cabin,** which was built by Chinese fishermen, there's a small cultural history museum, adjacent to the larger Whaling Station Museum. By the way, Point Lobos was supposedly the inspiration for Spyglass Hill in Robert Louis Stevenson's *Treasure Island,* and it also inspired Robinson Jeffers to write *Tamar.* Hours for the museum are the same as for the park, and access is included in your park admission.

Hours: Open daily, but actual hours change from month to month, depending on the availability of volunteers to staff the museum.

Among the trails here, my favorites are: the **North Shore Trail** between Whalers Cove and Sea Lion Point Parking Area (1.4 miles, 40 minutes one-way), which provides great cove views, the best view of Guillemot

Big Sur Coast

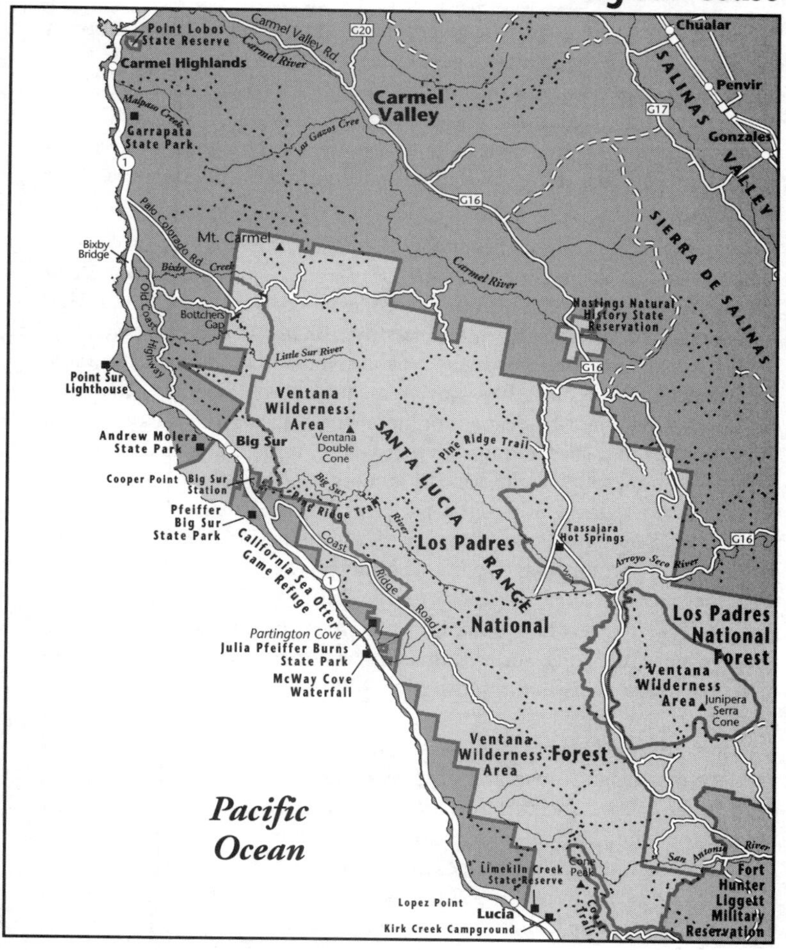

Island, where you can spot pigeon guillemots and both Brandt's and pelagic cormorants, and also of the Old Veteran Cypress at Cypress Cove (from a side trail); the **Sea Lion Point Trail** (.6 mile, 30 minutes), which affords great views of the offshore sea lion rocks; the **Bird Island Trail** (.8 mile, 30 minutes), which leaves from the Southern Parking area and provides access to China Cove and Gibson Beach, offering good views of Bird Island, a huge bird colony in spring and summer; the **Cypress Grove Trail** (.8 mile 30 minutes), which loops from Sea Lion Point Parking area to some great ocean views through stands of gnarled Monterey cypress; and the **Granite Point Trail** (1.3 miles, 60 minutes), from Whalers Cabin to Granite Point and back, which gives a glorious view of Carmel Bay and Pebble Beach and the terra-cotta rooftop of the Carmel Mission.

Guided tours of the area are given; inquire at the information station at the Sea Lion Parking area. The best time to visit is in spring, when wildflowers bloom everywhere and when seal pups are being raised and shore birds are nesting. No camping is allowed, nor are dogs.

Hours: 9am to 5pm, with extended hours in the summer. Access is limited so you may have to wait to gain entrance. *Admission:* $6 per vehicle.

Ten miles south of Carmel, beyond Yankee Point, you come upon the first of many state parks that line this famous coastline: **Garrapata State Park** (☎ 408/667-2315), which features 4 miles of coastline plus 2,879 adjacent acres. It's undeveloped, and in fact there is no formal entrance to the park. Instead, look for Soberanes Creek Canyon and the trails that lead off from it around the Point; they provide great views of the craggy, dramatic coastline. There's great tide-pooling here, and you may be lucky enough to see belted kingfishers along with many other birds. Rangers do conduct whale-watching tours in the park in January.

One or so miles south of the park you'll pass **Rocky Point,** where there's a restaurant of the same name with a great view (☎ 408/624-2933). Farther south, you'll cross two fragile **bridges,** the first over Rocky Creek and the second the bridge (formerly Rainbow Bridge) that spans Bixby Creek, 260 feet above the water. At one time lime was taken out of here on a 3-mile-long aerial tramway that operated from the canyon to a pier below. This is the setting for Robinson Jeffers poem "Thurso's Landing."

After you cross these and pass Hurricane Point, you will arrive at the landmark lighthouse at **Point Sur** (☎ 408/625-4419), which is set 360 feet above the surf and affords a great coastal view. It marks a treacherous point where many a ship has run aground, like the *Ventura* did in 1875. After the shipwreck, local doctor-hero John Roberts rode 30 miles from Monterey in 3½ hours to minister to the wounded and the dead. This shipwreck spurred the funding for a lighthouse, but even after it was opened in 1889 shipwrecks still occurred, such as those of the *Los Angeles* in 1894 and the *Howard Olson* in 1956. But the lighthouse keepers themselves lived a lonely existence. While their supplies were shipped in, they had to take a horse and wagon to Pfeiffer's Resort (now Pfeiffer Big Sur State Park) to pick up their mail. The last one left in 1974 when the light was automated. You can walk out to this light at low tide. On weekends (also Wednesdays during summer), you can take a 2- or 3-hour guided tour of the lighthouse, but you'll hike a half-mile each way to get there and climb 300 feet in elevation, so be prepared for the physical exertion and wear comfortable walking gear.

Tours: Sat at 10am and 2pm; Sun 10am; Wed 10am and 2pm (summer only). *Admission:* $5 adults, $3 youth 13–17, $2 children 5–12.

EXPLORING THE BIG SUR COAST

Three miles south of the Point Sur lighthouse lies **Andrew Molera State Park** (☎ 408/667-2315), a 4,800-acre park cut in half by the Big Sur River, which ambles out to sea at Molera Point. There are 16 miles of trails through the park. The **Spring Trail** leads down about a mile along the Big Sur River to Molera Beach, which is usually not crowded and is sheltered from the winds by the bluffs. Other trails include the **Bluff Trail,** which leads to the mouth of the river, and the **Rattlesnake Trail,** going up Pfeiffer Ridge to the Ridge Trail. There's also a trail along the west bank of the river and another that climbs up the East Side of the park for glorious ocean views.

A favorite pastime is trail-riding through the park, especially along the bluffs at sunset. These rides are organized from April to November by **Molera Big Sur Trail Rides** (☎ 408/625-8664). Several 2-hour rides are offered, costing $45 to $55. Otherwise, the park has few facilities except for a primitive camp area for 400 people.

Exit the park and continue down Highway 1; you'll come upon the Post Office and a cluster of the few businesses that operate in Big Sur. From here it's 1½ miles to the 807-acre **Pfeiffer Big Sur State Park** (☎ 408/667-2315), which is very popular in summer and geared to hosting families at its 200-plus sites along the Big Sur River. There are also a bike-in camp and two group sites plus Big Sur Lodge, which is described in the Lodging section below. You must make reservations for camping (☎ 800-444-7275).

Admission: $6 per vehicle.

Among the several trails in the park, the **Pfeiffer Falls Trail** (40 to 60 minutes) leads to a 60-foot waterfall; other trails follow the river or the gorge, while the **Buzzard's Roost Trail** (5 miles, 2 hours) leads to Pfeiffer Ridge up a rugged, steep course that brings you to a chaparral and great views of ocean and mountain. You can also access the Ventana Wilderness from this park.

Even though it is not in the park, make the effort to go down to **Pfeiffer Beach,** which is accessible from unmarked Sycamore Canyon Road, the only paved road off to the right between the Post Office and the entrance to Pfeiffer Big Sur State Park. Make a sharp right, and travel for 2 miles to the parking lot. Beyond, you will discover a lovely sand beach and an extraordinary sandstone arch carved out by the waves. If this beach seems familiar to you, it might be because it's been used in many movies, including Richard Burton and Elizabeth Taylor's *The Sandpiper.*

Clustered in this area about 28 miles south of Carmel are the major Big Sur resorts and restaurants—the Post Ranch Inn, Ventana, Nepenthe, and Deetjen's Big Sur Inn, all of which are described in the Lodging section below. You'll also find the **Coast Gallery,** which showcases the works of local artists and craftspeople.

Here, too, is the **Henry Miller Memorial Library,** on Highway 1 (☎ 408/667-2574). Visitors can see scores of Miller first editions and many of his watercolors. Miller arrived here in a taxicab and moved to Big Sur in 1944. He attracted many fellow travelers from the Beat Generation, including Jack Kerouac, Allen Ginsberg, Phillip Whalen, Gary Snyder, Lawrence Ferlinghetti, and Kenneth Rexroth. This collection, which was assembled by Miller's friend Emil White, has great personal warmth and obvious admiration.

Hours: Summer, daily 11am–5pm; Nov–Apr, weekends and holidays only. *Admission:* Free.

Before you reach another wonderful park, about 12 miles south of Pfeiffer Big Sur, you'll pass **Grimes and Partington Points.** Partington Cove is the site of an underwater canyon and a favorite scuba-diving destination. From the cove, the Tanbark Trail climbs up to the ridge above; a Loop Trail connects Partington and McWay canyons.

These trails are in **Julia Pfeiffer Burns State Park** (☎ 408/667-2315), which also contains the dramatic McWay Falls that drop 50 feet down onto the beach. The falls used to drop directly into the ocean, but recent road work extended the beach. You can view the falls at a distance from the road, or you can take the **Waterfall Trail,** which passes under the highway to an overlook. In spring this trail is lined with Indian paintbrush and morning glory. Two miles north of the main entrance to the park, a dirt road leads to a trailhead that goes down to Partington Cove, where the pioneers used to ship out tanbark, so called because it is rich in tannin, the main ingredient used in the tanneries at Santa Cruz and elsewhere. The next canyon over from McWay is Anderson's, which was the site where the convicts who built the highway in the 1930s were housed.

Three miles south of the park is the famous **Esalen Institute** (☎ 408/667-3000), which launched the human potential movement back in the 1960s. Named after the small tribe of Indians who had died out completely after the arrival of the Spanish, Esalen was started in 1961 by Michael Murphy and Richard Price, both Stanford graduates. Murphy was from Salinas and he and his brother Dennis were, it is believed, the models for Steinbeck's characters in *East of Eden.* Michael had dropped his premedical studies to concentrate on psychology, religion, and philosophy, then had dropped out all together and had gone to India to live at Sri Aurobindo's ashram in Pondicherry. Price, who was from the Midwest, had experienced his own harrowing journey through a nervous breakdown and hospitalization. Although they had both been at Stanford, they met in San Francisco. In 1961 they decided to move down to Big Sur and start something at Slate's Hot Springs, which Michael's family had bought in 1910. Even though the place was rented to an organization called the First Church of God of Prophecy, it was in a state of disrepair and malaise.

Back then Hunter Thompson was the caretaker, Joan Baez was living on the property, and Henry Miller was popping by daily to bathe at the springs. In the evenings and nights, though, the baths were being taken over by a group of gay men for their own purposes. That was until Thompson, Murphy, Baez, and Price confronted them with two Dobermans and scared them off so that programs could begin in Fall 1962.

After Alan Watts gave a seminar at the lodge, Michael began drawing up a series of programs that burgeoned over the years. Both Michael and Richard had a vision of developing human potential that was inspired by Aldous Huxley and others. Over the years, Esalen became known for encounter, Gestalt, and body work. At the institute, Fritz Perls conducted Gestalt therapy, William Schutz developed encounter therapy, and Bernard Gunther specialized in body work. Many famous philosophers and thinkers lectured or gave workshops here—Abraham Maslow, Paul Tillich, Linus Pauling, S.I. Hayakawa, Bishop James Pike, Norman O. Brown, Timothy Leary, B.F. Skinner, Arnold Toynbee, and more.

If you would like to have an Esalen experience, you can. Weekend and 5-day programs are still given year-round on all kinds of subjects, from biofeedback and lucid dreaming to Gestalt and martial arts. The grounds are spectacular, and the hot springs on top of the cliffs, from which you can look out at the ocean, are inspiring and rejuvenating. Sit out and enjoy these hot springs or have a massage outdoors. By the way, swimsuits are optional, and most everyone opts for nudity at the pool, the hot springs, and the massage tables. The charge for weekend workshops is anywhere from $200 to $400, depending on whether you choose sleeping space (which means simply that you put your own sleeping bag on the floor) or standard shared accommodations. Occasionally space is available for those who are not taking a workshop, and the charge is $95 to $150 for 2 weekend nights.

From Esalen it's about 10 miles to Lucia, which has a gas station and general store, then another 10 miles or so to Pacific Valley, which has a general store, cafe, and a few other facilities, as well as Sand Dollar Beach.

Sand Dollar Beach has good surf and offers a broad, crescent-shaped expanse of sand to stroll along. It's sheltered from the wind, offering picnicking facilities, fine tide-pooling, and great views of 5,155-foot Cone Peak to the northeast.

Two miles farther south, **Jade Cove** is a cobble-covered beach with plenty of schist and serpentine, which does yield some nephrite jade (usually found offshore by divers).

A mile farther on from Jade Grove is **Gorda,** which has a gas station and a few stores. From here it's another 12 miles to Ragged Point and San Carpoforo Creek, where the mountains retreat. It was here that Gaspar de Portolá turned inland in 1769 on his famous expedition.

The road continues on, skirting the lands that once comprised the 240,000-acre William Randolph Hearst family ranch. Eventually the road will bring you to the turnoff for San Simeon (65 miles south of Big Sur), site of the famous Hearst Castle.

A SIDE TRIP: THE VENTANA WILDERNESS

This wilderness area of 167,000-plus acres straddles the Santa Lucia Mountains. The terrain is characterized by steep, jagged ridges, separated by V-shaped valleys with elevations ranging from 600 to 5,750 feet. The climate is mild. Rain falls between November and April and ranges from 100 inches or more along the coastal ridge to less than 30 inches only a few miles inland. East of the coastal ridges, summers are hot and dry.

There are basically two ways into this backpacker's paradise. The first is by foot, and many people do hike in. One of the easiest trails in the park to access is the **Pine Ridge Trail,** which begins at Big Sur Station. There are 237 miles of trails through the wilderness, giving access to 55 trail camps. For information on camping or hiking, call ☎ 408/385-5434 in King City, ☎ 408/667-2315 in Big Sur station.

However, to get to the eastern side of the wilderness, you must go through Carmel Valley on the G16, which is also called the Carmel Valley Road as you leave the Monterey area. If you go this route, you will eventually reach the turnoff for Tassajara. On the way, you pass by the endpoint of the Pine Ridge Trail.

Anyone who lived through the '60s has probably heard of Tassajara, which is, literally, a place where jerked meat is hung up to cure. It's also the name of a Zen Monastery and a well-known bakery. Today summer vacationers still head to this haven, 45 miles south of Salinas in Los Padres National Forest, which is known as **Tassajara Hot Springs** (☎ 650/431-4438). It's still a Zen monastery where you can stay overnight (summer only) in one of the cabins for visitors, but only if you reserve by March. You can also arrange to drop in for the day, but you must book a week in advance. You can enjoy the hot springs, sunbathe on the decks extending out over a creek, and hike in the surrounding wilderness. Overnight guests are also invited to join the meditation sessions. The meals are, of course, vegetarian, and the charge is anywhere from $90 per person for dormitory-style accommodations to $200 in a private "stone room" equipped with wood stove. Prices include all meals. Breakfast will bring fruit, eggs, and the famous fresh whole-grain bread; lunch will be soup and salad; and dinner will be a meatless, often Asian-inspired, dish.

To reach Tassajara, take Highways 101 and 156 to Carmel. From Carmel take Carmel Valley Road 23 miles to Tassajara Road. Travel this road for 1½ miles to the small cluster of buildings that is Jamesburg. From there, the monastery is 14 miles down a dirt road suitable only for four-wheelers or stick shift cars only.

Big Sur Coast Lodging & Dining

Serenity, comfort, and a genuine concern for the environment are the hallmarks of the 98-acre **Post Ranch,** Highway 1, P.O. Box 219, Big Sur, CA 93920 (☎ 800/527-2200 for inn reservations only or 408/667-2200, fax 408/667 2824). The designers of the Post Ranch, the most recent cliff-top accommodation developed in the region, have done everything to minimize the impact of the resort on its surroundings. In fact, it's often referred to as the first "politically correct," resort and actually that's an appropriate enough name, since it took 8 years of botanical, biological, and environmental surveys before permission was granted to develop the site.

There are only 30 rooms and 1 suite available. The most spectacular are the singular Ocean Rooms, which are tucked into the cliff under sod roofs planted with flowers. They have unobstructed ocean views. The Coast Houses also have ocean views but are cylindrical in shape, and each contains two units with separate entrances. The Tree Houses are triangular-shaped single units built on stilts in the forest; only a few of these have ocean views. Six units are in a three-story, butterfly-shaped building. The interiors are all fashioned out of redwood and feature state-of-the-art music systems, minibars, fireplace, TVs, and VCRs. Bathrooms are faced with gray marble, which has been specially tumbled to create a natural look, and feature ceramic sinks and granite counters, plus deep, two-person Jacuzzi tubs made out of Indian slate. They are also equipped with hair dryers, robes, and windows that look out to forest, mountain, or ocean. Denim spreads cover the beds; the furniture is crafted from African woods, and doors are made from rusted steel, which has been waxed over to provide a smooth finish. Each unit also has a furnished terrace. Massage tables are tucked under every bed for use at most any time from early morning to midnight. Other special services include spa service, yoga, guided hikes, tarot reading, aromatherapy, and a library of books and CDs. The semi-circular hot tub/pool, which almost seems to spill off the cliff, is spectacular, too. Guests are provided with a continental breakfast, light appetizers, and gourmet picnics at lunch. Tours of this ecologically conscious resort are given Monday through Friday at 2pm.

The **Sierra Mar** restaurant (☎ 408/667-2200) has a dramatic, cliff-top setting and view and offers a four-course, prix-fixe menu for $60 per person. Your meal might open with Dungeness crab and basil potato salad with mussel vinaigrette, or roasted squab with parsnip mousse, chanterelles, and huckleberries. After soup or salad, you can choose among six main courses—grilled mahimahi with saffron aïoli and roasted Yukon golds, or grilled lamb tenderloin with pancetta, lentil ragout, and grilled bitter greens, to name two. Among the most celebrated dishes that might appear on the menu is the breast of duck with foie gras, quince, and walnuts. Desserts might run to Earl Grey parfait with espresso, toffee, and chocolate sauce, or a blackberry tartlet with a refreshing kiwi sorbet. The restaurant is open to the public only for dinner.

Rates (incl. breakfast and lunch but not dinner): Ocean Houses, $535–$560; Coast Houses, $460–$545; Tree Houses, $410–$435; Butterfly House, $295–$345. *Dining Hours:* Daily 5:30–9:30pm.

The Ventana Inn, Highway 1, Big Sur, CA 93920 (☎ 800/628-6500 or 408/667-2331, fax 408/667-2419), is set on top of the ridge with glorious, 50-mile ocean views from the flagstone dining terrace. The surrounding 243 acres are beautiful, the service unassuming, and the ambience comfortable. It's enchanting and idyllic—definitely a relaxing, contemplative place that, as its name implies, provides a window on nature and Big Sur in particular, without any busy social distractions like golf or tennis. In short, a place to restore the soul. There are only 60 rooms in about a dozen weathered cedar buildings, which are located up the hill, a distance from the restaurant, ensuring privacy and seclusion. Each room has walls of cedar and is elegantly furnished with comfortable seating and beds with hand-painted headboards and handsome quilts for covers. All the rooms have TV, VCR, and refrigerator, plus a private, latticed patio or balcony with an ocean or forest view. Those with forest views are, in fact, more secluded. Some have a fireplace or hot tub as well. The decor is easy on the eye—soft pastels and earth tones with wicker furnishings piled with pillows.

The **dining room** is located away from the lodgings. It's a serene place of stone and wood, with banquettes covered with Peruvian-patterned blanket fabric. The California cuisine is excellent. If it's offered, start with the Dungeness crab–cake salad made with wild greens, roasted bell peppers, browned butter, and capers, or the seared scallop and bacon salad with carmelized apple steak and a sherry reduction. Among the eight or so main courses, priced from $20 to $30, you might find a Petaluma chicken breast stuffed with garlic, herb croutons, and wild rice served with tomato-basil sauce; a perfectly oak-grilled filet mignon accompanied by caramelized apples and a warming, redolent zinfandel reduction; or delicious chestnut-crusted tuna in a ponzu sauce accompanied by sticky rice, bok choy, bell-pepper stir fry, and fried wontons. Lighter choices are also available. Desserts are equally enticing—go for the Bailey's chocolate cake enhanced by vanilla tuiles and fresh berries. The dining room is also lovely for lunch, and the cocktail lounge, warmed in winter by a fire in the stone hearth, is a welcoming place for a drink.

The Inn's facilities include two 75-foot pools, a bathhouse containing three Japanese hot baths, all with clothing optional areas, plus spa for massages, facials, herbal wraps, and more. There's also a worthy gift shop/gallery. Rates include a first-rate continental breakfast (fresh juices, melons, strawberries, pineapples, papayas, and other seasonal fruits, plus pastries and breads) and a wine-and-cheese buffet in the late afternoon served in the comfortable lobby in front of the large, stone fireplace.

Rates (incl. breakfast): Weekends, holidays, and high season $205–$280 standard; $295–$390 with fireplace; $460–$520 with fireplace and hot tub; $370–$500 standard suite; $500–$1,000 suite with fireplace and hot tub. Rates are about 10% less in low season. *Dining Hours:* Mon–Fri noon–3pm; Sat–Sun 11am–3pm; daily 6–9pm. Closed for 2 weeks in early Dec.

Deetjen's Big Sur Inn, Highway 1, Big Sur, CA 93920 (☎ 408/667-2377), contrasts dramatically with the lavish resorts of the area. It's not on the cliff top; it's in a canyon. It was originally built by Grandpa Deetjen, who came to Big Sur in the early 1930s from Norway. Until Highway 1 was completed, Castro Canyon was a stopover on the wagon trail, and Helmuth Deetjen welcomed overnight visitors. Over the years he added rooms, which he built in a very rustic style. The hostelry retains this earthy quality today with its heavy, hand-hewn doors, fireplaces, and wood-burning stoves, and lack of phones and TVs. Rooms range from small doubles with shared bath to larger rooms with fireplace and private bath. Because the rooms are not soundproofed, kids under 12 are not accepted unless you reserve both rooms in a two-room building.

The **restaurant** is equally atmospheric, with its four candlelit, low-beamed rooms warmed on cool nights by a fire. The food is classic—a rib eye grilled over oak with bordelaise sauce and fresh horseradish, pan-fried rock cod in an herb crust with the salsa of the night, and roasted duckling with a brandy peppercorn and molasses sauce. Prices range from $13.50 for the veggie platter to $23.

Rates: $95–$170 double weekends, $80–$145 midweek. For weekends you'll need to reserve a room 2–3 months in advance. *Dining Hours:* Daily 8–11am and 6pm–closing.

Big Sur Lodge, Pfeiffer Big Sur State Park, Highway 1, Big Sur, CA 93920 (☎ 800/424-4787 or 408/667-3100, fax 408/667-3110), is, obviously, right in the park and offers 61 cottage accommodations, all with porches or decks for getting close to nature. Some have fireplaces and/or kitchenettes. They are furnished with old-fashioned motel-style furnishings. The walls are paneled and the floors carpeted. Other facilities include a restaurant, outdoor fenced-in pool, and a convenience store.

Rates: Spring and fall, $99–$159; summer, $119–$189; winter, $89–$149 (higher prices are for cottages with kitchen and fireplace).

Big Sur Coast Dining Only

People come to **Rocky Point Restaurant** (☎ 408/624-2933) for the view. The food is strictly traditional steakhouse fare—filet mignon, prime rib, and porterhouse—plus fish—salmon and swordfish, for example—barbecued over charcoal flavored with mesquite. The sea scallops sautéed with tomato cilantro, jícama-citrus juices, olive oil, and garlic are worth trying, and so are the pork ribs with honey and soy sauce. Prices range from $18 to $27. Desserts are similarly traditional, consisting of cheesecake, apple pie, and ice cream.

Hours: Daily 11:30am–3pm and 5:30pm–closing.

Glen Oaks Restaurant, Highway 1, 26 miles south of Carmel (☎ 408/667-2264), is one place that the locals will frequent. The decor is plain but appealing, and the food, which combines a variety of cuisines, is a good value. To start, opt for the Castroville artichoke served with aïoli, or the goat cheese and roasted red pepper served with cilantro-infused olive oil and kalamata olives. Among the main courses, you'll find steaks alongside pork loin marinated in Szechuan peppercorns, soy sauce, ginger, garlic, and sesame oil; there's both chicken marsala and mushroom stroganoff. Prices range from $11 to $17.

Hours: Wed–Mon 6pm–closing (around 7:45pm in winter, 9pm in summer). Closed January.

If you climb the steps to **Nepenthe,** on Highway 1, 30 miles south of Carmel (☎ 408/667-2345), you're climbing to a legendary place, once the log cabin/bungalow Orson Welles built for his bride Rita Hayworth. On warm nights, you can dine at one of the tables set out around the perimeter of the cliff-hanging property overlooking the Pacific or inside on cooler evenings, when a central fire will be burning. From the decks there's a 40-mile view of the south coast of Big Sur. It is still operated by the fourth generation of the Fassett family, who bought the property for $15,000 in 1947 from Orson Welles.

Bill, who loved to drink, and Lolly Fassett, who could make a mean roast chicken, decided to open this redwood and glass restaurant 808 feet above the ocean and to open their door whenever anyone knocked. Instead of calling it something mundane, they were encouraged to give it an exotic name and so they did: Nepenthe, which they took from Norman Douglas' *South Wind and the Isle of Nepenthe,* where it refers to the island of Capri. The name means "isle of no sorrow" and is also the name given to a mythical Egyptian drug that was given to Helen, daughter of Jove, to induce forgetfulness and surcease from sorrow.

There's a convivial redwood bar up front, where many a famous figure has raised a glass or two—including Ted Turner and Jane Fonda, Elizabeth Taylor and Richard Burton, Dylan and Caitlin Thomas, Anaïs Nin and Man Ray, and, of course, Henry Miller, who was always trying to beat Bill Fassett at Ping Pong. Miller even showed up at 2am one morning in his bathrobe to challenge Bill to a game because he'd had a dream that his astrologer had predicted he would win.

The food is okay; you're paying more for the view, remember. At lunch the menu offers sandwiches, salads, and burgers. At dinner the fare consists of broiled fish and steak dishes and such lighter items as quiche. The burgers are popular and served with an ambrosia sauce, the specialty of the house, whose main ingredient is mayonnaise. Prices range from $10 to $24.

On a lower level, the **Cafe Kevah** also affords glorious views of the ocean, features light fare, and is open when the weather permits. It's a perfect, even preferable, place to linger over an iced tea or cappucino. **The Phoenix** offers some fine craft items by local artists plus clothing, jewelry, and books.

Hours: Daily 11:30am–10:30pm. Closed Jan–Feb.

Big Sur Coast
Special & Recreational Activities

Beaches: See the "Exploring" section above. Among the best (from north to south) are Molera Beach, Pfeiffer Beach, Sand Dollar Beach, and Jade Cove.

Camping: The major campgrounds are in the state parks, notably at **Andrew Molera** and **Pfeiffer Big Sur.** The former has only a hike-in campground, the latter 218 sites reachable by car.

There are also several National Forest Service camping facilities available. The first, as you travel south, is out along the Palo Colorado Road at **Bottcher's Gap,** with 11 tent sites only. It provides trailhead access into the Ventana Wilderness.

There are also two fine coastal campgrounds operated by the National Forest Service. The first is **Kirk Creek Campground,** which is located about 14 miles south of Esalen on an open bluff above the ocean; it has 33 sites with access to a beach via a steep trail. The second is **Plaskett Creek Campground,** on the eastern side of Highway 1 between Sand Dollar Beach and Jade Cove, which has 43 sites. For information on Forest Service Campgrounds call ☎ 408/667-2322 or 408/667-2315.

For information on additional campgrounds in the Los Padres National Forest or in Ventana Wilderness, write Monterey Ranger District, 406 S. Mildred Ave., King City, CA 93930 (☎ 408/385-5434). Camping fees vary from $5 to $15.

Fishing: Trout is the main catch in the coastal streams, although crayfish can be found, too. For detailed information contact the California Department of Fish and Game (☎ 408/649-2870).

Hiking: Seek information about the trails in the state parks by calling the parks themselves (they're all listed below and described in more detail in the "Exloring" section above). For information on the miles of trails in the Ventana Wilderness and Los Padres National Forest, contact the **Monterey Ranger District,** 406 S. Mildred Ave., King City, CA 93930 (☎ 408/385-5434). There are approximately 38 trails in the area's state parks and about 330 miles of trails in the Wilderness and National Forest.

Horseback Riding: Andrew Molera State Park is the place for horseback riding. To make arrangements, call **Molera Big Sur Trail Rides** (☎ 408/625-8664). The cost is $45 to $55 for 2 hours.

Picnicking: Plenty of picnicking opportunities are found in the state parks and also at the beaches listed above.

State Parks: The area is loaded with state parks and beaches. The following are discussed in more detail in the "Exploring" section above: **Point Lobos State Reserve,** Highway 1, 3 miles south of Carmel (☎ 408/624-3909); **Garrapata State Park,** Highway 1, 10 miles south of Carmel (☎ 408/667-2315); **Point Sur Lighthouse State Park,** Highway 1, 17 miles south of Carmel (☎ 408/667-4419); **Andrew Molera State Park,** Highway 1, 3 miles south of the Point Sur Light House ☎ (408/667-2315); **Pfeiffer Big Sur State Park,** Highway 1, 1½ miles south of Big Sur Station (☎ 408/667-2171); **Julia Pfeiffer Burns State Park,** Highway 1, 12 miles south of Pfeiffer Big Sur (☎ 408/667-2315).

Swimming: The ocean is not suitable for swimming here because of the temperature and the currents. Most of the resorts have pools, though.

INDEX